THE BOOK ®

Toyota Carina E
Service and Repair Manual

A K Legg LAE MIMI, Steve Rendle and John S Mead

Models covered

(3256 - 256)

Toyota Carina E Hatchback, Saloon and Estate models with petrol engines, including special/limited editions
1587 cc, 1762 cc and 1998 cc

Does not cover Diesel models

© Haynes Publishing 1997

ABCDE
FGHIJ
KLMN

Printed in the USA

A book in the **Haynes Service and Repair Manual Series**

Haynes Publishing
Sparkford, Yeovil, Somerset BA22 7JJ, England

Haynes North America, Inc
861 Lawrence Drive, Newbury Park, California 91320, USA

Editions Haynes
4, Rue de l'Abreuvoir
92415 COURBEVOIE CEDEX, France

Haynes Publishing Nordiska AB
Box 1504, 751 45 UPPSALA, Sweden

ISBN 1 85960 256 8

British Library Cataloguing in Publication Data
A catalogue record for this book is available from the British Library

Contents

LIVING WITH YOUR TOYOTA CARINA E

Roadside Repairs

Weekly Checks

Tyre pressures

Lubricants and fluids

MAINTENANCE

Routine Maintenance and Servicing

Contents

The Toyota Carina E was introduced to the UK in May 1992 in Saloon, Hatchback and Estate versions, with a choice of 1.6 or 2.0 litre engines. All models were fitted with power steering and a catalytic converter. Executive and GTi models were fitted with ABS as standard. From September 1994 all models were fitted with a driver's air bag, previous to this the driver's air bag was standard on Executive and GTi models.

All models are fitted with an independent McPherson-type front suspension incorporating a telescopic shock absorber and coil spring, and an independent dual-link strut rear suspension with integral shock absorbers and an anti-roll bar.

Provided that regular servicing is carried out in accordance with the manufacturer's recommendations, the Toyota Carina E should prove extremely reliable and economical. The engine compartment is well-designed, and most of the items needing frequent attention are easily accessible.

Your Toyota Carina E Manual

The aim of this manual is to help you get the best value from your vehicle. It can do so in several ways. It can help you decide what work must be done (even should you choose to get it done by a garage), provide information on routine maintenance and servicing, and give a logical course of action and diagnosis when random faults occur. However, it is hoped that you will use the manual by tackling the work yourself. On simpler jobs, it may even be quicker than booking the car into a garage and going there twice, to leave and collect it. Perhaps most important, a lot of money can be saved by avoiding the costs a garage must charge to cover its labour and overheads.

The manual has drawings and descriptions to show the function of the various components, so that their layout can be understood. Then the tasks are described and photographed in a clear step-by-step sequence.

Toyota Carina E Estates

Toyota Carina E GTi Saloon

The Toyota Carina E Team

Haynes manuals are produced by dedicated and enthusiastic people working in close co-operation. The team responsible for the creation of this book included:

Authors	Andy Legg
	Steve Rendle
	John Mead
Page make-up	Steve Churchill
Workshop manager	Paul Buckland
Photo Scans	John Martin
	Paul Tanswell
	Steve Tanswell
Cover illustration & Line Art	Roger Healing
Wiring diagrams	Matthew Marke

We hope the book will help you to get the maximum enjoyment from your car. By carrying out routine maintenance as described you will ensure your car's reliability and preserve its resale value.

Acknowledgements

Thanks are due to the Champion Spark Plug Company, who supplied the illustrations of various spark plug conditions. Thanks are also due to Sykes-Pickavant Limited, who provided some of the workshop tools, and to all those people at Sparkford who helped in the production of this manual.

This manual is not a direct reproduction of the vehicle manufacturers data, and its publication should not be taken as implying any technical approval by the vehicle manufacturers or importers.

We take great pride in the accuracy of information given in this manual, but vehicle manufacturers make alterations and design changes during the production run of a particular vehicle of which they do not inform us. No liability can be accepted by the authors or publishers for loss, damage or injury caused by any errors in, or omissions from, the information given.

Project vehicles

The main vehicle used in the preparation of this manual, and which appears in many of the photographic sequences, was a 1996 Toyota Carina E 1.6S Hatchback with a 1587 cc 4A-FE economy engine and manual transmission. Also used was a 1994 Toyota Carina E 2.0GLi with a 1998 cc 3S-FE engine and automatic transmission.

Working on your car can be dangerous. This page shows just some of the potential risks and hazards, with the aim of creating a safety-conscious attitude.

General hazards

Scalding

• Don't remove the radiator or expansion tank cap while the engine is hot.
• Engine oil, automatic transmission fluid or power steering fluid may also be dangerously hot if the engine has recently been running.

Burning

• Beware of burns from the exhaust system and from any part of the engine. Brake discs and drums can also be extremely hot immediately after use.

Crushing

• When working under or near a raised vehicle, always supplement the jack with axle stands, or use drive-on ramps. *Never venture under a car which is only supported by a jack.*
• Take care if loosening or tightening high-torque nuts when the vehicle is on stands. Initial loosening and final tightening should be done with the wheels on the ground.

Fire

• Fuel is highly flammable; fuel vapour is explosive.
• Don't let fuel spill onto a hot engine.
• Do not smoke or allow naked lights (including pilot lights) anywhere near a vehicle being worked on. Also beware of creating sparks (electrically or by use of tools).
• Fuel vapour is heavier than air, so don't work on the fuel system with the vehicle over an inspection pit.
• Another cause of fire is an electrical overload or short-circuit. Take care when repairing or modifying the vehicle wiring.
• Keep a fire extinguisher handy, of a type suitable for use on fuel and electrical fires.

Electric shock

• Ignition HT voltage can be dangerous, especially to people with heart problems or a pacemaker. Don't work on or near the ignition system with the engine running or the ignition switched on.

• Mains voltage is also dangerous. Make sure that any mains-operated equipment is correctly earthed. Mains power points should be protected by a residual current device (RCD) circuit breaker.

Fume or gas intoxication

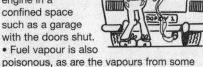

• Exhaust fumes are poisonous; they often contain carbon monoxide, which is rapidly fatal if inhaled. Never run the engine in a confined space such as a garage with the doors shut.
• Fuel vapour is also poisonous, as are the vapours from some cleaning solvents and paint thinners.

Poisonous or irritant substances

• Avoid skin contact with battery acid and with any fuel, fluid or lubricant, especially antifreeze, brake hydraulic fluid and Diesel fuel. Don't syphon them by mouth. If such a substance is swallowed or gets into the eyes, seek medical advice.
• Prolonged contact with used engine oil can cause skin cancer. Wear gloves or use a barrier cream if necessary. Change out of oil-soaked clothes and do not keep oily rags in your pocket.
• Air conditioning refrigerant forms a poisonous gas if exposed to a naked flame (including a cigarette). It can also cause skin burns on contact.

Asbestos

• Asbestos dust can cause cancer if inhaled or swallowed. Asbestos may be found in gaskets and in brake and clutch linings. When dealing with such components it is safest to assume that they contain asbestos.

Special hazards

Hydrofluoric acid

• This extremely corrosive acid is formed when certain types of synthetic rubber, found in some O-rings, oil seals, fuel hoses etc, are exposed to temperatures above 400°C. The rubber changes into a charred or sticky substance containing the acid. *Once formed, the acid remains dangerous for years. If it gets onto the skin, it may be necessary to amputate the limb concerned.*
• When dealing with a vehicle which has suffered a fire, or with components salvaged from such a vehicle, wear protective gloves and discard them after use.

The battery

• Batteries contain sulphuric acid, which attacks clothing, eyes and skin. Take care when topping-up or carrying the battery.
• The hydrogen gas given off by the battery is highly explosive. Never cause a spark or allow a naked light nearby. Be careful when connecting and disconnecting battery chargers or jump leads.

Air bags

• Air bags can cause injury if they go off accidentally. Take care when removing the steering wheel and/or facia. Special storage instructions may apply.

Diesel injection equipment

• Diesel injection pumps supply fuel at very high pressure. Take care when working on the fuel injectors and fuel pipes.

⚠️ *Warning: Never expose the hands, face or any other part of the body to injector spray; the fuel can penetrate the skin with potentially fatal results.*

Remember...

DO

• Do use eye protection when using power tools, and when working under the vehicle.

• Do wear gloves or use barrier cream to protect your hands when necessary.

• Do get someone to check periodically that all is well when working alone on the vehicle.

• Do keep loose clothing and long hair well out of the way of moving mechanical parts.

• Do remove rings, wristwatch etc, before working on the vehicle – especially the electrical system.

• Do ensure that any lifting or jacking equipment has a safe working load rating adequate for the job.

DON'T

• Don't attempt to lift a heavy component which may be beyond your capability – get assistance.

• Don't rush to finish a job, or take unverified short cuts.

• Don't use ill-fitting tools which may slip and cause injury.

• Don't leave tools or parts lying around where someone can trip over them. Mop up oil and fuel spills at once.

• Don't allow children or pets to play in or near a vehicle being worked on.

The following pages are intended to help in dealing with common roadside emergencies and breakdowns. You will find more detailed fault finding information at the back of the manual, and repair information in the main chapters.

If your car won't start and the starter motor doesn't turn

- ☐ If it's a model with automatic transmission, make sure the selector is in 'P' or 'N'.
- ☐ Open the bonnet and make sure that the battery terminals are clean and tight.
- ☐ Switch on the headlights and try to start the engine. If the headlights go very dim when you're trying to start, the battery is probably flat. Get out of trouble by jump starting (see next page) using a friend's car.

If your car won't start even though the starter motor turns as normal

- ☐ Is there fuel in the tank?
- ☐ Is there moisture on electrical components under the bonnet? Switch off the ignition, then wipe off any obvious dampness with a dry cloth. Spray a water-repellent aerosol product (WD-40 or equivalent) on ignition and fuel system electrical connectors like those shown in the photos. Pay special attention to the ignition coil wiring connector and HT leads.

A Check the security and condition of the battery connections

B Check that the spark plug HT leads are securely connected to the distributor cap by pushing them home

C Check that the ignition low tension wiring is securely connected to the distributor

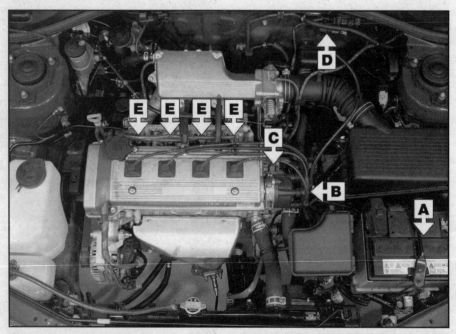

Check that electrical connections are secure (with the ignition switched off) and spray them with a water dispersant spray like WD40 if you suspect a problem due to damp

D Check that the HT lead is securely connected to the ignition coil, and spray with water-dispersant if necessary

E Check that the wiring plugs are securely connected to the injectors

Jump starting

HAYNES HINT *Jump starting will get you out of trouble, but you must correct whatever made the battery go flat in the first place. There are three possibilities:*

1 *The battery has been drained by repeated attempts to start, or by leaving the lights on.*

2 *The charging system is not working properly (alternator drivebelt slack or broken, alternator wiring fault or alternator itself faulty).*

3 *The battery itself is at fault (electrolyte low, or battery worn out).*

When jump-starting a car using a booster battery, observe the following precautions:

✔ Before connecting the booster battery, make sure that the ignition is switched off.

✔ Ensure that all electrical equipment (lights, heater, wipers, etc) is switched off.

✔ Make sure that the booster battery is the same voltage as the discharged one in the vehicle.

✔ If the battery is being jump-started from the battery in another vehicle, the two vehicles MUST NOT TOUCH each other.

✔ Make sure that the transmission is in neutral (or PARK, in the case of automatic transmission).

1 Connect one end of the red jump lead to the positive (+) terminal of the flat battery

2 Connect the other end of the red lead to the positive (+) terminal of the booster battery

3 Connect one end of the black jump lead to the negative (-) terminal of the booster battery

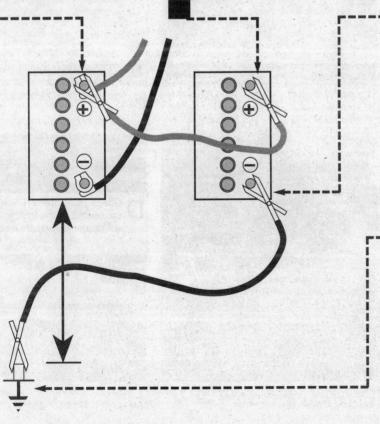

4 Connect the other end of the black jump lead to a bracket on the cylinder head, well away from the battery, on the vehicle to be started

5 Make sure that the jump leads will not come into contact with the fan, drivebelts or other moving parts of the engine

6 Start the engine using the booster battery, then with the engine running at idle speed, disconnect the jump leads in the reverse order of connection

Wheel changing

The details shown in the following photographs are from a Hatchback model, however the tools are located in the same location on all models.

⚠️ **Warning: Do not change a wheel in a situation where you risk being hit by another vehicle. On busy roads, try to stop in a lay-by or a gateway. Be wary of passing traffic while changing the wheel - it is easy to become distracted by the job in hand.**

Preparation

☐ When a puncture occurs, stop as soon as it is safe to do so.

☐ Park on firm level ground, if possible, and well out of the way of other traffic.

☐ Use hazard warning lights if necessary.

☐ If you have one, use a warning triangle to alert other drivers of your presence.

☐ Apply the handbrake and engage first or reverse gear (or Park on models with automatic transmission).

☐ Chock the wheel diagonally opposite the one being removed – a couple of large stones will do for this.

☐ If the ground is soft, use a flat piece of wood to spread the load under the jack.

Changing the wheel

1 The jack is positioned in the right-hand rear of the luggage compartment. The brace is located beneath the jack

2 Fold back the boot carpet and unscrew the plastic nut from the top of the spare wheel retaining stud

3 The jack handle is located on the underside of the spare wheel cover

4 Unscrew the stud and remove the retaining cup

5 Remove the spare wheel from the well in the rear luggage compartment (note that the outer side of the wheel is uppermost)

6 Use the end of the brace to prise off the wheel trim. Loosen the wheel nuts slightly before jacking up the car

7 Locate the jack head in the jacking point and raise the vehicle until the wheel is clear of the ground

8 Lift the wheel from the studs

9 Tighten the wheel nuts securely. Have them checked for tightness using a torque wrench at the earliest opportunity

Finally...

☐ Remove the wheel chocks.

☐ Stow the jack and tools in the correct locations in the car.

☐ Check the tyre pressure on the wheel just fitted. If it is low, or if you don't have a pressure gauge with you, drive slowly to the nearest garage and inflate the tyre to the right pressure.

☐ Have the damaged tyre or wheel repaired as soon as possible.

Identifying leaks

Puddles on the garage floor or drive, or obvious wetness under the bonnet or underneath the car, suggest a leak that needs investigating. It can sometimes be difficult to decide where the leak is coming from, especially if the engine bay is very dirty already. Leaking oil or fluid can also be blown rearwards by the passage of air under the car, giving a false impression of where the problem lies.

 Warning: Most automotive oils and fluids are poisonous. Wash them off skin, and change out of contaminated clothing, without delay.

HAYNES HiNT *The smell of a fluid leaking from the car may provide a clue to what's leaking. Some fluids are distinctively coloured. It may help to clean the car carefully and to park it over some clean paper overnight as an aid to locating the source of the leak.*
Remember that some leaks may only occur while the engine is running.

Sump oil

Engine oil may leak from the drain plug...

Oil from filter

...or from the base of the oil filter.

Gearbox oil

Gearbox oil can leak from the seals at the inboard ends of the driveshafts.

Antifreeze

Leaking antifreeze often leaves a crystalline deposit like this.

Brake fluid

A leak occurring at a wheel is almost certainly brake fluid.

Power steering fluid

Power steering fluid may leak from the pipe connectors on the steering rack.

Towing

When all else fails, you may find yourself having to get a tow home – or of course you may be helping somebody else. Long-distance recovery should only be done by a garage or breakdown service. For shorter distances, DIY towing using another car is easy enough, but observe the following points:
☐ Use a proper tow-rope – they are not expensive. The vehicle being towed must display an 'ON TOW' sign in its rear window.
☐ Always turn the ignition key to the ACC position when the vehicle is being towed, so that the steering lock is released, and that the direction indicator and brake lights will work.
☐ Only attach the tow-rope to the towing eyes provided at the front and rear of the car.
☐ Before being towed, release the handbrake and select neutral on the transmission.
☐ Note that greater-than-usual pedal pressure will be required to operate the brakes, since the vacuum servo unit is only operational with the engine running.
☐ On models with power steering, greater-than-usual steering effort will also be required.

☐ The driver of the car being towed must keep the tow-rope taut at all times to avoid snatching.
☐ Make sure that both drivers know the route before setting off.
☐ Only drive at moderate speeds and keep the distance towed to a minimum. Drive smoothly and allow plenty of time for slowing down at junctions.
☐ On models with automatic transmission, special precautions apply. If in doubt, do not tow, or transmission damage may result.

Introduction

There are some very simple checks which need only take a few minutes to carry out, but which could save you a lot of inconvenience and expense.

These "Weekly checks" require no great skill or special tools, and the small amount of time they take to perform could prove to be very well spent, for example;

☐ Keeping an eye on tyre condition and pressures, will not only help to stop them wearing out prematurely, but could also save your life.

☐ Many breakdowns are caused by electrical problems. Battery-related faults are particularly common, and a quick check on a regular basis will often prevent the majority of these.

☐ If your car develops a brake fluid leak, the first time you might know about it is when your brakes don't work properly. Checking the level regularly will give advance warning of this kind of problem.

☐ If the oil or coolant levels run low, the cost of repairing any engine damage will be far greater than fixing the leak, for example.

Underbonnet check points

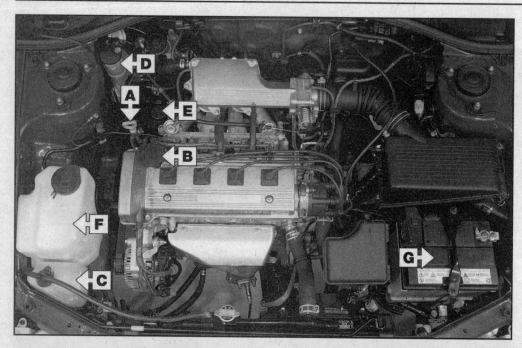

◀ **1.6 litre 4A-FE engine**

A *Engine oil level dipstick*

B *Engine oil filler cap*

C *Coolant expansion tank*

D *Brake fluid reservoir*

E *Power steering fluid reservoir*

F *Screen washer fluid reservoir*

G *Battery*

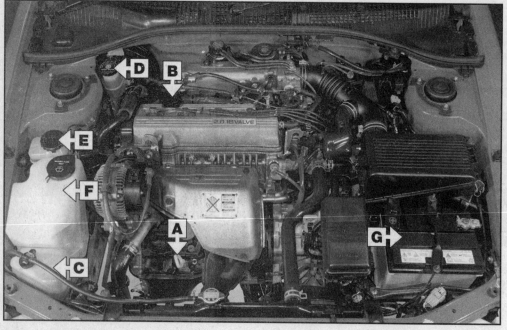

◀ **2.0 litre 3S-FE engine**

A *Engine oil level dipstick*

B *Engine oil filler cap*

C *Coolant expansion tank*

D *Brake fluid reservoir*

E *Power steering fluid reservoir*

F *Screen washer fluid reservoir*

G *Battery*

Engine oil level

Before you start

✔ Make sure that your car is on level ground.
✔ Check the oil level before the car is driven, or at least 5 minutes after the engine has been switched off.

 HAYNES HiNT *If the oil is checked immediately after driving the vehicle, some of the oil will remain in the upper engine components, resulting in an inaccurate reading on the dipstick!*

The correct oil

Modern engines place great demands on their oil. It is very important that the correct oil for your car is used (See "Lubricants and fluids")

Car Care

● If you have to add oil frequently, you should check whether you have any oil leaks. Place some clean paper under the car overnight, and check for stains in the morning. If there are no leaks, the engine may be burning oil *(see "Fault Finding").*

● Always maintain the level between the upper and lower dipstick marks (see photo 3). If the level is too low severe engine damage may occur. Oil seal failure may result if the engine is overfilled by adding too much oil.

1 The dipstick top is often brightly coloured for easy identification (see *"Underbonnet check points"* on page 0•10 for exact location). Withdraw the dipstick.

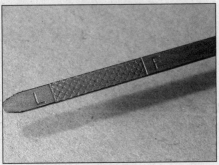

3 Note the oil level on the end of the dipstick, which should be between the upper (F) mark and lower (L) mark. Approximately 1.0 litre of oil will raise the level from the lower mark to the upper mark.

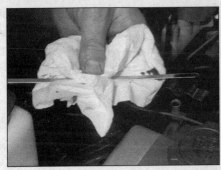

2 Using a clean rag or paper towel remove all oil from the dipstick. Insert the clean dipstick into the tube as far as it will go, then withdraw it again.

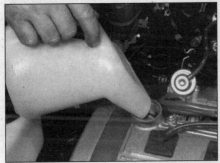

4 Oil is added through the filler cap. Unscrew the cap and top-up the level; a funnel may help to reduce spillage. Add the oil slowly, checking the level on the dipstick often. Don't overfill (see *"Car Care"* left).

Coolant level

 Warning: DO NOT attempt to remove the radiator pressure cap when the engine is hot, as there is a very great risk of scalding. Do not leave open containers of coolant about, as it is poisonous.

Car Care

● With a sealed-type cooling system, adding coolant should not be necessary on a regular basis. If frequent topping-up is required, it is likely there is a leak. Check the radiator, all hoses and joint faces for signs of staining or wetness, and rectify as necessary.

● It is important that antifreeze is used in the cooling system all year round, not just during the winter months. Don't top-up with water alone, as the antifreeze will become too diluted.

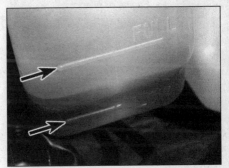

1 The coolant level varies with the temperature of the engine. When the engine is cold, the coolant level should be between the FULL and LOW marks.

2 If topping-up is necessary, wait until the engine is cold then remove the expansion tank cap. The expansion tank is not pressurised since the pressure cap is located in the top of the radiator, however the system should be topped up with the engine cold.

3 Add a mixture of water and antifreeze to the expansion tank until the coolant level is up to the FULL level mark, then refit the cap.

Clutch fluid level

Warning:
● **Brake fluid can harm your eyes and damage painted surfaces, so use extreme caution when handling and pouring it.**
● **Do not use fluid that has been standing open for some time, as it absorbs moisture from the air.**
● **Do not mix different types of fluid; mixing can cause damage to the system**

HAYNES HINT
• **Make sure that your car is on level ground.**
• **The fluid level in the reservoir will drop slightly but the fluid level must never be allowed to drop below the "MIN" mark.**

Safety First!

● If the reservoir requires repeated topping-up this is an indication of a fluid leak somewhere in the system, which should be investigated immediately.

1 The MAX and MIN marks are indicated on the clutch fluid reservoir filler neck. The fluid level must be kept within 5.0 mm of the MAX level mark.

2 If topping-up is necessary, first wipe clean the area around the filler cap to prevent dirt entering the hydraulic system.

3 Carefully prise off the cap using your fingers, and inspect the fluid and filler neck. If the fluid is dirty the hydraulic system should be drained and refilled (see Chapter 6).

4 Carefully add fluid, taking care not to spill it onto the surrounding components. Use only the specified fluid. After topping-up to the correct level, securely refit the cap and wipe off any spilt fluid. Note the special rubber float in the filler neck.

Brake fluid level

Warning:
● **Brake fluid can harm your eyes and damage painted surfaces, so use extreme caution when handling and pouring it.**
● **Do not use fluid that has been standing open for some time, as it absorbs moisture from the air, which can cause a dangerous loss of braking effectiveness.**

HAYNES HINT
• **Make sure that your car is on level ground.**
• **The fluid level in the reservoir will drop slightly as the brake pads wear down, but the fluid level must never be allowed to drop below the "MIN" mark.**

Safety First!

● If the reservoir requires repeated topping-up this is an indication of a fluid leak somewhere in the system, which should be investigated immediately.

● If a leak is suspected, the car should not be driven until the braking system has been checked. Never take any risks where brakes are concerned.

1 The MAX and MIN marks are indicated on the brake fluid reservoir filler neck. The fluid level must be kept within 10.0 mm of the MAX level mark.

2 If topping-up is necessary, first wipe clean the area around the filler cap to prevent dirt entering the hydraulic system.

3 Carefully prise off the cap using your fingers, and inspect the fluid and filler neck. If the fluid is dirty the hydraulic system should be drained and refilled (see Chapter 6).

4 Carefully add fluid, taking care not to spill it onto the surrounding components. Use only the specified fluid; mixing different types can cause damage to the system. After topping-up to the correct level, securely refit the cap and wipe off any spilt fluid.

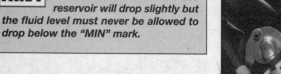

Power steering fluid level

Before you start:

✔ Park the vehicle on level ground.
✔ Set the steering wheel straight-ahead.
✔ The engine should be turned off.

 HAYNES HiNT *For the check to be accurate, the steering must not be turned once the engine has been stopped.*

Safety First!

● The need for frequent topping-up indicates a leak, which should be investigated immediately.

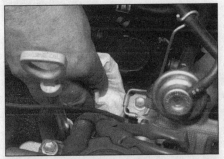

1 On models with the 4A-FE and 7A-FE engines, the power steering fluid reservoir is located behind the right-hand end of the engine. Wipe clean the area around the reservoir filler neck and unscrew the filler cap/dipstick from the reservoir.

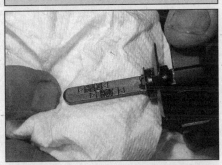

2 Wipe clean the dipstick (models with the 4A-FE and 7A-FE engines) then refit it and remove it again. When the engine is cold, the fluid level should be within the COLD range on the dipstick; if it is hot the level should be within the HOT range on the dipstick.

3 When topping-up the power steering fluid level (models with the 4A-FE and 7A-FE engines), use the specified type of fluid and do not overfill the reservoir. When the level is correct, securely refit the cap.

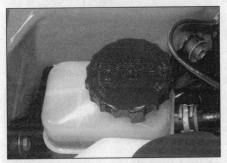

4 On models with the 3S-FE and 3S-GE engines, the reservoir is located on the right-hand side of the engine compartment behind the washer fluid reservoir.

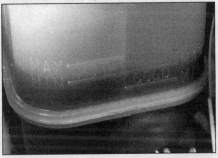

5 On models with the 3S-FE and 3S-GE engines, the level marks are on the side of the power steering fluid reservoir, and the fluid level can be seen through the translucent body. With the engine cold, the fluid level should be within the COLD range on the reservoir; if it is hot the level should be within the HOT range.

6 If topping-up is necessary (models with the 3S-FE and 3S-GE engines), first wipe clean the area around the filler cap to prevent dirt entering the hydraulic system, then unscrew and remove the cap. Use the specified type of fluid and do not overfill the reservoir. When the level is correct, screw on the cap securely.

Screen washer fluid level

Screenwash additives not only keep the winscreen clean during foul weather, they also prevent the washer system freezing in cold weather - which is when you are likely to need it most. Don't top up using plain water as the screenwash will become too diluted, and will freeze during cold weather.

 Warning: On no account use coolant antifreeze in the washer system - this could discolour or damage paintwork.

1 The screen washer fluid reservoir is located in the right-hand side of the engine compartment. The fluid level can be seen through the reservoir body. If topping-up is necessary, open the cap.

2 When topping-up the reservoir, add a screenwash additive in the quantities recommended on the bottle.

Tyre condition and pressure

It is very important that tyres are in good condition, and at the correct pressure - having a tyre failure at any speed is highly dangerous. Tyre wear is influenced by driving style - harsh braking and acceleration, or fast cornering, will all produce more rapid tyre wear. As a general rule, the front tyres wear out faster than the rears. Interchanging the tyres from front to rear ("rotating" the tyres) may result in more even wear. However, if this is completely effective, you may have the expense of replacing all four tyres at once! Remove any nails or stones embedded in the tread before they penetrate the tyre to cause deflation. If removal of a nail does reveal that the tyre has been punctured, refit the nail so that its point of penetration is marked. Then immediately change the wheel, and have the tyre repaired by a tyre dealer.

Regularly check the tyres for damage in the form of cuts or bulges, especially in the sidewalls. Periodically remove the wheels, and clean any dirt or mud from the inside and outside surfaces. Examine the wheel rims for signs of rusting, corrosion or other damage. Light alloy wheels are easily damaged by "kerbing" whilst parking; steel wheels may also become dented or buckled. A new wheel is very often the only way to overcome severe damage.

New tyres should be balanced when they are fitted, but it may become necessary to re-balance them as they wear, or if the balance weights fitted to the wheel rim should fall off. Unbalanced tyres will wear more quickly, as will the steering and suspension components. Wheel imbalance is normally signified by vibration, particularly at a certain speed (typically around 50 mph). If this vibration is felt only through the steering, then it is likely that just the front wheels need balancing. If, however, the vibration is felt through the whole car, the rear wheels could be out of balance. Wheel balancing should be carried out by a tyre dealer or garage.

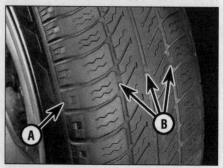

1 Tread Depth - visual check
The original tyres have tread wear safety bands (B), which will appear when the tread depth reaches approximately 1.6 mm. The band positions are indicated by a triangular mark on the tyre sidewall (A).

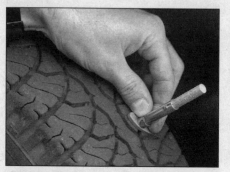

2 Tread Depth - manual check
Alternatively, tread wear can be monitored with a simple, inexpensive device known as a tread depth indicator gauge.

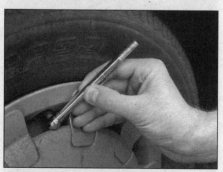

3 Tyre Pressure Check
Check the tyre pressures regularly with the tyres cold. Do not adjust the tyre pressures immediately after the vehicle has been used, or an inaccurate setting will result.

Tyre tread wear patterns

Shoulder Wear

Underinflation (wear on both sides)
Under-inflation will cause overheating of the tyre, because the tyre will flex too much, and the tread will not sit correctly on the road surface. This will cause a loss of grip and excessive wear, not to mention the danger of sudden tyre failure due to heat build-up.
Check and adjust pressures
Incorrect wheel camber (wear on one side)
Repair or renew suspension parts
Hard cornering
Reduce speed!

Centre Wear

Overinflation
Over-inflation will cause rapid wear of the centre part of the tyre tread, coupled with reduced grip, harsher ride, and the danger of shock damage occurring in the tyre casing.
Check and adjust pressures

If you sometimes have to inflate your car's tyres to the higher pressures specified for maximum load or sustained high speed, don't forget to reduce the pressures to normal afterwards.

Uneven Wear

Front tyres may wear unevenly as a result of wheel misalignment. Most tyre dealers and garages can check and adjust the wheel alignment (or "tracking") for a modest charge.
Incorrect camber or castor
Repair or renew suspension parts
Malfunctioning suspension
Repair or renew suspension parts
Unbalanced wheel
Balance tyres
Incorrect toe setting
Adjust front wheel alignment
Note: *The feathered edge of the tread which typifies toe wear is best checked by feel.*

Wiper blades

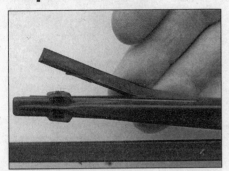

1 Check the condition of the wiper blades; if they are cracked or show any signs of deterioration, or if the glass swept area is smeared, renew them. Wiper blades should be renewed annually.

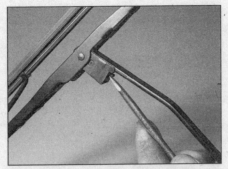

2 To remove a windscreen wiper blade. pull the arm fully away from the screen until it locks. Swivel the blade through 90°, and depress the locking tab with a screwdriver or your fingers.

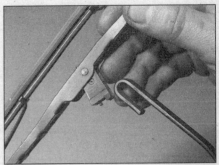

3 Slide the wiper blade out of the hooked end of the arm, then feed the arm through the hole in the blade.

Battery

Caution: *Before carrying out any work on the vehicle battery, read the precautions given in "Safety first" at the start of this manual.*

✔ Make sure that the battery tray is in good condition, and that the clamp is tight. Corrosion on the tray, retaining clamp and the battery itself can be removed with a solution of water and baking soda. Thoroughly rinse all cleaned areas with water. Any metal parts damaged by corrosion should be covered with a zinc-based primer, then painted.

✔ Periodically (approximately every three months), check the charge condition of the battery as described in Chapter 5A.

✔ If the battery is flat, and you need to jump start your vehicle, see *Roadside Repairs*.

1 The battery is located in the front left-hand side of the engine compartment. The exterior of the battery should be inspected periodically for damage such as a cracked case or cover.

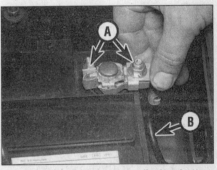

2 Check the tightness of the battery clamps (A) to ensure good electrical connections. You should not be able to move them. Also check each cable (B) for cracks and frayed conductors.

Battery corrosion can be kept to a minimum by applying a layer of petroleum jelly to the clamps and terminals after they are reconnected.

3 If corrosion (white, fluffy deposits) is evident, remove the cables from the battery terminals, clean them with a small wire brush, then refit them. Automotive stores sell a tool for cleaning the battery post . . .

4 . . . as well as the battery cable clamps

Bulbs and fuses

✔ Check all external lights and the horn. Refer to the appropriate Sections of Chapter 12 for details if any of the circuits are found to be inoperative.

✔ Visually check all accessible wiring connectors, harnesses and retaining clips for security, and for signs of chafing or damage.

 HAYNES HiNT *If you need to check your brake lights and indicators unaided, back up to a wall or garage door and operate the lights. The reflected light should show if they are working properly.*

1 If a single indicator light, stop light or headlight has failed, it is likely that a bulb has blown and will need to be replaced. Refer to Chapter 12 for details. If both stop lights have failed, it is possible that the switch has failed (see Chapter 9).

2 If more than one indicator light or tail light has failed it is likely that either a fuse has blown or that there is a fault in the circuit (see Chapter 12). The fuses are located behind a panel on the facia panel and in a fusebox located in the engine compartment (refer to Chapter 12).

3 To replace a fuse, pull it out using the plastic tweezers provided, and fit a new fuse of the correct rating (see Chapter 12). If the fuse blows again, it is important that you find out why - a complete checking procedure is given in Chapter 12.

Tyre pressures (cold) - bar/psi

	Front	Rear
Pressures with 1 to 4 passengers*:		
175/70R14 tyres	2.2/32	2.1/30
185/65R14 86H tyres	2.0/29	1.9/28
185/65R14 86V tyres	2.2/32	2.0/29
195/60 R15 tyres	2.1/30	1.9/28
Pressures with full load*:		
175/70R14 tyres	2.3/33	2.3/33
185/65R14 86H tyres	2.2/32	2.2/32
185/65R14 86V tyres	2.2/32	2.2/32
195/60 R15 tyres	2.1/30	2.1/30

*Note: Pressures apply only to original equipment tyres at speeds of up to 100 mph and may vary if any other make or type is fitted; check with the tyre manufacturer or supplier for correct pressures, if necessary. For pressures at higher speeds, consult the vehicle's handbook or your Toyota dealer.

Lubricants and fluids

Component or system	Lubricant type/specification
Engine	Multigrade engine oil, viscosity SAE 15W/40, 10W/30 or 20W/50 to API SG or better (Duckhams QXR, QS, Hypergrade Plus, Hypergrade or 10W/40 Motor Oil)
Cooling system	Ethylene glycol-based antifreeze and soft water (Duckhams Antifreeze and Summer Coolant)
Clutch system	Hydraulic fluid to SAE J1703F or DOT 4 (Duckhams Universal Brake and Clutch Fluid)
Manual gearbox	Hypoid gear oil, viscosity SAE 75W/90 gear oil to API GL-3 (Duckhams Hypoid 75W/90S)
Automatic transmission	Dexron type II automatic transmission fluid (ATF) (Duckhams Uni-Matic)
Braking system	Hydraulic fluid to SAE J1703F or DOT 4 (Duckhams Universal Brake and Clutch Fluid)
Power steering	Dexron type II automatic transmission fluid (ATF) (Duckhams Uni-Matic)

Choosing your engine oil

Oils perform vital tasks in all engines. The higher the engine's performance, the greater the demand on lubricants to minimise wear as well as optimise power and economy. Duckhams tailors lubricants to the highest technical standards, meeting and exceeding the demands of all modern engines.

HOW ENGINE OIL WORKS

• Beating friction

Without oil, the surfaces inside your engine which rub together will heat, fuse and quickly cause engine seizure. Oil, and its special additives, forms a molecular barrier between moving parts, to stop wear and minimise heat build-up.

• Cooling hot spots

Oil cools parts that the engine's water-based coolant cannot reach, bathing the combustion chamber and pistons, where temperatures may exceed 1000°C. The oil assists in transferring the heat to the engine cooling system. Heat in the oil is also lost by air flow over the sump, and via any auxiliary oil cooler.

• Cleaning the inner engine

Oil washes away combustion by-products (mainly carbon) on pistons and cylinders, transporting them to the oil filter, and holding the smallest particles in suspension until they are flushed out by an oil change. Duckhams oils undergo extensive tests in the laboratory, and on the road.

Note: It is antisocial and illegal to dump oil down the drain. To find the location of your local oil recycling bank, call this number free.

OIL CARE
FOLLOW THE CODE
OIL BANK LINE
0800 66 33 66

Engine oil types

Mineral oils are the "traditional" oils, generally suited to older engines and cars not used in harsh conditions. *Duckhams Hypergrade Plus* and *Hypergrade* are well suited for use in most popular family cars.

Diesel oils such as *Duckhams Diesel* are specially formulated for Diesel engines, including turbocharged models and 4x4s.

Synthetic oils are the state-of-the-art in lubricants, offering ultimate protection, but at a fairly high price. One such is *Duckhams QS*, for use in ultra-high performance engines.

Semi-synthetic oils offer high performance engine protection, but at less cost than full synthetic oils. *Duckhams QXR* is an ideal choice for hot hatches and hard-driven cars.

For help with technical queries on lubricants, call Duckhams Oils on 0181 290 8207

Chapter 1
Routine maintenance and servicing

Contents

Degrees of difficulty

Easy, suitable for novice with little experience	**Fairly easy,** suitable for beginner with some experience	**Fairly difficult,** suitable for competent DIY mechanic	**Difficult,** suitable for experienced DIY mechanic	**Very difficult,** suitable for expert DIY or professional

Lubricants and fluids

Refer to page 0•17 of *"Weekly checks"*

Capacities

Engine oil

	Excluding filter	Including filter
1587 cc (4A-FE) engines	2.8 litres	3.0 litres
1762 cc (7A-FE) engines	3.5 litres	3.7 litres
1998 cc (3S-FE) engines:		
Manual transmission models	4.2 litres	4.6 litres
Automatic transmission models	4.1 litres	4.5 litres
1998 cc (3S-GE) engines	4.0 litres	4.5 litres

Cooling system

1587 cc (4A-FE) engines	5.4 litres
1762 cc (7A-FE) engines	5.6 litres
1998 cc (3S-FE) engines:	
Manual transmission models	6.5 litres
Automatic transmission models	6.6 litres
1998 cc (3S-GE) engines	6.6 litres

Transmission

Manual transmission	2.6 litres
Automatic transmission:	
Drain and refill (approximate)	3.1 litres
From dry:	
4A-FE engine models:	
A240E transmissions	7.2 litres
A245E transmissions	7.6 litres
3S-FE engine models	8.0 litres

Fuel tank

All models	60 litres

Engine

Oil filter	Champion C138

Valve clearances (cold engine):

	Inlet	Exhaust
4A-FE and 7A-FE engines	0.15 to 0.25 mm	0.25 to 0.35 mm
3S-FE engines	0.19 to 0.29 mm	0.28 to 0.38 mm
3S-GE engines	0.15 to 0.25 mm	0.20 to 0.30 mm

Cooling system

Antifreeze mixture:

28% antifreeze	Protection down to -15°C
50% antifreeze	Protection down to -30°C

Note: *Refer to antifreeze manufacturer for latest recommendations.*

Fuel system

Air filter element	Champion U565
Fuel filter	Champion L149

Idle speed and mixture settings

Idle speed*

4A-FE engines:

Manual transmission models	750 ± 50 rpm
Automatic transmission models	800 ± 50 rpm
7A-FE engines	700 ± 50 rpm
3S-FE engine	700 ± 50 rpm
3S-GE engine	800 ± 50 rpm

Mixture*

All models - CO concentration	0 to 0.5%

* Non-adjustable - for checking purposes only

Ignition system

Ignition timing .... Refer to Chapter 5B

Spark plugs*:

	Champion type	Electrode gap
1587 cc (4A-FE) engines:		
Conventional engines	RC7YCC4	1.1 mm
Lean-burn engines	RC87PYX (Platinum tipped)	1.2 mm
1762 cc (7A-FE) engines	RC87PYX (Platinum tipped)	1.2 mm
1998 cc (3S-FE and 3S-GE) engines	RC6YCC	1.0 mm

Spark plug HT lead resistances .... 25 k ohms per HT lead maximum

Information on spark plug types and electrode gaps is as recommended by Champion Spark Plug. Where alternative types are used, refer to their manufacturer's recommendations.

Brakes

Brake pad lining minimum thickness .... 1.0 mm
Brake shoe friction material minimum thickness .... 1.0 mm
Handbrake lever travel .... 4 to 7 clicks of ratchet
Front brake disc minimum thickness:
    All except 3S-FE engine models .... 23.0 mm
    3S-FE engine models .... 26.0 mm
Rear brake disc minimum thickness .... 9.0 mm

Tyre pressures

Refer to page 0•16 of "Weekly checks"

Auxiliary drivebelt deflection

4A-FE and 7A-FE engines:
    Alternator/water pump drivebelt .... 11.5 to 13.5 mm
    Air conditioning compressor drivebelt .... 8.5 to 9.5 mm
    Power steering pump drivebelt .... 6.0 to 8.0 mm
3S-FE engine:
    Alternator drivebelt .... 13.0 to 17.0 mm
    Alternator/air conditioning compressor drivebelt .... 9.0 to 11.0 mm
    Power steering pump drivebelt .... 10.0 to 13.0 mm
3S-GE engine:
    Alternator drivebelt .... 12.0 to 18.0 mm
    Power steering pump drivebelt .... 10.0 to 13.0 mm
    Alternator/air conditioning compressor drivebelt .... 13.0 to 16.0 mm

Torque wrench settings

	Nm	lbf ft
Roadwheel nuts	103	76
Spark plugs	18	13
Sump drain plug	34	25
Manual transmission oil drain and filler plugs	49	36
Automatic transmission fluid drain plug	17	13
Alternator to mounting bracket bolts	54	40
Alternator to adjustment link:		
4A-FE and 7A-FE engines	19	14
3S-FE and 3S-GE engines	27	20
Camshaft cover:		
4A-FE and 7A-FE engines	6	4
3S-FE and 3S-GE engines	44	32

Notes

The maintenance intervals in this manual are provided with the assumption that you, not the dealer, will be carrying out the work. These are the minimum maintenance intervals recommended by us for vehicles driven daily. If you wish to keep your vehicle in peak condition at all times, you may wish to perform some of these procedures more often. We encourage frequent maintenance, because it enhances the efficiency, performance and resale value of your vehicle.

When the vehicle is new, it should be serviced by a factory-authorised dealer service department, in order to preserve the factory warranty.

It should be noted that for the 1993 model year, the service time/mileage intervals were extended by the manufacturer to the periods shown in this schedule. Although these intervals can be applied retrospectively, owners of earlier vehicles may notice a discrepancy between this schedule and the one shown in the Service Guide supplied with the vehicle.

Every 250 miles (400 km) or weekly
☐ Refer to "*Weekly checks*"

Every 4500 miles (7500 km) or 6 months - whichever comes first
Note: *Frequent oil and filter changes are good for the engine. We recommend changing the oil at the mileage specified here, or at least twice a year if the mileage covered is less.*
☐ Renew the engine oil and filter (Section 3)

Every 9000 miles (15 000 km) or 6 months - whichever comes first
☐ Check manual transmission oil level (Section 4)
☐ Check automatic transmission fluid level (Section 5)
☐ Check engine coolant strength (Section 6)
☐ Check the condition of the auxiliary drivebelt(s), and renew if necessary (Section 7)
☐ Check the idle speed and CO content (Section 8)
☐ Check the spark plugs and ignition system (Section 9)
☐ Check the evaporative loss emission control check valve (Section 10)
☐ Clean the air filter element (Section 11)
☐ Hose and fluid leak check (Section 12)
☐ Check and adjust the brake pedal (Section 13)
☐ Check the brake vacuum servo unit (Section 14)
☐ Check and adjust the handbrake (Section 15)
☐ Check the front and (where applicable) rear brake pads and discs and renew if necessary* (Section 16)
☐ Check the rear brake shoes and drums* (Section 17)
☐ Check the exhaust system (Section 18)
☐ Check the steering and suspension components for condition and security* (Section 19)
☐ Check the condition of the driveshaft rubber gaiters and CV joints* (Section 20)
☐ Check the battery (Section 21)
☐ Check the tightness of the roadwheel nuts (Section 22)
☐ Wheel alignment check (Section 23)
☐ Check the headlight beam alignment (Section 24)
☐ Lubricate door and bonnet hinges (Section 25)
☐ Adjust the washer jets (Section 26)
☐ Check the condition, operation and security of all seat belts (Section 27)
☐ Check the body for corrosion (Section 28)
☐ Renew the battery in the alarm remote control (Section 29)
☐ Carry out a road test (Section 30)
This should be performed more frequently if the vehicle is used in Severe Conditions (ie towing a trailer, repeated short distances, dusty conditions etc).

Every 18 000 miles (30 000 km) or 12 months - whichever comes first
In addition to the items listed above, carry out the following:
☐ Renew the spark plugs, except engines fitted with platinum-tipped spark plugs (Section 31)
☐ Renew the fuel filter* (Section 32)
☐ Renew the air filter element* (Section 33)
This should be performed more frequently if the vehicle is used in Severe Conditions (ie towing a trailer, repeated short distances, dusty conditions etc).

Every 24 months
In addition to the items listed above, carry out the following:
☐ Renew the brake fluid (Section 34)

Every 36 000 miles (60 000 km)
In addition to the items listed above, carry out the following:
☐ Change the transmission oil/fluid* (Section 35)
☐ Renew the engine coolant (Section 36)
This should be performed more frequently if the vehicle is used in Severe Conditions (ie towing a trailer, repeated short distances, dusty conditions etc).

Every 54 000 miles (90 000 km)
In addition to the items listed above, carry out the following:
☐ Check and adjust the valve clearances (Section 37)

Every 63 000 miles (105 000 km)
In addition to the items listed above, carry out the following:
☐ Renew the spark plugs, engines fitted with platinum-tipped spark plugs only (Section 31)
☐ Renew the timing belt (Section 38)

Underbonnet view of a 1.6 litre 4A-FE engine model with manual transmission

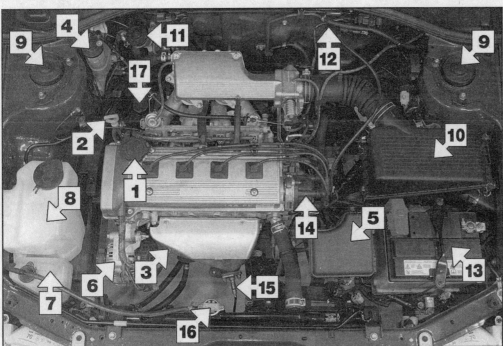

1 Engine oil filler cap
2 Engine oil dipstick
3 Oil filter
4 Brake master cylinder fluid reservoir
5 Engine compartment fuse and relay box
6 Alternator
7 Coolant expansion tank
8 Windscreen/tailgate washer fluid reservoir
9 Suspension strut upper mounting
10 Air cleaner housing
11 Clutch master cylinder fluid reservoir
12 Ignition HT coil
13 Battery
14 Distributor
15 Exhaust gas lean mixture sensor
16 Radiator pressure cap
17 Power steering pump

Underbonnet view of a 2.0 litre 3S-FE engine model with automatic transmission

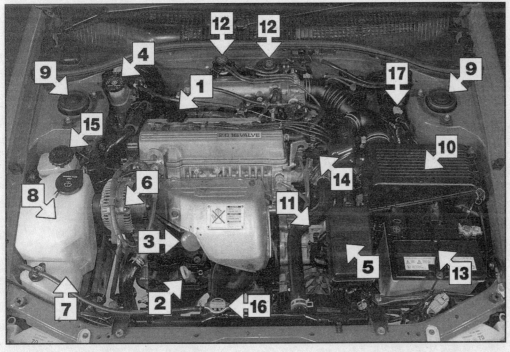

1 Engine oil filler cap
2 Engine oil dipstick
3 Oil filter
4 Brake master cylinder fluid reservoir
5 Engine compartment fuse and relay box
6 Alternator
7 Coolant expansion tank
8 Windscreen/tailgate washer fluid reservoir
9 Suspension strut upper mounting
10 Air cleaner housing
11 Automatic transmission fluid level dipstick
12 EGR valve and modulator
13 Battery
14 Distributor (with internal ignition HT coil)
15 Power steering fluid reservoir
16 Radiator pressure cap
17 Ignition igniter module

1

Underbonnet view of a 2.0 litre 3S-GE engine model with manual transmission

1 Engine oil filler cap
2 Engine oil dipstick
3 Oil filter
4 Brake master cylinder fluid reservoir
5 Engine compartment fuse and relay box
6 Alternator
7 Coolant expansion tank
8 Windscreen/tailgate washer fluid reservoir
9 Suspension strut upper mounting
10 Air cleaner housing
11 Clutch master cylinder fluid reservoir
12 Ignition HT coil
13 Battery
14 Radiator pressure cap

Front underbody view of a 1.6 litre 4A-FE engine model with manual transmission

1 Sump drain plug
2 Alternator
3 Exhaust front downpipe
4 Exhaust gas sensor
5 Radiator bottom hose
6 Manual transmission
7 Steering track rod
8 Front suspension lower arm
9 Front suspension subframe
10 Engine compartment longitudinal member
11 Driveshaft
12 Exhaust system intermediate section

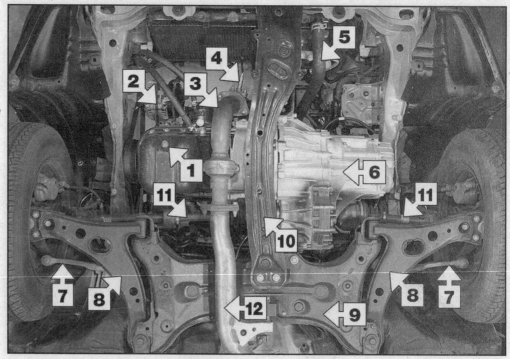

Front underbody view of a 2.0 litre 3S-FE engine model with automatic transmission

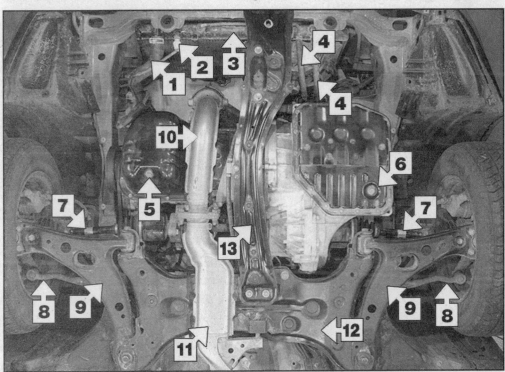

1 Radiator bottom hose
2 Cooling fan temperature switch
3 Radiator
4 Automatic transmission fluid cooler hoses
5 Sump drain plug
6 Automatic transmission fluid drain plug
7 Driveshaft
8 Steering track rod
9 Front suspension lower arm
10 Exhaust front downpipe
11 Exhaust system intermediate section
12 Front suspension subframe
13 Engine/transmission longitudinal crossmember

Rear underbody view (1.6 litre model shown - other models similar)

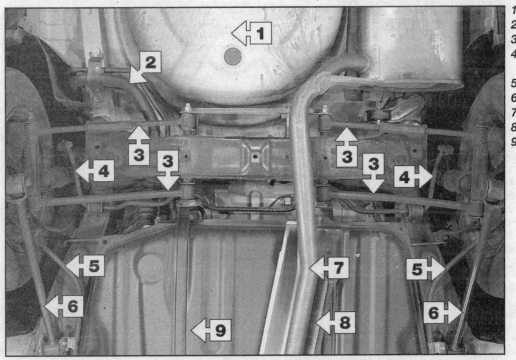

1 Spare wheel well
2 Fuel tank filler hose
3 Rear suspension lower arms
4 Rear suspension strut/shock absorber
5 Handbrake cables
6 Rear suspension radius rod
7 Exhaust tailpipe and silencer
8 Exhaust heat shield
9 Fuel tank

1 Introduction

1 This Chapter is designed to help the home mechanic maintain his/her vehicle for safety, economy, long life and peak performance.

2 The Chapter contains a master maintenance schedule, and Sections dealing specifically with each task in the schedule. Visual checks, adjustments, component renewal and other helpful items are included. Refer to the accompanying illustrations of the engine compartment and the underside of the vehicle for the locations of the various components.

3 Servicing your vehicle in accordance with the mileage/time maintenance schedule and the following Sections will provide a planned maintenance programme, which should result in a long and reliable service life. This is a comprehensive plan, so maintaining some items but not others at the specified service intervals, will not produce the same results.

4 As you service your vehicle, you will discover that many of the procedures can - and should - be grouped together, because of the particular procedure being performed, or because of the proximity of two otherwise-unrelated components to one another. For example, if the vehicle is raised for any reason, the exhaust can be inspected at the same time as the suspension and steering components.

5 The first step in this maintenance programme is to prepare yourself before the actual work begins. Read through all the Sections relevant to the work to be carried out, then make a list and gather all the parts and tools required. If a problem is encountered, seek advice from a parts specialist, or a dealer service department.

2 Intensive maintenance

1 If, from the time the vehicle is new, the routine maintenance schedule is followed closely, and frequent checks are made of fluid levels and high-wear items, as suggested throughout this manual, the engine will be kept in relatively good running condition, and the need for additional work will be minimised.

2 It is possible that there will be times when the engine is running poorly due to the lack of regular maintenance. This is even more likely if a used vehicle, which has not received regular and frequent maintenance checks, is purchased. In such cases, additional work may need to be carried out, outside of the regular maintenance intervals.

3 If engine wear is suspected, a compression test (refer to Chapter 2A) will provide valuable information regarding the overall performance of the main internal components. Such a test can be used as a basis to decide on the extent of the work to be carried out. If, for example, a compression test indicates serious internal engine wear, conventional maintenance as described in this Chapter will not greatly improve the performance of the engine, and may prove a waste of time and money, unless extensive overhaul work is carried out first.

4 The following operations are those most often required to improve the performance of a generally poor-running engine:

Primary operations

a) Clean, inspect and test the battery ("Weekly checks", Section 21 and Chapter 5A).
b) Check all the engine-related fluids ("Weekly checks").
c) Check the condition and tension of the auxiliary drivebelts (Section 7).
d) Renew the spark plugs (Section 31).
e) Inspect the ignition HT leads (Section 9).
f) Check the condition of the air filter, and renew if necessary (Section 11).
g) Check the fuel filter (Section 32).
h) Check the condition of all hoses, and check for fluid leaks (Section 12).
i) Check the exhaust gas emissions (Section 8).

5 If the above operations do not prove fully effective, carry out the following secondary operations:

Secondary operations

All items listed under Primary operations, plus the following:

a) Check the charging system (Chapter 5A).
b) Check the ignition system (Chapter 5B).
c) Check the fuel system (Chapter 4A and 4B).
d) Renew the ignition HT leads (Section 9 and Chapter 5B).

Every 4500 miles (7500 km) or 6 months

3 Engine oil and filter renewal

1 Frequent oil and filter changes are the most important preventative maintenance procedures which can be undertaken by the DIY owner. As engine oil ages, it becomes diluted and contaminated, which leads to premature engine wear.

2 Before starting this procedure, gather together all the necessary tools and materials. Also make sure that you have plenty of clean rags and newspapers handy, to mop up any spills. Ideally, the engine oil should be warm, as it will drain better, and more built-up sludge will be removed with it. Take care, however, not to touch the exhaust or any other hot parts of the engine when working under the vehicle. To avoid any possibility of scalding, and to protect yourself from possible skin irritants and other harmful contaminants in used engine oils, it is advisable to wear gloves when carrying out this work. Access to the underside of the vehicle will be greatly improved if it can be raised on a lift, driven onto ramps, or jacked up and supported on axle stands (see *Jacking and Vehicle Support*). Whichever method is chosen, make sure that the vehicle remains level or, if it is at an angle, that the drain plug is at the lowest point.

3 Remove the oil filler cap from the engine camshaft cover (twist it anti-clockwise and withdraw it) **(see illustration)**.

4 Using a spanner, or preferably a suitable socket and bar, slacken the drain plug about half a turn **(see illustration)**. Position the draining container under the drain plug, then remove the plug completely **(see Haynes Hint)**. Recover the sealing ring from the drain plug.

HAYNES HINT *Keep the drain plug pressed into the sump while unscrewing it by hand the last couple of turns. As the plug releases, move it away sharply so the stream of oil issuing from the sump runs into the container, not up your sleeve!*

3.3 Removing the oil filler cap (4A-FE engines)

3.4 Sump drain plug (4A-FE engines)

3.7 Oil filter on the 3S-FE engines

3.9 Using a chain strap to remove the oil filter (4A-FE engines)

3.11a Apply a light coating of clean engine oil to the sealing ring on the new filter

5 Allow some time for the oil to drain, noting that it may be necessary to reposition the container as the oil flow slows to a trickle.

6 After all the oil has drained, wipe the drain plug and the sealing washer with a clean rag. Examine the condition of the sealing washer - renew it if it shows signs of scoring or other damage which may prevent an oil-tight seal. Clean the area around the drain plug opening, and refit the plug complete with the washer. Tighten the plug securely - preferably to the specified torque, using a torque wrench.

7 The oil filter is located at the front right-hand side of the cylinder block - access is most easily obtained through the top of the engine compartment **(see illustration)**.

8 Move the container under the oil filter.

9 Use an oil filter removal tool (if required) to slacken the filter initially, then unscrew it by hand the rest of the way **(see illustration)**. Empty the oil from the old filter into the container.

10 Use a clean rag to remove all oil, dirt and sludge from the filter sealing area on the engine. Check the old filter to make sure that the rubber sealing ring has not stuck to the engine. If it has, carefully remove it.

11 Apply a light coating of clean engine oil to the sealing ring on the new filter, then screw the filter into position on the engine. Lightly tighten the filter until its sealing ring contacts the block, then tighten it through a further two-thirds of a turn **(see illustrations)**.

12 Remove the old oil and all tools from under the vehicle then, if applicable, lower the vehicle to the ground.

13 Fill the engine through the filler in the camshaft cover, using the correct grade and type of oil (refer to *"Weekly checks"* for details of topping-up). Pour in half the specified quantity of oil first, then wait a few minutes for the oil to drain into the sump. Continue to add oil, a small quantity at a time, until the level is up to the lower mark on the dipstick. Adding a further 1.0 litre will bring the level up to the upper mark on the dipstick.

14 Start the engine and run it for a few minutes, while checking for leaks around the oil filter seal and the sump drain plug. Note that there may be a delay of a few seconds before the low oil pressure warning light goes out when the engine is first started, as the oil circulates through the new oil filter and the engine oil galleries before the pressure builds

3.11b Screw on the new filter by hand

up. Do not run the engine above idle speed while the warning light is on.

15 Stop the engine, and wait a few minutes for the oil to settle in the sump once more. With the new oil circulated and the filter now completely full, recheck the level on the dipstick, and add more oil as necessary.

16 Dispose of the used engine oil safely, with reference to *General repair procedures* in the Reference Section at the end of this manual.

Every 9000 miles (15 000 km) or 6 months

4 Manual transmission oil level check

1 Park the car on a level surface. The oil level must be checked before the car is driven, or at least 5 minutes after the engine has been switched off. If the oil is checked immediately after driving the car, some of the oil will remain distributed around the transmission components, resulting in an inaccurate level reading. To improve access, position the car over an inspection pit, or raise the car off the ground and position it on axle stands, making sure the vehicle remains level to the ground.

2 Wipe clean the area around the filler/level plug, which is on the front face of the transmission. Unscrew the plug and clean it **(see illustration)**.

3 Check the oil level with your finger, or by inserting a home-made dipstick made from a short length of wire bent to shape. The oil

level should be no more than 5.0 mm below the lower edge of the filler/level hole. A certain amount of oil may have gathered behind the filler/level plug and will often trickle out when it is removed; this does **not** necessarily indicate that the level is correct. To ensure that a true level is established, wait until the

initial trickle has stopped, then add oil as necessary until a trickle of new oil can be seen emerging. The level will be correct when the flow ceases; use only good-quality oil of the specified type **(see illustration)**.

4 On completion refit the filler/level plug and tighten to the specified torque.

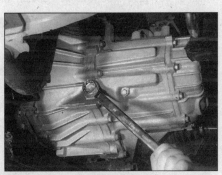

4.2 Unscrewing the filler/level plug from the front face of the transmission

4.3 Topping-up the manual transmission oil level

1

5.4 Withdraw the automatic transmission fluid dipstick from its tube

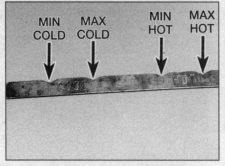

5.6 Automatic transmission fluid level markings on the dipstick

5.7 Topping up the automatic transmission fluid through the dipstick tube

5 Automatic transmission fluid level check

1 The level of the automatic transmission fluid should be carefully maintained. Low fluid level can lead to slipping or loss of drive, while overfilling can cause foaming, loss of fluid and transmission damage.

2 The transmission fluid level should only be checked when the transmission is hot (at its normal operating temperature). If the vehicle has just been driven over 10 miles (15 miles in a cold climate), and the fluid temperature is 160 to 175°F, the transmission is hot.

Caution: If the vehicle has just been driven for a long time at high speed or in city traffic in hot weather, or if it has been pulling a trailer, an accurate fluid level reading cannot be obtained. In these circumstances, allow the fluid to cool down for about 30 minutes.

3 Park the vehicle on level ground, apply the handbrake, and start the engine. While the engine is idling, depress the brake pedal and move the selector lever through all the gear positions, beginning and ending in P.

4 With the engine still idling, remove the dipstick from its tube **(see illustration)**. Note the condition and colour of the fluid on the dipstick.

5 Wipe the fluid from the dipstick with a clean rag, and re-insert it into the filler tube until the cap seats.

6 Pull the dipstick out again, and note the fluid level. The level should be between the two notches on the dipstick either side of the word HOT **(see illustration)**. Note that there are also two notches on the dipstick either side of the word COLD. If the car has not been driven for about five hours, and the fluid is at or below room temperature, the fluid should be between the two notches either side of the word COLD. Checking the level with the fluid cold should only be used for reference and the level must be checked again when the fluid is hot.

7 If the fluid level is near or below the appropriate lower notch, stop the engine, and add the specified automatic transmission fluid through the dipstick tube, using a clean funnel if necessary **(see illustration)**. It is important not to introduce dirt into the transmission when topping-up.

8 Add the fluid a little at a time, and keep checking the level as previously described until it is correct.

9 The need for regular topping-up of the transmission fluid indicates a leak, which should be found and rectified without delay.

10 The condition of the fluid should also be checked along with the level. If the fluid on the dipstick is black or a dark reddish-brown colour, or if it has a burned smell, the fluid should be changed. If you are in doubt about the condition of the fluid, purchase some new fluid, and compare the two for colour and smell.

6 Engine coolant level and strength check

 Warning: Wait until the engine is cold before starting this procedure.

1 The coolant antifreeze strength can be checked using a proprietary tester obtained from a car accessory shop. One type of tester acts similar to a battery hydrometer and has five small plastic balls within a clear tube - the coolant strength is determined by the number of balls floating in the coolant.

2 To use the tester, lift the cap from the coolant expansion tank and draw out some of the coolant. Hold the tester vertical and check the number of balls floating. After making the test disperse the coolant into the expansion tank and refit the cap.

7.2 Alternator and drivebelt (3S-FE engines without air conditioning)

3 If the strength of the coolant is low, drain the coolant and refill with the correct strength as described in Section 36.

4 Check the coolant level with reference to *"Weekly checks"*.

7 Auxiliary drivebelt(s) check and renewal

1 On 4A-FE and 7A-FE engines, two or three drivebelts are fitted. The main drivebelt drives the water pump and alternator from the crankshaft pulley. Where air conditioning is fitted, the compressor is driven by a separate drivebelt from the crankshaft pulley. Where power steering is fitted, a secondary drivebelt drives the pump from the water pump pulley.

2 On 3S-FE and 3S-GE engines, two drivebelts are fitted. The main drivebelt drives the alternator from the crankshaft pulley **(see illustration)**. On models with air conditioning the main drivebelt is longer and drives the air conditioning compressor in addition to the alternator. The power steering pump is driven by a separate drivebelt from the crankshaft pulley.

Checking the condition of the auxiliary drivebelts

3 For improved access to the auxiliary drivebelt on the right-hand side of the engine, remove the washer fluid reservoir as described in Chapter 12. If required the vehicle may be jacked up and supported on axle stands (see *Jacking and Vehicle Support*) and the right-hand roadwheel removed.

4 Using a socket and extension bar fitted to the crankshaft pulley bolt, rotate the crankshaft so that the entire length of each drivebelt can be examined. Examine the drivebelts for cracks, splitting, fraying or damage. Check also for signs of glazing (shiny patches) and for separation of the belt plies. Renew the belt if worn or damaged.

HAYNES HINT *Turning the engine will be much easier if the spark plugs are removed first (Section 31).*

5 If the condition of the belt is satisfactory, check the drivebelt tension as described below under the relevant sub-heading.

Alternator drivebelt (4A-FE and 7A-FE engines) - removal, refitting and tensioning

Removal

6 If not already done, proceed as described in paragraph 3.
7 Disconnect the battery negative (earth) lead (refer to Chapter 5A, Sections 1 and 3).
8 Slacken the alternator upper pivot bolt, then slacken the alternator lower adjusting lock bolt.
9 Back off the adjuster bolt (on the lower link bracket) to relieve the tension in the drivebelt, then slip the drivebelt from the pulleys.

Refitting

10 Fit the belt around the pulleys, ensuring that the belt is of the correct type if it is being renewed and is correctly engaged with the ribs on the pulley. Take up the slack in the belt by tightening the adjuster bolt. Tension the drivebelt as described in the following paragraphs.

Tensioning

11 If not already done, proceed as described in paragraph 3.
12 Correct tensioning of the drivebelt will ensure that it has a long life. Beware, however, of overtightening, as this can cause wear in the alternator or water pump bearings.
13 The belt tension is checked at the mid-point between the alternator and water pump pulleys on the upper belt run. Apply finger or thumb pressure by pressing down on the drivebelt, and check that it deflects by the amount given in the Specifications **(see illustration)**.
14 To adjust, with the upper pivot bolt and lower adjusting lock bolt loose, turn the adjuster bolt until the correct tension is achieved. Rotate the crankshaft a couple of times, recheck the tension, then securely tighten both the alternator mounting pivot and adjusting lock bolts.
15 Refit the washer fluid reservoir, and where removed refit the right-hand roadwheel and lower the vehicle to the ground.

7.13 Checking the tension of the alternator drivebelt (4A-FE and 7A-FE engines)

Alternator/air conditioning compressor drivebelt (3S-FE and 3S-GE engines) - removal, refitting and tensioning

Removal

16 If not already done, proceed as described in paragraph 3.
17 Disconnect the battery negative (earth) lead (refer to Chapter 5A, Sections 1 and 3).
18 On 3S-FE engines (with or without air conditioning), slacken the alternator upper pivot bolt, then slacken the alternator lower adjusting lock bolt. Back off the adjuster bolt (on the alternator bracket) to relieve the tension in the drivebelt, then slip the drivebelt from the pulleys.
19 On 3S-GE engines (with or without air conditioning), loosen the idler pulley lock bolt then back off the adjuster bolt (on the idler pulley bracket) to relieve the tension in the drivebelt, and slip the drivebelt from the pulleys. Note that on models without air conditioning, the idler pulley is ribbed to take the inner surface of the drivebelt, however on models with air conditioning the idler pulley is smooth to take the outer surface of the drivebelt.

Refitting

20 Fit the belt around the pulleys, ensuring that the belt is of the correct type if it is being renewed, and is correctly engaged with the ribs on the pulley. Take up the slack in the belt by tightening the adjuster bolt. Tension the drivebelt as described in the following paragraphs.

Tensioning

21 If not already done, proceed as described in paragraph 3.
22 Correct tensioning of the drivebelt will ensure that it has a long life. Beware, however, of overtightening, as this can cause wear in the alternator/compressor bearings.
23 The belt tension is checked at the mid-point between the alternator and crankshaft pulleys (except 3S-FE engines) or between the alternator and air conditioning compressor (3S-FE engines). Apply finger or thumb pressure by pressing on the drivebelt, and check that it deflects by the amount given in the Specifications.
24 To adjust, with the alternator or idler bolts loose, turn the adjuster bolt until the correct tension is achieved. Rotate the crankshaft a couple of times, recheck the tension, then securely tighten the alternator or idler bolts.
25 Refit the washer fluid reservoir, and where removed refit the right-hand roadwheel and lower the vehicle to the ground.

Air conditioning compressor drivebelt (4A-FE and 7A-FE engines)

26 If not already done, proceed as described in paragraph 3.
27 Remove the alternator drivebelt as described earlier in this Section.
28 Loosen the idler pulley bolt then back off the adjuster bolt (on the idler pulley bracket) to relieve the tension in the drivebelt, and slip the drivebelt from the pulleys.

Refitting

29 Fit the belt around the pulleys, ensuring that the belt is of the correct type if it is being renewed, and is correctly engaged with the ribs on the pulley. Take up the slack in the belt by tightening the adjuster bolt. Tension the drivebelt as described in the following paragraphs.

Tensioning

30 If not already done, proceed as described in paragraph 3.
31 Correct tensioning of the drivebelt will ensure that it has a long life. Beware, however, of overtightening, as this can cause wear in the compressor bearings.
32 The belt tension is checked at the mid-point between the compressor and crankshaft pulleys on the lower belt run. Apply finger or thumb pressure by pressing on the drivebelt, and check that it deflects by the amount given in the Specifications.
33 To adjust, with the idler pulley bolt loose, turn the adjuster bolt until the correct tension is achieved. Rotate the crankshaft a couple of times, recheck the tension, then securely tighten the idler pulley bolt.
34 Refit the washer fluid reservoir, and where removed refit the right-hand roadwheel and lower the vehicle to the ground.

Power steering pump drivebelt

35 If not already done, proceed as described in paragraph 3.
36 Disconnect the battery negative (earth) lead (see Chapter 5A, Sections 1 and 3). On 4A-FE and 3S-GE engines, remove the alternator drivebelt as described earlier in this Section.
37 Loosen the power steering pump pivot and adjuster lock bolts, then swivel the pump towards the engine and slip the drivebelt from the pulleys.

Refitting

38 Fit the belt around the pulleys, ensuring that the belt is of the correct type if it is being renewed, and is correctly engaged with the ribs on the pulley. Take up the slack in the belt by swivelling the pump away from the engine. Tension the drivebelt as described in the following paragraphs.

Tensioning

39 If not already done, proceed as described in paragraph 3.
40 Correct tensioning of the drivebelt will ensure that it has a long life. Beware, however, of overtightening, as this can cause wear in the power steering pump bearings.
41 The belt tension is checked at the mid-point between the pulleys on the upper belt run. Apply finger or thumb pressure by pressing on the drivebelt, and check that it deflects by the amount given in the Specifications.

1

42 To adjust, with the pump pivot bolt loose, swivel the pump away from the engine until the correct tension is achieved then tighten the adjuster lock bolt. Rotate the crankshaft a couple of times, then recheck the tension.

43 Refit the washer fluid reservoir, and where removed refit the right-hand roadwheel and lower the vehicle to the ground.

8 Idle speed and mixture check

Note: *A tachometer will be required to check the idle speed, and an exhaust gas analyser will be required to check the mixture.*

1 The following procedure is for *checking* the idle speed and mixture only. No adjustment is possible, and if the settings are incorrect, a diagnostic check should be carried out on the EFI system (see Chapter 4A and 4B).

2 Before checking the idle speed and mixture setting, always check first the following.
   a) *Check that the ignition timing is accurate (Chapter 5B).*
   b) *Check that the spark plugs are in good condition and correctly gapped (Sections 9 and 31 of this chapter).*
   c) *Check that the accelerator cable is correctly adjusted (Section 4A).*
   d) *Check that the crankcase breather hoses are secure, with no leaks or kinks (Chapter 4B).*
   e) *Check that the air cleaner filter element is clean and all air ducts correctly fitted (Section 11).*
   f) *Check that the exhaust system is in good condition (Section 18).*
   g) *If the engine is running very roughly, check the compression pressures as described in Chapter 2A.*

3 Turn off all electrical components including the air conditioning system (where fitted). On models fitted with power steering keep the front wheels pointing straight ahead during the checking and adjustment procedure. The check must be made with the cooling fan stopped and the transmission in neutral.

Idle speed

4 Connect a tachometer to the engine in accordance with the manufacturer's instructions.
Caution: Consult a dealer service department before connecting the tachometer - some tachometers may be incompatible with the types of ignition systems used on these vehicles.
5 Run the engine to normal operating temperature, then race the engine at 2500 rpm for approximately 90 seconds.
6 Check that the idle speed is within the limits given in the Specifications.
7 Stop the engine and disconnect the tachometer.

Mixture

8 Run the engine to normal operating temperature, then race the engine at 2500 rpm for approximately 180 seconds.
9 Allow the engine to idle, then connect the exhaust gas analyser probe in the exhaust tailpipe. Check that the CO content is within the limits given in the Specifications.
10 Stop the engine and remove the exhaust gas analyser.

9 Spark plug and ignition system check

 Warning: Voltages produced by an electronic ignition system are considerably higher than those produced by conventional ignition systems. Extreme care must be taken when working on the system with the ignition switched on. Persons with surgically-implanted cardiac pacemaker devices should keep well clear of the ignition circuits, components and test equipment.

Spark plug check

Note: *Standard spark plugs should be renewed at 18 000 miles, and platinum-tipped spark plugs should be renewed at 63 000 miles (see Section 31). The condition of the spark plugs over a period of time will reflect the general state of the engine; the following check will show up any problems with the engine which may require attention.*
1 Remove the spark plugs and check their condition with reference to Section 31.
2 Check each spark plug for excessive wear of the electrodes, and for damage to threads and insulators. If evident, refer to Section 31 for possible reasons.
3 Although Toyota recommend cleaning the spark plugs, certain spark plug manufacturers say this can cause damage to the insulator, especially if a wire brush is used. If there is no major build-up of carbon on the tip of the spark plug, do not clean it as it should be serviceable until it is due for renewal.
4 Check the spark plug electrode gaps and adjust them if necessary, then refit them as described in Section 31.

General component check

5 The spark plug (HT) leads should be checked whenever the spark plugs are removed.
6 Pull the leads from the plugs by gripping the end fitting, not the lead, otherwise the lead connection may be fractured.

 HAYNES HINT *Ensure that the leads are numbered before removing them, to avoid confusion when refitting*

7 Check inside the end fitting for signs of corrosion, which will look like a white crusty powder. Push the end fitting back onto the spark plug, ensuring that it is a tight fit on the plug. If not, remove the lead again and use pliers to carefully crimp the metal connector inside the end fitting until it fits securely on the end of the spark plug.
8 Using a clean rag, wipe the entire length of the lead to remove any built-up dirt and grease. Once the lead is clean, check for burns, cracks and other damage. Do not bend the lead excessively, nor pull the lead lengthwise - the conductor inside might break.
9 If an ohmmeter is available, check the resistance of the lead by connecting the meter across the ends of the lead and compare with the resistance given in the Specifications. Refit the lead securely on completion.
10 Check the remaining leads one at a time, in the same way.
11 If new spark plug (HT) leads are required, purchase a set for your specific car and engine.
12 Unscrew and remove the distributor cap retaining screws and remove the cap. Wipe the cap clean, and carefully inspect it inside and out for signs of cracks, carbon tracks (tracking) and worn, burned or loose contacts. Check that the cap's carbon brush is unworn and making good contact with the rotor arm. Inspect the cap seal for signs of wear or damage, and renew if necessary. Slacken the retaining screw where applicable, then remove the rotor arm from the distributor shaft, and inspect it. It is a good idea to renew the cap and rotor arm whenever new spark plug (HT) leads are fitted. When fitting a new cap, remove the leads from the old cap one at a time, and fit them to the new cap in the exact same location - do not simultaneously remove all the leads from the old cap, or firing order confusion may occur. On refitting, ensure that the rotor arm is pressed securely onto the distributor shaft, and securely tighten its retaining screw. Ensure that the cap seal is in position, then fit the cap and securely tighten its retaining screws.

Ignition timing check

13 Having performed the above checks, it is a good idea to also check the ignition timing. Refer to the procedures contained in Chapter 5B.

10 Evaporative loss system check

1 Refer to Chapter 4B and check that all wiring and hoses are correctly connected to the evaporative loss system components.

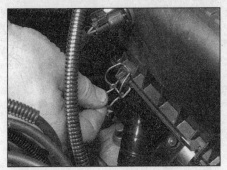

11.1a Release the toggle clips . . .

11.1b . . . and spring clips . . .

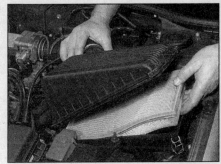

11.1c . . . then lift the cover from the air cleaner body and remove the element

11 Air filter element check and clean

1 Release the clips, then lift the cover from the air cleaner body and lift out the element **(see illustrations)**. There is no need to disconnect the air duct or inlet air temperature sensor wiring.
2 Check that the element is not damaged, oily or excessively dirty.
3 To clean the element, blow from its underside using compressed air then blow off its upper surfaces.
4 Refit the element using a reversal of the removal procedure.

12 Hose and fluid leak check

1 Visually inspect the engine joint faces, gaskets and seals for any signs of water or oil leaks. Pay particular attention to the areas around the camshaft cover, cylinder head, oil filter and sump joint faces. Bear in mind that, over a period of time, some very slight seepage from these areas is to be expected - what you are really looking for is any indication of a serious leak **(see Haynes Hint)**. Should a leak be found, renew the offending gasket or oil seal by referring to the appropriate Chapters in this manual.

HAYNES HINT

A leak in the cooling system will usually show up as white- or rust-coloured deposits on the area adjoining the leak.

2 Also check the security and condition of all the engine-related pipes and hoses. Ensure that all cable ties or securing clips are in place and in good condition. Clips which are broken or missing can lead to chafing of the hoses, pipes or wiring, which could cause more serious problems in the future.
3 Carefully check the radiator hoses and heater hoses along their entire length. Renew any hose which is cracked, swollen or deteriorated. Cracks will show up better if the hose is squeezed. Pay close attention to the hose clips that secure the hoses to the cooling system components. Hose clips can pinch and puncture hoses, resulting in cooling system leaks.
4 Inspect all the cooling system components (hoses, joint faces etc.) for leaks. Where any problems of this nature are found on system components, renew the component or gasket with reference to Chapter 3.
5 Where applicable, inspect the automatic transmission fluid cooler hoses for leaks or deterioration.
6 With the vehicle raised, inspect the fuel tank and filler neck for punctures, cracks and other damage. The connection between the filler neck and tank is especially critical. Sometimes a rubber filler neck or connecting hose will leak due to loose retaining clamps or deteriorated rubber.
7 Carefully check all rubber hoses and metal fuel lines leading away from the fuel tank. Check for loose connections, deteriorated hoses, crimped lines, and other damage. Pay particular attention to the vent pipes and hoses, which often loop up around the filler neck and can become blocked or crimped. Follow the lines to the front of the vehicle, carefully inspecting them all the way. Renew damaged sections as necessary.
8 From within the engine compartment, check the security of all fuel hose attachments and pipe unions, and inspect the fuel hoses and vacuum hoses for kinks, chafing and deterioration.
9 Where applicable, check the condition of the power steering fluid hoses and pipes.
10 With the vehicle raised, check all brake hydraulic pipes and hoses for deterioration and damage.

13 Brake pedal check and adjustment

Refer to the procedures in Chapter 9.

14 Brake vacuum servo unit check

Test the operation of the brake vacuum servo unit as follows. With the engine switched off, depress the footbrake four or five times to exhaust the vacuum, then hold the pedal depressed. Start the engine, and there should be a noticeable give in the brake pedal as vacuum builds up. Allow the engine to run for at least two minutes, and then switch it off. If the brake pedal is depressed again, it should be possible to detect a hiss from the servo as the pedal is depressed. After about four or five applications, no further hissing should be heard, and the pedal should feel considerably firmer.

15 Handbrake check and adjustment

In service, the handbrake should be fully applied within 4 to 7 clicks of the handbrake lever ratchet. On drum-brake models, the handbrake lever travel will normally be kept within these limits by the self-adjusting mechanism on the rear brake shoes. Periodic manual adjustment may be necessary however, to compensate for cable stretch, and this is carried out by means of the cable adjuster on the side of the handbrake lever. On disc-brake models, the handbrake shoes, located inside the rear brake disc/drum assemblies, must first be adjusted manually to compensate for lining wear, and then the handbrake cable can be adjusted by means of the adjuster on the handbrake lever, to provide the specified lever travel (ratchet clicks). Refer to Chapter 9 for the full adjustment procedure according to type.

1

16 Brake pad and disc check

Note: *For detailed photographs of the brake system, refer to Chapter 9.*

1 The work described in this Section should be carried out at the specified intervals, or whenever a defect is suspected in the braking system. Any of the following symptoms could indicate a potential brake system defect:
 a) *The vehicle pulls to one side when the brake pedal is depressed.*
 b) *The brakes make scraping or dragging noises when applied.*
 c) *Brake pedal travel is excessive.*
 d) *The brake fluid requires repeated topping-up.*

2 A thorough inspection should be made to confirm the thickness of the linings, as follows.

3 Jack up the front or rear of the vehicle, as applicable, and support it on axle stands (see *Jacking and Vehicle Support*). Where rear brake pads are fitted, also jack up the rear of the vehicle and support on axle stands.

4 For better access to the brake calipers, remove the wheels.

5 Look through the inspection window in the caliper, and check that the thickness of the friction lining material on each of the pads is not less than the recommended minimum thickness given in the Specifications **(see illustration). Note:** *Bear in mind that the lining material is normally bonded to a metal backing plate.*

6 If it is difficult to determine the exact thickness of the pad linings, or if you are at all concerned about the condition of the pads, then remove them from the calipers for further inspection (refer to Chapter 9).

7 Check the remaining brake caliper(s) in the same way.

8 If any one of the brake pads has worn down to, or below, the specified limit, *all four* pads at that end of the car must be renewed as a set (ie all the front pads or all the rear pads).

9 Measure the thickness of the discs with a micrometer, if available, to make sure that they still have service life remaining. If any disc is

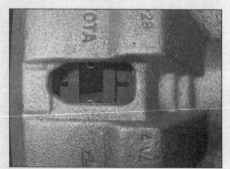

16.5 Check the brake pad friction material thickness by looking through the inspection window in the caliper

thinner than the specified minimum thickness, renew it (refer to Chapter 9). In any case, check the general condition of the discs. Look for excessive scoring and discolouration caused by overheating. If these conditions exist, remove the relevant disc and have it resurfaced or renewed (refer to Chapter 9).

10 Before refitting the wheels, check all brake lines and hoses (refer to Chapter 9). In particular, check the flexible hoses in the vicinity of the calipers, where they are subjected to most movement. Bend them between the fingers (but do not actually bend them double, or the casing may be damaged) and check that this does not reveal previously-hidden cracks, cuts or splits.

17 Rear brake shoe check

Note: *For detailed photographs of the brake system, refer to Chapter 9.*

1 The work described in this Section should be carried out at the specified intervals, or whenever a defect is suspected in the braking system. Any of the following symptoms could indicate a potential brake system defect:
 a) *The vehicle pulls to one side when the brake pedal is depressed.*
 b) *The brakes make scraping or dragging noises when applied.*
 c) *Brake pedal travel is excessive.*
 d) *The brake fluid requires repeated topping-up.*

2 Chock the front wheels then jack up the rear of the car and support it on axle stands (see *Jacking and Vehicle Support*). For better access, remove the rear roadwheels.

3 To check the brake shoe lining thickness without removing the brake drums, prise the inspection hole plugs from the backplates, and use an electric torch and mirror to inspect the linings of the leading brake shoes. Check that the thickness of the lining material on the brake shoes is not less than the recommendation given in the Specifications.

4 If it is difficult to determine the exact thickness of the brake shoe linings, or if you are at all concerned about the condition of the shoes, then remove the rear drums for a more comprehensive inspection (refer to Chapter 9).

5 With the drum removed, check the shoe return and hold-down springs for correct installation, and check the wheel cylinders for leakage of brake fluid. Check the friction surface of the brake drums for scoring and discoloration. If excessive, the drum should be resurfaced or renewed.

6 Before refitting the wheels, check all brake lines and hoses (refer to Chapter 9). On completion, fully apply the handbrake and check that the rear wheels are locked. The handbrake also requires periodic adjustment, and if its travel seems excessive, refer to Section 15.

18 Exhaust system check

1 With the engine cold (at least an hour after the vehicle has been driven), check the complete exhaust system from the engine to the end of the tailpipe. The exhaust system is most easily checked with the vehicle raised on a hoist, or suitably supported on axle stands, so that the exhaust components are readily visible and accessible.

2 Check the exhaust pipes and connections for evidence of leaks, severe corrosion and damage. Make sure that all brackets and mountings are in good condition, and that all relevant nuts and bolts are tight. Leakage at any of the joints or in other parts of the system will usually show up as a black sooty stain in the vicinity of the leak.

3 Rattles and other noises can often be traced to the exhaust system, especially the brackets and mountings. Move the pipes and silencers from side to side on the rubber mountings. If the components are able to come into contact with the body or suspension parts, secure the system with new mountings.

19 Steering, suspension and roadwheel check

Front suspension and steering check

1 Chock the rear wheels then jack up the front of the car and support it on axle stands (see *Jacking and Vehicle Support*).

2 Visually inspect the balljoint dust covers and the steering gear gaiters for splits, chafing or deterioration. Any wear of these components will cause loss of lubricant, together with dirt and water entry, resulting in rapid deterioration of the balljoints or steering gear.

3 Check the power-assisted steering fluid hoses (where fitted) for chafing or deterioration, and the pipe and hose unions for fluid leaks. Also check for signs of fluid leakage under pressure from the steering gear rubber gaiters, which would indicate failed fluid seals within the steering gear.

4 Grasp the roadwheel at the 12 o'clock and 6 o'clock positions, and try to rock it. Very slight free play may be felt, but if the movement is appreciable, further investigation is necessary to determine the source. Continue rocking the wheel while an assistant depresses the footbrake. If the movement is now eliminated or significantly reduced, it is likely that the hub bearings are at fault. If the free play is still evident with the footbrake depressed, then there is wear in the suspension joints or mountings.

5 Now grasp the wheel at the 9 o'clock and 3 o'clock positions, and try to rock it as before. Any movement felt now may again be caused

by wear in the hub bearings or the steering track rod balljoints. If the outer track rod end balljoint is worn, the visual movement will be obvious. If the inner joint is suspect, it can be felt by placing a hand over the rack-and-pinion rubber gaiter, and gripping the track rod. If the wheel is now rocked, movement will be felt at the inner joint if wear has taken place.

6 Using a large screwdriver or flat bar, check for wear in the suspension mounting bushes by levering between the relevant suspension component and its attachment point. Some movement is to be expected, as the mountings are made of rubber, but excessive wear should be obvious. Also check the condition of any visible rubber bushes, looking for splits, cracks or contamination of the rubber.

7 With the vehicle standing on its wheels, have an assistant turn the steering wheel back-and-forth, about an eighth of a turn each way. There should be very little, if any, lost movement between the steering wheel and roadwheels. If this is not the case, closely observe the joints and mountings previously described, but in addition, check the steering column universal joints for wear, and also check the rack-and-pinion steering gear itself.

Rear suspension check

8 Chock the front wheels then jack up the rear of the car and support it on axle stands (see *Jacking and Vehicle Support*). Remove the rear roadwheels.

9 Check the rear hub bearings for wear, using the method described for the front hub bearings (paragraph 4).

10 Using a large screwdriver or flat bar, check for wear in the suspension mounting bushes by levering between the relevant suspension component and its attachment point. Some movement is to be expected, as the mountings are made of rubber, but excessive wear should be obvious. Check the condition of the shock absorbers and their bushes/mountings.

Roadwheel check and balancing

11 Periodically remove the roadwheels, and clean any dirt or mud from the inside and outside surfaces. Examine the wheel rims for signs of rusting, corrosion or other damage. Light alloy wheels are easily damaged by kerbing whilst parking, and similarly, steel wheels may become dented or buckled. Renewal of the wheel is very often the only course of remedial action possible.

12 The balance of each wheel and tyre assembly should be maintained, not only to avoid excessive tyre wear, but also to avoid wear in the steering and suspension components. Wheel imbalance is normally signified by vibration through the vehicle's bodyshell, although in many cases it is particularly noticeable through the steering wheel. Conversely, it should be noted that wear or damage in suspension or steering components may cause excessive tyre wear. Out-of-round or out-of-true tyres, damaged wheels and wheel bearing wear/maladjustment also fall into this category. Balancing will not usually cure vibration caused by such wear.

13 Wheel balancing may be carried out with the wheel either on or off the vehicle. If balanced on the vehicle, ensure that the wheel-to-hub relationship is marked in some way prior to subsequent wheel removal, so that it may be refitted in its original position.

20 Driveshaft rubber gaiter and constant velocity (CV) joint check

1 With the vehicle raised and securely supported on stands, turn the steering onto full lock, then slowly rotate the roadwheel. Inspect the condition of the outer constant velocity (CV) joint rubber gaiters, squeezing the gaiters to open out the folds **(see illustration)**. Check for signs of cracking, splits or deterioration of the rubber, which may allow the grease to escape, and lead to water and grit entry into the joint. Also check the security and condition of the retaining clips. Repeat these checks on the inner CV joints. If any damage or deterioration is found, the gaiters should be renewed (see Chapter 8).

2 At the same time, check the general condition of the CV joints themselves by first holding the driveshaft and attempting to rotate the wheel. Repeat this check by holding the inner joint and attempting to rotate the driveshaft. Any appreciable movement indicates wear in the joints, wear in the driveshaft splines, or a loose driveshaft retaining nut.

21 Battery and electrolyte level check

1 The battery is located on the left-hand side of the engine compartment.

2 On batteries with removable cell covers, the electrolyte level in the battery should be checked (and if necessary topped up) at the interval given at the beginning of this Chapter; the check should be made more often if the car is operated in high ambient temperature conditions. Maintenance-free batteries (usually identifiable by a label on the battery top) do not require topping-up and the cell covers are not removable.

3 On some batteries, the case is translucent and incorporates minimum (or lower) and maximum (or upper) level marks; with the vehicle parked on level ground, the electrolyte level in each cell must be maintained between these marks **(see illustration)**. On batteries without a translucent case and level marks, the electrolyte level must be maintained just above the top of the cell plates.

4 If topping up is necessary, proceed as described in the following paragraph.

5 Remove the cell covers from the top of the battery then carefully add distilled or de-ionized water to raise the electrolyte level in each cell but do not overfill. With the electrolyte level replenished, refit the cell covers.

6 The exterior of the battery should be inspected periodically for damage such as a cracked case or cover.

7 Check the tightness of the battery cable terminal clamps to ensure good electrical connections, and check the entire length of each cable for cracks and frayed conductors.

8 If corrosion (visible as white, fluffy deposits) is evident, remove the cable terminal clamps from the battery terminals, clean them with a small wire brush then refit them. Corrosion can be kept to a minimum by applying a layer of petroleum jelly to the clamps and terminals after they are reconnected.

9 Make sure that the battery tray is in good condition and the retaining clamp is tight.

10 Corrosion or deposits on the tray, retaining clamp and the battery itself can be removed with a solution of water and baking soda. Thoroughly rinse all cleaned areas with cold water.

11 Any metal parts of the vehicle damaged by such corrosion should be covered with a zinc-based primer then painted.

12 Further information on the battery, charging and jump starting can be found in Chapter 5A and in the preliminary sections of this Manual.

22 Roadwheel nut tightness check

Using a torque wrench, check that the roadwheel nuts are tightened to the torque wrench setting given in the Specifications.

20.1 Checking the driveshaft gaiters for damage

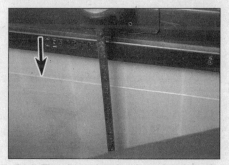

21.3 The electrolyte level can be viewed though the battery casing

1

23 Wheel alignment check

Refer to the procedure in Chapter 10.

24 Headlight beam adjustment check

1 Accurate adjustment of the headlight beam is only possible using optical beam-setting equipment, and this work should therefore be carried out by a Toyota dealer or suitably-equipped workshop.
2 Adjustment screws are located on the rear of the headlight units and access is gained by opening the bonnet. The outer screw (nearest the vehicle wing) is used to adjust the horizontal alignment, and the inner screw is used to adjust the vertical alignment. Note that on models with electric aim adjustment, the adjustment switch must be set to position 0 before carrying out beam alignment.
3 Certain models are equipped with a headlight beam adjustment switch, located on the centre console, which allows the aim of the headlights to be adjusted to compensate for the varying loads carried in the vehicle. The switch should be positioned according to the load being carried in the vehicle - eg; position 0 for driver with no passengers or luggage; up to position 3 for maximum load, or towing.

25 Door and bonnet hinge lubrication

1 All hinges and locks (doors, bonnet, tailgate, boot, and fuel filler flap) should be examined for correct operation and any defects rectified.
2 Lubricate the moving parts of the hinges and locks with a little engine oil, and apply a little multi-purpose grease to the contact surfaces of the locks and strikers.

26 Washer jet adjustment

1 While operating the windscreen washers, check that the upper limit of the jet is aimed at a point vertically above the jet and near the top of the area wiped by the wipers. The lower limit of the jet should be aimed on the windscreen near the bottom of the area wiped by the wipers but towards the driver's side.
2 If adjustment is required, use a pin or similar tool 0.7 to 0.75 mm in diameter to adjust the nozzle in the jet.

27 Seat belt check

1 All vehicles are fitted with three point, inertia reel front and outer rear seat belts, with a two point lap belt for the centre rear seat.
2 Inspect the belts for signs of fraying or other damage. Also check the operation of the buckles and retractor mechanisms, and ensure that all mounting bolts are securely tightened. Note that the bolts are shouldered so that the belt anchor points are free to rotate.
3 If there is any sign of damage, or any doubt about the condition of a belt, it must be renewed. If the vehicle has been involved in a collision, any belts in use at the time should be renewed as a matter of course, and all other belts should be checked carefully.
4 Use only warm water and non-detergent soap when cleaning the belt webbing. Never use chemicals that could attack the belt fabric and reduce its effectiveness. Keep the belts fully extended until they have dried - do not apply heat to accelerate drying.

28 Body corrosion check

1 Jack up the front and rear of the vehicle and support on axle stands (see *Jacking and Vehicle Support*).
2 Working from the front to the rear of the vehicle, check the condition of the entire vehicle structure for signs of corrosion, especially near the load-bearing areas. These include chassis box sections, side sills, cross-members, pillars, and all suspension, steering, braking system and seat belt mountings and anchorages.
3 Check that the anti-corrosion sealing materials on the underbody are intact. Where necessary re-apply the material.
4 In the engine compartment, examine the front suspension upper mountings and inner wing panels, also the lower areas of the front valance for signs of corrosion.
5 Inside the vehicle, lift the carpets where possible and check the floor and inner surfaces of the sills for signs of corrosion.
6 Check the drain holes in the doors for blockages and clear by probing with wire.
7 Where body corrosion is evident, consult a Toyota dealer to have it repaired.

29 Alarm remote control battery renewal

The alarm remote control battery should be renewed at the specified intervals to ensure correct operation of the alarm system. Obtain a new battery from a Toyota dealer and fit it in accordance with the instructions supplied.

30 Road test

Instruments and electrical equipment

1 Check the operation of all instruments and electrical equipment.
2 Make sure that all instruments read correctly, and switch on all electrical equipment in turn, to check that it functions properly.

Steering and suspension

3 Check for any abnormalities in the steering, suspension, handling or road feel.
4 Drive the vehicle, and check that there are no unusual vibrations or noises.
5 Check that the steering feels positive, with no excessive sloppiness, or roughness, and check for any suspension noises when cornering and driving over bumps.

Drivetrain

6 Check the performance of the engine, clutch (if applicable), transmission and driveshafts.
7 Listen for any unusual noises from the engine, clutch and transmission.
8 Make sure that the engine runs smoothly when idling, and that there is no hesitation when accelerating.
9 Check that, where applicable, the clutch action is smooth and progressive, that the drive is taken up smoothly, and that the pedal travel is not excessive. Also listen for any noises when the clutch pedal is depressed.
10 On manual transmission models, check that all gears can be engaged smoothly without noise, and that the gear lever action is not abnormally vague or notchy.
11 On automatic transmission models, make sure that all gearchanges occur smoothly, without snatching, and without an increase in engine speed between changes. Check that all the gear positions can be selected with the vehicle at rest. If any problems are found, they should be referred to a Toyota dealer.
12 Listen for a metallic clicking sound from the front of the vehicle, as the vehicle is driven slowly in a circle with the steering on full-lock. Carry out this check in both directions. If a clicking noise is heard, this indicates wear in a driveshaft joint, in which case the joint should be renewed.

Check the operation and performance of the braking system

13 Make sure that the vehicle does not pull to one side when braking, and that the wheels do not lock prematurely when braking hard.
14 Check that there is no vibration through the steering when braking.
15 Check that the handbrake operates correctly without excessive movement of the lever, and that it holds the vehicle stationary on a slope.

Every 18 000 miles (30 000 km) or 12 months

31 Spark plug renewal

Note: *On 4A-FE and 7A-FE (lean-burn) engines fitted with platinum-tipped spark plugs, the renewal interval is every 63 000 miles.*

1 The correct functioning of the spark plugs is vital for the correct running and efficiency of the engine. It is essential that the plugs fitted are appropriate for the engine (a suitable type is specified at the beginning of this Chapter). If this type is used and the engine is in good condition, the spark plugs should not need attention between scheduled replacement intervals. Spark plug cleaning is rarely necessary, and should not be attempted unless specialised equipment is available, as damage can easily be caused to the firing ends.

2 If the marks on the original-equipment spark plug (HT) leads cannot be seen, mark the leads 1 to 4, to correspond to the cylinder the lead serves (No 1 cylinder is at the timing belt end of the engine). Pull the leads from the plugs by gripping the end fitting, not the lead, otherwise the lead connection may be fractured. Note that as the spark plugs are deeply recessed, the HT lead end fittings are extended **(see illustration)**.

3 It is advisable to remove the dirt from the spark plug recesses using a clean brush, vacuum cleaner or compressed air before removing the plugs, to prevent dirt dropping into the cylinders.

⚠️ **Warning: Wear eye protection when using compressed air!**

4 Unscrew the plugs using a spark plug spanner, suitable box spanner or a deep socket and extension bar **(see illustration)**. Keep the socket aligned with the spark plug - if it is forcibly moved to one side, the ceramic insulator may be broken off, however since the spark plugs are deeply recessed this is not likely to be a problem until the plugs are being withdrawn. As each plug is removed, examine it as follows.

5 Examination of the spark plugs will give a good indication of the condition of the engine. If the insulator nose of the spark plug is clean and white, with no deposits, this is indicative of a weak mixture or too hot a plug (a hot plug transfers heat away from the electrode slowly, a cold plug transfers heat away quickly).

6 If the tip and insulator nose are covered with hard black-looking deposits, then this is indicative that the mixture is too rich. Should the plug be black and oily, then it is likely that the engine is fairly worn, as well as the mixture being too rich.

7 If the insulator nose is covered with light tan to greyish-brown deposits, then the mixture is correct and it is likely that the engine is in good condition.

8 The spark plug electrode gap is of considerable importance as, if it is too large or too small, the size of the spark and its efficiency will be seriously impaired. The gap should be set to the value given in the Specifications at the beginning of this Chapter.

9 To set the gap, measure it with a feeler blade or wire gauge, and then bend the outer plug electrode until the correct gap is achieved **(see illustrations)**. The centre electrode should never be bent, as this may crack the insulator and cause plug failure, if nothing worse. If using feeler blades, the gap is correct when the appropriate-size blade is a firm sliding fit.

10 Special spark plug electrode gap adjusting tools are available from most motor accessory shops, or from some spark plug manufacturers.

11 Before fitting the spark plugs, check that the threaded connector sleeves are tight, and that the plug exterior surfaces and threads are clean.

HAYNES HiNT

It is very often difficult to insert spark plugs into their holes without cross-threading them. To avoid this possibility, fit a short length of 5/16 inch internal diameter rubber hose over the end of the spark plug. The flexible hose acts as a universal joint to help align the plug with the plug hole. Should the plug begin to cross-thread, the hose will slip on the spark plug, preventing thread damage to the cylinder head.

12 Remove the rubber hose (if used), and tighten the plug to the specified torque using the spark plug socket and a torque wrench. Refit the remaining spark plugs in the same manner.

13 Connect the HT leads in their correct order, making sure they are located in the special support at the left-hand end of the camshaft cover.

1

31.2 Disconnecting the HT leads from the spark plugs

31.4 Removing the spark plugs

31.9a Measuring the spark plug gap with a feeler blade

31.9b Measuring the spark plug gap with a wire gauge

32.1 The fuel filter is located on the left-hand side of the engine compartment bulkhead

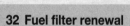

32 Fuel filter renewal

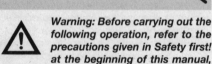

Warning: Before carrying out the following operation, refer to the precautions given in Safety first! at the beginning of this manual, and follow them implicitly. Petrol is a highly-dangerous and volatile liquid, and the precautions necessary when handling it cannot be overstressed.

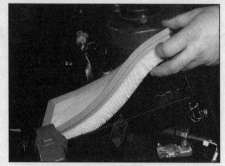

33.2 Removing the air cleaner element from the body

1 The fuel filter is located in the engine compartment, mounted on the left-hand side of the engine compartment bulkhead **(see illustration)**.
2 Open the bonnet, then refer to Chapter 4A and depressurise the fuel system.
3 To remove the filter, position a suitable container beneath the filter to catch spilt fuel, then slacken and remove the filter union bolts and disconnect the hoses. Recover the sealing washers. Tape or plug the hose ends to minimise fuel loss.
4 Unscrew the two retaining bolts and remove the fuel filter from the vehicle.

5 Fit the new filter using a reversal of the removal procedure. Position a new sealing washer on each side of the hose unions and ensure that the hose union is positioned between the locating pins on the filter. Tighten the union bolts securely.
6 Start the engine and check the filter hose connections for leaks. On completion, stop the engine.

33 Air filter element renewal

1 Release the air cleaner lid retaining clips, then lift off the lid and position it clear of the body. There is no need to disconnect the air duct or air temperature sensor wiring.
2 Note how the element is located in the air cleaner body, then lift it out **(see illustration)**.
3 Wipe the inside of the air cleaner body and lid with a clean cloth to remove all traces of dirt and debris.
4 Install the new filter element, ensuring that it is the right way up and is correctly seated in the housing.
5 Refit the air cleaner lid, and secure it in position with its retaining clips.

Every 24 months

34 Brake fluid renewal

The procedure is similar to that for the bleeding of the hydraulic system as described in Chapter 9, except that the brake fluid reservoir should be emptied by syphoning, and allowance should be made for the old fluid to be removed from the circuit when bleeding a section of the circuit.

Every 36 000 miles (60 000 km)

35 Transmission oil/fluid renewal

Refer to the procedures described in Chapter 7A (manual transmission) or 7B (automatic transmission).

36 Coolant renewal

Warning: Wait until the engine is cold before starting this procedure. Do not allow antifreeze to come in contact with your skin, or with the painted surfaces of the vehicle. Rinse off spills immediately with plenty of water. Never leave antifreeze lying around in an open container, or in a puddle in the driveway or on the garage floor. Children and pets are attracted by its sweet smell, but antifreeze can be fatal if ingested.

Draining

1 If the engine is cold, unscrew and remove the pressure cap from the radiator. If it is not possible to wait until the engine is cold, place a cloth over the pressure cap and slowly unscrew it. Wait until all pressure has escaped, then remove the cap.
2 Drain plugs are provided on the lower right-hand side of the radiator and the front or rear of the cylinder block, and suitable containers should be placed beneath these to catch the flow of escaping coolant prior to removing them **(see illustration)**.
3 With all the coolant drained into the containers, tighten the drain plugs; if the system needs to be flushed after draining refer to the following sub-section.
4 When draining the cooling system, do not forget about the coolant in the expansion tank. The heater hoses and matrix also contain engine coolant, although no recommendations are made to attend to this as the relatively small amount of coolant will circulate back into the main volume of coolant in the engine during heater usage.

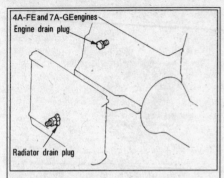

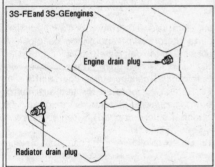

36.2 Radiator and cylinder block (engine) drain plug locations

Cooling system flushing

5 If coolant renewal has been neglected, or if the antifreeze mixture has become diluted then, in time, the cooling system may gradually lose efficiency, as the coolant passages become restricted due to rust, scale deposits, and other sediment. The cooling system efficiency can be restored by flushing the system clean.

6 The radiator should be flushed independently of the engine, to avoid unnecessary contamination.

Radiator flushing

7 To flush the radiator disconnect the top and bottom hoses from the radiator.

8 Insert a garden hose into the radiator top inlet. Direct a flow of clean water through the radiator, and continue flushing until clean water emerges from the radiator bottom outlet.

9 If after a reasonable period, the water still does not run clear, the radiator can be flushed with a good proprietary cooling system cleaning agent. It is important that the manufacturer's instructions are followed carefully. If the contamination is particularly bad, remove the radiator then insert the hose in the radiator bottom outlet, and reverse-flush the radiator.

Engine flushing

10 To flush the engine, remove the thermostat as described in Chapter 3 then temporarily refit the thermostat cover to enable the water to run out through the disconnected bottom hose and not all over the transmission.

11 With the top and bottom hoses disconnected from the radiator, insert a garden hose into the radiator top hose. Direct a clean flow of water through the engine, and continue flushing until clean water emerges from the radiator bottom hose.

12 On completion of flushing, refit the thermostat and reconnect the hoses with reference to Chapter 3.

Cooling system filling

13 Before attempting to fill the cooling system, reconnect all hoses and make sure that all clips are in good condition and tight. Note that an antifreeze mixture must be used all year round, to prevent corrosion of the engine components (see following sub-Section).

14 Fill the system slowly through the radiator filler until the level reaches the bottom of the filler neck. While filling, compress the radiator hoses frequently to purge air locks from the system.

15 Fill the expansion tank with coolant to the MAX level mark.

16 With the radiator cap still removed, start the engine and allow it to idle until heat can be felt through the radiator top hose. Accelerate the engine briefly several times, then switch off the ignition and allow the engine to cool (preferably for an hour).

17 Top up the level in the radiator to the filler neck and refit the radiator cap. Top up the level in the expansion tank to the MAX mark.

18 Start the engine and run it at 3000 rpm for half a minute. Stop the engine then remove the radiator cap and top up the level if necessary. Refit the cap.

19 Check for leaks, particularly around disturbed components.

Antifreeze mixture

20 The antifreeze should always be renewed at the specified intervals. This is necessary not only to maintain the antifreeze properties, but also to prevent corrosion which would otherwise occur as the corrosion inhibitors become progressively less effective.

21 Always use an ethylene-glycol based antifreeze which is suitable for use in mixed-metal cooling systems. The quantity of antifreeze and levels of protection are indicated in the Specifications.

22 Before adding antifreeze, the cooling system should be completely drained, preferably flushed, and all hoses checked for condition and security.

23 After filling with antifreeze, a label should be attached to the expansion tank, stating the type and concentration of antifreeze used, and the date installed. Any subsequent topping-up should be made with the same type and concentration of antifreeze.

24 Do not use engine antifreeze in the washer system, as it will cause damage to the vehicle paintwork. A screenwash additive should be added to the washer system in the quantities stated on the bottle.

Every 54 000 miles (90 000 km)

37 Valve clearance check and adjustment

1 The valve clearances must be checked and adjusted with the engine cold.

2 Remove the camshaft cover as described in Chapter 2A, Section 4.

3 Set No 1 piston at TDC compression as described in Chapter 2A, Section 3.

4 Using feeler blades, check and record the clearances of the following valves; the feeler blade should be a firm sliding fit between the shim on the follower and the camshaft lobe (see illustration).

Inlet camshaft	No 1 inlet valves
Inlet camshaft	No 2 inlet valves
Exhaust camshaft	No 1 exhaust valves
Exhaust camshaft	No 3 exhaust valves

5 Using a socket on the crankshaft pulley, turn the engine 360° clockwise and align the notch in the pulley with the 0° mark on the timing belt cover. This will set No 4 piston at TDC on compression.

6 Using feeler blades, check and record the clearances of the following valves; the feeler blade should be a firm sliding fit between the shim on the follower and the camshaft lobe.

Inlet camshaft	No 3 inlet valves
Inlet camshaft	No 4 inlet valves
Exhaust camshaft	No 2 exhaust valves
Exhaust camshaft	No 4 exhaust valves

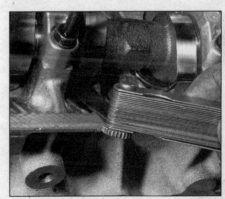

37.4 Checking the valve clearances with a feeler gauge

7 Compare the recorded clearances with the clearances given in the Specifications, and note the valves which require adjustment.

8 If adjustment is required on the inlet valves of 4A-FE and 7A-FE engines, it will be necessary to remove the inlet camshaft as described in Chapter 2A in order to remove existing shims and fit new ones. For the exhaust valves of these engines, and for all valves of other engines, the shims can be replaced without removing the camshafts provided that a special Toyota tool is obtained to depress and hold the camshaft followers down. With the camshaft follower held depressed, the shim is removed using a suitable screwdriver and a magnetic probe (possibly another magnetised screwdriver). It should be possible to use a suitable alternative tool to depress and hold the camshaft followers down, however, if the tool is not available the camshafts can be removed by following the procedure described in Chapter 2A and the shim removed using a small screwdriver **(see illustration)**. Adjustment should be made on each valve separately to ensure the shims are fitted in the correct locations.

37.8 Using a small screwdriver to remove a shim from the top of the follower

37.9 Measuring a shim with a micrometer

9 Measure the thickness of the removed shim using a micrometer **(see illustration)**, then calculate the thickness of the required shim using the following formula where the variables are T (the thickness of the removed shim), A (the valve clearance measured), V (the required valve clearance as given in the Specifications) and N (the thickness of the new shim required):

$$N = T + (A - V)$$

Shims are available in a variety of sizes, and the shim selected (from your Toyota dealer's parts department) should be as close as possible to the calculated value.

10 Install the new shim on the follower, with its thickness marking facing downwards.

11 Repeat the process for all the remaining shims that require renewal, then refit the camshafts (if removed) with reference to Chapter 2A.

12 On completion refit the camshaft cover as described in Chapter 2A, Section 4.

Every 63 000 miles (105 000 km)

38 Timing belt renewal

Refer to the procedures contained in Chapter 2A.

Chapter 2 Part A:
Engine in-car repair procedures

Contents

Degrees of difficulty

Easy, suitable for novice with little experience	**Fairly easy,** suitable for beginner with some experience	**Fairly difficult,** suitable for competent DIY mechanic	**Difficult,** suitable for experienced DIY mechanic	**Very difficult,** suitable for expert DIY or professional

2A

Specifications

General

Type	Four-cylinder, in-line, double-overhead camshafts, 16-valve

Engine code*
1.6 litre engine	4A-FE
1.8 litre engine	7A-FE
2.0 litre engine (single camshaft sprocket drive)	3S-FE
2.0 litre engine (double camshaft sprockets drive)	3S-GE

***Note:** See Buying Spare Parts and Vehicle Identification for the location of code marking on the engine.*

Capacity:
1.6 litre engine	1587 cc
1.8 litre engine	1762 cc
2.0 litre engines	1998 cc

Bore:
1.6 litre engine	81.0 mm
1.8 litre engine	81.0 mm
2.0 litre engine	86.0 mm

Stroke:
1.6 litre engine	77.0 mm
1.8 litre engine	85.5 mm
2.0 litre engine	86.0 mm
Direction of crankshaft rotation	Clockwise (viewed from right-hand side of vehicle)

Cylinder compression pressures:
Standard:
4A-FE and 7A-FE engines	13.5 bar
3S-FE and 3S-GE engines	13.0 bar

Minimum:
4A-FE and 7A-FE engines	10.0 bar
3S-FE and 3S-GE engines	9.5 bar
Maximum difference between cylinders	1.0 bar
Firing order	1-3-4-2
No 1 cylinder location	Timing belt (right-hand) end of the engine

Camshaft and followers

Drive:

4A-FE and 7A-FE engines	Toothed belt to exhaust camshaft sprocket, anti-backlash gears from exhaust to inlet camshaft
3S-FE engine	Toothed belt to inlet camshaft sprocket, anti-backlash gears from inlet to exhaust camshaft
3S-GE engine	Toothed belt to inlet and exhaust camshaft sprockets

Camshaft journal diameter:

4A-FE and 7A-FE engines:
Exhaust camshaft No 1 journal .... 24.949 to 24.965 mm
All other journals .... 22.949 to 22.965 mm
3S-FE and 3S-GE engines .... 26.959 to 26.975 mm

Camshaft journal-to-bearing running clearance:

	Standard	Service limit
4A-FE and 7A-FE engines	0.035 to 0.072 mm	0.10 mm
3S-FE engine	0.025 to 0.062 mm	0.10 mm
3S-GE engine	0.025 to 0.062 mm	0.08 mm

Camshaft endfloat:

	Standard	Service limit
4A-FE and 7A-FE engines:		
Inlet camshaft	0.030 to 0.085 mm	0.11 mm
Exhaust camshaft	0.035 to 0.090 mm	0.11 mm
3S-FE engine:		
Inlet camshaft	0.045 to 0.100 mm	0.12 mm
Exhaust camshaft	0.030 to 0.085 mm	0.10 mm
3S-GE engine	0.120 to 0.240 mm	0.30 mm

Maximum run-out - at centre (No 3) bearing journal:
Except 3S-GE engines .... 0.04 mm
3S-GE engines .... 0.06 mm

Gear backlash (4A-FE, 7A-FE and 3S-FE engines):
Standard .... 0.02 to 0.20 mm
Maximum .... 0.30 mm

Distance between free ends of inlet camshaft sub-gear spring:
4A-FE and 7A-FE engines .... 17.0 to 17.6 mm
3S-FE engine .... 22.5 to 22.9 mm

Follower-to-cylinder head bore clearance:

	Standard	Maximum
4A-FE and 7A-FE engines	0.024 to 0.059 mm	0.070 mm
3S-FE engine	0.024 to 0.052 mm	0.070 mm
3S-GE engine	0.015 to 0.046 mm	0.070 mm

Timing belt

Tensioner spring free length:
4A-FE engine .... 35.3 mm
7A-FE engine .... 31.8 mm
3S-FE engine .... 46.0 mm

Tensioner pushrod protrusion:
3S-GE engine .... 8.5 to 9.5 mm

Lubrication system

Oil pump type:
4A-FE and 7A-FE engines .... Bi-rotor driven from front of crankshaft
3S-FE and 3S-GE engines .... Trochoidal rotor, driven by timing belt

System pressure - at normal operating temperature:
At idle speed .... At least 0.3 bar
At 3000 rpm .... 5.0 bar

Oil pump clearances:

	Standard	Maximum
4A-FE and 7A-FE engines:		
Outer rotor-to-pump body clearance	0.080 to 0.180 mm	0.200 mm
Rotor side clearance (endfloat):		
4A-FE engine	0.025 to 0.075 mm	0.100 mm
7A-FE engine	0.025 to 0.085 mm	0.100 mm
Inner rotor-to-outer rotor tip clearance:		
4A-FE engine	0.060 to 0.180 mm	0.350 mm
7A-FE engine	0.025 to 0.085 mm	0.350 mm
3S-FE and 3S-GE engines:		
Outer rotor-to-pump body clearance	0.100 to 0.160 mm	0.200 mm
Inner rotor-to-outer rotor tip clearance	0.040 to 0.160 mm	0.200 mm

Torque wrench settings

	Nm	lbf ft
4A-FE and 7A-FE engines		
Camshaft bearing cap bolts	13	10
Camshaft cover	6	4
Camshaft sprocket bolt	59	44
Timing belt tensioner pulley bolt	37	27
Crankshaft pulley bolt	118	87
Cylinder head bolts:		
Stage 1	29	21
Stage 2	Angle-tighten a further 90°	
Stage 3	Angle-tighten a further 90°	
Alternator bracket bolts	26	20
Alternator adjusting bar to cylinder block	39	29
Engine lifting eye fasteners	27	20
Coolant inlet elbow (small) to cylinder head	15	11
Oil dipstick tube	9	7
Coolant inlet elbow to cylinder head	20	15
Coolant outlet elbow to cylinder head	15	11
Main bearing cap bolts	60	44
Connecting rod big-end cap nuts/bolts:		
Stage 1:		
4A-FE engine	29	21
7A-FE engine	25	18
Stage 2	Angle-tighten a further 90°	
Crankshaft rear (left-hand) oil seal housing bolts	9	7
Oil pump housing to cylinder block bolts	21	15
Oil pump cover screws	10	7
Oil pick-up tube/strainer nuts and bolts	9	7
Sump nuts and bolts:		
4A-FE engine	5	4
7A-FE engine:		
Main sump to cylinder block	16	12
Main sump to oil pump	8	6
Main sump to rear oil seal housing	8	6
Secondary sump to main sump	5	4
Oil cooler pipe union bolt	34	25
Oil filter housing/oil pressure regulator valve housing stud	54	40
Oil pressure relief valve plug on oil filter housing	37	27
Rear engine plate-to-cylinder block	6	4
Flywheel-to-crankshaft bolts - manual transmission	78	58
Driveplate-to-crankshaft bolts - automatic transmission	64	47
Engine-to-transmission attachment bolts:		
M12	64	47
M10	46	34
Engine/transmission mountings:		
Right-hand bracket-to-cylinder head (nut)	28	21
Right-hand bracket-to-cylinder block	51	38
Engine/transmission longitudinal crossmember bolts	35	26
Front engine/transmission mounting-to-crossmember	72	53
Rear engine/transmission mounting-to-crossmember	72	53
Engine-to-transmission reinforcing plate bolts	23	17
Rear engine/transmission mounting bracket through bolt	87	64
Rear engine/transmission mounting bracket-to-transmission	77	57
Left-hand engine/transmission mounting bracket-to-transmission:		
Bolts	64	47
Nuts	72	53
Roadwheel nuts	103	76
3S-FE and 3S-GE engines		
Oil pump sprocket:		
3S-FE engine	24	18
3S-GE engine	35	26
Idler pulley to cylinder block	42	31
Timing belt tensioner:		
3S-FE engine	42	31
3S-GE engine	21	15
Crankshaft pulley bolt	108	80

2A

Torque wrench settings (continued)

	Nm	lbf ft
3S-FE and 3S-GE engines (continued)		
Camshaft sprocket bolt:		
3S-FE engine	54	40
3S-GE engine	59	44
Cylinder head bolts:		
Stage 1	49	36
Stage 2	Angle-tighten a further 90°	
Spark plug tube	39	29
Camshaft bearing cap bolts	19	14
Camshaft cover	44	32
Alternator bracket to cylinder head	42	31
Engine lifting eye	25	18
Upper timing belt cover	3	2
Lower timing belt cover	8	6
Main bearing cap bolts	59	44
Connecting rod big-end cap nuts:		
Stage 1	25	18
Stage 2	Angle-tighten a further 90°	
Crankshaft rear (left-hand) oil seal housing bolts	13	9
Sump nuts and bolts	5	4
Oil pump housing to cylinder block bolts	9	7
Oil pump cover to housing	9	7
Oil cooler to cylinder block:		
Relief valve	78	58
Nut	8	6
Rear engine plate-to-cylinder block	9	7
Flywheel-to-crankshaft bolts - manual gearbox	88	65
Driveplate-to-crankshaft bolts - automatic transmission	83	61
Engine-to-transmission attachment bolts:		
M12	64	47
M10	46	34
Engine/transmission mountings:		
Right-hand engine mounting bracket to cylinder block	52	38
Engine/transmission longitudinal crossmember bolts	35	26
Front engine/transmission mounting-to-crossmember	72	53
Rear engine/transmission mounting-to-crossmember	72	53
Engine-to-transmission reinforcing plate bolts:		
M8 bolts	21	15
M10 bolts	44	32
Nuts	44	32
Rear engine/transmission mounting bracket through bolt	87	64
Rear engine/transmission mounting bracket-to-transmission	77	57
Left-hand engine/transmission mounting bracket-to-transmission:		
Bolts	64	47
Nuts	72	53
Roadwheel nuts	103	76

1 General information

Using this Chapter

Chapter 2 is divided into two Parts; A and B. Repair operations that can be carried out with the engine in the vehicle are described in Part A. Part B covers the removal of the engine/transmission as a unit, and describes the engine dismantling and overhaul procedures.

In Part A the assumption is made that the engine is installed in the vehicle, with all ancillaries connected. If the engine has been removed for overhaul, the preliminary dismantling information which precedes each operation may be ignored.

Engine description

Throughout this Chapter, engines are identified by their codes as given in the Specifications.

The engine is of in-line 4-cylinder design and is mounted transversely. A cast iron cylinder block and cast aluminium cylinder head are fitted.

The 4A-FE (1587 cc) and 7A-FE (1762 cc) engines have twin overhead camshafts, with two inlet valves and two exhaust valves per cylinder. Valve clearance adjustment is by means of shims located directly between the bucket-type camshaft followers and the camshaft lobes. The exhaust camshaft is driven from the crankshaft sprocket by the toothed timing belt, while the inlet camshaft is driven from the exhaust camshaft via a pair of gears; each camshaft is supported by five bearings. The pistons are attached to their connecting rods by semi-floating gudgeon pins. The distributor is driven from the left-hand end of the exhaust camshaft, whilst the oil pump is driven from the front of the crankshaft. The cast iron crankshaft runs in five main bearings; endfloat is controlled by semi-circular thrustwashers at the central main bearing. There are minor differences between the 4A-FE and 7A-FE engines; on the 7A-FE engine the sump is in two sections instead of one, and the connecting rod caps are secured with bolts instead of nuts.

The 3S-FE engine is similar to the 4A-FE and 7A-FE engines described in the previous paragraph, however the timing belt drives the inlet camshaft, and the exhaust camshaft is driven by gears from the inlet camshaft. The cylinder block is of a different casting and the oil pump is located in its own housing bolted to the front of the cylinder block and driven by the timing belt. The water pump is bolted to the cylinder block and is also driven by the timing belt.

The cylinder block on the 3S-GE engine is similar (though not the same) as the 3S-FE block, however the main difference between these two engines is that, on the 3S-GE unit, the pistons are of fully-floating type and the gudgeon pins are retained by circlips. The timing belt drives both the inlet and exhaust camshafts from sprockets located on the right-hand ends of the camshafts.

Repair operations possible with the engine in the car

The following work can be carried out with the engine in the car:

a) *Removal and refitting of the timing belt, sprockets and tensioner.*
b) *Renewal of the camshaft oil seal(s).*
c) *Removal and refitting of the camshafts and followers.*
d) *Removal and refitting of the cylinder head*.*
e) *Removal and refitting of the sump.*
f) *Removal and refitting of the oil pump.*
g) *Removal and refitting of the flywheel/driveplate.*
h) *Renewal of the crankshaft oil seals.*
i) *Renewal of the engine mountings.*

*Cylinder head dismantling procedures are detailed in Chapter 2B.

Note: *It is possible to remove the pistons and connecting rods (after removing the cylinder head and sump) without removing the engine, although this is not recommended. Work of this nature is more easily and thoroughly completed with the engine on the bench, as described in Chapter 2B.*

2 Compression test

1 When engine performance is down, or if misfiring occurs which cannot be attributed to the ignition or fuel systems, a compression test can provide diagnostic clues as to the engine's condition. If the test is performed regularly, it can give warning of trouble before any other symptoms become apparent.
2 The engine must be fully warmed-up to normal operating temperature, the battery must be fully charged, and all the spark plugs must be removed (Chapter 1). The aid of an assistant will also be required.
3 Depressurise the fuel system (see Chapter 4A), then temporarily remove the fuel injection relay in the engine compartment fusebox.
4 Disable the ignition system by disconnecting the wiring multiplug connector(s) at the distributor.
5 Fit a compression tester to the No 1 cylinder spark plug hole - the type of tester which screws into the plug thread is to be preferred.

6 Have the assistant hold the throttle wide open, and crank the engine on the starter motor; after one or two revolutions, the compression pressure should build up to a maximum figure, and then stabilise. Record the highest reading obtained.
7 Repeat the test on the remaining cylinders, recording the pressure in each.
8 All cylinders should produce very similar pressures; any difference greater than that specified indicates the existence of a fault. Note that the compression should build up quickly in a healthy engine; low compression on the first stroke, followed by gradually increasing pressure on successive strokes, indicates worn piston rings. A low compression reading on the first stroke, which does not build up during successive strokes, indicates leaking valves or a blown head gasket (a cracked head could also be the cause).
9 If the pressure in any cylinder is reduced to the specified minimum or less, carry out the following test to isolate the cause. Introduce 5 ml of clean oil into that cylinder through its spark plug hole and repeat the test.
10 If the addition of oil temporarily improves the compression pressure, this indicates that bore or piston wear is responsible for the pressure loss. No improvement suggests that leaking or burnt valves, or a blown head gasket, may be to blame.
11 A low reading from two adjacent cylinders is almost certainly due to the head gasket having blown between them. Renew the head gasket if this is the case.
12 If one cylinder is about 20 percent lower than the others and the engine has a slightly rough idle, a worn camshaft lobe could be the cause.
13 On completion of the test, refit the spark plugs and the fuel injection relay, then reconnect the distributor wiring.

3 Top dead centre (TDC) for No 1 piston - locating

1 Disconnect the battery negative (earth) lead (refer to Chapter 5A, Sections 1 and 3).
2 Trace No 1 spark plug HT lead from the plug back to the distributor cap, and use

chalk or similar to mark the distributor body or cylinder head nearest to the cap's No 1 terminal. No 1 cylinder is at the timing belt (right-hand) end of the engine. Unscrew the cap retaining screws, remove the cap and recover the seal.
3 The timing marks are marked on the lower timing belt cover at intervals of 5°, and the crankshaft pulley rim incorporates a notch for alignment with the timing marks. The 0° mark indicates TDC (top dead centre), and when the notch is aligned with this mark the pistons in cylinders 1 and 4 are at TDC **(see illustration).**
4 Using a spanner (or socket and extension bar) applied to the crankshaft pulley bolt, rotate the crankshaft clockwise until the notch on the crankshaft pulley rim is aligned with the 0° mark on the timing belt cover. Note that it will be necessary to remove the undershield from beneath the engine for access to the crankshaft pulley. Remove all four spark plugs; this will make the engine easier to turn; refer to Chapter 1 for details.
5 With the crankshaft in this position, Nos 1 and 4 cylinders are now at TDC, one of them on the compression stroke. If the distributor rotor arm is pointing at the previously-marked No 1 terminal position, then No 1 cylinder is correctly positioned; if the rotor arm is pointing at No 4 terminal, rotate the crankshaft one full turn (360°) clockwise until the arm points at the marked terminal. No 1 cylinder will then be at TDC on the compression stroke.
6 If necessary as a further check, remove the camshaft cover (4A-FE and 7A-FE engines) or upper timing belt cover (3S-FE and 3S-GE engines) and check that the hole (4A-FE, 7A-FE and 3S-FE engines) or mark (3S-GE engine) on the camshaft sprocket is aligned with the timing mark on the right-hand bearing cap (or inner timing belt cover - 3S-GE engine). Use a drill or dowel rod through the hole in the sprocket and check that it aligns with the cut-out in the bearing cap **(see illustration).**
7 Once No 1 cylinder has been positioned at TDC on the compression stroke, TDC for any of the other cylinders can then be located by rotating the crankshaft clockwise 180° at a time and following the firing order (see Specifications).

2A

3.3 Timing marks on the crankshaft pulley and lower timing belt cover

3.6 Check the camshaft is at TDC by inserting a dowel rod through the hole into the bearing cap cut-out

4.2 Disconnecting the crankcase ventilation hoses from the camshaft cover

4.3a Unscrew the bolts . . .

4.3b . . . and remove the wire harness protector

4 Camshaft cover - removal and refitting

4A-FE and 7A-FE engines

Removal

1 Disconnect the battery negative (earth) lead (refer to Chapter 5A, Sections 1 and 3).
2 Disconnect the crankcase ventilation hoses from the camshaft cover (see illustration).
3 Unbolt and remove the wire harness protector from the right-hand side of the camshaft cover (see illustrations).
4 Disconnect the HT leads from their locating clips and from their spark plugs; release the alternator wiring harness 'bridge' from the right-hand side of the camshaft cover (also

disconnect the wiring from the alternator and the oil pressure switch), and release any other relevant wiring/cable clips.
5 Unscrew the domed retaining nuts and washers, then remove the cover and gasket (see illustrations).

Refitting

6 Examine the condition of the cover gasket and spark plug tube seals, and renew if necessary. The tube seals may be prised or drifted out and the new ones fitted using a suitably-sized socket or section of tube (see illustrations).
7 Refitting is a reversal of the removal procedure, but apply a little sealant to the cylinder head as shown (see illustrations) and ensure that the gasket seats correctly in the cover before the cover is fitted; as the cover is being fitted, ensure that the spark plug tube seals seat correctly.

4.5a Remove the domed retaining nuts and washers . . .

4.5b . . . lift off the cover . . .

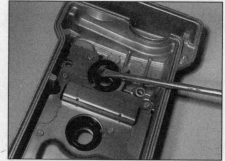

4.5c . . . and remove the gasket (4A-FE and 7A-FE engines)

4.6a Prise out the spark plug tube seals . . .

4.6b . . . and fit new ones

4.7a Apply sealant on each side of the distributor and right-hand exhaust camshaft mounting caps . . .

4.7b . . . and also over the semi-circular cover on the right-hand end of the inlet camshaft

4.13a Remove the special nuts . . .

4.13b . . . and seals . . .

4.13c . . . and remove the camshaft cover (3S-FE engines)

3S-FE and 3S-GE engines

Removal

8 Disconnect the battery negative (earth) lead (refer to Chapter 5A, Sections 1 and 3).

9 On 3S-GE engines remove the air inlet chamber from the inlet manifold (see Chapter 4A).

10 Where necessary, unbolt the accelerator cable and HT lead support brackets from the cylinder head cover and position them to one side.

11 Unclip the HT leads from their guides, then disconnect the leads from the spark plugs noting their locations.

12 Disconnect the PCV hoses from the left-hand end of the camshaft cover.

13 Unscrew the retaining nuts/bolts, then remove the cover and gasket. Note on 3S-FE engines the cover is retained with special nuts screwed onto the spark plug tubes together with seals **(see illustrations)**.

14 On 3S-GE engines, remove the semi-circular rubber inserts from the cut-outs in the top of the cylinder head.

Refitting

15 Examine the condition of the cover gasket and spark plug tube seals, and renew if necessary. The tube seals may be drifted out and the new ones fitted using a suitably-sized socket or section of tube. On 3S-GE engines also check the condition of the rubber inserts and obtain new ones if necessary.

4.16a Applying sealant to the cylinder head before refitting the camshaft cover

16 Refitting is a reversal of removal, but apply a little sealant where the camshaft bearing caps meet the cylinder head and over the semi-circular plugs at each end of the exhaust camshaft, and ensure that the gasket seats correctly in the cover before the cover is fitted; as the cover is being fitted, ensure that the spark plug tube seals seat correctly. On 3S-FE engines make sure that the special seals are located with their tabs pointing towards the timing belt end of the engine. On 3S-GE engines apply two beads of sealant to the grooves in the semi-circular rubber inserts before locating them in the cylinder head cut-outs. Tighten the retaining nuts/bolts to the specified torque **(see illustrations)**.

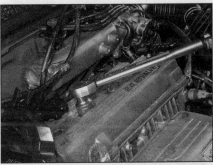

4.16b Tightening the special nuts on the 3S-FE engine

2A

5 Timing belt - removal, inspection and refitting

4A-FE and 7A-FE engines

Removal

1 Disconnect the battery negative (earth) lead (refer to Chapter 5A, Sections 1 and 3).

2 Syphon the fluid from the windscreen washer fluid reservoir on the right-hand side of the engine compartment, then unscrew the mounting screws, disconnect the tubing and wiring, and remove the reservoir **(see illustrations)**.

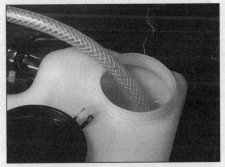

5.2a Syphon the washer fluid from the reservoir . . .

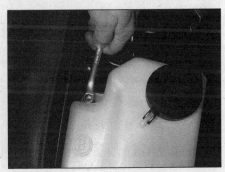

5.2b . . . before unbolting it . . .

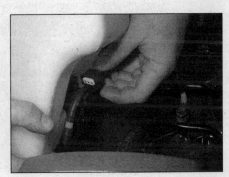

5.2c . . . and disconnecting the wiring from the pump

5.4 Loosening the water pump pulley bolts before removing the auxiliary drivebelts

5.7 Water pump pulley moved fully to the rear in order to remove the middle timing belt cover

5.11a Removing the crankshaft pulley bolt

5.11b Sliding the pulley off the end of the crankshaft

5.12a Removing the middle timing belt cover

5.12b Removing the lower timing belt cover

3 Remove the camshaft cover (see Section 4).
4 Loosen the bolts securing the drive pulley to the water pump one or two turns - the bolts are easier to loosen before actually removing the drivebelt **(see illustration)**. **Note:** *The pulley must be moved to one side later in order to remove the middle timing belt cover.*
5 Chock the rear wheels then jack up the front of the car and support it on axle stands (see *Jacking and Vehicle Support*). Remove the right-hand roadwheel, then unbolt and remove the splash guard from under the right-hand side of the engine compartment.
6 Remove the auxiliary drivebelt(s) (alternator, power steering and air conditioning, as applicable), as described in Chapter 1.
7 Unscrew the bolts securing the pulley to the water pump and move the pulley as far to the rear as possible **(see illustration)**. Note that there is insufficient room to remove the pulley

completely due to the body inner panel, however the pulley must be moved to one side to remove the middle timing belt cover.
8 Remove the spark plugs (see Chapter 1).
9 Set the engine at TDC for No 1 cylinder (nearest the timing belt) as described in Section 3.
10 The crankshaft must now be held stationary while the crankshaft pulley bolt is loosened. Toyota technicians use a special tool bolted to the crankshaft pulley to hold the crankshaft, and a similar tool can be fabricated out of flat metal bar. Alternatively, on manual transmission models have an assistant engage 4th gear and depress the brake pedal. On automatic transmission models, remove the cover/strengthener from the bottom of the transmission bellhousing and use a wide-bladed screwdriver engaged with the starter ring gear to hold the crankshaft stationary.

11 Unscrew the crankshaft pulley bolt and slide the pulley off of the end of the crankshaft. If it is tight, use a suitable puller to remove it **(see illustrations)**.
12 Unbolt and remove the upper, middle and lower timing belt covers **(see illustrations)**.
13 Slide the outer timing belt guide from the crankshaft noting which way round it is fitted **(see illustration)**.
14 If the timing belt is to be re-used, mark it with an arrow to indicate its direction of rotation. Also mark it in relation to the crankshaft and camshaft pulleys as an aid to refitting.
15 Loosen the bolt securing the timing belt tensioner to the cylinder block. Using a screwdriver and protective card, lever the tensioner rearwards to release the tension from the belt, then tighten the bolt to retain the tensioner in this position.
16 Slide the timing belt from the camshaft and crankshaft sprockets **(see illustration)**. To enable the timing belt to be fully removed, the weight of the engine must be taken off the right-hand engine/transmission mounting and the mounting separated (Section 15). Support the engine under the sump using a jack and block of wood before disconnecting the mounting.
17 Do **not** alter the position of the camshaft or crankshaft sprockets with the timing belt removed.

Inspection

18 With the timing belt removed, check it thoroughly for damage and deterioration. In particular check for cracking at the base of the teeth.

5.13 Slide the outer timing belt guide from the crankshaft key

5.16 Removing the timing belt from the camshaft sprocket

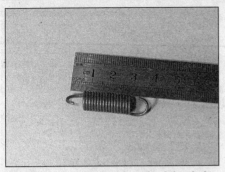

5.20 Checking the free length of the timing belt tensioner spring

19 In addition to the regular renewal called for as part of the service schedule (Chapter 1), the timing belt should be renewed, regardless of age or mileage, if it appears to be defective in any manner or if it has been in contact with water, oil or steam.

20 Check that the tensioner pulley turns smoothly without any signs of roughness. Also check that the free length of the pulley spring is as given in the Specifications - if it has stretched, renew it **(see illustration)**.

Refitting

21 Before refitting the timing belt, check that the small hole in the camshaft sprocket is in the 12 o'clock position and is centrally aligned with the mark on the camshaft right-hand bearing cap; also check that the TDC marks on the crankshaft sprocket and the oil pump housing are aligned (see Section 3).

22 Locate the timing belt on the crankshaft and camshaft sprockets, making sure that the sprockets remain at their TDC positions and the belt is taught between the front extremities of the camshaft and crankshaft sprockets. If the original belt is being refitted, ensure that the arrow marked on the belt during removal faces the correct way and that the belt-to-sprocket marks are correctly aligned. Refit the right-hand engine/transmission mounting and tighten the bolts.

23 Slacken the tensioner bolt and allow the tensioner to return with the spring pressure so that the pulley bears on the timing belt. Do not tighten the bolt at this stage.

24 Temporarily install the crankshaft pulley bolt.

25 Use a spanner or socket on the crankshaft pulley bolt to turn the crankshaft clockwise (viewed from the vehicle's right-hand side) through two full turns, then check that the camshaft and crankshaft sprocket timing marks remain aligned. If the marks are not correctly aligned, re-position the timing belt on the sprockets as previously described, then rotate the crankshaft through two further turns and recheck.

26 Tighten the tensioner pulley bolt to the specified torque, then use a spring balance to check that there is 5 to 6 mm of belt deflection midway between the front run of the belt when a load of 2 kg is applied. If adjustment is required, move the tensioner pulley slightly.

27 Remove the temporarily-installed crankshaft pulley bolt.

28 Refit the timing belt guide to the crankshaft, ensuring that its concave side is outermost, then refit the timing belt covers and tighten the bolts.

29 Slide the crankshaft pulley onto the end of the crankshaft, then tighten the bolt to the specified torque while holding the crankshaft stationary as described for the removal procedure.

30 Refit the splash guard and right-hand roadwheel and lower the vehicle to the ground.

31 Refit the spark plugs (see Chapter 1).

32 Locate the pulley on the water pump drive flange, and tighten the retaining bolts.

33 Refit and tension the auxiliary drivebelt(s) as described in Chapter 1

34 Refit the camshaft cover (Section 4).

35 Refit and fill the windscreen washer fluid reservoir, then reconnect the battery negative lead.

3S-FE and 3S-GE engines

Removal

36 Disconnect the battery negative (earth) lead (refer to Chapter 5A, Sections 1 and 3).

37 Remove the alternator as described in Chapter 5A. Also remove the power steering pump drivebelt as described in Chapter 1.

38 On 3S-GE engines remove the camshaft cover as described in Section 4.

39 Remove the spark plugs (see Chapter 1).

40 Set the engine at TDC for No 1 cylinder (nearest the timing belt) (Section 3).

41 Chock the rear wheels then jack up the front of the car and support it on axle stands (see *Jacking and Vehicle Support*). Remove the right-hand roadwheel, then unbolt and remove the splash guard from under the right-hand side of the engine compartment.

42 The crankshaft must now be held stationary while the crankshaft pulley bolt is loosened. Toyota technicians use a special tool bolted to the crankshaft pulley to hold the crankshaft, and a similar tool can be fabricated out of flat metal bar. Alternatively, on manual transmission models have an assistant engage 4th gear and depress the brake pedal. On automatic transmission models, remove the cover/strengthener from the bottom of the transmission bellhousing and use a wide-bladed screwdriver engaged with the starter ring gear to hold the crankshaft stationary.

43 Unscrew the crankshaft pulley bolt and slide the pulley off of the end of the crankshaft. If it is tight, use a suitable puller to remove it.

44 Unbolt and remove the upper and lower timing belt covers and, where fitted, recover the gaskets.

45 Slide the outer timing belt guide from the crankshaft.

46 If the timing belt is to be re-used, mark it with an arrow to indicate its direction of rotation. Also mark it in relation to the crankshaft and camshaft pulleys as an aid to refitting.

47 On 3S-FE engines, loosen the bolt securing the timing belt tensioner to the cylinder block. Using a screwdriver and protective card, lever the tensioner rearwards to release the tensioner from the belt, then tighten the bolt to retain the tensioner in this position.

48 On 3S-GE engines, note the position of the timing belt tensioner then unscrew the mounting bolts and remove it.

49 Slide the timing belt from the camshaft, crankshaft, oil pump and water pump sprockets. To enable the timing belt to be fully removed, the weight of the engine must be taken off the right-hand engine/transmission mounting and the mounting separated (see Section 15). Support the engine under the sump using a jack and block of wood before disconnecting the mounting.

50 Do **not** alter the position of the camshaft or crankshaft sprockets with the timing belt removed.

Inspection

51 With the timing belt removed, check it thoroughly for damage and deterioration. In particular check for cracking at the base of the teeth.

52 In addition to the regular renewal called for as part of the service schedule (Chapter 1), the timing belt should be renewed, regardless of age or mileage, if it appears to be defective in any manner or if it has been in contact with water, oil or steam.

53 Check that the tensioner pulley turns smoothly without any signs of roughness.

54 On 3S-FE engines, check that the free length of the pulley spring is as given in the Specifications - if it has stretched, renew it.

55 On 3S-GE engines, check the tensioner for signs of oil leakage from the pushrod seal. If evident, renew the tensioner. Check that it is not possible to move the pushrod when pressing the tensioner against the floor by hand. Using a steel rule check that the protrusion of the pushrod is within the limits given in the Specifications.

Refitting

56 Before refitting the timing belt, check that the timing marks on the camshaft sprocket(s) are aligned with the marks on the inner timing belt cover, and also check that the TDC marks on the crankshaft sprocket and the oil pump housing are aligned. As a further check, temporarily place the lower timing belt cover and the crankshaft pulley in position and check that the notch in the pulley is aligned with the 0° mark on the cover. Remove the pulley and cover after the check.

57 Fit the timing belt on the sprockets and idlers, ensuring that the sprocket positions do not alter and that the belt is taut on the front run between the camshaft, water pump and

2A

6.3a Remove the retaining bolt . . .

6.3b . . . and the camshaft sprocket

61 Refit the splash guard and right-hand roadwheel, then lower the vehicle to the ground.
62 Refit the spark plugs (see Chapter 1).
63 On 3S-GE engines refit the camshaft cover as described in Section 4.
64 Refit the alternator (Chapter 5A) and power steering pump drivebelt (Chapter 1).
65 Reconnect the battery negative lead.

6 Timing belt sprocket(s) and pulleys - removal, inspection and refitting

crankshaft sprockets. If the original belt is being refitted, ensure that the arrow marked on the belt during removal faces the correct way and that the belt-to-sprocket marks are correctly aligned. Refit the right-hand engine/transmission mounting, and tighten the bolts to the specified torque.

58 On 3S-FE engines, slacken the tensioner bolt and allow the tensioner to return against spring pressure so that the pulley bears on the timing belt. Do not tighten the bolt at this stage. Carry out the following procedure to set the tensioner.

a) Refit the outer timing belt guide concave side facing outwards, then refit the lower timing belt cover together with a new gasket (where applicable) and tighten the bolts.
b) Refit the crankshaft pulley, and tighten the bolt to the specified torque.
c) Turn the crankshaft clockwise nearly two complete revolutions, then turn it slowly to bring the TDC marks into alignment. Do not turn the crankshaft anti-clockwise. If the TDC marks do not align at this stage, remove the timing belt and carry out the refitting procedure again.
d) Turn the crankshaft clockwise one complete turn then continue turning until the timing mark is aligned with the 45° BTDC mark on the lower timing belt cover.
e) Tighten the tensioner bolt to the specified torque.

59 On 3S-GE engines, the tensioner pushrod must be pushed into the body with a press until it is possible to insert a suitable metal rod (a 1.27 mm Allen key is recommended)

through the holes in the body and pushrod The rod retains the pushrod in this position while the tensioner is being refitted. Carry out the following procedure to set the tensioner.

a) Refit the outer timing belt guide concave side facing outwards, then refit the lower timing belt cover together with a new gasket (where applicable) and tighten the bolts.
b) Refit the crankshaft pulley and tighten the bolt to the specified torque.
c) Apply a torque of 18 Nm to the tensioner idler pulley bolt in an anti-clockwise direction, then refit the tensioner and hand-tighten the bolts at this stage. Check that the timing marks are still correctly aligned.
d) Turn the crankshaft clockwise until the notch in the pulley is aligned with the 60° BTDC mark on the lower timing belt cover.
e) Insert a 1.9 mm feeler blade between the tensioner body and the idler pulley stopper.
f) Apply the torque as in paragraph c then push the tensioner and fully tighten the mounting bolts to the specified torque.
g) Remove the metal rod used to retain the tensioner pushrod, and turn the crankshaft one complete revolution until the 60° BTDC mark is aligned again.
h) Apply the torque as in paragraph c then use feeler blades to check that the clearance measured in paragraph e is between 1.8 and 2.2 mm. If not, carry out the procedure again.

60 Refit the upper timing belt cover together with a new gasket (where applicable), and tighten the retaining bolts.

Removal

1 Remove the timing belt as described in Section 5. Where only a camshaft sprocket is being removed, it is not necessary to remove the crankshaft pulley or the lower timing belt cover. Also it is not necessary to remove the right-hand engine mounting if the original timing belt is to be refitted.
2 On 3S-FE and 3S-GE engines remove the camshaft cover as described in Section 4.

Camshaft sprocket

3 Use a spanner on the flats provided to hold the camshaft stationary, then unscrew the bolt and remove the sprocket from the end of the camshaft (see illustrations).

Crankshaft sprocket

4 Slide the crankshaft sprocket from the key on the end of the crankshaft using two levers if necessary (see illustration). To prevent damage to the oil pump housing, position card or pieces of wood beneath the levers.
5 If necessary, remove the key from the groove in the crankshaft and place in a container for safe keeping.

Tensioner pulley (4A-FE, 7A-FE and 3S-FE engines)

6 Loosen the mounting bolt to release the spring tension, then unhook the spring, unscrew the mounting bolt and remove the tensioner from the oil pump housing or cylinder head as applicable (see illustration).

Tensioner pulley (3S-GE engine)

7 The tensioner body is removed during the removal of the timing belt. Unscrew the pulley arm shouldered mounting bolt, remove the pulley and arm from the cylinder head, and recover the washer.

Idler pulley (3S-GE engine)

8 Unscrew the bolt and remove the idler pulley from the oil pump housing.

Inspection

9 Inspect the teeth of the sprockets for signs of nicks and damage. The teeth are not prone to wear, and should normally last the life of the engine.
10 Spin the tensioner and idler pulleys by hand, and check for any roughness or tightness. Do not attempt to clean them with

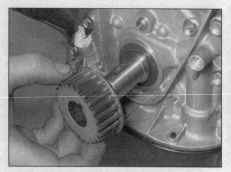

6.4 Removing the crankshaft sprocket

6.6 Removing the tensioner pulley

6.15 TDC marks on the crankshaft sprocket and oil pump housing

6.17a Locate the tensioner pulley on the oil pump housing . . .

6.17b . . . and insert the bolt

solvent, as this may enter the bearings. If wear is evident, renew the tensioner and/or idler wheel as necessary.

Refitting

Camshaft sprocket

11 Locate the camshaft sprocket on the end of the camshaft, making sure that the location pin engages with the groove in the sprocket.

12 Insert the bolt and tighten to the specified torque while holding the camshaft stationary with a spanner on the flats provided.

13 Refit the timing belt with reference to Section 5. On 3S-FE and 3S-GE engines refit the camshaft cover.

Crankshaft sprocket

14 If removed, locate the key in the groove in the crankshaft making sure that its top edge is parallel with the crankshaft.

15 Slide the crankshaft sprocket on the crankshaft, flanged side first. If the sprocket becomes tight on the key, remove it and check that the key is pressed fully into the groove. Check that the TDC mark is aligned correctly (see illustration).

16 Refit the timing belt with reference to Section 5. On 3S-FE and 3S-GE engines refit the camshaft cover.

Tensioner pulley (4A-FE, 7A-FE and 3S-FE engines)

17 Hook the spring onto the pulley and oil pump housing, then refit the pulley and insert the bolt (see illustrations).

18 Lever the pulley against the spring and retain in this position by tightening the bolt.

19 Refit the timing belt (see Section 5).

20 On 3S-FE engines, refit the camshaft cover.

Tensioner pulley (3S-GE engine)

21 Refit the pulley to the cylinder head together with the washer, then insert the shouldered bolt and tighten to the specified torque.

22 Refit the timing belt (see Section 5).

23 Refit the camshaft cover.

Idler pulley (3S-GE engine)

24 Apply locking fluid to the threads of the mounting bolt.

25 Locate the idler pulley on the oil pump housing then insert the mounting bolt and tighten to the specified torque.

26 Refit the timing belt (see Section 5).

27 Refit the camshaft cover.

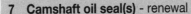

7 Camshaft oil seal(s) - renewal

4A-FE and 7A-FE engines

1 Remove the camshaft sprocket as described in Section 6.

2 Punch or drill two small holes opposite each other in the seal, but take care not to damage the surface of the camshaft. Screw a self-tapping screw into each hole and pull on the screws with pliers to extract the seal (see illustration).

3 Wipe clean the seal location and check the contact surface on the camshaft for excessive

wear. If a deep groove is evident, it will be necessary to renew the camshaft.

4 Lubricate the lips of the new seal with a little multi-purpose grease and ease the seal over the end of the camshaft. Using a socket as a drift which bears only on the seal's hard outer edge, drive the seal squarely into position until it seats on its locating shoulder, then wipe off any surplus grease (see illustrations).

5 Refit the camshaft sprocket with reference to Section 6.

3S-FE and 3S-GE engines

6 Remove the camshaft sprocket(s) and tensioner pulley as described in Section 6.

7 Unbolt and remove the inner timing belt cover from the end of the cylinder head.

8 Punch or drill two small holes opposite each other in the seal. Screw a self-tapping screw into each hole and pull on the screws with pliers to extract the seal.

9 Wipe clean the seal location and check the contact surface on the camshaft for excessive wear. If a deep groove is evident, it will be necessary to renew the camshaft.

10 Lubricate the lips of the new seal with a little multi-purpose grease and ease the seal over the end of the camshaft. Using a socket as a drift which bears only on the seal's hard outer edge, drive the seal squarely into position until it seats on its locating shoulder, then wipe off any surplus grease.

11 Refit the inner timing belt cover and tighten the bolts.

12 Refit the camshaft sprocket(s) and tensioner pulley with reference to Section 6.

2A

7.2 Drilling holes in the camshaft oil seal prior to removal

7.4a Ease the new oil seal over the end of the camshaft . . .

7.4b . . . and drive it into position with a socket

8.4 Using an adjustable spanner on the hexagonal section on the inlet camshaft

8.5 Removing the right-hand bearing cap from the inlet camshaft

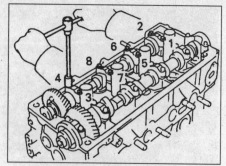

8.7a Inlet camshaft bearing cap bolt slackening sequence (4A-FE and 7A-FE engines)

8.7b Inlet camshaft caps are marked I and numbered, with an arrow towards the timing belt end of the engine

8.7c Removing the inlet camshaft

8 Camshafts and followers - removal, inspection and refitting

Removal

1 Remove the camshaft sprocket(s) as described in Section 6.

2 Remove the distributor as described in Chapter 5B. **Note:** *If the exhaust camshaft is not being removed then it is not necessary to remove the distributor.*

3 Before removing the camshafts, use a dial gauge to measure the endfloat of each camshaft. This must be within specification; if it exceeds its maximum permissible limit, the camshaft(s) and/or cylinder head must be renewed.

4A-FE and 7A-FE engines

4 Using an open-ended spanner or adjustable spanner on the camshaft hexagonal section, set the inlet camshaft drive gear service bolt hole to the 12 o'clock position; the lobes of numbers one and three cylinders should now be pushing evenly on their followers (see illustration).

5 Progressively slacken the inlet camshaft right-hand bearing cap retaining bolts, a little at a time, then remove the bearing cap (see illustration).

6 To release the pressure of the sub-gear spring, secure the inlet camshaft sub-gear to its main gear using a 6 mm bolt (16 to 20 mm long) inserted through the service bolt hole.

7 Progressively slacken the inlet camshaft bearing cap bolts, a little at a time, in the sequence shown until all valve spring pressure

has been relieved (see illustration). Remove the bearing caps, noting their correct fitted positions, then lift out the camshaft. The caps are marked with an I, and an arrow points to the timing belt end of the engine (see illustrations). Do not attempt to prise out the camshaft or it will be damaged; if the camshaft cannot be lifted out, re-tighten No 3 bearing cap then loosen each of its bolts alternately whilst pulling upwards the camshaft gear.

Caution: Make sure that the bolts are loosened progressively otherwise the force on the cylinder head thrust faces may damage the cylinder head and/or camshaft!

8 Rotate the exhaust camshaft so that the sprocket locating pin is at approximately the 7 o'clock position; the lobes of numbers one and three cylinders should be pushing evenly on their followers.

9 Progressively slacken the exhaust camshaft right-hand bearing cap retaining bolts, a little at a time, then remove the bearing cap. If it is tight, do not prise it out but leave it in position with the bolts removed.

10 Progressively slacken the exhaust camshaft bearing cap bolts, a little at a time, in the sequence shown until all valve spring pressure has been relieved (see illustration). Remove the bearing caps, noting their correct fitted positions, then lift out the camshaft (see illustrations). Do not attempt to prise it out or it will be damaged; if the camshaft cannot be lifted out, re-tighten No 3 bearing cap then loosen each of its bolts alternately whilst pulling upwards the camshaft gear.

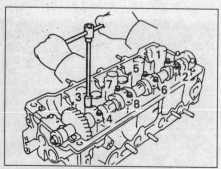

8.10a Exhaust camshaft bearing cap bolt slackening sequence (4A-FE and 7A-FE engines)

8.10b Exhaust camshaft caps are marked E and numbered, with an arrow towards the timing belt end of the engine

8.10c Remove the bolts . . .

8.10d . . . the bearing caps . . .

8.10e . . . and the exhaust camshaft

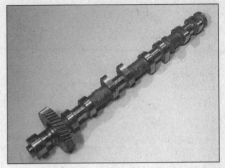

8.10f The exhaust camshaft removed from the cylinder head

Caution: Make sure that the bolts are loosened progressively otherwise the force on the cylinder head thrust faces may damage the cylinder head and/or camshaft!

8.11 Removing the camshaft followers

11 If necessary, lift out the shims and camshaft followers, keeping all components in order for refitting to their original locations **(see illustration)**.

12 The inlet camshaft sub-gear can be removed as follows. Mount the camshaft by its hexagonal section in a soft-jawed vice and screw in two further bolts to act as leverage points. Using a screwdriver between these bolts, apply pressure in a clockwise direction to hold the sub-gear against the torsional spring pressure, then remove the bolt inserted to secure the sub-gear to the main gear, and carefully allow the sub-gear to rotate anti-clockwise until all spring pressure is released. Remove the sub-gear securing circlip then remove the wave washer, sub-gear and spring **(see illustrations)**.

3S-FE engine

13 Using an open-ended spanner on its hexagonal section, set the inlet camshaft sprocket locating pin between 10° and 45° before TDC (camshaft angle); the lobes of numbers two and four cylinders should now be pushing evenly on their followers **(see illustration)**.

14 To release the pressure of the sub-gear spring, secure the exhaust camshaft sub-gear to its main gear using a 6 mm bolt (16 to 20 mm long).

15 Unbolt and remove the inner timing belt cover from the end of the cylinder head. Progressively slacken the exhaust camshaft left-hand bearing cap bolts, a little at a time, then remove the cap.

2A

8.12a Use two bolts to hold the inlet camshaft sub-gear tensioned while the retaining bolts is removed

8.12b Remove the circlip . . .

8.12c . . . the wave washer . . .

8.12d . . . the sub-gear . . .

8.12e . . . and the spring

8.13 Inlet and exhaust camshafts showing the drive gears (3S-FE engine)

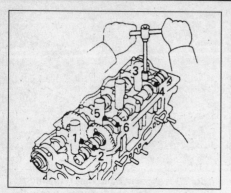

8.16 Exhaust camshaft bearing cap bolt slackening sequence (3S-FE engine)

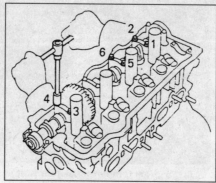

8.20 Inlet camshaft bearing cap bolt slackening sequence (3S-FE engine)

16 Working in several stages, in the sequence shown, progressively slacken the exhaust camshaft bearing cap bolts but leaving the bolts of No 3 cap engaged several threads **(see illustration)**. Remove the Nos 1, 2 and 4 bearing caps, having noted their markings and their correct fitted positions.

17 Unscrew the bolts of the No 3 cap, then remove the cap and lift out the exhaust camshaft keeping it level so that it does not bind on the cylinder head.

Caution: Make sure that the bolts are loosened progressively otherwise the force on the cylinder head thrust faces may damage the cylinder head and/or camshaft!

18 Using an open-ended spanner on the camshaft hexagonal section, set the inlet camshaft sprocket locating pin between 80° and 115° before TDC (camshaft angle); the lobes of numbers one and three cylinders should now be pushing evenly on their followers.

19 Progressively unscrew the bolts of the right-hand bearing cap, then remove the cap and oil seal.

20 Working in several stages in the sequence shown **(see illustration)**, progressively slacken the camshaft bearing cap bolts but leaving the bolts of No 2 cap engaged several threads.

Caution: Make sure that the bolts are loosened progressively otherwise the force on the cylinder head thrust faces may damage the cylinder head and/or camshaft!

21 Remove the Nos 1, 3 and 4 bearing caps, having noted their markings and their correct fitted positions.

22 Unscrew the bolts of the No 2 cap, then remove the cap and lift out the inlet camshaft keeping it level so that it does not bind on the cylinder head.

23 Lift out the shims and camshaft followers, keeping all components in order for refitting to their original locations.

24 The exhaust camshaft sub-gear can be removed as follows. Mount the camshaft by its hexagonal section in a soft-jawed vice and screw in two further bolts to act as leverage points. Using a screwdriver between these

bolts, apply pressure in a clockwise direction to hold the sub-gear against the torsional spring pressure, then remove the first bolt (inserted to secure the sub-gear to the main gear) and carefully allow the sub-gear to rotate anti-clockwise until all spring pressure is released. Remove the sub-gear securing circlip then remove the washer, sub-gear and spring.

3S-GE engine

25 Unbolt and remove the inner timing belt cover from the end of the cylinder head.

26 Working in several stages, progressively slacken the camshaft bearing cap bolts. Remove the bearing caps, having noted their markings and their correct fitted positions, then lift out the camshafts and remove the oil seals.

27 Lift out the shims and camshaft followers, keeping all components in order for refitting to their original locations.

Inspection

28 Examine the cam lobes and camshaft bearing surfaces for wear ridges and scoring, and the distributor drive for wear. Renew the camshaft(s) if any of these conditions are apparent. Supporting the ends of each camshaft on V-blocks and using a dial gauge at its centre journal, measure the camshaft runout. If the runout is outside specification, the camshaft(s) must be renewed.

29 Clean the bearing caps and the camshaft journals, then check the running clearances of each camshaft using Plastigauge, as follows. Place the camshaft in the cylinder head, then lay a strip of Plastigauge across each journal and refit the bearing caps as described later; do not rotate the camshaft. Remove the bearing caps, then compare the width of the compressed strips with the scale on the Plastigauge pack. If the running clearance on any journal is worn to the specified maximum or beyond, the camshaft and/or cylinder head must be renewed. Measure the camshaft journal diameters; if any is excessively worn the camshaft must be renewed. If the cylinder head bearing surfaces are worn excessively, the cylinder head must be renewed. Remove all traces of Plastigauge.

30 If the camshaft sub-gear has been removed, on 4A-FE, 7A-FE and 3S-FE engines, install the camshafts and check the gear backlash using a dial gauge. If the backlash is outside specification, the camshafts must be renewed. Remove the camshafts (as described above) upon completion of the check.

31 Using calipers, check that the distance between the ends of the sub-gear torsional spring is as specified (with the spring in a 'free state'); renew the spring if not.

32 Before reassembling the inlet camshaft gear, check that there are no signs of chipping or cracking on any of the teeth (check also the exhaust camshaft gear); the camshaft must be renewed if any such fault is evident.

33 Inspect the shims and camshaft followers for wear ridges or scoring. Renew any worn followers, but note that any shims required can be selected only when the cylinder head is reassembled and the valve clearances can be checked (Chapter 1).

34 Check the camshaft follower clearances as follows, taking great care not to mix them up; check each separately, noting the measurement. Measure the follower diameter, then measure its bore in the cylinder head; subtract the follower diameter from its bore diameter to obtain the clearance. If this is excessive, the follower(s) or the cylinder head (whichever is excessively worn) must be renewed.

Refitting

4A-FE and 7A-FE engines

35 If it was dismantled, reassemble the inlet camshaft sub-gear, reversing the method of dismantling; remove the two bolts used as leverage points once the single bolt is in place securing the sub-gear to the main gear.

36 Install the camshaft followers and shims to their original bores, having lightly oiled the bores; check that the followers can be rotated smoothly in the bores by hand.

37 Lightly oil the exhaust camshaft journals and cam lobes, then place the exhaust camshaft on the cylinder head so that the sprocket locating pin is positioned as described in paragraph 8; the cam lobes of number one and number three cylinders should push evenly on their followers.

38 Apply sealant to the camshaft right-hand bearing cap location on the cylinder head **(see illustration)**, then refit the camshaft bearing caps in their original fitted positions. Lightly oil the heads and threads of the bolts then insert and tighten them evenly and progressively to their specified torque setting in the sequence shown **(see illustrations)**.

39 Install a new camshaft oil seal as described in Section 7.

40 Lightly oil the inlet camshaft journals and cam lobes. Also lightly oil the camshaft bearing cap bolt threads and heads.

8.38a Apply sealant to the front edges of the exhaust camshaft right-hand bearing cap . . .

8.38b . . . then refit the cap on the cylinder head

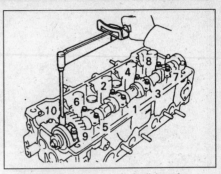

8.38c Bearing cap bolt tightening sequence for the exhaust camshaft (4A-FE and 7A-FE engines)

41 Set the exhaust camshaft locating pin to the 9 o'clock position just above the upper surface of the cylinder head, then engage the inlet camshaft gear with that of the exhaust camshaft so that their installation marks are aligned. Once the camshaft gears are correctly engaged, roll the inlet gear down the exhaust gear until the inlet camshaft is seated in the cylinder head **(see illustrations)**.

42 Refit the inlet camshaft bearing caps (with the exception of the right-hand cap), and their bolts, in their original fitted positions **(see illustration)**. Evenly and progressively, in the sequence shown **(see illustration)**, tighten the bolts to their specified torque setting.

43 Unscrew the bolt securing the sub-gear to the main gear **(see illustration)**.

44 Refit the inlet camshaft right-hand bearing

cap so that its arrow points toward the timing belt end of the engine, and tighten its retaining bolts (lightly oiled) alternately to their specified torque; if difficulty is experienced fitting the bearing cap, push the camshaft towards the cylinder head left-hand end.

45 Using an open-ended spanner, rotate the exhaust camshaft clockwise so that its locating pin is in the 12 o'clock position. Check that the TDC marks on the outer face of the camshaft gears align and that the installation marks are both in the 12 o'clock position.

46 If all is well, refit the camshaft sprocket as described in Section 6, and the distributor (Chapter 5B). Note that the valve clearances should be checked (see Chapter 1) before the camshaft cover is refitted.

3S-FE engine

47 If it was dismantled, reassemble the exhaust camshaft sub-gear, reversing the method of dismantling; remove the two bolts used as leverage points once the single bolt is in place securing the sub-gear to the main gear.

48 Install the camshaft followers and shims to their original bores, having lightly oiled the bores; check that the followers can be rotated smoothly in the bores by hand.

49 Lightly oil the inlet camshaft journals and cam lobes, then place the inlet camshaft on the cylinder head so that the camshaft sprocket locating pin is positioned as described in paragraph 18; the cam lobes of number one and number three cylinders should push evenly on their followers.

2A

8.38d Tightening the exhaust camshaft bearing cap bolts to the specified torque

8.41a Lowering the inlet camshaft into the cylinder head

8.41b Installation marks on the gears of the inlet and exhaust camshafts

8.42a Refitting the inlet camshaft bearing caps

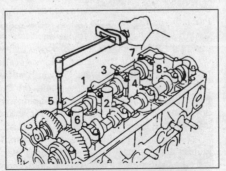

8.42b Bearing cap bolt tightening sequence for the inlet camshaft (4A-FE and 7A-FE engines)

8.43 Unscrewing the bolts securing the sub-gear to the main gear on the inlet camshaft

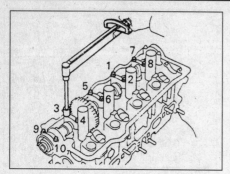

8.50 Inlet camshaft bearing cap bolt tightening sequence (3S-FE engine)

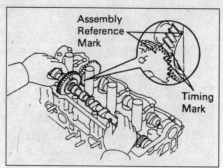

8.53 Assembly reference marks and timing marks on the camshaft gears (3S-FE engine)

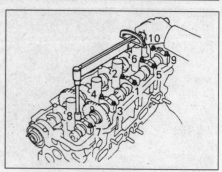

8.54 Exhaust camshaft bearing cap bolt tightening sequence (3S-FE engine)

50 Apply a bead of sealant to the camshaft right-hand bearing cap, then refit the camshaft bearing caps in their original fitted positions. Lightly oil the heads and threads of the bolts then insert and tighten them evenly and progressively to their specified torque setting in the sequence shown **(see illustration)**.

51 Install a new camshaft oil seal as described in Section 7.

52 Lightly oil the exhaust camshaft journals and cam lobes. Also lightly oil the camshaft bearing cap bolt threads and heads.

53 Set the inlet camshaft locating pin to the position described in paragraph 13, then engage the exhaust camshaft gear with that of the inlet camshaft so that their timing marks are aligned. Once the camshaft gears are correctly engaged, roll the exhaust gear down the inlet gear until the exhaust camshaft is seated in the cylinder head. Note that there are two sets of marks on the camshaft gears; assembly reference marks and timing marks. Ensure that the timing marks, **not** the assembly reference marks are aligned when engaging the gears **(see illustration)**.

54 Refit the exhaust camshaft bearing caps and their bolts in their original positions. Evenly and progressively, in the sequence shown **(see illustration)**, tighten the bolts to their specified torque setting.

55 Unscrew the bolt securing the sub-gear to the main gear.

56 Refit the inner timing belt cover and secure with the bolts.

57 Refit the camshaft sprocket as described in Section 6, and the distributor as described in Chapter 5B. Note that the valve clearances should be checked (see Chapter 1) before the camshaft cover is refitted.

3S-GE engine

58 Install the camshaft followers and shims to their original bores, having lightly oiled the bores; check that the followers can be rotated smoothly in their bores by hand.

59 Lightly oil the camshaft journals and cam lobes, then place the camshafts on the cylinder head with the No 1 camshaft lobes facing away from each other towards the front and rear of the engine. Ensure that the inlet and exhaust camshafts are correctly fitted; the exhaust camshaft has a distributor drive gear.

60 Apply a bead of sealant to the No 1 bearing caps, then place all the camshaft bearing caps in their original fitted positions.

61 Lightly oil the threads and under the heads of the bearing cap bolts, refit the bolts and tighten them evenly and progressively to the specified torque setting.

62 Install two new camshaft oil seals as described in Section 7.

63 Refit the inner timing belt cover and secure with the bolts.

64 Refit the camshaft sprockets as described in Section 6, and the distributor as described in Chapter 5B. Note that the valve clearances should be checked (see Chapter 1) before the camshaft cover is refitted.

9 Cylinder head - removal and refitting

To aid refitting, note the locations of all relevant brackets and the routing of hoses and cables before removal.

Removal

1 Disconnect the battery negative (earth) lead (refer to Chapter 5A, Sections 1 and 3).

2 Drain the cooling system (see Chapter 1).

3 On 4A-FE and 7A-FE engines, loosen the bolts securing the pulley to the water pump drive flange.

4 Remove the auxiliary drivebelt(s) (see Chapter 1).

5 Disconnect the wiring and remove the alternator as described in Chapter 5A.

6 Disconnect the wiring from the oil pressure switch, then unscrew the two bolts and remove the wiring loom harness and protector from the right-hand end of the cylinder head.

7 Remove the exhaust manifold (Chapter 4A).

8 Disconnect the HT leads from the spark plugs and release them from the support on the left-hand end of the cylinder head.

9 Remove the distributor (Chapter 5B).

10 Disconnect the wiring, bottom hose and heater hoses from the coolant inlet housing on the left-hand end of the cylinder head. Also disconnect the top hose from the outlet on the left-hand end of the cylinder head **(see illustrations)**. On 3S-FE engines disconnect

9.10a Removing the bottom hose . . .

9.10b . . . and top hose

9.10c Disconnecting the wiring from the temperature sensor

9.12 Removing the air duct from the throttle housing

9.14 Unbolting the support bracket from the rear of the inlet manifold

9.15 Unbolting the lifting eye and air chamber support bracket

the earth wiring, knock sensor wiring and EGR valve wiring.

11 On 3S-FE engines remove the EGR valve and vacuum modulator with reference to Chapter 4B.

12 Loosen the clips and remove the air duct from between the throttle housing and the air cleaner **(see illustration)**.

13 Disconnect the wiring and hoses, and accelerator cable, from the throttle housing.

14 Unbolt and remove the inlet manifold support bracket from the rear of the engine. Note that it is not necessary to completely remove the lower mounting bolt, but it must be loosened to enable the inlet manifold to be withdrawn from the studs on the cylinder head **(see illustration)**.

15 Unscrew the bolts securing the lifting eye and air chamber support bracket to the left-hand end of the cylinder head **(see illustration)**.

16 Unbolt the supports from the air chamber to release the fuel return hose and air pipe.

17 Identify the location of the wiring harness to the cylinder head and inlet manifold, then disconnect it and position to one side.

18 Disconnect the two PCV hoses from the camshaft cover.

19 Disconnect the vacuum hose from the right-hand end of the air chamber, then use an Allen key to unscrew the bolts securing the chamber to the inlet manifold. Lift off the chamber and remove the gasket **(see illustration)**.

20 Disconnect the fuel return hose from the pressure regulator on the fuel rail.

21 Unscrew the union bolt then disconnect the fuel inlet hose from the left-hand end of the fuel rail. Recover the copper washers.

22 Disconnect the wiring from the injectors.

23 Unscrew the mounting bolts and remove the fuel rail and injectors as described in

Chapter 4A. Recover the spacers from the inlet manifold **(see illustrations)**.

24 Unscrew the nuts and bolts and withdraw the inlet manifold from the studs on the cylinder head. On lean-burn engines also remove the intake air control valve assembly. Recover the gasket(s) **(see illustrations)**.

25 Remove the oil level dipstick, then unscrew the bolt securing the dipstick guide tube to the inlet manifold. Pull the tube from the oil pump housing and recover the O-ring seal.

26 At the rear of the engine, unscrew the nuts securing the water pump inlet to the cylinder head. Disconnect the hose from the water pump and remove the inlet and gasket.

27 Remove the spark plugs as described in Chapter 1.

28 Remove the camshaft cover as described in Section 4 of this Chapter.

2A

9.19 Removing the air chamber from the inlet manifold

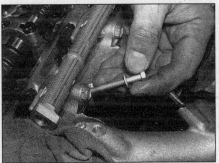

9.23a Unscrew the mounting bolts . . .

9.23b . . . and remove the fuel rail . . .

9.23c . . . then remove the long spacers . . .

9.23d . . . and short spacers

9.24a Removing the inlet manifold and gasket . . .

9.24b . . . the intake air control valve assembly . . .

9.24c . . . and the gasket

29 Unbolt and remove the upper (3S-FE and 3S-GE engines) or upper and middle (4A-FE and 7A-FE engines) timing belt covers.
30 Position the engine at TDC as described in Section 3 of this Chapter.
31 Mark the timing belt and camshaft sprocket(s) in relation to each other as an aid to refitting.
32 On 4A-FE, 7A-FE and 3S-FE engines, loosen the timing belt tensioner pulley retaining bolt, move the tensioner to the rear as far as possible and re-tighten the retaining bolt. For access to the tensioner pulley bolt on 4A-FE and 7A-FE engines, prise out the rubber grommet from the lower timing belt cover and slacken the bolt using a socket inserted through the hole in the cover. On 3S-GE engines, note the position of the timing belt tensioner then unscrew the mounting bolts

and remove it. Now unscrew the tensioner pulley arm shouldered mounting bolt, remove the pulley and arm from the cylinder head, and recover the washer.
33 Ease the timing belt from the camshaft sprocket(s) making sure that it remains engaged with the crankshaft sprocket. Tie the belt to one side but **do not** bend it excessively.
34 If necessary, unbolt the alternator mounting bracket from the front of the cylinder head. Note that the right-hand engine lifting eye is located on one of the mounting bolts.
35 Remove the inlet and exhaust camshafts as described in Section 8.
36 On 4A-FE, 7A-FE and 3S-FE engines, prise the semi-circular plug from the camshaft cut-out at the right-hand end of the cylinder head.

37 Working in the sequence shown, progressively slacken the cylinder head bolts by half a turn at a time, until all bolts can be unscrewed by hand **(see illustrations)**. A splined socket will be required for this procedure.
38 Lift out the cylinder head bolts and recover the washers **(see illustration)**.
39 Rock the cylinder head to release the gasket, then lift it from the two locating dowels on the cylinder block and position it on the bench. Remove the gasket from the top of the block **(see illustrations)**. If they are a loose fit in the block, remove the locating dowels and store them with the head for safe-keeping.
40 If the cylinder head is to be dismantled for overhaul, refer to Part B of this Chapter.

Preparation for refitting

41 Check the condition of the cylinder head bolts, and particularly their threads, whenever they are removed. Wash the bolts and wipe dry, then check each for any sign of visible wear or damage, renewing any bolt if necessary. Although Toyota do not actually specify that the bolts be renewed when disturbed, it is recommended that they are.
42 The mating faces of the cylinder head and cylinder block/crankcase must be perfectly clean before refitting the head. Use a hard plastic or wood scraper to remove all traces of gasket and carbon; also clean the piston crowns. Take particular care, as the surfaces

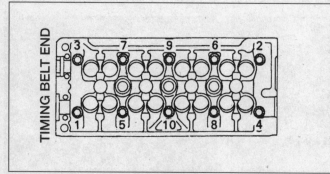

9.37a Cylinder head bolt slackening sequence (4A-FE engines)

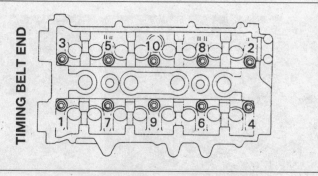

9.37b Cylinder head bolt slackening sequence (7A-FE, 3S-FE and 3S-GE engines)

9.37c Progressively slacken the cylinder bolts by half a turn at a time

9.38 Removing the cylinder head bolts

9.39a Lift the cylinder head from the block . . .

9.39b . . . and remove the gasket

9.46 Locating a new gasket on the cylinder block

9.49a 4A-FE and 7A-FE engines have the longer head bolts beneath the exhaust camshaft (4A-FE engine shown)

are damaged easily. Also, make sure that the carbon is not allowed to enter the oil and water passages - this is particularly important for the lubrication system, as carbon could block the oil supply to any of the engine's components. Using adhesive tape and paper, seal the water, oil and bolt holes in the cylinder block/crankcase. To prevent carbon entering the gap between the pistons and bores, smear a little grease in the gap. After cleaning each piston, use a small brush to remove all traces of grease and carbon from the gap, then wipe away the remainder with a clean rag. Clean all the pistons in the same way.

43 Check the mating surfaces of the cylinder block/crankcase and the cylinder head for nicks, deep scratches and other damage. If slight, they may be removed carefully with a

file, but if excessive, machining may be the only alternative to renewal.

44 If warpage of the cylinder head gasket surface is suspected, use a straight-edge to check it for distortion. Refer to Part B of this Chapter if necessary.

Refitting

45 Wipe clean the mating surfaces of the cylinder head and cylinder block/crankcase. Check that the two locating dowels are in position at each end of the cylinder block/crankcase surface. Check that the crankshaft is still at the TDC position.

46 Fit a new gasket to the cylinder block/crankcase surface, aligning it with the locating dowels **(see illustration)**.

47 Carefully refit the cylinder head to the block and align it with the locating dowels.

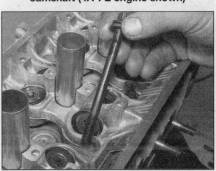

9.49b Refitting the cylinder head bolts and washers

48 Locate the washers on the cylinder head bolts, then lightly oil the threads of the bolts and the surfaces under the heads.

2A

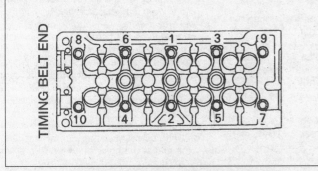

9.50a Cylinder head bolt tightening sequence (4A-FE, 3S-FE and 3S-GE engines)

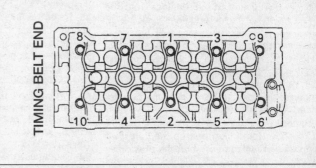

9.50b Cylinder head bolt tightening sequence (7A-FE engines)

9.50c Tightening the cylinder head bolts to the Stage 1 torque setting

9.51 Angle-tightening the cylinder head bolts to the Stage 2 angle

49 Enter each bolt into the holes (*do not drop them in*) and screw in, by hand until finger-tight. Note that on 4A-FE and 7A-FE engines, the longer bolts are located beneath the exhaust camshaft position **(see illustrations)**.

50 Working progressively and in the sequence shown, tighten the cylinder head bolts to their Stage 1 torque setting, using a torque wrench and socket **(see illustrations)**.

51 Go around again in the specified sequence and angle-tighten the head bolts through the specified Stage 2 angle. It is recommended that an angle-measuring gauge is used during this stage, to ensure accuracy **(see illustration)**. If an angle-

9.53a Apply sealant to the semi-circular plug . . .

9.53b . . . and put it in the cut-out at the right-hand end of the cylinder head with the protrusion on the outside

measuring gauge is not available, mark the side of each bolt with a dab of paint before angle-tightening them. If each bolt is marked on the side facing the timing belt end of the engine, it will be easy to determine when they have been tightened through the 90° Stage 2 angle (all the paint marks will be facing the inlet manifold side of the engine).

52 On the 4A-FE and 7A-FE engines only, and again working in the specified sequence, angle-tighten the bolts to the Stage 3 angle. Where used, the paint marks should .now be facing the flywheel end of the engine.

53 On 4A-FE, 7A-FE and 3S-FE engines, apply suitable sealant (consult a Toyota dealer) to the semi-circular plug and insert it in the cut-out at the right-hand end of the cylinder head **(see illustrations)**.

54 Refit the inlet and exhaust camshafts as described in Section 8.

55 On 3S-FE and 3S-GE engines, refit the inner timing belt cover. Additionally, on 3S-GE engines, position the timing belt tensioner pulley on the cylinder head, together with the washer, then insert the shouldered bolt and tighten to the specified torque.

56 Where removed, refit the alternator mounting bracket to the front of the cylinder head and tighten the bolts to the specified torque.

57 Locate the timing belt on the camshaft sprocket(s) making sure that the previously made marks are correctly aligned. Check that the TDC mark on the crankshaft pulley is still aligned.

58 Tension the timing belt with reference to the applicable paragraphs of Section 5 (according to engine type) then, on 4A-FE and 7A-FE engines, refit the rubber grommet to the lower timing belt cover.

59 Check that the TDC timing marks are correctly aligned with reference to Section 5.

60 Refit the upper, or upper and middle timing belt covers as applicable.

61 Refit the camshaft cover (see Section 4).

62 Refit the spark plugs (see Chapter 1).

63 Refit the water pump inlet together with a new gasket and tighten the nuts.

64 Reconnect the hose to the inlet.

65 Refit the oil level dipstick tube and tighten the bolt. Insert the dipstick in the tube.

66 Refit the inlet manifold together with a new gasket (refer to Chapter 4A if necessary). On lean-burn engines also refit the intake air control valve assembly and gasket.

67 Refit the fuel rail and injectors with reference to Chapter 4A.

68 Reconnect the injector wiring.

69 Refit the fuel inlet union to the left-hand end of the fuel rail together with new copper washers, and tighten the bolt.

70 Reconnect the fuel return hose to the pressure regulator on the fuel rail.

71 Refit the air chamber to the inlet manifold together with a new gasket and tighten the bolts.

72 Reconnect the PCV hoses to the camshaft cover.

73 Reconnect the wiring harness to the inlet manifold and cylinder head.

74 Refit the fuel return hose and air pipe supports.

75 Refit the lifting eye and air chamber support bracket to the cylinder head.

76 Refit the support bracket to the inlet manifold and tighten the bolts.

77 Reconnect the wiring and hoses, and accelerator cable, to the throttle housing.

78 Refit the air duct between the throttle housing and air cleaner.

79 On 3S-FE engines reconnect the earth wiring, knock sensor wiring and the EGR valve wiring.

80 Reconnect the wiring and hoses to the coolant inlet housing.

81 On 3S-FE engines refit the EGR valve and vacuum modulator (see Chapter 4B).

82 Refit the distributor with reference to Chapter 5B.

83 Reconnect the HT leads to the spark plugs and support.

84 Refit the exhaust manifold with reference to Chapter 4A.

85 Reconnect the oil pressure switch wiring, then refit the wiring loom harness and protector to the right-hand end of the cylinder head.

86 Refit the alternator with reference to Chapter 5A.

87 Refit the water pump pulley (4A-FE and 7A-FE engines) then refit and tension the auxiliary drivebelt(s) (see Chapter 1).

88 Refill the cooling system (see Chapter 1).

89 Reconnect the battery negative lead.

90 Start the engine and warm it up to normal operating temperature, and check for oil and coolant leaks.

10 Sump - removal and refitting

Removal

1 Disconnect the battery negative (earth) lead (refer to Chapter 5A, Sections 1 and 3).

2 Chock the rear wheels then jack up the front of the car and support it on axle stands (see *Jacking and Vehicle Support*).

3 Unbolt and remove the undershield from beneath the engine, then drain the engine oil as described in Chapter 1.

4 Connect a hoist and lifting tackle to the engine lifting bracket at the left-hand end of the cylinder head, and raise the hoist to just take the weight of the engine.

5 Remove the engine/transmission longi-tudinal crossmember as follows.

　a) *Unscrew the two securing bolts, and remove the shield from the crossmember.*

　b) *Prise out the cover plugs, and unscrew the three bolts securing the front engine/transmission mounting to the crossmember.*

　c) *Prise out the cover plug, and unscrew the bolt securing the rear engine/transmission mounting to the crossmember.*

　d) *Where applicable, unscrew the securing bolt and release the air conditioning pipe clamp from the crossmember.*

　e) *Unscrew the four securing bolts, and remove the crossmember.*

6 Remove the exhaust system front downpipe as described in Chapter 4A. Where applicable, unscrew the securing bolts and remove the engine-to-transmission reinforcing plate. Recover any spacers if fitted, noting their locations.

7 Where an oil cooler is fitted, unscrew the union bolt and recover the copper washers. Seal the end of the hose with tape to prevent entry of dust and dirt. Where necessary, disconnect the wiring from the oil temperature sensor **(see illustration)**.

10.7 Oil temperature sensor on the sump

10.8 Sump nuts and bolts

8 Unscrew and remove all the sump (secondary sump on 7A-FE engines) retaining bolts and nuts **(see illustration).**

9 Break the joint by striking the sump with the palm of your hand, then lower the sump and withdraw it from underneath the vehicle. If necessary use a suitable tool (such as a scraper blade) to free the sump from the sealant.

10 On 7A-FE engines if necessary the main sump may be unbolted from the cylinder block after removing the baffle plate and the pick-up tube and strainer with reference to Section 11.

Refitting

11 Clean all traces of sealant from the mating surfaces of the cylinder block/crankcase/ main sump, oil pump, rear oil seal housing and sump, then use a clean rag to wipe out the sump and the engine's interior.

12 Ensure that the sump and cylinder block/crankcase mating surfaces are clean and dry. Apply a continuous bead of suitable sealant (consult a Toyota dealer) to the mating surfaces of the sump making sure that the bead goes around the inner edges of the bolt holes. On 7A-FE engines, refit the main sump and oil pick-up tube first and tighten the bolts to the specified torque.

13 Offer up the sump and refit its retaining nuts and bolts. Tighten them evenly and progressively to the specified torque.

14 Where fitted, refit the oil cooler union together with new copper washers and tighten the union bolt.

15 Refit the engine-to-transmission reinforcing plate, together with the spacers where fitted.

16 Refit the exhaust system front downpipe section as described in Chapter 4A.

17 Refit the engine/transmission longitudinal crossmember, together with the engine mountings and tighten the bolts to the specified torque. Remove the engine support hoist and lifting tackle.

18 Refit the undershield and securely tighten the retaining screws.

19 Reconnect the battery and lower the vehicle to the ground.

20 Fill the engine with oil as described in Chapter 1.

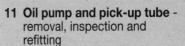

11 Oil pump and pick-up tube - removal, inspection and refitting

Removal

1 Remove the timing belt, tensioner, crankshaft sprocket and where applicable, the oil pump sprocket and idler pulleys as described in Sections 5 and 6. Remove the Woodruff key from the crankshaft and store it with the pulley for safe keeping **(see illustration).**

2 Remove the sump as described in Section 10, however, on 7A-FE engines only remove the secondary sump at this stage.

3 On 7A-FE engines unbolt the baffle plate from the main sump.

4 Undo the bolts/nuts securing the oil pick-up tube/strainer, then remove it with its gasket **(see illustrations).** On 3S-FE and 3S-GE engines remove the sump baffle plate at the same time.

5 On 7A-FE engines unbolt and remove the main sump with reference to Section 10.

6 Withdraw the engine oil dipstick, then on 4A-FE and 7A-FE engines unbolt and withdraw the guide tube and recover the rubber grommet from the oil pump housing.

7 Unscrew the pump retaining bolts, noting their correct fitted positions, then remove the pump and recover the gasket or rubber seal; if necessary carefully tap the pump with a soft-faced mallet to release it **(see illustrations).**

2A

11.1 Remove the Woodruff key from the front of the crankshaft

11.4a Removing the oil pick-up tube/strainer assembly

11.4b Oil pick-up tube/strainer assembly gasket on the oil pump housing

11.7a Unscrew the retaining bolts . . .

11.7b . . . remove the oil pump . . .

11.7c . . . and recover the gasket

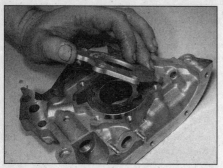

11.8a Remove the cover from the oil pump housing . . .

11.8b . . . and remove the drive rotor . . .

11.8c . . . and driven rotor

Inspection

8 Remove the screws securing the body cover to the pump housing then lift off the cover. Withdraw the drive and driven rotors **(see illustrations)**. On 3S-FE and 3S-GE engines recover the O-ring.

11.9a Removing the relief valve cap . . .

9 Dismantle the relief valve assembly after removing the spring retaining circlip; take care not to allow the spring to fly out and cause injury or damage, and note the order and orientation of the components as they are removed **(see illustrations)**.

10 Measure the oil pump clearances with a feeler blade. If the outer rotor-to-body clearance or side clearance is incorrect, the rotors and/or pump body must be renewed; if the rotor tip clearance is incorrect only the rotors need be renewed. If severe wear is evident, the oil pump assembly must be renewed complete **(see illustrations)**.

11 Check the relief valve components for wear and damage. Coat the valve piston with clean engine oil then check that it falls slowly into its bore under its own weight; if this is not the case, renew the complete valve assembly.

12 Renew the crankshaft right-hand oil seal as described in Section 13.

13 Reassemble the oil pump by lubricating the rotors then inserting them in the pump body, with their marks facing the pump body cover, then locate the body cover and tighten the screws to the specified torque.

14 The relief valve is reassembled by reversing the order of dismantling, ensuring that the valve piston is fitted the correct way around and that the circlip is securely located in its groove. When inserting the circlip use a screwdriver to depress the spring cap **(see illustration)**.

Refitting

15 Clean the sump and ensure that the oil pick-up pipe/strainer is clear.

16 Thoroughly clean the pump's sump mating face and ensure that the engine block-to-pump mating faces are clean.

17 Lightly oil the crankshaft oil pump drive and oil seal contact surfaces.

18 Position a new pump gasket on the cylinder block, or locate a new rubber seal in the pump body groove, according to engine,

11.9b . . . spring . . .

11.9c . . . and plunger

11.10a Using feeler blades to check the outer rotor-to-body clearance . . .

11.10b . . . the rotor tip clearance . . .

11.10c . . . and the side clearance

11.14 When refitting the circlip to the oil pump housing, depress the spring cap with a screwdriver

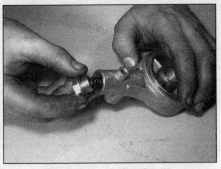

12.4a Remove the plug . . .

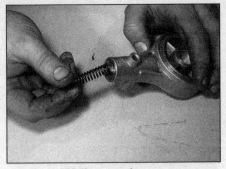

12.4b . . . spring . . .

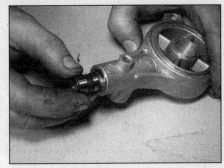

12.4c . . . and valve piston from the oil pressure regulating valve

then refit the pump. On 4A-FE and 7A-FE engines, ensure that the drive rotor engages with the crankshaft drive. Refit the pump bolts and tighten them to their specified torque.

19 On 4A-FE and 7A-FE engines, fit a new O-ring to the base of the engine oil dipstick guide tube, lubricating it with oil, then install the guide tube and tighten the bolt; refit the dipstick.

20 Refit the Woodruff key to the crankshaft, then refit the sprockets, pulleys and timing belt components as described in Sections 6 and 5.

21 On 7A-FE engines refit the main sump with reference to Section 10.

22 Using a new gasket, refit the oil pick-up pipe/strainer and tighten its nuts and bolts to their specified torque. On 3S-FE and 3S-GE engines refit the sump baffle plate at the same time.

23 On 7A-FE engines refit the baffle plate to the main sump.

24 Refit the sump as described in Section 10.

12 Oil cooler and pressure regulating valve - general information

Oil cooler

1 The oil cooler is mounted between the radiator and the radiator grille.

2 The oil cooler hose connections are secured by clips. If the unions on the sump and oil filter housing are to be removed, new washers (behind the union and behind its bolt) will be required on refitting; tighten the union bolts to the specified torque.

Oil pressure regulating valve

3 The valve is located in the combined oil filter housing/oil pressure regulator valve housing on the forward-facing side of the engine block.

4 To remove the valve, unscrew and remove the hexagon-headed plug on its base (with the washer) then withdraw the spring and valve piston noting their orientation; catch oil spillage in a container (see illustrations). Refitting is a reversal of the removal procedure, but fit a new washer and tighten the hexagon-headed plug to its specified torque.

12.5a Remove the stud securing the oil filter/oil pressure regulator valve housing to the cylinder block

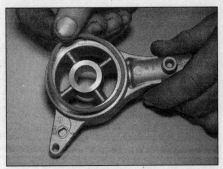

12.5b The O-ring in located in the housing groove

5 To remove the combined oil filter housing/oil pressure regulator valve housing, remove the oil filter (Chapter 1), then disconnect the union and remove the washers; catch oil spillage in a suitable container. Remove the filter mounting stud with its washer; remove the combined housing and its O-ring (see illustrations). The valve assembly can now be removed (paragraph 4), if required.

6 Test the pressure regulator by coating the valve piston with clean engine oil and checking that it falls into its housing bore under its own weight; if not, renew the complete assembly.

7 Refitting is a reversal of the removal procedure, but use a new O-ring and washers, and tighten all fastenings to the specified torques.

13 Crankshaft oil seals - renewal

Right-hand seal

1 To renew the seal with the oil pump removed from the vehicle, carefully prise out the old seal using a flat-bladed screwdriver (see illustration). Clean the seal housing and polish off any burrs or raised edges which may have caused the seal to fail in the first place. Apply multi-purpose grease to the new seal, then drive it squarely into position using a suitably-sized tubular drift, such as a socket, which bears only on the hard outer edge of the seal; the outer face of the seal should be flush with the pump face (see illustration).

13.1a Levering out the right-hand crankshaft seal from the oil pump housing

13.1b Using a hammer and socket to drive in the new oil seal

2A

13.5 Removing the oil seal from the left-hand (rear) oil seal housing

2 To renew the seal with the oil pump in place on the vehicle, first remove the timing belt, then remove the crankshaft sprocket.

3 Punch or drill two small holes opposite each other in the seal. Screw a self-tapping screw into each hole and pull on the screws with pliers to extract the seal. Clean the seal housing and polish off any burrs or raised edges which may have caused the seal to fail in the first place. Lubricate the lips of the new seal with clean engine oil and apply a smear of grease to the outer edge of the seal. Ease the seal over the end of the crankshaft and drive it squarely into position as described above.

4 Wipe off any excess grease then refit the crankshaft sprocket and install the timing belt as described earlier.

14.3 Using paint marks to mark the relationship of the flywheel/driveplate to its crankshaft flange

Left-hand seal

5 To renew the seal with its housing removed from the vehicle, work as described in paragraph 1 above **(see illustration)**.

6 To renew the seal with its housing in place in the vehicle, first remove the flywheel/driveplate (Section 14); the seal can then be renewed as described in paragraph 3.

7 Wipe off any excess grease, then refit the flywheel/driveplate.

14 Flywheel/driveplate - removal, inspection and refitting

Removal

1 Remove the transmission as described in Chapter 7A or 7B according to type.

2 On manual transmission models, remove the clutch assembly as described in Chapter 6.

3 Mark the relationship of the flywheel/driveplate to its crankshaft flange **(see illustration)**.

4 Prevent the flywheel from turning by locking the ring gear teeth with a large flat-bladed screwdriver or by bolting a home-made tool to one of the transmission mounting bolt holes in the cylinder block **(see illustration)**. Progressively slacken the flywheel/driveplate retaining bolts, then remove the bolts and lift off the flywheel/driveplate **(see illustration)**.

Inspection

5 Examine the flywheel for scoring on its clutch driven plate face; if evident it may be possible for a competent engineering works to machine the surface, but renewal is the preferable option. Check the flywheel/driveplate carefully for signs of distortion, or any hairline cracks around the bolt holes or cracks radiating outwards from the centre; renewal will be required if evident.

6 If the ring gear is worn or damaged it may be possible to renew it separately, but this job should be entrusted to a Toyota dealer or engineering works.

Refitting

7 Clean the flywheel/driveplate and crankshaft flange faces, and remove all traces of thread locking compound from the retaining bolts.

 HAYNES HINT *If a suitable tap is not available, cut two slots down the threads of one of the old bolts with a hacksaw, and use the bolt to remove the locking compound from the threads.*

8 Locate the flywheel/driveplate on its crankshaft flange, aligning the marks made on removal. Apply a little thread locking compound to the threads of the retaining bolts, then fit the bolts and progressively tighten them to the specified torque setting.

9 Remove the ring gear locking tool.

10 On manual transmission models refit the clutch as described in Chapter 6.

11 Refit the transmission as described in Chapter 7A or 7B.

15 Engine/transmission mountings - inspection and renewal

Inspection

1 If improved access is required, chock the rear wheels then jack up the front of the car and support it on axle stands (see *Jacking and Vehicle Support*).

2 Check the mounting rubber to see if it is cracked, hardened or separated from the metal at any point; renew the mounting if any such damage or deterioration is evident.

3 Check that all mounting fasteners are securely tightened; use a torque wrench to check if possible.

4 Using a large screwdriver or a crowbar, check for wear in the mounting by carefully levering against it to check for free play; where this is not possible, enlist the aid of an assistant to move the engine/transmission unit back and forth, or from side to side while

14.4a Home-made tool for locking the flywheel when loosening the retaining bolts

14.4b Removing the flywheel bolts

14.4d Removing the flywheel

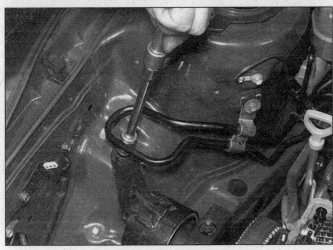

15.7a Unscrew the support bolt . . .

15.7b . . . and the nuts from the studs . . .

you watch the mounting. While some free play is to be expected even from new components, excessive wear should be obvious. If excessive free play is found, check first that the fasteners are correctly secured, then renew any worn components as described below.

Renewal

5 The engine/transmission mountings can be unbolted and removed once the weight of the engine/transmission unit is taken off them using either a suitable hoist, an engine support bar or a jack with an interposed block of wood. Lifting eyes are provided on the engine.

6 The mountings are located in the following positions:

a) Right-hand mounting, at the timing belt (right-hand) end of the engine.

b) Left-hand mounting, at the left-hand end of the transmission to the rear of the battery tray.

c) A front mounting between the cylinder block and the longitudinal crossmember.

d) A rear mounting between the rear of the transmission and the longitudinal crossmember and subframe.

7 Access to the right-hand mounting is gained by removing the windscreen washer reservoir on the right-hand side of the engine compartment. After removal of the through-bolt the brackets can be unbolted from the inner wing panel or cylinder block **(see illustrations)**.

8 Access to the left-hand mounting is gained by removing the battery and tray, followed by the engine compartment fusebox and air cleaner body. It will be necessary to move the engine wiring loom to one side in order to

reach all of the bolts. After removal of the through-bolt, unscrew the nuts and bolts and withdraw the mounting bracket from the top of the transmission.

9 It is necessary to raise and support the front of the vehicle in order to remove the front and rear engine mountings. After removal of the through-bolts the brackets may be unbolted from the longitudinal crossmember or subframe. Plastic blanking plates are fitted to the longitudinal crossmember to protect the heads of the bracket bolts.

10 There are a number of different versions of the mountings used according to engine size, so, when ordering replacement parts, ensure that full vehicle details are provided to enable the correct component(s) to be obtained. If possible, take the old component(s) along to your Toyota dealer for positive identification.

2A

15.7c . . . then withdraw the right-hand engine mounting

15.7d Right-hand engine mounting bracket on the cylinder block

Notes

Chapter 2 Part B:
Engine removal and overhaul procedures

Contents

Degrees of difficulty

Easy, suitable for novice with little experience	**Fairly easy,** suitable for beginner with some experience	**Fairly difficult,** suitable for competent DIY mechanic	**Difficult,** suitable for experienced DIY mechanic	**Very difficult,** suitable for expert DIY or professional

Specifications

Engine codes
See Chapter 2A.

2B

Cylinder head
Material	Cast aluminium alloy
Maximum gasket face warpage:	
Inlet and exhaust manifold faces:	
4A-FE and 7A-FE engines	0.10 mm
3S-FE engines	0.08 mm
3S-GE engines (inlet manifold)	0.20 mm
3S-GE engines (exhaust manifold)	0.30 mm
Cylinder head gasket face:	
Except 3S-GE engines	0.05 mm
3S-GE engines	0.20 mm
Valve seat angle	45°
Valve seat width	1.0 to 1.4 mm
Camshaft follower diameter:	
Except 3S-GE engines	30.966 to 30.976 mm
3S-GE engines	27.975 to 27.985 mm
Camshaft follower bore diameter:	
Except 3S-GE engines	31.00 to 31.025 mm
3S-GE engines	28.000 to 28.021 mm
Spark plug tube fitted height (except 3S-GE engines)	46.8 to 47.6 mm

Cylinder block
Material	Cast iron

4A-FE and 7A-FE engines
Bore diameter:	
Standard:	
Mark 1	81.00 to 81.01 mm
Mark 2	81.01 to 81.02 mm
Mark 3	81.02 to 81.03 mm
Oversize (0.5 mm)	81.50 to 81.53 mm
Bore diameter (maximum):	
Standard	81.23 mm
Oversize (0.5 mm)	81.73 mm
Maximum gasket face warpage	0.05 mm

3S-FE and 3S-GE engines

Bore diameter:
Standard:
    Mark 1 . . . . 86.00 to 86.01 mm
    Mark 2 . . . . 86.01 to 86.02 mm
    Mark 3 . . . . 86.02 to 86.03 mm
Bore diameter (maximum):
  Standard . . . . 86.23 mm
  Oversize (0.5 mm) . . . . 86.73 mm
Maximum gasket face warpage . . . . 0.05 mm

Pistons and piston rings

4A-FE engines

Piston diameter at right angles to gudgeon pin, 24.5 mm from crown:
Standard:
    Mark 1 . . . . 80.905 to 80.915 mm
    Mark 2 . . . . 80.915 to 80.925 mm
    Mark 3 . . . . 80.925 to 80.935 mm
  Oversize (0.50 mm) . . . . 81.405 to 81.435 mm

	Standard	Maximum
Piston-to-bore clearance	0.085 to 0.105 mm	0.13 mm
Piston ring installed end gaps - 87 mm from top of bore:		
Top compression ring	0.25 to 0.45 mm	1.05 mm
Second compression ring	0.35 to 0.60 mm	1.20 mm
Oil control ring	0.10 to 0.50 mm	1.10 mm
Piston ring-to-groove clearance:		
Top compression ring	0.045 to 0.085 mm	
Second compression ring	0.030 to 0.070 mm	

7A-FE engines

Note: *There are two types of piston assemblies fitted to these engines - Type A is identified by two indentations on the front of the piston crown; Type B is identified by a single indentation on the front of the piston crown.*

Piston diameter at right angles to gudgeon pin, 24.5 mm from piston crown:
Type A piston:
  Standard:
    Mark 1 . . . . 80.905 to 80.915 mm
    Mark 2 . . . . 80.915 to 80.925 mm
    Mark 3 . . . . 80.925 to 80.935 mm
    Oversize (0.50 mm) . . . . 81.405 to 81.435 mm
Type B piston:
  Standard:
    Mark 1 . . . . 80.925 to 80.935 mm
    Mark 2 . . . . 80.935 to 80.945 mm
    Mark 3 . . . . 80.945 to 80.955 mm
    Oversize (0.50 mm) . . . . 81.405 to 81.435 mm

	Standard	Maximum
Piston-to-bore clearance:		
Type A piston	0.085 to 0.105 mm	0.13 mm
Type B piston	0.065 to 0.085 mm	0.13 mm
Piston ring installed end gaps - 87 mm from top of bore:		
Piston rings with GOE marking:		
Top compression ring	0.25 to 0.41 mm	1.05 mm
Second compression ring	0.24 to 0.40 mm	1.20 mm
Oil control ring	0.10 to 0.40 mm	1.10 mm
Piston rings without GOE marking:		
Top compression ring	0.25 to 0.35 mm	1.05 mm
Second compression ring	0.35 to 0.50 mm	1.20 mm
Oil control ring	0.10 to 0.40 mm	1.10 mm
Piston ring-to-groove clearance:		
Piston rings with GOE marking:		
Top compression ring	0.035 to 0.080 mm	
Second compression ring	0.025 to 0.070 mm	
Piston rings without GOE marking:		
Top compression ring	0.045 to 0.085 mm	
Second compression ring	0.030 to 0.070 mm	

3S-FE engines

Piston diameter at right angles to gudgeon pin, 26 mm from piston crown:
- Standard:
  - Mark 1 .... 85.837 to 85.847 mm
  - Mark 2 .... 85.847 to 85.857 mm
  - Mark 3 .... 85.857 to 85.867 mm
- Oversize (0.50 mm) .... 86.337 to 86.367 mm

	Standard	Maximum
Piston-to-bore clearance	0.153 to 0.173 mm	0.190 mm
Piston ring installed end gaps - 110 mm from top of bore:		
Top compression ring	0.27 to 0.47 mm	1.07 mm
Second compression ring	0.45 to 0.65 mm	1.25 mm
Oil control ring (side rail)	0.10 to 0.45 mm	1.05 mm
Piston ring-to-groove clearance:		
Top compression ring	0.030 to 0.070 mm	
Second compression ring	0.030 to 0.070 mm	

3S-GE engines

Piston diameter at right angles to gudgeon pin, 30.1 mm from piston crown:
- Mark 1 .... 85.960 to 85.970 mm
- Mark 2 .... 85.970 to 85.980 mm
- Mark 3 .... 85.980 to 85.990 mm

	Standard	Maximum
Piston-to-bore clearance	0.030 to 0.050 mm	0.070 mm
Piston ring installed end gaps - 100 mm from top of bore:		
Top compression ring	0.33 to 0.55 mm	0.85 mm
Second compression ring	0.45 to 0.67 mm	0.97 mm
Oil control ring (side rail)	0.20 to 0.60 mm	0.90 mm
Piston ring-to-groove clearance:		
Top compression ring	0.040 to 0.080 mm	
Second compression ring	0.030 to 0.070 mm	

Crankshaft

Number of main bearings 5

	Standard	Undersize (0.25 mm)	Maximum
Main bearing journal diameter:			
4A-FE and 7A-FE engines	47.982 to 48.000 mm	47.745 to 47.755 mm	-
3S-FE and 3S-GE engines	54.988 to 55.003 mm	54.745 to 54.755 mm	-
Main bearing journal running clearance:			
4A-FE and 7A-FE engines	0.015 to 0.033 mm	0.016 to 0.056 mm	0.100 mm
3S-FE and 3S-GE engines:			
Except No 3 Standard	0.015 to 0.034 mm	0.019 to 0.059 mm	0.08 mm
No 3 Standard	0.025 to 0.044 mm	0.027 to 0.067 mm	0.08 mm
Crankpin (big-end) journal diameter:			
4A-FE engines	39.985 to 40.000 mm	39.745 to 39.755 mm	-
7A-FE engines	47.988 to 48.000 mm	47.745 to 47.555 mm	-
3S-FE engines	51.985 to 52.000 mm	51.745 to 51.755 mm	-
3S-GE engines	47.985 to 48.000 mm	47.745 to 47.755 mm	-
Crankpin (big-end) journal running clearance:			
4A-FE engines	0.020 to 0.051 mm	0.019 to 0.065 mm	0.080 mm
7A-FE engines	0.015 to 0.033 mm	0.016 to 0.056 mm	0.080 mm
3S-FE and 3S-GE engines	0.024 to 0.055 mm	0.023 to 0.069 mm	0.080 mm

Main bearing and crankpin (big-end) journals max taper and ovality:
- Except 7A-FE engines .... 0.02 mm
- 7A-FE engines .... 0.005 mm

Crankshaft endfloat:
- Standard .... 0.02 to 0.22 mm
- Maximum .... 0.30 mm
- Thrustwasher thickness .... 2.440 to 2.490 mm

Maximum run-out at centre main bearing journal:
- 4A-FE and 7A-FE engines .... 0.03 mm
- 3S-FE and 3S-GE engines .... 0.06 mm

	Standard	Maximum
Connecting rod big-end cap-to-crankshaft web thrust (side) clearance:		
4A-FE and 7A-FE engines	0.15 to 0.25 mm	0.30 mm
3S-FE and 3S-GE engines	0.160 to 0.312 mm	0.35 mm

2B

Valves

4A-FE and 7A-FE engines

Operation	Direct from camshaft lobes, via inverted camshaft followers (buckets), clearance adjusted by shims	
Face angle	44.5°	
Length:	**Standard**	**Minimum**
Inlet	87.45 mm	86.95 mm
Exhaust	87.84 mm	87.35 mm
Head margin (edge) thickness	0.8 to 1.2 mm	0.5 mm
Stem diameter:		
Inlet	5.970 to 5.985 mm	
Exhaust	5.965 to 5.980 mm	
Stem-to-guide clearance:	**Standard**	**Maximum**
Inlet	0.025 to 0.060 mm	0.080 mm
Exhaust	0.030 to 0.065 mm	0.100 mm
Spring free length	38.57 mm	
Guide internal diameter	6.01 to 6.03 mm	

3S-FE engines

Operation	Direct from camshaft lobes, via inverted camshaft followers (buckets), clearance adjusted by shims	
Face angle	44.5°	
Length:	**Standard**	**Minimum**
Inlet	97.60 mm	97.10 mm
Exhaust	98.45 mm	98.00 mm
Head margin (edge) thickness	0.8 to 1.2 mm	0.5 mm
Stem diameter:		
Inlet	5.970 to 5.985 mm	
Exhaust	5.965 to 5.980 mm	
Stem-to-guide clearance:	**Standard**	**Maximum**
Inlet	0.025 to 0.060 mm	0.080 mm
Exhaust	0.030 to 0.065 mm	0.100 mm
Spring free length	41.96 to 41.99 mm	
Guide internal diameter	6.01 to 6.03 mm	

3S-GE engines

Operation	Direct from camshaft lobes, via inverted camshaft followers (buckets), clearance adjusted by shims	
Face angle	44.5°	
Length:	**Standard**	**Minimum**
Inlet	105.50 mm	104.80 mm
Exhaust	99.55 mm	98.85 mm
Head margin (edge) thickness	0.8 to 1.2 mm	0.5 mm
Stem diameter:		
Inlet	5.960 to 5.975 mm	
Exhaust	5.955 to 5.970 mm	
Stem-to-guide clearance:	**Standard**	**Maximum**
Inlet	0.025 to 0.058 mm	0.080 mm
Exhaust	0.030 to 0.063 mm	
Maximum	0.100 mm	44.43 mm
Guide internal diameter	6.000 to 6.018 mm	

Torque wrench settings

See Chapter 2A.

1 General information

Included in this Part of Chapter 2 are details of removing the engine, and overhaul procedures for the cylinder head, cylinder block/ crankcase and all other engine internal components.

The information given ranges from advice concerning preparation for an overhaul and the purchase of replacement parts, to detailed step-by-step procedures covering removal, inspection, renovation and refitting of engine internal components.

After Section 8, all instructions are based on the assumption that the engine has been removed from the vehicle. For information concerning in-car engine repair, as well as the removal and refitting of those external components necessary for full overhaul, refer to Part A of this Chapter. Ignore any preliminary dismantling operations described in Part A that are no longer relevant once the engine has been removed from the vehicle.

Apart from torque wrench settings, which are given at the beginning of Part A, all specifications relating to engine overhaul are at the beginning of this Part of Chapter 2.

2 Engine overhaul - general information

It is not always easy to determine when, or if, an engine should be completely overhauled, as a number of factors must be considered.

High mileage is not necessarily an indication that an overhaul is needed, while low mileage does not preclude the need for an overhaul. Frequency of servicing is probably the most important consideration. An engine which has had regular and frequent oil and filter changes, as well as other required maintenance, should give many thousands of miles of reliable service. Conversely, a neglected engine may require an overhaul very early in its life.

Excessive oil consumption is an indication that piston rings, valve seals and/or valve guides are in need of attention. Make sure that oil leaks are not responsible before deciding that the rings and/or guides are worn. Perform a compression test, as described in Part A of this Chapter, to determine the likely cause of the problem.

Check the oil pressure with a gauge fitted in place of the oil pressure switch, and compare it with that specified. If it is extremely low, the main and big-end bearings, and/or the oil pump, are probably worn out.

Loss of power, rough running, knocking or metallic engine noises, excessive valve gear noise, and high fuel consumption may also point to the need for an overhaul, especially if they are all present at the same time. If a complete service does not remedy the situation, major mechanical work is the only solution.

An engine overhaul involves restoring all internal parts to the specification of a new engine. During an overhaul, the pistons and the piston rings are renewed. New main and big-end bearings are generally fitted; if necessary, the crankshaft may be reground, to restore the journals. The valves are also serviced as well, since they are usually in less-than-perfect condition at this point. While the engine is being overhauled, other components, such as the distributor, starter and alternator, can be overhauled as well. The end result should be an as-new engine that will give many trouble-free miles.

Cooling system components such as the hoses, thermostat and water pump should be renewed when an engine is overhauled. The radiator should be checked carefully, to ensure that it is not clogged or leaking. Also, it is a good idea to renew the oil pump whenever the engine is overhauled.

Before beginning the engine overhaul, read through the entire procedure, to familiarise yourself with the scope and requirements of the job. Overhauling an engine is not difficult if you follow carefully all of the instructions, have the necessary tools and equipment, and pay close attention to all specifications. It can, however, be time-consuming. Plan on the car being off the road for a minimum of two weeks, especially if parts must be taken to an engineering works for repair or reconditioning. Check on the availability of parts, and make sure that any necessary special tools and equipment are obtained in advance. Most work can be done with typical hand tools, although a number of precision measuring tools are required for inspecting parts to determine if they must be renewed. Often, the engineering works will handle the inspection of parts, and can offer advice concerning reconditioning and renewal.

Always wait until the engine has been completely dismantled, and until all components (especially the cylinder block/crankcase and the crankshaft) have been inspected, before deciding what service and repair operations must be performed by an engineering works. The condition of these components will be the major factor to consider when determining whether to overhaul the original engine, or to buy a reconditioned unit. Do not, therefore, purchase parts or have overhaul work done on other components until they have been thoroughly inspected. As a general rule, time is the primary cost of an overhaul, so it does not pay to fit worn or sub-standard parts.

As a final note, to ensure maximum life and minimum trouble from a reconditioned engine, everything must be assembled with care, in a spotlessly-clean environment.

3 Engine removal - methods and precautions

If you have decided that the engine must be removed for overhaul or major repair work, several preliminary steps should be taken.

Locating a suitable place to work is extremely important. Adequate work space, along with storage space for the vehicle, will be needed. If a workshop or garage is not available, at the very least, a flat, level, clean work surface is required.

Cleaning the engine compartment and engine/transmission before beginning the removal procedure will help keep tools clean and organised.

An engine hoist or A-frame will also be necessary. Make sure that the equipment is rated in excess of the combined weight of the engine and transmission. Safety is of primary importance, considering the potential hazards involved in removing the engine/transmission from the vehicle.

If this is the first time you have removed an engine, an assistant should ideally be available. Advice and aid from someone more experienced would also be helpful. There are many instances when one person cannot simultaneously perform all of the operations required when lifting the engine out of the vehicle.

Plan the operation ahead of time. Before starting work, arrange for the hire of, or obtain, all of the tools and equipment you will need. Some of the equipment necessary to perform engine/transmission removal and installation safely and with relative ease (in addition to an engine hoist) is as follows: a heavy-duty trolley jack, complete sets of spanners and sockets as described at the end of this manual, wooden blocks, and plenty of rags and cleaning solvent for mopping up spilled oil, coolant and fuel. If the hoist must be hired, make sure that you arrange for it in advance, and perform all of the operations possible without it beforehand. This will save you money and time.

Plan for the vehicle to be out of use for quite a while. An engineering works will be required to perform some of the work which the do-it-yourselfer cannot accomplish without special equipment. These places often have a busy schedule, so it would be a good idea to consult them before removing the engine, in order to accurately estimate the amount of time required to rebuild or repair components that may need work.

Always be extremely careful when removing and refitting the engine/transmission. Serious injury can result from careless actions. Plan ahead and take your time, and a job of this nature, although major, can be accomplished successfully.

The engine and transmission can be removed as an assembly either upwards or downwards from the engine compartment depending primarily on the lifting equipment available.

4 Engine and transmission - removal, separation and refitting

 Warning: Petrol is extremely flammable, so take extra precautions when disconnecting any part of the fuel system. *Don't smoke, or allow naked flames or bare light bulbs, in or near the work area, and don't work in a garage where a natural-gas appliance (such as a clothes dryer or water heater) is installed. If you spill petrol on your skin, rinse it off immediately. Have a fire extinguisher rated for petrol fires handy, and know how to use it.*
Note: *The engine and transmission assembly can be removed either upwards or downwards from the engine compartment. The method used will depend primarily on the equipment available. On cars equipped with ABS brakes, it may be found that the restricted clearance between the engine/transmission and the ABS actuator may make removal downwards preferable. If it is decided to remove the assembly upwards, make sure that the hoist used is able to lift the assembly high enough.*

Removal

1 Chock the rear wheels then jack up the front of the car and support it on axle stands (see *Jacking and Vehicle Support*). **Note:** *If the engine and transmission is to be lowered from the engine compartment, allow sufficient clearance between the front bumper and the ground. If a low trolley is being used to move the assembly from under the vehicle, additional height will be required.*
2 Remove both front roadwheels, and remove the splash guards from under the engine compartment **(see illustration)**.
3 Remove the bonnet as described in Chapter 11.
4 Depressurise the fuel system as described in Chapter 4A.

2B

4.2 Unbolting the splash guards from under the engine compartment

5 Remove the battery and tray as described in Chapter 5A.
6 Drain the cooling system (see Chapter 1), saving the coolant if it is fit for re-use.
7 Drain the transmission oil/fluid with reference to Chapter 7A or 7B (as applicable). Refit and tighten the drain and filler plugs.
8 If the engine is to be dismantled, working as described in Chapter 1, drain the oil and if required remove the oil filter. Clean and refit the drain plug, tightening it to the specified torque (Chapter 1).
9 On models fitted with air conditioning, remove the air conditioning compressor (Chapter 3) however leave the air conditioning system lines connected. Tie the compressor to one side.
10 Unbolt the windscreen washer fluid reservoir from the right-hand side of the engine compartment and position it to one side. If necessary, syphon the fluid from the reservoir first, disconnect the wiring and remove the reservoir completely.
11 Unscrew the bolts securing the power steering pump to the bracket on the rear of the cylinder block, then swivel the pump towards the engine and disconnect the drivebelt. Note there is insufficient room to remove the lower bolt at this stage, however if necessary the bracket may be unbolted from the cylinder block. Alternatively leave the lower bolt in position until the engine is being lifted out. Do not disconnect the hydraulic fluid hoses from the power steering pump.
12 Unbolt the fusebox and bracket from the battery support **(see illustration)**.
13 Loosen the clips and disconnect the air

4.12 Unbolting the fusebox and bracket from the battery support

inlet hose from the throttle housing and air cleaner. Remove the air cleaner body with reference to Chapter 4A.
14 The wiring loom must now be disconnected from the engine and transmission, and positioned to one side on the left-hand side of the engine compartment. It is not possible to disconnect the loom and leave the wiring on the engine. To ensure correct refitting, work methodically and make notes. Start at the alternator position and disconnect the wiring from the oil pressure switch, then unbolt the small cover at the right-hand end of the cylinder head and release the wiring from the groove in the camshaft cover. Disconnect the wiring from the injectors, then note the location of the wiring on the rear of the engine. Disconnect the wiring from the transmission (speedometer sensor and reverse switch), the manifold absolute pressure sensor on the bulkhead, the starter motor, the exhaust gas oxygen sensor, and the temperature sensors on the thermostat housing, then finally position it on the left-hand side of the engine compartment. Also unbolt the earth cable from the top of the transmission.

> **HAYNES HiNT** *Whenever you disconnect any vacuum lines, coolant or emissions hoses, wiring connectors and fuel lines, always label them clearly, so that they can be correctly reassembled. Masking tape and/or a touch-up paint applicator work well for marking items. Take instant photos, or sketch the locations of components and brackets.*

15 Detach the accelerator cable from the throttle housing with reference to Chapter 4A, and position the cable to one side. On automatic transmission models also disconnect the kick-down cable.
16 Position a suitable container beneath the front of the engine, then unscrew the union bolts securing the oil cooler hoses to the oil filter housing and sump. Recover the washers.
17 Unscrew the nuts securing the exhaust front downpipe to the exhaust manifold, then lower the downpipe and recover the sealing ring. **Note:** *If the engine and transmission is being lowered from the engine compartment, it will be necessary to completely remove the front section of the exhaust system with reference to Chapter 4A.*
18 Remove the radiator as described in Chapter 3, then disconnect and remove the top and bottom hoses from the engine.
19 Disconnect the HT lead from the ignition coil on the bulkhead.
20 Note the location of the heater hoses on the left-hand side of the cylinder head, then loosen the clips and disconnect them. Also disconnect the wiring from the connectors on the throttle housing.
21 Disconnect the vacuum hoses from the inlet manifold, throttle housing and air chamber noting their fitted locations.
22 Unscrew the union bolt and detach the fuel supply hose from the end of the fuel rail. Also disconnect the fuel return hose. Position both hoses to one side and cover their ends to prevent entry of dust and dirt.
23 On manual transmission models, unbolt the clutch slave cylinder from the front of the transmission and release it from the support bracket. Position it to one side. Also disconnect the gearchange selector cables with reference to Chapter 7A.
24 On automatic transmission models, disconnect the selector cable and starter inhibitor switch wiring from the transmission with reference to Chapter 7B. Also disconnect the transmission fluid cooler hoses.
25 Remove the right-hand driveshaft completely as described in Chapter 8.
26 On all except 3S-GE engine models, unscrew the bolt and two nuts, and disconnect the suspension lower balljoint from the lower arm **(see illustrations)**. On 3S-GE engine models, unscrew the nut and two bolts, and disconnect the suspension lower balljoint from the hub carrier. Lever the inner end of the driveshaft from the transmission taking care not to damage the transmission housing. Swivel the driveshaft forwards and support it away from the engine compartment on an axle stand.
27 Manoeuvre the engine hoist into position, and attach it to the engine using suitable lifting brackets on the cylinder head **(see illustration)**. To keep the balance of the assembly, attach the hoist to the left-hand rear and right-hand front of the cylinder head. Raise the hoist until it is supporting the weight of the engine/transmission assembly.

4.26a Unscrew the bolts/nuts . . .

4.26b . . . and lever the lower suspension arm downwards

28 Unscrew and remove the through-bolts from the front and rear engine mountings, then unbolt the mounting brackets from the cylinder block and transmission. Also unbolt the front mounting rubber from the centre member - the rear mounting rubber can remain on the subframe.

29 Unbolt the right-hand engine mounting from the inner wing panel and from the bracket on the cylinder block as described in Chapter 2A.

30 Unbolt the left-hand engine mounting stay from the top of the transmission, then unscrew the nuts and bolts and remove the mounting bracket from the transmission.

31 If the assembly is to be lowered to the ground, unbolt the longitudinal crossmember from the underbody. If available, a low trolley should be placed under the engine/transmission assembly.

32 Make a final check that everything has been disconnected. Ensure that components such as the gearchange cables and driveshafts are secured so that they cannot be damaged on removal.

33 Either lift or lower the engine/transmission assembly from the engine compartment, making sure that nothing is trapped or damaged **(see illustration)**. Enlist the help of an assistant during this procedure, as it will be necessary to tilt the assembly slightly to clear the body panels. This is particularly relevant when lifting the assembly as it must be initially raised at the right-hand end in order to clear the left-hand side of the engine compartment.

Separation

34 With the engine/transmission assembly removed, support the assembly on suitable blocks of wood, on a workbench or failing that, on a clean area of the workshop floor.

35 On automatic transmission models unbolt the cover/strengthener from the transmission and cylinder block for access to the torque converter-to-driveplate bolts. Turn the crankshaft as necessary for access, and unscrew the six bolts.

36 Unscrew the retaining bolts, and remove the starter motor from the transmission (refer to Chapter 5A if necessary).

37 Ensure that both engine and transmission are adequately supported, then slacken and remove the bolts securing the transmission to the engine. Note the correct fitted positions of each bolt (and, where fitted, the relevant brackets) as they are removed, to use as a reference on refitting.

38 With the help of an assistant, withdraw the transmission from the engine. On manual transmission models, ensure that the weight of the transmission is not allowed to hang on the input shaft while it is engaged with the clutch disc. On automatic transmission models ensure that the torque converter remains fully engaged with the transmission.

39 If they are loose, remove the locating dowels from the engine or transmission, and keep them in a safe place.

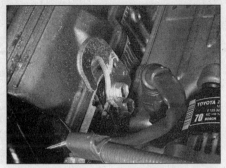

4.27 Engine lifting eye on the 3S-FE engine

Refitting

40 If the engine and transmission have been separated, perform the operations described below in paragraphs 41 to 46. If not, proceed as described from paragraph 47 onwards.

41 On manual transmission models, apply a smear of high-melting-point grease to the splines of the transmission input shaft. Do not apply too much, otherwise there is a possibility of the grease contaminating the clutch friction plate. Also ensure that the clutch release bearing is correctly engaged with the fork.

42 On automatic transmission models make sure that the torque converter is fully engaged with the transmission (see Chapter 7B).

43 Ensure that the locating dowels are correctly positioned in the engine or transmission. Carefully offer the transmission to the engine, until the locating dowels are engaged. On manual transmission models, ensure that the weight of the transmission is not allowed to hang on the input shaft.

44 Refit the transmission housing-to-engine bolts, ensuring that all the necessary brackets are correctly positioned, and tighten them to the specified torque setting.

45 Refit the starter motor and tighten the retaining bolts.

46 On automatic transmission models align the holes in the driveplate and torque converter then insert the bolts and tighten them to the specified torque (Chapter 7A). Refit the cover and tighten the bolts.

47 Where necessary, position the engine/transmission assembly under the vehicle ready to be lifted into position.

4.33 Lifting the engine/transmission assembly from the engine compartment

48 Reconnect the hoist and lifting tackle to the engine lifting brackets. With the aid of an assistant, lift the assembly into the engine compartment, making sure that it clears the surrounding components.

49 Refit the right-hand and left-hand engine mountings with reference to Chapter 2A.

50 Where removed, refit the longitudinal crossmember to the underbody.

51 Refit the front and rear engine mountings with reference to Chapter 2A. Remove the engine hoist.

52 The remainder of the refitting procedure is a direct reversal of the removal sequence, with reference to the relevant Chapters and noting the following points:

a) *Ensure that the wiring harness is correctly routed and all connectors are correctly and securely reconnected.*

b) *Refill the transmission oil/fluid with reference to Chapter 7A or 7B (as applicable).*

c) *Adjust the auxiliary drivebelts as described in Chapter 1.*

d) *On automatic transmission models adjust the kick-down cable and selector cable with reference to Chapter 7B, and top up the fluid with reference to Chapter 1.*

e) *Refill the engine with oil with reference to Chapter 1.*

f) *Refill the cooling system as described in Chapter 1.*

g) *On completion, start the engine and check for leaks.*

5 Engine overhaul - dismantling sequence

1 It is much easier to dismantle and work on the engine if it is mounted on a portable engine stand. These stands can often be hired from a tool hire shop. Before the engine is mounted on a stand, the flywheel/driveplate should be removed, so that the stand bolts can be tightened into the end of the cylinder block/crankcase.

2 If a stand is not available, it is possible to dismantle the engine with it blocked up on a sturdy workbench, or on the floor. Be extra-careful not to tip or drop the engine when working without a stand.

3 If you are going to obtain a reconditioned engine, all the external components must be removed first, to be transferred to the replacement engine (just as they will if you are doing a complete engine overhaul yourself). These components include the following:

a) *Alternator, power steering pump and/or air conditioning compressor mounting brackets (as applicable).*

b) *Distributor, HT leads and spark plugs (Chapters 1 and 5B).*

c) *Water pump and thermostat/coolant outlet housing(s) (Chapter 3).*

d) *The fuel injection system components (see Chapter 4A).*

2B

6.1a Removing the coolant outlet . . .

6.1b . . . the thermostat housing . . .

6.1c . . . and the alternator upper mounting bracket from the cylinder head

e) All electrical switches and sensors, and the engine wiring harness.

f) Inlet and exhaust manifolds (see Chapter 4A).

g) Engine mountings (Part A of this Chapter).

h) Flywheel/driveplate (Part A of this Chapter).

Note: When removing the external components from the engine, pay close attention to details that may be helpful or important during refitting. Note the fitted position of gaskets, seals, spacers, pins, washers, bolts, and other small items.

4 If you are obtaining a short engine (which consists of the engine cylinder block/crankcase, crankshaft, pistons and connecting rods all assembled), then the cylinder head, sump, oil pump, and timing belt will have to be removed also.

5 If you are planning a complete overhaul, the engine can be dismantled, and the internal components removed, in the order given.

a) Timing belt covers, timing belt, sprockets, tensioner and idler pulleys (see Part A of this Chapter).

b) Inlet and exhaust manifolds (Chapter 4A).

c) Cylinder head (see Part A of this Chapter).

d) Sump (see Part A of this Chapter).

e) Piston/connecting rod assemblies (Section 9).

f) Flywheel/driveplate (see Part A of this Chapter).

g) Oil pump (see Part A of this Chapter).

h) Crankshaft (Section 10).

6 Before beginning the dismantling and overhaul procedures, make sure that you have all of the correct tools necessary. Refer to *Tools and working facilities* at the end of this manual for further information.

6 Cylinder head - dismantling

Note: New and reconditioned cylinder heads can be obtained from the manufacturer and engine overhaul specialists. Be aware that some specialist tools are required for the dismantling and inspection procedures, and new components may not be readily available. It may therefore be more practical and economical for the home mechanic to purchase a reconditioned head, rather than dismantle, inspect and recondition the original head.

1 Remove the cylinder head as described in Part A of this Chapter. This procedure includes removal of the camshafts, followers, and the inlet and exhaust manifolds. Unbolt and remove the coolant outlet and thermostat housing, also the alternator upper mounting bracket **(see illustrations)**.

2 Using a valve spring compressor, compress each valve spring in turn until the split collets can be removed. Release the compressor, and lift off the spring retainer, spring and spring seat. Using a pair of pliers or special removal tool, carefully extract the valve stem seal from the top of the guide **(see illustrations)**.

3 If, when the valve spring compressor is screwed down, the spring retainer refuses to free and expose the split collets, gently tap the top of the tool, directly over the retainer, with a light hammer. This will free the retainer.

6.2a Using a compressor tool to compress the valve springs

6.2b Remove the spring retainer . . .

6.2c . . . spring . . .

6.2d . . . and spring seat

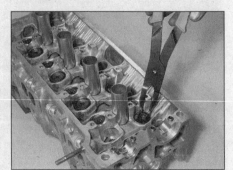

6.2e Using a special removal tool . . .

6.2f ... to remove the valve stem seals from the tops of the guides

4 Withdraw the valve through the combustion chamber **(see illustration)**.

5 It is essential that each valve is stored together with its collets, retainer, spring, and spring seat. The valves should also be kept in their correct sequence, unless they are so badly worn that they are to be renewed. If they are going to be kept and used again, place each valve assembly in a labelled polythene bag or similar small container. Note that the valves of No 1 cylinder are nearest to the timing belt end of the engine.

7 Cylinder head and valves - cleaning and inspection

1 Thorough cleaning of the cylinder head and valve components, followed by a detailed inspection, will enable you to decide how much valve service work must be carried out during the engine overhaul. **Note:** *If the engine has been severely overheated, it is best to assume that the cylinder head is warped - check carefully for signs of this.*

Cleaning

2 Scrape away all traces of old gasket material from the cylinder head.

3 Scrape away the carbon from the combustion chambers and ports, then wash the cylinder head thoroughly with paraffin or a suitable solvent.

4 Scrape off any heavy carbon deposits that may have formed on the valves, then use a power-operated wire brush to remove deposits from the valve heads and stems.

6.4 Removing a valve from the combustion chamber

Inspection

Note: *Be sure to perform all the following inspection procedures before concluding that the services of a machine shop or engine overhaul specialist are required. Make a list of all items that require attention.*

Cylinder head

5 Inspect the head very carefully for cracks, evidence of coolant leakage, and other damage. If cracks are found, a new cylinder head should be obtained.

6 Use a straight-edge and feeler blade to check that the cylinder head surface is not distorted **(see illustration)**. If it is, it may be possible to have it machined by an engine overhaul specialist.

7 Examine the valve seats in each of the combustion chambers. If they are severely pitted, cracked, or burned, they will need to be renewed or re-cut by an engine overhaul specialist. If they are only slightly pitted, this can be removed by grinding-in the valve heads and seats with fine valve-grinding compound, as described below.

8 Check the valve guides for wear by inserting the relevant valve, and checking for side-to-side movement of the valve. A very small amount of movement is acceptable, however, if excessive remove the valve and measure the valve stem diameter (see below) and renew the valve if it is worn. If the valve stem is not worn, the wear must be in the valve guide, and it must be renewed. The renewal of valve guides is best carried out by a Toyota dealer or engine overhaul specialist, who will have the necessary tools available.

9 If renewing the valve guides, the valve seats must be re-cut or re-ground only *after* the guides have been fitted.

Valves

10 Examine the head of each valve for pitting, burning, cracks, and general wear. Check the valve stem for scoring and wear ridges. Rotate the valve, and check for any obvious indication that it is bent. Look for pits and excessive wear on the tip of each valve stem. Renew any valve that shows any signs of wear or damage.

11 If the valve appears satisfactory at this stage, measure the valve stem diameter at several points using a micrometer **(see illustration)**. Any significant difference in the readings obtained indicates wear of the valve stem. Should any of these conditions be apparent, the valve(s) must be renewed.

12 If the valves are in satisfactory condition, they should be ground (lapped) into their respective seats, to ensure a smooth, gas-tight seal. If the seat is only lightly pitted, or if it has been re-cut, fine grinding compound *only* should be used to produce the required finish. Coarse valve-grinding compound should *not* be used, unless a seat is badly burned or deeply pitted. If this is the case, the cylinder head and valves should be inspected by an expert, to decide whether seat re-cutting, or even the renewal of the valve or seat insert is required.

13 Valve grinding is carried out as follows. Place the cylinder head upside-down on a bench.

14 Smear a trace of the appropriate grade of valve-grinding compound on the seat face, and press a suction grinding tool onto the valve head. With a semi-rotary action, grind the valve head to its seat, lifting the valve occasionally to redistribute the grinding compound **(see illustration)**. A light spring placed under the valve head will greatly ease this operation.

15 If coarse grinding compound is being used, work only until a dull, matt even surface is produced on both the valve seat and the valve, then wipe off the used compound, and repeat the process with fine compound. When a smooth unbroken ring of light grey matt finish is produced on both the valve and seat, the grinding operation is complete. *Do not grind-in the valves any further than absolutely necessary.*

2B

7.6 Checking the cylinder head surface for distortion

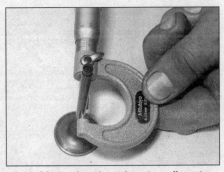

7.11 Measuring the valve stem diameter

7.14 Grinding-in the valves

7.17 Measuring the free length of the valve springs

16 When all the valves have been ground-in, carefully wash off *all* traces of grinding compound using paraffin or a suitable solvent, before reassembling the cylinder head.

Valve components

17 Examine the valve springs for signs of damage and discoloration. The specified Toyota procedure for checking the condition of valve springs involves measuring the force necessary to compress each spring to a specified height. This is not possible without the use of the Toyota special test equipment, and therefore spring checking must be entrusted to a Toyota dealer. A rough idea of the condition of the spring can be gained by measuring the spring free length, and comparing it to the length given in this Chapter's Specifications **(see illustration)**.

18 Stand each spring on a flat surface, and position a square alongside the edge of the

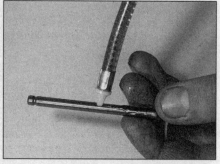

8.1 Lubricate the stems of the valves before inserting them in their guides

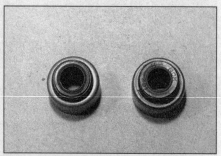

8.2 The inlet valve stem oil seals are brown or grey (left) and the exhaust valve seals are black (right)

spring. Measure the gap between the upper and lower edges of the spring and the square.
19 If any of the springs are damaged, distorted or have lost their tension, obtain a complete new set of springs. It is normal to renew the valve springs as a matter of course if a major overhaul is being carried out.
20 Renew the valve stem oil seals regardless of their apparent condition. They are supplied in the engine gasket set.

8 Cylinder head - reassembly

1 Lubricate the stems of the valves, and insert the valves into their original locations in the cylinder head. If new valves are being fitted, insert them into the locations to which they have been ground **(see illustration)**.
2 Working on the first valve, dip the new valve stem seal in fresh engine oil and ease it over the valve stem onto the guide. Use a suitable socket or metal tube to press the seal firmly onto the guide. Note that the seals are colour-coded on their top surface for identification purposes. On all engines the black seals are fitted to the exhaust valve guides, the seals for the inlet valve guides are either brown or grey **(see illustration)**.
3 Refit the spring seat, then locate the valve spring on top of its seat and refit the spring retainer.
4 Compress the valve spring with the valve spring compressor tool, and locate the split collets in the recess in the valve stem. Release the compressor, then repeat this procedure on the remaining valves **(see illustration)**.

 HAYNES HINT *Use a little dab of grease on a screwdriver and on the collets while locating them on the valve recess.*

5 With all the valves installed, place the cylinder head flat on the bench and, using a hammer and interposed block of wood, tap the end of each valve stem to settle the components.
6 The cylinder head and associated components may now be refitted as described in Part A of this Chapter.

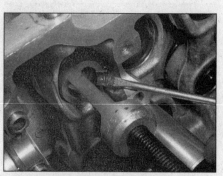

8.4 Using a dab of grease to retain the collets on the valve stems

9 Pistons/connecting rods - removal

1 Remove the timing belt, cylinder head, sump and oil pump pick-up tube, as described in Part A of this Chapter.
2 If there is a pronounced wear ridge at the top of any bore, it may be necessary to remove it with a scraper or ridge reamer, to avoid piston damage during removal. Such a ridge indicates excessive wear of the cylinder bore.
3 Each connecting rod and bearing cap should be identified for its respective cylinder, however the markings do not include the cylinder number. Make a note of the markings and the respective cylinders, or alternatively use a hammer and centre-punch, paint or similar, to mark each connecting rod and big-end bearing cap with its respective cylinder number on the flat machined surface provided.
4 Turn the crankshaft to bring pistons 1 and 4 to BDC (bottom dead centre).
5 Before removing the pistons and connecting rods, use a feeler gauge to measure the big-end bearing side clearances, and compare with the limit given in the Specifications. Unless the engine has completed a very high mileage, it is unusual to find excessive side wear of the connecting rods.
6 Unscrew the nuts/bolts from No 1 piston big-end bearing cap. Take off the cap, and recover the bottom half bearing shell. If the bearing shells are to be re-used, tape the cap and the shell together **(see illustrations)**.
7 Where necessary, to prevent the possibility of damage to the crankshaft bearing journals, tape over the connecting rod bolt threads or fit a length of plastic hose to them.
8 Using a hammer handle, push the piston up through the bore, and remove it from the top of the cylinder block. Recover the bearing shell, and tape it to the connecting rod for safe-keeping **(see illustration)**.
9 Loosely refit the big-end cap to the connecting rod, and secure with the nuts/bolts - this will help to keep the components in their correct order.

9.6a Unscrewing the nuts/bolts from No 1 piston big-end bearing cap

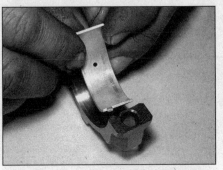

9.6b Recovering the bottom half bearing shell from the big-end bearing cap

9.8 Recovering the upper half bearing shell from the connecting rod

10 Remove No 4 piston assembly in the same way.

11 Turn the crankshaft through 180° to bring pistons 2 and 3 to BDC (bottom dead centre), and remove them in the same way.

10 Crankshaft - removal

1 Remove the timing belt, sump, oil pump and pick-up tube and flywheel/driveplate with reference to Part A of this Chapter (the engine must be removed from the vehicle), then unbolt the rear engine plate and rear oil seal housing and recover the gasket **(see illustrations)**.

2 Remove the pistons and connecting rods, as described in Section 9. **Note:** *If no work is to be done on the pistons and connecting rods, there is no need to remove the cylinder head, or to push the pistons out of the cylinder bores. The pistons should just be pushed far enough up the bores to position them clear of the crankshaft journals.*

3 Check and note the crankshaft endfloat as described in Section 13, then proceed as follows.

4 Working in the sequence shown, slacken the main bearing cap retaining bolts by a turn at a time **(see illustration)**. Once all bolts are loose, unscrew and remove them from the cylinder block. Note that the caps are numbered from the timing belt end of the engine, and in addition an arrow points to the timing end **(see illustrations)**.

5 Remove the main bearing caps and recover the lower main bearing shells. Tape each shell to its relevant cap for safe-keeping. Also recover the thrust washers either side of the centre main bearing cap keeping them identified for position.

6 Carefully lift out the crankshaft, taking care not to displace the upper main bearing shells.

7 Recover the upper bearing shells from the cylinder block, and tape them to their respective positions on the main bearing caps. Remove the thrustwasher halves from the side of centre main bearing, and store them with the main bearing cap.

2B

10.1a Remove the rear engine plate . . .

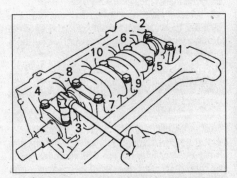

10.4a Main bearing cap bolt slackening sequence

10.4b Loosening the main bearing cap bolts

10.1b . . . then unscrew the bolts . . .

10.1c . . . remove the rear oil seal housing . . .

10.1d . . . and recover the gasket

10.4c Main bearing caps are numbered and marked with an arrow towards the timing end of the engine

11.1a Removing the oil pressure sensor from the cylinder block

11.1b Power steering pump lower mounting bracket

11.1c Alternator adjustment bracket on the right-hand end of the cylinder block

11 Cylinder block/crankcase - cleaning and inspection

Cleaning

1 Remove all external components and electrical switches/sensors from the block, and unbolt the alternator and power steering pump brackets as applicable **(see illustrations)**.

2 For complete cleaning, the core plugs should ideally be removed. Drill a small hole in the plugs, then insert a self-tapping screw into the hole. Pull out the plugs by pulling on the screw with a pair of grips, or by using a slide hammer.

3 Scrape all traces of sealant from the cylinder block/crankcase, taking care not to damage the gasket/sealing surfaces.

4 Remove all oil gallery plugs (where fitted). The plugs are usually very tight - they may have to be drilled out, and the holes re-tapped. Use new plugs when the engine is reassembled.

5 If any of the castings are extremely dirty, all should be steam-cleaned.

6 After the castings are returned, clean all oil holes and oil galleries one more time. Flush all internal passages with warm water until the water runs clear. Dry thoroughly, and apply a light film of oil to all mating surfaces and the cylinder bores, to prevent rusting. If you have access to compressed air, use it to speed up the drying process, and to blow out all the oil holes and galleries.

 Warning: Wear eye protection when using compressed air!

7 If the castings are not very dirty, you can do an adequate cleaning job with hot (as hot as you can stand!), soapy water and a stiff brush. Take plenty of time, and do a thorough job. Regardless of the cleaning method used, be sure to clean all oil holes and galleries very thoroughly, and to dry all components well. Protect the cylinder bores as described above, to prevent rusting.

8 All threaded holes must be clean, to ensure accurate torque readings during reassembly.

To clean the threads, run the correct-size tap into each of the holes to remove rust, corrosion, thread sealant or sludge, and to restore damaged threads. If possible, use compressed air to clear the holes of debris produced by this operation.

 Warning: Wear eye protection when cleaning out these holes in this way!

9 Apply suitable sealant to the new oil gallery plugs, and insert them into the holes in the block. Tighten them securely.

10 If the engine is not going to be reassembled right away, cover it with a large plastic bag to keep it clean; protect all mating surfaces and the cylinder bores as described above, to prevent rusting.

Inspection

11 Visually check the casting for cracks and corrosion. Look for stripped threads in the threaded holes. If there has been any history of internal water leakage, it may be worthwhile having an engine overhaul specialist check the cylinder block/crankcase with special equipment. If defects are found, have them repaired if possible, or obtain a new block.

12 Check each cylinder bore for scuffing and scoring. Check for signs of a wear ridge at the top of the cylinder, indicating that the bore is excessively worn.

13 Measure the diameter of each cylinder bore 20 mm from the top of the bore, both parallel to the crankshaft axis and at right-angles to it. Repeat the procedure measuring the bore diameter 60 mm from the top, and then 100 mm from the top, so that a total of six measurements are taken. Using the measurements obtained, calculate the cylinder bore at these positions. **Note:** *The bore grade is stamped both on the bottom of the cylinder block and on the piston crown. There are three sizes of standard cylinder bore diameter.*

14 Check the pistons and rings as described in Section 12. The piston-to-bore clearance can be calculated by subtracting the piston diameter from the cylinder bore diameter measurement.

15 Compare all results with the Specifications at the beginning of this Chapter. If any measurement exceeds the

service limit specified, the cylinders must be rebored, where possible, to the next oversize and new pistons fitted, or the cylinder block must be renewed. Seek the advice of an engine overhaul specialist as to the best course of action. Pistons are available in only one oversize - 0.5 mm.

16 If the cylinder bores and pistons are in reasonably good condition, and not worn to the specified limits, and if the piston-to-bore clearances are not excessive, then it may only be necessary to renew the piston rings.

17 If this is the case, the bores should be honed, to allow the new rings to bed in correctly and provide the best possible seal. The conventional type of hone has spring-loaded stones, and is used with a power drill. You will also need some paraffin, or honing oil, and rags. The hone should be moved up and down the bore to produce a cross-hatch pattern, and plenty of honing oil should be used. Ideally the cross-hatch lines should intersect at approximately a 60° angle. Do not take off more material than is necessary to produce the required finish. If new pistons are being fitted, the piston manufacturers may specify a finish with a different angle, so their instructions should be followed. Do not withdraw the hone from the bore while it is still being turned - stop it first. After honing a bore, wipe out all traces of the honing oil. If equipment of this type is not available, or if you are not sure whether you are competent to undertake the task yourself, an engine overhaul specialist will carry out the work at moderate cost.

18 After all work has been carried out on the cylinder block/crankcase, refit all the external components and electrical switches/sensors removed from the block.

12 Pistons/connecting rods - inspection

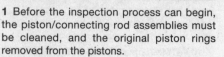

1 Before the inspection process can begin, the piston/connecting rod assemblies must be cleaned, and the original piston rings removed from the pistons.

2 Carefully expand the old rings over the top of the pistons - note that the oil control ring

12.2 Carefully expand the rings from the top of the piston

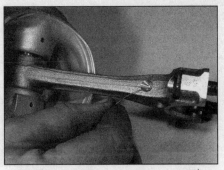

12.5 Checking the connecting rod oil jet hole for blockage

12.6 The piston size grade is stamped onto the piston crown

assembly incorporates two rails and an expander. The use of two or three old feeler blades will be helpful in preventing the rings dropping into empty grooves **(see illustration)**. Be careful not to scratch the piston with the ends of the ring. The rings are brittle, and will snap if they are spread too far. They're also very sharp - protect your hands and fingers. Always remove the rings from the top of the piston. Keep each set of rings with its piston if the old rings are to be re-used.

3 Scrape away all traces of carbon from the top of the piston. A hand-held wire brush (or a piece of fine emery cloth) can be used, once the majority of the deposits have been scraped away.

4 Remove the carbon from the ring grooves in the piston, using an old ring. Break the ring in half to do this (be careful not to cut your fingers - piston rings are sharp). Be careful to remove only the carbon deposits - do not remove any metal, and do not nick or scratch the sides of the ring grooves.

5 Once the deposits have been removed, clean the piston/connecting rod assembly with paraffin or a suitable solvent, and dry thoroughly. Make sure that the oil return holes in the ring grooves are clear, and check that the oil jet holes are also clear **(see illustration)**.

6 Using a micrometer, measure the piston diameter at right-angles to the gudgeon pin axis (at the specified distance up from the bottom of the skirt - see Specifications). The piston size grade is stamped onto the piston crown **(see illustration)**. Renew any piston which has worn beyond its specified limits.

7 To check the ring-to-groove clearance, hold a new piston ring in the appropriate groove and measure the ring clearance using a feeler blade **(see illustration)**. If the ring-to-groove clearance is excessive, renew the rings and recheck the clearance. If the clearance is still excessive, even with new piston rings, then the piston must be renewed.

8 Check the ring end gaps by inserting each ring into the cylinder bore and pushing it in with the piston crown to ensure that it is square in the bore. Push the ring down into the bore the specified distance, then withdraw the piston. Using feeler blades, measure the

piston ring end gap. If the ring end gap is excessive, renew the rings and repeat the checking procedure. If the clearance is still excessive, even with new piston rings, then the cylinder bores must be rebored (see Section 11).

9 Carefully inspect each piston for cracks around the skirt, around the gudgeon pin holes, and at the piston ring lands (between the ring grooves).

10 Look for scoring and scuffing on the piston skirt, holes in the piston crown, or burned areas at the edge of the crown. If the skirt is scored or scuffed, the engine may have been suffering from overheating, and/or abnormal combustion which caused excessively-high operating temperatures. The cooling and lubrication systems should be checked thoroughly. Scorch marks on the sides of the pistons show that blow-by has occurred. A hole in the piston crown, or burned areas at the edge of the piston crown, indicates that abnormal combustion (pre-ignition, knocking, or detonation) has been occurring. If any of the above problems exist, the causes must be investigated and corrected, or the damage will occur again. The causes may include incorrect ignition timing or inlet air leaks.

11 Corrosion of the piston, in the form of pitting, indicates that coolant has been leaking into the combustion chamber and/or the crankcase. Again, the cause must be corrected, or the problem may persist in the rebuilt engine.

12 Examine each connecting rod carefully for signs of damage, such as cracks around the

12.7 Checking the piston-to-ring groove clearance

big-end and small-end bearings. Check that the rod is not bent or distorted. Damage is highly unlikely, unless the engine has been seized or badly overheated. Detailed checking of the connecting rod assembly can only be carried out by a Toyota dealer or engine repair specialist with the necessary equipment.

13 On 4A-FE, 7A-FE and 3S-FE engines the pistons and connecting rods can only be separated by a Toyota dealer or engine repair specialist with suitable equipment to press the gudgeon pins from the connecting rods. If the pistons are being renewed on these engines, have the new pistons fitted by the specialist. On 3S-GE engines the gudgeon pins are fully floating in the pistons and connecting rods and may be removed after removal of the end circlips.

14 The connecting rods themselves should not need renewal, unless seizure or some other major mechanical failure has occurred. Check the alignment of the connecting rods visually, and if the rods are not straight, take them to an engine overhaul specialist for a more detailed check.

15 Measure the diameter of the big-end cap retaining bolts, using vernier calipers, at a point approximately 15 mm below the underside of the bolt head. If the diameter of any bolt is less than 7.60 mm (3S-FE and 3S-GE engines) or 8.60 mm (4A-FE and 7A-FE engines), the bolt must be renewed. If any of the bolts have reached this minimum diameter, it is a wise precaution to renew all the connecting rod bolts as a set.

2B

13 Crankshaft - inspection

Checking crankshaft endfloat

1 If the crankshaft endfloat is to be checked, this must be done when the crankshaft is still installed in the cylinder block/crankcase, but is free to move (see Section 10).

2 Check the endfloat using a dial gauge in contact with the end of the crankshaft **(see illustration)**. Push the crankshaft fully one way, and then zero the gauge. Push the crankshaft fully the other way, and check the

13.2 Checking the crankshaft endfloat with a dial gauge

13.3 Checking the crankshaft endfloat with feeler blades on the centre (No 3) main bearing

13.11 Using a micrometer to check the diameter of the big-end bearing journals

endfloat. The result can be compared with the specified amount, and will give an indication as to whether new thrustwashers are required.

3 If a dial gauge is not available, feeler blades can be used. First push the crankshaft fully towards the flywheel end of the engine, then use feeler blades to measure the gap between the centre crankpin web and centre main bearing thrustwasher **(see illustration)**.

Inspection

4 Clean the crankshaft using paraffin or a suitable solvent, and dry it, preferably with compressed air if available.

 Warning: Wear eye protection when using compressed air!

5 Check the main and big-end bearing journals for uneven wear, scoring, pitting and cracking.

6 Big-end bearing wear is accompanied by distinct metallic knocking when the engine is running (particularly noticeable when the engine is pulling from low speed) and some loss of oil pressure.

7 Main bearing wear is accompanied by severe engine vibration and rumble - getting progressively worse as engine speed increases - and again by loss of oil pressure.

8 Check the bearing journal for roughness by running a finger lightly over the bearing surface. Any roughness (which will be accompanied by obvious bearing wear) indicates that the crankshaft requires regrinding (where possible) or renewal.

9 Crankshaft run-out can be checked by supporting each end of the crankshaft on V-blocks, and measuring any run-out at the centre of the shaft using a dial gauge. If the run-out exceeds the specified limit, a new crankshaft will be required.

10 If the crankshaft has been reground, check for burrs around the crankshaft oil holes (the holes are usually chamfered, so burrs should not be a problem unless regrinding has been carried out carelessly). Remove any burrs with a fine file or scraper, and thoroughly clean the oil holes as described previously.

11 Using a micrometer, measure the

diameter of the main and big-end bearing journals, and compare the results with the Specifications **(see illustration)**. By measuring the diameter at a number of points around each journal's circumference, you will be able to determine whether or not the journal is out-of-round. Take the measurement at each end of the journal, near the webs, to determine if the journal is tapered. Compare the results obtained with those given in the Specifications.

12 Check the oil seal contact surfaces at each end of the crankshaft for wear and damage. If the seal has worn a deep groove in the surface of the crankshaft, consult an engine overhaul specialist. Repair may be possible, but otherwise a new crankshaft will be required.

13 Toyota produce undersize bearing shells for both the main bearings and big-end bearings as given in the Specifications. Refer to your Toyota dealer for further information on parts availability. If undersize bearing shells are available, and the crankshaft has worn beyond the specified limits, providing that the crankshaft journals have not already been reground, it may be possible to have the crankshaft reconditioned, and to fit the undersize shells. Seek the advice of your Toyota dealer or engine specialist on the best course of action.

14 Main and big-end bearings - inspection

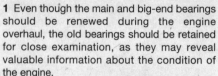

1 Even though the main and big-end bearings should be renewed during the engine overhaul, the old bearings should be retained for close examination, as they may reveal valuable information about the condition of the engine.

2 Bearing failure can occur due to lack of lubrication, the presence of dirt or other foreign particles, overloading the engine, or corrosion. Regardless of the cause of bearing failure, the cause must be corrected (where applicable) before the engine is reassembled, to prevent it from happening again **(see illustration)**.

3 When examining the bearing shells, remove them from the cylinder block/crankcase, the main bearing caps, the connecting rods and the connecting rod big-end bearing caps. Lay them out on a clean surface in the same general position as their location in the engine. This will enable you to match any bearing problems with the corresponding crankshaft journal. *Do not* touch any shell's bearing surface with your fingers while checking it, or the delicate surface may be scratched.

4 Dirt and other foreign matter gets into the engine in a variety of ways. It may be left in the engine during assembly, or it may pass through filters or the crankcase ventilation system. It may get into the oil, and from there into the bearings. Metal chips from machining operations and normal engine wear are often present. Abrasives are sometimes left in engine components after reconditioning, especially when parts are not thoroughly cleaned using the proper cleaning methods. Whatever the source, these foreign objects often end up embedded in the soft bearing

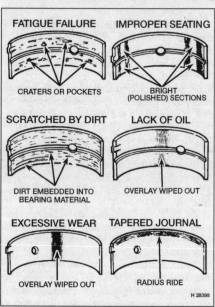

14.2 Typical bearing failures

material, and are easily recognised. Large particles will not embed in the bearing, and will score or gouge the bearing and journal. The best prevention for this cause of bearing failure is to clean all parts thoroughly, and keep everything spotlessly-clean during engine assembly. Frequent and regular engine oil and filter changes are also recommended.

5 Lack of lubrication (or lubrication breakdown) has a number of interrelated causes. Excessive heat (which thins the oil), overloading (which squeezes the oil from the bearing face) and oil leakage (from excessive bearing clearances, worn oil pump or high engine speeds) all contribute to lubrication breakdown. Blocked oil passages, which usually are the result of misaligned oil holes in a bearing shell, will also oil-starve a bearing, and destroy it. When lack of lubrication is the cause of bearing failure, the bearing material is wiped or extruded from the steel backing of the bearing. Temperatures may increase to the point where the steel backing turns blue from overheating.

6 Driving habits can have a definite effect on bearing life. Full-throttle, low-speed operation (labouring the engine) puts very high loads on bearings, tending to squeeze out the oil film. These loads cause the bearings to flex, which produces fine cracks in the bearing face (fatigue failure). Eventually, the bearing material will loosen in pieces, and tear away from the steel backing.

7 Short-distance driving leads to corrosion of bearings, because insufficient engine heat is produced to drive off the condensed water and corrosive gases. These products collect in the engine oil, forming acid and sludge. As the oil is carried to the engine bearings, the acid attacks and corrodes the bearing material.

8 Incorrect bearing installation during engine assembly will lead to bearing failure as well. Tight-fitting bearings leave insufficient bearing running clearance, and will result in oil starvation. Dirt or foreign particles trapped behind a bearing shell result in high spots on the bearing, which lead to failure.

9 *Do not* touch any shell's bearing surface with your fingers during reassembly; there is a risk of scratching the delicate surface, or of depositing particles of dirt on it.

10 As mentioned at the beginning of this Section, the bearing shells should be renewed as a matter of course during engine overhaul; to do otherwise is false economy. Refer to Section 16 for details of bearing shell selection.

15 Engine overhaul - reassembly sequence

1 Before reassembly begins, ensure that all new parts have been obtained, and that all necessary tools are available. Read through the entire procedure, to familiarise yourself

16.2a Press the bearing shells into their correct locations in the cylinder block . . .

with the work involved, and to ensure that all items necessary for reassembly of the engine are at hand. In addition to all normal tools and materials, thread-locking compound will be needed. A suitable tube of liquid sealant will also be required for the joint faces that are fitted without gaskets; it is recommended that Toyota sealant (available from your Toyota dealer) is used.

2 In order to save time and avoid problems, engine reassembly can be carried out in the following order:
a) *Crankshaft (Section 16).*
b) *Piston/connecting rod assemblies (Sections 17 and 18).*
c) *Oil pump, oil pump pick-up tube and rear oil seal housing (see Part A of this Chapter).*
d) *Sump (see Part A of this Chapter).*
e) *Flywheel/driveplate (see Part A of this Chapter).*
f) *Cylinder head (see Part A of this Chapter).*
g) *Timing belt, tensioner, sprockets and idler pulleys (see Part A of this Chapter).*
h) *Inlet and exhaust manifolds (Chapter 4A).*
i) *Engine external components.*

3 At this stage, all engine components should be absolutely clean and dry, with all faults repaired. The components should be laid out (or in individual containers) on a completely clean work surface.

16 Crankshaft - refitting and main bearing running clearance check

1 Clean the backs of the bearing shells and the bearing recesses in both the cylinder block and main bearing caps.
2 Press the bearing shells into their correct locations in the cylinder block and caps, ensuring that the shells with oil holes align with the oil holes in the cylinder block; the tags on the bearing shells must engage in their respective notches **(see illustrations)**. On 3S-FE and 3S-GE engines the centre (No 3) upper and lower main bearing shells are 22.9 mm wide and all the others are 19.2 mm wide - ensure that the shells are fitted accordingly. Note that if the original main bearing shells are being re-used these must

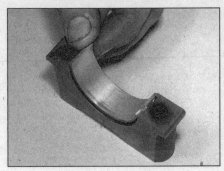

16.2b . . . and caps

be refitted to their original locations in the block and caps.

Main bearing running clearance check

3 Before the crankshaft can be permanently installed, the main bearing running clearance should be checked; this can be done in either of two ways. One method is to fit the main bearing caps to the cylinder block, with shells in place. With the cap bolts tightened to the specified torque, measure the internal diameter of each assembled pair of bearing shells using a vernier dial indicator or internal micrometer. If the diameter of each corresponding crankshaft journal is measured and then subtracted from the bearing internal diameter, the result will be the main bearing running clearance. The second (and more accurate) method is to use a product known as Plastigauge. This consists of a fine thread of perfectly round plastic which is compressed by the action of tightening down the main bearing caps with the crankshaft in position. When the cap is removed, the plastic is deformed and the running clearance can be measured with a special card gauge supplied with the kit.

4 With the upper main bearing shells in position on the cylinder block, ensure that the crankshaft journals and bearing shells are perfectly clean and dry, then carefully lower the crankshaft into position.

5 Cut several lengths of Plastigauge and place one on each crankshaft journal **(see illustration)**.

16.5 Cut several lengths of Plastigauge and place one on each crankshaft journal

2B

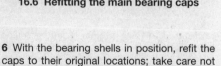

16.6 Refitting the main bearing caps

16.9 Using the Plastigauge scale to measure the main bearing running clearance

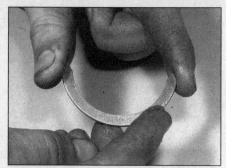

16.15 Use a dab of grease to hold the thrustwashers in position each side of the centre main bearing

6 With the bearing shells in position, refit the caps to their original locations; take care not to disturb the Plastigauge **(see illustration)**.

7 Progressively tighten the cap bolts to their specified torque setting; do **not** rotate the crankshaft at any time during this operation.

8 Unscrew the bolts and carefully lift off the bearing caps whilst taking great care not to disturb the Plastigauge or rotate the crankshaft.

9 Compare the width of the crushed Plastigauge on each journal to the scale printed on the Plastigauge envelope to obtain the main bearing running clearance **(see illustration)**.

10 If the clearance is not as specified, the bearing shells may be the wrong size (or excessively worn if the original shells are being re-used). Before deciding that different size shells are needed, make sure that no dirt or oil was trapped between the bearing shells and the caps or block when the clearance was measured. If the Plastigauge was wider at one end than at the other, the journal may be tapered.

11 Carefully scrape away all traces of the Plastigauge material from the crankshaft and bearing shells using your fingernail or other object which is unlikely to score the shells.

Final crankshaft refitting

12 If necessary, obtain new bearing shells which carry the same number as that stamped on the reverse side of the defective ones (unless the crankshaft has been reground); if the number is not visible, select a

bearing from the table below, according to the numbers imprinted on the crankshaft and cylinder block. The numbers are stamped on the sump face of the cylinder block at the rear of the engine, and also on the crankshaft webs. On 4A-FE and 7A-FE engines, No 1 bearing is on the 1st web, Nos 2 and 3 on the 4th web and Nos 4 and 5 on the 5th web. On 3S-FE and 3S-GE engines, the numbers are all stamped on the 3rd web.

Cylinder block number	Crankshaft number	Correct shell
1	0	1
2	0	2
3	0	3
1	1	2
2	1	3
3	1	4
1	2	3
2	2	4
3	2	5

13 With any protective grease removed from the new bearing shells and the bearing shells correctly positioned, the running clearance should be checked (as described above) whenever the bearings shells have been renewed. If the running clearance is outside specification with the new bearings fitted, consult your Toyota dealer or engine overhaul specialist regarding crankshaft regrinding/renewal.

14 Check that the bearing shells are correctly installed to their cylinder block and cap locations as described in paragraph 2.

15 Install the upper thrustwashers on either

16.16 Lubricate the main bearing journals . . .

side of the centre (No 3) main bearing in the cylinder block so that their oil grooves are facing outwards. If necessary they can be held in position using a smear of grease **(see illustration)**.

16 Lubricate the main bearing journals, the upper bearing shell-to-journal contact faces and the upper thrustwashers with clean engine oil **(see illustration)**.

17 Carefully lay the crankshaft in position on the cylinder block; be careful not to dislodge the upper thrustwashers **(see illustration)**.

18 Lubricate the lower bearing shell faces and the lower thrustwashers, then install the bearing caps to their original locations; ensure that the arrows on the caps face the timing end of the engine, and that the lower thrustwashers are fitted to the centre (No 3) main bearing cap with their oil grooves facing outwards **(see illustration)**.

16.17 . . . then lower the crankshaft into the cylinder block

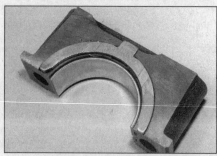

16.18 Make sure that the thrustwashers are correctly located each side of the centre main bearing cap

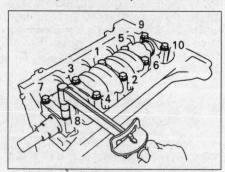

16.19a Main bearing cap tightening sequence

19 Fit the main bearing cap bolts, having applied a light coating of clean engine oil to their threads and under their heads, then progressively tighten them to the specified torque in the sequence shown **(see illustrations)**. Check that the crankshaft is free to turn, then recheck the endfloat.

17 Piston rings - refitting

1 Before fitting new piston rings, the ring end gaps must be checked as described in Section 12. Keep the rings identified for position so that they are refitted correctly.
2 Measure the end gap using feeler gauges, and compare the measurements with the figures given in the Specifications.
3 If the gap is too small (unlikely if genuine Toyota parts are used), it must be enlarged, or the ring ends may contact each other during engine operation, causing serious damage. Ideally, new piston rings providing the correct end gap should be fitted. As a last resort, the end gap can be increased by filing the ring ends very carefully with a fine file. Mount the file in a vice with soft jaws, slip the ring over the file with the ends contacting the file face, and slowly move the ring to remove material from the ends. Take care, as piston rings are sharp, and are easily broken.
4 With new piston rings, it is unlikely that the end gap will be too large. If the gaps are too large, check that you have the correct rings for your engine and for the particular cylinder bore size.
5 Repeat the checking procedure for each ring in the first cylinder, and then for the rings in the remaining cylinders. Remember to keep rings, pistons and cylinders matched up.
6 Once the ring end gaps have been checked and if necessary corrected, the rings can be fitted to the pistons. **Note:** *Always follow any instructions supplied with the new piston ring sets - different manufacturers may specify different procedures. Do not mix up the top and second compression rings, as they have different cross-sections.*
7 The oil control ring (lowest on the piston) is installed first. It is composed of three separate components. Slip the expander into the

16.19b Insert the main bearing cap bolts . . .

16.19c . . . then progressively tighten them to the specified torque

groove, then install the upper side rail into the groove between the expander and the ring land, then install the lower side rail in the same manner.
8 Install the second ring next taking care not to expand the ring any more than is necessary. Making sure the ring is the correct way up with any markings facing upwards, fit the ring into the middle groove on the piston, taking care not to expand the ring any more than is necessary.
9 Install the top ring in the same way, making sure the ring is the correct way up with its identification marking facing upwards.
10 With all the rings in position on the piston, space the ring end gaps as shown **(see illustrations)**.
11 Repeat the above procedure for the remaining pistons and rings.

18 Pistons/connecting rods - refitting and bearing running clearance check

Selection of new bearing shells

1 There are two sizes of big-end bearing shell produced by Toyota; a standard size for use with the standard crankshaft, and an undersize for use once the crankshaft journals have been reground. The standard size is graded into three sub-sizes with the marks 1, 2 and 3.
2 Consult your Toyota dealer for the latest information on parts availability. If possible quote the diameter of the crankshaft big-end crankpins when ordering bearing shells.

3 Prior to refitting the piston/connecting rod assemblies, it is recommended that the big-end bearing running clearance is checked as follows.

Big-end bearing running clearance check

4 Clean the backs of the bearing shells, and the bearing locations in both the connecting rod and bearing cap.
5 Press the bearing shells into their locations, ensuring that the tab on each shell engages in the recess in the connecting rod and cap. Take care not to touch any shell's bearing surface with your fingers, and ensure that the shells are correctly installed. If the original bearing shells are being used for the check, ensure that they are refitted in their original locations. The clearance can be checked in either of two ways.
6 One method is to refit the big-end bearing cap to the connecting rod, ensuring that they are fitted the correct way round, with the bearing shells in place. With the cap retaining nuts/bolts correctly tightened, use an internal micrometer or vernier caliper to measure the internal diameter of each assembled pair of bearing shells. If the diameter of each corresponding crankshaft journal is measured and then subtracted from the bearing internal diameter, the result will be the big-end bearing running clearance.
7 The second, and more accurate, method is to use Plastigauge (see Section 16).
8 Ensure that the bearing shells are correctly fitted. Place a strand of Plastigauge on each (cleaned) crankpin journal.

2B

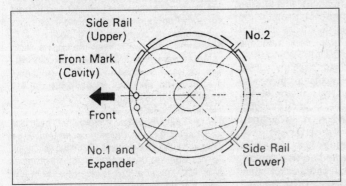
17.10a Piston ring end gap spacing (4A-FE and 7A-FE engines)

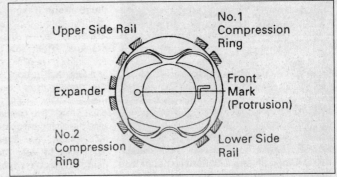
17.10b Piston ring end gap spacing (3S-FE and 3S-GE engines)

18.20 Using a hammer handle to tap the piston into its bore

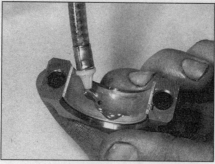

18.21a Lubricate the lower big-end bearing shell before refitting the cap

18.21b Refitting the big-end bearing cap nuts

9 Refit the (clean) piston/connecting rod assemblies to the crankshaft, and refit the big-end bearing caps, using the marks made or noted on removal to ensure that they are fitted the correct way round.

10 Tighten the bearing cap nuts/bolts in the specified two Stages as described below. Take care not to disturb the Plastigauge, nor to rotate the connecting rod during the tightening sequence.

11 Dismantle the assemblies without rotating the connecting rods. Use the scale printed on the Plastigauge envelope to obtain the big-end bearing running clearance.

12 If the clearance is not as specified, the bearing shells may be the wrong size (or excessively worn, if the original shells are being re-used). Make sure that no dirt or oil was trapped between the bearing shells and the caps or connecting rods when the clearance was measured. If the Plastigauge was wider at one end than at the other, the crankpins may be tapered.

13 If the clearance is not as specified with the original bearing shells, repeat the checking procedure using new bearing shells. If the clearance is not as specified even with new bearing shells, then seek the advice of a Toyota dealer or engine overhaul specialist. They will be able to advise you on the best course of action, and whether or not it will be necessary to have the crankpin journals reground and fit undersize shells.

14 Where necessary, obtain the required grades of bearing shell, and repeat the running clearance checking procedure as described above.

18.22 Using an angle-tightening gauge to tighten the big-end bearing cap bolts to their Stage 2 angle

15 On completion, carefully scrape away all traces of the Plastigauge material from the crankshaft and bearing shells. Use your fingernail, or a wooden or plastic scraper which is unlikely to score the bearing surfaces.

Final piston/connecting rod refitting

16 Note that the following procedure assumes that the crankshaft and main bearing caps are in place (see Section 16).

17 Ensure that the bearing shells are correctly fitted as described in paragraphs 4 and 5. If new shells are being fitted, ensure that all traces of the protective grease are cleaned off using paraffin. Wipe dry the shells and connecting rods with a lint-free cloth.

18 Lubricate the cylinder bores, the pistons, and piston rings, then lay out each piston/connecting rod assembly in its respective position **(see illustration)**.

19 Start with assembly No 1. Make sure that the piston rings are still spaced as described in Section 17, then clamp them in position with a piston ring compressor.

20 Insert the piston/connecting rod assembly into the top of cylinder No 1. Ensure that the piston front marking (in the form of one or two indentations or a single protrusion) on the piston crown is on the timing belt side of the bore. Using a block of wood or hammer handle against the piston crown, tap the assembly into the cylinder until the piston crown is flush with the top of the cylinder **(see illustration)**.

21 Ensure that the bearing shell is still correctly installed. Liberally lubricate the crankpin and both bearing shells **(see illustration)**. Taking care not to mark the cylinder bores, tap the piston/connecting rod assembly down the bore and onto the crankpin. Refit the big-end bearing cap, tightening its retaining nuts/bolts finger-tight at first **(see illustration)**. Note that the faces with the identification marks must match (which means that the bearing shell locating tabs abut each other). The cast landing on the cap must face the timing belt end of the engine.

22 Tighten the bearing cap retaining nuts/bolts to their Stage 1 torque setting, using a torque wrench and socket, then tighten them through the specified Stage 2 angle setting **(see illustration)**.

23 Rotate the crankshaft and check that it turns freely; some stiffness is to be expected if new components have been fitted, but there should be no signs of binding or tight spots.

24 Refit the remaining three piston/connecting rod assemblies in the same way.

25 Refit the cylinder head, timing belt, oil pump, oil pump pick-up tube, sump, rear engine plate, rear oil seal housing, flywheel/driveplate and the remainder of the external components with reference to Part A and earlier Sections of this Chapter.

19 Engine - initial start-up after overhaul

1 With the engine refitted in the vehicle, double-check the engine oil and coolant levels. Make a final check that everything has been reconnected, and that there are no tools or rags left in the engine compartment.

2 Remove the spark plugs, and disable the fuel injection system by temporarily removing the EFI relay from the engine compartment fusebox. Disable the ignition system by disconnecting the wiring multiplug connector(s) at the distributor.

3 Turn the engine on the starter until the oil pressure warning light goes out. Refit the spark plugs, refit the EFI relay and reconnect the distributor.

4 Start the engine, noting that this may take a little longer than usual, due to the fuel system components having been disturbed.

5 While the engine is idling, check for fuel, water and oil leaks. Don't be alarmed if there are some odd smells and smoke from parts getting hot and burning off oil deposits.

6 Assuming all is well, keep the engine idling until hot water is felt circulating through the radiator top hose, then switch off the engine.

7 After a few minutes, recheck the oil and coolant levels as described in Chapter 1, and top-up as necessary.

8 If new pistons, rings or crankshaft bearings have been fitted, the engine must be treated as new, and run-in for the first 500 miles (800 km). *Do not* operate the engine at full-throttle, or allow it to labour at low engine speeds in any gear. It is recommended that the oil and filter be changed at the end of this period.

Chapter 3
Cooling, heating and air conditioning systems

Contents

Degrees of difficulty

Easy, suitable for novice with little experience	**Fairly easy,** suitable for beginner with some experience	**Fairly difficult,** suitable for competent DIY mechanic	**Difficult,** suitable for experienced DIY mechanic	**Very difficult,** suitable for expert DIY or professional

Specifications

General
Radiator cap opening pressure	0.75 to 1.05 bars (10.7 to 14.9 psi)
Coolant mixture type and capacity	See Chapter 1

Thermostat
Opening temperature	80° to 84°C
Minimum valve lift at 95°C	8.0 mm

Cooling fan temperature switch resistance

4A-FE and 7A-FE engines
93°C and above	0 ohms
Below 83°C	Infinity

3S-FE and 3S-GE engines
No 1 switch:	
93°C and above	0 ohms
Below 83°C	Infinity
No 2 switch:	
102°C and above	0 ohms
Below 93°C	Infinity

Engine temperature sensor resistance

4A-FE, 7A-FE and 3S-FE engines
20°C	2 to 3 k ohms
40°C	0.9 to 1.3 k ohms
80°C	0.2 to 0.4 k ohms

3S-GE engine
20°C	2 to 7 k ohms
40°C	0.9 to 1.3 k ohms
80°C	0.2 to 0.4 k ohms

Torque wrench settings
	Nm	lbf ft
Cylinder block drain plug	29	21
Thermostat cover/inlet	9	7
Water pump to cylinder block:		
4A-FE and 7A-FE engines	14	10
3S-FE and 3S-GE engines	8	6
Water pump body to cover	9	7
Water pump elbow nuts	15	11

3

1 General information and precautions

General information

The cooling system is of pressurised type, comprising a water pump, a crossflow radiator, a coolant expansion tank, an electric cooling fan, a thermostat, heater matrix, and all associated hoses and switches. On 4A-FE and 7A-FE engines the water pump is driven by a ribbed drivebelt from the crankshaft pulley; the water pump pulley also drives the power steering pump where fitted. On 3S-FE and 3S-GE engines the water pump is driven by the engine timing belt.

The system functions as follows. The water pump pumps cold water around the cylinder block and head passages, and through the throttle body and heater matrix. On 3S-GE engines the water is also circulated through the oil cooler on the front of the cylinder block.

When the engine is cold, the coolant is returned from the thermostat housing to the water pump. When the coolant reaches a predetermined temperature, the thermostat opens, and the coolant passes through the top hose to the radiator. As the coolant circulates through the radiator, it is cooled by the inrush of air when the car is in forward motion. The airflow is supplemented by the action of the electric cooling fan when necessary. Upon reaching the bottom of the radiator, the coolant has now cooled, and the cycle is repeated.

When the engine is at normal operating temperature, the coolant expands, and some of it is released through the valve in the radiator pressure cap, and displaced into the expansion tank. Coolant collects in the tank, and is returned to the radiator when the system cools. The expansion tank is not pressurised.

The electric cooling fan is mounted on the rear of the radiator. At a predetermined coolant temperature, the cooling fan temperature switch contacts close and the fan is actuated via a relay.

Precautions

 Warning: Do not attempt to remove the radiator pressure cap, or to disturb any part of the cooling system, while the engine is hot, as there is a high risk of scalding. If the radiator pressure cap must be removed before the engine and radiator have fully cooled (even though this is not recommended), the pressure in the cooling system must first be relieved. Cover the cap with a thick layer of cloth, to avoid scalding, and slowly unscrew the pressure cap until a hissing sound is heard. When the hissing has stopped, indicating that the pressure has reduced, slowly unscrew the pressure cap until it can be removed; if

more hissing sounds are heard, wait until they have stopped before unscrewing the cap completely. At all times, keep your face well away from the pressure cap opening, and protect your hands.

 Warning: Do not allow antifreeze to come into contact with your skin, or with the painted surfaces of the vehicle. Rinse off spills immediately, with plenty of water. Never leave antifreeze lying around in an open container, or in a puddle in the driveway or on the garage floor. Children and pets are attracted by its sweet smell, but antifreeze can be fatal if ingested.

 Warning: Refer to Section 10 for precautions to be observed when working on models equipped with air conditioning.

2 Cooling system hoses - disconnection and renewal

Note: *Refer to the warnings given in Section 1 of this Chapter before proceeding. Hoses should only be disconnected once the engine has cooled sufficiently to avoid scalding.*

1 If the checks described in Chapter 1 reveal a faulty hose, it must be renewed as follows.

2 First drain the cooling system (see Chapter 1). If the coolant is not due for renewal, it may be re-used if it is collected in a clean container. Squirt a little penetrating oil onto the hose clips if they are corroded.

3 To disconnect a hose, release its retaining clips, then move them along the hose, clear of the stubs. Carefully work the hose free. **Do not** attempt to disconnect any part of the system while it is still hot.

4 Note that the radiator stubs are fragile; do not use excessive force when attempting to remove the hoses. If a hose is difficult to remove, try to release it by twisting it.

 If all else fails, cut the hose with a sharp knife, then slit it so that it can be peeled off in two pieces. Although this may prove expensive if the hose is otherwise undamaged, it is preferable to buying a new radiator.

5 When fitting a hose, first slide the clips onto the centre of the hose, then engage the hose with its union. If clamp type clips were originally fitted and they have lost their tension, it is a good idea to replace them with screw type clips when refitting the hose.

 If the hose is stiff, use a little soapy water as a lubricant, or soften the hose by soaking it in hot water. Do not use oil or grease, which may attack the rubber.

6 Work the hose fully into place, checking that it is correctly routed, then slide each clip along the hose until it passes over the flared end of the relevant outlet, before securing it in position.

7 Refill the cooling system with reference to Chapter 1.

8 Check thoroughly for leaks as soon as possible after disturbing any part of the cooling system.

3 Radiator - removal, inspection and refitting

Note: *Refer to the warnings given in Section 1 of this Chapter before starting work.*

Removal

 If leakage is the reason for removing the radiator, bear in mind that minor leaks can often be cured using a radiator sealant with the radiator in situ.

1 Disconnect the battery negative (earth) lead (refer to Chapter 5A, Sections 1 and 3). If necessary for improved access, chock the rear wheels then jack up the front of the car and support it on axle stands (see *Jacking and Vehicle Support*). Remove the splash guards from under the engine compartment.

2 Drain the cooling system as described in Chapter 1.

3 Disconnect the top and bottom hoses from the radiator **(see illustration)**.

4 Disconnect the expansion tank hose from the top of the radiator **(see illustration)**.

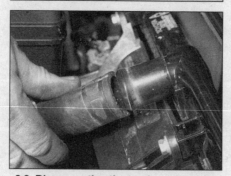

3.3 Disconnecting the top hose from the radiator

3.4 Disconnecting the expansion tank hose from the radiator

3.5 Cooling fan temperature switch on the radiator bottom tank (3S-FE and 3S-GE engines)

3.7 Automatic transmission fluid cooler line on the radiator bottom tank

3.8 Unbolting the radiator upper mounting brackets from the crossmember

5 On 3S-FE and 3S-GE engines disconnect the wiring from the cooling fan temperature switch(es) on the radiator lower tank **(see illustration)**.

6 Remove the cooling fan and shroud assembly as described in Section 5.

7 On models with automatic transmission, disconnect the fluid cooler lines from the bottom of the radiator **(see illustration)**.

8 Unbolt the upper mounting brackets from the front engine compartment crossmember and remove them from the top of the radiator **(see illustration)**.

9 Lift the radiator from the lower rubber mountings and remove it from the engine compartment **(see illustration)**.

10 If necessary remove the mounting rubbers from the front valance.

Inspection

11 If the radiator has been removed due to suspected blockage, reverse-flush it as described in Chapter 1. Clean dirt and debris from the radiator fins, using an air line (in which case, wear eye protection) or a soft brush. Be careful, as the fins are sharp, and can also be easily damaged.

12 If necessary, a radiator specialist can perform a flow test on the radiator, to establish whether an internal blockage exists.

13 A leaking radiator must be referred to a specialist for permanent repair. Do not attempt to weld or solder a leaking radiator, as damage to the plastic components may result.

14 In an emergency, minor leaks from the radiator can be cured by using a suitable radiator sealant, in accordance with its manufacturer's instructions, with the radiator *in situ*.

15 If the radiator is to be sent for repair, or is to be renewed, remove all hoses first.

16 Inspect the condition of the upper and lower radiator mounting rubbers, and renew them if necessary.

Refitting

17 Refitting is a reversal of removal, but on completion, refill and bleed the cooling system as described in Chapter 1.

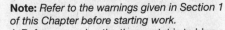

4 Thermostat - removal, testing and refitting

Note: *Refer to the warnings given in Section 1 of this Chapter before starting work.*

1 Before assuming the thermostat is to blame for a cooling system problem, check the coolant level, auxiliary drivebelt tension and condition (see Chapter 1) and temperature gauge operation.

2 If the engine seems to be taking a long time to warm up (based on heater output or temperature gauge operation), the thermostat is probably stuck open. Renew the thermostat.

3 If the engine runs hot, use your hand to check the temperature of the radiator top hose. If the hose isn't hot, but the engine is, the thermostat is probably stuck closed, preventing the coolant inside the engine from escaping to the radiator - renew the thermostat.

Caution: Don't drive the vehicle without a thermostat. The lack of a thermostat will slow warm-up time. The engine management system's ECU will then stay in warm-up mode for longer than necessary, causing emissions and fuel economy to suffer.

4 If the radiator top hose is hot, it means that the coolant is flowing and the thermostat is open. Consult the *Fault finding* section at the end of this manual to assist in tracing possible cooling system faults.

Removal

5 On 4A-FE and 7A-FE engines the thermostat is located in a housing bolted to the transmission end of the cylinder head. On 3S-FE and 3S-GE engines it is located on the water pump at the front right-hand end of the cylinder block.

6 Drain the cooling system as described in Chapter 1.

7 Disconnect the radiator top hose from the thermostat cover/inlet.

8 On 4A-FE and 7A-FE engines disconnect the wiring from the cooling fan temperature switch on the thermostat cover/inlet.

9 On the 3S-GE engine remove the alternator lower bracket with reference to Chapter 5A.

10 Unscrew the nuts and remove the thermostat cover/inlet from the studs on the housing **(see illustrations)**.

3

3.9 Lifting the radiator from the engine compartment

4.10a Removing the thermostat cover/inlet (4A-FE and 7A-FE engines)

4.10b Thermostat cover/inlet (3S-FE engine)

11 Note that the jiggle pin on the thermostat is facing upwards, then withdraw the thermostat from the thermostat housing (4A-FE and 7A-FE engines) or cover/inlet (3S-FE and 3S-GE engines). Ease the rubber sealing ring from the edge of the thermostat **(see illustrations)**.

Testing

12 Suspend the thermostat on a length of string in a container full of cold water. Heat the water to bring it to the boil - the thermostat must open by the time the water boils. If not, renew it.
13 If a thermometer is available, the opening temperature of the thermostat may be determined; compare with the figures given in the Specifications. The opening temperature is also marked on the thermostat.
14 If the thermostat fails to close as the water cools, it must be renewed.

Refitting

15 Commence refitting by thoroughly cleaning the mating faces and seating of the cover/inlet and the housing.
16 Fit a new rubber sealing ring to the thermostat.
17 Locate the thermostat in the housing or inlet (as applicable) making sure that the jiggle pin is facing upwards. On 3S-FE and 3S-GE engines the cover/inlet has a protrusion for aligning the jiggle pin.
18 Refit the cover/inlet on the studs and tighten the mounting nuts progressively to the specified torque. Reconnect the wiring to the temperature sensor on 4A-FE and 7A-FE engines.
19 Reconnect the radiator top hose.
20 Refill the cooling system as described in Chapter 1.

5 Electric cooling fan(s) - testing, removal and refitting

Note: *Refer to the warnings given in Section 1 of this Chapter before starting work.*

Testing

1 Current supply to the cooling fan is via the radiator fan relay which is triggered by the cooling fan temperature switch located on the thermostat cover/inlet (4A-FE and 7A-FE engines) or on the bottom tank of the radiator (3S-FE and 3S-GE engines). On 4A-FE and 7A-FE engine models with air conditioning, an air conditioning pressure switch is incorporated in the circuit upstream of the temperature switch. There are two cooling fans on 3S-FE and 3S-GE engine models, and where air conditioning is fitted, the magnetic clutch relay is linked to the No 1 cooling fan circuit.
2 Detailed fault diagnosis can be carried out by a Toyota dealer using suitable test equipment, but basic diagnosis can be carried out as follows.

4.11a The thermostat jiggle pin must face upwards

3 If the fan does not appear to work, run the engine until normal operating temperature is reached, then allow it to idle. The fan should cut in within a few minutes (before the temperature gauge needle enters the red section).
4 The motor can be tested by disconnecting it from the wiring loom, and connecting a 12-volt supply directly to it. The motor should operate - if not, the motor or wiring is faulty.
5 If the motor operates when tested as described in paragraph 4, the fault must lie in the engine wiring harness, the relay, or the temperature switch. The temperature switch can be tested as described in Section 6. Any further fault diagnosis should be referred to a suitably-equipped Toyota dealer.

Removal

6 Make sure that the ignition is switched off, then disconnect the wiring to the cooling fan at the connector.
7 Unscrew the mounting bolts securing the cooling fan assembly to the rear of the radiator, then lift the assembly upwards taking care not to damage the radiator fins **(see illustration)**.
8 If necessary unscrew the nuts and remove the fan from the cowl.

Refitting

9 Refitting is a reversal of removal, but take care not to damage the radiator fins.

5.7 Removing the electric cooling fan assembly (4A-FE and 7A-FE engines)

4.11b Removing the rubber sealing ring from the thermostat

6 Cooling system electrical sensors - testing, removal and refitting

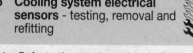

Note: *Refer to the warnings given in Section 1 of this Chapter before starting work.*

Cooling fan temperature switch

Testing

1 The cooling fan temperature switch controls the electric cooling fan(s) located on the rear of the radiator. The switch is located on the thermostat cover/inlet (4A-FE and 7A-FE engines) or on the bottom tank of the radiator (3S-FE and 3S-GE engines).
2 Testing may be carried out (after the switch has been removed) by immersing its temperature sensing end, with a thermometer, in a pan of cold water and testing for continuity as the water is heated. Connect an ohmmeter to the switch terminals. Check that the internal contacts operate in accordance with the information given in Specifications.

Removal

3 Drain the cooling system as described in Chapter 1.
4 Disconnect the wiring, then unscrew the switch from the thermostat cover/inlet (4A-FE and 7A-FE engines) or radiator bottom tank (3S-FE and 3S-GE engines).

Refitting

5 Refitting is a reversal of removal. Refill the cooling system with reference to Chapter 1.

Engine temperature sensor

Testing

6 The engine temperature sensor provides information to the engine management electronic control unit to control the fuel and ignition systems.
7 The sensor is located on the thermostat housing on the left-hand end of the cylinder head on 4A-FE and 7A-FE engines, and in the water outlet elbow on the left-hand end of the cylinder head on 3S-FE and 3S-GE engines. The sensor contains a thermistor - an electronic component whose electrical resistance decreases at a predetermined rate as its temperature rises.

8 The fuel injection/engine management ECU supplies the sensor with a set voltage and then, by measuring the current flowing in the sensor circuit, determines the engine temperature. This information is then used, in conjunction with other inputs, to control the fuel injection/engine management system.

9 If the sensor circuit should fail to provide adequate information, the ECU back-up facility will override the sensor signal. In this event, the ECU assumes a predetermined setting which will allow the fuel injection/engine management system to run, albeit at reduced efficiency. When this occurs, the engine warning light on the instrument panel will come on, and the advice of a Toyota dealer should be sought. The sensor itself can be tested by removing it, and checking the resistances at various temperatures using an ohmmeter (heat the sensor in a container of water, and monitor the temperature with a thermometer). The resistance values are given in the Specifications. *Do not* attempt to test the circuit with the sensor fitted to the engine, and the wiring connector fitted, as there is a high risk of damaging the ECU.

10 Refer to Chapter 4A for further details of the fuel injection/engine management system.

Removal

11 For improved access, remove the air cleaner body as described in Chapter 4A.

12 Drain the cooling system as described in Chapter 1.

13 Disconnect the wiring plug from the sensor.

14 Unscrew the sensor from the housing.

Refitting

15 Refitting is a reversal of removal, but tighten the sensor securely and refill the cooling system as described in Chapter 1.

Coolant temperature gauge sender

Testing

16 The sender is located on the water pump rear elbow on 4A-FE and 7A-FE engines, and on the left-hand end of the cylinder head on 3S-FE and 3S-GE engines.

17 The temperature gauge is fed with a voltage from the instrument panel feed (via the ignition switch and a fuse). The gauge earth is controlled by the sender. The sender contains a thermistor - an electronic component whose electrical resistance decreases at a predetermined rate as its temperature rises. When the coolant is cold, the sender resistance is high, current flow through the gauge is reduced, and the gauge needle points towards the cold end of the scale. As the coolant temperature rises and the sender resistance falls, current flow increases, and the gauge needle moves towards the upper end of the scale. If the sender is faulty, it must be renewed.

18 If the gauge develops a fault, first check the other instruments; if they do not work at all, or work erratically, check the instrument panel electrical feed. If the fault lies in the temperature gauge alone, check it as follows.

19 If the gauge needle remains at the cold end of the scale when the engine is hot, disconnect the sender wiring plug and earth the wire to the cylinder head. If the needle then deflects when the ignition is switched on, the sender unit is proved faulty, and should be renewed. If the needle still does not move, remove the instrument panel (Chapter 12) and check the continuity of the wire between the sender unit and the gauge, and the feed to the gauge unit. If continuity is shown, and the fault still exists, then the gauge is faulty, and the gauge should be renewed.

20 If the gauge needle remains at the hot end of the scale when the engine is cold, disconnect the sender wire. If the needle then returns to the cold end of the scale when the ignition is switched on, the sender unit is proved faulty, and should be renewed. If the needle still does not move, check the remainder of the circuit as described previously.

Removal and refitting

21 The procedure is similar to that described previously in this Section for the engine temperature sensor.

Air conditioning system pressure switch

Testing

22 The sensor is located on the right-hand side of the engine compartment, in the A/C line. Testing should be entrusted to a Toyota dealer.

Removal and refitting

23 Removal and refitting should be entrusted to a Toyota dealer suitably equipped to test the unit.

---

7 Water pump - removal, inspection and refitting

Note: *Refer to the warnings given in Section 1 of this Chapter before starting work.*

4A-FE and 7A-FE engines

Removal

1 Disconnect the battery negative (earth) lead (refer to Chapter 5A, Sections 1 and 3).

2 Drain the cooling system as described in Chapter 1.

3 Syphon the fluid from the windscreen washer fluid reservoir on the right-hand side of the engine compartment, then unscrew the mounting screws, disconnect the tubing and wiring, and remove the reservoir.

4 Remove the camshaft cover as described in Chapter 2A.

5 Disconnect the wiring loom from the alternator and oil pressure sender, then position the loom away from the right-hand side of the engine.

7.10a Unscrew the mounting bolt . . .

6 Loosen the bolts securing the drive pulley to the water pump one or two turns - the bolts are easier to loosen before actually removing the drivebelt.

7 Loosen the alternator pivot and adjustment lock bolts then back off the adjustment bolt and slip the auxiliary drivebelt from the pulleys. On models with power steering also remove the power steering pump drivebelt (see Chapter 1).

8 Fully unscrew the bolts securing the pulley to the water pump. **Note:** *It is not possible to completely remove the pulley as there is insufficient room between the pulley and inner wing panel. The pulley is removed together with the pump, however it must be moved to the rear as far as possible at this stage in order to remove the middle timing cover.*

9 Unbolt and remove the upper and middle timing belt covers.

10 Unscrew the bolt securing the engine oil level dipstick tube to the water pump rear elbow, then withdraw the tube from the rear of the oil pump housing and remove from the engine compartment. Check that the O-ring is still located on the bottom end of the tube **(see illustrations)**.

11 Where fitted, unscrew the bolt securing the power steering pump bracket to the cylinder head, then loosen the pump mounting bolts and move the pump as far to the rear as possible **(see illustration)**.

12 Disconnect the wiring from the temperature gauge sender on the water pump-to-cylinder head elbow.

13 Unbolt and remove the support from the rear elbow.

7.10b . . . and remove the oil dipstick tube from the rear of the oil pump housing

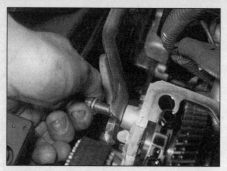

7.11 Removing the bolt securing the power steering pump bracket to the cylinder head

7.14a Removing the water pump rear elbow . . .

7.14b . . . and gasket

14 Unscrew the two nuts securing the water pump rear elbow to the cylinder head, pull the elbow from the studs, and recover the gasket **(see illustrations)**.

15 Unscrew the bolts securing the water pump to the right-hand end of the cylinder block, then withdraw the assembly upwards while guiding it from behind the timing belt. Recover the water pump pulley then remove the O-ring from the cylinder block **(see illustrations)**.

16 With the assembly on the bench, release the clips and disconnect the elbow and hose from the rear of the water pump **(see illustration)**.

17 Unscrew the bolts and separate the rear cover from the water pump. Recover the gasket **(see illustrations)**.

Inspection

18 Check the pump body and impeller for signs of excessive corrosion. Turn the impeller, and check for stiffness due to corrosion, or roughness due to excessive end play. If the pump bearings are worn excessively, it is possible to fit new bearings, however this work is best entrusted to a Toyota dealer or overhaul specialist who will have a press required to both remove and fit the bearings.

Refitting

19 Refitting is a reversal of the removal procedure, however always fit new gaskets to the cover and elbow, and fit a new O-ring to the cylinder block. The rear elbow gasket must be located on the studs with the protrusion facing upwards. Tighten all nuts

and bolts to the specified torque settings. *Do not* forget to locate the pulley on the water pump before refitting the pump to the cylinder block - tighten the pulley bolts moderately and fully tighten them after adjusting the auxiliary drivebelt as described in Chapter 1. Refit the camshaft cover with reference to Chapter 2A. Refill the cooling system with reference to Chapter 1, then start the engine and check all disturbed joints for leaks as soon as the engine is fully warmed up.

3S-FE and 3S-GE engines

Removal

20 Drain the cooling system as described in Chapter 1. Disconnect the radiator top hose from the thermostat cover elbow on the water pump.

7.15a Removing the water pump . . .

7.15b . . . and O-ring

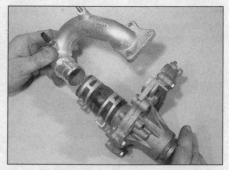

7.16 Removing the elbow and hose from the rear of the water pump

7.17a Unscrew the bolts . . .

7.17b . . . separate the cover . . .

7.17c . . . and remove the gasket

21 Remove the timing belt and idler pulley(s) as described in Chapter 2A.

22 Remove the alternator as described in Chapter 5A, then unbolt the lower alternator mounting bracket.

23 Unscrew the two nuts securing the bypass pipe to the water pump on the front of the engine.

24 Unscrew the three mounting bolts securing the water pump to the cylinder block, then withdraw the pump from the bypass pipe and remove from the engine compartment. Recover the O-ring from the bypass pipe and the gasket from the cylinder block.

25 With the assembly on the bench, unbolt the water pump from the cover and recover the gasket. If necessary, remove the thermostat with reference to Section 4.

Inspection

26 Clean all mating surfaces thoroughly then inspect the water pump for wear and damage.

27 Check the pump body and impeller for signs of excessive corrosion. Turn the impeller, and check for stiffness due to corrosion, or roughness due to excessive end play. Renew the pump if the bearings are worn excessively.

Refitting

28 Refitting is a reversal of removal, but fit a new O-ring and gaskets and tighten all nuts and bolts to the specified torque wrench settings. Refit the timing belt as described in Chapter 2A, and adjust the alternator drivebelt with reference to Chapter 1. Refill the cooling system with reference to Chapter 1, then start the engine and check all disturbed joints for leaks as soon as the engine is fully warmed up.

8 Heating and ventilation system - general information

The heater/ventilation system consists of a blower motor (housed beneath the left-hand side of the facia), face level vents in the centre and at each end of the facia, and air ducts to the front footwells.

The control unit is located in the facia, and the controls operate flap valves to deflect and mix the air flowing through the various parts of the heating/ventilation system. The flap valves are contained in the air distribution housing, which acts as a central distribution unit, passing air to the various ducts and vents.

Cold air enters the system through the grille at the rear of the engine compartment. If required, the airflow is boosted by the blower fan, and then flows through the various ducts, according to the settings of the controls. Stale air is expelled through ducts at the rear of the vehicle. If warm air is required, the cold air is passed over the heater matrix, which is heated by the engine coolant.

On models fitted with air conditioning, a recirculation switch enables the outside air supply to be closed off, while the air inside the vehicle is recirculated. This can be useful to prevent unpleasant odours entering from outside the vehicle, but should only be used briefly, as the recirculated air inside the vehicle will soon become stale.

9 Heating and ventilation system components - removal and refitting

Heater/ventilation control panel

Removal

1 Remove the radio as described in Chapter 12.

2 Using a screwdriver, carefully prise out the surround from the centre of the facia. To prevent damage to the facia, lever against card or cloth rags. Disconnect the wiring from the rear of the surround.

3 Remove the screws and withdraw the heater/ventilation control panel from the facia **(see illustration)**.

4 Disconnect the wiring and cables having noted their position, then withdraw the panel **(see illustration)**.

Refitting

5 Refitting is a reversal of removal, but reconnect the control cables in their previously noted positions. Check the operation of the control panel before refitting the surround and radio.

Heater assembly

Warning: On models fitted with air conditioning, do not attempt to remove the cooling unit, which is located between the heater blower motor casing and the main heater assembly. Removal of the cooling unit entails disconnection of refrigerant lines - refer to Section 10 for precautions to be observed. If in any doubt as to the procedure to follow on models with air conditioning, consult a Toyota dealer for advice.

Removal

6 Remove the instrument panel as described in Chapter 12.

7 Remove the steering column as described in Chapter 10.

8 Unscrew the nuts and bolts and remove the reinforcement bar.

9 Drain the cooling system as described in Chapter 1. Position cloth rags or absorbent material in the front footwells to catch spilt coolant from the heater.

10 Disconnect the control cable from the water valve.

11 In the engine compartment, disconnect the two heater hoses on the bulkhead.

12 Pull the rear compartment air ducts from the bottom of the heater assembly.

13 Note the location of all wiring connectors, then disconnect them from the assembly.

14 Unscrew the mounting nuts and bolts and withdraw the assembly from inside the vehicle. Be prepared for some loss of coolant from the heater matrix stubs.

15 If necessary the heater motor and housing can be removed from the passenger side of the vehicle at this stage after disconnecting the wiring and cables.

Refitting

16 Refitting is a reversal of removal, but note the following:

a) Make sure that all wiring and cables are routed as noted during dismantling.

b) Make sure that all air ducts are securely reconnected.

c) Refit the instrument panel with reference to Chapter 12.

d) On completion, refill and bleed the cooling system as described in Chapter 1.

Heater matrix

Removal

17 Drain the cooling system as described in Chapter 1.

18 In the engine compartment, disconnect the heater hoses on the bulkhead noting their location.

19 Inside the vehicle pull the plastic cover from the right-hand side of the heater assembly.

20 Remove the centre console as described in Chapter 11.

21 Position cloth rags or absorbent material in the right-hand footwell to catch any spilt coolant.

3

9.3 Remove the heater/ventilation control panel . . .

9.4 . . . and disconnect the control cables

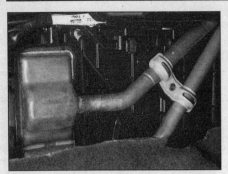

9.22 Heater matrix and pipe clamp

9.27a Lowering the blower motor from the facia

9.27b The blower motor

22 Unscrew the screw securing the matrix pipe clamp to the heater assembly and remove the clamp **(see illustration)**.
23 Pull the carpet down, then withdraw the matrix from the heater assembly while guiding the pipes from the bulkhead.

Refitting

24 Refitting is a reversal of removal, and refill the cooling system with reference to Chapter 1.

Heater blower motor

Removal

25 Working beneath the left-hand side of the facia, remove the glovebox from the facia panel.
26 Disconnect the wiring leading to the heater blower motor.
27 Unscrew the mounting screws and lower the blower motor from the facia **(see illustrations)**.

Refitting

28 Refitting is a reversal of removal.

10 Air conditioning system - general information and precautions

General information

An air conditioning system is available on certain models. It enables the temperature of incoming air to be lowered, and also dehumidifies the air, which makes for rapid demisting and increased comfort.

The cooling side of the system works in the same way as a domestic refrigerator. Refrigerant gas is drawn into a belt-driven compressor, and passes into a condenser mounted on the front of the radiator, where it loses heat and becomes liquid. The liquid passes through an expansion valve to an evaporator, where it changes from liquid under high pressure to gas under low pressure. This change is accompanied by a drop in temperature, which cools the evaporator. The refrigerant returns to the compressor, and the cycle begins again.

Air blown through the evaporator passes to the air distribution unit, where it is mixed with hot air blown through the heater matrix to achieve the desired temperature in the passenger compartment.

The heating side of the system works in the same way as on models without air conditioning.

The system is electronically-controlled. Any problems with the system should be referred to a Toyota dealer.

Precautions

With an air conditioning system, it is necessary to observe special precautions whenever dealing with any part of the system, or its associated components. If for any reason the system must be disconnected, entrust this task to your Toyota dealer or a refrigeration engineer.

Do not operate the air conditioning system if it is known to be short of refrigerant, as this may damage the compressor.

⚠ *Warning: The refrigeration circuit contains a liquid refrigerant (R134a). The refrigerant is potentially dangerous, and should only be handled by qualified persons. If it is splashed onto the skin, it can cause frostbite. It is not itself poisonous, but in the presence of a naked flame (including a cigarette), it forms a poisonous gas. Uncontrolled discharging of the refrigerant is dangerous, and potentially damaging to the environment. For all these reasons, it is dangerous to disconnect any part of the system without specialised knowledge and equipment.*

11 Air conditioning system components - removal and refitting

⚠ *Warning: Do not attempt to open the refrigerant circuit. Refer to the precautions given in Section 10.*

1 The only operation which can be carried out easily without discharging the refrigerant is renewal of the auxiliary (compressor) drivebelt as described in Chapter 1. All other operations must be referred to a Toyota dealer or an air conditioning specialist.
2 If necessary for access to other components, the compressor can be unbolted and moved aside, *without disconnecting its flexible hoses*, after removing the drivebelt.

Chapter 4 Part A:
Fuel and exhaust systems

Contents

Degrees of difficulty

Easy, suitable for novice with little experience	**Fairly easy,** suitable for beginner with some experience	**Fairly difficult,** suitable for competent DIY mechanic 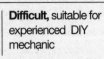	**Difficult,** suitable for experienced DIY mechanic	**Very difficult,** suitable for expert DIY or professional 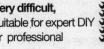

Specifications

General
System type . . . .   Electronic Fuel Injection (EFI), controlled by Toyota Computer Control System (TCCS)

Fuel system data
Idle speed and mixture settings . . . .   See Chapter 1
Fuel pump type . . . .   Electric, immersed in tank
Fuel system regulated pressure . . . .   2.7 to 3.1 bars

Fuel system component test data
Injectors:
  Resistance . . . .   13.4 to 14.2 ohms
  Maximum fuel leakage . . . .   One drop per minute
Cold start injector (3S-GE engines):
  Resistance . . . .   2.0 to 4.0 ohms
  Maximum fuel leakage . . . .   One drop per minute
Cold start injector time switch resistance (3S-GE engines):
  Terminal STA to STJ:
    Below 10°C . . . .   30 to 50 ohms
    Above 25°C . . . .   70 to 90 ohms
  Terminal STA to Ground . . . .   30 to 90 ohms
Idle speed control valve resistance . . . .   19.3 to 22.3 ohms
Air conditioning idle-up valve resistance (cold) . . . .   30 to 34 ohms
Inlet air temperature sensor resistance:
  At -20°C . . . .   10 to 20 k ohms
  At 0°C . . . .   4 to 7 k ohms
  At 20°C . . . .   2 to 3 k ohms
  At 40°C . . . .   0.9 to 1.3 k ohms
  At 60°C . . . .   0.4 to 0.7 k ohms
  At 80°C . . . .   0.2 to 0.4 k ohms

Inlet manifold
Maximum gasket face distortion . . . .   0.2 mm

Exhaust manifold
Maximum gasket face distortion . . . .   0.3 mm

4A

Air control valve (lean-burn engines)
Maximum gasket face distortion .... 0.2 mm

Recommended fuel
All models .... 95 RON unleaded. Leaded fuel (eg UK 4-star) must **not** be used

Torque wrench settings

	Nm	lbf ft
Camshaft cover		
4A-FE and 7A-FE engines	6	4
3S-FE and 3S-GE engines	44	33
Fuel pump	3.4	2.5
Fuel tank	39	29
Inlet manifold	19	14
Fuel rail:		
4A-FE conventional engines	15	11
4A-FE and 7A-FE lean-burn engines	9	7
3S-FE engines	13	9
3S-GE engines	19	14
Fuel inlet hose to rail:		
4A-FE, 7A-FE and 3S-GE engines	29	22
3S-FE engines	34	25
Pulsation damper to fuel rail	34	25
Air inlet chamber to inlet manifold	19	14
Cold start injector mounting bolt	5.9	4.3
Cold start injector union bolt	18	13
Inlet manifold stay to inlet manifold:		
4A-FE and 7A-FE engines	19	14
3S-FE engines	42	31
3S-GE engines	39	29
Inlet manifold stay to cylinder head:		
4A-FE and 7A-FE engines	39	29
3S-FE engines	42	31
3S-GE engines	39	29
Air inlet chamber support bracket (3S-GE engines)	19	14
Throttle housing to inlet manifold:		
4A-FE and 7A-FE engines	22	16
3S-FE and 3S-GE engines	19	14
Exhaust manifold:		
4A-FE and 7A-FE engines	34	25
3S-FE and 3S-GE engines	49	36
Exhaust manifold stay to exhaust manifold:		
4A-FE and 7A-FE engines	39	29
3S-FE and 3S-GE engines	42	31
Exhaust manifold stay to cylinder block		
4A-FE and 7A-FE engines	59	43
3S-FE and 3S-GE engines	42	31
Heat shield to exhaust manifold	9	7
Knock sensor to cylinder block:		
4A-FE engines	37	27
7A-FE and 3S-FE engines	44	32
Cold start injector (3S-GE engines)	5.9	4.3

1 General information and precautions

General information

The fuel system consists of a fuel tank mounted under the rear of the car, an electric fuel pump and the various fuel injection components.

Fuel is supplied from the tank by an electric fuel pump, located inside the tank, via a pressure regulator, to the fuel rail. The fuel rail acts as a reservoir for the four fuel injectors, which inject fuel into the cylinder inlet tracts.

A fuel filter is incorporated in the fuel supply line to ensure that the fuel supplied to the injectors is clean.

The Electronic Fuel Injection (EFI) system is controlled by the Toyota Computer Control System (TCCS) engine management system; further information on the emission control and ignition system components of the TCCS system may be found in Chapters 4B and 5B respectively, while further information regarding the EFI system is given in Section 6.

Precautions

 Warning: Petrol is extremely flammable - great care must be taken when working on any part of the fuel system. Do not smoke or allow any naked flames or uncovered light bulbs near the work area. Note that gas powered domestic appliances with pilot flames, such as heaters, boilers and tumble dryers, also present a fire hazard - bear this in mind if you are working in an area where such appliances are present. Always keep a suitable fire extinguisher close to the work area and familiarise yourself with its operation before starting work. Wear eye protection when working on fuel systems and wash off any fuel spilt on bare skin immediately with soap and water. Note that fuel vapour is just as dangerous as liquid fuel; a vessel that has just been

2.3a Unscrew the mounting bolts . . .

2.3b . . . and remove the air cleaner body

2.4 Air inlet duct arrangement (3S-FE engines)

emptied of liquid fuel will still contain vapour and can be potentially explosive. Petrol is a highly dangerous and volatile liquid, and the precautions necessary when handling it cannot be overstressed.

⚠ Many of the operations described in this Chapter involve the disconnection of fuel lines, which may cause an amount of fuel spillage. Before commencing work, refer to the above Warning and the information in Safety first at the beginning of this manual.

⚠ When working with fuel system components, pay particular attention to cleanliness - dirt entering the fuel system may cause blockages which will lead to poor running.

Note: Residual pressure will remain in the fuel lines long after the vehicle was last used. When disconnecting any fuel line, first depressurise the fuel system as described in Section 7.

2 Air cleaner and inlet ducts - removal and refitting

Removal

Air cleaner

1 Unclip and remove the cover from the air cleaner body, then remove the element.
2 Disconnect the wiring from the inlet air temperature sensor on the cover, loosen the clip and remove the cover from the inlet duct.
3 Unscrew and remove the mounting bolts from inside the air cleaner body, then disconnect the body from the inlet duct on the front left-hand side of the engine compartment and remove the body **(see illustrations)**.

Inlet ducts

4 Loosen the clips and disconnect the inlet duct from the throttle housing and air cleaner cover **(see illustration)**.
5 If applicable disconnect the air tube, then remove the inlet duct from the engine compartment.

6 On 3S-FE and 3S-GE engines loosen the clip and remove the resonance extension from the air duct.
7 The front inlet duct can be removed after removing the air cleaner body as previously described, then unscrewing the mounting bolt(s) and withdrawing the front inlet duct from the left-hand side of the engine compartment.

Refitting

8 Refitting is a reversal of removal, ensuring that all clips and mounting bolts are tightened securely.

3 Accelerator cable - removal, refitting and adjustment

Removal

1 Working in the engine compartment, turn the throttle valve segment on the throttle housing to release the tension on the accelerator inner cable, then disconnect the cable end fitting **(see illustrations)**.

3.1a Disconnecting the accelerator cable from the throttle valve segment (4A-FE and 7A-FE engines)

3.1b Disconnecting the accelerator cable from the throttle valve segment (3S-FE engines)

3.2a Unbolting the accelerator cable support (4A-FE and 7A-FE engines)

3.2b Unbolting the accelerator cable support (3S-FE engines)

3.3a Releasing the accelerator cable from the support (4A-FE and 7A-FE engines)

2 Loosen the two adjustment nuts on the cable support bracket, and remove the cable from the support. If necessary the support can be unbolted from the inlet manifold or air inlet chamber as applicable **(see illustrations)**.

3 Release the cable from the support clip on the inlet manifold **(see illustrations)**.

4 Working inside the vehicle, reach up behind the facia and disconnect the inner cable from the top of the accelerator pedal. If necessary, for improved access, unscrew the retaining screws and withdraw the lower trim panel located beneath the steering column. Detach the bonnet pull lever (2 screws) then disconnect the wiring from the instrument panel illumination rheostat. Remove the lower trim panel.

5 Unbolt the plate from the bulkhead, then withdraw the cable through the bulkhead inside the vehicle.

Refitting

6 Feed the cable through the bulkhead from inside the vehicle, then reconnect the inner cable to the top of the accelerator pedal and tighten the plate bolts securely. If removed, refit the facia lower trim panel.

7 In the engine compartment, locate the cable in the support clip and bracket and reconnect the inner cable end fitting to the throttle valve segment.

8 Where removed, refit the support bracket and tighten the mounting bolts, then refit the trim panel beneath the steering column.

Adjustment

9 With both adjusting nuts loose check that the inner cable is slack. Unscrew the nut nearest the throttle valve segment several turns.

10 Tighten the nut furthest from the segment until the segment just starts to move, then back off the nut 1.5 to 2.0 turns to provide the correct amount of play. Tighten the locknut to retain the ferrule in this position.

11 Have an assistant depress the accelerator pedal, and check that the throttle valve segment opens fully and returns smoothly to its stop.

4 Accelerator pedal - removal and refitting

Removal

1 Working inside the vehicle, reach up behind the facia and disconnect the inner cable from the top of the accelerator pedal **(see illustration)**. If necessary for improved access, unscrew the retaining screws and withdraw the lower trim panel located beneath the steering column. Detach the bonnet pull lever (2 screws) then disconnect the wiring from the instrument panel illumination rheostat. Remove the lower trim panel.

2 Unbolt the accelerator pedal from the bulkhead **(see illustration)**.

3 Examine the mounting bracket and pedal pivot for signs of wear, and renew as necessary.

Refitting

4 Refitting is a reversal of the removal procedure, applying a little multi-purpose grease to the pedal pivot shaft. On completion, adjust the accelerator cable as described in Section 3.

5 Unleaded petrol - general information and usage

The fuel recommended by Toyota is given in the Specifications Section of this Chapter.

3.3b Releasing the accelerator cable from the support (3S-FE engines)

All Toyota Carina E models are designed to run on unleaded fuel with a minimum octane rating of 95 (RON). Under no circumstances should leaded fuel (UK 4-star) be used, as this may damage the catalytic converter.

Super unleaded petrol, 98 (RON) can also be used in all models if wished, though there is no advantage in doing so.

6 Fuel injection system - general information

The Electronic Control Unit (ECU), which controls both the ignition system Electronic Spark Advance (ESA) and Electronic Fuel Injection (EFI) functions of the Toyota Computer Control System (TCCS), is located inside the vehicle, behind the facia, together with the circuit opening relay. On 4A-FE and

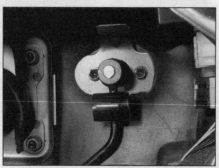

4.1 Accelerator inner cable connection to the top of the accelerator pedal

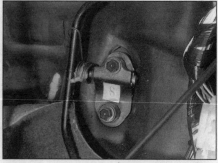

4.2 Accelerator pedal mounting on the bulkhead

7A-FE engine models it is located behind the left-hand side of the facia on RHD models, or behind the right-hand side of the facia on LHD models. On 3S-FE engine models, it is located behind the right-hand side of the facia, and on 3S-GE engine models it is located beneath the facia in front of the centre console. In addition to its control of the fuel injection and ignition functions, the ECU also provides electronic control of the automatic transmission on models so equipped.

The ECU is supplied with data from sensors which monitor inlet manifold pressure, inlet air temperature, coolant temperature, engine speed, throttle valve opening angle and exhaust oxygen content. The data is compared with pre-programmed values stored in the ECU memory to determine the appropriate electrical signals to operate the injectors. The injectors are supplied with fuel at constant pressure by means of an electric fuel pump and a pressure regulator, therefore the quantity of fuel injected is determined by the time that the injectors remain open. An additional cold start injector is fitted to the 3S-GE engine.

Under certain conditions, engine idle speed can be regulated by the idle speed control valve under the control of the ECU. The valve opens and closes an air passage to allow intake air to bypass the throttle valve in the throttle housing. Additionally, on models with air conditioning, further control of the idle speed is provided by an idle-up valve. This unit compensates for power drain when the air conditioning compressor switches on.

A fail-safe function is incorporated in the ECU so that if one of the sensors fails, a back-up circuit will take over to allow the vehicle to be driven, albeit at reduced power and efficiency. A Check Engine warning lamp will light to indicate that this condition is present, and a fault code will be stored in the ECU relating to the circuit affected. The fault codes can be accessed by the DIY mechanic (see Section 12), or the vehicle can be taken to a Toyota dealer for further investigation.

All 7A-FE, and certain 4A-FE engines are equipped with the Toyota Lean Combustion System and are referred to in this Chapter as Lean-Burn engines. On these engines,

modifications to the inlet manifold configuration and fuel injector positioning allow a lean air/fuel mixture ratio to be used without sacrificing engine performance. This arrangement enhances fuel economy and significantly reduces toxic exhaust emissions. The obvious visual difference between the lean-burn and conventional version of the 4A-FE engine is the location of the fuel injectors; in the lean-burn version they are located directly in the cylinder head, whereas on the conventional version they are situated in the inlet manifold.

7 Fuel injection system - depressurisation

![warning triangle] *Warning: Refer to the warning in Section 1 before proceeding. The following procedure will merely relieve the pressure in the fuel system - remember that fuel will still be present in the system components, and take precautions accordingly before disconnecting any of them.*

1 The fuel system referred to in this Section consists of the tank-mounted fuel pump, the fuel filter, the fuel rail and injectors, the fuel pressure regulator, and the metal pipes and flexible hoses of the fuel lines between these components. All these contain fuel which will be under pressure while the engine is running and/or while the ignition is switched on. The pressure will remain for some time after the ignition has been switched off, and must be relieved before any of these components are disturbed for servicing work.

2 Remove the rear seat cushion as described in Chapter 11.

3 Unscrew the crosshead screws and move the fuel pump cover to one side.

4 Disconnect the fuel pump/fuel gauge sender wiring from the top of the fuel pump assembly and tape it to the vehicle body **(see illustration 8.3)**.

5 Start the engine, and allow it to run until it stalls.

6 Try to start the engine at least twice more, to ensure that all residual pressure has been relieved then switch off the ignition.

7 Reconnect the wiring to the fuel pump/fuel gauge sender and refit the cover, followed by the rear seat cushion. **Do not** switch on the ignition until completion of work.

8 Fuel pump - removal and refitting

![warning triangle] *Warning: Refer to the warning in Section 1 before proceeding. Since a fuel tank drain plug is not provided, it is preferable to carry out this work when the tank is nearly empty.*

Removal

1 Remove the rear seat cushion as described in Chapter 11.

2 Unscrew the crosshead screws and move the fuel pump cover to one side **(see illustration)**.

3 Disconnect the fuel pump/fuel gauge sender wiring from the top of the fuel pump assembly, and tape it to the vehicle body **(see illustration)**.

4 Depressurise the fuel system with reference to the relevant paragraphs in Section 7.

5 Disconnect the battery negative (earth) lead (refer to Chapter 5A, Sections 1 and 3).

6 To prevent fuel flowing out of the supply line, remove the cap from the filter located in the engine compartment with reference to Chapter 1.

7 Slacken the union bolt and disconnect the supply line from the fuel pump. Counterhold the union with a further spanner while loosening the bolt. Tape or cover the end of the line **(see illustration)**.

8 Using a pair of pliers, release the clip then disconnect the return hose from the top of the fuel pump **(see illustrations)**.

9 Unscrew the crosshead screws securing the pump to the fuel tank **(see illustration)**.

10 Carefully withdraw the fuel pump/fuel gauge assembly from the top of the tank, taking care not to damage the float and arm **(see illustration)**.

11 Recover the gasket from the top of the fuel tank.

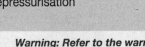

4A

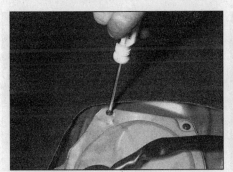

8.2 Removing the fuel pump cover

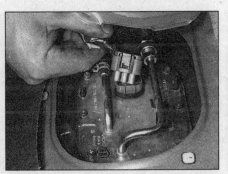

8.3 Disconnecting the wiring from the fuel pump/fuel gauge sender unit

8.7 Disconnecting the fuel supply line union from the fuel pump

8.8a Release the clip . . .

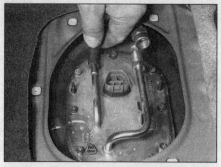

8.8b . . . and disconnect the return hose from the top of the fuel pump

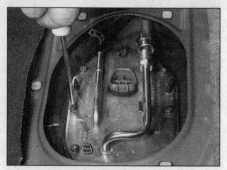

8.9 Unscrew the crosshead screws . . .

8.10 . . . and withdraw the fuel pump/fuel gauge sender unit assembly from the top of the fuel tank

8.12 Release the clips . . .

8.13 . . . and pull the fuel pump from the hose

12 Remove the fuel gauge sender unit with reference to Section 9, then release the clips securing the small hose to the pump **(see illustration)**.

13 Release the pump from the bottom of the bracket by moving it sideways, then pull it from the hose. Remove the hose and recover the seat from the bracket. If necessary, prise out the clip and remove the filter from the pump **(see illustration)**.

Refitting

14 Refitting is a reversal of removal, but make sure the fuel pump is securely located in the bracket before tightening the hose clips. Always fit a new gasket. Before refitting the cover, switch on the ignition and check for fuel leaks at the supply and return pipes.

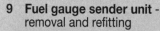
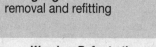

9 Fuel gauge sender unit - removal and refitting

> ⚠ **Warning: Refer to the warning in Section 1 before proceeding. Since a fuel tank drain plug is not provided, it is preferable to carry out this work when the tank is nearly empty.**

Removal

1 Remove the fuel pump (see Section 8).
2 Disconnect the fuel gauge sender unit wiring plug **(see illustration)**.
3 Unscrew the crosshead screws, and withdraw the fuel gauge sender unit from the bracket on the fuel pump assembly **(see illustrations)**.

Refitting

4 Refitting is a reversal of removal , but tighten the crosshead screws securely. Refit the fuel pump with reference to Section 8.

10 Fuel tank - removal, inspection and refitting

> ⚠ **Warning: Refer to the warning in Section 1 before proceeding. Since a fuel tank drain plug is not provided, it is preferable to carry out this work when the tank is nearly empty.**

Removal

1 Depressurise the fuel system as described in Section 7.

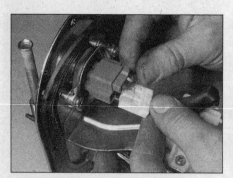

9.2 Disconnect the wiring plug . . .

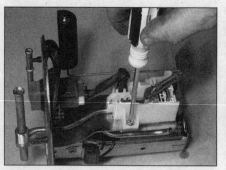

9.3a . . . then unscrew the screws . . .

9.3b . . . and withdraw the fuel gauge sender unit from the bracket

10.13 Fuel filler hose connection to the rear of the tank

10.14 Breather hose connection to the top of the tank

10.16 Fuel tank mounting strap bolt on the underbody

2 Disconnect the battery negative (earth) lead (refer to Chapter 5A, Sections 1 and 3).
3 Remove the rear seat cushion as described in Chapter 11.
4 Unscrew the crosshead screws and move the fuel pump cover to one side.
5 Disconnect the fuel pump/fuel gauge sender wiring from the top of the fuel pump assembly, and tape it to the vehicle body.
6 To prevent fuel flowing out of the supply line, remove the cap from the fuel filter located in the engine compartment with reference to Chapter 1.
7 Slacken the union bolt and disconnect the supply line from the fuel pump. Counterhold the union with a further spanner while loosening the bolt. Tape or cover the end of the line.
8 Using a pair of pliers, release the clip then disconnect the return hose from the top of the fuel pump.
9 If the tank is not empty at this stage, remove the fuel pump completely (Section 8) and syphon or hand-pump the remaining fuel into a suitable container. Refit the fuel pump to prevent entry of dust and dirt.
10 Chock the front wheels then jack up the rear of the car and support it on axle stands (see *Jacking and Vehicle Support*).
11 Remove the rear section of the exhaust system with reference to Section 16.
12 Unbolt the heat insulator from under the fuel tank.
13 Loosen the clip and disconnect the filler hose from the rear of the tank **(see illustration)**.

14 Loosen the clip and disconnect the breather hose from the tank **(see illustration)**.
15 Place a trolley jack with an interposed block of wood beneath the tank, then raise the jack until it is supporting the weight of the tank.
16 Unscrew and remove the retaining strap rear bolts, then pivot each strap away from the tank **(see illustration)**.
17 Slowly lower the fuel tank to the ground, and remove it from underneath the vehicle.

Inspection

18 Whilst removed, the fuel tank can be inspected for damage or deterioration. Removal of the fuel pump (Section 8) will allow a partial inspection of the interior. If the tank is contaminated with sediment or water, swill it out with clean petrol. Do not under any circumstances undertake any repairs on a leaking or damaged fuel tank; this work must be carried out by a professional who has experience in this critical and potentially-dangerous work.
19 Whilst the fuel tank is removed from the vehicle, it should not be placed in an area where sparks or open flames could ignite the fumes coming out of the tank. Be especially careful inside garages where a natural-gas type appliance is located, because the pilot light could cause an explosion.
20 If necessary, the filler and ventilation hoses may be removed by unbolting the retaining clamp from the underbody, then unbolting the collar and plate from under the filler flap. Remove the mudguard and hose

cover, then disconnect the hose from the collar **(see illustrations)**.

Refitting

21 Refitting is a reversal of the removal procedure, noting the following points:
a) *When lifting the tank back into position, take care to ensure that the supply and return hoses are not trapped between the tank and vehicle body. Tighten the fuel tank mounting bolts to the specified torque setting.*
b) *Ensure that all pipes and hoses are correctly routed, and securely held in position with their retaining clips.*
c) *On completion refill the tank with fuel, run the engine, and check for signs of leakage prior to taking the vehicle out on the road.*

11 Throttle housing - removal and refitting

4A

 Warning: Refer to the warning in Section 1 before proceeding.

Removal

1 Disconnect the battery negative (earth) lead (refer to Chapter 5A, Sections 1 and 3), then drain the cooling system as described in Chapter 1.
2 Loosen the clips and disconnect the air inlet duct from the throttle housing and air cleaner cover.
3 Turn the segment on the throttle housing to open the throttle, then disconnect the inner accelerator cable. On automatic transmission models, also disconnect the kick-down cable.
4 Disconnect the wiring from the throttle position sensor on the upper rear of the throttle housing.
5 Disconnect the wiring from the idle speed control valve on the lower front of the throttle housing **(see illustration)**.
6 Identify the positions of the vacuum, coolant, air and, where fitted, the evaporation loss and EGR hoses, then disconnect them **(see illustration)**.

10.20a Fuel tank filler and ventilation hose retaining clamp on the underbody

10.20b Fuel tank filler collar and plate beneath the filler flap

11.5 Disconnecting the idle speed control valve wiring

11.6 Disconnecting a coolant hose from the bottom of the throttle housing

11.7a Removing the throttle housing . . .

7 Progressively unscrew the two bolts and two nuts, or four bolts (as applicable), and withdraw the throttle housing. Remove the gasket **(see illustrations)**. Do not disturb the throttle position sensor unless absolutely necessary.

Refitting

8 Refitting is a reverse of the removal sequence, noting the following points.
a) Clean the mating surfaces and fit a new gasket to the throttle housing with the protrusion facing downwards.
b) Tighten the retaining nuts/bolts to their specified torque settings.
c) Adjust the accelerator cable (Section 3), and on automatic transmission models the kick-down cable (Chapter 7B).
d) Adjust the throttle position sensor (Section 12) if disturbed.
e) Refill the cooling system (Chapter 1).

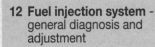

12 Fuel injection system - general diagnosis and adjustment

General diagnosis

1 If a fault appears in the fuel injection/ignition system, first ensure that all the system wiring connectors are securely connected and free of corrosion. Then ensure that the fault is not due to poor maintenance - ie, check that the air cleaner filter element is clean, that the spark plugs are in good condition and correctly gapped, that the valve clearances are correctly adjusted, the cylinder compression pressures are correct, and that the emission control systems are operating correctly, referring to Chapters 1, 2A, 4B and 5B for further information.
2 If these checks fail to reveal the cause of the problem, it is possible to extract fault codes which may be held in the ECU memory (CHECK engine warning light illuminated). After repair, the fault codes can be erased from memory by removing the EFI fuse (fuse 24 or 25 according to engine) for 10 seconds or more with the ignition switched off. They can also be erased by disconnecting the battery negative lead, however in this case any radio security codes will have to be re-entered on reconnecting the lead.

Setting the self-diagnostic test modes

3 The ECU self-diagnosis system has a normal mode and a test mode. If a fault is detected while the engine is running and the ECU is in *Normal* mode, the CHECK engine warning light is illuminated and the fault code is stored in memory. The fault code can be read in *Normal* mode by counting the number of blinks of the CHECK engine warning light as described later. The light goes off when the fault is repaired, but the code remains in memory until it is cleared by removing the EFI fuse as described in paragraph 2. The *Test* mode is used to identify a fault as it occurs while driving the vehicle, and is useful if the fault occurs during certain conditions.
4 Before entering either mode, check that the battery is in a good state of charge, all accessories are turned off and the engine is at normal operating temperature. The transmission should be in neutral before starting the check.
5 To carry out a Normal Mode check, proceed as follows:
a) Make sure that the throttle valve is closed then switch on the ignition but do not start the engine.
b) Lift the diagnostic socket cover in the left-hand side of the engine compartment, and use a bridging wire or length of welding rod to connect the terminals TE1 and E1 (the terminals are indicated on the inside of the cover).
c) Observe the CHECK engine warning light. If the system has no fault codes in memory the light will blink regularly every 0.26 seconds, however if the memory has codes stored in it, the light will output the two-digit codes one after another with a 2.5 second pause between them. A 1.5 second pause occurs between the first and second digits of the code.
d) On completion, remove the bridging wire and switch off the ignition.
6 To carry out a Test Mode check, proceed as follows in the order given:
a) Lift the diagnostic socket cover in the left-hand side of the engine compartment, and use a bridging wire or length of welding rod to connect the terminals TE2 and E1 (the terminals are indicated on the inside of the cover).

11.7b . . . and gasket

b) Switch on the ignition but do not start the engine at this stage. The CHECK engine warning light will start flashing.
c) Now start the engine and drive the vehicle at a speed of 6 mph or higher. If possible try to simulate the conditions which cause the fault to occur.
d) With the vehicle stationary, use a second bridging wire or length of welding rod to connect the terminals TE1 and E1 of the diagnostic socket (terminals TE2 and E1 should remain connected by the first bridging wire).
e) Observe the CHECK engine warning light. If the system has no fault codes in memory the light will blink regularly every 0.26 seconds, however if the memory has codes stored in it, the light will output the two-digit codes one after another with a 2.5 second pause between them. A 1.5 second pause occurs between the first and second digits of the code.
f) On completion, remove the bridging wire and switch off the ignition.
7 The fault codes are as follows:

Code number	Faulty circuit
12	RPM signal
13	RPM signal
14	Ignition igniter signal
16	ECU control signal
21	Oxygen sensor/lean mixture sensor signal
22	Engine (coolant) temperature sensor signal
24	Inlet air temperature sensor signal
25	Air-fuel ratio Lean malfunction
31	Vacuum sensor signal

13.16 Disconnecting the fuel return hose from the fuel pressure regulator

13.17 Removing the fuel inlet hose

33	Idle speed control valve signal
41	Throttle position sensor signal
42	Vehicle speed sensor signal
43	Starter signal
52	Knock sensor signal
51	Switch condition signal

8 If a more detailed check of the fuel injection/ignition system is required, take the vehicle to a Toyota dealer. They will have access to the special electronic diagnostic test unit which is plugged into the system's diagnostic connector, and can carry out a full check of the system components.

Adjustment

9 On all models covered by this manual, the idle speed and mixture are controlled by the engine management ECU. The mixture is regulated by altering the injector opening time, and the idle speed is regulated by altering the ignition timing and/or opening and

13.18 Disconnecting the wiring plugs from the injectors

closing the air bypass channels in the throttle housing by means of the idle speed control valve. Although it is possible to check the idle speed and mixture (see Chapter 1), no adjustment is possible. Any deviation from the specified settings indicates a fault in the idle speed control valve circuit or the oxygen sensor/lean mixture sensor circuit as applicable.

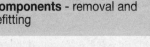

13 Fuel injection system components - removal and refitting

 Warning: Refer to the warning in Section 1 before proceeding.

Note: Some test procedures are included in this Section.

Fuel rail and injectors (4A-FE and 7A-FE engines)

Note: If a faulty injector is suspected, before condemning the injector it is worth trying the effect of one of the proprietary injector-cleaning treatments.

Removal - conventional engine

1 Depressurise the fuel system as described in Section 7.
2 Disconnect the battery negative (earth) lead (refer to Chapter 5A, Sections 1 and 3).
3 Remove the throttle housing as described in Section 11.
4 Unbolt the air pipe and fuel inlet hose from the air inlet chamber.

5 Unbolt and remove the engine lifting eye, and the inlet chamber stay and gasket.
6 Disconnect the PCV hoses and vacuum sensing hose, then unscrew the socket headed bolts and nuts and remove the air inlet chamber cover and gasket.
7 Release the clip and disconnect the fuel return hose from the fuel pressure regulator.
8 Unscrew the union bolt and disconnect the fuel inlet hose from the left-hand end of the fuel rail. Recover the two washers.
9 Disconnect the wiring plugs from the injectors.
10 Unscrew the mounting bolts and carefully remove the fuel rail together with the injectors. Recover the insulators and spacers from the inlet manifold.
11 Withdraw the injectors from the fuel rail and remove the sealing rings and O-rings. Discard the seals; new ones must be used on refitting.

Removal - lean burn engine

12 Depressurise the fuel system as described in Section 7.
13 Disconnect the battery negative lead.
14 Disconnect the PCV hoses from the camshaft cover and air inlet chamber.
15 Disconnect the vacuum sensing hose from the fuel pressure regulator on the right-hand end of the fuel rail.
16 Release the clip and disconnect the fuel return hose from the fuel pressure regulator **(see illustration)**.
17 Unscrew the union bolt and disconnect the fuel inlet hose from the left-hand end of the fuel rail. Recover the two washers **(see illustration)**.
18 Disconnect the wiring plugs from the injectors **(see illustration)**.
19 On RHD models, unbolt the accelerator cable support bracket from the air inlet chamber.
20 Unscrew the mounting bolts and carefully remove the fuel rail together with the injectors. Recover the rubber insulators and spacers from the cylinder head **(see illustration)**.
21 Withdraw the injectors from the fuel rail and remove the sealing rings and O-rings. Discard the seals; new ones must be used on refitting **(see illustrations)**.

4A

13.20 Removing the fuel rail

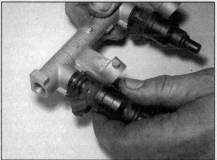

13.21a Withdrawing the injectors from the fuel rail

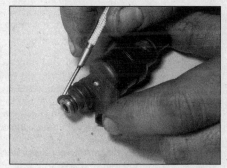

13.21b Removing the O-rings from the injectors

Refitting

22 Refitting is a reversal of the removal procedure, noting the following points:

a) *Fit new O-rings and sealing rings to all injectors, and fit new injector seals to the manifold or cylinder head as applicable.*

b) *Apply a smear of engine oil to the O-rings to aid installation, then ease the injectors into the fuel rail together with new sealing rings.*

c) *Ease the injectors and fuel rail assembly into position on the manifold or cylinder head. Fit the spacers, then insert the mounting bolts and tighten to the specified torque setting.*

d) *On completion, start the engine and check for fuel leaks.*

Fuel rail and injectors (3S-FE engines)

Note: *If a faulty injector is suspected, before condemning the injector, it is worth trying the effect of one of the proprietary injector-cleaning treatments.*

Removal

23 Depressurise the fuel system (Section 7).
24 Disconnect the battery negative (earth) lead (refer to Chapter 5A, Sections 1 and 3).
25 Remove the throttle housing as described in Section 11.
26 Unbolt and remove the engine lifting eye, together with the inlet manifold stay.
27 Identify the hoses and disconnect them from the EGR valve located on the left-hand rear of the inlet manifold. Unscrew the union nut securing the EGR tube to the connecting tube near the distributor, then unscrew the mounting nuts and remove the EGR valve from the inlet manifold. Recover the gasket.
28 Unbolt and remove the remaining inlet manifold stay at the left-hand end of the manifold.
29 Unbolt the accelerator cable support bracket from the inlet manifold and position the bracket and cable(s) to one side.
30 Unclip the HT leads from their guides, then disconnect the leads from the spark plugs noting their locations.
31 Disconnect the PCV hose from the inlet manifold.
32 Release the power steering fluid return hose from the clip on the engine wiring loom cover.
33 Disconnect the engine wiring loom cover from the upper timing belt cover by releasing the rear attachment first, then the front attachment.
34 Unscrew the retaining nuts, then remove the camshaft cover and gasket. Note that the cover is retained with special nuts screwed onto the spark plug tubes together with seals.
35 Disconnect the retaining clips and release the engine wiring loom from the support bracket and inlet manifold.
36 Unscrew the pulsation damper and disconnect the fuel inlet hose from the left-hand end of the fuel rail. Recover the two washers.

37 Release the clip and disconnect the fuel return hose from the return pipe.
38 Disconnect the vacuum sensing hose from the fuel pressure regulator.
39 Disconnect the wiring plugs from the injectors.
40 Unscrew the two bolts securing the fuel rail to the cylinder head.
41 Carefully withdraw the fuel rail, together with the injectors, from the cylinder head. As soon as the injectors are clear of their locations, turn the fuel rail so that the injectors are horizontal and facing forward, then remove the assembly over the top of the engine. Recover the insulators and spacers from the cylinder head.
42 Withdraw the injectors from the fuel rail and remove the sealing rings and O-rings. Discard the seals; new ones must be used on refitting.

Refitting

43 Refitting is a reversal of the removal procedure, noting the following points:

a) *Fit new O-rings and sealing rings to all injectors, and fit new injector seals to the cylinder head.*

b) *Apply a smear of engine oil to the O-rings to aid installation, then ease the injectors into the fuel rail together with new sealing rings.*

c) *Ease the injectors and fuel rail assembly into position on cylinder head. Insert the mounting bolts and tighten to the specified torque setting.*

d) *Examine the condition of the camshaft cover gasket and renew if necessary.*

e) *When refitting the camshaft cover, apply a little sealant where the camshaft bearing caps meet the cylinder head and over the semi-circular plugs at each end of the exhaust camshaft and ensure that the gasket seats correctly in the cover before the cover is fitted; as the cover is being fitted, ensure that the spark plug tube seals seat correctly. Tighten the retaining nuts to the specified torque.*

f) *Refit the throttle housing as described in Section 11.*

g) *On completion, start the engine and check for fuel leaks.*

Fuel rail and injectors (3S-GE engines)

Note: *If a faulty injector is suspected, before condemning the injector it is worth trying the effect of one of the proprietary injector-cleaning treatments.*

Removal

44 Depressurise the fuel system (Section 7).
45 Remove the inlet manifold as described in Section 14.
46 Unscrew the union bolts and disconnect the fuel inlet hose and cold start injector fuel hose from the fuel rail. Recover the two washers at each union.
47 Disconnect the wiring plugs from the injectors.

48 Unscrew the two nuts and remove the wiring loom cover.
49 Unscrew the three bolts securing the fuel rail to the cylinder head.
50 Carefully withdraw the fuel rail, together with the injectors, from the cylinder head. Recover the insulators and spacers from the cylinder head.
51 Withdraw the injectors from the fuel rail and remove the sealing rings and O-rings. Discard the seals; new ones must be used on refitting.

Refitting

52 Refitting is a reversal of the removal procedure, noting the following points:

a) *Fit new O-rings and sealing rings to all injectors, and fit new injector seals to the cylinder head.*

b) *Apply a smear of engine oil to the O-rings to aid installation, then ease the injectors into the fuel rail together with new sealing rings.*

c) *Ease the injectors and fuel rail assembly into position on cylinder head. Insert the mounting bolts and tighten to the specified torque setting.*

d) *Refit the inlet manifold as described in Section 14.*

e) *On completion, start the engine and check for fuel leaks.*

Fuel pressure regulator (4A-FE and 7A-FE engines)

Removal

53 Depressurise the fuel system as described in Section 7.
54 Disconnect the battery negative (earth) lead (refer to Chapter 5A, Sections 1 and 3).
55 Disconnect the vacuum sensing hose from the fuel pressure regulator, which is mounted on the right-hand end of the fuel rail.
56 Slacken the retaining clip and disconnect the fuel return hose from the regulator.
57 Undo the two retaining bolts, and remove the regulator from the end of the fuel rail. Recover the sealing ring fitted to the regulator and discard it; a new one must be used on refitting.

Refitting

58 Refitting is the reverse of removal, using a new sealing ring. On completion, start the engine and check for fuel leaks.

Fuel pressure regulator (3S-FE engines)

Removal

59 Depressurise the fuel system as described in Section 7.
60 Disconnect the battery negative (earth) lead (refer to Chapter 5A, Sections 1 and 3).
61 Unbolt the accelerator cable support bracket from the inlet manifold and position the bracket and cable(s) to one side.
62 Unclip the HT leads from their guides, then disconnect the leads from the spark plugs noting their locations.

63 Disconnect the PCV hoses from the inlet manifold and throttle housing.
64 Release the power steering fluid return hose from the clip on the engine wiring loom cover.
65 Disconnect the engine wiring loom cover from the upper timing belt cover by releasing the rear attachment first, then the front attachment.
66 Unscrew the retaining nuts, then remove the camshaft cover and gasket. Note that the cover is retained with special nuts screwed onto the spark plug tubes together with seals.
67 Disconnect the vacuum sensing hose from the fuel pressure regulator, which is mounted on the right-hand end of the fuel rail.
68 Unscrew the union bolt and disconnect the fuel return hose from the fuel pressure regulator. Recover the two washers
69 Undo the two retaining bolts, and remove the regulator from the end of the fuel rail. Recover the sealing ring fitted to the regulator and discard it; a new one must be used on refitting.

Refitting

70 Refitting is a reversal of the removal procedure, noting the following points:
a) *Use a new sealing ring on the fuel pressure regulator and tighten the mounting bolts to the specified torque.*
b) *Examine the condition of the camshaft cover gasket and renew if necessary.*
c) *When refitting the camshaft cover, apply a little sealant where the camshaft bearing caps meet the cylinder head and over the semi-circular plugs at each end of the exhaust camshaft and ensure that the gasket seats correctly in the cover before the cover is fitted; as the cover is being fitted, ensure that the spark plug tube seals seat correctly. Tighten the retaining nuts to the specified torque.*
d) *Adjust the accelerator cable (Section 3), and on automatic transmission models the kick-down cable (Chapter 7B).*
e) *On completion, start the engine and check for fuel leaks.*

Fuel pressure regulator (3S-GE engines)

Removal

71 Depressurise the fuel system as described in Section 7.
72 Remove the inlet manifold as described in Section 14.
73 Release the clip and disconnect the fuel return hose and pipe from the fuel pressure regulator which is mounted on the right-hand end of the fuel rail.
74 If not already done, disconnect the vacuum sensing hose from the fuel pressure regulator.
75 Unbolt and remove the engine lifting eye adjacent to the fuel pressure regulator.
76 Slacken the locknut and remove the fuel pressure regulator from the fuel rail. Recover the sealing ring fitted to the regulator and

discard it; a new one must be used on refitting.

Refitting

77 Refitting is a reversal of the removal procedure, noting the following points:
a) *Fully slacken the locknut then fit a new sealing ring on the fuel pressure regulator.*
b) *Install the regulator on the fuel rail and turn it anticlockwise so that the vacuum sensing pipe stub is facing the rear of the car. Hold the regulator in this position and tighten the locknut.*
c) *Refit the inlet manifold as described in Section 14.*
d) *On completion, start the engine and check for fuel leaks.*

Throttle position sensor

Removal

78 Disconnect the throttle position sensor wiring connector.
79 Using a dab of white paint or a suitable marker pen, make alignment marks between the throttle position sensor body and the throttle housing.
80 Undo the two retaining screws then remove the throttle position sensor along with its gasket (where fitted).

Refitting

81 Fit a new gasket (where necessary) to the throttle position sensor and refit the sensor to the throttle housing. Align the marks made on removal and tighten the retaining screws securely. Before reconnecting the wiring connector check the sensor adjustment as described in the following sub-Sections, according to engine type.

Adjustment (4A-FE and 7A-FE engines)

82 Using an ohmmeter, measure between the terminals given in the following table and check that the resistance is within the specified range for each particular clearance. The small throttle lever-to-stop screw clearances are set by inserting a feeler blade of the required thickness (0.40 mm or 0.90 mm) between the stop and lever. The top terminal is E2, and the terminals beneath are IDL, VTA, and VC (bottom).

Terminals	Clearance (mm)	Resistance (W)
VTA to E2	0	200 to 6000
IDL to E2	0.40	2300 or less
IDL to E2	0.90	Infinity
VTA to E2	Throttle valve fully open	3300 to 10000
VC to E2	—	4000 to 8500

83 If the resistances are not as specified, connect the ohmmeter between the terminals IDL and E2 then adjust the position of the throttle position sensor as follows. Slacken the retaining screws then, insert a 0.70 mm feeler gauge between the stop screw and the throttle lever. Turn the sensor body fully anti-clockwise then turn it slowly clockwise until continuity is just present between the

terminals. Hold the switch in this position then tighten the retaining screws securely and recheck the switch terminal resistances. If the resistances are still outside those given in the above table, renewal of the throttle position sensor will be required.
84 Once the throttle position sensor is correctly adjusted reconnect the throttle position sensor wiring connector.

Adjustment (3S-FE and 3S-GE engines)

85 On 3S-FE engines, disconnect the throttle opener vacuum hose at the throttle housing and apply vacuum to the hose to retract the throttle opener.
86 Using an ohmmeter, measure between the terminals given in the following table and check that the resistance is within the specified range for each particular clearance. The small throttle lever to stop screw clearances are set by inserting a feeler blade of the required thickness (0.50 mm or 0.70 mm) between the stop and lever. The top terminal is VC, and the terminals beneath are VTA, IDL, and E2 (bottom).

Terminals	Clearance (mm)	Resistance (W)
VTA to E2	0	200 to 5700 (3S-FE) 200 to 8000 (3S-GE)
IDL to E2	0.50	2300 or less
IDL to E2	0.70	Infinity
VTA to E2	Throttle valve fully open	2000 to 10200 (3S-FE), 3300 to 10000 (3S-GE)
VC to E2	—	2500 to 5900 (3S-FE) 3000 to 7000 (3S-GE)

87 If the resistances are not as specified, connect the ohmmeter between the terminals IDL and E2 then adjust the position of the throttle position sensor as follows. Slacken the retaining screws then, insert a 0.60 mm feeler gauge between the stop screw and the throttle lever. Turn the sensor body fully anti-clockwise then turn it slowly clockwise until continuity is just present between the terminals. Hold the switch in this position then tighten the retaining screws securely and recheck the switch terminal resistances. If the resistances are still outside those given in the above table, renewal of the throttle position sensor will be required.
88 Once the throttle position sensor is correctly adjusted reconnect the throttle position sensor wiring connector. On 3S-FE engines, reconnect the throttle opener vacuum hose to the throttle housing.

Throttle opener (3S-FE engines)

Removal

89 Remove the throttle housing as described in Section 11.
90 Disconnect the vacuum hose at the throttle opener.

4A

91 Undo the bolts securing the throttle opener mounting bracket to the base of the throttle housing then remove the throttle opener and bracket.

Refitting

92 Refit the throttle opener and mounting bracket to the throttle housing and tighten its retaining bolts securely, then refit the throttle housing as described in Section 11.
93 On completion of refitting, check the throttle opener adjustment as follows.
94 Start the engine and warm it up to normal operating temperature.
95 Switch the engine off and connect a tachometer in accordance with the maker's instructions.
96 Start the engine again and allow it to idle. Disconnect the vacuum hose at the throttle opener and plug its end.
97 Increase the engine speed to 2500 rpm then release the throttle. The throttle opener should hold the engine speed at 1300 to 1500 rpm when the throttle is released. If the engine speed is not as specified, turn the adjusting screw on the throttle opener plunger to set the engine speed at 1400 rpm. Reconnect the vacuum hose and check that the engine speed returns to the specified idle setting given in Chapter 1.
98 Switch the engine off and disconnect the tachometer.

Idle speed control valve

Removal

99 Remove the throttle housing as described in Section 11.
100 Undo the screws securing the valve to the base of the throttle housing then remove the valve, noting the correct fitted position of its gasket.

Refitting

101 Ensure the mating surfaces are clean then fit a new gasket to the valve.
102 Refit the idle speed control valve to the throttle housing and tighten its retaining screws securely, then refit the throttle housing as described in Section 11.

Air conditioning idle-up valve

Removal

103 The idle-up valve is located on the bulkhead in the engine compartment. Disconnect the wiring connector, then note the location of the hoses and disconnect them.
104 Remove the valve from the bulkhead.

Refitting

105 Refitting is a reversal of removal.

Vacuum switching valve

Removal

106 On 4A-FE and 7A-FE lean-burn engines and 3S-GE engines, the inlet manifold air control valve assembly is controlled by a

13.106 Disconnecting the wiring from the air control valve vacuum switching valve (4A-FE lean-burn engines)

vacuum switching valve located at the rear of the engine, either on or beneath the manifold. Disconnect the wiring connector, then note the location of the hoses and disconnect them **(see illustration)**.
107 Unbolt the valve from the bracket on the cylinder block.

Refitting

108 Refitting is a reversal of removal.

Manifold absolute pressure sensor

Removal

109 The MAP sensor is mounted on the engine compartment bulkhead. Disconnect the vacuum hose and wiring plug and remove the mounting bracket retaining bolt **(see illustration)**.

Refitting

110 Refitting is a reversal of the removal procedure.

Inlet air temperature sensor

Removal

111 Disconnect the wiring connector and withdraw the sensor from the air cleaner housing grommet.

Refitting

112 Refitting is a reverse of the removal procedure.

Engine temperature sensor

113 Refer to Chapter 3.

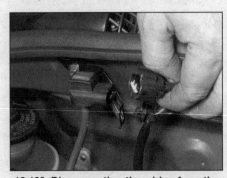

13.109 Disconnecting the wiring from the MAP sensor

Cold start injector (3S-GE engines)

Removal

114 The injector is located on the air inlet chamber above the inlet manifold.
115 Depressurise the fuel system as described in Section 7.
116 Disconnect the wiring plug from the cold start injector.
117 Unscrew the union bolt and disconnect the fuel supply line. Recover the sealing washers.
118 Unscrew the mounting bolts and remove the cold start injector from the air inlet chamber. Recover the gasket.
119 The injector may be tested using an ohmmeter connected to the two terminals. Check that the resistance is as given in the Specifications and renew the component if necessary.

Refitting

120 Refitting is the reverse of the removal procedure, but fit a new gasket and tighten the mounting bolts and union bolt to the specified torque wrench setting.

Cold start injector time switch (3S-GE engine)

Removal

121 The switch is located in the heater outlet housing on the left-hand end of the engine, next to the engine temperature sensor.
122 Testing may be carried out (after disconnecting the switch multi-plug) by measuring the resistance at the switch terminal pins. First measure the resistance between switch terminal pins STA and STJ; this should be as given in the Specifications. Now measure the resistance between switch terminal pin STA and a good earth point and compare with the Specifications. If any measurement obtained differs significantly from those specified, the switch must be renewed.
123 The component is removed (with the engine cold) by first disconnecting, then unscrewing it; plug its location to prevent excessive coolant loss. Note whether an O-ring is fitted, or if sealant is evident on the threads.

Refitting

124 Refitting is the reverse of the removal procedure, noting the following points.
 a) If an O-ring was originally fitted this should be renewed.
 b) If sealant was noted on the component's threads on removal, the threads must be cleaned and a suitable sealant applied on refitting.
 c) Top up the coolant level (Chapter 1).

Knock sensor (4A-FE, 7A-FE and 3S-FE engines)

Removal

125 The knock sensor is located on the rear right-hand side of the cylinder block on 7A-FE engines, or on the rear left-hand side of the cylinder block on 3S-FE engines. On the 4A-FE (conventional) engine, the sensor is located on the rear right-hand side of the cylinder block; a knock sensor is not fitted to 4A-FE lean-burn engines.

126 Disconnect the battery negative (earth) lead (refer to Chapter 5A, Sections 1 and 3).

127 Where the sensor does not have hexagon flats, Toyota technicians use a special tool to locate on the serrations. If necessary, obtain this tool. Unscrew the sensor from the cylinder block.

Refitting

128 Refitting is a reversal of removal, but tighten the sensor to the specified torque.

Electronic Control Unit (ECU)

Removal

129 On 4A-FE, 7A-FE and 3S-GE engine models, the ECU is located behind the left-hand side of the facia on right-hand drive models and behind the right-hand side of the facia on left-hand drive models. On 3S-GE engine models, it is located in front of the centre console beneath the middle of the facia.

130 To remove the ECU on 4A-FE, 7A-FE and 3S-GE engine models, remove the glovebox as described in Chapter 11.

131 On 3S-GE engine models, remove the centre console as described in Chapter 11.

132 On all models, disconnect the wiring connector then unscrew the mounting bracket

bolts and withdraw the ECU **(see illustration)**. **Do not** attempt to check the internal circuits of the ECU - if necessary, there are electronic specialists who can test the ECU for you.

Refitting

133 Refitting is a reversal of removal, but make sure that the wiring connector is fully entered on the ECU terminals.

---

14 Inlet manifold - removal and refitting

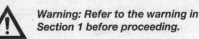

> ⚠️ **Warning: Refer to the warning in Section 1 before proceeding.**

4A-FE and 7A-FE engines

Removal

1 Remove the throttle housing as described in Section 11.

2 Remove the fuel rail and injectors as described in Section 13.

3 Unscrew the mounting bolts and remove the engine lifting eye and air inlet chamber support bracket. Also unbolt the hose support. Remove the gasket.

4 Unbolt the inlet manifold rear support bracket from the manifold and cylinder block.

5 Unbolt the fuel return hose and air pipe supports from the inlet manifold, then unbolt the wiring conduit and air pipe assembly from the inlet manifold.

13.132 Electronic Control Unit (ECU)

6 Disconnect the manifold and air inlet chamber hoses and unbolt the air inlet chamber cover. Recover the gasket **(see illustrations)**.

7 Unscrew the nuts and bolts securing the inlet manifold to the cylinder head, then withdraw the manifold from the studs and remove from the engine compartment. Remove the gasket **(see illustrations)**.

8 On lean-burn engines, disconnect the vacuum hose then remove the air control valve assembly and gasket **(see illustrations)**.

9 Clean the surfaces of the inlet manifold (and air control valve assembly where applicable) and cylinder head and check the inlet manifold for distortion using a straight-edge and feeler blade. If the distortion exceeds the specified maximum, renew the manifold. **Do**

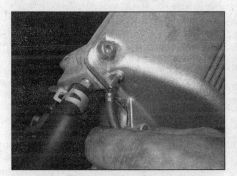

14.6a Disconnecting the pressure regulator vacuum sensing hose from the air inlet chamber cover

14.6b Removing the air inlet chamber cover . . .

14.6c . . . and gasket

14.7a Unscrew the mounting nuts . . .

14.7b . . . and bolts . . .

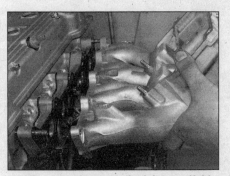

14.7c . . . and remove the inlet manifold from the cylinder head studs

4A

14.8a On lean-burn engines, remove the air control valve assembly . . .

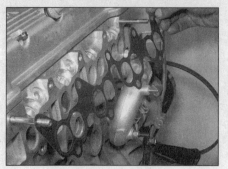

14.8b . . . and gasket

14.8c The air control valve, vacuum switching valve and vacuum reservoir components

not disturb the vacuum adjustment screw on the air control valve assembly **(see illustration)**.

Refitting

10 Refitting is a reversal of the removal procedure with reference to Sections 13 and 11, but fit new gaskets and tighten the mounting nuts and bolts progressively to the specified torque settings.

3S-FE engines

Removal

11 Remove the throttle housing as described in Section 11.

12 Remove the fuel rail and injectors as described in Section 13.

13 Disconnect the air and vacuum hoses, labelling them for reconnection, then unbolt the air pipe assembly from underside of the inlet manifold.

14 Unbolt the EGR vacuum switching valve from the underside of the inlet manifold.

15 Disconnect the remaining hose and wire connections at the manifold then undo the six bolts and two nuts securing the manifold to the cylinder head. Withdraw the manifold from the studs and remove from the engine compartment. Remove the gasket.

Refitting

16 Refitting is a reversal of the removal procedure with reference to Sections 13 and 11, but fit new gaskets and tighten the mounting nuts and bolts progressively to the specified torque settings.

14.9 Vacuum adjustment screw on the air control valve assembly (do not adjust)

3S-GE engines

Removal

17 Depressurise the fuel system as described in Section 7.

18 Disconnect the battery negative (earth) lead (refer to Chapter 5A, Sections 1 and 3)

19 Drain the cooling system as described in Chapter 1.

20 Loosen the clips and disconnect the air inlet duct from the throttle housing and air cleaner cover.

21 Turn the segment on the throttle housing to open the throttle, then disconnect the inner accelerator cable. On automatic transmission models, also disconnect the kick-down cable.

22 Disconnect the wiring from the throttle position sensor on the upper rear of the throttle housing.

23 Disconnect the wiring from the idle speed control valve on the lower front of the throttle housing.

24 Identify the positions of the vacuum, coolant, air and evaporation loss hoses, then disconnect them from the throttle housing.

25 Disconnect the wiring plug from the cold start injector at the rear of the manifold air inlet chamber.

26 Unscrew the cold start injector union bolt and disconnect the fuel supply line. Recover the sealing washers.

27 Undo the four bolts and remove the air inlet chamber support bracket.

28 Undo the bolts and nuts securing the air inlet chamber to the inlet manifold and remove the air inlet chamber. Remove the gasket.

29 Undo the bolts and remove the inlet manifold support brackets at the rear of the engine.

30 Disconnect the vacuum hoses from the air pipe assembly, labelling them for reconnection.

31 Disconnect the earth lead and wiring connectors at the vacuum switching valves on the rear of the inlet manifold. Unbolt the vacuum switching valve and air control valve assembly mounting bracket from the rear of the inlet manifold.

32 Check that all wiring, air and vacuum

connections at the manifold have been disconnected then undo the four bolts and three nuts securing the manifold to the cylinder head. Remove the manifold and gasket.

Refitting

33 Refitting is a reversal of the removal procedure, but fit new gaskets and tighten the mounting nuts and bolts progressively to the specified torque settings. Adjust the accelerator cable and, where applicable the automatic transmission kick-down cable with reference to Section 3 of this Chapter and Chapter 7B respectively. Refill the cooling system as described in Chapter 1 on completion.

15 Exhaust manifold - removal and refitting

Removal

1 On lean-burn engines, disconnect the lean mixture sensor wiring connector.

2 Unscrew the nuts securing the exhaust downpipe to the exhaust manifold, then lower the downpipe and remove the gasket **(see illustration)**. On the 3S-FE engine it is difficult to lower the downpipe as it jams on the studs, therefore disconnection can be left until the manifold is removed.

3 Unbolt and remove the heat shield **(see illustrations)**.

15.2 Separating the exhaust downpipe from the exhaust manifold

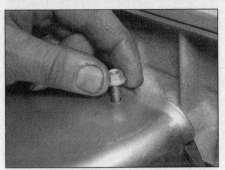

15.3a Unscrew the bolts . . .

15.3b . . . and remove the heat shield from the exhaust manifold

15.4 Removing the bolt from the exhaust manifold stay

15.5a Progressively loosen the mounting nuts . . .

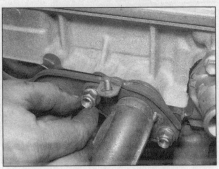

15.5b . . . then remove the nuts . . .

15.5c . . . and withdraw the exhaust manifold from the cylinder head studs

4 Unbolt and remove the exhaust manifold stay **(see illustration)**. Note that on 3S-GE engines there are two stays.
5 Progressively unscrew the mounting nuts, and withdraw the exhaust manifold from the studs on the cylinder head **(see illustrations)**. Remove the gasket.
6 Where a heat shield is fitted underneath, unbolt it from the manifold.
7 Clean the surfaces of the exhaust manifold and cylinder head and check the exhaust manifold for distortion using a straight-edge and feeler blade. If the distortion exceeds the specified maximum, renew the manifold.

Refitting

8 Refitting is a reversal of the removal procedure, but fit new gaskets to the cylinder head and exhaust downpipe, and tighten the mounting nuts to the specified torque.

16 Exhaust system - general information, removal and refitting

General information

1 The exhaust system consists of three sections, the front downpipe, the catalytic converter and intermediate pipe with resonator, and the tailpipe and rear silencer.
2 The system is suspended throughout its entire length by rubber mountings, and all exhaust sections are joined by flanged joints

which are secured together by studs and nuts.

Removal

3 Each exhaust section can be removed individually or, alternatively, the complete system can be removed as a unit.
4 First jack up the vehicle, and support it on axle stands. Alternatively, position the car over an inspection pit, or on car ramps.

Front downpipe section

5 Where the exhaust gas oxygen sensor is located in the downpipe, disconnect the sensor wiring connector. Unscrew the nuts securing the downpipe to the exhaust manifold, then lower the downpipe and recover the gasket **(see illustration)**.
6 Unbolt the downpipe from the intermediate section, and remove it from under the vehicle.

16.5 Exhaust downpipe and gasket

Intermediate section and catalytic converter

> **Warning:** The catalytic converter operates at very high temperatures - make sure it is cool before attempting to remove it!

7 Unbolt the front downpipe exhaust section from the intermediate section.
8 Unbolt the intermediate section from the rear silencer and tailpipe.
9 Support the intermediate section and release it from the mounting rubbers. Remove the exhaust section from under the vehicle **(see illustration)**.

Tailpipe and silencer

10 Unbolt the intermediate exhaust section from the rear silencer and tailpipe.

4A

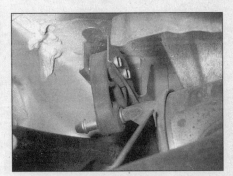

16.9 Intermediate exhaust section mounting rubber

11 Support the tailpipe and rear silencer and release it from the mounting rubbers. Remove the exhaust section from under the vehicle **(see illustration).**

Complete exhaust system

12 Unscrew the nuts securing the downpipe to the exhaust manifold, then lower the downpipe and recover the gasket.

13 Support the exhaust system, then release the rubber mountings and lower the system to the ground.

Heat shields

14 Heat shields are riveted to the underbody and may be removed by drilling out the securing rivets. In most instances there is sufficient clearance to carry out this operation with the exhaust system in place.

Refitting

15 Each section is refitted by a reversal of the removal sequence, noting the following points:

a) *Ensure that all traces of corrosion have been removed from the flanges, and renew the gasket(s).*

b) *Inspect the rubber mountings for signs of damage or deterioration, and renew as necessary.*

c) *Prior to tightening the exhaust system fasteners to the specified torque, ensure that all rubber mountings are correctly located, and that there is adequate clearance between the exhaust system and vehicle underbody/suspension components, etc.*

d) *When refitting the heat shields, use new pop rivets to secure them to the underbody.*

16.11 Tailpipe and silencer mounting rubbers

Chapter 4 Part B:
Emissions control systems

Contents

Degrees of difficulty

Easy, suitable for novice with little experience	Fairly easy, suitable for beginner with some experience	Fairly difficult, suitable for competent DIY mechanic	Difficult, suitable for experienced DIY mechanic	Very difficult, suitable for expert DIY or professional

Specifications

General

Exhaust gas oxygen sensor/lean mixture sensor resistance (at 20°C):	
Conventional engine	5.1 to 6.3 ohms
Lean-burn engine	1.10 to 1.44 ohms
EGR vacuum switching valve resistance	33 to 39 ohms

Torque wrench settings

	Nm	lbf ft
EGR valve to inlet manifold	13	9
EGR pipe to cylinder head	59	43
Exhaust gas oxygen sensor/lean mixture sensor	20	14

1 General information

1 Models covered in this manual are fitted with the following emission control systems.
a) Crankcase emission control
b) Catalytic converter
c) Evaporative emission control
d) Exhaust gas recirculation (3S-FE engine only)
The systems operate as follows.

Crankcase emissions control

2 To reduce the emission of unburned hydrocarbons from the crankcase into the atmosphere, the engine is sealed, and the blow-by gases and oil vapour are drawn from inside the crankcase, through the PCV valve, into the inlet manifold, to be burned by the engine during normal combustion.
3 Under conditions of high manifold vacuum, the gases will be sucked positively out of the crankcase. Under conditions of low manifold vacuum, the gases are forced out of the crankcase by the (relatively) higher crankcase pressure; if the engine is worn, the raised crankcase pressure (due to increased blow-by) will cause some of the flow to return under all manifold conditions.

Catalytic converter

4 To minimise the amount of pollutants which escape into the atmosphere, a catalytic converter is fitted in the intermediate section of the exhaust system. The system is of closed-loop type, in which an exhaust gas oxygen sensor (or lean mixture sensor on lean-burn engines) provides the engine management ECU constant feedback, enabling the unit to adjust the mixture to provide the best possible conditions for the converter to operate.
5 The exhaust gas sensor's tip is sensitive to oxygen, and sends the control unit a varying voltage depending on the amount of oxygen in the exhaust gases; if the intake air/fuel mixture is too rich, the sensor sends a high-voltage signal. The voltage falls as the mixture weakens. Peak conversion efficiency of all major pollutants occurs if the intake air/fuel mixture is maintained at the chemically-correct ratio for the complete combustion of petrol - 14.7 parts (by weight) of air to 1 part of fuel (the stoichiometric ratio). The sensor output voltage alters in a large step at this point, the control unit using the signal change as a reference point, and correcting the intake air/fuel mixture accordingly by altering the fuel injector pulse width (injector opening time). The sensor has a built-in heating element (controlled by the ECU), to quickly bring the sensor's tip to an efficient operating temperature.

Evaporative emissions control system

6 An evaporative emissions control system is fitted in order to minimise the escape of unburned hydrocarbons into the atmosphere. The fuel tank filler cap is sealed, and a carbon canister collects the petrol vapours generated in the tank when the car is parked. It stores the vapours until they can be cleared into the inlet manifold when the engine is running. To ensure that the engine runs correctly when it is cold and/or idling, and to protect the catalytic converter from the effects of an over-rich mixture, the system is designed to operate only when the engine has warmed up and is under load.
7 The system is controlled by a Bi-metal Vacuum Switching Valve (BVSV) located on the left-hand end of the cylinder head. At coolant temperatures below 35°C the valve is closed and the system is disabled, however at temperatures above 54°C the valve is open and the system is enabled.

Exhaust gas recirculation system

8 An Exhaust Gas Recirculation (EGR) system is fitted to 3S-FE engines. This reduces the level of nitrogen oxides produced during combustion by introducing a proportion of the exhaust gas back into the inlet manifold under certain engine operating conditions. The

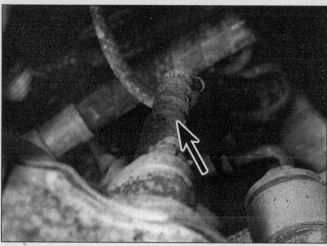

2.6a Exhaust gas oxygen sensor location (arrowed) on top of the exhaust downpipe on conventional engines

2.6b Disconnecting the lean mixture sensor wiring (lean-burn engines)

system is controlled by a Vacuum Switching Valve (VSV) through the engine management ECU. The VSV supplies vacuum to the EGR valve which then opens and allows a proportion of exhaust gases to flow into the inlet manifold. With the throttle valve closed the system is inactive since there is no vacuum available to open the EGR valve, however when the throttle valve is opened initially the first vacuum port is opened and the EGR valve will open provided that the ECU has energised the VSV. Further opening of the throttle valve causes a second vacuum port to be influenced by engine vacuum. This causes the vacuum modulator to increase the amount of exhaust gases entering the engine. The modulator has an internal diaphragm which is subject to exhaust gas pressure on one side, and to atmospheric pressure through a filter on the other side.

---

2 Emissions control systems - testing and component renewal

Crankcase emissions control system

1 Disconnect the crankcase ventilation hoses

and check that they are clear and undamaged then refit them.

2 With the engine idling, disconnect the PCV valve from the rubber seal on the rear of the camshaft cover. A hissing noise should be heard and vacuum should be felt when a finger is placed over the valve inlet. Switch off the engine after making the check and refit the valve to the seal in the camshaft cover.

3 Renew the PCV valve if it is blocked.

Catalytic converter (exhaust emissions control system)

Testing

4 If the CO level at the tailpipe is too high, the operation of the exhaust gas oxygen sensor/lean mixture sensor should be tested using the ECU self-diagnosis facility as described in Chapter 4A. Detailed testing must be left to a Toyota dealer.

Catalytic converter - renewal

5 Refer to Chapter 4A.

Exhaust gas oxygen sensor/lean mixture sensor - renewal

Note: *The sensor is delicate, and it will not work if it is dropped or knocked, if its power supply is disrupted, or if any cleaning materials are used on it.*

6 The exhaust gas oxygen sensor (used on conventional engines) is located on the exhaust downpipe and the lean mixture sensor (used on lean-burn engines) is located on exhaust manifold. First trace the wiring back to the connector and disconnect it **(see illustrations)**.

7 Unscrew the mounting nuts, then remove the sensor and recover the gaskets **(see illustrations)**.

8 Refitting is a reversal of the removal procedure, but prior to installing the sensor, apply a smear of high-temperature grease to the sensor mounting stud threads. Tighten the nuts to the specified torque. Check that the wiring is correctly routed, and in no danger of contacting either the exhaust system or the engine.

Evaporative emissions control system

Testing

9 To test the system, disconnect the hoses between the carbon canister (located in the left-hand rear corner of the engine compartment), BVSV valve (left-hand end of the cylinder head) and throttle housing, and check that they are clear by blowing through them **(see illustration)**.

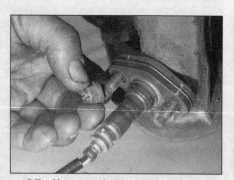

2.7a Unscrew the mounting nuts . . .

2.7b . . . then remove the lean mixture sensor . . .

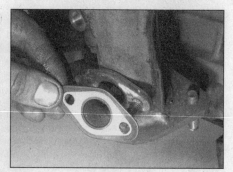

2.7c . . . and gasket (lean-burn engines)

2.9 The EVAP system BVSV valve located on the left-hand end of the cylinder head (3S-FE engines)

2.14 The carbon canister (arrowed) is located in the left-hand rear corner of the engine compartment

10 Check the fuel tank filler cap for a deformed or damaged seal.

11 Using low air pressure on the carbon canister port with the long stub, check that air flows through the canister freely and exits through the short stub.

12 Using air pressure on the carbon canister port with the short stub, check that no air flows from the long stub.

13 The BVSV valve may be tested by immersing it in water being heated. Connect an air supply to one of the outlets. At temperatures below 35°C the valve should be closed, however at temperatures above 54°C it should be open.

Carbon canister - renewal

14 The canister is located in the left-hand rear corner of the engine compartment **(see illustration)**. First remove the air inlet duct with reference to Chapter 4A.

15 Make a note of the correct fitted location of each hose on the canister **(see illustration)**.

16 Release the retaining clips (where fitted) and disconnect the two hoses from the top of the canister, then disconnect the atmosphere hose from the bottom of the canister.

17 Free the canister from its mounting bracket, and remove it from the engine compartment.

18 Refitting is a reverse of the removal procedure, ensuring that the hoses are correctly reconnected.

Exhaust gas recirculation system components

Testing

19 Detailed testing of the exhaust gas recirculation system should be entrusted to a Toyota dealer as it entails the use of a vacuum gauge.

Removal

20 To remove the EGR vacuum modulator, identify the hoses and disconnect them from the unit which is located on the air inlet chamber on the top of the inlet manifold **(see illustration)**. Unscrew the mounting nut and remove the modulator.

21 To remove the EGR valve, identify the hoses and disconnect them from the unit which is located on the left-hand rear of the inlet manifold. Unscrew the union nut securing the EGR tube to the exhaust manifold, then unscrew the mounting nuts and remove the EGR valve from the inlet manifold. Recover the gasket.

22 The VSV valve is located in the rear of the cylinder block, and access is best from under the vehicle. Chock the rear wheels then jack up the front of the car and support it on axle stands (see *Jacking and Vehicle Support*). Identify the hoses then disconnect them from the valve. Disconnect the wiring plug, then unbolt the valve and bracket.

Refitting

23 Refitting is a reversal of removal, but make sure that the hoses are correctly refitted.

2.20 The EGR vacuum modulator (3S-FE engines)

3 Catalytic converter - general information and precautions

The catalytic converter is a reliable and simple device which needs no maintenance in itself, but there are some facts of which an owner should be aware to ensure the converter functions properly for its full service life.

a) DO NOT use leaded petrol in a vehicle with a catalytic converter - the lead will coat the precious metals, reducing their converting efficiency, and will eventually destroy the converter.

b) Always keep the ignition and fuel systems well-maintained in accordance with the manufacturer's schedule.

c) If the engine develops a misfire, do not drive the car at all (or at least as little as possible) until the fault is cured.

d) DO NOT push- or tow-start the car - this will soak the catalytic converter in unburned fuel, causing it to overheat when the engine does start.

e) DO NOT switch off the ignition at high engine speeds.

f) DO NOT use fuel or engine oil additives - these may contain substances harmful to the catalytic converter.

g) DO NOT continue to use the car if the engine burns oil to the extent of leaving a visible trail of blue smoke.

h) Remember that the catalytic converter operates at very high temperatures. DO NOT, therefore, park the car in dry undergrowth, over long grass, or over piles of dead leaves, after a long run.

i) Remember that the catalytic converter is FRAGILE - do not strike it with tools during servicing work.

4B

Chapter 5 Part A:
Starting and charging systems

Contents

Degrees of difficulty

| Easy, suitable for novice with little experience | | Fairly easy, suitable for beginner with some experience | | Fairly difficult, suitable for competent DIY mechanic | | Difficult, suitable for experienced DIY mechanic | | Very difficult, suitable for expert DIY or professional | |

Specifications

General
System type .... 12 volt, negative earth

Battery
Type .... Low-maintenance or maintenance-free
Charge condition:
 Poor .... 12.5 volts
 Normal .... 12.6 volts
 Good .... 12.7 volts

Alternator

Nippondenso
Rating .... 70 amp
Brush exposed length:
 Standard .... 10.5 mm
 Minimum .... 1.5 mm
Rotor coil resistance .... 2.8 to 3.0 ohms
Slip ring diameter (minimum) .... 12.8 mm

Bosch
Rating .... 70 amp
Brush exposed length:
 Standard .... 10.0 to 11.0 mm
 Minimum .... 5.0 mm
Rotor coil resistance .... 2.3 to 2.9 ohms
Slip ring diameter (minimum) .... 10.5 mm

Starter motor
Type .... Pre-engaged
Output:
 4A-FE and 7A-FE engines .... 0.8 kW
 3S-FE and 3S-GE engines .... 1.2 or 1.4 kW
Minimum brush length:
 4A-FE and 7A-FE engines .... 9.0 mm
 3S-FE and 3S-GE engines .... 8.5 mm

Torque wrench settings

	Nm	lbf ft
Alternator to mounting bracket bolts	54	40
Alternator to adjustment link:		
4A-FE and 7A-FE engines	19	14
3S-FE and 3S-GE engines	27	20
Alternator pulley nut:		
Nippondenso	110	81
Bosch	65	48
Starter-mounting bolts	39	29

1 General information, precautions and battery disconnection

General information

This Part of Chapter 5 includes the charging and starting systems. Because of their engine-related functions, these components are covered separately from the body electrical devices such as the lights, instruments, etc (which are covered in Chapter 12). Refer to Part B of this Chapter for information on the ignition system.

The electrical system is of 12-volt negative earth type.

The battery is of low-maintenance or maintenance-free (sealed for life) type, and is charged by the alternator, which is belt-driven from the crankshaft pulley.

The starter motor is of pre-engaged type incorporating an integral solenoid. On starting, the solenoid moves the drive pinion into engagement with the flywheel/driveplate ring gear before the starter motor is energised. Once the engine has started, a one-way clutch prevents the motor armature being driven by the engine until the pinion disengages.

Further details of the various systems are given in the relevant Sections of this Chapter. While some repair procedures are given, the usual course of action is to renew the component concerned. The owner whose interest extends beyond mere component renewal should obtain a copy of the *Automobile Electrical & Electronic Systems Manual*, available from the publishers of this manual.

Precautions

It is necessary to take extra care when working on the electrical system to avoid damage to semi-conductor devices (diodes and transistors), and to avoid the risk of personal injury. In addition to the precautions given in *Safety first!* at the beginning of this manual, observe the following when working on the system:

Always remove rings, watches, etc before working on the electrical system. Even with the battery disconnected, capacitive discharge could occur if a component's live terminal is earthed through a metal object. This could cause a shock or nasty burn.

Do not reverse the battery connections. Components such as the alternator, electronic control units, or any other components having semi-conductor circuitry could be irreparably damaged.

If the engine is being started using jump leads and a slave battery, connect the batteries positive-to-positive and negative-to-negative (see Jump starting). This also applies when connecting a battery charger but in this case both of the battery terminals should first be disconnected.

Never disconnect the battery terminals, the alternator, any electrical wiring or any test instruments when the engine is running.

Do not allow the engine to turn the alternator when the alternator is not connected.

Never test for alternator output by flashing the output lead to earth.

Never use an ohmmeter of the type incorporating a hand-cranked generator for circuit or continuity testing.

Always ensure that the battery negative lead is disconnected when working on the electrical system.

Before using electric-arc welding equipment on the car, disconnect the battery, alternator and components such as the fuel injection/ignition electronic control unit to protect them from the risk of damage.

Battery disconnection

Several systems fitted to the vehicle require battery power to be available at all times, either to ensure their continued operation (such as the clock) or to maintain control unit memories (such as that in the engine management system's ECU) which would be wiped if the battery were to be disconnected. Whenever the battery is to be disconnected therefore, first note the following, to ensure that there are no unforeseen consequences of this action:

a) First, on any vehicle with central locking, it is a wise precaution to remove the key from the ignition, and to keep it with you, so that it does not get locked in if the central locking should engage accidentally when the battery is reconnected.

b) The engine management system's ECU will lose any fault code information stored in its memory when the battery is disconnected. if it is thought likely that the system has developed a fault for which the corresponding fault code has been logged, the code(s) must first be recorded for future fault diagnosis before the battery is disconnected. Refer to Chapter 4A for further information on the engine management system.

c) Where an audio system incorporating an anti-theft security code is fitted, if the power source to the unit is cut, the anti-theft system will activate. Even if the power source is immediately reconnected, the radio/cassette unit will not function until the correct security code has been entered. Therefore, if you do not know the correct security code for the radio/cassette unit do not disconnect the negative terminal of the battery or remove the radio/cassette unit from the car. Refer to the Owner's Manual, the audio system operating manual, or your Toyota dealer for further information on security codes.

Devices known as memory-savers (or code-savers) can be used to avoid some of the above problems. Precise details vary according to the device used. Typically, it is plugged into the cigarette lighter, and is connected by its own wires to a spare battery; the vehicle's own battery is then disconnected from the electrical system, leaving the memory-saver to pass sufficient current to maintain audio unit security codes and ECU memory values, and also to run permanently-live circuits such as the clock, all the while isolating the battery in the event of a short-circuit occurring while work is carried out.

⚠️ *Warning: Some of these devices allow a considerable amount of current to pass, which can mean that many of the vehicle's systems are still operational when the main battery is disconnected. If a memory-saver is used, ensure that the circuit concerned is actually dead before carrying out any work on it!*

2.9a Minimum electrolyte level mark on the front of the battery

2.9b Removing the cell covers . . .

2.9c . . . and topping up the electrolyte level

2 Battery - testing and charging

Standard and low maintenance battery - testing

1 If the vehicle covers a small annual mileage, it is worthwhile checking the specific gravity of the electrolyte every three months to determine the state of charge of the battery. Use a hydrometer to make the check and compare the results with the following table. Note that the specific gravity readings assume an electrolyte temperature of 15°C; for every 10°C below 15°C subtract 0.007. For every 10°C above 15°C add 0.007.

	Ambient temperature	
	above 25°C	below 25°C
Fully-charged	1.210 to 1.230	1.270 to 1.290
70% charged	1.170 to 1.190	1.230 to 1.250
Discharged	1.050 to 1.070	1.110 to 1.130

2 If the battery condition is suspect, first check the specific gravity of electrolyte in each cell. A variation of 0.040 or more between any cells indicates loss of electrolyte or deterioration of the internal plates.
3 If the specific gravity variation is 0.040 or more, the battery should be renewed. If the cell variation is satisfactory but the battery is discharged, it should be charged as described later in this Section.

Maintenance-free battery - testing

4 In cases where a sealed for life maintenance-free battery is fitted, topping-up and testing of the electrolyte in each cell is not possible. The condition of the battery can therefore only be tested using a battery condition indicator or a voltmeter.
5 Some models may be fitted with a maintenance-free battery with a built-in charge condition indicator. The indicator is located in the top of the battery casing, and indicates the condition of the battery from its colour. Consult your battery supplier for specific information concerning charge condition indicator colours acording to battery type.
6 If testing the battery using a voltmeter, connect the voltmeter across the battery and compare the result with those given in the Specifications under charge condition. The test is only accurate if the battery has not been subjected to any kind of charge for the previous six hours. If this is not the case, switch on the headlights for 30 seconds, then wait four to five minutes before testing the battery after switching off the headlights. All other electrical circuits must be switched off, so check that the doors and tailgate are fully shut when making the test.
7 If the voltage reading is less than 12.2 volts, then the battery is discharged, whilst a reading of 12.2 to 12.4 volts indicates a partially discharged condition.
8 If the battery is to be charged, remove it from the vehicle (Section 3) and charge it as described later in this Section.

Standard and low maintenance battery - charging

Note: *The following is intended as a guide only. Always refer to the manufacturer's recommendations (often printed on a label attached to the battery) before charging a battery.*
9 Before charging the battery check the level of the electrolyte which is visible through the translucent battery casing. If the level is not up to the minimum mark on the front of the battery, remove the cell covers and add distilled or de-ionised water as necessary (see illustrations).
10 Charge the battery at a rate of 3.5 to 4 amps and continue to charge the battery at this rate until no further rise in specific gravity is noted over a four hour period. Alternatively, a trickle charger charging at the rate of 1.5 amps can safely be used overnight.
11 Specially rapid boost charges which are claimed to restore the power of the battery in 1 to 2 hours are not recommended, as they can cause serious damage to the battery plates through overheating.
12 While charging the battery, note that the temperature of the electrolyte should never exceed 38°C.

Maintenance-free battery - charging

Note: *The following is intended as a guide only. Always refer to the manufacturer's recom-*
mendations *(often printed on a label attached to the battery) before charging a battery.*
13 This battery type takes considerably longer to fully recharge than the standard type, the time taken being dependent on the extent of discharge, but it can take anything up to three days.
14 A constant voltage type charger is required, to be set, when connected, to 13.9 to 14.9 volts with a charger current below 25 amps. Using this method, the battery should be usable within three hours, giving a voltage reading of 12.5 volts, but this is for a partially discharged battery and, as mentioned, full charging can take considerably longer.
15 If the battery is to be charged from a fully discharged state (condition reading less than 12.2 volts), have it recharged by your local automotive electrician, as the charge rate is higher and constant supervision during charging is necessary.

3 Battery - removal and refitting

Note: *Refer to the precautions in Section 1 before starting work.*

Removal

1 The battery is located in the left-hand front corner of the engine compartment.
2 Loosen the clampbolt, and disconnect the clamp from the battery negative terminal (see illustration). Alternatively leave the clamp on the battery terminal and unscrew the nut securing the cable to the clamp.

3.2 Disconnecting the battery negative terminal

3.3 The battery positive terminal

3.4 Battery retaining clamp and rod

3 Lift the insulation cover and disconnect the positive clamp in the same way **(see illustration)**.
4 Unscrew the nuts, and remove the battery retaining clamp from the tops of the metal rods. Unhook and remove the metal rods **(see illustration)**.
5 Lift the battery out of the engine compartment, and if necessary remove the plastic tray from the battery platform.

Refitting

6 Refitting is a reversal of removal; always reconnect the positive lead first followed by the negative lead.
7 Smear petroleum jelly on the terminals after reconnecting the leads to prevent corrosion - corroded connections are amongst the most frequent causes of electrical system faults.

---

4 Charging system - testing

Note: *Refer to the precautions in Section 1 before starting work.*

1 If the ignition warning light fails to illuminate when the ignition is switched on, first check the alternator wiring connections for security. If satisfactory, check that the warning light bulb has not blown, and that the bulbholder is secure in its location in the instrument panel. If the light still fails to illuminate, check the continuity of the warning light feed wire from the alternator to the bulbholder. If all is satisfactory, the alternator is at fault and should be renewed or taken to an auto-electrician for testing and repair.
2 If the ignition warning light illuminates when the engine is running, stop the engine and

check that the drivebelt is correctly tensioned (see Chapter 1) and that the alternator connections are secure. If all is so far satisfactory, have the alternator checked by an auto-electrician.
3 If the alternator output is suspect even though the warning light functions correctly, the regulated voltage may be checked as follows.
4 Connect a voltmeter across the battery terminals and start the engine.
5 Increase the engine speed to 1500 rpm and check that the reading is between 13 and 15 volts and no more.
6 Switch on as many electrical accessories (eg, the headlights, heated rear window and heater blower) as possible, and check that the alternator maintains the regulated voltage at around 13 to 15 volts.
7 If the regulated voltage is not as stated, the fault may be due to worn brushes, weak brush springs, a faulty voltage regulator, a faulty diode, a severed phase winding or worn or damaged slip rings. The alternator should be renewed or taken to an auto-electrician for testing and repair.

---

5 Alternator - removal and refitting

Removal

1 Disconnect the battery negative (earth) lead (refer to Sections 1 and 3).
2 Loosen the auxiliary drivebelt tension with reference to Chapter 1, and disengage it from the alternator pulley **(see illustration)**.
3 Note the location of the wiring on the rear of the alternator, then disconnect it.
4 Unscrew and remove the alternator lower mounting bolt from the adjustment link bracket **(see illustration)**.
5 Unscrew and remove the upper mounting bolt, then withdraw the alternator from the engine compartment **(see illustrations)**.

Refitting

6 Refitting is a reversal of removal, tensioning the auxiliary drivebelt as described in Chapter 1, and ensuring that the alternator mounting and adjustment bolts are securely tightened.

5.2 Disconnecting the auxiliary drivebelt from the alternator

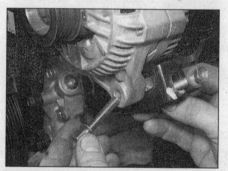

5.4 Remove the lower mounting bolt . . .

5.5a . . . upper mounting bolt . . .

5.5b . . . and withdraw the alternator (4A-FE and 7A-FE engine)

5.5c Alternator upper mounting bolt (3S-FE engine)

6.2 Unscrew the nut from the main terminal . . .

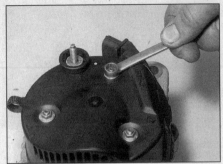

6.3a . . . unscrew the cover nuts . . .

6.3b . . . remove the plastic cover . . .

6 Alternator - brush holder/regulator renewal

Note: *The following paragraphs describe the brush holder/regulator removal on a Bosch alternator, however the procedure is similar for a Nippondenso alternator.*

1 Remove the alternator as described in Section 5.

2 Unscrew the nut from the main terminal **(see illustration)**.

3 Unscrew the nuts, then carefully lift the plastic cover from the alternator **(see illustrations)**. On some alternator types it is necessary to remove an additional bolt.

4 Using a crosshead screwdriver, remove the mounting screws from the brush holder/ regulator **(see illustrations)**.

5 Carefully withdraw the brush holder/ regulator taking care not to damage or break the carbon brushes **(see illustration)**.

6 Using a steel rule check the length of the brushes. If less than the minimum amount given in Specifications, the complete brush holder assembly should be renewed. **Note:** *It may be possible to obtain the brushes separately, in which case the brush leads should be unsoldered from the terminals and* the new brush leads carefully soldered onto the terminals.

7 Check the slip rings for excessive wear and clean them with a rag and suitable solvent.

8 Fit the new holder using a reversal of the removal procedure but make sure that each brush moves freely first.

7 Starting system - testing

Note: *Refer to the precautions in Section 1 before starting work.*

1 If the starter motor fails to operate when the ignition key is turned to the appropriate position, the following possible causes may be to blame.

 a) *The battery is faulty.*
 b) *The electrical connections between the switch, solenoid, battery and starter motor are somewhere failing to pass the necessary current from the battery through the starter to earth.*
 c) *The solenoid is faulty.*
 d) *The starter motor is mechanically or electrically defective.*

2 To check the battery, switch on the headlights. If they dim after a few seconds,

6.4a . . . then unscrew the mounting screws . . .

this indicates that the battery is discharged - recharge (see Section 2) or renew the battery. If the headlights glow brightly, operate the starter motor on the ignition switch and observe the lights. If they dim, then this indicates that current is reaching the starter motor, therefore the fault must lie in the starter motor. If the lights continue to glow brightly (and no clicking sound can be heard from the starter motor solenoid), this indicates that there is a fault in the circuit or solenoid - see following paragraphs. If the starter motor turns slowly when operated, but the battery is in good condition, then this indicates that

5A

6.4b . . . remove them . . .

6.5 . . . and withdraw the brush holder/regulator (Bosch alternator)

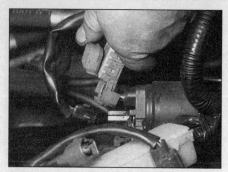

8.5a Disconnecting the main battery lead from the starter motor (4A-FE and 7A-FE engines)

8.5b Disconnecting the trigger lead from the starter motor (4A-FE and 7A-FE engines)

8.6 Lowering the starter motor from the rear of the engine (4A-FE and 7A-FE engines)

either the starter motor is faulty, or there is considerable resistance somewhere in the circuit.

3 If a fault in the circuit is suspected, disconnect the battery leads (including the earth connection to the body), the starter/solenoid wiring and the engine/transmission earth strap. Thoroughly clean the connections, and reconnect the leads and wiring, then use a voltmeter or test lamp to check that full battery voltage is available at the battery positive lead connection to the solenoid, and that the earth is sound. Smear petroleum jelly around the battery terminals to prevent corrosion - corroded connections are amongst the most frequent causes of electrical system faults.

4 If the battery and all connections are in good condition, check the circuit by disconnecting the wire from the solenoid blade terminal. Connect a voltmeter or test lamp between the wire end and a good earth (such as the battery negative terminal), and check that the wire is live when the ignition switch is turned to the start position. If it is, then the circuit is sound - if not, the circuit wiring can be checked as described in Chapter 12.

5 The solenoid contacts can be checked by connecting a voltmeter or test lamp across the solenoid. When the ignition switch is turned to the start position, there should be a reading or lighted bulb, as applicable. If there is no reading or lighted bulb, the solenoid is faulty and should be renewed.

6 If the circuit and solenoid are proved sound, the fault must lie in the starter motor. In this event, it may be possible to have the starter motor overhauled by a specialist, but check on the cost of spares before proceeding, as it may prove more economical to obtain a new or exchange motor.

8 Starter motor - removal and refitting

Note: *Refer to the precautions in Section 1 before starting work.*

Removal

1 Disconnect the battery negative (earth) lead (refer to Sections 1 and 3).
2 Chock the rear wheels then jack up the front of the car and support it on axle stands (see *Jacking and Vehicle Support*).
3 For access to the upper mounting bolts on 4A-FE and 7A-FE engines, remove the air cleaner body and inlet air duct as described in Chapter 4A. On 3S-FE and 3S-GE engines remove the battery and fuse/relay box from

the left-hand side of the engine compartment.
4 Where necessary, unbolt the engine compartment splash guard.
5 Disconnect the battery lead and trigger wire from the starter solenoid terminals **(see illustrations)**.
6 Unscrew the mounting bolts and withdraw the starter motor from the engine compartment **(see illustration)**. On 4A-FE and 7A-FE engines the starter motor is best lowered from the rear of the engine, however on 3S-FE and 3S-GE engines it can be lifted from the front of the engine.

Refitting

7 Refitting is a reversal of removal but tighten the mounting bolts to the specified torque.

9 Starter motor - testing and overhaul

If the starter motor is thought to be suspect, it should be removed from the vehicle and taken to an auto-electrician for testing. Most auto-electricians will be able to supply and fit brushes at a reasonable cost. However, check on the cost of repairs before proceeding as it may prove more economical to obtain a new or exchange motor.

Chapter 5 Part B:
Ignition system

Contents

Degrees of difficulty

Easy, suitable for novice with little experience	Fairly easy, suitable for beginner with some experience	Fairly difficult, suitable for competent DIY mechanic	Difficult, suitable for experienced DIY mechanic	Very difficult, suitable for expert DIY or professional 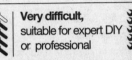

Specifications

General

Ignition system type . . . . Breakerless electronic ignition controlled by ECU
Firing order . . . . 1-3-4-2 (No 1 cylinder at timing belt end)

Ignition system data

4A-FE and 7A-FE engines with integrated (IIA) ignition system

Ignition timing (with diagnostic terminals connected - see text) . . . . . . 10° BTDC
Ignition timing (with diagnostic terminals disconnected - see text) . . . . 5° to 15° BTDC
Ignition HT coil resistances:
  Primary windings:
    Cold (below 50°C) . . . . 1.11 to 1.75 ohms
    Hot (above 50°C) . . . . 1.41 to 2.05 ohms
  Secondary windings:
    Cold (below 50°C) . . . . 9.0 to 15.7 k ohms
    Hot (above 50°C) . . . . 11.4 to 18.4 k ohms
Air gap . . . . 0.2 to 0.4 mm
Pick-up coil resistance:
  Cold:
    G+ to G– . . . . 185 to 275 ohms
    NE+ to NE– . . . . 370 to 550 ohms
  Hot:
    G+ to G– . . . . 240 to 325 ohms
    NE+ to NE– . . . . 475 to 650 ohms

4A-FE engine with Lean Burn ignition system

Ignition timing (with diagnostic terminals connected - see text) . . . . . . 10° BTDC
Ignition timing (with diagnostic terminals disconnected - see text) . . . . 14° to 24° BTDC
Ignition HT coil resistances:
  Primary windings:
    Cold (below 50°C) . . . . 0.36 to 0.55 ohms
    Hot (above 50°C) . . . . 0.45 to 0.65 ohms
  Secondary windings:
    Cold (below 50°C) . . . . 9.0 to 15.4 k ohms
    Hot (above 50°C) . . . . 11.4 to 18.1 k ohms
Air gap . . . . 0.2 to 0.5 mm
Pick-up coil resistance:
  Cold:
    G1 to G– . . . . 125 to 200 ohms
    G2 to G– . . . . 125 to 200 ohms
    NE to G– . . . . 155 to 250 ohms
  Hot:
    G1 to G– . . . . 160 to 235 ohms
    G2 to G– . . . . 160 to 235 ohms
    NE to G– . . . . 195 to 290 ohms

3S-FE engine

Ignition timing (with diagnostic terminals connected - see text)	10° BTDC
Ignition timing (with diagnostic terminals disconnected - see text)	10° to 20° BTDC
Ignition HT coil resistances:	
Primary windings:	
Cold (below 50°C)	0.36 to 0.55 ohms
Hot (above 50°C)	0.45 to 0.65 ohms
Secondary windings:	
Cold (below 50°C)	9.0 to 15.4 k ohms
Hot (above 50°C)	11.4 to 18.1 k ohms
Air gap	0.2 to 0.4 mm
Pick-up coil resistance:	
Cold:	
G+ to G−	185 to 275 ohms
NE+ to NE−	370 to 550 ohms
Hot:	
G+ to G−	240 to 325 ohms
NE+ to NE−	475 to 650 ohms

3S-GE engine

Ignition timing (with diagnostic terminals connected - see text)	10° BTDC
Ignition timing (with diagnostic terminals disconnected - see text)	9° to 21° BTDC
Ignition HT coil resistances (cold):	
Primary windings	0.40 to 0.50 ohms
Secondary windings	10.2 to 13.8 k ohms
Air gap	0.2 to 0.4 mm
Pick-up coil resistance:	
G1 to G−	140 to 180 ohms
G2 to G−	140 to 180 ohms
NE to G−	180 to 220 ohms

Torque wrench setting

	Nm	lbf ft
Distributor mounting bolts	20	15

---

1 General information and precautions

General information

The ignition system is integrated with the fuel system, to form a combined engine management system which is controlled by the electronic control unit (ECU). The ignition system arrangement differs for each type of engine, although all operate in the same way. In the Integrated Ignition Assembly (or IIA) ignition system, fitted to 4A-FE and 7A-FE engines, the distributor contains two rotors and pick-up coils, an ignition coil, a condensor, and an igniter. In the Lean Burn ignition system, fitted to the 4A-FE Lean Burn engine, the ignition coil and igniter are mounted remotely, and the distributor contains two rotors and pick-up coils. In the ignition system fitted to the 3S-FE engine, the distributor contains two rotors and pick-up coils and an ignition coil, however the igniter is located remotely in the engine compartment. In the ignition system fitted to the 3S-GE engine, the ignition coil and igniter are mounted remotely, and the distributor contains two rotors and pick-up coils. In all the systems, each component is connected to the ECU. The NE pick-up coil detects crankshaft angle, and the G pick-up coil detects camshaft angle.

The engine management ECU is programmed to provide the correct ignition timing under all engine operating conditions. Sensors on the engine monitor speed, temperature, inlet air volume and load, and from this information the ECU sends a signal to the igniter at the appropriate time. The igniter controls the ignition coil primary circuit by switching it on and off. This causes a high voltage to be induced in the coil secondary (HT) windings, which is then transferred through the distributor cap to the rotor arm and onto the relevant spark plug.

Precautions

Refer to the precautions given in Chapter 5A, Section 1, and the following:

a) *Do not keep the ignition switch on for more than 10 minutes with the engine stopped.*

b) *If a separate tachometer is ever required for servicing work, consult a dealer service department before buying a tachometer for use with this vehicle - some tachometers may be incompatible with these types of ignition systems - and always connect it in accordance with the equipment manufacturer's instructions.*

c) *Never connect the ignition coil terminals to earth. This could result in damage to the coil and/or the ECU.*

d) *Do not disconnect the battery when the engine is running.*

e) *Refer to the warning at the beginning of the next Section concerning HT voltage.*

2 Ignition system - testing

Warning: Voltages produced by an electronic ignition system are considerably higher than those produced by conventional ignition systems. Extreme care must be taken when working on the system with the ignition switched on. Persons with surgically-implanted cardiac pacemaker devices should keep well clear of the ignition circuits, components and test equipment.
Note: *Refer to the precautions given in Section 1 of Part A of this Chapter before starting work. Always switch off the ignition before disconnecting or connecting any component and when using a multi-meter to check resistances.*

1 If a fault appears in the ignition system (eg misfiring), first ensure that the fault is not due to a poor electrical connection or poor maintenance; check that the air cleaner filter element is clean, that the spark plugs are in good condition and correctly gapped, and that the engine breather hoses are clear and undamaged, referring to Chapter 1 for further information. If the engine is running very

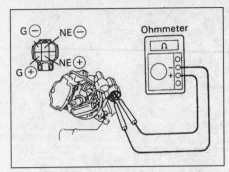

4.6a Pick-up coil resistance check (4A-FE and 7A-FE engines with IIA ignition system)

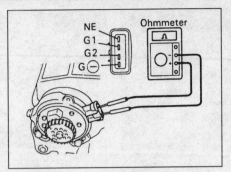

4.6b Pick-up coil resistance check (4A-FE engine with Lean Burn ignition system)

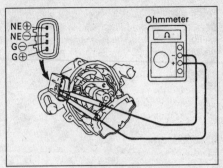

4.6c Pick-up coil resistance check (3S-FE engine)

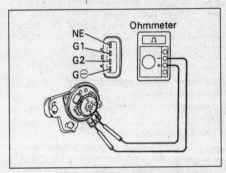

4.6d Pick-up coil resistance check (3S-GE engine)

roughly, check the compression pressures and the valve clearances, as described in Chapter 2A and Chapter 1.

2 Refer to Chapter 4A and carry out a self-diagnosis check on the engine management system - individual component fault codes will show up if there are faults in these circuits. For more information refer also to the removal and refitting procedures for these components in Chapter 4A.

3 Check the ignition coil with reference to Section 3 of this Chapter.

4 Check the distributor cap with reference to Chapter 1.

5 If these checks fail to reveal the cause of the problem, the vehicle should be taken to a Toyota dealer for testing. A wiring block connector is incorporated in the engine management circuit (left-hand rear corner of the engine compartment) into which a special electronic diagnostic tester can be plugged. The tester will locate the fault quickly and simply, alleviating the need to test all the system components individually which is a time consuming operation that carries a high risk of damaging the ECU.

6 If necessary, the system wiring and wiring connectors can be checked with reference to Chapter 12 ensuring that the ECU wiring connectors have first been disconnected.

3 Ignition HT coil - testing

Ignition system with coil in distributor

1 With the ignition switched off, disconnect the wiring connector from the side of the distributor.

2 Unscrew the retaining screws and carefully remove the cap from the end of the distributor. Recover the O-ring seal.

3 Slide the rotor from the driveshaft, then remove the dust cover.

4 Connect an ohmmeter between the low tension terminals and check that the resistance is as given in the Specifications.

5 Connect the ohmmeter between the positive low tension terminal and the high tension

terminal on top of the coil and check that the resistance is as given in the Specifications.

6 If the resistances are not as specified, renew the ignition coil as described in Section 5.

7 Refit the dust cover, rotor, and cap, and reconnect the wiring.

Ignition system with remote-mounted coil

8 With the ignition switched off, disconnect the low tension wiring from the ignition coil mounted on the bulkhead.

9 Disconnect the HT lead from the coil.

10 Connect an ohmmeter between the low tension terminals and check that the resistance is as given in the Specifications.

11 Connect the ohmmeter between the positive low tension terminal and the high tension terminal on the coil and check that the resistance is as given in the Specifications.

12 If the resistances are not as specified, renew the ignition coil.

13 Reconnect the wiring.

4 Distributor air gap and pick-up coils - testing

Air gap

1 With the ignition switched off, disconnect the wiring connector from the side of the distributor.

2 Unscrew the retaining screws and carefully remove the cap from the end of the distributor. Recover the O-ring seal.

3 Remove the rotor from the driveshaft, then remove the dust cover. On the IIA ignition system the rotor is simply withdrawn from the driveshaft, however on all other systems it is necessary to unscrew the retaining screws.

4 Using a feeler blade (preferably anti-magnetic), measure the gap between the pick-up coil projection and the rotor.

5 If the gap is not as given in the Specifications, it will be necessary to renew the distributor.

Pick-up coils

6 The pick-up coil resistances may be checked by disconnecting the wiring from the

distributor, then connecting an ohmmeter to the terminals. Check that the resistances are as given in the Specifications **(see illustration)**. If not it will be necessary to renew the distributor as the coils are not available separately.

5 Distributor - removal, overhaul and refitting

Removal

1 With the ignition switched off, disconnect the wiring from the distributor body **(see illustration)**.

2 Where the ignition coil is remotely located on the bulkhead, disconnect the HT lead from the coil **(see illustration)**.

5.1 Disconnecting the wiring from the distributor body

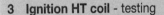

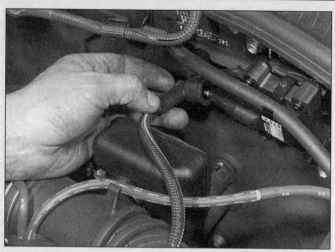

5.2 Disconnecting the HT lead from the remotely mounted ignition coil

5.3 Marking the position of the distributor by painting a mark before removing it

3 Using a dab of paint or a scriber, mark the position of the distributor in relation to the cylinder head. This is necessary in order to retain the approximate ignition timing position **(see illustration)**.

4 Unscrew the mounting bolts, then remove the distributor from the left-hand end of the cylinder head **(see illustration)**. Be prepared for some loss of oil as the distributor is being withdrawn, and have some cloth rags ready to mop it up.

5 Remove the O-ring from the groove at the bottom of the distributor **(see illustration)**.

Overhaul

6 Unscrew the retaining screws and carefully remove the cap from the distributor. Recover the O-ring seal. If necessary the HT leads may be removed from the cap by prising out the special retainers and pulling out the leads.

IIA ignition system

7 Slide the rotor from the driveshaft, then remove the dust cover.

8 Unscrew the nuts and disconnect the wires from the ignition coil terminals, then unscrew the bolts and remove the ignition coil.

9 Unscrew the bolts and disconnect the wires from the igniter, then unscrew the bolts and remove the igniter.

10 If necessary remove the wire and grommet by removing the retaining screw.

11 Unscrew the single screw and remove the condensor.

12 Check the driveshaft for wear by turning it by hand. If it feels rough or worn, or there is excessive sideplay, renew the distributor; parts are not available separately.

13 Reassemble the distributor in reverse order, however, before refitting the ignition coil, clean away the old sealant and apply a little new sealant (consult a Toyota dealer).

Except IIA ignition system

14 Remove the two screws and slide the rotor arm from the top of the driveshaft **(see illustration)**.

15 Check the driveshaft for wear by turning it by hand. If it feels rough or worn, or there is excessive sideplay, renew the distributor; parts are not available separately.

16 Reassemble the distributor in reverse order, however, locate the rotor arm on the rotor making sure that the location tab is correctly aligned. Insert and tighten the two screws.

Refitting

17 Clean the contact faces of the distributor and cylinder head, then apply a little engine oil to the O-ring and fit it to the groove in the distributor body.

18 Align the drive dog on the distributor with the cut-out in the end of the camshaft then insert the distributor. Note that the distributor can only be fitted in one position.

19 Turn the distributor to align the marks made previously, then tighten the mounting bolts. If a new distributor is being fitted, position it centrally between the flange cut-

5.4 Unscrew the mounting bolts and remove the distributor from the cylinder head

5.5 Removing the O-ring from the bottom of the distributor

5.14 Rotor arm retaining screw locations (lean burn ignition)

5.19a Refit the O-ring . . .

outs as a temporary measure so that the engine can be started. Refit the O-ring seal and the distributor cap (see illustrations).

20 Check and, if necessary, adjust the ignition timing as described in Section 6.

6 Ignition timing - checking and adjustment

1 To check the ignition timing, a stroboscopic timing light will be required, preferably the type which clips over the No 1 HT lead. If this type is not available, an adapter must be fitted between No 1 HT lead and the terminal in the distributor cap so that the timing light trigger wire can be connected to it. Due to the depth of the spark plugs in the cylinder head, it is not feasible to connect an adapter to the spark plugs.

2 The timing marks are in the form of a notch in the crankshaft pulley and marks on the lower timing belt cover (see illustration). The marks are at 5° intervals before top dead centre (BTDC) with the 10° and 0° marked

clearly. The 0° indicates top dead centre (TDC).

3 Start the engine and warm it up to normal operating temperature, then check the idle speed as described in Chapter 1. Switch off the engine.

4 Open the diagnostic socket cover on the left-hand rear corner of the engine compartment, and connect a bridging wire or similar connector between terminals TE1 and E1. The terminal positions are marked on the inside of the cover (see illustrations).

5 Connect the timing light to No 1 cylinder plug lead (nearest the timing belt end) as described in the timing light manufacturer's instructions.

6 Start the engine, allowing it to idle, and point the timing light at the crankshaft pulley. The notch on the pulley should be aligned with the specified mark on the lower timing belt cover.

7 If adjustment is necessary, slacken the two distributor mounting bolts, then slowly rotate the distributor body as required until the crankshaft pulley marks are correctly positioned. Tighten the bolts.

5.19b . . . and the distributor cap

> ⚠ **Warning:** Avoid touching the HT leads, and keep loose clothing, long hair, etc, well away from the moving parts of the engine.

8 Remove the bridging wire from the diagnostic socket, then repeat the procedure given in paragraph 6 and check that the timing falls within the tolerance range given in the Specifications.

9 Switch off the engine and disconnect the timing light from the engine.

5B

6.2 Ignition timing marks on the crankshaft pulley and timing belt cover (4A-FE and 7A-FE engines)

6.4a Bridging the TE1 and E1 terminals of the diagnostic socket

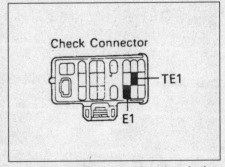

6.4b TE1 and E1 terminal locations in the diagnostic socket

Chapter 6
Clutch

Contents

Degrees of difficulty

| Easy, suitable for novice with little experience | | Fairly easy, suitable for beginner with some experience | | Fairly difficult, suitable for competent DIY mechanic | | Difficult, suitable for experienced DIY mechanic | | Very difficult, suitable for expert DIY or professional | |

Specifications

General

Type	Diaphragm spring, single dry plate, hydraulic operation
Minimum clutch disc rivet head depth	0.3 mm
Clutch pedal height (from pedal pad to asphalt sheet):	
Right-hand drive models	152.0 to 162.0 mm
Left-hand drive models	161.1 to 171.1 mm
Master cylinder pushrod play	1.0 to 5.0 mm
Clutch pedal free play	5.0 to 15.0 mm

Torque wrench settings

	Nm	lbf ft
Clutch cover-to-flywheel bolts	19	14
Master cylinder-to-bulkhead	8	6
Slave cylinder-to-transmission	12	9
Release lever pivot stud	39	29
Hydraulic pipe union nuts	15	11
Slave cylinder bleed screw	8	6

1 General information

All manual transmission models are equipped with an hydraulically-operated single dry plate diaphragm spring clutch assembly. The unit consists of a clutch disc (or driven plate), a steel cover (doweled and bolted to the rear face of the flywheel, it contains the pressure plate and diaphragm spring) and a release mechanism.

The clutch disc is free to slide along the splines of the transmission input shaft, and is held in position, between the flywheel and the pressure plate, by the pressure exerted on the pressure plate by the diaphragm spring. Friction lining material is riveted to the clutch disc, which has a spring-cushioned hub to absorb transmission shocks and help ensure a smooth take-up of the drive.

The diaphragm spring is mounted on pins, and is held in place in the cover by annular fulcrum rings.

The release bearing is located on a guide sleeve at the front of the transmission, and the bearing is free to slide on the sleeve, under the action of the release lever which pivots inside the clutch bellhousing.

The release mechanism is operated by the clutch pedal, using hydraulic pressure. The pedal acts on the hydraulic master cylinder pushrod, and a slave cylinder, mounted on the transmission bellhousing, operates the clutch release lever via a pushrod.

When the clutch pedal is depressed, the release lever pushes the release bearing forwards, to bear against the centre of the diaphragm spring, thus pushing the centre of the diaphragm spring inwards. The diaphragm spring acts against the fulcrum rings in the cover, and so as the centre of the spring is pushed in, the outside of the spring is pushed out, so allowing the pressure plate to move backwards away from the clutch disc.

When the clutch pedal is released, the diaphragm spring forces the pressure plate into contact with the friction linings on the clutch disc, and simultaneously pushes the disc forwards on its splines, forcing it against the flywheel. The clutch disc is now firmly sandwiched between the pressure plate and the flywheel, and drive is taken up.

The clutch is self-adjusting. As wear takes place on the clutch disc friction linings over a period of time, the pressure plate automatically moves closer to the clutch disc to compensate.

2.4 Removing the clutch disc

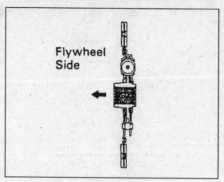

2.11 Clutch disc orientation

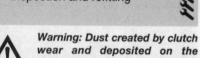

2 Clutch assembly - removal, inspection and refitting

⚠️ **Warning: Dust created by clutch wear and deposited on the clutch components may contain asbestos, which is a health hazard. DO NOT blow it out with compressed air, or inhale any of it. DO NOT use petrol (or petroleum-based solvents) to clean off the dust. Brake system cleaner or methylated spirit should be used to flush the dust into a suitable receptacle. After the clutch components are wiped clean with rags, dispose of the contaminated rags and cleaner in a sealed, marked container.**

Removal

1 Remove the transmission, as described in Chapter 7A.

2 If the original clutch is to be refitted, make alignment marks between the clutch cover and the flywheel, so that the clutch can be refitted in its original position.

3 Unscrew and remove the clutch cover retaining bolts, working in a diagonal sequence and slackening the bolts only a few turns at a time. If necessary, the flywheel may be held stationary using a wide-bladed screwdriver, inserted in the teeth of the starter ring gear and resting against a suitable bolt or part of the cylinder block **(see illustration 2.16)**.

4 Ease the clutch cover off its locating dowels. Be prepared to catch the clutch disc, which will drop out as the cover is removed **(see illustration)**. Note which way round the disc is fitted.

Inspection

5 With the clutch assembly removed, clean off all traces of dust using a dry cloth. Although most clutch discs now have asbestos-free linings, some do not, and it is wise to take suitable precautions; *asbestos dust is harmful, and must not be inhaled.*

6 Examine the friction linings of the clutch disc for wear and loose rivets, and the disc for distortion, cracks, broken cushioning springs and worn splines. The surface of the friction linings may be highly glazed, but, as long as

the friction material pattern can be clearly seen, this is satisfactory. If there is any sign of oil contamination, indicated by a continuous, or patchy, shiny black discolouration, the disc must be renewed. The source of the contamination must be traced and rectified before fitting new clutch components; typically, a leaking crankshaft rear oil seal or transmission input shaft oil seal - or both - will be to blame (renewal procedures are given Chapter 2A and Chapter 7A respectively). The disc must also be renewed if the lining thickness has worn down to, or just above, the level of the rivet heads. Check that the rivet head depth is greater than the minimum figure given in the Specifications.

7 Check the machined faces of the flywheel and pressure plate. If either is grooved, or heavily scored, renewal is necessary. The pressure plate must also be renewed if any cracks are apparent, or if the diaphragm spring is damaged or its pressure suspect.

8 With the clutch removed, it is advisable to check the condition of the release bearing, as described in Section 3.

Refitting

9 If new clutch components are to be fitted, where applicable, ensure that all anti-corrosion preservative is cleaned from the contact surfaces of the pressure plate.

10 It is important to ensure that no oil or grease gets onto the clutch disc linings, or the pressure plate and flywheel faces. It is advisable to refit the clutch assembly with

clean hands, and to wipe down the pressure plate and flywheel faces with a **clean, dry** rag before assembly begins.

11 Begin reassembly by placing the clutch disc against the flywheel, the two sides of the disc may be marked *Engine side* and/or *Transmission side*. If no identification markings are visible, the greater projecting side of the cushioning springs (not the splined hub) on clutch disc must face away from the flywheel **(see illustration)**. Hold the clutch disc against the flywheel while the cover assembly is offered into position. If a clutch-aligning tool is available (see paragraph 15) this can be used to hold the disc in place as the cover is fitted.

12 Fit the clutch cover assembly, where applicable aligning the marks on the flywheel and cover **(see illustration)**. Ensure that the clutch cover locates over the dowels on the flywheel. Insert the securing bolts and tighten them finger-tight, so that the clutch disc is gripped, but can still be moved.

13 The clutch disc must now be centralised, so that when the engine and transmission are mated, the transmission input shaft splines will pass through the splines in the clutch disc hub.

14 Centralisation can be carried out by inserting a round bar or a long screwdriver through the hole in the centre of the clutch disc, so that the end of the bar rests in the hole in the end of the crankshaft. Moving the bar sideways or up and down as necessary, move the clutch disc in whichever direction is necessary to achieve centralisation. With the bar removed, view the clutch disc hub in relation to the hole in the centre of the crankshaft and the circle created by the ends of the diaphragm spring fingers. When the hub appears exactly in the centre, all is correct.

15 An alternative and more accurate method of centralisation is to use a commercially-available clutch-aligning tool, obtainable from most accessory shops.

16 Once the clutch is centralised, progressively tighten the cover bolts in a diagonal sequence to the torque setting given in the Specifications **(see illustration)**. Remove the alignment tool.

2.12 Fitting the clutch cover assembly. Note the clutch-aligning tool being used to hold the clutch disc in position

2.16 Tighten the clutch cover retaining bolts, while holding the flywheel stationary with a screwdriver

3.4 Release lever pivot stud (arrowed) in the transmission bellhousing

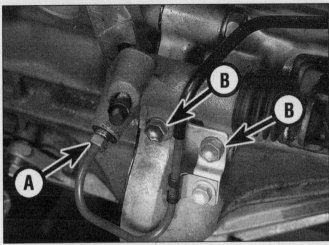

4.6 Clutch slave cylinder fluid pipe union (A) and mounting bolts (B)

17 Ensure that the input shaft splines, clutch disc splines and release bearing guide sleeve are clean. Apply a thin smear of molybdenum disulphide grease to the input shaft splines and the release bearing guide sleeve. Only use a very small amount of grease, otherwise the excess will inevitably find its way onto the friction linings when the vehicle is in use.
18 Refit the transmission (see Chapter 7A).

3 Clutch release bearing and lever - removal, inspection and refitting

Note: *Refer to the warning at the beginning of Section 2 before proceeding.*

Removal

1 Remove the transmission, as described in Chapter 7A.
2 Release the spring clip securing the release lever to the pivot stud, then withdraw the release lever, complete with the bearing, from the guide sleeve in the transmission bellhousing. Recover the rubber dust cover if it is loose.
3 Slide the release bearing from the lever, releasing the spring clip if fitted.
4 If desired, the release lever pivot stud can be unscrewed from the bellhousing **(see illustration)**.

Inspection

5 Spin the release bearing, and check it for excessive roughness. Hold the outer race, and attempt to move it laterally against the inner race. If any excessive movement or roughness is evident, renew the bearing.

 If a new clutch has been fitted, it is wise to renew the release bearing as a matter of course.

Refitting

6 Where applicable, screw the pivot stud into position in the bellhousing and tighten to the specified torque.
7 Lightly lubricate the release bearing and slave cylinder pushrod contact surfaces on the release lever, the release bearing guide sleeve, the transmission input shaft splines, and the release lever pivot stud with molybdenum disulphide grease.
8 Locate the release bearing into position in the lever and, where applicable, secure with the spring clip. Slide the assembly over the guide sleeve.
9 Secure the fork to the pivot stud with the spring clip. Refit the rubber dust cover, where applicable.
10 Refit the transmission as described in Chapter 7A.

4 Clutch slave cylinder - removal, overhaul and refitting

⚠️ **Warning:** *Hydraulic fluid is poisonous; wash off immediately and thoroughly in the case of skin contact, and seek immediate medical advice if any fluid is swallowed or gets into the eyes. Certain types of hydraulic fluid are inflammable, and may ignite when allowed into contact with hot components; when servicing any hydraulic system, it is safest to assume that the fluid is inflammable, and to take precautions against the risk of fire as though it is petrol that is being handled. Hydraulic fluid is also an effective paint stripper, and will attack plastics; if any is spilt, it should be washed off immediately, using copious quantities of fresh water. Finally, it is hygroscopic (it absorbs moisture from the air) - old fluid may be contaminated and unfit for further use.*

When topping-up or renewing the fluid, always use the recommended type, and ensure that it comes from a freshly-opened sealed container.

Removal

1 Chock the rear wheels then jack up the front of the car and support it on axle stands (see *Jacking and Vehicle Support*).
2 The slave cylinder is located on the top of the transmission bellhousing at the front.
3 On models with the 3S-GE engine, unscrew the two securing bolts, and remove the slave cylinder heat shield.
4 Where applicable, unscrew the bolt securing the hydraulic fluid pipe bracket to the cylinder or transmission.
5 Place a suitable container beneath the slave cylinder to catch escaping hydraulic fluid.
6 Unscrew the fluid pipe union, and disconnect the fluid pipe from the slave cylinder **(see illustration)**. Once the fluid had drained, plug the open ends of the pipe and slave cylinder to prevent dirt ingress.
7 Unscrew the two bolts securing the slave cylinder to the transmission bellhousing, then withdraw the cylinder, complete with the pushrod, and the pipe bracket, where applicable.

Overhaul

Note: *Before attempting to overhaul the assembly, check on the price and availability of spare parts, and the price of a new unit, as overhaul may not be viable on economic grounds alone.*

8 Remove the pushrod and rubber boot, then unscrew the bleed screw from the cylinder body **(see illustration)**.
9 Apply compressed air (from a foot pump or bicycle tyre pump) to the bleed screw hole, to force the piston from the cylinder. The piston will be ejected with the spring.
10 Wash all the parts in clean hydraulic fluid, then lay them out for inspection.

6

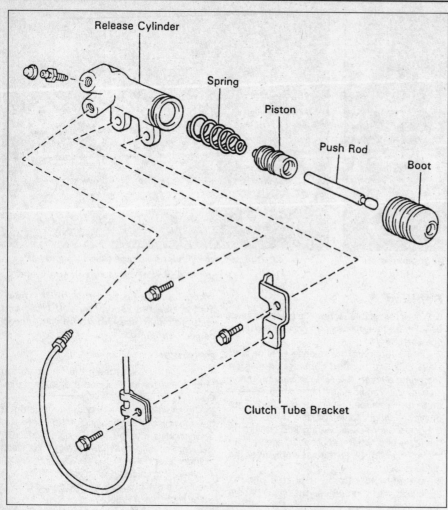

Release Cylinder

Spring

Piston

Push Rod

Boot

Clutch Tube Bracket

4.8 Exploded view of the clutch slave cylinder

5 Clutch master cylinder - removal, overhaul and refitting

Note: *Refer to the warning at the beginning of Section 4 before proceeding.*

Removal

1 The clutch master cylinder is located on the engine compartment bulkhead, next to the brake servo/master cylinder assembly.
2 To reduce fluid loss, draw off as much fluid as possible from the clutch hydraulic fluid reservoir.

> **HAYNES HiNT**
> *An ideal way to remove fluid from the master cylinder reservoir is to use a clean syringe or an old poultry baster.*

3 On left-hand-drive models, disconnect the fluid reservoir hose connecting the reservoir to the master cylinder **(see illustration)**. If necessary, unclip the reservoir from its bracket to improve access.
4 Place a suitable container beneath the master cylinder fluid pipe union to catch escaping fluid, then unscrew the union and disconnect the fluid pipe from the cylinder.
5 Working in the driver's footwell, reach up behind the pedals, and pull the securing clip from the clutch pedal-to-master cylinder pushrod clevis pin. Slide out the clevis pin.
6 Again working in the footwell, unscrew the two nuts securing the master cylinder to the bulkhead.
7 Withdraw the master cylinder from the engine compartment.

Overhaul

Note: *Before attempting to overhaul the assembly, check on the price and availability of spare parts, and the price of a new unit, as overhaul may not be viable on economic grounds alone. New seals and a new master cylinder end cap will be required on reassembly. On right-hand-drive models, a new fluid reservoir seal and reservoir securing roll-pin will be required on reassembly.*

8 With the master cylinder removed, proceed as follows.
9 On right-hand-drive models, remove the fluid reservoir from the top of the master cylinder as follows.
a) *Using a pin-punch and hammer, drive out the roll-pin.*
b) *Slide the reservoir from the master cylinder, and recover the rubber seal. Discard the seal, a new one must be used on refitting.*
10 On left-hand-drive models, proceed as follows.
a) *Disconnect the fluid reservoir connecting hose from the master cylinder, if not already done.*

11 Examine the cylinder bore and piston carefully for signs of scoring or wear ridges. If these are apparent, renew the complete slave cylinder. If the condition of the components appears satisfactory, a repair kit containing new rubber seals should be obtained. Never re-use the old seals.
12 Remove the old seals from the piston, noting the orientation of the seal lips to aid fitting of the new seals.
13 Fit new seals to the piston, using the fingers only. To ease fitting of the seals, lubricate them with clean hydraulic fluid of the specified type (see *Lubricants and fluids*). Ensure that the sealing lip edge of the main seal is towards the spring end of the piston.
14 Lubricate the cylinder bore with clean hydraulic fluid and insert the spring, with the larger coils towards fluid union end of the cylinder.
15 Carefully insert the piston, engaging the locating lug into the centre of the spring.

16 If necessary, fit a new rubber boot to the pushrod, then insert the pushrod assembly into the cylinder. The notched end of the pushrod should face away from the piston. Ensure that the rubber boot locates in the groove in the end of the cylinder.
17 Refit the bleed screw to the cylinder body.

Refitting

18 Offer the slave cylinder into position on the transmission bellhousing, and engage the pushrod with the recess in the clutch release lever. Refit and tighten the cylinder securing bolts.
19 Reconnect the fluid pipe to the cylinder and tighten the union.
20 Where applicable, refit and tighten the bolt securing the hydraulic fluid pipe bracket to the cylinder or transmission.
21 Where applicable, refit the slave cylinder heat shield and tighten the securing bolts.
22 Bleed the clutch hydraulic system as described in Section 6.

b) Remove the securing screw, and withdraw the fluid inlet union from the master cylinder. Recover the O-ring seal.

11 Using a small screwdriver, prise up the locking tabs, and pull the end cap from the pushrod end of the master cylinder. Discard the end cap - a new one should be used on refitting. Where applicable, recover the spacer ring.

12 Withdraw the pushrod and piston assembly from the cylinder bore, followed by the piston spring.

13 Wash all components in clean hydraulic fluid, then lay them out for inspection.

14 Examine the cylinder bore and piston carefully for signs of scoring or wear ridges. If these are evident, renew the complete master cylinder. If the condition of the components is satisfactory, a new set of rubber seals must be obtained. Never re-use the old seals.

15 Remove the old seals from the piston, noting the orientation of the seal lips to aid fitting of the new seals.

16 Fit the new seals to the piston, using the fingers only. To ease fitting of the seals, lubricate them with clean hydraulic fluid of the specified type (see *Lubricants and fluids*). Ensure that the sealing lip edge of the main seal is towards the spring end of the piston.

17 Lubricate the cylinder bore and the piston with hydraulic fluid, then insert the spring into the bore.

18 Carefully insert the piston and pushrod assembly into the cylinder bore, ensuring that the threaded end of the pushrod is furthest away from the piston.

19 Fit a new end cap to the cylinder, ensuring that the locking tabs lock the cap in position.

20 On left-hand-drive models, refit the fluid reservoir as follows.

a) Examine the O-ring and renew if necessary, then refit the fluid inlet union, and tighten the securing screw.

b) Reconnect the fluid hose to the master cylinder. Note that the end of the hose with the yellow mark connects to the master cylinder, and the yellow mark should face upwards.

21 On right-hand-drive models, fit a new rubber seal to the master cylinder fluid inlet, then refit the fluid reservoir, and secure with a new roll-pin.

Refitting

22 Refitting is a reversal of removal, bearing in mind the following points.

a) Ensure that the master cylinder pushrod clevis pin and securing clip are correctly refitted.

b) On left-hand-drive models, note that when reconnecting the fluid hose to the reservoir, the white mark on the hose should face upwards.

c) On completion, bleed the clutch hydraulic system as described in Section 6.

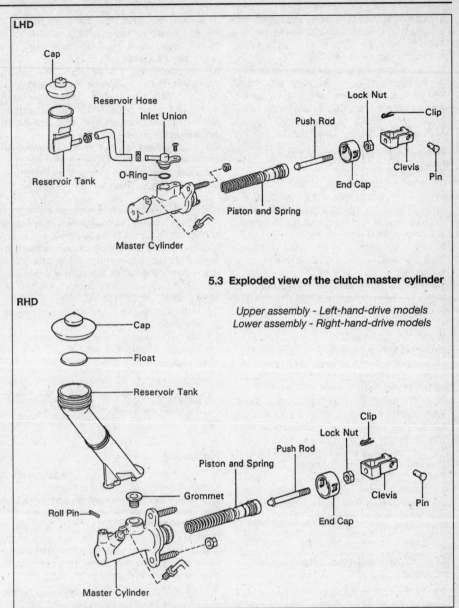

5.3 Exploded view of the clutch master cylinder

Upper assembly - Left-hand-drive models
Lower assembly - Right-hand-drive models

6 Hydraulic system - bleeding

Note: *Refer to the warning at the beginning of Section 4 before proceeding.*

1 The correct operation of any hydraulic system is only possible after removing all air from the components and circuit; this is achieved by bleeding the system.

2 During the bleeding procedure, add only clean, unused hydraulic fluid of the specified type (see *Lubricants and fluids*); never re-use fluid that has already been bled from the system. Ensure that sufficient fluid is available before starting work.

3 If there is any possibility of incorrect fluid being already in the system, the clutch hydraulic components and circuit must be flushed completely with uncontaminated, correct fluid, and new seals should be fitted to the various components.

4 If hydraulic fluid has been lost from the system, or air has entered because of a leak, ensure that the fault is cured before proceeding further.

5 Unscrew the clutch fluid reservoir cap, and top up the reservoir to the MAX level line. Refit the cap loosely, and remember to maintain the fluid level at least above the MIN level line throughout the procedure, otherwise there is a risk of further air entering the system.

6 There are a number of one-man, do-it-yourself, hydraulic bleeding kits currently available from motor accessory shops. It is recommended that one of these kits is used wherever possible, as they greatly simplify the bleeding operation, and also reduce the risk

6

of expelled air and fluid being drawn back into the system. If such a kit is not available, the basic (two-man) method must be used, which is described in detail below.

7 If a one-man kit is to be used, prepare the vehicle as described previously, and follow the kit manufacturer's instructions, as the procedure may vary slightly according to the type being used; generally, they are as outlined below in the relevant sub-section.

Bleeding - basic (two-man) method

8 Collect a clean glass jar and a suitable length of plastic or rubber tubing, which is a tight fit over the bleed screw on the slave cylinder, and a ring spanner to fit the screw. The help of an assistant will also be required.

9 Where applicable, remove the dust cap from the bleed screw and fit the bleed tube to the screw.

10 Immerse the other end of the bleed tube in the jar, which should contain enough fluid to cover the end of the tube.

11 Ensure that the reservoir fluid level is maintained at least above the MIN level line throughout the procedure.

12 Open the bleed screw approximately half a turn, and have your assistant depress the clutch pedal with a smooth steady stroke down to the floor, and then hold it there. When the flow of fluid through the tube stops, tighten the bleed screw and have your assistant release the pedal slowly.

13 Repeat this operation (paragraph 14) until clean fluid, free from air bubbles, can be seen flowing from the end of the tube.

14 When no more air bubbles appear, tighten the bleed screw, remove the bleed tube and refit the dust cap (where applicable). Check that the clutch pedal feels firm when depressed.

Bleeding - using a one-way valve kit

15 As their name implies, these kits consist of a length of tubing with a one-way valve fitted, to prevent expelled air and fluid being drawn back into the system; some kits incorporate a translucent container, which can be positioned so that the air bubbles can be more easily seen flowing from the end of the tube.

16 The kit is connected to the bleed screw, which is then opened. The user returns to the driver's seat, depresses the clutch pedal with a smooth steady stroke, and slowly releases it; this is repeated until the expelled fluid is clear of air bubbles.

17 Note that these kits simplify work so much that it is easy to forget the reservoir fluid level; ensure that this is maintained at least above the MIN level line at all times.

Bleeding - using a pressure-bleeding kit

18 These kits are usually operated by the reserve of pressurised air contained in the spare tyre. However, note that it will probably be necessary to reduce the pressure to a lower level than normal; refer to the instructions supplied with the kit.

19 By connecting a pressurised, fluid-filled container to the fluid reservoir, bleeding is then carried out by simply opening the bleed screw and allowing the fluid to run out, rather like turning on a tap, until no air bubbles can be seen in the expelled fluid.

20 This method has the advantage that the large reservoir of fluid provides an additional safeguard against air being drawn into the system during bleeding.

All methods

21 When bleeding is completed, check and top up the fluid level in the reservoir.

22 Check the feel of the clutch pedal. If it feels at all spongy, air must still be present in the system, and further bleeding is indicated. Failure to bleed satisfactorily after a reasonable repetition of the bleeding operations may be due to worn master cylinder seals.

23 Discard hydraulic fluid which has been bled from the system; it will not be fit for re-use.

7 Clutch pedal - removal, refitting and adjustment

Removal

1 Disconnect the battery negative (earth) lead (refer to Chapter 5A, Sections 1 and 3).

2 Unscrew the retaining screws and withdraw the lower trim panel located beneath the steering column. Detach the bonnet pull lever (2 screws) then disconnect the wiring from the instrument panel illumination rheostat. Remove the lower trim panel. Remove the air duct for access to the top of the pedal.

3 Detach the helper spring from the upper part of the pedal arm.

4 Disconnect the pushrod from the pedal arm by removing the clevis pin securing clip and the clevis pin.

5 Unscrew the nut from the end of the pedal pivot bolt and remove the washer. Remove the bolt then withdraw the pedal arm.

Refitting

6 Refitting is the reverse of the removal procedure, but carry out the following adjustments before refitting the facia trim panel and air duct.

Adjustment

Pedal height

7 Peel back the carpet below the pedals and measure the clutch pedal height (see illustration). Note that the measurement should be taken from the upper face of the pedal rubber to the asphalt sheet on the floorpan. If the height is not within the specified tolerance range, slacken the pedal height adjusting bolt locknut and turn the adjusting bolt until the correct height is achieved. Tighten the locknut on completion and refit the carpet.

8 Once the pedal height is correct, check the free play as follows.

Pushrod play and pedal free play

9 While gently depressing the clutch pedal with the fingers, measure the pedal travel (at the pedal pad) until the resistance increases very slightly. This measurement is the master cylinder pushrod play. Now depress the pedal further until the beginning of clutch resistance is felt. This second measurement, from the pedal at rest position to the beginning of clutch resistance is the pedal free play.

10 Compare the measurements obtained with those given in the Specifications. If adjustment is required, slacken the clevis locknut and turn the pushrod until the settings are correct. Recheck the pedal height on completion and repeat the adjustment procedures if necessary. When all is correct, tighten the clevis locknut.

11 Refit the air duct and facia trim panel, then reconnect the battery if not already done.

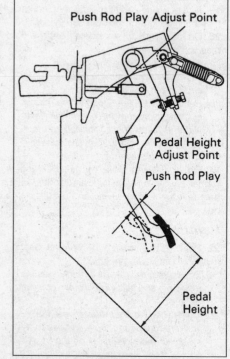

7.7 Measurement points for the clutch pedal free play

Chapter 7 Part A:
Manual transmission

Contents

Degrees of difficulty

| Easy, suitable for novice with little experience | | Fairly easy, suitable for beginner with some experience | | Fairly difficult, suitable for competent DIY mechanic | | Difficult, suitable for experienced DIY mechanic | | Very difficult, suitable for expert DIY or professional | |

Specifications

General

Type .... Five forward speeds and reverse, synchromesh on all forward gears, final drive integral with transmission

Application:
4A-FE and 7A-FE engine models C50, C52
3S-FE engine models S54, S55
3S-GE engine models S54

Torque wrench settings

	Nm	lbf ft
Oil filler/level and drain plugs:		
C50, C52 transmissions	39	29
S54, S55 transmissions	49	36
Gear lever housing base plate-to-floor	16	12
Release bearing guide sleeve bolts:		
C50, C52 transmissions	11	8
S54, S55 transmissions	7	5
Engine-to-transmission attachment bolts:		
M12	64	47
M10	46	34
Engine/transmission longitudinal crossmember bolts	35	26
Front engine/transmission mounting-to-crossmember	72	53
Rear engine/transmission mounting-to-crossmember	72	53
Engine-to-transmission reinforcing plate bolts:		
C50, C52 transmissions	23	17
S54, S55 transmissions:		
M8 bolts	21	15
M10 bolts	44	32
Nuts	44	32
Rear engine/transmission mounting bracket through bolt	87	64
Rear engine/transmission mounting bracket-to-transmission	77	57
Left-hand engine/transmission mounting bracket-to-transmission:		
Bolts	64	47
Nuts	72	53
Roadwheel nuts	103	76

7A

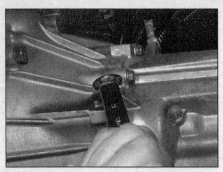

2.2 Manual transmission oil filler/level plug

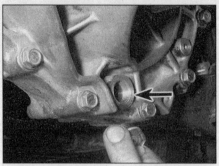

2.3 Manual transmission oil drain plug

7 Where applicable, refit the lower splash guard(s), then lower the vehicle to the ground.

3 Gearchange components - removal, refitting and adjustment

Gearchange control cables

Removal

1 Two control cables are used: the select control cable, and the shift control cable. Both cables are removed and refitted together as an assembly.

2 Disconnect the battery negative (earth) lead (refer to Chapter 5A, Sections 1 and 3).

3 Unbolt the engine compartment fuse/relay box, and move it to one side, taking care not to strain the wiring harnesses.

4 Remove the air cleaner assembly, and the air intake hose, as described in Chapter 4A.

5 Working at the transmission end of the cables, prise out the clip, and remove the washer securing each inner cable end to the gearchange levers on the transmission **(see illustration)**.

6 Extract the two outer cable retainers, securing the cables to the transmission bracket **(see illustration)**.

7 Working back along the cables toward the bulkhead, undo the retaining screws and release the cable support bracket and clips.

8 Working inside the vehicle, remove the centre console as described in Chapter 11.

9 Prise out the clip, and remove the washer securing the select control cable inner cable end to the bellcrank on the side of the gear lever housing **(see illustration 3.17)**. Extract the retainer securing the outer cable to the gear lever housing.

10 Unbolt the gear lever housing from the base plate, and lift it for access to the shift control cable inner cable end at the bottom of the gear lever. Disconnect the cable as described previously for the select control cable.

11 Chock the rear wheels then jack up the front of the car and support it on axle stands (see *Jacking and Vehicle Support*).

12 Refer to Chapter 4A and remove the exhaust system heat shield below the gear lever housing.

13 Undo the nut securing the cable grommet retainer to the front face of the gear lever housing base plate. Withdraw the cable grommet and the two cables from the base plate and remove the cable assembly from under the car.

Refitting

14 Refitting is a reversal of removal.

Gearchange lever mechanism

Removal

15 Disconnect the battery negative (earth) lead (refer to Chapter 5A, Sections 1 and 3).

1 General information

All manual transmission models are fitted with a 5-speed transmission contained in a casing bolted to the left-hand end of the engine. All the transmission types are similar, the main differences being in the gear selector mechanism, gear ratios, and the casing design to suit the different engines in the range.

Drive is transmitted from the crankshaft via the clutch to the transmission input shaft, which has a splined extension to accept the clutch disc hub. The input shaft runs parallel to the mainshaft, and the input shaft and mainshaft gears are in constant mesh. Selection of gears is by sliding synchromesh hubs, which lock the appropriate mainshaft gears to the mainshaft.

The 5th speed components are located in an extension housing at the end of the transmission.

Reverse gear is obtained by sliding an idler gear into mesh with two straight-cut gears on the input shaft and mainshaft.

All the forward gear teeth are helically cut, to reduce noise and improve wear characteristics.

The differential is mounted in the main transmission casing, and drive is transmitted to the differential by a pinion gear on the end of the mainshaft. The inboard ends of the driveshafts locate directly into the differential.

Gear selection is by a floor-mounted gearchange lever, via two control cables.

2 Manual transmission oil - draining and refilling

Draining

1 To improve access, jack up the vehicle and support on axle stands (see *Jacking and Vehicle Support*), but ensure that the vehicle is level. If necessary, remove the lower splash guard(s), with reference to Chapter 11.

2 Working at the front of the transmission, unscrew the filler/level plug from the forward facing side of the transmission casing **(see illustration)**.

3 Position a suitable container beneath the oil drain plug, located below the left-hand driveshaft constant velocity joint, then unscrew the drain plug **(see illustration)**. Try to hold the plug in as it is unscrewed the last few turns, then move it away sharply so that the oil flows into the container and not up your sleeve!

4 Once the oil has drained fully (it may be necessary to reposition the container as the flow slows down), refit the drain plug, using a new sealing washer (where applicable), and tighten it securely.

Filling

5 Fill the transmission with the specified type and quantity of oil through the filler/level hole. Add the oil slowly until it begins to trickle out of the hole.

6 Allow the oil to settle, then refit and tighten the filler/level plug.

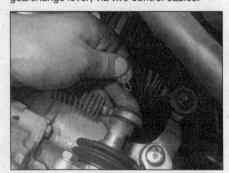

3.5 Removing the gearchange control cable retaining clip and washer at the transmission end

3.6 Extract the retainers securing the gearchange control outer cables to the bracket

16 Remove the centre console (Chapter 11).
17 Prise out the clip, and remove the washer securing the select control cable inner cable end to the bellcrank on the side of the gear lever housing **(see illustration)**. Extract the retainer securing the outer cable to the gear lever housing.

18 Unbolt the gear lever housing from the base plate, and lift it for access to the shift control cable inner cable end at the bottom of the gear lever. Disconnect the cable as described previously for the select control cable, then remove the housing from the car.
19 If necessary the housing base plate can

be removed as follows.
20 Chock the rear wheels then jack up the front of the car and support it on axle stands (see *Jacking and Vehicle Support*).
21 Refer to Chapter 4A and remove the exhaust system heat shield below the gear lever housing.

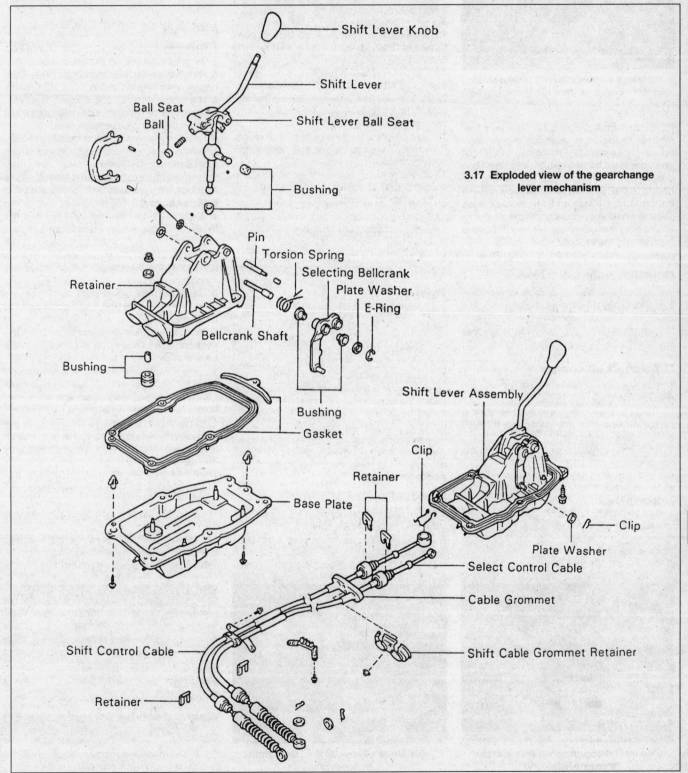

3.17 **Exploded view of the gearchange lever mechanism**

7A

4.2 Using a screwdriver to prise out the driveshaft oil seal from the transmission

22 Undo the nut securing the cable grommet retainer to the front face of the gear lever housing base plate. Withdraw the cable grommet and the two cables from the base plate.
23 Undo the bolts securing the base plate to the underbody floor and remove the base plate and gasket from under the car.
24 Inspect the gasket and renew it if there is any sign of deterioration.

Refitting

25 Refitting is a reversal of removal.

4 Oil seals - renewal

Driveshaft oil seals

1 Remove the relevant driveshaft as described in Chapter 8.
2 Using a screwdriver, carefully prise out the oil seal, taking care not to damage the seal housing **(see illustration)**.
3 Thoroughly clean the oil seal housing in the transmission.
4 Dip the new oil seal in clean transmission oil, then press it into the housing as far as possible by hand.
5 Using a tube or socket of suitable diameter, carefully tap the seal into place. Ensure that the seal is fitted square, and take care not to damage the seal lip.
6 Refit the driveshaft as described in Chapter 8.

Input shaft oil seal

7 With the transmission removed as described in Section 6, remove the clutch release lever and bearing, as described in Chapter 6.
8 Unbolt the guide sleeve from the bellhousing, then carefully prise out the seal, taking care not to scratch the seal housing.
9 Thoroughly clean the oil seal housing.
10 Wrap tape around the input shaft splines, to protect the lips of the new seal as it is installed.
11 Dip the new seal in clean transmission oil, then use a tube or socket of suitable diameter to tap the seal into position. Ensure that the seal is fitted square, and take care not to damage the seal lip.
12 Remove the tape from the input shaft, then refit the guide sleeve and tighten the securing bolts.
13 Refit the clutch release lever and bearing as described in Chapter 6, then refit the transmission as described in Section 6.

5 Reversing light switch - testing, removal and refitting

Testing

1 The reversing light circuit is controlled by a plunger-type switch located on top of the transmission casing in the engine compartment. If a fault develops in the circuit, first ensure that the circuit fuse has not blown.
2 To test the switch, disconnect the wiring connector, and use a multimeter (set to the resistance function) or a battery-and-bulb test circuit to check that there is continuity between the switch terminals only when reverse gear is selected. If this is not the case, and there are no obvious breaks or other damage to the wires, the switch is faulty, and must be renewed.

Removal

3 Disconnect the battery negative (earth) lead (refer to Chapter 5A, Sections 1 and 3).
4 Disconnect the switch wiring plug **(see illustration 6.5)**.
5 Unscrew the switch from the transmission.

Refitting

6 Refitting is a reversal of removal.

6 Manual transmission - removal and refitting

Removal

1 Disconnect the battery negative (earth) lead (refer to Chapter 5A, Sections 1 and 3).
2 Remove the battery, and unclip the battery tray as described in Chapter 5A.
3 Unbolt the engine compartment fuse/relay box, and move it to one side, taking care not to strain the wiring harnesses.
4 Remove the air cleaner assembly, and the air intake hose, as described in Chapter 4A.
5 Disconnect the wiring plug from the reversing light switch **(see illustration)**.
6 Unbolt the earth lead from the transmission **(see illustration)**.
7 Remove the clutch slave cylinder from the transmission, as described in Chapter 6, but note that there is no need to disconnect the fluid pipe. Extract the pipe support clip from the top of the transmission then move the cylinder to one side.
8 Disconnect the gearchange control cables from the transmission, as described in Section 3.
9 Disconnect the wiring connector from the speedometer sensor at the rear of the transmission.
10 Working at the top of the transmission casing, unscrew the upper engine-to-transmission mounting bolts, and the upper starter motor mounting bolt **(see illustration)**.
11 Chock the rear wheels then jack up the front of the car and support it on axle stands (see *Jacking and Vehicle Support*). Remove the front roadwheels.
12 Remove the engine lower splash guard(s), where applicable, with reference to Chapter 11.
13 Drain the transmission oil as described in Section 2.
14 Where applicable, unscrew the securing bolts and remove the engine-to-transmission reinforcing plate **(see illustration)**.

6.5 Disconnect the wiring plug from the reversing light switch

6.6 Unbolt the earth lead from the transmission

6.10 Unscrew the upper engine-to-transmission mounting bolts

6.14 Removing the engine-to-transmission reinforcing plate

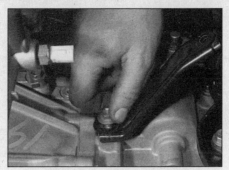

6.24 Removing the left-hand engine/transmission mounting stay

6.27 Removing the transmission from the engine

15 Where applicable, unscrew the securing bolts, and remove the clutch bellhousing cover plate.

16 Disconnect the exhaust front section from the manifold as described in Chapter 4A.

17 Remove the driveshafts as described in Chapter 8.

18 Connect a hoist and lifting tackle to the engine lifting bracket at the left-hand end of the cylinder head, and raise the hoist to just take the weight of the engine.

19 Remove the engine/transmission longitudinal crossmember as follows.

a) Unscrew the two securing bolts, and remove the shield from the crossmember.

b) Prise out the cover plugs, and unscrew the three bolts securing the front engine/transmission mounting to the crossmember.

c) Prise out the cover plug, and unscrew the bolt securing the rear engine/transmission mounting to the crossmember.

d) Where applicable, unscrew the securing bolt and release the air conditioning pipe clamp from the crossmember.

e) Unscrew the four securing bolts, and remove the crossmember.

20 Disconnect the wiring from the starter motor.

21 Unscrew the lower securing bolt, and remove the starter motor.

22 Unscrew the through-bolt securing the rear engine/transmission mounting bracket to the mounting rubber.

23 Unscrew the three bolts securing the rear engine/transmission mounting bracket to the transmission.

24 Unscrew the nut and bolt (or two bolts on some models), and remove the left-hand engine/transmission mounting stay from the top of the mounting and transmission **(see illustration)**.

25 Unscrew the nuts and bolts, and remove the left-hand engine/transmission mounting bracket from the transmission.

26 Support the transmission using a jack, and a block of wood, then unscrew the lower engine-to-transmission bolts.

27 Lower the engine and transmission, then slide the transmission from the engine, taking care not to allow the transmission to hang on the input shaft **(see illustration)**. Lower the transmission from under the vehicle. Take care - the transmission is heavy!

Refitting

28 Before attempting to refit the transmission, ensure that the clutch disc is centralised, as described in Chapter 6.

29 Further refitting is a reversal of removal, bearing in mind the following points.

a) Tighten all fixings to the specified torque, where applicable.

b) Refit the driveshafts as described in Chapter 8.

c) Reconnect the exhaust front section as described in Chapter 4A.

d) Fill the transmission with oil as described in Section 2.

---

7 Manual transmission overhaul - general information

Overhauling a manual transmission is a difficult and involved job for the DIY home mechanic. In addition to dismantling and reassembling many small parts, clearances must be precisely measured and, if necessary, changed by selecting shims and spacers. Internal transmission components are also often difficult to obtain, and, in many instances, extremely expensive. Because of this, if the transmission develops a fault or becomes noisy, the best course of action is to have the unit overhauled by a specialist repairer, or to obtain an exchange reconditioned unit. Be aware that some transmission repairs can be carried out with the transmission in the car.

Nevertheless, it is not impossible for the more experienced mechanic to overhaul the transmission, provided the special tools are available, and the job is done in a deliberate step-by-step manner, so that nothing is overlooked.

The tools necessary for an overhaul include internal and external circlip pliers, bearing pullers, a slide hammer, a set of pin punches, a dial test indicator, and possibly a hydraulic press. In addition, a large, sturdy workbench and a vice will be required.

During dismantling of the transmission, make careful notes of how each component is fitted, to make reassembly easier and more accurate.

Before dismantling the transmission, it will help if you have some idea what area is malfunctioning. Certain problems can be closely related to specific areas in the transmission, which can make component examination and replacement easier. Refer to the Fault finding Section at the end of this manual for more information.

7A

Chapter 7 Part B:
Automatic transmission

Contents

Degrees of difficulty

| **Easy,** suitable for novice with little experience | | **Fairly easy,** suitable for beginner with some experience | | **Fairly difficult,** suitable for competent DIY mechanic | | **Difficult,** suitable for experienced DIY mechanic | | **Very difficult,** suitable for expert DIY or professional | |

Specifications

General

Type	Fully electronic, four-speed with torque converter lock-up
Application:	
4A-FE engine models	A240E, A245E
3S-FE engine models	A241E

Torque converter fitted position

Distance from bellhousing face to torque converter retaining bolt lugs:

A240E, A245E transmissions	13.0 mm (minimum)
A241E transmissions	22.8 mm (minimum)

Torque wrench settings

	Nm	lbf ft
Transmission fluid drain plug	17	13
Torque converter-to-driveplate	27	20
Engine-to-transmission attachment bolts	64	47
Transmission mountings-to-transmission:		
Bolts	64	47
Nuts	72	53
Transmission mounting bracket through bolt	78	58
Engine-to-transmission reinforcing plate bolts	23	17
Roadwheel nuts	103	76

7B

1 General information

A four-speed, fully electronic, automatic transmission is available as an option on 1.6 litre (4A-FE) and 2.0 litre (3S-FE) engine models.

The transmission comprises a torque converter, an epicyclic geartrain, hydraulically-operated clutches and brakes, and an electronic control system controlled by the Toyota Computer Control System (TCCS) engine management electronic control unit (ECU).

Drive is taken from the engine to the transmission by a torque converter. This is a type of fluid-coupling between engine and transmission, which acts as a clutch, and also provides a degree of torque multiplication when accelerating. The torque converter is mechanically locked to the engine, under the control of the ECU, when the transmission is operating in certain gear positions, thus eliminating losses due to slip, and improving fuel economy.

The epicyclic geartrain provides either of the four forward or one reverse gear ratio, according to which of its component parts are held stationary or allowed to turn. The components of the geartrain are held or

released by brakes and clutches which are hydraulically activated. A fluid pump within the transmission provides the necessary hydraulic pressure to operate the brakes and clutches.

Driver control of the transmission is by a selector lever and two, two-position switches. The selector lever has a drive position, and a hold facility on 1st and 2nd gear. The drive position (D) provides automatic changing throughout the range of all forward gear ratios, and is the position selected for normal driving. An automatic kick-down facility shifts the transmission down a gear if the accelerator pedal is fully depressed. The hold facility is similar to the drive position, but limits the number of gear ratios available - ie, when the selector lever is in the 2 position, only the first two ratios can be selected; and in the L position, only the first ratio can be selected. The lower ratio hold (L) is useful when travelling down steep gradients, or for preventing unwanted selection of high gears on twisty roads. Two driving programs are provided for selection by a switch; Normal or Power. With the switch in the Normal (NORM) position, the transmission will change gear normally, at an engine speed which is biased towards fuel economy. With the switch in the Power (PWR) position, the gearchanges will take place at a higher engine speed, giving improved acceleration.

The transmission also has an overdrive switch which allows the transmission to operate as a four-speed or a three-speed transmission. When the overdrive switch is in the ON position, the transmission will use all four speeds for greater economy. With the switch in the OFF position, only the first three speeds will be selected. Note that when the engine coolant temperature is low, only the first three speeds can be selected, even if the overdrive switch is in the ON position.

Automatic control of the transmission is by the engine management ECU which receives signal inputs from the engine management sensors relating to engine and transmission operating conditions. From this data, the ECU can establish the optimum gear shifting speeds and lock-up engagement points according to transmission mode selected, and driver inputs.

In addition to control of the engine management system and transmission, the ECU incorporates a built-in fault diagnosis facility. A fault is signalled to the driver by the flashing of the O/D OFF indicator light on the instrument panel. If a fault of this nature does occur, the ECU stores a series of signals (or fault codes) for subsequent read-out during fault diagnosis.

Due to the complexity of the automatic transmission, any repair or overhaul work must be left to a Toyota dealer with the necessary special equipment for fault diagnosis and repair. The contents of the following Sections are therefore confined to supplying general information, and any service information and instructions that can be used by the owner.

2 Automatic transmission fluid – draining and refilling

Draining

1 To improve access, jack up the car and support it on axle stands (see *Jacking and Vehicle Support*), but ensure that it is level.
2 If necessary, unscrew the mounting screws and remove the splash guard(s) from the underbody.
3 Position a suitable container beneath the transmission fluid drain plug, then wipe clean the area all around the plug and unscrew it **(see illustration)**. Try to hold the plug in as it is unscrewed the last few turns, then move it away sharply so that the fluid flows into the container and not up your sleeve!
Caution: If the vehicle has just been run, the transmission fluid may be very hot.
4 Once the fluid has drained fully, refit the drain plug, using a new sealing washer (where applicable), and tighten it securely.

Filling

5 Where applicable, refit the underbody splash guards, then lower the car to the ground.
6 Open the bonnet and remove the transmission fluid dipstick from its tube.
7 Slowly fill the transmission with the specified fluid (see *Lubricants and fluids*) through the dipstick tube, using a clean funnel if necessary. Continue filling the transmission until the level reaches the upper of the two notches on the dipstick, either side of the word COLD.
8 Refit the dipstick to its tube then, with the handbrake applied and the selector lever in the P position, start the engine. While the engine is idling, depress the brake pedal and move the selector lever through all the gear positions, beginning and ending in P.
9 With the engine still idling, recheck the fluid level and add further fluid as necessary to bring the level up to the upper of the two notches on the dipstick, either side of the word COLD.
10 Final checking of the fluid level should be carried out after the car has been driven for approximately 10 miles, and with reference to the procedures contained in Chapter 1.

3 Gear selector cable – adjustment, removal and refitting

Adjustment

1 Move the gear selector lever through the full range of positions, and check that the gear position indicator correctly indicates the relevant gear position. If the indicator is not aligned with the correct position, carry out the following adjustment procedure.
2 Chock the rear wheels then jack up the front of the car and support it on axle stands (see *Jacking and Vehicle Support*). If necessary, unscrew the mounting screws and remove the splash guard(s) from the underbody.
3 Working at the gear selector lever on the transmission, loosen the nut securing the cable to the selector lever **(see illustration)**.
4 Push the transmission selector lever fully towards the right-hand side of the car.
5 Move the lever back two notches to the neutral position.
6 Move the gear selector lever inside the vehicle to the N position.
7 Hold the transmission selector lever lightly towards the R side of N, then tighten the securing nut.
8 Where applicable, refit the splash guard(s), then lower the car to the ground.

Removal

9 Chock the rear wheels then jack up the front of the car and support it on axle stands (see *Jacking and Vehicle Support*). If necessary, unscrew the mounting screws and remove the splash guard(s) from the underbody.
10 Unscrew the retaining nut and disconnect the selector cable from the transmission selector lever.
11 Extract the retaining clip and disconnect the selector outer cable from the support bracket **(see illustration)**.
12 Working backwards along the cable until it enters the passenger compartment, release it from its securing clips.
13 Remove the centre console as described in Chapter 11.

2.3 Automatic transmission fluid drain plug location on the sump pan

3.3 Gear selector cable-to-transmission selector lever retaining nut (arrowed)

3.11 Extract the retaining clip (arrowed) to disconnect the selector outer cable from the bracket

14 Remove the gear position indicator panel retaining screws, lift up the panel and disconnect the illumination bulbholder. Lift the panel up as far as the gear lever knob will allow and tie it in this position.

15 Extract the retaining clip and disconnect the cable from the lower end of the selector lever.

16 Extract the clip securing the outer cable to the selector lever base and withdraw the cable.

17 Release the cable grommet and retaining plate (where fitted) on the bulkhead, and remove the cable assembly from the engine compartment.

Refitting

18 Refitting is the reversal of removal, but adjust the cable as described previously before tightening the cable-to-transmission selector lever retaining nut.

4 Kick-down cable - general information and adjustment

General information

1 The kick-down cable (or more precisely, the throttle valve control cable) connects the throttle linkage on the engine with the valve block inside the transmission, thus regulating the opening of the valve block fluid passages according to throttle position.

2 The lower end of the cable is connected to a cam inside the transmission which actuates the valves in the valve block. To gain access to the attachment, it is necessary to remove the transmission sump pan and valve block assembly, together with other transmission internal components. As this work carries a very high risk of dirt entry and possible future transmission malfunction if not carried out under scrupulously clean conditions, removal, refitting or complete cable renewal should be entrusted to a Toyota dealer.

Adjustment

3 Ensure that the accelerator cable is correctly adjusted as described in Chapter 4A.

4 With the accelerator pedal released (throttle fully closed) check that the crimped metal stopper on the inner cable protrudes from the end of the rubber sleeve on the outer cable by between 0 and 1.0 mm **(see illustration)**.

5 If the stopper protrusion is incorrect, slacken the outer cable locknuts at the support bracket and adjust the position of the outer cable as necessary. Tighten the locknuts on completion.

5 Starter inhibitor switch - removal, refitting and adjustment

Removal

1 To improve access, apply the handbrake, then jack up the front of the car and support on axle stands (see *Jacking and Vehicle Support*).

2 If necessary, unscrew the mounting screws and remove the splash guard(s) from the underbody.

3 Working at the gear selector lever on the transmission, unscrew the nut securing the gear selector cable to the selector lever, and disconnect the cable.

4 Unscrew the securing nut, recover the washer, and remove the gear selector lever from the switch.

5 Using a screwdriver, prise back the tab on the lockwasher under the nut securing the switch to the valve shaft.

6 Unscrew the nut, and recover the lockwasher and shim(s).

7 Unscrew the two securing bolts, and withdraw the switch from the transmission.

Refitting

8 Offer the switch into position over the valve shaft, then refit the shim(s), lockwasher, and securing nut. Tighten the securing nut.

9 Temporarily refit the gear selector lever to the switch. Turn the gear selector lever clockwise to its stop, then turn it back, anti-clockwise, by three notches.

10 Remove the gear selector lever.

11 Align the groove in the valve shaft with the neutral basic line marked on the switch body, then refit and tighten the switch securing bolts **(see illustration)**.

12 Using a screwdriver, bend up the tab on the lockwasher to lock the switch-to-valve shaft nut in position.

13 Where applicable, refit the underbody splash guard(s) and lower the car to the ground.

Adjustment

14 If the engine can be started with the transmission selector lever in any position other than N or P, the starter inhibitor switch requires adjustment.

15 For improved access, apply the handbrake, then jack up the front of the car and support on axle stands (see *Jacking and Vehicle Support*). Where applicable, remove the underbody splash guard(s).

16 Loosen the two starter inhibitor switch securing bolts.

17 Set the transmission selector lever to the N position.

18 Align the groove in the valve shaft with the neutral basic line marked on the switch body, then refit and tighten the switch securing bolts **(see illustration 5.11)**.

19 Where applicable, refit the underbody splash guard(s) and lower the car to the ground.

6 Oil seals - renewal

The procedure for renewal of the driveshaft oil seals is the same as that described for the manual transmission in Part A, Section 4.

7 Automatic transmission - removal and refitting

Removal

1 Disconnect the battery negative (earth) lead (refer to Chapter 5A, Sections 1 and 3).

2 Remove the battery, and unclip the battery tray as described in Chapter 5A.

3 Unbolt the engine compartment fuse/relay box, and move it to one side, taking care not to strain the wiring harnesses.

4 Remove the air cleaner assembly, and the air intake hose, as described in Chapter 4A.

5 On models equipped with anti-lock brakes, remove the ABS hydraulic modulator as described in Chapter 9.

6 Pull out the automatic transmission fluid level dipstick.

7 Remove the bolt securing the automatic transmission fluid level dipstick, then remove the dipstick tube.

8 Turn the segment on the throttle housing to open the throttle, then disconnect the kick-down cable end **(see illustration)**. Unscrew the locknut and release the outer cable from the bracket.

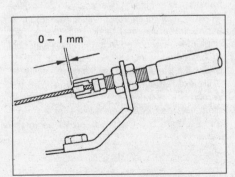

4.4 Kick-down cable adjustment

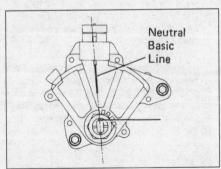

5.11 Setting the starter inhibitor switch

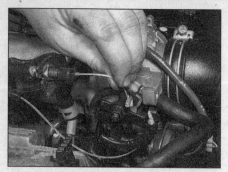

7.8 Disconnecting the kick-down cable from the throttle segment

9 Chock the rear wheels then jack up the front of the car and support it on axle stands (see *Jacking and Vehicle Support*). Remove the front roadwheels.

10 Unscrew the mounting screws and remove the splash guard(s) from the underbody.

11 Connect a suitable hoist and lifting tackle to the engine lifting brackets, and raise the hoist to just take the weight of the engine and transmission.

12 Working at the left-hand end of the transmission, unscrew the nuts and bolts securing the transmission mounting to the transmission.

13 Disconnect the transmission earth cable from the transmission.

14 Release the kick-down cable from the clamp.

15 Remove the driveshafts as described in Chapter 8.

16 Remove the exhaust front downpipe and intermediate section as described in Chapter 4A.

17 Disconnect the steering column universal joint from the steering gear pinion as described in Chapter 10.

18 Position a container beneath the power steering fluid unions on the steering gear, then disconnect the power steering fluid supply pipe and return hose from the steering gear.

Allow the fluid to drain into the container, then plug the open ends of the steering gear, pipe and hose to prevent dirt ingress and further fluid loss.

19 Unbolt the power steering pipe and hose support brackets.

20 Remove the front subframe as described in Chapter 10.

21 Disconnect the solenoid, speedometer sensor, and the starter inhibitor switch wiring plugs from the transmission.

22 Disconnect the gear selector cable from the selector lever on the transmission as described in Section 3.

23 Place a container beneath the fluid cooler hose connections at the transmission, then release the securing clips, and disconnect the hoses from the transmission.

24 Remove the starter motor as described in Chapter 5A.

25 Unscrew the securing bolts and remove the engine-to-transmission reinforcing plate.

26 Using a spanner on the crankshaft pulley bolt, turn the engine for access to each torque converter-to-driveplate bolt in turn. Unscrew the six torque converter-to-driveplate bolts.

27 Support the transmission, using a jack and block of wood.

28 Work around the transmission bellhousing, and unscrew the engine-to-transmission bolts.

29 According to model, unscrew the remaining transmission mounting bolts.

30 Carefully manipulate the transmission away from the engine, then lower the assembly, and withdraw it from under the car. As the transmission is removed, take great care not to allow the torque converter to fall out.

31 To prevent the torque converter from falling out of the transmission after removal, bolt a metal plate or bar across the end of the bellhousing.

Refitting

32 Commence refitting by removing the plate used to retain the torque converter on the transmission.

33 Check the torque converter fitted position as follows:
 a) Place a straight-edge across the end of the transmission bellhousing.
 b) Using a steel rule or calipers, measure the distance between the straight-edge and the torque converter-to-driveplate bolt lugs at the edge of the torque converter **(see illustration)**.
 c) The distance measured should be as given in the Specifications. If the distance is less than the minimum specified, it is probable that the torque converter is not fully engaged with the transmission. Try pushing the torque converter further into the bellhousing.

34 Turn the torque converter so that, when the transmission is installed, the torque converter-to-driveplate bolt holes in the torque converter align with the corresponding bolt holes in the driveplate.

35 Lift the transmission into position, and offer it up to the engine.

36 Refit the engine-to-transmission bolts, and tighten them to the specified torque.

37 Refit and tighten the transmission mounting retaining bolts.

38 Thoroughly clean the threads of the torque converter-to-driveplate bolts, then coat them with thread-locking compound.

39 Refit the torque converter-to-driveplate bolts, and tighten them evenly to the specified torque.

40 Refit the engine-to-transmission reinforcing plate.

41 Refit the front subframe (Chapter 10).

42 Further refitting is a reversal of removal, bearing in mind the following points.
 a) Tighten all fixings to the specified torque where given.
 b) Refit the starter motor with reference to Chapter 5A.
 c) Reconnect and adjuster the gear selector cable as described in Section 3.
 d) Reconnect the steering column universal joint to the steering gear pinion with reference to Chapter 10.
 e) Refit the exhaust front downpipe and intermediate section as described in Chapter 4A.
 f) Refit the driveshafts as described in Chapter 8.
 g) Reconnect the kick-down cable then adjust it as described in Section 4.
 h) On completion, top up the automatic transmission fluid level as described in Chapter 1.
 i) Refill and bleed the power steering system as described in Chapter 10.

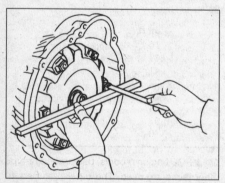

7.33 Checking the torque converter fitted position

8 Automatic transmission overhaul - general information

In the event of a fault occurring with the transmission, it is first necessary to determine whether it is of an electrical, mechanical or hydraulic nature, and to do this special test equipment is required. It is therefore essential to have the work carried out by a Toyota dealer if a transmission fault is suspected.

Do not remove the transmission from the vehicle for repair before professional fault diagnosis has been carried out, since most tests require the transmission to be in the vehicle.

Chapter 8
Driveshafts

Contents

Degrees of difficulty

Easy, suitable for novice with little experience	Fairly easy, suitable for beginner with some experience	Fairly difficult, suitable for competent DIY mechanic 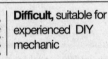	Difficult, suitable for experienced DIY mechanic 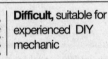	Very difficult, suitable for expert DIY or professional

Specifications

General
Type . . . . Unequal length steel with constant velocity (CV) joint at each end

Overhaul
Standard length setting dimension:
  4A-FE and 7A-FE engine models:
    Left-hand driveshaft . . . . 541.3 ± 5.0 mm
    Right-hand driveshaft . . . . 855.8 ± 5.0 mm
  3S-FE engine models:
    Left-hand driveshaft . . . . 558.2 ± 5.0 mm
    Right-hand driveshaft . . . . 844.6 ± 5.0 mm
  3S-GE engine models:
    Left-hand driveshaft . . . . 554.2 ± 5.0 mm
    Right-hand driveshaft . . . . 841.8 ± 5.0 mm
Lubricant type . . . . Special grease supplied with gaiter repair kits - joints are otherwise pre-packed with grease, and sealed
Lubricant quantity:
  All except 3S-FE engine models:
    Inner and outer CV joints . . . . 100 to 120 g
  3S-FE engine models:
    Inner CV joint . . . . 180 to 190 g
    Outer CV joint . . . . 120 to 130 g

Torque wrench settings

	Nm	lbf ft
Hub/driveshaft retaining nut	226	167
Driveshaft intermediate bearing housing-to-bracket bolts	64	47
Track rod end balljoint-to-hub carrier	56	41
Anti-roll bar drop link-to-suspension strut	44	32
Suspension lower balljoint-to-lower arm (all except 3S-GE engine models)	127	94
Suspension lower balljoint-to-hub carrier (3S-GE engine models)	91	67
Roadwheel nuts	103	76

8

1 General information

Drive is transmitted from the differential to the front wheels by means of two unequal length steel driveshafts incorporating constant velocity (CV) joints at each end.

On all models, the driveshafts are fitted with ball-and-cage-type constant velocity joints at their outer ends. These outer joints cannot be dismantled. Each joint has an outer member, which is splined at its outer end to accept the wheel hub, and is threaded so that the hub can be fastened by a large nut.

On all except 3S-GE engine models, tripod-type inner constant velocity joints are used.

On 3S-GE engine models, ball-and-cage-type inner joints are used. The outer members of the inner joints are splined, and engage directly with the differential sunwheels.

On 3S-FE and 3S-GE engine models, the inner section of the right-hand driveshaft is supported by an intermediate bearing located in a bracket bolted to the engine.

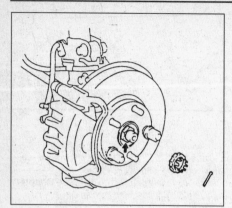

2.2 Extract the hub/driveshaft retaining nut split pin and remove the locking cap over the nut (arrowed)

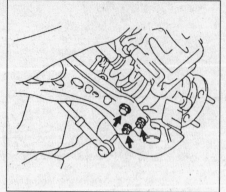

2.8a On all except 3S-GE engine models, unscrew the bolt and two nuts (arrowed), and disconnect the suspension lower balljoint from the lower arm

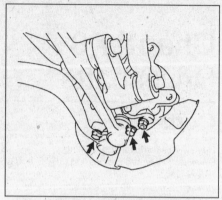

2.8b On 3S-GE engine models, unscrew the nut and two bolts (arrowed), and disconnect the suspension lower balljoint from the hub carrier

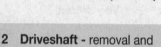

2 Driveshaft - removal and refitting

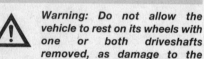

Warning: Do not allow the vehicle to rest on its wheels with one or both driveshafts removed, as damage to the wheel bearing(s) may result. If moving the vehicle is unavoidable, temporarily insert the outer ends of the driveshaft(s) in the hub(s) and tighten the hub nut(s). In this case the inner end(s) of the driveshaft(s) must be supported, for example by suspending with string from the vehicle underbody.

All except right-hand driveshaft on 3S-FE and 3S-GE engine models

Removal

1 Chock the rear wheels then jack up the front of the car and support it on axle stands (see *Jacking and Vehicle Support*). Remove the relevant front roadwheel.
2 Extract the hub/driveshaft retaining nut split pin and remove the locking cap over the nut **(see illustration)**.
3 Have an assistant firmly depress the brake pedal to prevent the front hub from rotating.

Using a socket and a long extension bar, slacken and remove the hub/driveshaft retaining nut. Alternatively, a tool can be fabricated from two lengths of steel strip (one long, one short) and a nut and bolt; the nut and bolt forming the pivot of a forked tool. Bolt the tool to the hub using two wheel nuts, and hold the tool to prevent the hub from rotating as the hub/driveshaft retaining nut is undone. This nut is very tight; make sure that there is no risk of pulling the car off the axle stands.
4 Where applicable, remove the lower splash guard(s) to improve access.
5 Drain the transmission oil/fluid as described in Chapter 7A or B as applicable.
6 Extract the split pin from the track rod end balljoint, and unscrew the balljoint nut as far as the end of the balljoint shank threads. Using a balljoint separator tool, release the track rod end balljoint tapered shank. Once the taper has separated, unscrew the nut and detach the track rod end from the hub carrier.
7 On models with an anti-roll bar drop link attached to the suspension strut, unscrew the securing nut, and disconnect the drop link from the strut. Note that it may be necessary to counterhold the drop link pin using an Allen key or bit.
8 On all except 3S-GE engine models, unscrew the bolt and two nuts, and

disconnect the suspension lower balljoint from the lower arm **(see illustration)**. On 3S-GE engine models, unscrew the nut and two bolts, and disconnect the suspension lower balljoint from the hub carrier **(see illustration)**.
9 Hold the hub carrier, and release the driveshaft outer CV joint from the hub bearings by tapping it towards the transmission with a soft-faced mallet.
10 Using a metal lever, prise the driveshaft inner CV joint from the transmission. Locate the lever on the lug provided on the side of the joint.
11 Once the inner CV joint has been released from the transmission, withdraw the outer joint from the hub carrier and remove the driveshaft from under the vehicle **(see illustration)**.
12 Remove the snap-ring from the splined end of the inner CV joint **(see illustration)**. *This snap-ring must be renewed each time the driveshaft is withdrawn from the transmission. The hub/driveshaft retaining nut split pin and the track rod end balljoint nut split pin must also be renewed when refitting the driveshaft.*

Refitting

13 Before installing the driveshaft, examine the driveshaft oil seal in the transmission for signs of damage or deterioration and, if necessary, renew it, referring to the appropriate Part of Chapter 7 for further information. (Having got this far it is worth renewing the seal as a matter of course.)
14 Thoroughly clean the driveshaft splines, and the apertures in the transmission and hub assembly. Apply a thin film of grease to the oil seal lips, and to the driveshaft splines and shoulders. Check that all gaiter clips are securely fastened.
15 Fit a new snap-ring to the splined end of the inner CV joint.
16 With the opening in the snap-ring facing downwards, offer the inner end of the driveshaft up to the opening in the transmission then, using a soft metal drift, and a hammer, tap the CV joint into position until the snap-ring engages with the differential.

2.11 Removing the driveshaft outer CV joint from the hub carrier

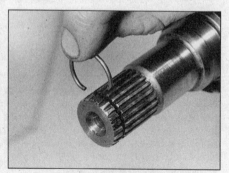

2.12 Remove the snap-ring from the splined end of the inner CV joint

2.22a Refit the hub/driveshaft nut locking cap . . .

2.22b . . . then fit a new split pin and bend over the legs to secure

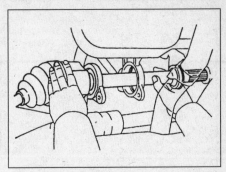

2.29 Removing the right-hand driveshaft on 3S-FE and 3S-GE engine models

17 Check that the inner CV joint is fully engaged with the differential by pulling on the joint. There should be 2 to 3 mm of movement, but it should not be possible to pull the joint out by hand.

18 Engage the driveshaft outer CV joint with the hub carrier, then reconnect the suspension lower balljoint to the lower arm or hub carrier. Secure with the nut(s) and bolt(s), tightened to the specified torque.

19 Reconnect the anti-roll bar drop link to the suspension strut, then tighten the securing nut to the specified torque, counterholding the drop link pin as during removal if necessary.

20 Engage the track-rod end balljoint shank with the hub carrier, and screw on the balljoint nut. Tighten the nut to the specified torque, fit a new split pin and bend over the split pin legs to secure. If the castellations in the nut do not line up with the hole in the balljoint shank, tighten the nut a little more until the split pin can be fitted.

21 Refit the hub/driveshaft retaining nut and, using the method employed on removal to prevent the hub from rotating, tighten the hub/driveshaft retaining nut to the specified torque. Check that the hub rotates freely.

22 Refit the hub/driveshaft nut locking cap, fit a new split pin and bend over the split pin legs to secure **(see illustrations)**.

23 Refill the transmission with oil/fluid as described in the relevant Part of Chapter 7.

24 Where applicable, refit the lower splash guard(s).

25 Refit the roadwheel, and lower the vehicle to the ground.

26 On completion, have the front wheel alignment checked at the earliest opportunity (see Chapter 10).

Right-hand driveshaft on 3S-FE and 3S-GE engine models

Removal

27 Proceed as described in paragraphs 1 to 9.

28 Unscrew the two bolts securing the driveshaft intermediate bearing housing to the bracket on the engine.

29 Pull the hub carrier and suspension strut assembly outwards and withdraw the driveshaft outer CV joint from the hub carrier.

Pull the inner end of the driveshaft from the transmission, and withdraw the driveshaft through the bearing housing bracket, complete with the intermediate bearing assembly **(see illustration)**.

Refitting

30 Before installing the driveshaft, examine the driveshaft oil seal in the transmission for signs of damage or deterioration and, if necessary, renew it, referring to the appropriate Part of Chapter 7 for further information. (Having got this far it is worth renewing the seal as a matter of course.)

31 Coat the driveshaft oil seal with a little grease, then slide the inner end of the driveshaft into the differential, simultaneously engaging the intermediate bearing with the bracket on the engine. Take care not to damage the differential oil seal.

32 Refit the bolts securing the driveshaft intermediate bearing housing to the bracket, and tighten them to the specified torque.

33 Proceed as described in paragraphs 18 to 26.

3 Driveshaft rubber gaiters - renewal

Inner CV joint gaiter

All except 3S-GE engine models

Note: *Before proceeding, obtain a suitable gaiter repair kit which should include grease,*

3.4 Alignment marks on the driveshaft, tripod and driveshaft joint outer member

new gaiter securing clips, and new CV joint circlips.

1 With the driveshaft removed as described in Section 2, proceed as follows.

2 Using a screwdriver, prise up the locking tabs and release the metal clips securing the gaiter to the driveshaft joint and the driveshaft.

3 Slide the gaiter back from the joint along the driveshaft.

4 Using quick-drying paint, make alignment marks on the driveshaft and the driveshaft joint outer member **(see illustration)**. **Do not** use a punch to make the marks.

5 Slide the joint outer member from the driveshaft.

6 Make alignment marks on the driveshaft tripod and the end of the driveshaft. Again, do not use a punch to make the marks.

7 Using a pair of circlip pliers, remove the circlip from the end of the driveshaft **(see illustration)**.

8 Similarly, release the circlip located behind the joint tripod, and slide it down the driveshaft, away from the tripod.

9 Using a hammer and a soft metal drift, tap the tripod from the end of the driveshaft.

10 Slide the circlip from the driveshaft.

11 Slide the gaiter from the driveshaft, complete with the securing clips.

12 Thoroughly clean the driveshaft joint components and the end of the driveshaft.

13 Wrap a little tape over the driveshaft splines to prevent damage to the new gaiter as it is fitted, then slide the new gaiter, complete with the securing clips onto the inner end of the driveshaft.

3.7 Removing the tripod retaining circlip

8

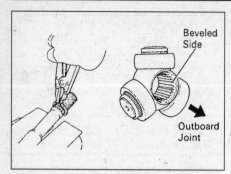
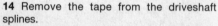

3.15 Fit a new circlip then fit the tripod with its bevelled side toward the outer (roadwheel) end of the driveshaft

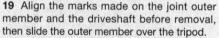

3.18 Pack the joint outer member with the grease supplied in the repair kit

3.20 Fit the clip by bending its tongue back, then secure the tongue with the retaining tags (arrowed)

14 Remove the tape from the driveshaft splines.

15 Fit a new circlip to the driveshaft groove nearest the gaiter. Align the marks made on the joint tripod and the end of the driveshaft before removal. Note that the bevelled edge of the tripod hub must face towards the outer end of the driveshaft **(see illustration)**.

16 Tap the tripod into position on the splines using a hammer and soft metal drift. Tap on the tripod hub, **not** the rollers.

17 Fit a new circlip to secure the tripod.

18 Pack the joint outer member with the grease supplied in the repair kit **(see illustration)**. Use any surplus grease to pack the gaiter.

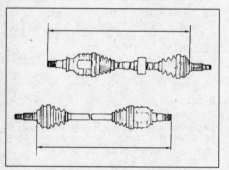

3.21a Measuring points for setting driveshaft standard length (4A-FE and 7A-FE engine models)

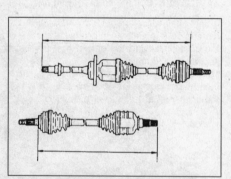

3.21b Measuring points for setting driveshaft standard length (3S-FE engine models)

19 Align the marks made on the joint outer member and the driveshaft before removal, then slide the outer member over the tripod.

20 Slide the gaiter over the joint outer member, and secure it using the larger clip **(see illustration)**.

21 Move the joints in or out slightly to set the driveshaft to the standard length setting dimension as given in the Specifications **(see illustrations)**. Ensure that the gaiter is located in its grooves and not stretched or contracted. Secure the smaller end to the driveshaft using the new clip.

3S-GE engine models

Note: *Before proceeding, obtain a suitable gaiter repair kit which should include grease, new gaiter securing clips, and new CV joint circlips and snap-ring.*

22 Proceed as described in paragraphs 1 to 4.

23 Using a screwdriver, prise out the snap-ring, and pull the inner joint outer member from the end of the shaft **(see illustration)**. Leave the joint ball bearings and cage on the end of the driveshaft at this stage.

24 Make alignment marks on the end of the driveshaft, the ball bearing inner race, and the ball bearing cage **(see illustration)**.

25 Remove the ball bearings and the cage from the bearing inner race.

26 Using circlip pliers, remove the circlip from the end of the driveshaft.

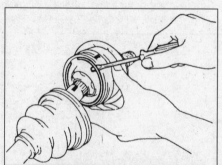

3.23 Prise out the snap-ring, and pull the inner joint outer member from the end of the shaft (3S-GE engine models)

27 Clamp the driveshaft in a soft-jawed vice, and then tap the ball bearing inner race from the driveshaft splines using a hammer and soft metal drift.

28 Again using circlip pliers, remove the remaining circlip from the end of the driveshaft, then slide off the gaiter, complete with the securing clips.

29 Thoroughly clean the driveshaft joint components and the end of the driveshaft.

30 Wrap a little tape over the driveshaft splines to prevent damage to the new gaiter as it is fitted, then slide the new gaiter, complete with the securing clips onto the inner end of the driveshaft.

31 Remove the tape from the driveshaft splines.

32 Fit a new circlip to the driveshaft groove nearest the gaiter.

33 Slide the ball bearing cage onto the end of the driveshaft, with its smaller diameter towards the outer end of the driveshaft.

34 Align the marks made on the ball bearing inner race and the end of the driveshaft before removal, then tap the race onto the driveshaft splines using a hammer and soft metal drift.

35 Fit a new circlip to the groove in the driveshaft end to secure the ball bearing inner race.

36 Pack the joint outer member with the new grease. Save some grease to hold the ball bearings in place, and to pack the driveshaft gaiter.

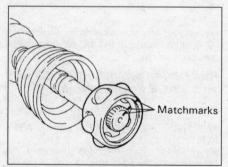

3.24 Alignment marks on the end of the driveshaft, the ball bearing inner race, and the ball bearing cage (3S-GE engine models)

37 Align the marks made on the ball bearing cage, inner race and driveshaft, then slide the cage over the inner race.

38 Fit the ball bearings to the cage and inner race, using a little grease (use the grease from the repair kit) to hold them in place.

39 Align the marks made on the joint outer member and the driveshaft, then slide the outer member onto the end of the driveshaft, and secure it using a new snap-ring.

40 Pack any surplus grease into the gaiter, then secure the outer end of the gaiter to the driveshaft using the smaller clip.

41 Move the joints in or out slightly to set the driveshaft to the standard length setting dimension as given in the Specifications (see illustration 3.21b). Ensure that the gaiter is not stretched or contracted. Secure the inner end to the joint outer member using the larger clip.

Outer CV joint gaiter

Note: *Do not attempt to dismantle the driveshaft outer CV joints. Before proceeding, obtain a suitable gaiter repair kit which should include grease and new gaiter securing clips. New CV joint circlips and a new snap-ring (where applicable) will be required for the inner joint.*

42 Remove the inner joint gaiter as described previously in this Section.

43 If working on the right-hand driveshaft of a model fitted with a vibration damper, mark the position of the damper, then prise up the locking tab, and remove the metal clip securing the damper (see illustration). Note which way round the damper is fitted to ensure correct refitting, then slide the damper from the end of the driveshaft.

44 Using a screwdriver, prise up the locking tabs, and release the metal clips securing the gaiter to the CV joint and the driveshaft.

45 Slide the gaiter along the driveshaft, and remove it from the inner end. Do not attempt to dismantle the outer driveshaft CV joint.

46 Using old rags, clean away as much of the old grease as possible from the outer CV joint. Do not use any solvents to clean the joint.

47 Fill the driveshaft joint with the new grease supplied in the repair kit. Save any surplus grease to push into the new gaiter.

48 Wind a little tape around the driveshaft inner CV joint splines to protect the gaiter as it is fitted.

49 Slide the new gaiter onto the inner end of the driveshaft, along with the securing clips, then slide it along the driveshaft.

50 Remove the tape from the driveshaft splines.

51 Secure the gaiter to the outer CV joint using the larger clip, then move the joints in or out slightly to set the driveshaft to the standard length (see illustrations 3.21a and 3.21b). Ensure that the gaiter is located in its grooves and not stretched or contracted. Secure it to the driveshaft using the smaller clip.

52 Where applicable, refit the vibration damper, ensuring that it is fitted in its original position (align the marks made before removal). Secure the damper using a new clip.

53 Refit the inner joint gaiter as described previously in this Section.

4 Driveshaft overhaul - general information

1 If any of the checks described in Chapter 1 reveal wear in a driveshaft constant velocity joint, first check that the hub/driveshaft retaining nut is still correctly tightened with reference to the procedures contained in Section 2 relating to removal and refitting of the hub/driveshaft nut.

2 Road test the vehicle, and listen for a metallic clicking from the front as the vehicle is driven slowly in a circle on full-lock. If a clicking noise is heard, this indicates wear in the outer constant velocity joint.

3 If vibration, consistent with road speed, is felt through the vehicle when accelerating, there is a possibility of wear in the inner constant velocity joints.

4 Inner constant velocity joints can be dismantled and inspected for wear as described in Section 3. Check on the availability of components before dismantling a joint. Outer joints are only supplied as an assembly complete with the relevant driveshaft.

5 Driveshaft intermediate bearing (3S-FE and 3S-GE engine models) - renewal

Note: *A suitable press will be required for this operation. A new bearing securing snap-ring will be required on refitting.*

1 Remove the right-hand driveshaft as described in Section 2, then proceed as follows.

2 Remove the driveshaft inner CV joint outer member as described in Section 3.

3 Support the differential dust cover at the inner end of the driveshaft on a suitable metal plate, then press the end of the driveshaft from the dust cover.

4 Using a screwdriver at the outer end of the bearing housing, prise out the snap-ring securing the bearing in the bearing housing.

5 Support the bearing housing on a metal plate, then press the driveshaft from the bearing housing.

6 Similarly, support the bearing dust cover, and press the driveshaft from the dust cover.

7 Using circlip pliers, release the circlip securing the intermediate bearing to the driveshaft.

8 Support the bearing, and press the driveshaft from the bearing. Alternatively, it may be possible to use a long-reach bearing puller.

9 Thoroughly clean the bearing housing, and the contact faces of the driveshaft.

10 Using a press, with a suitable adapter to push on the outer bearing race, press the new bearing into the bearing housing.

11 Fit a new snap-ring to secure the bearing in the housing.

12 Support the bearing housing using a suitable tube or socket then, using a soft metal mandrel resting on the inner surface of the driveshaft joint outer member, press the end of the driveshaft into the bearing.

13 Fit a new circlip to secure the assembly to the driveshaft.

14 Support the bearing dust cover, then press the end of the driveshaft into the dust cover, using the mandrel on the joint outer member, as described previously.

15 Similarly, press the driveshaft into the differential dust cover, to achieve the dimension shown between the outer face of the dust cover and the end of the driveshaft splines (see illustration).

16 Refit the driveshaft inner joint outer member as described in Section 3, then refit the driveshaft as described in Section 2.

8

3.43 Right-hand driveshaft vibration damper and retaining clip (arrowed)

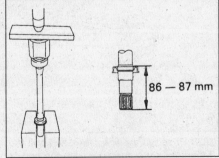

5.15 Dust cover setting dimension (3S-FE and 3S-GE engine models)

86 — 87 mm

Chapter 9
Braking system

Contents

Degrees of difficulty

Easy, suitable for novice with little experience	**Fairly easy,** suitable for beginner with some experience	**Fairly difficult,** suitable for competent DIY mechanic 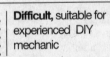	**Difficult,** suitable for experienced DIY mechanic	**Very difficult,** suitable for expert DIY or professional

Specifications

Front brakes
Type . . . . Ventilated disc, with single or twin piston sliding calipers
Minimum disc thickness:
  All except 3S-FE engine models . . . . 23.0 mm
  3S-FE engine models . . . . 26.0 mm
Maximum disc run-out (disc fitted) . . . . 0.05 mm
Minimum brake pad thickness . . . . 1.0 mm

Rear drum brakes
Type . . . . Drum with leading and trailing shoes and automatic adjusters
Maximum drum diameter . . . . 201.0 mm
Minimum brake lining thickness . . . . 1.0 mm
Brake shoe-to-drum clearance . . . . 0.6 mm

Rear disc brakes
Type . . . . Solid disc with single piston sliding calipers
Minimum disc thickness . . . . 9.0 mm
Maximum disc run-out (disc fitted) . . . . 0.15 mm
Minimum brake pad thickness . . . . 1.0 mm

Handbrake (rear disc brake models)
Maximum disc internal diameter . . . . 171.0 mm
Handbrake shoe minimum thickness . . . . 1.0 mm

9

Brake pedal

Brake pedal height (from pedal pad to asphalt sheet):
Right-hand drive models	159.0 to 169.0 mm
Left-hand drive models	138.0 to 148.0 mm
Brake pedal free play	1.0 to 6.0 mm

Brake pedal reserve travel:

Right-hand drive models:
4A-FE, 7A-FE and 3S-FE engine models without ABS	90.0 mm
4A-FE, 7A-FE and 3S-FE engine models with ABS	85.0 mm
3S-GE engine models	90.0 mm

Left-hand drive models:
4A-FE, 7A-FE and 3S-FE engine models without ABS	70.0 mm
4A-FE, 7A-FE and 3S-FE engine models with ABS	65.0 mm
3S-GE engine models	70.0 mm

Torque wrench settings

	Nm	lbf ft
Master cylinder to servo	13	10
Master cylinder piston stopper bolt	10	7
Servo unit to bulkhead	13	10
Front brake caliper:		
Anchor bracket to hub carrier	94	69
Guide pin bolts	34	25
Rear brake caliper:		
Anchor bracket bolts	47	35
Lower guide bolt	20	15
Upper guide pin	27	20
Rear wheel cylinder to backplate	10	7
Brake hose banjo union bolts	30	22
Load-sensing proportioning valve bracket to body	39	29
ABS wheel sensor bolts	8	6
Roadwheel nuts	103	76

1 General information

The braking system is of the dual-circuit hydraulic type, with servo assistance to the front disc brakes and rear drum/disc brakes. The dual-circuit hydraulic system is a safety feature - in the event of a malfunction somewhere in one of the hydraulic circuits, the other circuit continues to operate, providing at least some braking effort. Under normal circumstances, both brake circuits operate in unison, to provide efficient braking.

A load-sensing proportioning valve is fitted in the rear brake circuit hydraulic line, its function being to regulate the braking force available at each rear wheel, reducing the possibility of the rear wheels locking up under heavy braking.

The front brakes are of the ventilated disc type on all models. The front brake calipers are of single or twin piston sliding type mounted on the front hub carriers each side.

Rear drum brakes are fitted to all models without an anti-lock braking system (ABS), while models with ABS are fitted with rear disc brakes.

On drum brake models, each rear brake shoe assembly is operated by a twin-piston wheel cylinder. To take up the brake adjustment as the linings wear, each rear brake assembly incorporates an automatic adjuster mechanism.

The handbrake operates the rear brake shoes by means of a floor-mounted lever and two cables.

On models fitted with rear disc brakes, the brake calipers are of single piston sliding type, with handbrake operation by means of separate handbrake shoes operating within a drum-in-disc arrangement.

An anti-lock braking system is available on some models, and has many of the components in common with the conventional braking system. Further details on ABS can be found later in this Chapter.

Note: *When servicing any part of the system, work carefully and methodically; also observe scrupulous cleanliness when overhauling any part of the hydraulic system. Always renew components (in axle sets, where applicable) if in doubt about their condition, and use only genuine Toyota replacement parts, or at least those of known good quality. Note the warnings given in Safety first and at relevant points in this Chapter concerning the dangers of asbestos dust and hydraulic fluid.*

2 Hydraulic system - bleeding

⚠ *Warning: Hydraulic fluid is poisonous; wash off immediately and thoroughly in the case of skin contact, and seek immediate medical advice if any fluid is swallowed or gets into the eyes. Certain types of hydraulic fluid are inflammable, and may ignite when allowed into contact with hot components; when servicing any hydraulic system, it is safest to assume that the fluid IS inflammable, and to take precautions against the risk of fire as though it is petrol that is being handled. Hydraulic fluid is also an effective paint stripper, and will attack plastics; if any is spilt, it should be washed off immediately, using copious quantities of clean water. Finally, it is hygroscopic (it absorbs moisture from the air). The more moisture is absorbed by the fluid, the lower its boiling point becomes, leading to a dangerous loss of braking under hard use. Old fluid may be contaminated and unfit for further use. When topping-up or renewing the fluid, always use the recommended type, and ensure that it comes from a freshly-opened sealed container.*

General

1 The correct functioning of the brake hydraulic system is only possible after removing all air from the components and circuit; this is achieved by bleeding the system.

2 During the bleeding procedure, add only clean, fresh hydraulic fluid of the specified type (see *Lubricants and fluids*); never re-use fluid that has already been bled from the system. Ensure that sufficient fluid is available before starting work.

3 If there is any possibility of incorrect fluid being used in the system, the brake lines and components must be completely flushed with uncontaminated fluid and new seals fitted to the components.

4 If brake fluid has been lost from the master cylinder due to a leak in the system, ensure that the cause is traced and rectified before proceeding further.

5 Park the car on level ground, switch off the ignition and select first gear (manual transmission) or Park (automatic transmission) then chock the wheels and release the handbrake.

6 Check that all pipes and hoses are secure, unions tight, and bleed screws closed. Remove the dust caps and clean any dirt from around the bleed screws.

7 Unscrew the master cylinder reservoir cap, and top up the reservoir to the MAX level line. Refit the cap loosely, and remember to maintain the fluid level at least above the MIN level line throughout the procedure, otherwise there is a risk of further air entering the system.

8 There are a number of one-man, do-it-yourself, brake bleeding kits currently available from motor accessory shops. It is recommended that one of these kits is used wherever possible, as they greatly simplify the bleeding operation, and also reduce the risk of expelled air and fluid being drawn back into the system. If such a kit is not available, the basic (two-man) method must be used, which is described in detail below.

9 If a kit is to be used, prepare the car as described previously, and follow the kit manufacturer's instructions, as the procedure may vary slightly according to the type being used; generally, they are as outlined below in the relevant sub-section.

10 Whichever method is used, the same sequence must be followed (paragraphs 11 and 12) to ensure the removal of all air from the system. Note that if the master cylinder has been disconnected or if the fluid reservoir has been emptied, the master cylinder should be bled first.

Bleeding sequence

11 If the hydraulic system has only been partially disconnected and suitable precautions were taken to minimise fluid loss, it should only be necessary to bleed that part of the system (ie the primary or secondary circuit).

12 If the complete system is to be bled, then it should be done in the following sequence:

a) *Master cylinder**
b) *Left-hand rear brake.*
c) *Right-hand front brake.*
d) *Right-hand rear brake.*
e) *Left-hand front brake.*

*Only necessary if the master cylinder has been disconnected or if the fluid reservoir has been emptied.

Master cylinder bleeding

13 The master cylinder must be bled if it has been disconnected or if the fluid reservoir has been emptied.

14 Take adequate precautions to ensure that hydraulic fluid is not ejected with force from the master cylinder (which could cause damage or injury) during the following procedure.

15 Disconnect the hydraulic pipes from the master cylinder and place a container under it to catch the fluid that will be ejected. Use plenty of clean rags to prevent fluid spraying on to surrounding components. Ensure that the reservoir is topped-up with clean fluid of the specified type and engage the help of an assistant.

16 Have your assistant **slowly** depress the brake pedal and hold it down. Cover the master cylinder fluid outlets with your fingers and have your assistant slowly release the brake pedal so that fluid is drawn forcibly from the reservoir and into the cylinder body. Repeat this procedure three or four times to expel all air from the master cylinder, topping-up the reservoir as necessary throughout.

17 When the master cylinder is completely primed, have your assistant hold the pedal down, and while it is held down, reconnect the hydraulic pipes to the master cylinder fluid outlets and tighten them securely.

18 Top-up the reservoir and continue bleeding the hydraulic circuits using the following procedures.

Bleeding - basic (two-man) method

19 Collect a clean glass jar of reasonable size and a suitable length of plastic or rubber tubing, which is a tight fit over the bleed screw, and a ring spanner to fit the screws. The help of an assistant will also be required.

20 If not already done, remove the dust cap from the bleed screw of the first wheel to be bled and fit the spanner and bleed tube to the screw. Place the other end of the tube in the jar, and pour in sufficient fluid to cover the end of the tube.

21 Ensure that the master cylinder reservoir fluid level is maintained at least above the MIN level line throughout the procedure.

22 Have the assistant fully depress the brake pedal several times to build up pressure, then maintain it on the final downstroke.

23 While pedal pressure is maintained, unscrew the bleed screw (approximately one turn) and allow the compressed fluid and air to flow into the jar. The assistant should maintain pedal pressure, following it down to the floor if necessary, and should not release it until instructed to do so. When the flow stops, tighten the bleed screw again have the assistant release the pedal slowly, and recheck the reservoir fluid level.

24 Repeat the steps given in paragraphs 22 and 23) until the fluid emerging from the bleed screw is free from air bubbles.

25 When no more air bubbles appear, tighten the bleed screw securely, remove the tube and spanner and refit the dust cap. **Do not overtighten the bleed screw**.

26 Repeat these procedures on the remaining calipers in sequence until all air is removed from the system and the brake pedal feels firm again.

Bleeding - using a one-way valve kit

27 As their name implies, these kits consist of a length of tubing with a one-way valve fitted, to prevent expelled air and fluid being drawn back into the system; some kits include a translucent container, which can be positioned so that the air bubbles can be more easily seen flowing from the end of the tube.

28 The kit is connected to the bleed screw, which is then opened **(see illustration)**. The user returns to the driver's seat, depresses the brake pedal with a smooth steady stroke, and slowly releases it; this is repeated until the expelled fluid is clear of air bubbles.

29 Note that these kits simplify work so much that it is easy to forget the master cylinder fluid level; ensure that this is maintained at least above the MIN level line at all times.

Bleeding - using a pressure-bleeding kit

30 These kits are usually operated by the reserve of pressurised air contained in the spare tyre. However, note that it will probably be necessary to reduce the pressure to a lower level than normal; refer to the instructions supplied with the kit.

31 By connecting a pressurised, fluid-filled container to the master cylinder reservoir, bleeding is then carried out by simply opening each bleed screw in turn (in the specified sequence) and allowing the fluid to run out, until no more air bubbles can be seen in the expelled fluid.

32 This method has the advantage that the large reservoir of fluid provides an additional safeguard against air being drawn into the system during bleeding.

2.28 One-way valve brake bleeding kit connected to a rear wheel cylinder bleed screw

9

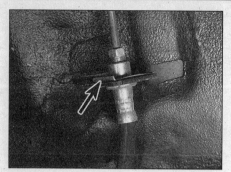

3.2a Brake flexible hose spring clip attachment (arrowed) . . .

3.2b . . . and hose support bracket attachment bolt (arrowed)

33 Pressure bleeding is particularly effective when bleeding difficult systems, or when bleeding the complete system at the time of routine fluid renewal.

All methods

34 When bleeding is complete, and firm pedal feel is restored, wash off any spilt fluid, tighten the bleed screws securely, and refit their dust caps.

35 Check the hydraulic fluid level in the master cylinder reservoir and top-up if necessary.

36 Discard any hydraulic fluid that has been bled from the system; it will not be fit for re-use.

37 Check the feel of the brake pedal. If it feels at all spongy, air must still be present in the system, and further bleeding is required. Failure to bleed satisfactorily after a reasonable repetition of the bleeding operations may be due to worn master cylinder seals.

3 Hydraulic pipes and hoses - renewal

Note: *Before starting work, refer to the warning at the beginning of Section 2 concerning the dangers of hydraulic fluid.*

1 If any pipe or hose is to be renewed, minimise hydraulic fluid loss by removing the master cylinder reservoir cap, placing a piece of plastic film over the reservoir and sealing it with an elastic band. Alternatively, flexible

hoses can be sealed, if required, using a proprietary brake hose clamp; metal brake pipe unions can be plugged (if care is taken not to allow dirt into the system) or capped immediately they are disconnected. Place a wad of rag under any union that is to be disconnected, to catch any spilt fluid.

2 If a flexible hose is to be disconnected, unscrew the brake pipe union nut before removing the spring clip or undoing the hose support bracket retaining bolts which secure the hose to its mounting **(see illustrations)**.

3 To unscrew the union nuts, it is preferable to obtain a brake pipe spanner of the correct size; these are available from most large motor accessory shops. Failing this, a close-fitting open-ended spanner will be required, though if the nuts are tight or corroded, their flats may be rounded-off if the spanner slips. In such a case, a self-locking wrench is often the only way to unscrew a stubborn union, but it follows that the pipe and the damaged nuts must be renewed on reassembly. Always clean a union and surrounding area before disconnecting it. If disconnecting a component with more than one union, make a careful note of the connections before disturbing any of them.

4 If a brake pipe is to be renewed, it can be obtained, cut to length and with the union nuts and end flares in place from Toyota dealers. All that is then necessary is to bend it to shape, following the line of the original, before fitting it to the car. Alternatively, most motor accessory shops can make up brake pipes from kits, but this requires very careful measurement of the original, to ensure that

the replacement is of the correct length. The safest answer is usually to take the original to the shop as a pattern.

5 Before refitting, blow through the new pipe or hose with dry compressed air. Do not overtighten the union nuts. It is not necessary to exercise brute force to obtain a sound joint.

6 If flexible rubber hoses are renewed, ensure that the pipes and hoses are correctly routed, with no kinks or twists, and that they are secured in the clips or brackets provided.

7 After fitting, bleed the hydraulic system as described in Section 2, wash off any spilt fluid, and check carefully for fluid leaks.

4 Front brake pads - renewal

⚠️ *Warning: Disc brake pads must be renewed on both front wheels at the same time - never renew the pads on only one wheel as uneven braking may result. Dust created by wear of the pads may contain asbestos, which is a health hazard. Never blow it out with compressed air and do not inhale any of it. DO NOT use petroleum-based solvents to clean brake parts. Use brake cleaner or methylated spirit only. DO NOT allow any brake fluid, oil or grease to contact the brake pads or disc. Also refer to the warning at the start of Section 2 concerning the dangers of hydraulic fluid.*

1 Chock the rear wheels then jack up the front of the car and support it on axle stands (see *Jacking and Vehicle Support*). Remove the front roadwheels.

All except GTi models

2 Push in the caliper piston by sliding the caliper body towards the outside of the vehicle by hand.

3 Unscrew the caliper lower guide pin bolt using a ring spanner while counterholding the guide pin with an open-ended spanner. Remove the guide pin bolt and swing the caliper upwards to allow access to the brake pads; tie the caliper up in the raised position **(see illustrations)**.

4 Remove the two anti-rattle springs then withdraw the inner and outer brake pads, with

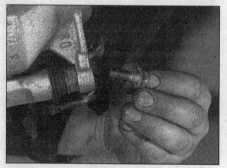

4.3a Remove the brake caliper lower guide pin bolt . . .

4.3b . . . and swing the caliper upwards for access to the brake pads

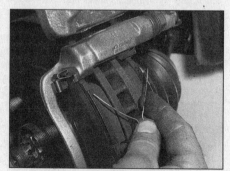

4.4a Remove the anti-rattle springs . . .

4.4b . . . then withdraw the inner brake pad and shims . . .

4.4c . . . and the outer brake pad and shims from the anchor bracket

4.5 Remove the four brake pad support plates

their anti-squeal shims, from the anchor bracket **(see illustrations)**. If the old pads are to be refitted, ensure that they are identified so that they can be returned to their original positions.

5 Remove the four brake pad support plates from their locations in the anchor bracket **(see illustration)**.

6 Measure the thickness of the pad friction linings. If any one pad lining has worn down to the specified minimum, or if any are fouled with oil or grease, all four pads must be renewed. Do not interchange pads in an attempt to even out wear.

7 Brush the dust and dirt from the caliper, piston and disc.

 Warning: Take great care not to inhale the dust as it is injurious to health.

8 Inspect the dust cover around the piston for damage and for evidence of fluid leaks, which if found will necessitate caliper overhaul as described in Section 5. Inspect the disc for signs of cracks, scoring or severe abrasions with reference to Section 6.

9 If new brake pads are to be fitted, the caliper piston will need to be pushed back into its housing, to allow for the extra pad thickness - use a G-clamp to do this. Note that, as the piston is pressed back into the bore, it will displace the fluid in the system, causing the fluid level in the brake master cylinder reservoir to rise and possibly overflow. To avoid this possibility, a small quantity of fluid should be syphoned from the reservoir. If any brake fluid is spilt onto the bodywork, hoses or adjacent components in the engine compartment, wipe it clean without delay.

 HAYNES HiNT *An ideal way to remove fluid from the master cylinder reservoir is to use a clean syringe or an old poultry baster.*

10 Prior to refitting, check that the pads and the disc are clean. Where new pads are to be installed, peel the protective backing paper (where fitted) from them. If the old pads are to be refitted, ensure that they are correctly located as noted during their removal.

11 Fit the four brake pad support plates to their upper and lower locations in the anchor bracket.

12 Locate the inner and outer brake pads, together with their anti-squeal shims into position in the anchor bracket.

13 Refit the two anti-rattle springs then lower the caliper down over the pads.

14 Screw in the lower guide pin bolt then tighten the bolt to the specified torque while counterholding the guide pin with a spanner.

15 Repeat the procedure on the opposite front brake.

16 Before lowering the vehicle, check the that the fluid level in the brake master cylinder reservoir is up to the Maximum level mark, and top-up with the specified fluid type if required (see *Weekly Checks*). Depress the brake pedal a few times to position the pads against the disc, then recheck the fluid level in the reservoir and further top-up the fluid level if necessary.

17 Refit the roadwheels, then lower the vehicle to the ground. Tighten the roadwheel retaining nuts to the specified torque.

18 To allow the new brake pads to bed-in and reach full efficiency, a running-in period of approximately 100 miles or so should be observed before hard use and heavy braking.

3S-GE engine models (GTi)

19 Push in the caliper piston by sliding the caliper body towards the outside of the vehicle by hand.

20 Unscrew the caliper upper and lower guide pin bolts using a ring spanner while counterholding the guide pins with an open-ended spanner. Remove the guide pin bolts and lift the caliper assembly off the brake pads and anchor bracket. Suspend the caliper from the front suspension coil spring using string or wire, but take care not to stretch or kink the flexible brake hydraulic hose.

21 Remove the two anti-rattle springs then withdraw the inner and outer brake pads, with their anti-squeal shims (two on the outside of each pad) from the anchor bracket. Remove the pad wear indicator from the top of the inner pad. If the old pads are to be refitted, ensure that they are identified so that they can be returned to their original positions.

22 Remove the four brake pad support plates from their locations in the anchor bracket.

23 Inspect the brake pads and disc as described in paragraphs 6 to 8.

24 If new brake pads are to be fitted, the caliper pistons will need to be pushed back into their housings, to allow for the extra pad thickness - use a G-clamp to do this. Note that, as the pistons are pressed back into their bores, they will displace the fluid in the system, causing the fluid level in the brake master cylinder reservoir to rise and possibly overflow. To avoid this possibility, a small quantity of fluid should be syphoned from the reservoir. If any brake fluid is spilt onto the bodywork, hoses or adjacent components in the engine compartment, wipe it clean without delay.

 HAYNES HiNT *An ideal way to remove fluid from the master cylinder reservoir is to use a clean syringe or an old poultry baster.*

25 Prior to refitting, check that the pads and the disc are clean. Where new pads are to be installed, peel the protective backing paper (where fitted) from them. If the old pads are to be refitted, ensure that they are correctly located as noted during their removal.

26 Fit the four brake pad support plates to their upper and lower locations in the anchor bracket.

27 Apply a smear of copper-based high melting point brake grease to both sides of the inner (perforated) anti squeal shims, and place the shims against the pad backing plates. Place the solid shim over the perforated shim on each pad **(see illustration)**.

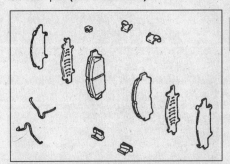

4.27 Front brake pads, anti-squeal shims, support plates and anti-rattle shims on GTi models

9

5.4 Unscrew the brake hose-to-caliper banjo union bolt, and recover the copper sealing washers

28 Fit the pad wear indicator to the top of the inner pad and locate the inner and outer brake pads, with the pad wear indicator on the inner pad facing upwards, together with their anti-squeal shims into position in the caliper anchor bracket.

29 Refit the two anti-rattle springs then place the caliper in position over the pads.

30 Screw in the upper and lower guide pin bolts and tighten the bolts to the specified torque while counterholding the guide pins with a spanner.

31 Repeat the procedure on the opposite front brake.

32 Before lowering the vehicle, check the that the fluid level in the brake master cylinder reservoir is up to the Maximum level mark, and top-up with the specified fluid type if required (see *Weekly Checks*). Depress the brake pedal a few times to position the pads against the disc, then recheck the fluid level in the reservoir and further top-up the fluid level if necessary.

33 Refit the roadwheels, then lower the vehicle to the ground. Tighten the wheel nuts to the specified torque.

34 To allow the new brake pads to bed-in and reach full efficiency, a running-in period of approximately 100 miles or so should be observed before hard use and heavy braking.

5 Front brake caliper - removal, overhaul and refitting

Note: *Before starting work, refer to the warning at the beginning of Section 2 concerning the dangers of hydraulic fluid, and to the warning at the beginning of Section 4 concerning the dangers of asbestos dust.*

Removal

1 Chock the rear wheels then jack up the front of the car and support it on axle stands (see *Jacking and Vehicle Support*). Remove the roadwheel.

2 Push in the caliper piston slightly by sliding the caliper body towards the outside of the vehicle by hand.

3 To minimise fluid loss, unscrew the master cylinder reservoir filler cap and place a piece of polythene over the filler neck. Secure the polythene with an elastic band ensuring that an airtight seal is obtained. Alternatively, use a brake hose clamp, a G-clamp, or a similar tool with protected jaws, to clamp the front flexible hydraulic hose.

4 Unscrew the brake hose-to-caliper banjo union bolt, then recover the copper sealing washers **(see illustration)**. Note that new washers will be needed for refitting. Cover or plug the open hydraulic unions to keep them clean.

5 Unscrew the caliper upper and lower guide pin bolts using a ring spanner while counterholding the guide pins with an open-ended spanner. Remove the guide pin bolts and lift the caliper off the brake pads and anchor bracket.

6 To remove the caliper anchor bracket, first remove the brake pads with reference to Section 4. If they are likely to be re-used, mark them for identification (inner and outer, right- or left-hand as applicable) to ensure that they are installed in their original locations when refitting.

7 Unscrew the two anchor bracket mounting bolts, and withdraw the anchor bracket from the hub carrier **(see illustrations)**.

Overhaul

8 With the caliper removed, clean it externally with methylated spirit and a soft brush.

9 Remove the bleed screw and empty any remaining hydraulic fluid out of the caliper.

10 Remove the piston dust boot retaining ring(s) and the dust boot(s) and pull the piston(s) out of the caliper bore(s). If a piston is reluctant to move, refit the bleed screw and apply **low** air pressure (eg from a foot pump) to the fluid inlet, but note that the piston may be ejected with some force.

11 Hook out the piston seal(s) from the bore(s) using a blunt instrument.

12 Withdraw the two guide pins from the anchor bracket then remove the guide pin dust boots by tapping them off using a screwdriver and small hammer.

13 Clean the piston(s) and caliper bore(s) with a lint-free rag and some clean brake fluid or methylated spirit. Slight imperfections may be polished out with steel wool. If any pitting, scoring or wear ridges are evident, the caliper must be renewed.

14 Renew all rubber components (seal(s) and dust boots).as a matter of course. Blow through the fluid inlet and bleed screw hole with compressed air.

15 Fit the new guide pin dust boots to the anchor bracket by tapping them into place using a hammer and 19 mm socket bit. Lubricate the guide pins sparingly with high-melting-point brake grease and insert them through the dust boots into the anchor bracket. Note that the pin with the guide bush locates in the bottom hole.

16 Lubricate the new piston seal(s) with clean brake fluid. Insert the seal(s) into the groove(s) in the bore, using your fingers only.

17 Lubricate the piston(s) and bore(s) with clean brake fluid, then install the piston(s) in the caliper.

5.7a Unscrew the two anchor bracket mounting bolts . . .

5.7b . . . and withdraw the anchor bracket from the hub carrier

18 Fit a new dust boot to the piston(s) and caliper and secure with the retaining ring(s)

19 Refit the caliper bleed screw.

Refitting

20 If removed, refit the caliper anchor bracket and tighten the bolts to the specified torque.

21 Refit the brake pads to the anchor bracket with reference to Section 4.

22 Place the caliper over the brake pads and screw in the guide pin bolts. Hold the guide pins with a spanner and tighten the guide pin bolts to the specified torque.

23 Reconnect the flexible hydraulic hose banjo union using new copper washers and ensuring that the hose is not kinked. Tighten the union bolt to the specified torque.

24 Remove the brake hose clamp or polythene, where fitted, and bleed the hydraulic system as described in Section 2.

25 Apply the footbrake two or three times to settle the pads then refit the roadwheel and lower the car. Tighten the wheel nuts to the specified torque.

6 Front brake disc - inspection, removal and refitting

Note: *Before starting work, refer to the warning at the beginning of Section 4 concerning the dangers of asbestos dust.*

Inspection

Note: *If either disc requires renewal, BOTH should be renewed at the same time, to ensure even and consistent braking. New brake pads should also be fitted.*

1 Remove the front brake pads as described in Section 4.

2 With the brake pads removed, temporarily secure the disc to the wheel hub using three wheel nuts.

3 Inspect the disc friction surfaces for cracks

or deep scoring (light grooving is normal and may be ignored). A cracked disc must be renewed; a scored disc can be reclaimed by machining provided that the thickness is not reduced below the specified minimum.

4 Check the disc run-out using a dial test indicator with its probe positioned 10.0 mm from the outer edge of the disc. If the run-out exceeds the figures given in the Specifications, check the axial play of the hub bearings as described in Chapter 10. If the hub bearings are satisfactory, reposition the disc on the wheel hub, one fifth of a turn from its original position. Secure with three wheel nuts and repeat the run-out check. Continue repositioning the disc, one fifth of a turn at a time, checking the run-out in each position. If the run-out is still excessive after all disc positions have been tried, machining may be possible, otherwise disc renewal will be necessary.

> **HAYNES HiNT**
> *If a dial test indicator is not available, check the run-out by positioning a fixed pointer near the outer edge, in contact with the disc face. Rotate the disc and measure the maximum displacement of the pointer with feeler blades.*

5 Excessive disc thickness variation can also cause judder. Check this using a micrometer **(see illustration)**. If the thickness variation exceeds the figures given in the Specifications, machining may be possible, otherwise disc renewal will be necessary.

Removal

6 If not already done, chock the rear wheels then jack up the front of the car and support it on axle stands (see *Jacking and Vehicle Support*). Remove the roadwheel.

7 If the brake pads have not been removed, push in the caliper piston slightly by sliding the caliper body towards the outside of the vehicle by hand.

8 Undo the two bolts securing the brake caliper anchor bracket to the hub carrier. Withdraw the caliper and anchor bracket, complete with brake pads and suspend the caliper from the front suspension coil spring using string or wire, but take care not to stretch or kink the flexible brake hydraulic hose.

9 Check whether the position of the disc in relation to the hub is marked, and if not, make your own mark as an aid to refitting. Where applicable, remove the wheel nuts temporarily fitted to hold the disc during the inspection procedure, and lift off the disc **(see illustration)**.

Refitting

10 Ensure that the hub and disc mating faces are spotlessly clean. Clean rustproofing compound off a new disc with methylated spirit and a rag.

11 Locate the disc on the hub with the orientation marks made on removal aligned.

12 Refit the brake caliper and anchor bracket and tighten the bolts to the specified torque.

13 Apply the footbrake two or three times to settle the pads then refit the roadwheel and lower the car. Tighten the wheel nuts to the specified torque.

7 Rear brake drum - removal, inspection and refitting

Note: *Before starting work, refer to the warning at the beginning of Section 8 concerning the dangers of asbestos dust.*

Removal

1 Chock the front wheels then jack up the rear of the car and support it on axle stands (see *Jacking and Vehicle Support*). Remove the appropriate rear roadwheel, and release the handbrake.

6.5 Using a micrometer to measure the disc thickness

6.9 Front brake disc removal

9

7.2 If the rear drum is tight on the hub, use two screws to help release it

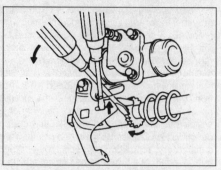

7.3 Use two screwdrivers as shown to release the automatic brake adjuster

2 It should now be possible to simply slide the drum off the rear hub and brake shoes. If the drum is tight on the hub or wheel studs due to corrosion, insert two suitable screws or bolts into the threaded holes on the drum face. Tighten the bolts evenly, a little at a time until the drum releases **(see illustration)**.

3 If the brake drum is stuck on the brake shoes due to a severe internal wear ridge, remove the rubber access plug from the upper rear of the brake backplate, just below the wheel cylinder. Release the automatic brake adjuster by inserting a screwdriver through the access hole and easing the adjuster lever away from the adjuster wheel. Insert a second screwdriver through the hole and turn the adjuster wheel to back off the brake shoe adjustment **(see illustration)**. Withdraw the drum and refit the rubber plug to the access hole.

4 With the brake drum removed, brush or wipe the dust from the drum, brake shoes, wheel cylinder and backplate.

> ⚠ **Warning: Take great care not to inhale the dust as it is injurious to health.**

Inspection

Note: *If a brake drum requires renewal, BOTH rear drums should be renewed at the same time to ensure even and consistent braking. New brake shoes should also be fitted.*

5 Examine the internal surface of the brake drum for signs of scoring, cracks or a severe wear ridge. If any deterioration of the friction surface is evident, it may be possible to reclaim it by machining provided that the drum diameter does not exceed the specified maximum. If any cracks are apparent, the drum must be renewed.

Refitting

6 Check that the automatic brake adjuster is fully retracted, then fit the drum over the wheel studs.

7 With the brake drum refitted, operate the handbrake several times, to actuate the rear brake adjuster and take up the adjustment. It should be possible to hear a clicking noise as the adjuster operates. When no further clicking can be heard, release the handbrake.

8 Withdraw the drum from the wheel studs once more, and measure the drum internal diameter. Now measure the diameter of the brake shoes at their widest point. Subtract the brake shoe diameter from the brake drum internal diameter to give the brake shoe-to-drum clearance. If the clearance is significantly greater than the dimension given in the Specifications, check the operation of the automatic adjuster mechanism and the associated brake shoe components.

9 When all is satisfactory, refit the drum and roadwheel, check that the rear wheels spin freely when the brakes are released, then apply the handbrake, lower the vehicle and tighten the wheel nuts to the specified torque.

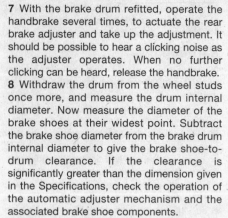

8 Rear brake shoes - renewal

> ⚠ **Warning: Drum brake shoes MUST be renewed on both rear wheels at the same time - NEVER renew the shoes on only one wheel, as uneven braking may result. Also, the dust created by wear of the shoes may contain asbestos, which is a health hazard. Never blow it out with compressed air, and don't inhale any of it. An approved filtering mask should be worn when working on the brakes. DO NOT use petroleum-based solvents to clean brake parts - use brake cleaner or methylated spirit only.**

Early models

1 Remove the rear brake drum with reference to Section 7.

2 Note the fitted positions of the springs and the adjuster mechanism **(see illustration)**.

3 Using pliers, unhook the brake shoe upper return spring from the slot in the leading brake shoe.

4 Unhook the upper return spring from the slot in the trailing shoe and remove the spring and the front portion of the adjuster mechanism

5 Remove the leading shoe hold-down springs by depressing and turning the outer cup through 90° using pliers, while holding the pin in place from behind the backplate. Remove the outer cup, spring, inner cup and pin.

6 Pull the leading brake shoe from the bottom anchor, disconnect the lower return spring and remove the leading shoe. Remove the lower return spring from the trailing shoe.

7 Remove the trailing shoe hold-down spring, cups and pin using the same procedure as for the leading shoe.

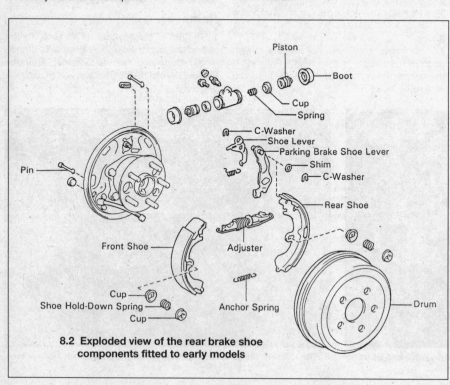

8.2 Exploded view of the rear brake shoe components fitted to early models

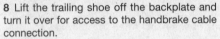

8.11 Using an elastic band to retain the rear wheel cylinder pistons

8.28a Depress and remove the brake shoe hold-down spring . . .

8.28b . . . then remove the hold-down pins from the rear of the backplate

8 Lift the trailing shoe off the backplate and turn it over for access to the handbrake cable connection.

9 Using pointed-nose pliers, push the handbrake cable spring away from the brake shoe and disengage the handbrake cable end from the lever on the trailing shoe.

10 With the trailing shoe removed, unhook the adjuster lever spring from the shoe. Remove the rear portion of the adjuster mechanism.

11 To prevent the wheel cylinder pistons from being accidentally ejected with the brake shoes removed, fit a suitable elastic band (or wire) lengthwise over the cylinder/pistons **(see illustration)**.

12 Prise off the retaining C-clip, withdraw the shim then remove the adjuster lever and handbrake lever from the shoe.

13 Clean the adjuster mechanism and its associated components, then lay all the parts out and check them thoroughly for signs of wear, loss of tension of any of the springs and brake shoe friction lining condition. Measure the thickness of the friction linings noting that If any one shoe lining has worn down to the specified minimum, or if any are fouled with oil or grease, all four shoes must be renewed.

14 Clean the brake backplate, then apply a little high-melting-point grease to the shoe contact points on the backplate and lower anchor, and to the adjuster thread and contact end.

15 Attach the handbrake lever and adjuster lever to the new trailing brake shoe and secure with the C-clip. Make sure that the shim is in place under the C-clip. Using feeler blades check that the clearance between the handbrake lever and the brake shoe web is less than 0.35 mm. If the clearance is excessive, obtain a new shim; different thicknesses are available.

16 Engage the rear portion of the adjuster mechanism with the slot in the adjuster lever. Move the adjuster lever back against the handbrake lever while at the same time engaging the forked end of the adjuster mechanism with the handbrake lever.

17 Attach the short end of the adjuster lever spring to the lever, then connect the other end to the slot in the brake shoe.

18 Attach the handbrake cable to the handbrake lever on the trailing shoe using the same procedure as for removal.

19 Remove the elastic band (or wire retainer) from the wheel cylinder. Locate the trailing shoe in position on the backplate and refit the hold-down pin, inner cup, spring and outer cup. Hold the pin from behind, push the outer cup in against spring pressure, and turn through 90° to secure.

20 Engage the front portion of the adjuster mechanism, together with the upper return spring into the adjuster mechanism rear portion.

21 Attach one end of the lower return spring to the trailing shoe, then hook the other end of the spring into the hole in the leading shoe. Locate the leading shoe in place on the backplate, engaging the front portion of the adjuster mechanism with the shoe web.

22 Connect both ends of the upper return spring into their respective holes in the leading and trailing shoes.

23 Refit the leading shoe hold-down pin, inner cup, spring and outer cup. Hold the pin from behind, push the outer cup in against spring pressure, and turn through 90° to secure.

24 Check that the brake shoes and their associated components are correctly refitted, then refit the brake drum (refer to Section 7).

25 Repeat the procedure on the remaining rear brake.

Later models

26 Remove the rear brake drum with reference to Section 7.

27 Note the fitted positions of the springs and the adjuster mechanism.

28 Remove the shoe hold-down springs and pins by depressing the spring and sliding it off the pin while holding the pin from behind. Remove the pins from the rear of the backplate **(see illustrations)**.

29 Using pliers, ease the leading brake shoe from the bottom anchor, and disconnect the lower return spring from both shoes **(see illustrations)**.

8.29a Using pliers, ease the leading brake shoe from the bottom anchor . . .

8.29b . . . then disconnect the lower return spring from both shoes

9

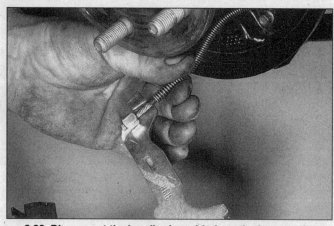

8.33 Disconnect the handbrake cable from the lever on the trailing brake shoe

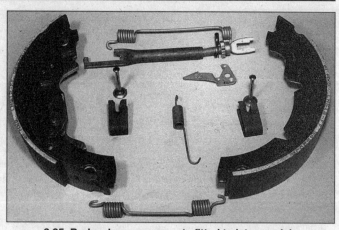

8.35 Brake shoe components fitted to later models

30 Move the bottom ends of the brake shoes towards each other, then disconnect the tops of the shoes from the wheel cylinder. Be careful not to damage the wheel cylinder rubber boots. To prevent the wheel cylinder pistons from being accidentally ejected, fit a suitable elastic band (or wire) lengthwise over the cylinder/pistons.

31 Disconnect the upper return spring from the brake shoes, disengage the adjuster strut from the handbrake lever on the trailing shoe, then remove the leading shoe and adjuster assembly.

32 Lift the trailing shoe off the backplate and turn it over for access to the handbrake cable connection.

8.36 Applying a little high-melting-point grease to the shoe contact points on the backplate

33 Using pointed-nose pliers, push the handbrake cable spring away from the brake shoe and disengage the handbrake cable end from the lever on the trailing shoe and remove the shoe (see illustration).

34 Unhook the adjuster lever spring from the leading shoe then lift off the adjuster lever and adjuster strut.

35 Clean the adjuster mechanism and its associated components, then lay all the parts out and check them thoroughly for signs of wear, loss of tension of any of the springs and brake shoe friction lining condition (see illustration). Measure the thickness of the friction linings noting that if any one shoe lining has worn down to the specified minimum, or if any are fouled with oil or grease, all four shoes must be renewed.

36 Clean the brake backplate, then apply a little high-melting-point grease to the shoe contact points on the backplate and lower anchor, and to the adjuster thread and contact ends (see illustration).

37 Place the adjuster lever on the peg of the new leading brake shoe then refit the adjuster strut so that the forked end engages over the adjuster lever (see illustrations).

38 Attach the handbrake cable to the handbrake lever on the trailing shoe using the same procedure as for removal.

39 Remove the elastic band (or wire retainer) from the wheel cylinder and locate the trailing shoe in position on the backplate.

40 Place the leading shoe and adjuster mechanism in position on the backplate and connect the upper return spring to both the brake shoes, while at the same time engaging the adjuster strut with the trailing shoe handbrake lever.

41 Engage the tops of both brake shoes with the wheel cylinder pistons, taking care not to damage the wheel cylinder rubber boots.

42 Connect the lower return spring to both brake shoes then engage the trailing shoe with the bottom anchor. Using pliers ease the leading brake shoe into place in the bottom anchor.

43 Refit the hold-down pin to the trailing brake shoe, then slide the hold-down spring into place. Push down on the spring while at the same time turning the T-shaped end of the pin through 90° with pliers to secure. Refit the pin and spring to the leading shoe in the same way.

44 Attach the short end of the adjuster lever spring to the adjuster lever then pull the long end down and engage it with the hole in the brake shoe (see illustration).

45 Check that the brake shoes and their associated components are correctly refitted, then refit the brake drum with reference to Section 7.

46 Repeat the procedure on the remaining rear brake.

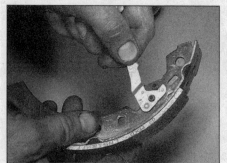

8.37a Place the adjuster lever on the peg of the new leading brake shoe . . .

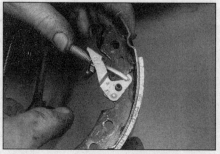

8.37b . . . then refit the adjuster strut so that the forked end engages over the adjuster lever

8.44 Attaching the adjuster lever spring to the brake shoe

9 Rear wheel cylinder - removal, overhaul and refitting

Note: *Before starting work, refer to the warning at the beginning of Section 2 concerning the dangers of hydraulic fluid.*

Removal

1 Remove the rear brake shoes (Section 8).
2 Using a brake hose clamp or self-locking wrench with protected jaws, clamp the flexible brake hose near its support bracket on the underbody. This will minimise brake fluid loss during subsequent operations.
3 Wipe away all traces of dirt around the brake pipe union at the rear of the wheel cylinder, then unscrew the union nut.
4 Unscrew the two retaining bolts and withdraw the wheel cylinder from the backplate. Plug the brake pipe, to prevent the possible ingress of dirt and to minimise further fluid loss whilst the cylinder is detached from it.

Overhaul

5 Clean the external surfaces of the cylinder, then pull free the rubber boots from each end of the cylinder **(see illustration)**.
6 The pistons and spring will probably shake out; if not, use a foot pump to apply air pressure through the hydraulic union and eject them.
7 Remove the cup seals from the pistons then clean the pistons and the cylinder by washing in fresh hydraulic fluid or methylated spirits (not petrol, paraffin or any other mineral-based fluid). Examine the surfaces of the pistons and the cylinder bores. Look for any signs of rust, scoring or metal-to-metal rubbing, which if evident, will necessitate renewal of the wheel cylinder.
8 Begin reassembly by lubricating the first piston in clean hydraulic fluid. Manipulate its new seal into position so that its raised lip faces away from the brake shoe bearing face of the piston.
9 Insert the piston into the cylinder from the opposite end of the cylinder body, and push it through to its normal location in the bore.
10 Insert the spring into the cylinder, then fit the second new seal into position on the second piston (as described for the first) and fit the second piston into the wheel cylinder. Take care not to damage the lip of the seal as the piston is inserted into the cylinder - additional lubrication and a slight twisting action may help. Only use fingers (no tools) to manipulate the piston and seal into position.
11 Fit the new rubber boots to each end of the piston.

Refitting

12 Wipe clean the backplate, and remove the plug from the end of the hydraulic pipe. Place the wheel cylinder in position and engage the pipe union. Screw the union nut in by a few turns to ensure that the threads engage.

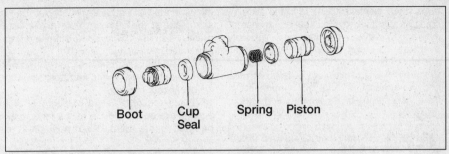

Boot   Cup   Spring   Piston
       Seal

9.5 Exploded view of the rear wheel cylinder components

13 Refit the two retaining bolts and tighten to the specified torque.
14 Tighten the brake pipe union nut securely.
15 Remove the clamp from the flexible brake hose then refit the brake shoes as described in Section 8.
16 Bleed the brake hydraulic system as described in Section 2. Providing suitable precautions were taken to minimise loss of fluid, it should only be necessary to bleed the relevant rear brake.

10 Rear brake pads - renewal

 Warning: Disc brake pads must be renewed on both rear wheels at the same time - never renew the pads on only one wheel as uneven braking may result. Dust created by wear of the pads may contain asbestos, which is a health hazard. Never blow it out with compressed air and do not inhale any of it. DO NOT use petroleum-based solvents to clean brake parts. Use brake cleaner or methylated spirit only. DO NOT allow any brake fluid, oil or grease to contact the brake pads or disc. Also refer to the warning at the start of Section 2 concerning the dangers of hydraulic fluid.

1 Chock the front wheels then jack up the rear of the car and support it on axle stands (see *Jacking and Vehicle Support*). Remove the rear roadwheels.
2 Push in the caliper piston by sliding the caliper body towards the outside of the vehicle by hand.
3 Undo the bolt and release the flexible brake hose support bracket from the suspension strut.
4 Unscrew the caliper lower guide bolt and swing the caliper upwards to allow access to the brake pads; tie the caliper up in the raised position.
5 Withdraw the inner and outer brake pads, with their anti-squeal shims from the anchor bracket. Note that there are two anti-squeal shims fitted behind the outer pad, and a single anti-squeal shim fitted behind the inner pad **(see illustration)**. If the old pads are to be refitted, ensure that they are identified so that they can be returned to their original positions.

6 Remove the four brake pad support plates or anti-rattle springs from their locations in the anchor bracket.
7 Measure the thickness of the pad friction linings. If any one pad lining has worn down to the specified minimum, or if any are fouled with oil or grease, all four pads must be renewed. Do not interchange pads in an attempt to even out wear.
8 Brush the dust and dirt from the caliper, piston and disc.

 Warning: Take great care not to inhale the dust as it is injurious to health.

9 Inspect the dust cover around the piston for damage and for evidence of fluid leaks, which if found will necessitate caliper overhaul as described in Section 11. Inspect the disc for signs of cracks, scoring or severe abrasions with reference to Section 12.
10 If new brake pads are to be fitted, the caliper piston will need to be pushed back into its housing, to allow for the extra pad thickness - use a G-clamp to do this. Note that, as the piston is pressed back into the

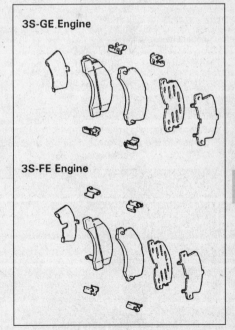

3S-GE Engine

3S-FE Engine

10.5 Rear brake pad and shim details

9

bore, it will displace the fluid in the system, causing the fluid level in the brake master cylinder reservoir to rise and possibly overflow. To avoid this possibility, a small quantity of fluid should be syphoned from the reservoir. If any brake fluid is spilt onto the bodywork, hoses or adjacent components in the engine compartment, wipe it clean without delay.

HAYNES HINT *An ideal way to remove fluid from the master cylinder reservoir is to use a clean syringe or an old poultry baster.*

11 Prior to refitting, check that the pads and the disc are clean. Where new pads are to be installed, peel the protective backing paper (where fitted) from them. If the old pads are to be refitted, ensure that they are correctly located as noted during their removal.

12 Fit the four brake pad support plates or anti-rattle springs to their upper and lower locations in the anchor bracket.

13 Apply a smear of copper-based high-melting-point brake grease to both sides of the perforated anti-squeal shim, and place the shim against the backing plate of the outer brake pad. Place the solid shim over the perforated shim on the outer pad.

14 Locate the outer brake pad, together with the two anti-squeal shims into position in the caliper anchor bracket.

15 Place the other solid anti-squeal shim against the backing plate of the inner brake pad and locate the pad into position in the anchor bracket.

16 Lower the caliper down over the pads, screw in the lower guide bolt then tighten the bolt to the specified torque.

17 Reconnect the flexible brake hose support bracket to the suspension strut.

18 Repeat the procedure on the opposite rear brake.

19 Before lowering the vehicle, check the that the fluid level in the brake master cylinder reservoir is up to the Maximum level mark, and top-up with the specified fluid type if required (see *Weekly Checks*). Depress the brake pedal a few times to position the pads against the disc, then recheck the fluid level in the reservoir and further top-up the fluid level if necessary.

20 Refit the roadwheels, then lower the vehicle to the ground. Tighten the roadwheel retaining nuts to the specified torque.

21 To allow the new brake pads to bed-in and reach full efficiency, a running-in period of approximately 100 miles or so should be observed before hard use and heavy braking.

11 Rear brake caliper - removal, overhaul and refitting

Note: *Before starting work, refer to the warning at the beginning of Section 2 concerning the dangers of hydraulic fluid, and to the warning at the beginning of Section 10 concerning the dangers of asbestos dust.*

Removal

1 Chock the front wheels then jack up the rear of the car and support it on axle stands (see *Jacking and Vehicle Support*). Remove the relevant rear roadwheel.

2 Push in the caliper piston slightly by sliding the caliper body towards the outside of the vehicle by hand.

3 To minimise fluid loss, unscrew the master cylinder reservoir filler cap and place a piece of polythene over the filler neck. Secure the polythene with an elastic band ensuring that an airtight seal is obtained. Alternatively, use a brake hose clamp, a G-clamp, or a similar tool with protected jaws, to clamp the front flexible hydraulic hose.

4 Unscrew the brake hose-to-caliper banjo union bolt, and recover the copper sealing washers. Note that new washers will be needed for refitting. Cover or plug the open hydraulic unions to keep them clean.

5 Unscrew the caliper lower guide bolt, swing the caliper upwards clear of the brake pads, then slide it off the upper guide pin.

6 To remove the caliper anchor bracket, first remove the brake pads with reference to Section 10. If they are likely to be re-used, mark them for identification (inner and outer, right- or left-hand as applicable) to ensure that they are installed in their original locations when refitting.

7 Unscrew the two anchor bracket mounting bolts, and withdraw the anchor bracket from the rear axle carrier.

Overhaul

8 This is essentially the same procedure as that described for the front caliper (see Section 5) except that the guide pin dust boots and bushings are a simple push-fit in their caliper locations **(see illustration)**.

Refitting

9 If removed, refit the caliper anchor bracket and tighten the bolts to the specified torque.

10 Refit the brake pads to the anchor bracket with reference to Section 10.

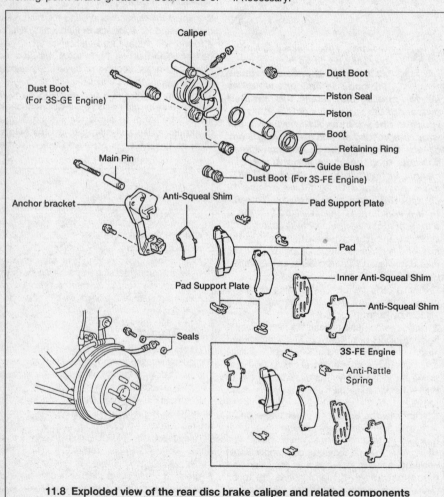

11.8 Exploded view of the rear disc brake caliper and related components

Labels: Caliper; Dust Boot; Dust Boot (For 3S-GE Engine); Piston Seal; Piston; Boot; Retaining Ring; Main Pin; Guide Bush; Dust Boot (For 3S-FE Engine); Anchor bracket; Anti-Squeal Shim; Pad Support Plate; Pad; Inner Anti-Squeal Shim; Pad Support Plate; Anti-Squeal Shim; Seals; 3S-FE Engine; Anti-Rattle Spring

11 Engage the caliper with the upper guide pin, lower it down over the brake pads and screw in the lower guide bolt. Tighten the guide bolt to the specified torque.

12 Reconnect the flexible hydraulic hose banjo union using new copper washers and ensuring that the hose is not kinked. Tighten the union bolt to the specified torque.

13 Remove the brake hose clamp or polythene, where fitted, and bleed the hydraulic system as described in Section 2.

14 Apply the footbrake two or three times to settle the pads then refit the roadwheel and lower the car. Tighten the wheel nuts to the specified torque.

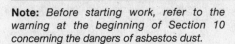

12 Rear brake disc - inspection, removal and refitting

Note: *Before starting work, refer to the warning at the beginning of Section 10 concerning the dangers of asbestos dust.*

Inspection

Note: *If either disc requires renewal, BOTH should be renewed at the same time, to ensure even and consistent braking. New brake pads should also be fitted.*

1 With the rear brake pads removed (Section 10), the inspection procedures are the same as for the front brake disc, and reference should be made to Section 6, paragraphs 2 to 5 inclusive. Additionally, after removal, check the condition of the handbrake drums - refinishing limits are given in the Specifications. The drums are unlikely to wear unless the handbrake is habitually used to stop the car.

Removal

2 If not already done, chock the front wheels then jack up the rear of the car and support it on axle stands (see *Jacking and Vehicle Support*). Remove the relevant roadwheel.

3 If the brake pads have not been removed, push in the caliper piston slightly by sliding the caliper body towards the outside of the vehicle by hand.

4 Undo the two bolts securing the brake caliper anchor bracket to the rear axle carrier. Withdraw the caliper and anchor bracket, complete with brake pads and suspend the caliper from the rear suspension coil spring using string or wire, but take care not to stretch or kink the flexible brake hydraulic hose.

5 Check whether the position of the disc in relation to the hub is marked, and if not, make your own mark as an aid to refitting. Where applicable, remove the wheel nuts, temporarily fitted to hold the disc during the inspection procedure, and lift off the disc. If the disc is tight due to it binding on the handbrake shoes, remove the access plug from the front face of the disc and turn the disc so that the access hole is at the bottom. Insert a screwdriver through the hole and turn the handbrake shoe adjuster wheel to back off the shoe adjustment **(see illustration)**.

Refitting

6 Ensure that the hub and disc mating faces are spotlessly clean. Clean rustproofing compound off a new disc with methylated spirit and a rag.

7 Locate the disc on the hub with the orientation marks made on removal aligned.

8 Refit the brake caliper and anchor bracket and tighten the bolts to the specified torque.

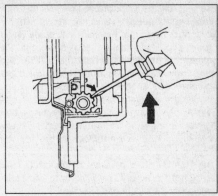

12.5 Slackening the handbrake shoe adjuster wheel to allow removal of the rear brake disc

9 Apply the footbrake two or three times to settle the pads then adjust the handbrake as described in Section 19.

10 Refit the roadwheel and lower the car. Tighten the wheel nuts to the specified torque.

13 Handbrake shoes (rear disc brake models) - inspection and renewal

Inspection

1 Remove the rear brake disc as described in Section 12.

2 Measure the thickness of the shoe friction linings noting that if any one shoe lining has worn down to the specified minimum, or if any are fouled with oil or grease, all four shoes must be renewed. Check the condition of all remaining components and renew as necessary.

Renewal

3 Unhook the handbrake shoe return springs from the upper anchor post and from the shoes, then remove the shoe strut and spring **(see illustration)**.

4 Prise the shoes apart at the bottom and remove the adjuster. Unhook the lower return spring from the front shoe then slide the shoe out from between the backplate and the inner hold-down cup.

5 Slide out the rear shoe and remove the lower return spring.

6 Using pointed-nose pliers, push the handbrake cable spring away from the rear shoe and disengage the handbrake cable end from the lever on the shoe.

7 Prise off the retaining C-clip, withdraw the shim, then remove the handbrake lever from the rear shoe.

8 If required, the hold-down pins, springs and cups can now be removed from the backplate.

9 Clean the backplate, the inside of the brake disc and the adjuster mechanism. Make sure that the adjuster wheel turns freely on its threads.

9

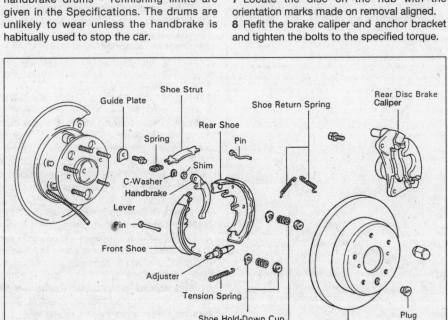

13.3 Exploded view of the rear handbrake shoe components on models fitted with rear disc brakes

Guide Plate
Shoe Strut
Shoe Return Spring
Rear Disc Brake Caliper
Rear Shoe
Spring
Pin
Shim
C-Washer
Handbrake Lever
Pin
Front Shoe
Adjuster
Tension Spring
Shoe Hold-Down Cup
Shoe Hold-Down Spring
Disc
Plug

10 Attach the handbrake lever to the new rear handbrake shoe and secure with the C-clip. Make sure that the shim is in place under the C-clip. Using feeler blades check that the clearance between the handbrake lever and the shoe web is less than 0.35 mm. If the clearance is excessive, obtain a new shim, noting that different thicknesses are available.

11 Apply a smear of high-melting-point grease to the shoe contact areas on the brake backplate, and to the threads of the adjuster mechanism.

12 Refitting is a reversal of removal. Take care not to get grease or oil onto the brake linings or the disc friction surface.

13 Refit the brake disc as described in Section 12, then adjust the handbrake as described in Section 19.

14 Brake master cylinder - removal and refitting

Note: *Before starting work, refer to the warning at the beginning of Section 2 concerning the dangers of hydraulic fluid.*

Removal

1 Disconnect the wiring connector from the fluid level warning indicator. Unscrew the filler cap and remove the brake fluid from the reservoir.

> **HAYNES HINT** *An ideal way to remove fluid from the reservoir is to use a clean syringe or an old poultry baster.*

2 Identify each brake pipe and its connection to the master cylinder. Unscrew the brake pipe union nuts and disconnect the pipes. Plug the connections and tape over the pipe ends, to prevent the entry of dust and dirt.

3 Unscrew the mounting nuts and withdraw the master cylinder and gasket from the servo unit.

Overhaul

4 With the master cylinder removed, empty any remaining fluid from it, and clean it externally.

5 Using a screwdriver, prise off the boot from the end of the master cylinder body **(see illustration)**.

6 Undo the retaining screw at the base of the hydraulic fluid reservoir, then withdraw the reservoir from the top of the master cylinder by pulling and rocking it free from its retaining seals.

7 Extract the reservoir seals from the top face of the master cylinder.

8 Mount the cylinder in a soft-jawed vice, push the pistons in all the way using a screwdriver then unscrew the stopper bolt from the end of the cylinder body.

9 With the pistons still pushed in, extract the piston retaining snap-ring from the cylinder bore.

10 Release the pistons and remove the cylinder from the vice.

11 Pull free the primary (No 1) piston and spring assembly from the rear end of the master cylinder bore. Pull the piston straight out, not at an angle, otherwise there is a risk of scoring the cylinder bore.

12 Extract the secondary (No 2) piston and spring assembly by shaking or lightly tapping the cylinder body on a block of wood.

13 Wash all components of the cylinder in methylated spirit or clean hydraulic brake fluid of the specified type. Do not use any other type of cleaning fluid.

14 Inspect the master cylinder and piston assemblies for any signs of excessive wear or damage. Deep scoring in the cylinder bore and/or on the piston surfaces will necessitate a new master cylinder being fitted.

15 If the cylinder is in a serviceable condition, obtain a cylinder repair kit which comprises pre-assembled primary and secondary piston assemblies.

16 Check that all components are perfectly clean before they refitted. Smear them in new brake fluid of the specified type as they are assembled. *Do not allow grease, old fluid or any other lubricant to contact the components during reassembly.*

17 Lubricate the pistons before refitting them to the cylinder and as they are inserted, use a twisting action to assist in pushing them into position.

18 With the secondary and primary pistons in position, fit the snap-ring and the stopper bolt while pushing the pistons into the bore as was done for removal. Fit the boot to the end of the cylinder with the UP mark facing upwards.

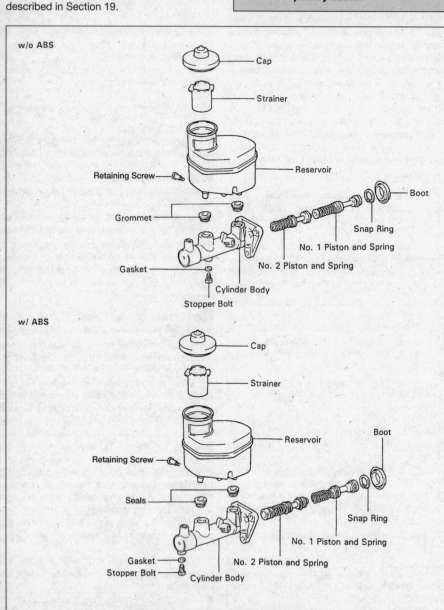

14.5 Brake master cylinder components

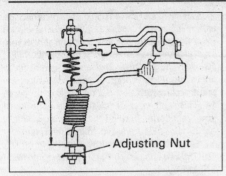

15.8 Load sensing proportioning valve initial set-up dimension

A = 172.7 to 173.6 mm

19 Using new seals, refit the reservoir and secure with the retaining screw.

Refitting

20 Before refitting the master cylinder, clean the mounting faces of the cylinder and vacuum servo unit then place a new gasket in position over the master cylinder mounting studs on the servo.

21 Refitting is a reversal of removal. Tighten the master cylinder retaining nuts to the specified torque and bleed the hydraulic system as described in Section 2 on completion.

15 Load-sensing proportioning valve - removal and refitting

Note: *Due to the specialised equipment required to check and accurately adjust the brake fluid pressure after refitting (or reconnecting) the valve, you are advised to entrust this task to a Toyota dealer or suitably equipped specialist. The following procedure is given for circumstances where the task must be undertaken, but it is vitally important that the brake fluid pressure is checked and adjusted as necessary by a dealer (or other suitably equipped specialist) upon completion.*

 Warning: If the fluid pressure is not checked and accurately adjusted, braking system performance may be severely impaired.

Note: *Before starting work, refer to the warning at the beginning of Section 2 concerning the dangers of hydraulic fluid.*

Removal

1 Position the car over an inspection pit or raise it on a hoist. Alternatively car ramps may be used at the front and rear but the car must be level and with its weight on the roadwheels.

2 To minimise fluid loss, unscrew the master cylinder reservoir filler cap and place a piece of polythene over the filler neck. Secure the polythene with an elastic band ensuring that an airtight seal is obtained.

3 Wipe clean the brake pipe unions at the load-sensing proportioning valve and place absorbent rags beneath them to collect any spilled fluid.

4 Unscrew the brake pipe union nuts and carefully withdraw the pipes from the valve.

5 Accurately measure and record the distance from the adjusting nut bracket to the valve mounting bracket **(see illustration 15.8)**. Undo the locknut below the adjusting nut and detach the bracket from the suspension member.

6 Undo the three mounting bracket retaining bolts and remove the valve and bracket assembly.

Refitting

7 Install the valve and tighten the three mounting bolts to the specified torque.

8 Install the adjusting nut bracket and temporarily tighten the locknut below the adjusting nut. Measure the distance from the adjusting nut bracket to the valve mounting bracket then if necessary turn the adjusting nut to obtain the dimension recorded during removal **(see illustration)**. If an accurate measurement was not obtained during removal, set the spring length to the initial set-up dimension of 172.7 to 173.6 mm.

9 Reconnect the brake pipes then bleed the brake hydraulic system as described in Section 2.

10 Lower the vehicle to the ground and have the brake fluid pressure checked and if necessary adjusted by a Toyota dealer.

16 Brake pedal - check and adjustment

Pedal height

1 Peel back the carpet below the pedals and measure the brake pedal height **(see illustration)**. Note that the measurement should be taken from the upper face of the pedal rubber to the asphalt sheet on the floorpan.

2 If the height is not within the specified tolerance range, unscrew the retaining screws and withdraw the lower trim panel located beneath the steering column. Detach the bonnet pull lever (2 screws) then disconnect the wiring from the instrument panel illumination rheostat. Remove the lower trim panel. Remove the air duct for access to the top of the pedal.

3 Disconnect the wiring connector at the stop light switch, then slacken the locknut and unscrew the switch. Slacken the pedal height adjusting bolt locknut and turn the adjusting bolt until the correct height is achieved then tighten the locknut.

4 With the pedal height correctly set, refit the stop light switch and locknut and screw in the switch until it just contacts the pedal stopper.

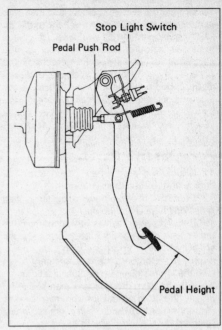

16.1 Brake pedal height adjustment details

5 Unscrew the stop light switch one turn, then measure the distance between the switch and the pedal stopper **(see illustration)**. Reposition the switch as necessary until the specified clearance is obtained then tighten the switch locknut and reconnect the wiring.

6 Check that the stop lights come on when the brake pedal is depressed slightly, and go off when it is released.

7 Once the pedal height and stop light switch adjustment are correct, check the free play as follows.

Pedal free play

8 With the engine switched-off, depress the brake pedal several times to exhaust the vacuum in the servo unit.

9 While gently depressing the brake pedal with the fingers, measure the pedal travel (at the pedal pad) until the resistance is felt to increase. This measurement, from the pedal at rest position to the beginning of firm resistance is the pedal free play.

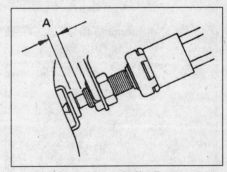

16.5 Stop light switch adjustment

A = 0.5 to 2.4 mm

 9

10 Compare the measurement obtained with that given in the Specifications. If the stop light switch has been correctly adjusted, the pedal free play should also be correct. If the clearance is not as specified, recheck the pedal height and stop light switch adjustments as described previously. If the clearance is still incorrect, it is likely that there is either air in the hydraulic system which should be bled out as described in Section 2, or a fault in the master cylinder or vacuum servo unit.

Pedal reserve travel

11 Chock the rear wheels then start the engine and release the handbrake.
12 Depress the brake pedal a few times then press down hard and hold it.
13 Pedal reserve travel is measured from the upper face of the pedal rubber to the asphalt sheet on the floorpan with the pedal depressed. Compare the measurement taken with the figures given in the Specifications.
14 If the reserve travel is less than specified, check the adjustment of the rear brakes (Sections 8 and 10) and the vacuum servo unit pushrod dimension (Section 18). If the brake pedal feels spongy when depressed, bleed the hydraulic system as described in Section 2.
15 When all the checks and adjustments are complete, refit the air duct and facia trim panel.

17 Brake pedal - removal and refitting

Removal

1 Disconnect the battery negative (earth) lead (refer to Chapter 5A, Sections 1 and 3).
2 Unscrew the retaining screws and withdraw the lower trim panel located beneath the steering column. Detach the bonnet pull lever (2 screws) then disconnect the wiring from the instrument panel illumination rheostat. Remove the lower trim panel. Remove the air duct for access to the top of the pedal.
3 Detach the return spring from the upper part of the pedal arm.
4 Disconnect the vacuum servo unit pushrod from the pedal arm by removing the clevis pin securing clip and the pin (see illustration).

17.4 Vacuum servo unit pushrod clevis pin attachment (arrowed) at the brake pedal

5 Unscrew the nut from the end of the pedal pivot bolt and remove the washer. Remove the bolt then withdraw the pedal arm.

Refitting

6 Refitting is the reverse of the removal procedure, but carry out the checks and adjustments described in Section 16 before refitting the facia trim panel and air duct.

18 Brake vacuum servo unit - removal and refitting

Removal

1 Disconnect the battery negative (earth) lead (refer to Chapter 5A, Sections 1 and 3).
2 Remove the brake master cylinder as described in Section 14.
3 On left-hand drive models with anti-lock brakes, remove the ABS hydraulic modulator as described in Section 25.
4 Disconnect the servo vacuum hose at the connection on the servo unit.
5 Unscrew the retaining screws and withdraw the lower trim panel located beneath the steering column. Detach the bonnet pull lever (2 screws) then disconnect the wiring from the instrument panel illumination rheostat. Remove the lower trim panel.
6 Detach the return spring from the upper part of the brake pedal arm.
7 Disconnect the vacuum servo unit pushrod from the brake pedal arm by removing the clevis pin securing clip and the clevis pin.
8 Undo the four nuts then remove the servo from the engine compartment. Recover the gasket between the servo and the bulkhead.

Refitting

9 If a new servo unit is being fitted, the clearance between the master cylinder piston and the servo unit pushrod must be checked and, if necessary, adjusted. Toyota technicians use a special tool to check and adjust this clearance, but an alternative method can be used as follows.
10 Slacken the servo unit-to-master cylinder pushrod locknut and unscrew the pushrod end approximately one turn.
11 Place a new gasket on the servo unit then locate the master cylinder over the mounting studs and slide it gently into position against the gasket. The pushrod should seat in its location in the master cylinder piston before the cylinder mounting flange contacts the gasket. If not, unscrew the pushrod a little more until it does.
12 Using a trial and error process, screw in the pushrod, a little at a time, until the point is reached where the pushrod seats in the piston just as the mounting flange seats firmly on the gasket. The correct adjustment of the pushrod is when there is no clearance between the pushrod and piston with the

master cylinder fitted, but no interference either. If there is clearance, then there will be excessive brake pedal free play; if there is interference, the brakes may not release fully.
13 Continue the procedure until the adjustment is correct, then tighten the pushrod locknut.
14 The remainder of refitting is a reversal of removal bearing in mind the following points:
   a) Ensure that the servo-to-bulkhead gasket is in position before fitting the servo.
   b) Tighten all nuts and bolts to the specified torque.
   c) Refit the master cylinder as described in Section 14.
   d) Where applicable, refit the ABS hydraulic modulator assembly as described in Section 25.
   e) Bleed the hydraulic system as described in Section 2.
   f) Carry out the brake pedal check and adjustment as described in Section 16.

19 Handbrake - adjustment

1 The handbrake lever, when correctly adjusted, should travel four to seven clicks of the ratchet when a moderate pulling force is applied. If it travels less than the specified number of clicks, there is a possibility that the handbrake may not release completely and the brake shoes may drag on the drum. If the lever can be pulled up more than the specified amount the handbrake may not hold properly on a slope.

Rear drum brake models

2 Chock the rear wheels and release the handbrake.
3 Remove the centre console as described in Chapter 11.
4 Locate the handbrake cable adjuster on the side of the handbrake lever and slacken the locknut (the upper nut) while holding the adjuster nut.
5 Turn the adjuster nut as necessary until the desired lever travel is obtained then tighten the locknut (see illustration).
6 Refit the centre console.

19.5 Adjusting the handbrake cable at the adjuster nut on the handbrake lever

20.4 Unscrew the handbrake cable locknut and adjuster nut (arrowed) on the side of the lever

Rear disc brake models

7 To adjust the handbrake shoe clearance, chock the front wheels then jack up the rear of the car and support it on axle stands (see *Jacking and Vehicle Support*). Remove the rear roadwheels and temporarily refit three wheel nuts each side to hold the brake discs in place.

8 Remove the plug from the access hole on the front face of each rear disc. With the handbrake fully released, turn one of the rear discs until the access hole is in its lowest position and the handbrake shoe internal adjuster wheel can be seen through the hole. Insert a screwdriver through the hole and turn the adjuster wheel as necessary until the disc is locked. Now back off the adjuster wheel by 8 notches until the disc is again free to turn without any trace of binding. Refit the access plug then repeat this procedure on the other rear brake.

9 Refit the roadwheels and lower the car to the ground. Tighten the wheel nuts to the specified torque.

10 Settle the handbrake shoes by driving the car slowly on a safe quiet road for about 400 metres with the handbrake lightly applied. This will clean any rust and deposits from the handbrake shoes and drum. Release the handbrake then apply it again and repeat the procedure.

11 With the handbrake shoe clearance correctly set, adjust the handbrake lever travel as described above in paragraphs 2 to 6.

20.5 Handbrake primary cable attachment (arrowed) at the equaliser yoke

20 Handbrake cable - removal and refitting

Removal

1 Chock the front wheels then jack up the rear of the car and support it on axle stands (see *Jacking and Vehicle Support*).
2 Remove the exhaust tailpipe and silencer and the heat shield below the handbrake lever as described in Chapter 4A.

Primary cable

3 Remove the centre console as described in Chapter 11.
4 With the handbrake off, unscrew the cable locknut and adjuster nut on the side of the handbrake lever **(see illustration)**. Detach the primary cable from the lever.
5 From under the car, turn the primary cable end through 90° and disconnect it from the equaliser yoke **(see illustration)**.
6 Extract the cable entry grommet from the floorpan and pull the cable out through the hole.

Secondary cable

7 Remove the rear brake shoes (drum brake models) or handbrake shoes (disc brake models) on the relevant side as described in Section 8 or 13 respectively.

8 Undo the cable retaining bolts from the brake backplate and pull the cable end through the backplate **(see illustration)**.
9 Undo the cable support bracket nuts and bolts from the suspension components and underbody **(see illustrations)**.
10 Pull the nylon bushing out of the front mounting bracket and disconnect the cable from the equaliser.

Refitting

11 Refitting is a reversal of removal, but adjust the handbrake as described in Section 19 on completion.

21 Handbrake lever - removal and refitting

Removal

1 Remove the centre console as described in Chapter 11.
2 With the rear wheels chocked and the handbrake off, unscrew the cable locknut and adjuster nut on the side of the handbrake lever **(see illustration 20.4)**. Detach the primary cable from the lever.
3 Disconnect the wiring connector from the handbrake warning light switch.
4 Undo the warning light switch mounting screw and remove the switch.
5 Undo the bolts securing the lever assembly to the floor and remove the lever from the car.

Refitting

6 Refitting is a reversal of removal. Adjust the handbrake as described in Section 19 on completion.

22 Handbrake warning light switch - removal and refitting

Removal

1 Remove the centre console as described in Chapter 11.

20.8 Handbrake secondary cable retaining bolts (arrowed) on the brake backplate

20.9a Undo the secondary cable support bracket from the suspension components (arrowed) . . .

20.9b . . . and the underbody attachments (arrowed)

22.2 Handbrake warning light switch location on the side of the handbrake lever

2 Disconnect the wiring connector from the warning light switch on the side of the handbrake lever **(see illustration)**.
3 Undo the switch mounting screw and remove the switch.

Refitting

4 Refitting is a reversal of removal.

23 Stop light switch - removal and refitting

Removal

1 Unscrew the retaining screws and withdraw the lower trim panel located beneath the steering column. Detach the bonnet pull lever (2 screws) then disconnect the wiring from the instrument panel illumination rheostat. Remove the lower trim panel. Remove the air duct for access to the top of the pedal.
2 Disconnect the wiring connector at the stop light switch located on the brake pedal bracket, then slacken the locknut and unscrew the switch **(see illustration)**.

Refitting

3 Refitting of the switch is carried out as part of the brake pedal check and adjustment procedures contained in Section 16.

24 Anti-lock braking system (ABS) - general information

The anti-lock braking system, available as an option on certain models, monitors the rotational speed of the wheels under braking. Sudden deceleration of one wheel, indicating that lock-up is occurring, causes the hydraulic pressure to that wheel's brake to be reduced or interrupted momentarily.

The main components of the system are the wheel sensors, the electronic control unit (ECU) and the hydraulic modulator assembly.

One sensor is fitted to each wheel, together with a pulse wheel integral with the driveshaft outer CV joint or rear wheel hub. The sensors monitor the rotational speeds of the wheels, and are able to detect when there is a risk of wheel locking (low rotational speed).

Information from the sensors is fed to the ECU which operates solenoid valves in the hydraulic modulator. The solenoid valves restrict the hydraulic fluid supply to any caliper detected to be on the verge of locking.

Should a fault develop in the system, the ECU illuminates a warning light on the instrument panel. To facilitate fault diagnosis, the system is provided with an on-board diagnostic facility. In the event of a fault, the ECU stores a series of signals (or fault codes) for subsequent read-out and diagnosis by a Toyota dealer.

25 Anti-lock braking system (ABS) components - removal and refitting

Removal

Front wheel sensor

1 Chock the rear wheels then jack up the front of the car and support it on axle stands (see *Jacking and Vehicle Support*). Remove the roadwheel.
2 Remove the wheel arch liner and disconnect the wheel sensor wiring connector. Undo the bolts or release the supports securing the wiring to the suspension components.
3 Undo the bolt which secures the sensor to the hub carrier and withdraw the sensor.

Rear wheel sensor

4 Chock the front wheels then jack up the rear of the car and support it on axle stands (see *Jacking and Vehicle Support*). Remove the roadwheel.
5 Undo the bolt which secures the sensor to the rear hub carrier, and the bolt securing the wiring support clip under the wheel arch.
6 Release the wiring and grommet from the cable entry point under the wheel arch.
7 Remove the rear seat base and seat back as described in Chapter 11.
8 Trace the wiring back until the connector inside the car is located then disconnect it.
9 Pull the wiring through the cable entry point and remove the sensor from under the wheel arch.

23.2 Brake stop light switch location on the brake pedal bracket

Electronic control unit (ECU)

10 Wipe clean the area around the wiring connector on the ECU and disconnect it.
11 Undo the three retaining bolts and carefully lift the ECU from its location.

Hydraulic modulator

Note: *Before starting work, refer to the warning at the beginning of Section 2 concerning the dangers of hydraulic fluid.*
12 Disconnect the battery negative (earth) lead (refer to Chapter 5A, Sections 1 and 3).
13 On left-hand drive models, remove the brake master cylinder as described in Section 14.
14 Wipe clean all the brake pipe unions at the hydraulic modulator then unscrew the union nuts and carefully ease the pipes clear. Place absorbent rags beneath the pipe unions to catch any spilled fluid and label the pipes as an aid to refitting.
15 Identify the wiring connectors at the hydraulic modulator and disconnect them.
16 Undo the bolts securing the hydraulic modulator mounting bracket and remove the modulator, complete with bracket from the engine compartment.
17 Note that the modulator is a sealed precision assembly and must not under any circumstances be dismantled.

Refitting

18 In all cases, refitting is a reversal of the removal operations but note the following points:
 a) *Clean off all dirt from the wheel sensors and mounting locations before refitting and also clean the pulse wheels with a stiff brush.*
 b) *Bleed the hydraulic system as described in Section 2 after refitting the hydraulic modulator.*

Chapter 10
Suspension and steering

Contents

Degrees of difficulty

| **Easy,** suitable for novice with little experience | **Fairly easy,** suitable for beginner with some experience | **Fairly difficult,** suitable for competent DIY mechanic 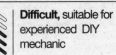 | **Difficult,** suitable for experienced DIY mechanic | **Very difficult,** suitable for expert DIY or professional |

Specifications

Front wheel alignment and steering angles

Toe setting . . . . 0° ± 0.2° (0 ± 2.0 mm) toe-in
Camber (non-adjustable):
  All except 3S-GE engine models . . . . -20 ± 45'
  3S-GE engine models . . . . -5 ± 45'
Castor (non-adjustable):
  All except 3S-GE engine models:
    With power steering . . . . 0°30 ± 45'
    Without power steering . . . . 0° ± 45'
  3S-GE engine models . . . . 2°35 ± 45'
Steering axis inclination (non-adjustable):
  All except 3S-GE engine models . . . . 13°25 ± 45'
  3S-GE engine models . . . . 5°15 ± 45'

Rear wheel alignment

Toe setting . . . . 0.4° ± 0.2° (4.0 ± 2.0 mm) toe-in
Camber (non-adjustable):
  All except 3S-GE engine models . . . . -30'
  3S-GE engine models . . . . -1° ± 45'

10

Torque wrench settings

	Nm	lbf ft
Front suspension (all except 3S-GE engine models)		
Hub/driveshaft retaining nut	226	167
Anti-roll bar drop link-to-suspension lower arm	64	47
Anti-roll bar drop link-to-anti-roll bar	64	47
Anti-roll bar clamp plates	19	14
Brake hose bracket to suspension strut	29	21
Brake caliper anchor bracket to hub carrier	94	69
Suspension strut-to-hub carrier	275	203
Suspension strut upper mounting-to-body	64	47
Suspension strut piston rod nut	47	35
Lower balljoint-to-lower arm	127	94
Lower balljoint-to-hub carrier	123	91
Suspension lower arm front pivot bolt	235	173
Suspension lower arm rear mounting bolts:		
Forward bolt	165	122
Rear bolt	176	130
Subframe-to-body	181	134
Engine/transmission mounting-to-subframe	58	43
Engine/transmission longitudinal crossmember bolts	35	26
Rear engine/transmission mounting through bolt	87	64
Front suspension (3S-GE engine models)		
Hub/driveshaft retaining nut	226	167
Anti-roll bar drop link-to-suspension strut	44	32
Anti-roll bar drop link-to-anti-roll bar	64	47
Anti-roll bar clamp plates	19	14
Brake caliper anchor bracket to hub carrier	94	69
Suspension strut upper mounting-to-body	64	47
Suspension strut piston rod nut	47	35
Suspension strut upper balljoint-to-hub carrier	124	92
Suspension lower No 1 arm-to-lower balljoint attachment	59	44
Suspension lower No 1 arm-to-camber control arm	118	87
Suspension lower No 1 arm-to-subframe	235	173
Suspension lower No 2 arm-to-lower balljoint attachment	118	87
Suspension lower No 2 arm-to-subframe	165	122
Lower balljoint attachment-to-hub carrier	91	67
Camber control arm-to-suspension strut	113	83
Subframe-to-body	181	134
Engine/transmission mounting-to-subframe	58	43
Engine/transmission longitudinal crossmember bolts	35	26
Rear engine/transmission mounting through bolt	87	64
Rear suspension		
Hub carrier-to-rear axle carrier	80	59
Rear wheel hub retaining nut	123	91
Suspension strut-to-rear axle carrier	255	188
Suspension strut upper mounting-to-body	39	29
Suspension strut piston rod nut	49	36
Longitudinal link mounting bolts/nuts	113	83
Transverse link mounting bolts/nuts	181	134
Subframe-to-body	64	47
Anti-roll bar drop link-to-suspension strut	64	47
Anti-roll bar drop link-to-anti-roll bar	64	47
Anti-roll bar clamp plates	19	14
Steering		
Track rod end balljoint-to-hub carrier	56	41
Steering wheel-to-column shaft nut	35	26
Steering shaft/intermediate shaft universal joint clamp bolts	35	26
Steering column mounting nuts	25	19
Steering gear mounting bolts (all except 3S-GE engine)	59	43
Steering gear mounting bolts (3S-GE engine):		
Mounting bolts at pinion housing end	59	44
Mounting through bolt and nut	127	94
Engine/transmission mounting-to-subframe	58	43
Hydraulic pipe union banjo bolts	51	38
Hydraulic pipe flare union nuts	44	32
Steering pump mounting and adjustment bolts	39	29
Roadwheel nuts		
All models	103	76

1 General information

On all except 3S-GE engine models, the front suspension is of the conventional MacPherson strut type, incorporating coil springs and integral telescopic shock absorbers. The MacPherson struts are located by transverse lower suspension arms, which utilise rubber inner mounting bushes and incorporate a balljoint at the outer ends. The front hub carriers, which carry the hub bearings, brake calipers and the hub/disc assemblies, are bolted to the MacPherson struts and connected to the lower arms via the balljoints (see illustration). A front anti-roll bar is fitted to all models. The anti-roll bar is rubber-mounted onto the subframe, and connects both the lower arms, via drop links.

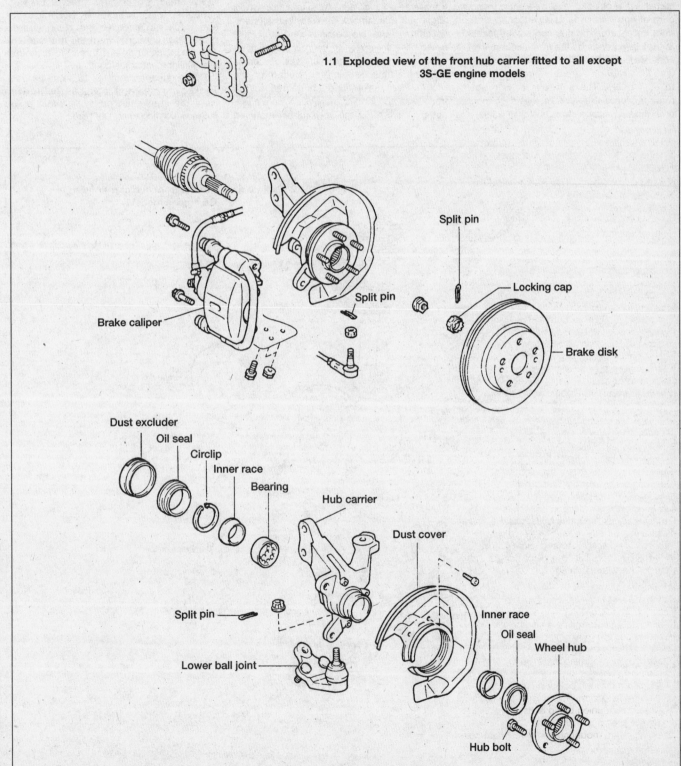

1.1 Exploded view of the front hub carrier fitted to all except 3S-GE engine models

10

On 3S-GE engine models, the front suspension is a variation of the MacPherson strut layout and designated Super strut by Toyota. The struts incorporate coil springs and integral telescopic shock absorbers in the conventional way, but the lower end of each strut is located by the upper end of the hub carrier, via a balljoint, and by a short camber control arm, which is itself attached to the front lower arm. The hub carriers are located at their lower ends by the front and rear lower arms, via balljoints on the ends of the lower arms **(see illustration)**. A front anti-roll bar is fitted to all models. The anti-roll bar is rubber-mounted onto the subframe, and connects both the suspension struts, via drop links.

The rear suspension is of the MacPherson strut type, incorporating coil springs and integral telescopic shock absorbers. The MacPherson struts are located laterally by two transverse links each side, bolted to the subframe at their inner ends, and longitudinally by a single longitudinal link each side. The rear transverse links are adjustable to enable wheel alignment adjustment. The rear hub carriers, which carry the hub bearings, and drum/disc assemblies are bolted to the rear axle carriers which carry the rear brake shoes or disc brake calipers. These are in turn bolted to the MacPherson struts and connected to the transverse and longitudinal links. Where a rear anti-roll bar is fitted, the bar is rubber-mounted onto the chassis side members, and connects both the suspension struts via drop links.

The steering column is connected by a universal joint to an intermediate shaft, which has a second universal joint at its lower end. The lower universal joint is attached to the steering gear pinion by means of a clamp bolt.

The steering gear is mounted on the front subframe. It is connected by two track-rods and track rod ends to the steering arms projecting rearwards from the hub carriers. The track-rod ends are threaded to enable wheel alignment adjustment.

Power steering is fitted to some models. The power steering pump is belt-driven from the crankshaft pulley or water pump pulley according to engine type.

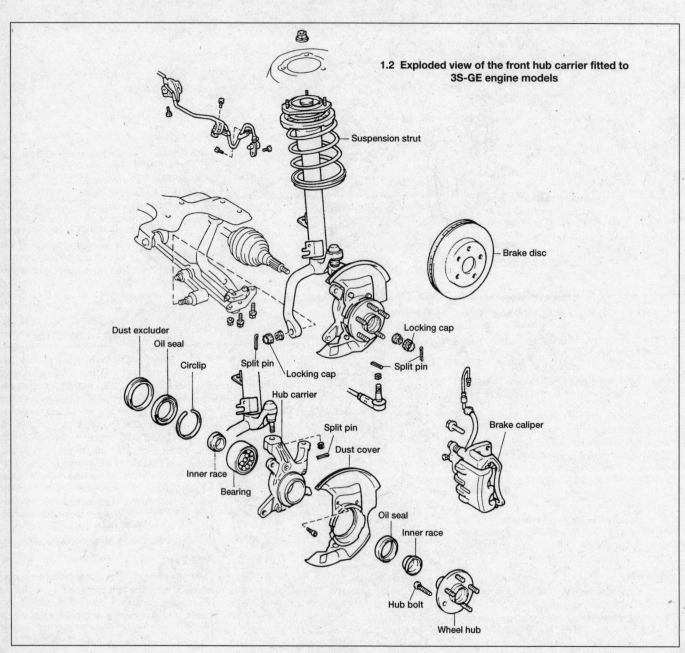

1.2 Exploded view of the front hub carrier fitted to 3S-GE engine models

- Suspension strut
- Brake disc
- Dust excluder
- Oil seal
- Circlip
- Split pin
- Locking cap
- Locking cap
- Split pin
- Hub carrier
- Inner race
- Split pin
- Bearing
- Dust cover
- Brake caliper
- Oil seal
- Inner race
- Hub bolt
- Wheel hub

2 Front hub carrier - removal and refitting

All except 3S-GE engine models

Removal

1 Chock the rear wheels then jack up the front of the car and support it on axle stands (see *Jacking and Vehicle Support*). Remove the relevant front roadwheel.

2 On models with ABS, it is advisable to remove the ABS wheel sensor as described in Chapter 9, to avoid any possibility of damage during the removal procedure.

3 Extract the hub/driveshaft retaining nut split pin and remove the locking cap over the nut.

4 Have an assistant firmly depress the brake pedal to prevent the front hub from rotating. Using a socket and a long extension bar, slacken and remove the hub/driveshaft retaining nut. Alternatively, a tool can be fabricated to prevent the hub from rotating (see Chapter 8, Section 2). This nut is very tight; make sure that there is no risk of pulling the car off the axle stands.

5 Undo the two bolts securing the brake caliper anchor bracket to the hub carrier. Withdraw the caliper and anchor bracket, complete with brake pads and suspend the assembly from a suitable place under the wheel arch using string or wire. To avoid straining the flexible brake hose or metal pipes, release the flexible hose from its support bracket(s) on the suspension strut.

6 Mark the relationship of the brake disc to the wheel hub with quick-drying paint then remove the disc.

7 Loosen the nuts securing the hub carrier to the suspension strut. If necessary, counter-hold the bolts. Do not remove the bolts at this stage.

8 Extract the split pin from the track rod end balljoint nut, and unscrew the nut as far as the end of the balljoint shank threads. Using a balljoint separator tool, release the track rod end balljoint tapered shank. Once the taper has separated, unscrew the nut and detach the track rod end from the hub carrier.

9 Unscrew the bolt and two nuts, and disconnect the suspension lower balljoint from the lower arm.

10 Hold the hub carrier, and release the driveshaft outer CV joint from the hub bearings by tapping it towards the transmission with a soft-faced mallet.

11 Unscrew the nuts securing the hub carrier to the suspension strut, then withdraw the bolts, and remove the hub carrier.

Refitting

12 Refitting is a reversal of removal, bearing in mind the following points.

  a) *Tighten all fixings to the specified torque.*
  b) *Do not fully tighten the hub carrier-to-suspension strut nuts until the lower arm*

and track rod end balljoints have been reconnected.

  c) *Use new split pins to secure the track rod end balljoint nut, and the hub/driveshaft nut and locking cap, and bend over the split pin legs to secure.*
  d) *When refitting the brake disc, align the marks made on removal.*
  e) *Refit the ABS wheel sensor (where fitted), as described in Chapter 9.*
  f) *On completion, have the front wheel alignment checked at the earliest opportunity.*

3S-GE engine models

Removal

13 The hub carrier must be removed complete with the suspension strut as an assembly, as described in the following paragraphs.

14 Proceed as described in paragraphs 1 to 6.

15 Extract the split pin from the track rod end balljoint nut, and unscrew the nut as far as the end of the balljoint shank threads. Using a balljoint separator tool, release the track rod end balljoint tapered shank. Once the taper has separated, unscrew the nut and detach the track rod end from the hub carrier.

16 Unscrew the securing nut, and disconnect the anti-roll bar drop link from the suspension strut. It will be necessary to counterhold the drop link pin using an Allen key or hexagon bit as the nut is unscrewed.

17 Remove the split pin from the camber control arm-to-suspension strut balljoint. Loosen the balljoint nut, and unscrew it as far as the end of the threads on the joint.

18 Using a suitable puller, disconnect the suspension strut from the camber control arm.

19 Unscrew the nut and two bolts, and disconnect the hub carrier from the suspension lower balljoint attachment.

20 Hold the hub carrier, and release the driveshaft outer CV joint from the hub bearings by tapping it towards the transmission with a soft-faced mallet.

21 Have an assistant support the lower end of the strut/hub carrier assembly. Alternatively, support the lower end of the strut/hub carrier assembly using a jack and a block of wood.

22 Working in the engine compartment, unscrew the three nuts securing the top of the suspension strut to the vehicle body. Ensure that the strut is adequately supported before fully unscrewing the nuts.

23 Lower the strut/hub carrier assembly, and withdraw it from under the wheel arch.

24 The hub carrier can now be removed from the strut as follows.

25 Clamp the assembly in a soft-jawed vice.

26 Remove the split pin from the suspension strut-to-hub carrier balljoint nut. Loosen the balljoint nut, and unscrew it as far as the end of the threads on the balljoint.

27 Using a balljoint separator tool, free the suspension strut-to-hub carrier balljoint. Unscrew the nut, and disconnect the suspension strut from the hub carrier.

Refitting

28 Refitting is a reversal of removal, bearing in mind the following points.

  a) *Tighten all fixings to the specified torque.*
  b) *Use new split-pins to secure the camber control arm-to-suspension strut balljoint nut, the track rod end balljoint nut, and the hub/driveshaft nut and locking cap, and bend over the split pin legs to secure.*
  c) *When refitting the brake disc, align the marks made on removal.*
  d) *Refit the ABS wheel sensor (where fitted), as described in Chapter 9.*
  e) *On completion, have the front wheel alignment checked at the earliest opportunity (see Section 25).*

3 Front hub bearing - checking and renewal

Checking

1 Chock the rear wheels then jack up the front of the car and support it on axle stands (see *Jacking and Vehicle Support*). Remove the relevant front roadwheel.

2 Undo the two bolts securing the brake caliper anchor bracket to the hub carrier. Withdraw the caliper and anchor bracket, complete with brake pads and suspend the assembly from a suitable place under the wheel arch using string or wire. To avoid straining the flexible brake hose or metal pipes, release the flexible hose from its support bracket(s) on the suspension strut.

3 Mark the relationship of the brake disc to the wheel hub with quick-drying paint then remove the disc.

4 Wear in the front hub bearings can be checked by measuring the amount of side play present. To do this, a dial gauge should be fixed so that its probe is in contact with the disc contact face of the wheel hub, near the centre of the hub. The axial play should be between 0 and 0.05 mm. If the play is greater than specified, the bearings are worn excessively and must be renewed.

5 At the same time, check the run-out of the wheel hub by repositioning the dial gauge probe towards the outside edge of the hub. Rotate the hub, and observe the deviation in the reading. If the run-out is greater than 0.07 mm, the wheel hub should be renewed.

Renewal

Note: *The front hub bearings should only be removed from the hub carrier if they are to be renewed. The removal procedure renders the bearings unserviceable, and they must not be re-used. Prior to dismantling, it should be noted that a hub/bearing puller, a slide*

10

hammer and adaptor and an assortment of metal tubes of various diameters (and preferably, a press) will be required. Unless these tools are available, the renewal of the hub bearings will have to be entrusted to a Toyota dealer or suitably equipped garage. Under no circumstances attempt to tap the hub bearings into position, as this will render them unserviceable.

6 Remove the hub carrier as described in Section 2.

7 Working at the inboard side of the hub carrier, prise off the dust excluder, using a screwdriver **(see illustrations 1.1 and 1.2).**

8 Prise the oil seal from the inboard side of the hub carrier. It may be necessary to use a suitable puller or a slide hammer and adaptor if the seal is very tight.

9 Using circlip pliers, extract the bearing retaining circlip from the inboard side of hub carrier.

10 On all except 3S-GE engine models, remove the split pin from the hub carrier lower balljoint nut. Loosen the balljoint nut, and unscrew it as far as the end of the threads on the balljoint. Using a suitable balljoint separator tool, disconnect the balljoint from the hub carrier.

11 Using a puller, or a slide hammer and adaptor, pull the wheel hub from the bearing in the hub carrier. The bearing outer race will be withdrawn with the wheel hub during this procedure.

12 Using a thin metal plate, support the bearing outer race (still attached to the wheel hub), then drive or press the hub from the outer race, using a socket or tube of the correct diameter.

13 Unscrew the securing bolts, and remove the brake disc shield from the hub carrier.

14 Prise the oil seal from the outboard side of the hub carrier. Again, it may be necessary to use a suitable puller or a slide hammer and adaptor if the seal is very tight.

15 Support the inboard side of the hub carrier, then drive or press out the bearing, using a socket or tube acting on the bearing outer race.

16 Thoroughly clean the bearing contact face of the hub carrier.

17 Support the outboard side of the hub carrier, then press in the new bearing up to the shoulder in the hub carrier, using a socket or tube acting on the bearing outer race.

18 Secure the bearing using a new retaining circlip, ensuring that the circlip locates fully in its groove.

19 Fit a new outboard oil seal using a socket or tube of suitable diameter to tap the seal into the hub carrier.

20 Refit the brake disc shield, and securely tighten the four bolts.

21 Support the outboard side of the wheel hub (do not support the hub on the wheel studs), then press the hub carrier onto the wheel hub, using a socket or tube acting on the bearing inner race.

22 Where applicable, fit the lower balljoint to the hub carrier, then refit the nut, and tighten to the specified torque. Insert a new split pin and bend over the split pin legs to secure the nut.

23 Using a suitable socket or tube, fit a new inboard oil seal to the hub carrier then tap a new dust excluder into position. Where applicable, ensure that the holes for the ABS wheel sensor in the dust excluder and the hub carrier are aligned.

24 Refit the hub carrier as described in Section 2.

4 Front suspension strut - removal, overhaul and refitting

All except 3S-GE engine models

Removal

1 Chock the rear wheels then jack up the front of the car and support it on axle stands (see *Jacking and Vehicle Support*). Remove the relevant front roadwheel.

2 Where necessary unscrew the bolts securing the wiring/hose bracket to the suspension strut, and release the flexible brake hose and, where applicable, the ABS wheel sensor wiring from the suspension strut **(see illustration).**

3 Loosen the nuts securing the hub carrier to the suspension strut. If necessary, counterhold the bolts. Remove the nuts and the bolts, and release the suspension strut from the hub carrier **(see illustration)**.

4 Ensure that the lower end of the strut is supported then, working in the engine compartment, unscrew the three nuts securing the top of the suspension strut to the vehicle body. Remove the nuts and stiffener plate, then withdraw the strut from under the wheel arch **(see illustrations)**.

Overhaul

Warning: Before attempting to dismantle the suspension strut, a suitable tool to hold the coil spring in compression must be obtained. Adjustable coil spring compressors which can be positively secured to the spring coils are readily available, and are recommended for this operation. Any attempt to dismantle the strut without such a tool is likely to result in damage or personal injury.

4.2 Removing the flexible brake hose bracket from the suspension strut

4.3 Remove the nuts and the bolts, and release the suspension strut from the hub carrier

4.4a Unscrew the three nuts securing the top of the suspension strut to the vehicle body . . .

4.4b . . . remove the nuts and stiffener plate . . .

4.4c . . . then withdraw the strut from under the wheel arch

4.6 Fit the compressor and compress the spring until all tension is relieved from the upper mounting

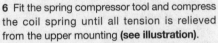

4.8 Unscrew the central piston rod nut while holding the upper spring seat

4.10a Lift off the upper mounting . . .

Note: *When holding the strut during the following procedure, with the coil spring removed, do not hold the strut by the lower spring seat, and avoid knocking the lower spring seat.*

5 With the strut removed from the car as described previously, clean away all external dirt then mount the strut upright in a vice.

HAYNES HiNT *Screw a bolt and two nuts into one of the hub carrier-to-suspension strut bolt holes in the strut to enable the strut to be clamped in place in the vice. Clamp the strut against the bolt head and outer nut.*

6 Fit the spring compressor tool and compress the coil spring until all tension is relieved from the upper mounting **(see illustration)**.

7 Prise off the dust cap from the top of the strut, then securely clamp the upper spring seat using a pair of grips or similar reaction tool so that it cannot rotate in relation to the strut.

8 Unscrew the central piston rod nut **(see illustration)**.

9 Note the orientation and location of all components to aid refitting.

10 Lift off the upper mounting, dust seal, upper spring seat, and upper mounting rubber **(see illustrations)**.

11 Lift off the spring and compressor tool **(see illustration)**. Do not remove the tool from the spring unless the spring is to be renewed.

12 Withdraw the bump rubber and the lower mounting rubber **(see illustrations)**.

13 With the strut assembly now completely dismantled, examine all the components for wear, damage or deformation. Check the rubbers for cracks and splits. Renew any of the components as necessary.

14 Examine the strut for signs of fluid leakage. Check the strut piston rod for signs of pitting along its entire length and check the strut body for signs of damage or elongation of the mounting bolt holes. Test the operation of the strut, while holding it in an upright position, by moving the piston rod through a full stroke and then through short strokes of 50 to 100 mm. In both cases the resistance felt should be smooth and continuous. If the resistance is jerky, or uneven, or if there is any visible sign of wear or damage to the strut, renewal is necessary.

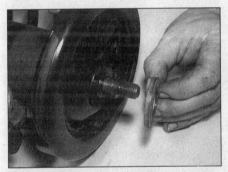

4.10b . . . the dust seal. . .

4.10c . . . the upper spring seat . . .

4.10d . . . and the upper mounting rubber

4.11 Withdraw the spring and compressor tool . . .

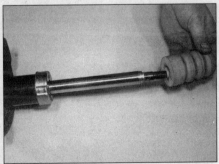

4.12a . . . followed by the bump rubber . . .

4.12b . . . and lower mounting rubber

10

5.6 Anti-roll bar drop link-to-lower arm bracket attachment (arrowed)

15 If any doubt exists about the condition of the coil spring, gradually release the spring compressor, and check the spring for distortion and signs of cracking. Since no minimum free length is specified by Toyota, the only way to check the tension of the spring is to compare it to a new component. Renew the spring if it is damaged or distorted, or if there is any doubt as to its condition.

16 Inspect all other components for signs of damage or deterioration, and renew any that are suspect.

17 Reassembly is a reversal of dismantling, bearing in mind the following points.

a) If a new strut is being fitted, prime the strut before refitting the spring, by compressing and extending the piston rod several times.
b) Ensure that all components are correctly orientated and positioned, as noted before dismantling.
c) Ensure that the locating lug on the lower mounting rubber engages with the corresponding cut-out in the lower spring seat.
d) Make sure that the spring ends are correctly located in the upper and lower seats.
e) Ensure that the upper spring seat is correctly orientated, with the arrow and OUT marking positioned on the outboard side of the strut.
f) Tighten the piston rod nut to the specified torque.
g) Pack grease around the top of the piston rod before refitting the dust cap.

Refitting

18 Refitting is a reversal of removal, but tighten all fixings to the specified torque and, on completion, have the front wheel alignment checked at the earliest opportunity (see Section 25).

3S-GE engine models

Removal and refitting

19 The procedure is described as part of the front hub carrier removal and refitting procedure in Section 2.

Overhaul

20 The procedure is as described in paragraphs 5 to 17 of this Section, but additionally, if desired, the balljoint at the lower end of the strut can be renewed as follows.

a) Using circlip pliers, remove the retaining circlip from the top of the balljoint.
b) Support the strut on a vice, then drive the balljoint from the housing in the strut. Drive the balljoint out downwards.
c) Thoroughly clean the housing in the strut.
d) Drive in the new balljoint from the bottom of the strut, then fit a new retaining circlip.

---

5 Front suspension lower arm(s) - removal and refitting

All except 3S-GE engine models

Note: If removing the left-hand lower arm on models equipped with automatic transmission, it will be necessary to remove the front subframe as described in Section 8; the left-hand lower arm can then be detached once the subframe is removed.

Removal

1 Chock the rear wheels then jack up the front of the car and support it on axle stands (see *Jacking and Vehicle Support*). Remove the relevant front roadwheel.

2 Extract the hub/driveshaft retaining nut split pin and remove the locking cap over the nut.

3 Have an assistant firmly depress the brake pedal to prevent the front hub from rotating. Using a socket and a long extension bar, slacken and remove the hub/driveshaft retaining nut. Alternatively, a tool can be fabricated to prevent the hub from rotating (see Chapter 8, Section 2). This nut is very tight; make sure that there is no risk of pulling the car off the axle stands.

4 Where applicable, remove the lower splash guard(s) to improve access.

5 Extract the split pin from the track rod end balljoint, and unscrew the balljoint nut as far as the end of the balljoint shank threads. Using a balljoint separator tool, release the track rod end balljoint tapered shank. Once the taper has separated, unscrew the nut and detach the track rod end from the hub carrier.

6 Unscrew the securing nut, and disconnect the anti-roll bar drop link from the bracket on the lower arm **(see illustration)**. Note that it may be necessary to counterhold the drop link pin using an Allen key or bit.

7 Unscrew the bolt and two nuts, and disconnect the suspension lower balljoint from the lower arm **(see illustration)**.

8 Unscrew the lower arm front pivot bolt and the two rear mounting bolts **(see illustration)**. Remove the rear mounting stiffener bracket and withdraw the lower arm from the subframe.

9 If the mounting and pivot bushes are found to be in poor condition, the complete arm must be renewed. The suspension arm must also be renewed if it has suffered any form of structural damage.

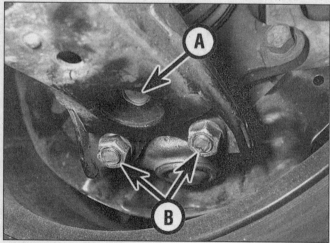

5.7 Suspension lower balljoint retaining bolt (A) and nuts (B)

5.8 Suspension lower arm front pivot bolt (arrowed)

Refitting

10 Locate the lower arm in position in the subframe and fit the front pivot bolt and the two mounting bolts. Tighten the bolts moderately tight only at this stage.

11 Reconnect the suspension lower balljoint to the lower arm and secure with the bolt and two nuts, tightened to the specified torque.

12 Reconnect the anti-roll bar drop link, then tighten the securing nut to the specified torque, counterholding the drop link pin as during removal, if necessary.

13 Engage the track-rod end balljoint shank with the hub carrier, and screw on the balljoint nut. Tighten the nut to the specified torque, fit a new split pin and bend over the split pin legs to secure. If the castellations in the nut do not line up with the hole in the balljoint shank, tighten the nut a little more until the split pin can be fitted.

14 Refit the hub/driveshaft retaining nut and, using the method employed on removal to prevent the hub from rotating, tighten the hub/driveshaft retaining nut to the specified torque. Check that the hub rotates freely.

15 Refit the driveshaft nut locking cap, fit a new split pin and bend over the split pin legs to secure.

16 Where applicable, refit the splash guards.

17 Refit the roadwheel, and lower the vehicle to the ground. Tighten the wheel nuts to the specified torque.

18 Bounce the car up and down several times to allow the suspension to settle.

19 Tighten the lower arm pivot and mounting bolts to the specified torque, starting with the front pivot bolt, then the forward mounting bolt and finally the rear mounting bolt.

20 On completion, have the wheel alignment checked as soon as possible (see Section 25).

3S-GE engine models

Note: *On 3S-GE engine models there are two suspension lower arms on each side. For the purposes of identification, the arm nearest the front of the car will be referred to as the No 1 arm, and the arm nearest the rear of the car will be referred to as the No 2 arm, throughout the following procedure* **(see illustration)**.

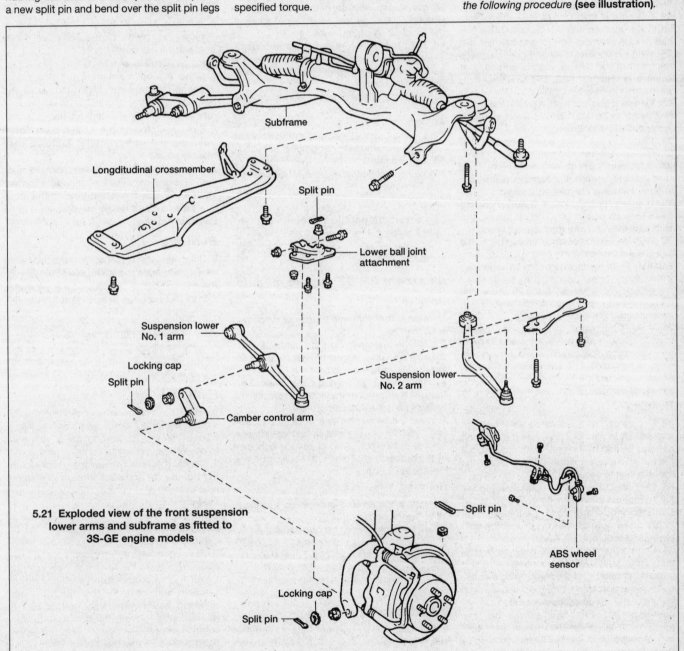

5.21 Exploded view of the front suspension lower arms and subframe as fitted to 3S-GE engine models

10

Removal

Note: *If removing the left-hand No 1 arm on models equipped with automatic transmission, it will be necessary to remove the front subframe as described in Section 8; the left-hand No 1 arm can then be detached once the subframe is removed.*

21 Chock the rear wheels then jack up the front of the car and support it on axle stands (see *Jacking and Vehicle Support*). Remove the relevant front roadwheel.

22 On models with ABS, remove the ABS wheel sensor from the hub carrier as described in Chapter 9, and release the sensor wiring from the suspension components.

23 Where applicable, remove the lower splash guard(s) to improve access.

24 Extract the split pin, remove the locking cap and unscrew the nut securing the hub carrier to the camber control arm balljoint.

25 Using a small two-legged puller, release the taper of the camber control arm balljoint shank and separate the suspension strut from the camber control arm balljoint.

26 Unscrew the nut and remove the pinch bolt securing the No 1 arm to the suspension lower balljoint attachment.

27 Undo the No 1 arm inner pivot bolt and remove the arm from the subframe.

28 Unscrew the nut and two bolts, and disconnect the hub carrier from the suspension lower balljoint attachment.

29 Unscrew the two No 2 arm inner mounting bolts. Remove the stiffener bracket and withdraw the No 2 arm from the subframe.

30 With the two lower arms removed from the car, the suspension lower balljoint attachment and the camber control arm may be separated from their arms using the procedures described in paragraphs 24 and 25 noting that a locking cap is not fitted to the suspension lower balljoint attachment.

31 If the suspension arm balljoints, or the mounting and pivot bushes are found to be in poor condition, the complete suspension arm must be renewed. The suspension arm must also be renewed if it has suffered any form of structural damage.

Refitting

32 Reconnect the suspension lower balljoint attachment to the No 2 arm, refit the retaining nut and tighten to the specified torque. Lock the nut with a new split pin and bend over the split pin legs to secure.

33 Reconnect the camber control arm to the No 1 arm, refit the retaining nut and tighten to the specified torque. Refit the locking cap, insert a new split pin and bend over the split pin legs to secure.

34 Locate the No 2 arm in position on the subframe, refit the two mounting bolts and stiffener bracket and moderately tighten the bolts. Final tightening is carried out with the weight of the car on its roadwheels.

35 Reconnect the hub carrier to the suspension lower balljoint attachment and secure with the nut and two bolts tightened to the specified torque.

36 Engage the No 1 arm with its subframe location while at the same time guiding the camber control arm balljoint into engagement with the suspension strut. Refit the No 1 arm inner pivot bolt and tighten it moderately tight only at this stage.

37 Connect the No 1 arm to the suspension lower balljoint attachment, refit the pinch bolt and nut and tighten the nut to the specified torque.

38 Refit the nut securing the camber control arm balljoint to the suspension strut and tighten the nut to the specified torque. Refit the locking cap, insert a new split pin and bend over the split pin legs to secure.

39 On models with ABS, refit the ABS wheel sensor to the hub carrier as described in Chapter 9, and re-attach the sensor wiring to the suspension components.

40 Refit the splash guard (s), where applicable, then refit the roadwheel and lower the car to the ground. Tighten the wheel nuts to the specified torque.

41 Settle the suspension by bouncing the car up and down several times.

42 Tighten the No 1 arm inner pivot bolt to the specified torque, followed by the No 2 arm mounting bolt and stiffener bracket bolt.

43 On completion, have the front wheel alignment checked at the earliest opportunity (see Section 25).

6 Front suspension lower balljoint - renewal

All except 3S-GE engine models

Removal

1 Remove the front hub carrier as described in Section 2.

2 With the hub carrier on the bench, extract the split pin and unscrew the nut securing the lower balljoint to the hub carrier.

3 Using a small two-legged puller, release the taper of the balljoint shank and separate the balljoint from the hub carrier.

4 Move the balljoint shank from side to side and check for any signs of excessive stiffness, binding or free play. Also check the condition of the rubber boot. Renew the balljoint if any defects are found.

Refitting

5 Refitting is a reversal of removal, bearing in mind the following points:
a) Tighten the balljoint-to-hub carrier retaining nut to the specified torque and insert a new split pin. Bend over the split pin legs to secure.
b) Refit the hub carrier as described in Section 2.

3S-GE engine models

6 The suspension balljoints are all integral with the suspension arms on 3S-GE engine models and cannot be renewed separately.

The suspension arms can be removed as described in Section 5, to allow the condition of the balljoints to be carefully examined, but if any defects are found, the relevant suspension arm must be renewed.

7 Front anti-roll bar components - removal and refitting

Removal

1 Remove the front subframe as described in Section 8.

2 On all except 3S-GE engine models, unscrew the securing nut, and disconnect the anti-roll bar drop links from the brackets on the lower suspension arms. Note that it may be necessary to counterhold the drop link pin using an Allen key or bit.

3 Undo the bolts securing the two clamp plates to the subframe, lift off the plates and remove the anti-roll bar. Remove the two rubber bushes from the anti-roll bar.

4 If required, the drop links can be removed from the anti-roll bar after undoing their retaining nuts.

5 Inspect the condition of the rubber bushes and renew if any signs of deterioration are visible. Check the condition of the drop link balljoints and renew the drop links if the balljoints are worn.

Refitting

6 Refitting is a reversal of removal, tightening all nuts and bolts to the specified torque. With the anti-roll bar in position on the subframe, refit the subframe as described in Section 8

8 Front subframe - removal and refitting

Removal

Note: *The following procedure depicts models equipped with power steering. Where manual steering is fitted, ignore all reference to power steering components.*

1 Chock the rear wheels then jack up the front of the car and support it on axle stands (see *Jacking and Vehicle Support*). Remove the front roadwheels.

2 Extract the left-hand hub/driveshaft retaining nut split pin and remove the locking cap over the nut.

3 Have an assistant firmly depress the brake pedal to prevent the front hub from rotating. Using a socket and a long extension bar, slacken and remove the hub/driveshaft retaining nut. Alternatively, a tool can be fabricated to prevent the hub from rotating (see Chapter 8, Section 2). This nut is very tight; make sure that there is no risk of pulling the car off the axle stands.

4 Repeat the operations described in paragraphs 2 and 3 on the right-hand side.

5 Where applicable, remove the underbody shield(s) to improve access.

6 Extract the split pin from the left-hand track rod end balljoint, and unscrew the balljoint nut as far as the end of the balljoint shank threads. Using a balljoint separator tool, release the track rod end balljoint tapered shank. Once the taper has separated, unscrew the nut and detach the track rod end from the hub carrier. Repeat this operation on the right-hand track rod end balljoint.

All except 3S-GE engine models

7 Unscrew the securing nuts, and disconnect the anti-roll bar drop links from the brackets on the lower suspension arms. Note that it may be necessary to counterhold the drop link pins using an Allen key or bit.

8 Unscrew the bolt and two nuts each side, and disconnect the suspension lower balljoint from each lower suspension arm.

3S-GE engine models

9 On models with ABS, remove the ABS wheel sensor from the hub carrier as described in Chapter 9, and release the sensor wiring from the suspension components.

10 Extract the split pin, remove the locking cap and unscrew the nut securing the hub carrier to the camber control arm balljoint.

11 Using a small two-legged puller, release the taper of the camber control arm balljoint shank and separate the suspension strut from the camber control arm balljoint.

12 Unscrew the nut and two bolts, and disconnect the hub carrier from the suspension lower balljoint attachment.

All models

13 Disconnect the fluid return hose from the power steering fluid reservoir and allow the fluid to drain into a suitable container.

14 Clean the area around the power steering pressure and return pipe unions on the steering gear pinion housing. Unscrew the pipe union nuts or banjo union bolts and where fitted, recover the sealing washers. Note that new sealing washers must be obtained for refitting.

15 Make alignment marks on the steering column intermediate shaft universal joint and the steering gear pinion shaft to ensure correct alignment when refitting. Undo the universal joint clamp bolt and separate the joint from the steering gear pinion shaft.

16 Refer to Chapter 4A and remove the exhaust downpipe and intermediate section.

17 Disconnect the power steering return hose at the support bracket above the steering gear.

18 Connect a hoist and lifting tackle to the engine lifting bracket at the left-hand end of the cylinder head, and raise the hoist to just take the weight of the engine.

19 From under the car, remove the engine/transmission longitudinal crossmember as follows.

a) Unscrew the two securing bolts, and remove the shield from the crossmember.
b) According to model, detach any additional pipe/cable support brackets from the crossmember.
c) Prise out the cover plugs, and unscrew the three bolts securing the front engine/transmission mounting to the crossmember.
d) Prise out the cover plug, and unscrew the bolt securing the rear engine/transmission mounting to the crossmember.
e) Where applicable, unscrew the securing bolt and release the air conditioning pipe clamp from the crossmember.
f) Unscrew the four securing bolts, and remove the crossmember.

20 Undo the power steering fluid cooler clamp retaining bolt.

21 Undo the nut and remove the rear engine/transmission mounting through bolt.

22 Position a jack under the subframe and just take the subframe weight.

23 Unscrew the subframe mounting bolts and nuts and slowly lower the subframe, steering gear and suspension arm assemblies to the ground. Withdraw the unit from under the car for further dismantling.

24 If required, the suspension arm(s) and steering gear can be unbolted from the subframe and removed, with reference to the relevant Sections of this Chapter.

Refitting

25 Refit the steering gear and suspension arm(s) to the subframe. Tighten the steering gear mounting bolts to the specified torque, but only tighten the suspension arm bolts moderately tight at this stage. Final tightening is carried out with the weight of the car on its roadwheels.

26 Manoeuvre the subframe assembly into position on the car and refit the retaining nuts and bolts. Tighten the mountings to the specified torque.

27 Refit the engine/transmission mounting through bolt and tighten the nut to the specified torque.

28 Refit the power steering fluid cooler clamp retaining bolt.

29 Refit the engine/transmission longitudinal crossmember and refit the retaining bolts, cover plugs and related components in the reverse of the removal sequence given in paragraph 19. Tighten all fastenings to the specified torque. Remove the hoist and lifting tackle once the crossmember is secure.

30 Reconnect the power steering return hose at the support bracket above the steering gear.

31 Refit the exhaust sections as described in Chapter 4A.

32 Attach the steering column intermediate shaft universal joint to the steering gear pinion shaft ensuring that the marks made on removal are aligned. If new components have been fitted and no marks are present, set the roadwheels, steering gear and steering wheel in the straight-ahead position, then reconnect the universal joint. Refit the clamp bolt and tighten to the specified torque.

33 Reconnect the power steering pressure and return pipe unions to the pinion housing using new sealing washers where applicable.

34 Reconnect the fluid return hose to the power steering fluid reservoir.

All except 3S-GE engine models

35 Reconnect the suspension lower balljoints to the lower arms and secure with the bolt and two nuts each side, tightened to the specified torque.

36 Reconnect the anti-roll bar drop links, then tighten the securing nuts to the specified torque, counterholding the drop link pins as during removal if necessary.

3S-GE engine models

37 Reconnect the hub carrier to the suspension lower balljoint attachment and secure with the nut and two bolts tightened to the specified torque.

38 Refit the nut securing the camber control arm balljoint to the suspension strut and tighten the nut to the specified torque. Refit the locking cap, insert a new split pin and bend over the split pin legs to secure.

39 On models with ABS, refit the ABS wheel sensor to the hub carrier as described in Chapter 9, and re-attach the sensor wiring to the suspension components.

All models

40 Engage the track-rod end balljoint shank with the hub carrier on each side, and screw on the balljoint nuts. Tighten the nuts to the specified torque, fit new split pins and bend over the split pin legs to secure. If the castellations in the nuts do not line up with the holes in the balljoint shanks, tighten the nuts a little more until the split pins can be fitted.

41 Refit the hub/driveshaft retaining nut each side and, using the method employed on removal to prevent the hub from rotating, tighten the hub/driveshaft retaining nuts to the specified torque. Check that the hubs rotate freely.

42 Refit the driveshaft nut locking caps, fit new split pins and bend over the split pin legs to secure.

43 Where applicable, refit the underbody shields.

44 Refit the roadwheel, and lower the vehicle to the ground. Tighten the roadwheel nuts to the specified torque.

45 Bounce the car up and down several times to allow the suspension to settle.

46 Tighten the lower arm pivot and mounting bolts to the specified torque, starting with the front pivot bolt, then the forward mounting bolt and finally the rear mounting bolt.

47 Fill the power steering fluid reservoir with the specified fluid (see *Lubricants and fluids*) then bleed the power steering gear as described in Section 22.

48 On completion, have the front wheel alignment checked at the earliest opportunity (see Section 25).

10

9.3 Two of the four hub carrier-to-rear axle carrier retaining bolts (arrowed)

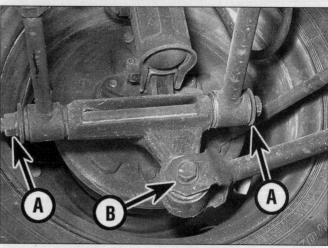

11.5 Rear transverse arm-to-axle carrier through-bolt and nut (A), and longitudinal arm attachment (B)

9 Rear hub carrier - removal and refitting

Removal

1 Chock the front wheels then jack up the rear of the car and support it on axle stands (see *Jacking and Vehicle Support*). Remove the relevant rear roadwheel.
2 Refer to Chapter 9 and remove the rear brake drum or rear brake disc, as applicable.
3 Undo the four bolts securing the hub carrier to the rear axle carrier **(see illustration)**. The bolts can be accessed by inserting a socket and extension bar through the hole in the wheel hub.
4 Withdraw the hub carrier assembly from the axle carrier and recover the sealing O-ring.

Refitting

5 Refitting is a reversal of removal, bearing in mind the following points:
a) Use a new sealing O-ring lightly lubricated with multi-purpose grease.
b) Tighten the hub carrier retaining bolts to the specified torque.
c) Refit the rear brake drum or disc as described in Chapter 9.

10 Rear hub bearing - checking and renewal

Checking

1 Chock the front wheels then jack up the rear of the car and support it on axle stands (see *Jacking and Vehicle Support*). Remove the rear roadwheels.
2 Refer to Chapter 9 and remove the rear brake drum or rear brake disc, as applicable.
3 Wear in the rear hub bearings can be checked by measuring the amount of side

play present. To do this, a dial gauge should be fixed so that its probe is in contact with the drum or disc contact face of the wheel hub, near the centre of the hub. The axial play should be between 0 and 0.05 mm. If the play is greater than specified, the bearings are worn excessively and must be renewed.
4 At the same time, check the run-out of the wheel hub by repositioning the dial gauge probe towards the outside edge of the hub. Rotate the hub, and observe the deviation in the reading. If the run-out is greater than 0.07 mm, the wheel hub and bearings should be renewed.

Renewal

Note: *The following procedure is only applicable to models without anti-lock brakes (ABS). On models with ABS the wheel sensor pulse wheels are an integral part of the wheel hub, and the wheel hub cannot be separated from the carrier/bearing assembly. On models so equipped, if renewal of the hub bearings is necessary a complete hub carrier and wheel hub assembly must be obtained.*

5 Remove the rear hub carrier as described in Section 9.
6 Mount the assembly in a vice with the wheel hub retaining nut at the rear of the hub carrier uppermost.
7 Using a small chisel, release the staking securing the retaining nut in place then undo the nut. Note that a new nut will be required for refitting.
8 Engage the legs of a two or three-legged puller behind the hub carrier flange and press the wheel hub out of the bearing in the hub carrier. The bearing outer race will be withdrawn with the hub during this procedure.
9 Using a thin metal plate, support the bearing outer race (still attached to the wheel hub), then drive or press the hub from the outer race, using a socket or tube of the correct diameter.
10 Obtain a new hub carrier/bearing assembly and a new wheel hub retaining nut.

11 Support the outboard side of the wheel hub (do not support the hub on the wheel studs), then press the hub carrier onto the wheel hub, using a socket or tube acting on the bearing inner race.
12 Fit the new wheel hub retaining nut and tighten the nut to the specified torque. Stake the nut in place to secure.
13 Refit the hub carrier as described in Section 9.

11 Rear axle carrier - removal and refitting

Removal

1 Remove the rear hub carrier as described in Section 9.
2 Withdraw the brake backplate from the axle carrier and tie the backplate to the rear coil spring using string or wire. To avoid straining the flexible brake hydraulic hose, disconnect it from the support bracket on the suspension strut.
3 On models with anti-lock brakes, undo the retaining bolt and remove the ABS wheel sensor from the axle carrier.
4 Where a load-sensing proportioning valve is fitted, unscrew the locknut securing the valve lower spring anchor to the right-hand rear suspension transverse link. Take care not to alter the position of the adjusting nut fitted just above. It is advisable to mark the adjusting nut and the spring anchor threads with quick drying paint so that the relative positions can be maintained.
5 Slacken the two nuts and bolts securing the suspension strut, and the nut and through-bolt securing the two transverse arms to the axle carrier **(see illustration)**.
6 Undo the nut and bolt and disconnect the longitudinal arm from the base of the axle carrier.

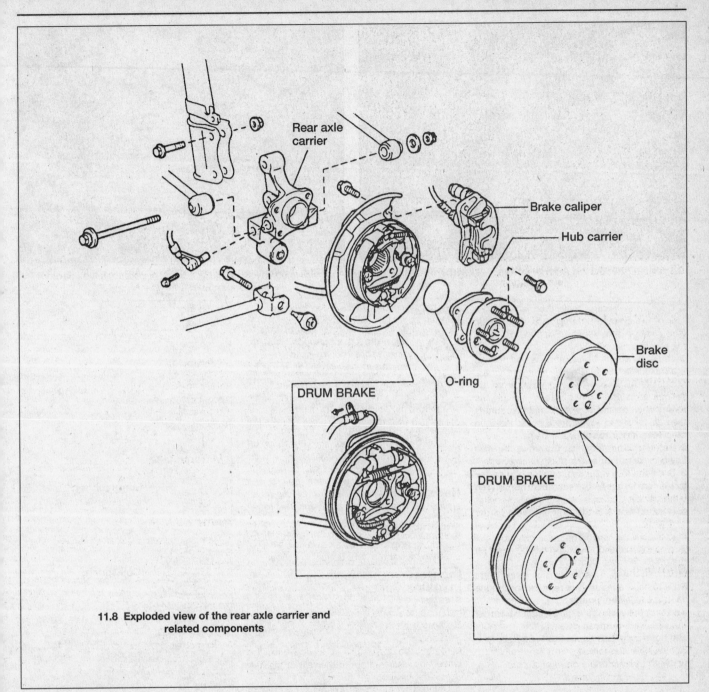

Rear axle carrier

Brake caliper

Hub carrier

Brake disc

O-ring

DRUM BRAKE

DRUM BRAKE

11.8 Exploded view of the rear axle carrier and related components

7 Remove the three previously slackened nuts and bolts and remove the axle carrier from the car.

Refitting

8 Connect the suspension strut, transverse arms and longitudinal arm to the axle carrier and tighten the nuts and bolts moderately tight only at this stage **(see illustration)**.
9 With the carrier in place, tighten the suspension strut-to-axle carrier nuts and bolts to the specified torque. The transverse and longitudinal arm securing nuts are tightened when the weight of the car is standing on its roadwheels.

10 Where applicable, refit the ABS wheel sensor and secure with the retaining bolt.
11 Reconnect the load sensing proportioning valve spring anchor and tighten the locknut without disturbing the position of the adjusting nut.
12 Place the brake backplate in position then refit the rear hub carrier (see Section 9).
13 Reconnect the brake hose support bracket to the suspension strut.
14 Refit the roadwheel, and lower the car to the ground. Tighten the wheel nuts to the specified torque.
15 Bounce the car up and down several times to allow the suspension to settle.

16 Tighten the longitudinal arm and transverse arm securing nuts and bolts to the specified torque.

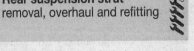

12 Rear suspension strut - removal, overhaul and refitting

10

Removal

1 Remove the rear seat as described in Chapter 11 then, where necessary for access, remove the screws and clips and lift out the rear parcel shelf.

12.4 Rear anti-roll bar drop link attachment (arrowed) to the rear suspension strut

12.5 Suspension strut-to-rear axle carrier retaining bolts (arrowed)

2 Chock the front wheels then jack up the rear of the car and support it on axle stands (see *Jacking and Vehicle Support*). Remove the relevant rear roadwheel.

3 Undo the support bracket bolts and remove the flexible brake hydraulic hose and where fitted, the ABS speed sensor wiring from the suspension strut.

4 Unscrew the securing nut, and disconnect the anti-roll bar drop link from the suspension strut **(see illustration)**. It will be necessary to counterhold the drop link pin using an Allen key or hexagon bit as the nut is unscrewed.

5 Slacken the two nuts and bolts securing the suspension strut to the rear axle carrier **(see illustration)**.

6 Position a jack under the rear axle carrier and raise the jack to just take the weight of the suspension assembly.

7 Working in the luggage compartment, lift off the protective cap from the centre of the strut mounting then unscrew the three nuts securing the top of the suspension strut to the vehicle body **(see illustration)**.

8 Lower the jack under the rear axle carrier then remove the previously slackened nuts and bolts securing the strut to the axle carrier. Remove the suspension strut assembly from under the wheel arch.

12.7 Rear suspension strut-to-body retaining nuts (arrowed)

Overhaul

  Warning: Before attempting to dismantle the suspension strut, a suitable tool to hold the coil spring in compression must be obtained. Adjustable coil spring compressors which can be positively secured to the spring coils are readily available, and are recommended for this operation. Any attempt to dismantle the strut without such a tool is likely to result in damage or personal injury.

Note: *When holding the strut during the following procedure, with the coil spring removed, do not hold the strut by the lower spring seat, and avoid knocking the lower spring seat.*

9 With the strut removed from the car as described previously, clean away all external dirt then mount the strut upright in a vice.

HAYNES HiNT *Screw a bolt and two nuts into one of the axle carrier-to-suspension strut bolt holes in the strut to enable the strut to be clamped in place in the vice. Clamp the strut against the bolt head and outer nut.*

10 Fit the spring compressor tool and compress the coil spring until all tension is relieved from the upper mounting.

11 Securely clamp the upper spring seat using a pair of grips so that it cannot rotate in relation to the strut.

12 Unscrew the central piston rod nut and remove the nut and collar **(see illustration)**.

13 Note the orientation and location of all components to aid refitting.

14 Lift off the upper mounting and upper spring seat, the spring and compressor tool. Do not remove the tool from the spring unless the spring is to be renewed.

15 Withdraw the bump rubber and the lower mounting rubber.

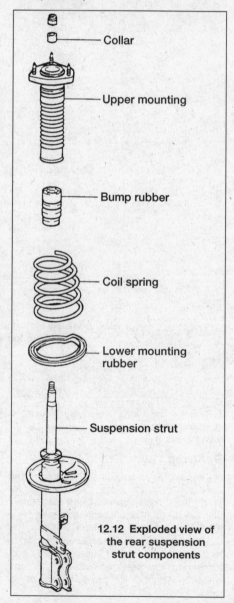

— Collar

— Upper mounting

— Bump rubber

— Coil spring

— Lower mounting rubber

— Suspension strut

12.12 Exploded view of the rear suspension strut components

16 With the strut assembly now completely dismantled, examine all the components for wear, damage or deformation. Check the rubbers for cracks and splits. Renew any of the components as necessary.

17 Examine the strut for signs of fluid leakage. Check the strut piston rod for signs of pitting along its entire length and check the strut body for signs of damage or elongation of the mounting bolt holes. Test the operation of the strut, while holding it in an upright position, by moving the piston rod through a full stroke and then through short strokes of 50 to 100 mm. In both cases the resistance felt should be smooth and continuous. If the resistance is jerky, or uneven, or if there is any visible sign of wear or damage to the strut, renewal is necessary.

18 If any doubt exists about the condition of the coil spring, gradually release the spring compressor, and check the spring for distortion and signs of cracking. Since no minimum free length is specified by Toyota, the only way to check the tension of the spring is to compare it to a new component. Renew the spring if it is damaged or distorted, or if there is any doubt as to its condition.

19 Inspect all other components for signs of damage or deterioration, and renew any that are suspect.

20 Reassembly is a reversal of dismantling, bearing in mind the following points.

 a) *If a new strut is being fitted, prime the strut before refitting the spring, by compressing and extending the piston rod several times.*

 b) *Ensure that all components are correctly orientated and positioned, as noted before dismantling.*

 c) *Make sure that the spring ends are correctly located in the upper and lower seats.*

 d) *Ensure that the upper spring seat is correctly orientated, with the pointed edge of the upper mounting positioned on the outboard side of the strut (see illustration).*

 e) *Tighten the piston rod nut to the specified torque.*

Refitting

21 Refitting is a reversal of removal, tightening all fixings to the specified torque.

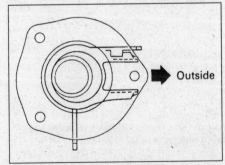

12.20 Correct orientation of the rear suspension strut upper spring seat

---

13 Rear suspension longitudinal links - removal and refitting

Removal

1 Chock the front wheels then jack up the rear of the car and support it on axle stands (see *Jacking and Vehicle Support*). Remove the rear roadwheel.

2 Undo the nut and bolt and disconnect the longitudinal arm from the base of the axle carrier.

3 Undo the nut and bolt and disconnect the longitudinal arm from its forward chassis mounting then remove the arm from car.

Refitting

4 Engage the arm in its chassis and axle carrier locations, fit the mounting nuts and bolts and tighten the nuts moderately tight only at this stage.

5 Refit the roadwheel, and lower the car to the ground. Tighten the wheel nuts to the specified torque.

6 Bounce the car up and down several times to allow the suspension to settle.

7 Tighten the longitudinal arm mounting nuts and bolts to the specified torque.

---

14 Rear suspension transverse links - removal and refitting

Removal

1 Remove both rear suspension longitudinal links as described in Section 13.

2 Where a load sensing proportioning valve is fitted, unscrew the locknut securing the valve lower spring anchor to the right-hand transverse link. Take care not to alter the position of the adjusting nut fitted just above. It is advisable to mark the adjusting nut and the spring anchor threads with quick drying paint so that the relative positions can be maintained.

3 Undo the two nuts and washers each side, withdraw the stiffener plate then remove the adjustable transverse links from the mounting through bolts at the rear axle carrier and subframe **(see illustration overleaf)**. Remove the links from under the car.

4 Refer to Chapter 4A and remove the exhaust intermediate section and tailpipe.

5 Place a jack under the centre of the rear subframe and raise the jack until it just contacts the subframe.

6 Undo the three bolts each side securing the subframe to the underbody.

7 Slowly lower the jack and subframe assembly until sufficient clearance exists for the transverse link inner mounting through bolts to be withdrawn.

8 Remove the mounting through bolts and washers securing the transverse links to the subframe and rear axle carriers, then remove the links from under the car.

9 To dismantle the adjustable transverse links, slacken the locknuts and unscrew the two link ends from the centre section.

10 Check the condition of all components and renew any that shoe evidence of damage or distortion. Note that if the mounting bushes in the links are worn, a new link must be obtained; the bushes are not available separately.

11 Prior to refitting, measure the length of the adjustable links between the centres of the mounting bolt holes. Set the length of each link to 493.3 ± 1.5 mm by slackening the locknuts and turning the centre section. Once the link length is set, check that there are the same number of exposed threads visible next to the locknuts on each side. If not, turn the links themselves in relation to the centre section, as necessary, until the length is correct and the same number of threads are visible each side. Tighten the locknuts when all is correct.

Refitting

12 Refitting is a reversal of removal, bearing in mind the following points:

 a) *Position the links with their paint marks toward the outside of the car and facing to the rear.*

 b) *Secure the links with the mounting through bolts, washers and nuts, but only tighten the nuts moderately tight at this stage. Final tightening is carried out with the weight of the car on its roadwheels.*

 c) *Locate the subframe in position and tighten the six mounting bolts to the specified torque.*

 d) *Where fitted, reconnect the load sensing proportioning valve spring anchor and tighten the locknut without disturbing the position of the adjusting nut.*

 e) *Refit the longitudinal links as described in Section 13.*

 f) *Refit the exhaust sections as described in Chapter 4A.*

 g) *With the car on its roadwheels, bounce it up and down several times to allow the suspension to settle then tighten the longitudinal arm and transverse link mounting nuts and bolts to the specified torque.*

 h) *On completion have the rear wheel alignment checked at the earliest opportunity (see Section 25).*

---

15 Rear anti-roll bar components - removal and refitting

Removal

1 Chock the front wheels then jack up the rear of the car and support it on axle stands (see *Jacking and Vehicle Support*). Remove the rear roadwheels.

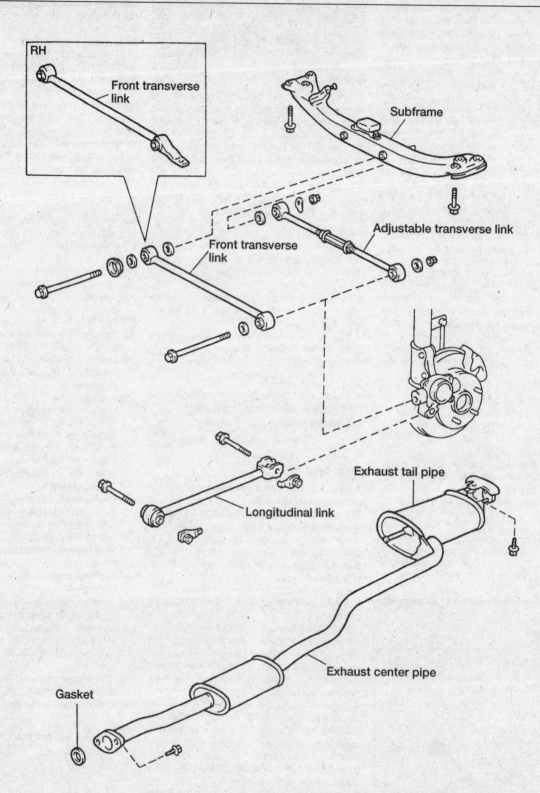

RH

Front transverse link

Subframe

Front transverse link

Adjustable transverse link

Longitudinal link

Exhaust tail pipe

Exhaust center pipe

Gasket

14.3 Exploded view of the rear suspension transverse links and related components

2 Unscrew the securing nuts, and disconnect the anti-roll bar drop links from the rear suspension struts **(see illustration)**. Note that it may be necessary to counterhold the drop link pins using an Allen key or bit.

3 Disconnect the drop links from the anti-roll bar in the same way and remove the links.

4 Undo the bolts securing the two clamp plates to the chassis members each side and lift off the plates.

5 Turn the anti-roll bar as necessary and manoeuvre it out from under the car. Withdraw the two bushes from the anti-roll bar after removal.

6 Inspect the condition of the rubber bushes and renew if any signs of deterioration are visible. Check the condition of the drop link balljoints and renew the drop links if the balljoints are worn.

Refitting

7 Refitting is a reversal of removal, tightening all nuts and bolts to the specified torque.

16 Rear subframe - removal and refitting

Rear subframe removal and refitting is part of the rear transverse link removal and refitting operations. Refer to Section 14 for the full procedure.

17 Steering wheel - removal and refitting

Removal

Models without air bag

1 Disconnect the battery negative (earth) lead (refer to Chapter 5A, Sections 1 and 3).

2 Turn the ignition key to release the steering

15.2 Rear anti-roll bar drop link attachments

lock, then set the front roadwheels in the straight-ahead position. Move the ignition key to the OFF position.

3 Undo the screw(s) securing the centre pad to the steering wheel. These are located either underneath the steering wheel or at the side.

4 Lift off the centre pad from the steering wheel and disconnect the horn wiring connector.

5 Unscrew the retaining nut from the centre of the steering wheel, then mark the position of the steering wheel in relation to the column shaft using quick drying paint. Grip the wheel each side, pull and withdraw it from the column shaft. If the wheel is tight, use a suitable puller. Threaded holes are provided in the steering wheel hub for this purpose.

Models with air bag

 Warning: Handle the air bag with extreme care as a precaution against personal injury, and always hold it with the cover facing away from your body. If in doubt concerning any proposed work involving the air bag or its control circuitry, consult a Toyota dealer or other qualified specialist.

6 Turn the ignition key to release the steering lock, then set the front roadwheels in the straight-ahead position. Move the ignition key to the OFF position.

17.8 Using a suitable Torx bit, undo the screws securing the air bag module to the steering wheel . . .

7 Disconnect the battery negative (earth) lead (refer to Chapter 5A, Sections 1 and 3).

 Warning: Before proceeding, wait a minimum of 15 minutes, as a precaution against accidental firing of the air bag. This period ensures that any stored energy in the back-up capacitor is dissipated.

8 Using a suitable Torx bit, undo the screws securing the air bag module to the steering wheel **(see illustration)**. These are located or at the side of the steering wheel and may be concealed behind trim cappings. Do not remove the screws completely, only unscrew them until the groove in the circumference of the screw catches on the screw case.

9 Pull the air bag module off the steering wheel and disconnect the module electrical connector **(see illustration)**.

 Warning: Position the air bag module in a safe place, with the mechanism facing downwards as a precaution against accidental operation.

10 Mark the position of the steering wheel in relation to the column shaft using quick drying paint, then unscrew the retaining nut from the centre of the steering wheel **(see illustration)**.

10

17.9 . . . then lift off the module and disconnect the wiring connector

17.10 Make alignment marks between the steering wheel and column shaft then undo the retaining nut

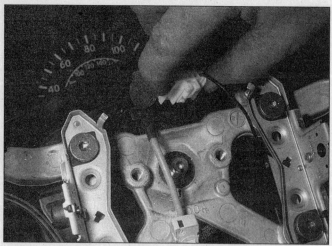

17.11 Disconnect the horn wiring connector and remove the steering wheel

18.2a Undo the two screws . . .

11 Disconnect the horn wiring at the connector then grip the wheel each side, pull and withdraw it from the column shaft **(see illustration)**. If the wheel is tight use a suitable puller. Threaded holes are provided in the steering wheel hub for this purpose.

Refitting

Models without air bag

12 Refitting is a reversal of removal. Align the marks made on removal when engaging the steering wheel with the column shaft and tighten the retaining nut to the specified torque.

Models with air bag

13 Make sure that the front wheels are in the straight-ahead position. Turn the contact ring assembly at the top of the column behind the steering wheel location, anti-clockwise until it becomes tight. Now turn it clockwise two complete turns and align the arrow markers on the lower left of the contact ring face.

14 Align the marks on the steering wheel and column shaft made on removal and locate the wheel in position.
15 Refit the retaining nut and tighten it to the specified torque.
16 Reconnect the horn wiring connector.
17 Reconnect the air bag module wiring connector and place the module over the steering wheel. Make sure that the wiring is positioned correctly and not trapped by the module as it is fitted.
18 Tighten the module retaining screws and reconnect the battery.

18 Steering column and intermediate shaft - removal, inspection and refitting

Removal

1 Remove the steering wheel as described in Section 17.

2 Undo the two screws securing the upper and lower steering column shrouds and lift off the upper shroud **(see illustrations)**.
3 Undo the lower shroud retaining screw(s) and lift off the lower shroud **(see illustration)**.
4 Unscrew the retaining screws and withdraw the lower trim panel located beneath the steering column. Detach the bonnet pull lever (2 screws) then disconnect the wiring from the instrument panel illumination rheostat. Remove the lower trim panel. Remove the heater air duct for access to the base of the steering column.
5 Unclip the large wiring connector from the steering column then disconnect the combination switch and ignition switch loom plate connectors.
6 Undo the screws securing the combination switch and remove the switch from the steering column.
7 Mark the relative positions of the steering column shaft to the intermediate shaft upper universal joint, then remove the clamp bolt and washer **(see illustration)**.

18.2b . . . then lift off the upper steering column shroud

18.3 Undo the screw and lift off the lower steering column shroud

18.7 Intermediate shaft universal joint clamp bolt (arrowed)

18.8 The steering column is attached to its mounting under the facia by four studs and nuts like these

8 Undo the four nuts securing the steering column to its mounting under the facia and release the column shaft from the intermediate shaft upper universal joint **(see illustration)**. Remove the steering column assembly from the car.

9 To remove the intermediate shaft, release the retaining clip and remove the intermediate shaft rubber dust cover from the floor.

10 Undo the clamp bolt securing the intermediate shaft lower universal joint to the steering gear pinion shaft **(see illustration)**.

11 Carefully lever the lower universal joint up the pinion shaft until the relationship of the joint to the shaft can be marked, then separate the joint from the shaft. Remove the intermediate shaft from inside the car.

Refitting

12 Refitting is a reversal of removal, bearing in mind the following points:

a) Tighten all nuts and bolts to the specified torque (where given).

b) Ensure that the alignment marks made during removal between the steering gear pinion, steering column shaft and intermediate shaft universal joints are aligned.

c) Refit the steering wheel as described in Section 17.

19 Ignition switch/steering column lock - removal and refitting

Removal

1 Undo the two screws securing the upper and lower steering column shrouds and lift off the upper shroud.

2 Undo the lower shroud retaining screw(s) and lift off the lower shroud.

3 Unscrew the retaining screws and withdraw the lower trim panel located beneath the steering column. Detach the bonnet pull lever (2 screws) then disconnect the wiring from the instrument panel illumination rheostat. Remove the lower trim panel. Remove the heater air duct for access to the base of the steering column.

4 Insert the ignition key into the lock and turn it to the ACC position.

5 Depress the lock barrel securing plunger, using a thin rod (welding rod or similar) inserted through the access hole in the lock housing, while pulling the key to withdraw the lock barrel.

Refitting

6 Refitting is a reversal of removal. Ensure that the barrel is correctly aligned so that its shaft engages with the loom plate, and ensure that the plunger positively secures it.

18.10 Intermediate shaft lower universal joint-to-steering gear pinion clamp bolt (arrowed)

10

20.3a Typical steering gear-to-subframe left-hand mounting . . .

20.3b . . . and right-hand mounting (right-hand drive version shown)

20 Steering gear assembly - removal and refitting

Removal

1 Remove the front subframe as described in Section 8.
2 Undo the bolts securing the engine/ transmission mounting bracket to the subframe and remove the bracket and mounting.
3 Undo the steering gear mounting bolts and nuts and remove the steering gear from the subframe **(see illustrations)**.

Refitting

4 Refitting is a reversal of removal. Tighten the steering gear and engine/transmission mounting bracket nuts and bolts to the specified torque then refit the subframe as described in Section 8.

21 Steering gear rubber gaiters - renewal

1 Remove the track rod end from the track rod as described in Section 24.
2 Count and record the number of exposed threads from the back of the track rod end locknut to the beginning of the threaded portion of the track rod. Now unscrew the locknut.
3 Release the rubber gaiter retaining clips and withdraw the gaiter from the steering gear and track rod **(see illustration)**.
4 Liberally apply molybdenum disulphide grease (manual steering gear) or power steering fluid (power steering gear) to the rack teeth, bush and track rod inner balljoint.
5 Fit the new gaiter and its new inner clip to the steering gear ensuring that they are correctly located, then fasten the clip to secure. Secure the small end of the gaiter with a new outer clip.

6 Screw the track rod end locknut back onto the track rod positioning it in the exact location as noted during removal.
7 Refit the track rod end as described in Section 24.

22 Power steering hydraulic system - bleeding

1 This will normally only be required if any part of the hydraulic system has been disconnected.
2 Referring to *Weekly Checks*, remove the fluid reservoir filler cap, and top-up with the specified fluid to the maximum level mark.
3 Start the engine and allow it to idle, slowly moving the steering wheel from lock-to-lock three or four times to purge out the air. Hold the steering wheel at full lock each way, for two to three seconds before turning to full lock the other way.
4 With the engine still running, note the reservoir fluid level and check that the fluid is not foaming or cloudy. Stop the engine and check that the fluid level does not rise by more than 5.0 mm above the level noted with the engine running. If a problem is found, proceed as follows.

21.3 Steering gear rubber gaiter outboard retaining clip

5 Disconnect the fluid return hose from the reservoir and plug the reservoir connection. Top-up the reservoir with fresh fluid of the specified type and engage the help of an assistant to start and stop the engine as required. Also have a container ready to collect the fluid which will be discharged from the disconnected return hose.
6 Have your assistant start the engine and run it at 1000 rpm. After one or two seconds, fluid should begin to discharge from the return hose; when it does, have your assistant stop the engine immediately.
7 Top up the fluid reservoir and repeat the procedure in paragraph 6 (keeping the fluid reservoir topped up) until there is no air in the fluid being discharged.
8 Remove the temporarily fitted plug and reconnect the fluid return hose to the reservoir. Work as quickly as possible to minimise fluid loss and prevent the need to repeat the procedure.
9 Repeat the bleeding procedure described in paragraph 1 to 4.

23 Power steering pump - removal and refitting

Removal

1 Remove the auxiliary (power steering pump) drivebelt as described in Chapter 1.
2 On 3S-FE and 3S-GE engine models, remove the right-hand driveshaft as described in Chapter 8.
3 Slacken the hose clip and disconnect the fluid return hose from the pump. Allow the fluid to drain into a suitable container.
4 Undo the banjo union bolt and disconnect the fluid feed (pressure) pipe from the pump, collecting the sealing washers as the union is disconnected. Note that new sealing washers will be required for refitting.

5 Where fitted, disconnect the fluid cooler feed and return pipe unions from the pump and the small bore hoses from the air control valve.

6 Undo the pump mounting bolt and adjuster bolt and remove the pump assembly from the engine.

Refitting

7 Refitting is a reversal of removal, bearing in mind the following points:

a) *Tighten all fastenings to the specified torque.*

b) *Use new sealing washers on the fluid feed pipe union.*

c) *On 3S-FE and 3S-GE engine models, refit the driveshaft as described in Chapter 8.*

d) *Refit and adjust the auxiliary drive belt as described in Chapter 1.*

e) *On completion, bleed the power steering hydraulic system as described in Section 22.*

24 Track rod end - removal and refitting

Removal

1 Chock the rear wheels then jack up the front of the car and support it on axle stands (see *Jacking and Vehicle Support*). Remove the relevant front roadwheel.

2 Use a wire brush to scrub clean the exposed track rod threads, then use a straight edge and a scriber, or similar, to mark the relationship of the track rod end to the track rod.

3 Holding the track rod end, unscrew its locknut by one quarter of a turn.

4 Extract the split pin from the track rod end balljoint nut, and unscrew the nut as far as the end of the balljoint shank threads **(see illustration)**. Using a balljoint separator tool, release the track rod end balljoint tapered shank. Once the taper has separated, unscrew the nut and detach the track rod end from the hub carrier.

5 Counting the exact number of turns necessary to do so, unscrew the track rod end from the track rod.

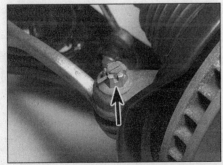

24.4 Track rod end balljoint retaining nut and split pin (arrowed)

Refitting

6 Screw the track rod end onto the track rod the number of turns noted during removal. This should return the track rod end to within a quarter turn of the locknut and, if the original component is being refitted, bring the marks made on removal into alignment. Now tighten the locknut while holding the track rod end securely.

7 Engage the shank of the track rod end balljoint with the hub carrier, and refit the locknut. Tighten the locknut to the specified torque then fit a new split pin. If the castellations in the nut do not line up with the holes in the balljoint shank, tighten the nuts a little more until the split pin can be fitted. Bend over the split pin legs to secure.

8 Refit the roadwheel, and lower the car to the ground. Tighten the wheel nuts to the specified torque.

9 Finally, have the front wheel alignment checked (see Section 25).

25 Wheel alignment and steering angles - general information

General

1 A car's steering and suspension geometry is defined in four basic settings - all angles are expressed in degrees (toe settings are also expressed as a measurement); the relevant settings are camber, castor, steering axis inclination, and toe-setting. With the exception of front and rear wheel toe-setting, none of these settings are adjustable on Carina E models.

Front wheel toe setting - checking and adjustment

2 Due to the special measuring equipment necessary to accurately check the wheel alignment, and the skill required to use it properly, checking and adjustment is best left to a Toyota dealer or similar expert. Note that most tyre-fitting shops now possess sophisticated checking equipment. The following is provided as a guide, should the owner decide to carry out a DIY check.

3 The front wheel toe setting is checked by measuring the distance between the front and rear inside edges of the roadwheel rims. Proprietary toe measurement gauges are available from motor accessory shops. Adjustment is made by screwing the track rods in or out of their track rod ends, to alter the effective length of the track rod assemblies.

4 For **accurate** checking, the vehicle **must** be at the kerb weight, ie unladen and with a full tank of fuel.

5 Before starting work, check the tyre pressures and tread wear (see Chapter 1), the condition of the hub bearings, the steering wheel free play, and the condition of the front suspension components. Correct any faults found.

6 Park the vehicle on level ground, check that the front roadwheels are in the straight-ahead position, then rock the rear and front ends to settle the suspension. Release the handbrake, and roll the vehicle backwards 1 metre, then forwards again, to relieve any stresses in the steering and suspension components.

7 Measure the distance between the front edges of the wheel rims and the rear edges of the rims. Subtract the smallest measurement from the largest, and check that the result is within the specified range.

8 If adjustment is necessary, apply the handbrake, then jack up the front of the vehicle and support it securely on axle stands (see *Jacking and Vehicle Support*). Turn the steering wheel onto full-left lock, and record the number of exposed threads on the right-hand track rod. Now turn the steering onto full-right lock, and record the number of threads on the left-hand side. If there are the same number of threads visible on both sides, then subsequent adjustment should be made equally on both sides. If there are more threads visible on one side than the other, it will be necessary to compensate for this during adjustment. **Note:** *It is most important that after adjustment, the same number of threads are visible on each track rod end.*

9 First clean the track rod end threads; if they are corroded, apply penetrating fluid before starting adjustment. Release the rubber gaiter outboard clips (where necessary), and peel back the gaiter; apply a smear of grease to the inside of the gaiter, so that both are free, and will not be twisted or strained as their respective track rods are rotated.

10 Use a straight-edge and a scriber or similar to mark the relationship of each track rod to its track rod end then, holding each track rod in turn, unscrew its locknut fully.

11 Alter the length of the track rods, bearing in mind the note made in paragraph 8. Screw them into or out of the track rod ends, rotating the track rods using a self-grip wrench. Shortening the track rods (screwing them into their track rod end balljoints) will reduce toe-in/increase toe-out.

12 When the setting is correct, hold the track rods and securely tighten the track rod end locknuts. Count the exposed threads to check the length of both track rods. If they are not the same, then the adjustment has not been made equally, and problems will be encountered with tyre scrubbing in turns; also, the steering wheel spokes will no longer be horizontal when the wheels are in the straight-ahead position.

13 If the track rod lengths are the same, lower the vehicle to the ground and re-check the toe setting; re-adjust if necessary. When the setting is correct, securely tighten the track rod end locknuts. Ensure that the rubber gaiters are seated correctly, and are not twisted or strained, and secure them in position with new retaining clips (where necessary).

10

Rear wheel toe setting - checking and adjustment

14 The measuring procedure for the rear wheel toe setting is essentially the same as described above for the front wheels but the adjustment is carried out by altering the length of the adjustable rear transverse links.

15 If, after measuring the toe setting, adjustment is required, first measure the length of the left and right-hand adjustable transverse links, between the centres of their two mounting bolts. If the length difference between the two is greater than 1.0 mm, slacken the locknuts on either side of the centre (adjusting) portion on one of the transverse links, and turn the adjusting portion as necessary until the length is equal to the length of the other transverse link **(see illustration)**.

16 Recheck the toe setting and make any corrections necessary by turning the adjusting portion of each transverse link by equal amounts. Recheck the toe setting after each adjustment and continue until the correct adjustment is obtained. When the setting is correct, securely tighten the locknuts on each side of the adjusting portion on each transverse link.

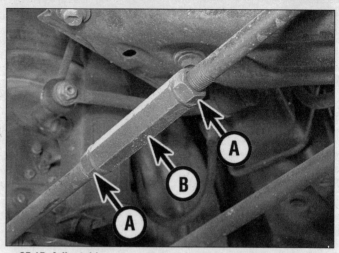

25.15 Adjustable rear transverse link locknuts (A) and centre (adjusting) portion (B)

Chapter 11
Bodywork and fittings

Contents

Degrees of difficulty

Easy, suitable for novice with little experience	**Fairly easy,** suitable for beginner with some experience	**Fairly difficult,** suitable for competent DIY mechanic 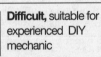	**Difficult,** suitable for experienced DIY mechanic	**Very difficult,** suitable for expert DIY or professional

Specifications

Torque wrench settings	Nm	lbf ft
Door hinges	29	21
Front seat mounting bolts	37	27
Rear seat mounting bolts	19	14
Seat belt mounting bolt	43	32
Hinge to tailgate	13	10
Tailgate hinge to body	21	15

1 General information

The bodyshell is made of pressed-steel sections, and is available in four-door Saloon, 5-door Hatchback and 5-door Estate versions. Most components are welded together, but some use is made of structural adhesives and the front wings are bolted on.

The front and rear body sections incorporate crumple zones and the doors are fitted with side bars. From September 1994, all models are fitted with a driver's air bag and a passenger airbag can be fitted as an option. The lower areas of the body and doors are coated with an anti-stone chipping protective material.

Extensive use is made of plastic materials, mainly in the interior, but also in exterior components. The outer sections of the front and rear bumpers are injection-moulded from a synthetic material which is very strong, and yet light. Plastic components such as wheel arch liners are fitted to the underside of the vehicle, to improve the body's resistance to corrosion.

2 Maintenance - bodywork and underframe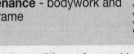

The general condition of a vehicle's bodywork is the one thing that significantly affects its value. Maintenance is easy, but needs to be regular. Neglect, particularly after minor damage, can lead quickly to further deterioration and costly repair bills. It is important also to keep watch on those parts of the vehicle not immediately visible, for instance the underside, inside all the wheel arches, and the lower part of the engine compartment.

The basic maintenance routine for the bodywork is washing - preferably with a lot of water, from a hose. This will remove all the loose solids which may have stuck to the vehicle. It is important to flush these off in such a way as to prevent grit from scratching the finish. The wheel arches and underframe need washing in the same way, to remove any accumulated mud, which will retain moisture and tend to encourage rust. Paradoxically enough, the best time to clean the underframe and wheel arches is in wet weather, when the mud is thoroughly wet and soft. In very wet weather, the underframe is usually cleaned of large accumulations automatically, and this is a good time for inspection.

Periodically, except on vehicles with a wax-based underbody protective coating, it is a good idea to have the whole of the underframe of the vehicle steam-cleaned, engine compartment included, so that a thorough inspection can be carried out to see what minor repairs and renovations are

11

necessary. Steam-cleaning is available at many garages, and is necessary for the removal of the accumulation of oily grime, which sometimes is allowed to become thick in certain areas. If steam-cleaning facilities are not available, there are some excellent grease solvents available which can be brush-applied; the dirt can then be simply hosed off. Note that these methods should not be used on vehicles with wax-based underbody protective coating, or the coating will be removed. Such vehicles should be inspected annually, preferably just prior to Winter, when the underbody should be washed down, and any damage to the wax coating repaired. Ideally, a completely fresh coat should be applied. It would also be worth considering the use of such wax-based protection for injection into door panels, sills, box sections, etc, as an additional safeguard against rust damage, where such protection is not provided by the vehicle manufacturer.

After washing paintwork, wipe off with a chamois leather to give an unspotted clear finish. A coat of clear protective wax polish will give added protection against chemical pollutants in the air. If the paintwork sheen has dulled or oxidised, use a cleaner/polisher combination to restore the brilliance of the shine. This requires a little effort, but such dulling is usually caused because regular washing has been neglected. Care needs to be taken with metallic paintwork, as special non-abrasive cleaner/polisher is required to avoid damage to the finish. Always check that the door and ventilator opening drain holes and pipes are completely clear, so that water can be drained out. Brightwork should be treated in the same way as paintwork. Windscreens and windows can be kept clear of the smeary film which often appears, by the use of proprietary glass cleaner. Never use any form of wax or other body or chromium polish on glass.

3 Maintenance - upholstery and carpets

Mats and carpets should be brushed or vacuum-cleaned regularly, to keep them free of grit. If they are badly stained, remove them from the vehicle for scrubbing or sponging, and make quite sure they are dry before refitting. Seats and interior trim panels can be kept clean by wiping with a damp cloth. If they do become stained (which can be more apparent on light-coloured upholstery), use a little liquid detergent and a soft nail brush to scour the grime out of the grain of the material. Do not forget to keep the headlining clean in the same way as the upholstery. When using liquid cleaners inside the vehicle, do not over-wet the surfaces being cleaned. Excessive damp could get into the seams and padded interior, causing stains, offensive odours or even rot.

> **HAYNES HiNT** *If the inside of the vehicle gets wet accidentally, it is worthwhile taking some trouble to dry it out properly, particularly where carpets are involved. Do not leave oil or electric heaters inside the vehicle for this purpose.*

4 Minor body damage - repair

Repairs of minor scratches in bodywork

If the scratch is very superficial, and does not penetrate to the metal of the bodywork, repair is very simple. Lightly rub the area of the scratch with a paintwork renovator, or a very fine cutting paste, to remove loose paint from the scratch, and to clear the surrounding bodywork of wax polish. Rinse the area with clean water.

Apply touch-up paint to the scratch using a fine paint brush; continue to apply fine layers of paint until the surface of the paint in the scratch is level with the surrounding paintwork. Allow the new paint at least two weeks to harden, then blend it into the surrounding paintwork by rubbing the scratch area with a paintwork renovator or a very fine cutting paste. Finally, apply wax polish.

Where the scratch has penetrated right through to the metal of the bodywork, causing the metal to rust, a different repair technique is required. Remove any loose rust from the bottom of the scratch with a penknife, then apply rust-inhibiting paint to prevent the formation of rust in the future. Using a rubber or nylon applicator, fill the scratch with bodystopper paste. If required, this paste can be mixed with cellulose thinners to provide a very thin paste which is ideal for filling narrow scratches. Before the stopper-paste in the scratch hardens, wrap a piece of smooth cotton rag around the top of a finger. Dip the finger in cellulose thinners, and quickly sweep it across the surface of the stopper-paste in the scratch; this will ensure that the surface of the stopper-paste is slightly hollowed. The scratch can now be painted over as described earlier in this Section.

Repairs of dents in bodywork

When deep denting of the vehicle's bodywork has taken place, the first task is to pull the dent out, until the affected bodywork almost attains its original shape. There is little point in trying to restore the original shape completely, as the metal in the damaged area will have stretched on impact, and cannot be reshaped fully to its original contour. It is better to bring the level of the dent up to a point which is about 3 mm below the level of the surrounding bodywork. In cases where the dent is very shallow anyway, it is not worth

trying to pull it out at all. If the underside of the dent is accessible, it can be hammered out gently from behind, using a mallet with a wooden or plastic head. Whilst doing this, hold a suitable block of wood firmly against the outside of the panel, to absorb the impact from the hammer blows and thus prevent a large area of the bodywork from being belled-out.

Should the dent be in a section of the bodywork which has a double skin, or some other factor making it inaccessible from behind, a different technique is called for. Drill several small holes through the metal inside the area - particularly in the deeper section. Then screw long self-tapping screws into the holes, just sufficiently for them to gain a good purchase in the metal. Now the dent can be pulled out by pulling on the protruding heads of the screws with a pair of pliers.

The next stage of the repair is the removal of the paint from the damaged area, and from an inch or so of the surrounding sound bodywork. This is accomplished most easily by using a wire brush or abrasive pad on a power drill, although it can be done just as effectively by hand, using sheets of abrasive paper. To complete the preparation for filling, score the surface of the bare metal with a screwdriver or the tang of a file, or alternatively, drill small holes in the affected area. This will provide a really good key for the filler paste.

To complete the repair, see the Section on filling and respraying.

Repairs of rust holes or gashes in bodywork

Remove all paint from the affected area, and from an inch or so of the surrounding sound bodywork, using an abrasive pad or a wire brush on a power drill. If these are not available, a few sheets of abrasive paper will do the job most effectively. With the paint removed, you will be able to judge the severity of the corrosion, and therefore decide whether to renew the whole panel (if this is possible) or to repair the affected area. New body panels are not as expensive as most people think, and it is often quicker and more satisfactory to fit a new panel than to attempt to repair large areas of corrosion.

Remove all fittings from the affected area, except those which will act as a guide to the original shape of the damaged bodywork (eg headlight shells etc). Then, using tin snips or a hacksaw blade, remove all loose metal and any other metal badly affected by corrosion. Hammer the edges of the hole inwards, in order to create a slight depression for the filler paste.

Wire-brush the affected area to remove the powdery rust from the surface of the remaining metal. Paint the affected area with rust-inhibiting paint, if the back of the rusted area is accessible, treat this also.

Before filling can take place, it will be necessary to block the hole in some way. This can be achieved by the use of aluminium or plastic mesh, or aluminium tape.

Aluminium or plastic mesh, or glass-fibre matting, is probably the best material to use for a large hole. Cut a piece to the approximate size and shape of the hole to be filled, then position it in the hole so that its edges are below the level of the surrounding bodywork. It can be retained in position by several blobs of filler paste around its periphery.

Aluminium tape should be used for small or very narrow holes. Pull a piece off the roll, trim it to the approximate size and shape required, then pull off the backing paper (if used) and stick the tape over the hole; it can be overlapped if the thickness of one piece is insufficient. Burnish down the edges of the tape with the handle of a screwdriver or similar, to ensure that the tape is securely attached to the metal underneath.

Bodywork repairs - filling and respraying

Before using this Section, see the Sections on dent, deep scratch, rust holes and gash repairs.

Many types of bodyfiller are available, but generally speaking, those proprietary kits which contain a tin of filler paste and a tube of resin hardener are best for this type of repair. A wide, flexible plastic or nylon applicator will be found invaluable for imparting a smooth and well-contoured finish to the surface of the filler.

Mix up a little filler on a clean piece of card or board - measure the hardener carefully (follow the maker's instructions on the pack), otherwise the filler will set too rapidly or too slowly. Using the applicator, apply the filler paste to the prepared area; draw the applicator across the surface of the filler to achieve the correct contour and to level the surface. As soon as a contour that approximates to the correct one is achieved, stop working the paste - if you carry on too long, the paste will become sticky and begin to pick-up on the applicator. Continue to add thin layers of filler paste at 20-minute intervals, until the level of the filler is just proud of the surrounding bodywork.

Once the filler has hardened, the excess can be removed using a metal plane or file. From then on, progressively-finer grades of abrasive paper should be used, starting with a 40-grade production paper, and finishing with a 400-grade wet-and-dry paper. Always wrap the abrasive paper around a flat rubber, cork, or wooden block - otherwise the surface of the filler will not be completely flat. During the smoothing of the filler surface, the wet-and-dry paper should be periodically rinsed in water. This will ensure that a very smooth finish is imparted to the filler at the final stage.

At this stage, the dent should be surrounded by a ring of bare metal, which in turn should be encircled by the finely feathered edge of the good paintwork. Rinse the repair area with clean water, until all of the dust produced by the rubbing-down operation has gone.

Spray the whole area with a light coat of primer - this will show up any imperfections in the surface of the filler. Repair these imperfections with fresh filler paste or bodystopper, and once more smooth the surface with abrasive paper. Repeat this spray-and-repair procedure until you are satisfied that the surface of the filler, and the feathered edge of the paintwork, are perfect. Clean the repair area with clean water, and allow to dry fully.

 If bodystopper is used, it can be mixed with cellulose thinners to form a really thin paste which is ideal for filling small holes.

The repair area is now ready for final spraying. Paint spraying must be carried out in a warm, dry, windless and dust-free atmosphere. This condition can be created artificially if you have access to a large indoor working area, but if you are forced to work in the open, you will have to pick your day very carefully. If you are working indoors, dousing the floor in the work area with water will help to settle the dust which would otherwise be in the atmosphere. If the repair area is confined to one body panel, mask off the surrounding panels; this will help to minimise the effects of a slight mis-match in paint colours. Bodywork fittings (eg chrome strips, door handles etc) will also need to be masked off. Use genuine masking tape, and several thicknesses of newspaper, for the masking operations.

Before commencing to spray, agitate the aerosol can thoroughly, then spray a test area (an old tin, or similar) until the technique is mastered. Cover the repair area with a thick coat of primer; the thickness should be built up using several thin layers of paint, rather than one thick one. Using 400-grade wet-and-dry paper, rub down the surface of the primer until it is really smooth. While doing this, the work area should be thoroughly doused with water, and the wet-and-dry paper periodically rinsed in water. Allow to dry before spraying on more paint.

Spray on the top coat, again building up the thickness by using several thin layers of paint. Start spraying at one edge of the repair area, and then, using a side-to-side motion, work until the whole repair area and about 2 inches of the surrounding original paintwork is covered. Remove all masking material 10 to 15 minutes after spraying on the final coat of paint.

Allow the new paint at least two weeks to harden, then, using a paintwork renovator, or a very fine cutting paste, blend the edges of the paint into the existing paintwork. Finally, apply wax polish.

Plastic components

With the use of more and more plastic body components by the vehicle manufacturers (eg bumpers. spoilers, and in some cases major body panels), rectification of more serious damage to such items has become a matter of either entrusting repair work to a specialist in this field, or renewing complete components. Repair of such damage by the DIY owner is not really feasible, owing to the cost of the equipment and materials required for effecting such repairs. The basic technique involves making a groove along the line of the crack in the plastic, using a rotary burr in a power drill. The damaged part is then welded back together, using a hot-air gun to heat up and fuse a plastic filler rod into the groove. Any excess plastic is then removed, and the area rubbed down to a smooth finish. It is important that a filler rod of the correct plastic is used, as body components can be made of a variety of different types (eg polycarbonate, ABS, polypropylene).

Damage of a less serious nature (abrasions, minor cracks etc) can be repaired by the DIY owner using a two-part epoxy filler repair material. Once mixed in equal proportions, this is used in similar fashion to the bodywork filler used on metal panels. The filler is usually cured in twenty to thirty minutes, ready for sanding and painting.

If the owner is renewing a complete component himself, or if he has repaired it with epoxy filler, he will be left with the problem of finding a suitable paint for finishing which is compatible with the type of plastic used. At one time, the use of a universal paint was not possible, owing to the complex range of plastics encountered in body component applications. Standard paints, generally speaking, will not bond to plastic or rubber satisfactorily. However, it is now possible to obtain a plastic body parts finishing kit which consists of a pre-primer treatment, a primer and coloured top coat. Full instructions are normally supplied with a kit, but basically, the method of use is to first apply the pre-primer to the component concerned, and allow it to dry for up to 30 minutes. Then the primer is applied, and left to dry for about an hour before finally applying the special-coloured top coat. The result is a correctly-coloured component, where the paint will flex with the plastic or rubber, a property that standard paint does not normally possess.

5 Major body damage - repair

Where serious damage has occurred, or large areas need renewal due to neglect, it means that complete new panels will need welding-in, and this is best left to professionals. If the damage is due to impact, it will also be necessary to check completely the alignment of the bodyshell, and this can only be carried out accurately by a Toyota dealer using special jigs. If the body is left misaligned, it is primarily dangerous, as the car will not handle properly, and secondly, uneven stresses will be imposed on the steering, suspension and possibly transmission, causing abnormal wear, or complete failure, particularly to such items as the tyres.

11

6.6 Removing the wheelarch liner-to-front bumper screws

6.7 Front bumper lower mounting bolt removal

6.8 Front bumper upper mounting bolt removal

6 Bumpers - removal and refitting

Front bumper

Removal

1 To improve access, apply the handbrake, then jack up the front of the vehicle and support on axle stands (see *Jacking and Vehicle Support*).

2 Unbolt and remove the splash guards from the underbody.

3 Remove the radiator grille as described in Section 7.

4 Remove the front indicator light units as described in Chapter 12.

5 Where applicable, remove the fog and driving lights from the front bumper.

6 Working under the front wheelarches, unscrew the screws securing the wheelarch liners to the front bumper (**see illustration**). Carefully pull out the liner for access to the bolts securing the rear of the front bumper to the body. Unscrew and remove the bolts.

7 Unscrew and remove the bolts securing the bottom of the front bumper to the underbody (**see illustration**).

8 Support the front bumper then unscrew and remove the upper mounting bolts (**see illustration**).

9 Remove the special plastic clips securing the corners of the front bumper to the body. To remove the clips, depress the centre pin which will release the clip (**see illustration**).

Reset the clips for fitting by pushing the centre pin fully upwards.

10 Withdraw the front bumper from the body taking care not to damage the paintwork.

Refitting

11 Refitting is a reversal of removal.

Rear bumper

Removal

12 To improve access chock the front wheels, then jack up the rear of the vehicle and support on axle stands (see *Jacking and Vehicle Support*).

13 Unscrew and remove the screws securing the rear wheelarch liners to the rear bumper.

14 Carefully pull back the liners and unscrew the mounting bolts from the front upper edge of the rear bumper.

15 Unscrew and remove the special clips from the front lower edge of the rear bumper (**see illustration**).

16 Unscrew and remove the lower mounting bolts (**see illustration**).

17 Support the rear bumper then unscrew and remove the upper mounting bolts (**see illustration**).

18 Withdraw the rear bumper from the body taking care not to damage the paintwork (**see illustration**).

Refitting

19 Refitting is a reversal of removal.

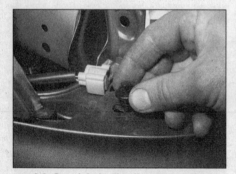

6.9 Special plastic clips secure the corners of the front bumper to the body

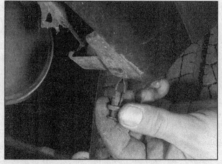

6.15 Removing the special clips from the front lower edge of the rear bumper

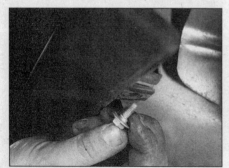

6.16 Rear bumper lower mounting bolt removal

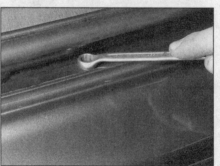

6.17 Removing the rear bumper upper mounting bolts

6.18 Withdrawing the rear bumper from the body

7.1 Unscrew the upper mounting screws . . .

7.2 . . . and withdraw the radiator grille

7 Radiator grille - removal and refitting

Removal

1 Open the bonnet and unscrew the mounting screws from the radiator grille (see illustration).
2 Withdraw the radiator grille upwards from the lower mounting rubbers and remove from the body (see illustration).

Refitting

3 Refitting is a reversal of removal.

8 Bonnet - removal, refitting and adjustment

Removal

1 Open the bonnet and have an assistant support it. Using a pencil or felt tip pen, mark the outline of each bonnet hinge relative to the bonnet, to use as a guide on refitting.
2 Disconnect the windscreen washer fluid supply hose from the connector under the bonnet, and release it from the clips (see illustration).
3 Unscrew the bolts securing the bonnet to the hinges (see illustration) and, with the help of an assistant, carefully lift the bonnet clear. Store the bonnet out of the way in a safe place.

4 Inspect the bonnet hinges for signs of wear and free play at the pivots, and if necessary renew.

Refitting

5 With the aid of an assistant, offer up the bonnet, and loosely fit the retaining bolts. Align the hinges with the marks made on removal, then tighten the retaining bolts securely.
6 Reconnect the windscreen washer fluid supply hose.
7 Adjust the alignment of the bonnet as follows.

Adjustment

8 Close the bonnet, and check for alignment with the adjacent panels. If necessary, slacken the hinge bolts and re-align the bonnet to suit. Once the bonnet is correctly aligned, tighten the relevant hinge bolts securely.
9 Once the bonnet is correctly aligned, check that the bonnet fastens and releases in a satisfactory manner. If adjustment is necessary, slacken the bonnet lock retaining bolts, and adjust the position of the lock to suit. Once the lock is operating correctly, securely tighten its retaining bolts. Make sure that the bonnet striker enters the lock centrally.
10 If necessary, align the front edge of the bonnet with the wing panels by turning the rubbers screwed into the body front panel, to raise or lower the front edge as required.

9 Bonnet release cable - removal and refitting

Removal

1 Open the bonnet. For improved access remove the radiator grille.
2 Unscrew the three securing bolts, and remove the lock assembly from the cross panel.
3 Unhook the end of the bonnet release cable from the lock lever. Withdraw the lock assembly from the vehicle.
4 Release the cable from the clips in the engine compartment.
6 Working inside the vehicle on the driver's side, remove the screws securing the lower trim panel to the facia and remove the panel.
7 Unscrew the screws and remove the bonnet release cable from the lower trim panel (see illustration). Release the cable from the clips on the bulkhead.
8 Note the routing of the cable, and release it from any clips in the engine compartment, then feed the cable through the bulkhead grommet into the vehicle interior. On some models, it may be necessary to move certain components in the engine compartment to one side, to gain access to the cable clips. It is advisable to tie a length of string to the cable before removal, to aid fitting. Pull the cable through the bulkhead, then untie the string and leave it in place until the cable is to be fitted.

Refitting

9 Refitting is a reversal of removal, but use the string to pull the cable into position, and ensure that the bulkhead grommet is securely located. Make sure that the cable is routed as noted before removal, and reposition the cable in its securing clips in the engine compartment. Check the bonnet release mechanism for correct operation on completion.

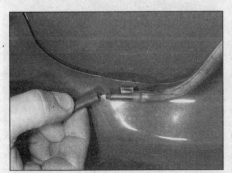

8.2 Disconnecting the windscreen washer fluid supply hose

8.3 Unscrewing the bonnet-to-hinge mounting bolts

9.7 Bonnet release cable removed from the lower trim panel

11

10.2 Bonnet lock on the cross panel

11.4 Front door upper hinge

11.8 Adjusting the door striker

10 Bonnet lock - removal and refitting

Removal

1 Open the bonnet. For improved access, remove the radiator grille.
2 Unscrew the three securing bolts, and remove the lock assembly from the cross panel **(see illustration)**.
3 Pull the return spring to one side, then unhook the end of the bonnet release cable from the lock lever, and withdraw the assembly from the vehicle.

Refitting

4 Refitting is a reversal of removal. If necessary, adjust the position of the lock, as described in Section 8.

11 Door - removal, refitting and adjustment

Removal

1 Disconnect the battery negative lead.
2 If the door is to be dismantled, remove the relevant door inner trim panel (Section 12). Disconnect, and draw out the wiring to the electrical components inside the door; also

ensure that earth lead wiring is disconnected. If the door is being removed intact, the wiring can be disconnected from inside the vehicle by removing the applicable trim from the footwell or B pillar.
3 Drive out the roll pin securing the door check arm to its body bracket.
4 Use a marker pen to mark around the door hinge positions as an aid to correct refitting **(see illustration)**.
5 With the aid of an assistant to support the door, remove the bolts and detach the door. If necessary, the door hinges can be unbolted from the body.

Refitting

6 Refitting is the reverse of the removal procedure, noting the following points.
 a) *Align the hinges with the marks made on removal and lightly tighten the hinge bolts, then gently close the door and check that it fits correctly in its aperture, with equal gaps at all points between it and the surrounding bodywork; if adjustment is required see below. Securely tighten the bolts.*
 b) *When the door fits correctly in its aperture, check that it fits flush with the surrounding bodywork; if adjustment is required, move the striker (see below).*

Adjustment

7 To adjust the doors in a forwards, rearwards and/or vertical direction slacken the

hinge-to-body bolts; to adjust them in a left, right and/or vertical direction slacken the hinge-to-door bolts. Securely tighten the bolts when the fit is correct.
8 The striker alignment should be checked after either the door or the lock has been disturbed. To adjust a striker, slacken its screws, reposition it and securely tighten the screws **(see illustration)**.

12 Door inner trim panel - removal and refitting

Front door trim panel (without electric windows)

Removal

1 Disconnect the battery negative lead.
2 Remove the screw securing the inner trim panel to the interior door handle **(see illustration)**.
3 Remove the screw and lift out the door grip **(see illustration)**.
4 Remove the plastic clip from the front upper corner of the inner trim panel.
5 Fully close the window, and note the position of the window regulator handle. Using a length of bent welding rod or similar, release the retaining spring from the window regulator handle and withdraw the handle from the splines. Recover the washer **(see illustrations)**.

12.2 Removing the screw securing the front door inner trim panel to the interior door handle

12.3 Front door grip removal

12.5a Using a length of welding rod to release the window regulator handle retaining spring

12.5b Removing the window regulator handle washer

12.6a Prise off the grille . . .

12.6b . . . then unscrew the screws . . .

6 Carefully prise away the grille from the loudspeaker, then unscrew the screws and withdraw the loudspeaker sufficient to disconnect the wiring **(see illustrations)**.

12.6c . . . and disconnect speaker the wiring

7 Remove the remaining clips and screws securing the trim panel to the door. The plastic clip on the rear edge of the door is removed by depressing the centre pin.

8 Using a wide-blade screwdriver, carefully prise out the trim panel clips and lift it from the upper shoulder. Withdraw the trim panel from the door, while guiding it over the inner door handle.

9 If necessary the membrane can be removed by first unbolting the inner door handle from the door **(see illustration)**. Peel away the membrane taking care not to tear it. Try to keep the sealant intact as far as possible, to ease refitting.

Refitting

10 Refitting is a reversal of removal, but make sure that the regulator handle is pointing upwards 30° to the rear with the window fully closed.

Front door trim panel (with electric windows)

Removal

11 Disconnect the battery negative lead.

12 Remove the screw securing the inner trim panel to the interior door handle **(see illustration)**.

13 Remove the armrest cover, then unscrew the screws securing the trim panel to the door **(see illustrations)**.

14 Prise the exterior mirror control panel from the trim panel and disconnect the wiring.

15 Prise the power window switch panel from the armrest, and disconnect the wiring plug **(see illustrations)**.

16 Prise the exterior mirror triangular trim panel from the front of the door, then remove the trim panel upper mounting bolt **(see illustration)**.

12.9 Unbolting the inner door handle

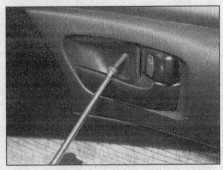

12.12 Removing the screw securing the inner trim panel

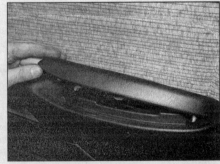

12.13a Remove the armrest cover . . .

12.13b . . . and unscrew the trim panel screws

12.15a Prise the power window switch panel from the armrest . . .

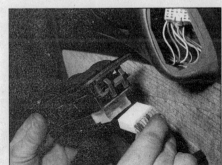

12.15b . . . and disconnect the wiring plug

11

12.16 Trim panel upper mounting bolt removal

12.17a Prise off the grille . . .

12.17b . . . remove the speaker mounting screws . . .

17 Carefully prise away the grille from the speaker, then unscrew the screws and withdraw the speaker sufficient to disconnect the wiring **(see illustrations).**

18 Remove the remaining clips and screws securing the trim panel to the door **(see illustration).** The plastic clip on the rear edge of the door is removed by depressing the centre pin.

19 Using a wide-blade screwdriver, carefully prise out the trim panel clips and lift it from the upper shoulder. Withdraw the trim panel from the door, while guiding it over the inner door handle.

20 If necessary the membrane can be removed by first unbolting the inner door handle from the door. Peel away the membrane taking care not to tear it. Try to keep the sealant intact as far as possible, to ease refitting.

Refitting

21 Refitting is a reversal of removal.

Rear door trim panel

Removal

22 Disconnect the battery negative lead.

23 On models with manual windows, fully close the window and note the position of the window regulator handle. Using a length of bent welding rod or similar, release the retaining spring from the window regulator handle and withdraw the handle from the splines. Recover the washer.

24 On models with electric windows, prise out the switch panel and disconnect the wiring.

25 Remove the screw securing the inner trim panel to the interior door handle **(see illustration).**

26 On early models remove the screws and withdraw the armrest; on later models remove the screw and withdraw the door grip **(see illustration).**

27 Using a wide-blade screwdriver, carefully prise out the trim panel clips and lift it from the upper shoulder. Withdraw the trim panel from the door, while guiding it over the inner door handle.

28 If necessary the membrane can be removed by first unbolting the inner door handle from the door. Peel away the membrane taking care not to tear it. Try to keep the sealant intact as far as possible, to ease refitting **(see illustrations).**

Refitting

29 Refitting is a reversal of removal, but on manual window models make sure that the regulator handle is pointing upwards 30° to the rear with the window fully closed.

12.17c . . . and disconnect the wiring

12.18 One of the trim panel mounting screws is located in the exterior mirror control panel aperture

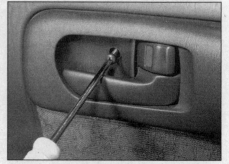

12.25 Rear door inner trim panel retaining screw removal

12.26 Rear door grip removal

12.28a Unbolt the inner door handle . . .

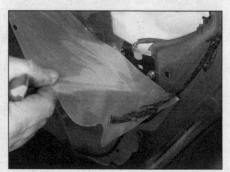

12.28b . . . and peel away the membrane

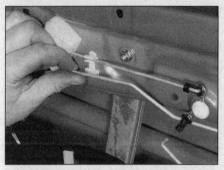

13.6 Disconnecting the front door lock operating rods from the guides

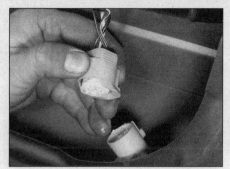

13.7 Disconnecting the central locking wiring

13.8a Unscrew the crosshead mounting screws . . .

---

13 Door handle and lock components - removal and refitting

Interior door handle

Removal

1 Remove the door trim panel (Section 12).
2 Unscrew the mounting bolts and disconnect the operating rods, then remove the interior door handle from the door.

Refitting

3 Refitting is a reversal of removal.

Front door lock

Removal

4 Remove the door inner trim panel, inner

door handle and membrane as described in Section 12.
5 Unbolt the security bracket from over the door lock.
6 Reach into the door and disconnect the operating rods from the lock. Alternatively, leave them attached and disconnect them from the guides and pivot **(see illustration)**.
7 Disconnect the central locking wiring from the lock, and detach the connector from the door **(see illustration)**.
8 Unscrew the crosshead screws from the rear edge of the door, then withdraw the lock assembly from inside the door **(see illustrations)**.

Refitting

9 Refitting is a reversal of removal, but check the operation of the lock before refitting the door inner trim panel.

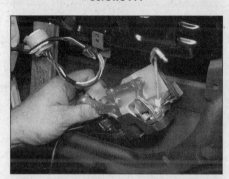

13.8b . . . then withdraw the lock assembly from inside the door

Rear door lock

Removal

10 Remove the door trim panel, inner door handle and membrane (see Section 12).
11 Prise out the child safety lock control **(see illustration)**.
12 Unbolt and remove the security bracket; the rear mounting bolt is on the rear edge of the door and the front bolt is near the operating rod pivot **(see illustrations)**.
13 Reach into the door and disconnect the operating rods from the lock. Alternatively, leave them attached and disconnect them from the guides and pivot.
14 Disconnect the central locking wiring from the lock.
15 Unscrew the crosshead screws from the rear edge of the door, then withdraw the lock assembly from inside the door **(see illustrations)**.

13.11 Prise out the child safety lock control

13.12a Remove the bolts . . .

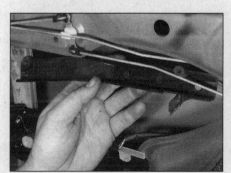

13.12b . . . and remove the security bracket

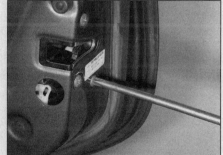

13.15a Unscrew the mounting screws . . .

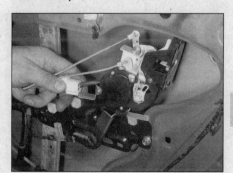

13.15b . . . and withdraw the rear door lock from inside the door

11

13.19 Removing the front door exterior handle and lock cylinder

Refitting

16 Refitting is a reversal of removal, but make sure that the lock lever is correctly entered in the lever on the exterior handle. Check the operation of the lock before refitting the door inner trim panel. Make sure that the child safety lock control is engaged with the lock correctly.

Front door exterior handle and lock cylinder

Removal

17 Remove the door lock as described in paragraphs 4 to 8 of this Section.
18 Disconnect the lock cylinder operating rod from the exterior handle.
19 Using a socket inserted through the special holes, unscrew the bolts securing the exterior handle to the door. Withdraw the handle and lock cylinder taking care not to

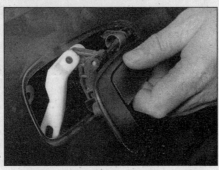

13.22 Removing the rear door exterior handle

damage the paintwork. Separate the lock cylinder from the handle **(see illustration)**.

Refitting

20 Refitting is a reversal of removal, with reference to paragraph 9 of this Section.

Rear door exterior handle

Removal

21 Remove the door lock as described in paragraphs 10 to 15 of this Section.
22 Using a socket inserted through the special holes, unscrew the bolts securing the exterior handle to the door. Withdraw the handle and lever assembly taking care not to damage the paintwork **(see illustration)**.

Refitting

23 Refitting is a reversal of removal, with reference to paragraph 16 of this Section.

14 Door window regulator and glass - removal and refitting

Front door window regulator

Removal

1 Remove the door inner trim panel and membrane as described in Section 12.
2 Temporarily reconnect the electric window switch, and the battery negative lead, or refit the window regulator handle, as applicable. Fully lower the window.
3 Mark the position of the window glass mounting bolts on the regulator bracket using a marker pen. Support the glass, then remove the two bolts **(see illustration)**. Fully raise the window and support in the raised position using strong adhesive tape. Ensure that the glass cannot drop into the door.
4 On models with power windows, disconnect the wiring **(see illustration)**.
5 Unscrew the mounting bolts and nuts, then manipulate the complete motor/regulator assembly out through the aperture in the door **(see illustrations)**.

Refitting

6 Refitting is a reversal of removal, but align the window glass mounting bolts with the marks made on the regulator bracket before tightening them. Check that the top edge of the window aligns correctly with the weatherstrip. If necessary, adjust the glass on the bracket to correct the alignment.

14.3 Removing the front window glass-to-regulator bracket bolts

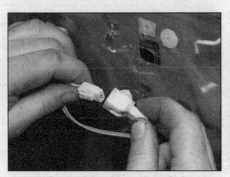

14.4 On models with power windows, disconnect the wiring

14.5a Front door window regulator mounting bolt removal (models with manual windows)

14.5b Front door window regulator mounting bolts (models with power windows)

14.5c Front window regulator lower mounting bolt

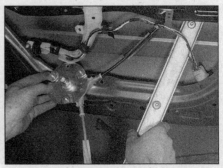

14.5d Removing the window regulator from inside the front door

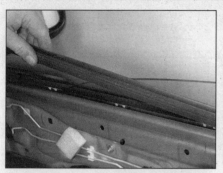

14.9 Removing the inner weatherstrip from the upper edge of the front door

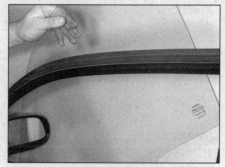

14.10 Tilt and lift the glass through the top of the front door

14.14 Removing the rear door window glass-to-regulator bracket bolts

Front door window glass

Removal

7 Remove the front door window regulator as described previously.

8 Unscrew the window glass rear channel mounting bolts.

9 Lower the glass into the door, then remove the inner weatherstrip from the upper edge of the door **(see illustration)**.

10 Tilt and lift the glass out through the top of the door, manipulating the glass past the outer weatherstrip as it is withdrawn **(see illustration)**.

Refitting

11 Refitting is a reversal of removal with reference to paragraph 6, but check the operation of the window before refitting the door inner trim panel.

14.16 Removing the rear door window regulator mounting nuts

Rear door window regulator

Removal

12 Remove the door inner trim panel and membrane as described in Section 12.

13 Temporarily reconnect the electric window switch, and the battery negative lead, or refit the window regulator handle, as applicable. Fully lower the window.

14 Mark the position of the window glass mounting bolts on the regulator bracket using a marker pen. Support the glass, then remove the two bolts **(see illustration)**. Fully raise the window and support in the raised position using strong adhesive tape. Ensure that the glass cannot drop into the door.

15 On models with power windows, disconnect the wiring.

16 Unscrew the mounting bolts and nuts, then manipulate the complete motor/regulator assembly out through the aperture in the door **(see illustration)**.

Refitting

17 Refitting is a reversal of removal, but align the window glass mounting bolts with the marks made on the regulator bracket before tightening them. Check that the top edge of the window aligns correctly with the weatherstrip. If necessary, adjust the glass on the bracket to correct the alignment.

Rear door window glass

Removal

18 Remove the rear door window regulator as described previously.

19 Unscrew the screws and bolts securing the window glass rear division bar/channel to the door. The upper screws are located on the upper edge of the door **(see illustration)**. On some models it is necessary to remove a cover for access to the lower mounting bolts.

20 Lower the glass into the door, then remove the inner weatherstrip from the upper edge of the door.

21 Ease the rubber weatherstrip away and remove the division bar (4-door models) or rear channel/plate (5-door models) from inside the door **(see illustration)**.

22 On 4-door models ease the rear quarter window and weather strip from the door and place to one side.

23 Tilt and lift the glass out through the top of the door, manipulating the glass past the outer weatherstrip as it is withdrawn **(see illustration)**.

Refitting

24 Refitting is a reversal of removal with reference to paragraph 17, but check the operation of the window before refitting the door inner trim panel.

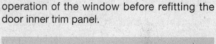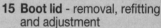

15 Boot lid - removal, refitting and adjustment

Removal

1 Disconnect the battery negative lead.

2 Open the boot and disconnect the wiring from the rear lighting (see Chapter 12).

14.19 Remove the mounting screws . . .

14.21 . . . and remove the rear channel/plate from the door

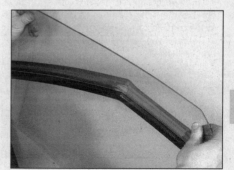

14.23 Tilt and lift the window glass from the rear door

11

3 Use a marker pen to mark around the boot hinge positions as an aid to correct refitting.
4 With the aid of an assistant, undo the bolts securing the boot lid to its hinges, then remove the boot lid. **Do not** attempt to remove the hinges until the torsion bars have been removed (Section 16).

Refitting

5 Refitting is a reversal of removal, but if necessary adjust the position of the boot as follows.

Adjustment

6 Close the boot and ensure that it sits flush with the surrounding panels and that there is an equal gap between the boot lid and each rear wing; the lid should close smoothly and positively, with no excessive force being applied. If this is not the case, adjustment is required.
7 Remove the rear seat as described in Section 25.
8 Unscrew the bolts and remove the rear seat side cushions.
9 Remove the trim panel from the rear quarter pillars, then remove the rear shelf trim.
10 Loosen the hinge bolts on the rear shelf panel, then reposition the boot and tighten the bolts.
11 Refit the removed components, then check that the boot lock engages centrally with the striker on the rear panel. If necessary, remove the trim and loosen the striker screws, then reposition the striker and tighten the screws.

16 Boot lid torsion bar - removal and refitting

Note: *A Toyota special tool is recommended for carrying out the following procedure, as the torsion bars may whip out and cause injury or damage if attempts are made to remove them without it; if this tool is not available, or an alternative cannot be fabricated from a long bar with a cranked, padded end, the task is best entrusted to your Toyota dealer.*

Removal

1 Remove the carpet from the rear luggage compartment then remove the trim for access to the boot lid torsion bars.
2 Release the torsion bars from the centre bracket.
3 Have an assistant support the boot lid, then attach the special tool to the first torsion bar and press down to release the bar from the hinge extension.
4 Release the special tool slowly then disengage the torsion bar from the anchor-end bracket. Withdraw the bar from the luggage compartment.
5 Repeat the procedure on the second torsion bar and withdraw it from the luggage compartment.

Refitting

7 Refitting is the reverse of the removal procedure.

17 Boot lid lock and lock cylinder - removal and refitting

Removal

1 Open the boot lid, then remove the trim for access to the lock.
2 Disconnect the lock cylinder operating rod from the lock.
3 Unbolt the lock and withdraw from the boot lid.
4 To remove the lock cylinder pull out the retaining plate and withdraw together with the operating rod.

Refitting

5 Refitting is a reversal of removal.

18 Boot lid/tailgate and fuel filler flap release mechanism - removal and refitting

Removal

1 The mechanism is cable-operated, with levers mounted on the floor next to the driver's seat and release catches on the boot lid/tailgate and the fuel filler flap.
2 To remove the lever unit, peel up the carpet, unscrew the mounting bolt and release the unit's locating tag. Withdraw the unit and disconnect the cables.
3 The cables are routed through the inside of the vehicle, with the fuel filler flap cable crossing to the opposite side. Remove the rear seat and trim components and peel back the carpet as necessary to reach the cables if they are to be renewed.
4 To remove the fuel filler flap release catch, open the flap and unscrew the retaining nut, then remove the relevant interior trim and withdraw the catch into the luggage compartment. Disconnect the cable and remove the catch.

5 To remove the boot lid/tailgate release catch open the boot lid/tailgate and remove, where fitted, the trim panel covering the lock striker. Unscrew the striker bolts, withdraw the striker/catch assembly and disconnect the cable.

Refitting

6 Refitting is the reverse of the removal procedure.

19 Tailgate and support struts - removal, refitting and adjustment

Tailgate

Removal

1 Disconnect the battery negative lead. Open the tailgate.
2 Withdraw the grommet/protector from the top left-hand side of the tailgate, then disconnect the hose from the tailgate washer jet.
3 Remove the tailgate interior trim panel, then disconnect the tailgate wiring and attach drawstrings to the multi-plugs; withdraw the remaining grommet/protector from the top right-hand side of the tailgate and remove the wiring, leaving the drawstrings in place in the tailgate **(see illustration)**. An alternative method is to unclip the rear of the headlining and remove the side quarter trim from the right-hand side of the rear passenger compartment, then disconnect the wiring plug - the tailgate can then be removed together with the wiring.
4 With an assistant supporting the tailgate, disconnect the support struts as described later in this Section.
5 With the aid of an assistant, unbolt the tailgate from its hinges and remove it **(see illustration)**.

Refitting

6 Refitting is the reverse of the removal procedure, but check that the tailgate sits flush with the surrounding panels when closed and that there is an equal gap between it and each rear wing. If necessary, adjust the tailgate as follows.

19.3 Prising out the grommet/protector from the top right-hand side of the tailgate

19.5 Tailgate hinge

Adjustment

7 If adjustment is required, remove the rear seat and side cushions followed by the rear side quarter trim panels. Carefully prise the rear section of the headlining away from the clips on the roof.

8 Loosen the tailgate hinge mounting nuts slightly, then reposition the tailgate as necessary and tighten the nuts.

9 Slowly close the tailgate and check that the lock engages with the striker centrally. If not, remove the trim from the rear luggage compartment, then loosen the mounting bolts and reposition the striker. Tighten the mounting bolts on completion, and refit the headlining and removed trim.

Support strut

Removal

10 Open the tailgate and support it using suitable wooden props.

11 Note which way round the strut is fitted - the piston rod end is located on the rear body pillar.

12 Remove the relevant trim from the rear luggage compartment for access to the strut lower mounting nuts, then unscrew the nuts **(see illustration)**.

13 Unbolt the strut from the tailgate and remove from the vehicle.

Refitting

14 Refitting is a reversal of removal.

19.12 Tailgate support strut mounting on the rear body panel

20 Tailgate lock components - removal and refitting

Tailgate lock

Removal

1 Open the tailgate then remove the trim panel.

2 Working through the aperture in the inner panel, hold the operating rod stationary while it is disconnected from the lock. Use a screwdriver to release the rod clip **(see illustration)**.

3 Unbolt and remove the lock from the tailgate **(see illustration)**.

Refitting

4 Refitting is a reversal of removal, but make

sure that clip is firmly attached to the operating rod.

Tailgate lock cylinder

Removal

5 Open the tailgate then remove the trim panel.

6 Working through the aperture in the inner panel, disconnect the operating rod from the lock cylinder **(see illustration)**.

7 Unbolt and remove the lock cylinder from the tailgate **(see illustration)**.

Refitting

8 Refitting is a reversal of removal, but check the operation of the lock cylinder before refitting the trim panel.

Tailgate lock striker

Removal

9 Remove the trim panel from the rear of the luggage compartment.

10 Using a marker pen, mark the position of the lock striker as a guide for refitting.

11 Unscrew the mounting screws, then disconnect the wiring and control cable **(see illustrations)**.

Refitting

12 Refitting is a reversal of removal, but check the operation of the tailgate release mechanism before refitting the trim. If necessary adjust the position of the lock striker with reference to Section 19.

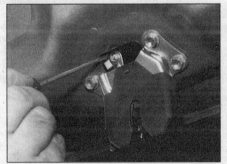

20.2 Disconnect the operating rod . . .

20.3 . . . then unbolt the tailgate lock

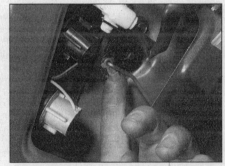

20.6 Disconnect the operating rod . . .

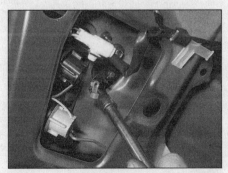

20.7 . . . then unbolt the lock cylinder from the tailgate

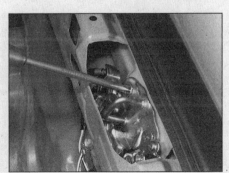

20.11a Tailgate lock striker removal

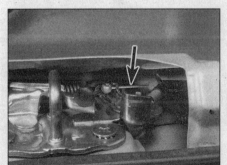

20.11b Control cable on the tailgate lock striker

11

21.3 Remove the triangular trim . . .

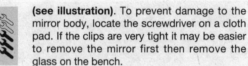

21.5a . . . then unscrew the mounting bolts . . .

21.5b . . . and remove the mirror assembly

21 Exterior mirror and glass - removal and refitting

Mirror assembly

Removal

1 Disconnect the battery negative lead if an electrically-adjustable mirror is being removed.

2 If a manual remote-control mirror is being removed, undo the operating lever securing screw, then disconnect the lever.

3 Carefully prise away the triangular trim from the inner door **(see illustration)**.

4 If an electrically-adjustable mirror is being removed, remove the relevant door inner trim panel and peel back the protective plastic membrane on the inside of the door until the mirror multi-plug can be disconnected.

5 Unscrew the mounting screws and remove the mirror assembly; where an electrically-adjustable mirror is being removed, ensure that its wiring and multi-plug are not trapped as the assembly is withdrawn **(see illustrations)**.

Refitting

6 Refitting is a reversal of removal.

Mirror glass

Removal

7 Insert a thin screwdriver between the mirror glass and the mirror body, and lever out the glass to release it from the securing clips

 (see illustration). To prevent damage to the mirror body, locate the screwdriver on a cloth pad. If the clips are very tight it may be easier to remove the mirror first then remove the glass on the bench.

8 Where applicable, disconnect the heating wiring from the rear of the glass.

Refitting

9 Where applicable, reconnect the wires to the rear of the mirror glass, then push the glass into position to engage the securing clips.

 HAYNES HiNT *To aid refitting, lightly grease the securing clips on the rear of the mirror glass.*

22 Windscreen, rear window glass and rear quarter window glass - general information

Windscreen and rear window

1 The windscreen and rear window are bonded in position with special adhesive. In addition, the tailgate window is retained in a rubber moulding. Renewal of these windows is a difficult, messy and time-consuming task, which is beyond the scope of the home mechanic. It is difficult, unless one has plenty of practice, to obtain a secure, waterproof fit. Furthermore, the task carries a high risk of breakage. In view of this, owners are strongly advised to have this work carried out by one of the many specialist windscreen fitters.

Rear quarter window glass

Removal

2 The rear quarter window glass is secured by four mounting nuts. First remove the rear quarter trim panel then support the glass from the outside and unscrew the mounting nuts. Withdraw the window glass from the aperture in the body **(see illustration)**.

Refitting

3 Refitting is a reversal of removal.

23 Sunroof components - general information

1 Removal, refitting and adjustment of the sunroof components is best left to a Toyota dealer who will have the necessary equipment and expertise to carry out the work.

2 For the experienced home mechanic who wishes to carry out the work, it is necessary to remove all side trim panels from the passenger compartment, then remove the headlining complete. The rear edge of the glass should be adjusted 0.5 mm above the level of the roof, and the front edge should be 0.5 mm below the level of the roof.

3 The correct operation time for the sunroof to open is approximately 6 seconds with the engine running.

24 Body exterior fittings - removal and refitting

Engine compartment lower splash guards

Removal

1 Apply the handbrake then jack up the front of the vehicle and support on axle stands (see *Jacking and Vehicle Support*).

2 Unscrew the mounting screws and remove the splash guard(s) from the underbody.

Refitting

3 Refitting is a reversal of removal.

21.7 Removing the mirror glass

22.2 Rear quarter window glass mounting nuts

25.1 Front seat front mounting bolts removal

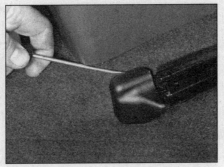

25.2 Prise the covers from the front seat runner rear ends

25.4 Prise the covers from the rear seat front mounting bolts

Wheel arch liners

4 The wheel arch liners are secured by a combination of self-tapping screws and plastic clips, and the removal/refitting procedure is self-evident.

Body trim strips and badges

5 The various body trim strips and badges are held in position with a special adhesive tape. Removal requires the trim/badge to be heated, to soften the adhesive, and then cut away from the surface. Due to the high risk of damage to the vehicle paintwork during this operation, it is recommended that this task should be entrusted to a Toyota dealer.

Roof drip moulding

6 Remove the rear quarter inner trim panel for access to the moulding retaining nuts. Unscrew and remove the nuts.

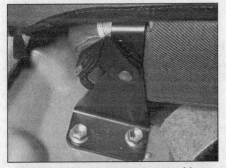

25.6a Fold-down rear seat centre hinge and mounting bolts

25.6b Fold-down rear seat side hinge and mounting bolt

7 Carefully prise away the roof drip moulding.
8 Fit the new moulding using a reversal of the removal procedure.

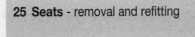

25 Seats - removal and refitting

Removal

Front

1 Slide the seat as far back as possible, then unbolt the seat runner forward ends **(see illustration)**.
2 Slide the seat as far forward as possible, then remove the covers from the seat runner rear ends **(see illustration)**.
3 Unbolt the seat runner rear ends from the floor, then remove the seat from inside the vehicle. Where fitted, disconnect the wiring for the seat heaters.

Rear

4 The seat base is secured at its forward edge by sockets on 4-door models and by bolts on 5-door models. On 4-door models lift the front edge of the seat base and remove it. On 5-door models prise off the covers then unscrew the mounting bolts and remove the seat base **(see illustration)**.
5 If the seat back is fixed, it can be removed (after the seat base has been removed) by undoing the bolts at its base and unhooking it from its upper mountings.
6 If the seat back is of the fold-down type the section(s) can be removed, after disengaging

25.7 Removing the mounting bolt from a rear seat side cushion

the upper mounting(s), by undoing the seat back-to-hinge securing bolts **(see illustrations)**.
7 The rear seat side cushions can be removed by first removing the seat base, then pulling back the carpet and unscrewing the lower mounting bolts **(see illustration)**.

Refitting

7 Refitting is the reverse of the removal procedure, but tighten the mounting bolts to the specified torque.

26 Seat belt components - removal and refitting

Caution: On later models, the retractor units on the B pillars are linked to the SRS system. Observe the warning given on the side of the units, and if necessary have the work carried out by a Toyota dealer.
Note: *Note of the positions of any washers and spacers on the seat belt anchors, and ensure that they are refitted in their original positions.*

Removal

Front

1 If the belt inner stalk is to be removed, remove the relevant front seat then remove the plastic trim and unbolt the stalk from the seat **(see illustrations)**.
2 If the outer belt is to be removed, first slide the seat as far forward as possible.

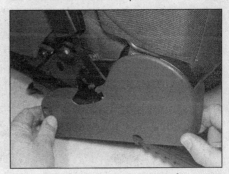

26.1a With the front seat removed, remove the plastic trim . . .

11

26.1b . . . for access to the inner stalk and mounting bolt

26.3 Front seat belt retractor unit at the base of the B pillar.

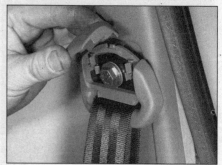

26.4 Prise the plastic cover from the front seat belt upper anchor bolt

26.5 Front seat belt lower mounting bolt

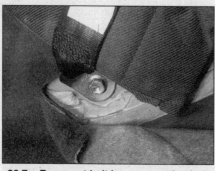

26.7a Rear seat belt lower mounting bolt

26.7b Rear seat belt retractor and mounting bolt

3 Remove the trim from the base of the B pillar for access to the retractor unit. Unscrew the mounting bolts and remove the retractor unit **(see illustration)**.

4 Prise off the plastic cover from the belt upper anchor bolt, then unscrew the bolt noting the location of the spacers. If necessary, the height adjustment slider may be unbolted from the B pillar **(see illustration)**.

5 Unscrew the bolt securing the lower mounting to the inner sill panel, and withdraw the seat belt from inside the vehicle. Note the location of the spacers **(see illustration)**.

Rear

6 Remove the rear seat components as necessary to reach the rear seat belt mountings.

7 To remove the outer belt, unscrew the

lower mounting bolt located under the carpet beneath the side seat cushions. Remove the luggage compartment interior trim panels as necessary, then unscrew the mounting bolt for the retractor and withdraw the outer belt from inside the vehicle **(see illustrations)**.

8 To remove the centre lap belts and the outer belt buckles, note their locations then unbolt them from the floor **(see illustration)**.

Refitting

9 Refitting is the reverse of the removal procedure, but make sure that the belts are correctly routed and tighten the mounting bolts to the specified torque.

27 Interior trim panels - general information

Note: *Take extra care when removing plastic clips from interior trim panels, as the clips and panels are easily damaged or broken.*

1 Most interior trim panels are secured by clips and/or screws; before attempting to remove a panel always inspect it closely to check where all fasteners are located and to decide on the correct approach for removal. Remember that if the panel is being removed for access to another component, it may only be necessary to lift one end of the panel.

2 A wide variety of clip types are used; hidden clips may be prised free, but some visible clips will require a different method.

Some plastic clips require their centres to be depressed before withdrawal. When prising free a panel secured by hidden clips, always wrap tape around the blade of the tool used, to protect the paintwork.

3 It may be necessary to remove components, such as seats, handles etc before a given panel can be removed. Refer to the relevant Section of this Chapter for details.

4 The A (windscreen) pillar trims are each secured by clips. To remove, carefully prise out the trim.

8 To remove the B pillar trim first prise up the front and rear scuff plates, then pull away the weatherstrips and prise out the trim panel.

9 To remove the C pillar and luggage compartment trim, first remove the rear seat and side cushions. The trim is secured by clips and screws **(see illustrations)**.

26.8 Rear seat centre lap belts and mounting bolt

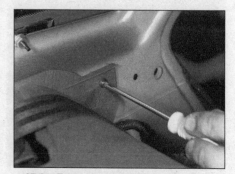

27.9a Removing the side trim from the luggage compartment

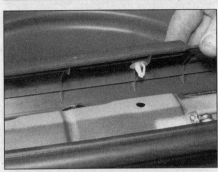

27.9b Prise up the protector cover . . .

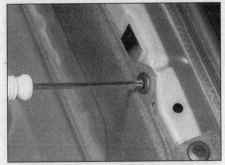

27.9c . . . and remove the trim retaining screws from the rear of the luggage compartment

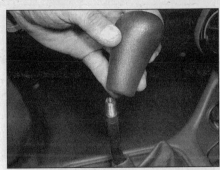

28.1 Removing the gear lever knob

28 Centre console - removal and refitting

Removal

1 On manual transmission models, unscrew and remove the gear lever knob (see illustration).
2 On automatic transmission models, remove the selector lever with reference to Chapter 7B.
3 Remove the screw and withdraw the cover from the top of the handbrake lever (see illustrations).
4 Unscrew the retaining screws located inside the oddments tray and on the sides of the console, then withdraw the console until it

is possible to disconnect the cigar lighter wiring at the front. Withdraw the centre console from inside the vehicle (see illustrations).

Refitting

5 Refitting is a reversal of removal.

29 Facia panel and glovebox - removal and refitting

⚠ Warning: Where a passenger air bag is fitted, make sure that the safety recommendations given in Chapter 12 are followed, to prevent personal injury. Refer to Chapter 10 when removing the steering wheel and air bag module.

Facia panel

Removal

1 Disconnect the battery negative lead.
2 Remove the steering wheel as described in Chapter 10.
3 Carefully prise the trim from the A pillars.
4 Prise out the entry scuff plates from the front door apertures, then remove the footwell side trim panels (see illustration).
5 Remove the steering column shrouds.
6 Remove the instrument panel as described in Chapter 12.
7 Remove the glovebox as described later in this Section.
8 Remove the centre console as described in Section 28.
9 Unscrew the retaining screws and withdraw the lower trim panel located beneath the

28.3a Remove the screw . . .

28.3b . . . and withdraw the cover from the top of the handbrake lever

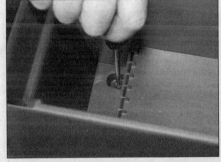

28.4a Remove the retaining screws . . .

28.4b . . . withdraw the console . . .

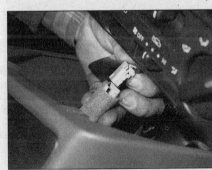

28.4c . . . and disconnect the wiring from the cigar lighter

29.4 Footwell side trim panel removal

11

29.9 Disconnecting the wiring from the instrument panel illumination rheostat

29.10a Use a screwdriver to prise out the centre surround . . .

29.10b . . . and remove it from the facia

steering column. Detach the bonnet pull lever (2 screws) then disconnect the wiring from the instrument panel illumination rheostat **(see illustration)**. Remove the lower trim panel.
10 Carefully prise the centre surround from the facia noting that the air ducts are located behind the centre vents **(see illustrations)**.
11 Remove the radio/cassette player as

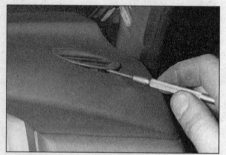

29.13 Prising out the defroster nozzles

described in Chapter 12, and the heater control panel as described in Chapter 3.
12 Under the driver's side of the facia, remove the air duct leading from the heater unit to the side vent.
13 Prise the defroster nozzles from each side of the facia **(see illustration)**.
14 Remove the rubber grommet from the ignition switch/lock **(see illustration)**.
15 Prise the side covers from each end of the facia, then unscrew and remove the side mounting bolts **(see illustrations)**.
16 Unscrew the mounting nuts located on the bottom of the instrument panel aperture **(see illustration)**.
17 Unscrew the mounting bolts located on the outer lower corners of the facia.
18 Unscrew the centre mounting screw from under the heater control panel location.
19 Unscrew the mounting nut located behind the glovebox location.
20 With the help of an assistant, withdraw the facia panel from the bulkhead, and at the

same time identify and disconnect the wiring.
21 Withdraw the facia panel from inside the vehicle.
22 With the facia panel removed, the passenger air bag module can be unbolted after removing the air ducting. Store the air bag in a safe place to prevent possible personal injury **(see illustration)**.

Refitting

23 Refitting is a reversal of removal, but make sure that all electrical wiring is correctly reconnected to the relevant components and tighten the facia mounting screws securely.

Glovebox

Removal

24 Working under the glovebox unscrew the mounting screws and withdraw the glovebox from the facia **(see illustration)**.

Refitting

25 Refitting is a reversal of removal.

29.14 Removing the rubber grommet from the ignition switch/lock

29.15a Prise out the side covers . . .

29.15b . . . and unscrew the facia side mounting bolts

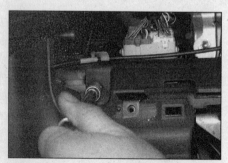

29.16 Removing the facia mounting bolts on the bottom of the instrument panel aperture

29.22 Passenger bag removal from the facia panel

29.24 Removing the glovebox from the facia panel

Chapter 12
Body electrical systems

Contents

Degrees of difficulty

| Easy, suitable for novice with little experience | | Fairly easy, suitable for beginner with some experience | | Fairly difficult, suitable for competent DIY mechanic | | Difficult, suitable for experienced DIY mechanic | | Very difficult, suitable for expert DIY or professional | |

Specifications

Bulb ratings

	Watts
Headlamp	60/55
Front sidelamp	5
Front foglamp	55
Direction indicator	21
Front direction indicator side repeater	5
Stop/tail lamps	21/5
Rear foglamp	21
Reversing lamp	21
Number plate lamp	5
Interior lamp:	
With sunroof	8
Without sunroof	10
Personal lamp	8
Glovebox lamp	1.4
Luggage compartment lamp	5
Trunk lamp	3.8

Torque wrench settings

	Nm	lbf ft
Wiper arm retaining nut:		
Windscreen wiper	22	16
Tailgate wiper	5	4

12

1 General information and precautions

Warning: Before carrying out any work on the electrical system, read through the precautions given in Safety first! at the beginning of this manual, and in Chapter 5. Most models are equipped with an air bag system. When working on the electrical system, refer to the precautions given in Section 23, to avoid the possibility of personal injury.

The electrical system is of 12-volt negative earth type. Power for the lights and all electrical accessories is supplied by a lead/acid type battery, which is charged by the alternator.

This Chapter covers repair and service procedures for the various electrical components not associated with the engine. Information on the battery, alternator and starter motor can be found in Chapter 5A.

It should be noted that, prior to working on any component in the electrical system, the battery negative terminal should first be disconnected, to prevent the possibility of electrical short-circuits and/or fires.

Caution: If the radio/cassette player fitted to the vehicle is one with an anti-theft security code, refer to the information given in the Reference Section at the rear of this manual before disconnecting the battery.

2 Electrical fault-finding - general information

Note: *Refer to the precautions given in Safety first! and in Section 1 of this Chapter before starting work. The following tests relate to testing of the main electrical circuits, and should not be used to test delicate electronic circuits (such as anti-lock braking systems), particularly where an electronic control module is used.*

General

1 A typical electrical circuit consists of an electrical component, any switches, relays, motors, fuses, fusible links or circuit breakers related to that component, and the wiring and connectors which link the component to both the battery and the bodyshell. To help pinpoint a problem in an electrical circuit, wiring diagrams are included at the end of this manual.

2 Before attempting to diagnose an electrical fault, first study the appropriate wiring diagram, to obtain a more complete understanding of the components included in the particular circuit concerned. The possible sources of a fault can be narrowed down by noting whether other components related to the circuit are operating properly. If several components or circuits fail at one time, the problem is likely to be related to a shared fuse or earth connection.

3 Electrical problems usually stem from simple causes, such as loose or corroded connections, a faulty earth connection, a blown fuse, a melted fusible link, or a faulty relay (refer to Section 3 for details of testing relays). Visually inspect the condition of all fuses, wires and connections in a problem circuit before testing the components. Use the wiring diagrams to determine which terminal connections will need to be checked, in order to pinpoint the trouble-spot.

4 The basic tools required for electrical fault-finding include a circuit tester or voltmeter (a 12-volt bulb with a set of test leads can also be used for certain tests); a self-powered test light (sometimes known as a continuity tester); an ohmmeter (to measure resistance); a battery and set of test leads; and a jumper wire, preferably with a circuit breaker or fuse incorporated, which can be used to bypass suspect wires or electrical components. Before attempting to locate a problem with test instruments, use the wiring diagram to determine where to make the connections.

5 To find the source of an intermittent wiring fault (usually due to a poor or dirty connection, or damaged wiring insulation), a wiggle test can be performed on the wiring. This involves wiggling the wiring by hand, to see if the fault occurs as the wiring is moved. It should be possible to narrow down the source of the fault to a particular section of wiring. This method of testing can be used in conjunction with any of the tests described in the following sub-Sections.

6 Apart from problems due to poor connections, two basic types of fault can occur in an electrical circuit - open-circuit, or short-circuit.

7 Open-circuit faults are caused by a break somewhere in the circuit, which prevents current from flowing. An open-circuit fault will prevent a component from working, but will not cause the relevant circuit fuse to blow.

8 Short-circuit faults are caused by a short somewhere in the circuit, which allows the current flowing in the circuit to escape along an alternative route, usually to earth. Short-circuit faults are normally caused by a breakdown in wiring insulation, which allows a feed wire to touch either another wire, or an earthed component such as the bodyshell. A short-circuit fault will normally cause the relevant circuit fuse to blow.

Finding an open-circuit

9 To check for an open-circuit, connect one lead of a circuit tester or voltmeter to either the negative battery terminal or a known good earth.

10 Connect the other lead to a connector in the circuit being tested, preferably nearest to the battery or fuse.

11 Switch on the circuit, bearing in mind that some circuits are live only when the ignition switch is moved to a particular position.

12 If voltage is present (indicated either by the tester bulb lighting or a voltmeter reading, as applicable), this means that the section of the circuit between the relevant connector and the battery is problem-free.

13 Continue to check the remainder of the circuit in the same fashion.

14 When a point is reached at which no voltage is present, the problem must lie between that point and the previous test point with voltage. Most problems can be traced to a broken, corroded or loose connection.

Finding a short-circuit

15 To check for a short-circuit, first disconnect the load(s) from the circuit (loads are the components which draw current from a circuit, such as bulbs, motors, heating elements, etc).

16 Remove the relevant fuse from the circuit, and connect a circuit tester or voltmeter to the fuse connections.

17 Switch on the circuit, bearing in mind that some circuits are live only when the ignition switch is moved to a particular position.

18 If voltage is present (indicated either by the tester bulb lighting or a voltmeter reading, as applicable), this means that there is a short-circuit.

19 If no voltage is present, but the fuse still blows with the load(s) connected, this indicates an internal fault in the load(s).

Finding an earth fault

20 The battery negative terminal is connected to earth - the metal of the engine/transmission and the car body - and most systems are wired so that they only receive a positive feed, the current returning via the metal of the car body. This means that the component mounting and the body form part of that circuit. Loose or corroded mountings can therefore cause a range of electrical faults, ranging from total failure of a circuit, to a puzzling partial fault. In particular, lights may shine dimly (especially when another circuit sharing the same earth point is in operation), motors (eg wiper motors or the radiator cooling fan motor) may run slowly, and the operation of one circuit may have an apparently-unrelated effect on another. Note that on many vehicles, earth straps are used between certain components, such as the engine/transmission and the body, usually where there is no metal-to-metal contact between components, due to flexible rubber mountings, etc.

21 To check whether a component is properly earthed, disconnect the battery, and connect one lead of an ohmmeter to a known good earth point. Connect the other lead to the wire or earth connection being tested. The resistance reading should be zero; if not, check the connection as follows.

3.3a For access to the engine compartment fusebox, release the clips . . .

3.3b . . . and remove the cover

3.6 Using the plastic tweezers provided to remove a fuse

22 If an earth connection is thought to be faulty, dismantle the connection, and clean back to bare metal both the bodyshell and the wire terminal or the component earth connection mating surface. Be careful to remove all traces of dirt and corrosion, then use a knife to trim away any paint, so that a clean metal-to-metal joint is made. On reassembly, tighten the joint fasteners securely; if a wire terminal is being refitted, use serrated washers between the terminal and the bodyshell, to ensure a clean and secure connection. When the connection is remade, prevent the onset of corrosion in the future by applying a coat of petroleum jelly or silicone-based grease, or by spraying on (at regular intervals) a proprietary ignition sealer.

3 Fuses, fusible links and relays - general information

Fuses

1 Fuses are designed to break a circuit when a predetermined current is reached, in order to protect the components and wiring which could be damaged by excessive current flow. Any excessive current flow will be due to a fault in the circuit, usually a short-circuit.

2 Fuses and relays are located behind the driver's side of the facia, and in a fuse and relay box in the left-hand side of the engine compartment next to the battery. On models with air conditioning, a relay box is located on the right-hand side of the radiator. On LHD models the headlight dip relay and relevant fuses are located on the right-hand side of the engine compartment by the coolant expansion tank.

3 For access to the facia-mounted fuses, pull off the cover. For access to the fuses in the engine compartment, unclip and remove the cover **(see illustrations)**.

4 A blown fuse can be recognised from its melted or broken wire.

5 To remove a fuse, first ensure that the relevant circuit is switched off.

6 To remove a standard current fuse, use the plastic tweezers supplied and pull the fuse from its location **(see illustration)**. To remove a medium current fuse (30 and 40 amp) simply pull the fuse from its socket.

7 Spare fuses are provided in the fusebox.

8 Before renewing a blown fuse, trace and rectify the cause, and always use a fuse of the correct rating (fuse ratings are specified on the inside of the fusebox cover). Never substitute a fuse of a higher rating, or make temporary repairs using wire or metal foil; more serious damage, or even fire, could result.

9 The radio/cassette player fuse is located in the rear of the unit, and can be accessed after removing the radio/cassette player.

10 The facia-mounted fusebox is best removed by first removing the facia panel as described in Chapter 11 **(see illustration)**.

Fusible links

11 Main fusible links are located next to the battery in the engine compartment. The links are designed to melt in the event of a serious wiring fault, thus protecting the main wiring loom from damage; in the event of a link melting, the fault must be traced and rectified before the link is renewed. When renewing a fusible link, use **only** a genuine Toyota replacement part.

3.10 Facia-mounted fusebox (shown with the facia removed from the vehicle)

Relays

12 A relay is an electrically-operated switch, which is used for the following reasons:
a) A relay can switch a heavy current remotely from the circuit in which the current is flowing, therefore allowing the use of lighter-gauge wiring and switch contacts.
b) A relay can receive more than one control input, unlike a mechanical switch.
c) A relay can have a timer function - for example, the intermittent wiper relay.

13 The various relays are located behind the right-hand side of the facia and in the engine compartment. Most of the engine-related relays are in the engine compartment.

14 If a circuit or system controlled by a relay develops a fault, and the relay is suspect, operate the system. If the relay is functioning, it should be possible to hear it click as it is energised. If this is the case, the fault lies with the components or wiring of the system. If the relay is not being energised, then either the relay is not receiving a main supply or a switching voltage, or the relay itself is faulty. Testing is by the substitution of a known good unit, but be careful - while some relays are identical in appearance and in operation, others look similar but perform different functions.

15 To remove a relay, first ensure that the relevant circuit is switched off. The relay can then simply be pulled out from the socket, and pushed back into position.

4 Switches - removal and refitting

Note: *Disconnect the battery negative lead before removing any switch, and reconnect the lead after refitting the switch. Refer to the caution in Section 1 if a security-coded radio/cassette player is fitted.*

Ignition switch/steering column lock

1 Refer to Chapter 10.

12

4.3a Unscrew the mounting screws . . .

4.3b . . . and remove the wiper switch

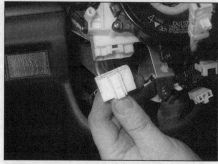

4.3c Disconnect the wiring . . .

Steering column combination switches

Removal

2 Remove the steering wheel and shrouds as described in Chapter 10.

3 Where the switch is mounted separately on the body, disconnect the wiring then unscrew the side mounting screws and withdraw the switch from the steering column. If necessary, disconnect the wiring plugs then unscrew the mounting screw and remove the switch base from the steering column. On models with a driver's air bag, use adhesive tape to hold the contact ring assembly in its central position **(see illustrations)**.

4 Where the switch forms part of the wiring, disconnect the connectors and remove the switch body from the steering column

Refitting

5 Refitting is a reversal of removal.

Facia-mounted switches

Removal

6 Carefully prise out the switch, then disconnect the wiring. Where necessary on the surround mounted switches, remove the surround first as described in Chapter 11 **(see illustrations)**.

Refitting

7 Refitting is a reversal of removal.

Centre console-mounted switches

Removal

8 Remove the centre console (see Chapter 11).

9 Release the securing clips, then push the switch out of the centre console **(see illustration)**.

Refitting

10 Refitting is a reversal of removal.

Courtesy light/door ajar warning switch

Removal

11 Open the door to expose the switch in the door pillar.

12 Remove the securing bolt, then withdraw the switch from the door pillar and remove the rubber gaiter. Disconnect the wiring connector as it becomes accessible **(see illustration)**.

> **HAYNES HINT** *Tape the wiring to the door pillar, or tie a length of string to the wiring, to retrieve it if it falls back into the door pillar.*

Refitting

13 Refitting is a reversal of removal.

5 Bulbs (exterior lights) - renewal

General

1 Whenever a bulb is renewed, note the following points:

a) Make sure the electrical circuit is switched off.

b) Remember that, if the light has just been in use, the bulb may be extremely hot.

c) Always check the bulb contacts and holder, ensuring that there is clean metal-

4.3d . . . then unscrew the switch base mounting screw

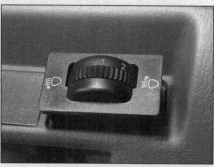

4.6a Prise the headlight leveller switch from the facia . . .

4.6b . . . and disconnect the wiring

4.9 Removing a switch from the centre console

4.12 Removing the courtesy light/door ajar warning switch

5.3 Moving the coolant expansion tank to one side

5.4 Disconnect the wiring plug . . .

5.5 . . . remove the plastic cover . . .

to-metal contact between the bulb and its live contact(s) and earth. Clean off any corrosion or dirt before fitting a new bulb.

d) Wherever bayonet-type bulbs are fitted, ensure that the live contact(s) bear firmly against the bulb contact.

e) Always ensure that the new bulb is of the correct rating (see Specifications), and that it is completely clean before fitting.

Headlight

2 Open the bonnet.

3 If removing the right-hand headlight bulb, first unbolt the coolant expansion tank and position to one side **(see illustration)**.

4 Disconnect the wiring plug from the rear of the headlight **(see illustration)**.

5 Unscrew and remove the plastic cover **(see illustration)**.

6 Pull the rubber dust cover from the rear of the headlight. Note that the pull tag is positioned uppermost **(see illustration)**.

7 Squeeze the retaining spring clip ends, and release the clip from the rear of the bulb **(see illustration)**.

8 Withdraw the bulb **(see illustration)**.

9 When handling the new bulb, use a tissue or clean cloth, to avoid touching the glass with the fingers; moisture and grease from the skin can cause blackening and rapid failure of this type of bulb.

> **HAYNES HINT** *If the headlight bulb glass is accidentally touched, wipe it clean using methylated spirit.*

10 Install the new bulb, ensuring that its locating tabs are located in the light unit cut-outs. Secure the bulb in position with the retaining clip, then refit the dust cover and plastic cover, and reconnect the wiring plug. If necessary, refit the coolant expansion tank.

Front sidelight

11 Open the bonnet.

12 If removing the right-hand sidelight bulb, first unbolt the coolant expansion tank and position to one side.

13 Twist the sidelight bulbholder and remove it from the headlight unit **(see illustration)**.

14 Pull the wedge-type bulb from the bulbholder.

15 Push the new bulb into the bulbholder, then insert the bulbholder in the headlight unit and twist to secure.

16 Where necessary, refit the coolant expansion tank.

Front direction indicator

17 Open the bonnet.

18 Unscrew the screw securing the front direction indicator unit to the headlight, then withdraw the unit noting the location of the guides. **(see illustration)**.

19 Twist the bulbholder and remove it from the unit, then twist the bulb to remove it from the holder **(see illustrations)**.

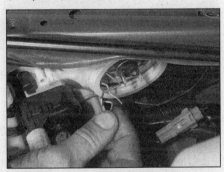

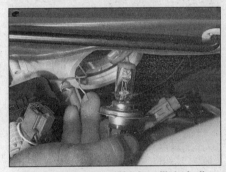

5.6 . . . remove the dust cover . . .

5.7 . . . release the spring clip . . .

5.8 . . . and remove the headlight bulb

5.13 Removing the front sidelight bulbholder from the headlight

5.18 Removing the front direction indicator retaining screw

5.19a Twist the bulbholder from the front direction indicator unit . . .

12

5.19b ... then depress and twist the bulb to remove it

20 Fit the new bulb using a reversal of the removal procedure.

Front direction indicator side repeater

21 Push the front direction indicator side repeater lens forwards, and release the unit from the front wing **(see illustration)**.
22 Twist the bulbholder from the unit, then pull out the wedge-type bulb **(see illustrations)**.
23 Fit the new bulb using a reversal of the removal procedure.

Front driving light/foglight

24 Where fitted, the front driving light/foglight is located in the front bumper.
25 Unscrew the retaining screw located on the inner upper corner of the light unit. Withdraw the unit from the location pins on the front bumper.
26 Disconnect the wiring plug and remove the light unit from the vehicle.

5.21 Press forward and remove the front direction indicator side repeater

27 Twist and remove the connector from the rear of the light, then disconnect the two wires.
28 Squeeze the spring ends and pivot the spring away from the bulb. Remove the bulb.
29 Fit the new bulb using a reversal of the removal procedure. If necessary, the light beam may be adjusted by turning the screw located on the inner lower corner.

Rear direction indicator and stop/tail light cluster

30 Open the tailgate or boot lid as applicable.
31 Unscrew the retaining screws and withdraw the light unit from the rear wing. Note the location pegs on Saloon models.
32 Twist the relevant bulbholder and remove it from the light unit.
33 Depress and twist the bulb and remove it from the bulbholder.
34 Fit the new bulb noting that the stop/tail light bulb has offset pins, to ensure correct installation.

Rear fog and reversing lights

Saloon models

35 Open the boot lid then, where applicable, unclip the trim covering for access to the relevant light.
36 Twist and remove the bulbholder, then depress and twist the bulb to remove it.
37 Fit the new bulb using a reversal of the removal procedure.

Hatchback and Estate models

38 Open the tailgate then remove the relevant outer access cover from the trim panel.
39 Twist and remove the bulbholder, then depress and twist the bulb to remove it **(see illustrations)**.
40 Fit the new bulb using a reversal of the removal procedure.

Rear number plate light

Saloon models

41 Open the boot lid then, where applicable, unclip the trim covering for access to the light unit.
42 Twist and remove the bulbholder then pull out the wedge-type bulb.
43 Fit the new bulb using a reversal of the removal procedure.

Hatchback models

44 Open the tailgate then remove the inner access cover from the trim panel.
45 Twist and remove the bulbholder, then pull out the wedge-type bulb **(see illustrations)**.

5.22a Twist the bulbholder from the light unit ...

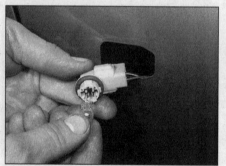

5.22b ... then pull out the wedge-type bulb

5.39a Remove the rear fog/reversing light bulbholder ...

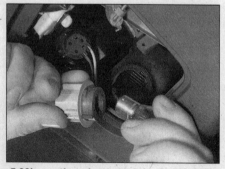

5.39b ... then depress and twist the bulb to remove it

5.45a Remove the rear number plate light bulbholder ...

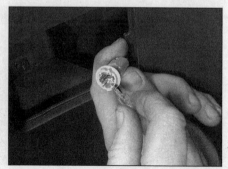

5.45b ... then pull out the wedge-type bulb

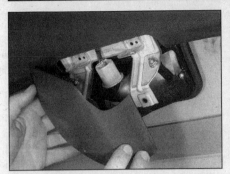

5.50 Remove the high-mounted stop light cover . . .

5.51a . . . then twist the bulbholder from the body . . .

5.51b . . . and remove the bulb

46 Fit the new bulb using a reversal of the removal procedure.

Estate models

47 Unscrew the retaining screws and remove the lens cover.
48 Pull out the wedge-type bulb from the light unit.
49 Fit the new bulb using a reversal of the removal procedure.

High-mounted stop light

50 Open the tailgate then unscrew the retaining screws and remove the cover from the high-mounted stop light (see illustration).
51 Twist and remove the bulbholder, then depress and twist the bulb to remove it (see illustrations).
52 Fit the new bulb using a reversal of the removal procedure.

6 Bulbs (interior lights) - renewal

General

1 Refer to Section 5, paragraph 1.

Roof front console light

2 Using a small screwdriver, prise the lens from the light unit (see illustration).
3 Depress and twist the bulb to remove it (see illustration).
4 Fit the new bulb using a reversal of the removal procedure.

Interior and luggage compartment lights

5 Using a small screwdriver, prise the lens from the light unit (see illustrations).
6 Remove the festoon-type bulb from the light contacts (see illustrations).
7 Fit the new bulb using a reversal of the removal procedure, but make sure the bulb is held firmly between the contacts. Bend the contacts if necessary.

Instrument panel lights

8 Remove the instrument panel, as described in Section 8.
9 Twist the relevant bulbholder anti-clockwise to remove it from the rear of the instrument panel (see illustration).
10 Pull the wedge-type bulb from the bulbholder (see illustration).
11 Fit the new bulb using a reversal of the removal procedure, with reference to Section 8 when refitting the instrument panel.

6.2 Prise out the roof front console light lens . . .

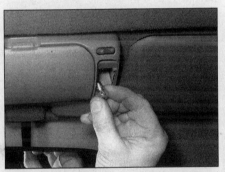

6.3 . . . then depress and twist the bulb to remove it

6.5a Prising the lens from the interior light . . .

6.5b . . . and luggage compartment light

6.6a Removing the festoon-type bulb from the interior light . . .

6.6b . . . and luggage compartment light

12

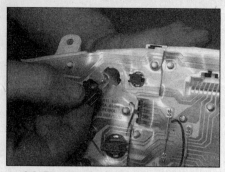

6.9 Remove the bulbholder from the instrument panel . . .

6.10 . . . and pull out the wedge-type bulb

6.14 Removing the illumination bulb from the heater control panel

Heater control panel illumination bulbs

12 Remove the heater/ventilation control panel as described in Chapter 3, however leave the control cables connected.
13 Twist the relevant bulbholder anti-clockwise, and withdraw the bulbholder.
14 Pull the wedge-type bulb from the bulbholder **(see illustration)**.
15 Fit the new bulb using a reversal of the removal procedure.

Switch illumination bulb

16 Remove the switch as described in Section 4.
17 Twist the bulbholder anti-clockwise to remove it from the switch. The bulb is integral with the bulbholder **(see illustrations)**.
18 Fit the new bulb using a reversal of the removal procedure.

6.17a Removing an illumination bulb from the rear foglight switch . . .

6.17b . . . and clock

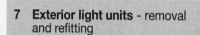

7 Exterior light units - removal and refitting

Headlight unit

Removal

1 Where fitted remove the headlight wiper arm.
2 Remove the front direction indicator light as described later in this Section.
3 Remove the radiator grille as described in Chapter 11.
4 Disconnect the headlight and sidelight wiring from the rear of the headlight unit. Also where fitted, disconnect the wiring from the headlight beam level motor **(see illustration)**.
5 Unscrew the outer mounting bolts **(see illustration)**.
6 Unscrew the upper mounting bolt and

withdraw the headlight unit from the front of the vehicle **(see illustrations)**.
7 If necessary the lens can be removed separately by prising off the retaining clips.

Refitting

8 Refitting is a reversal of removal, but if necessary adjust the headlight beam alignment as described in Chapter 1.

Front direction indicator light

9 The procedure is described as part of the bulb renewal procedure in Section 5.

Front direction indicator side repeater light

10 The procedure is described as part of the bulb renewal procedure in Section 5.

Front driving light/foglight

11 The procedure is described as part of the bulb renewal procedure in Section 5.

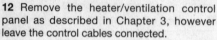

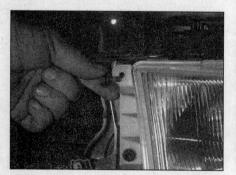

7.4 Disconnect the wiring from the rear of the headlight . . .

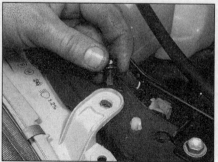

7.5 . . . then unscrew the outer mounting bolts . . .

7.6a . . . and upper mounting bolt . . .

7.6b . . . and withdraw the headlight unit from the front of the vehicle

Rear direction indicator and stop/tail light cluster

12 The procedure is described as part of the bulb renewal procedure in Section 5.

Rear fog and reversing lights

Removal

13 Open the boot lid/tailgate and remove the trim panel.
14 Disconnect the wiring.
15 Remove the rear number plate light unit as described later.
16 Unscrew the mounting nuts and withdraw the light unit from the outside.

Refitting

17 Refitting is a reversal of removal.

Rear number plate light holder

Removal

18 Open the boot lid/tailgate and remove the trim panel.
19 Working through the access holes in the boot lid/tailgate, disconnect the wiring and unscrew the mounting nuts.
20 Withdraw the rear number plate light holder.

Refitting

21 Refitting is a reversal of removal.

Roof front console light

Removal

22 Remove the light bulbs as described in Section 6.

7.23 Remove the roof front console light from the headlining and disconnect the wiring

23 Unscrew the mounting screws and lower the light unit from the headlining (see illustration).
24 Disconnect the wiring.

Refitting

25 Refitting is a reversal of removal.

Luggage compartment light

Removal

26 Carefully prise the light unit from the luggage compartment trim panel, then disconnect the wiring.

Refitting

27 Refitting is a reversal of removal.

---

8 Instrument panel - removal and refitting

Removal

1 Disconnect the battery negative lead.
2 Remove the steering wheel as described in Chapter 10.
3 Unscrew the crosshead screws, and withdraw the surround from the facia (see illustrations).
4 Unscrew the mounting screws and withdraw the instrument panel from the facia (see illustration).
5 Disconnect the wiring multiplugs and remove the panel (see illustration).

Refitting

8 Refitting is a reversal of removal, but make sure that the wiring connectors are fully engaged.

---

9 Instrument panel components - removal and refitting

Caution: The instrument panel components are delicate and should be treated with care. Do not place gauges face down, as the needles may be bent and/or damaged resulting in them being inaccurate. Work in a clean environment to prevent dust and dirt entering the instrument panel.

Removal

Printed circuit

1 Remove all bulbholders, then unscrew the printed circuit securing screws and release any clips; note that, where applicable, the printed circuit will have to be freed from its instrument terminal pins, and it may be necessary to separate the panel as the screws holding the printed circuit also secure the instruments in the panel. Note the number of different types of screw fitted.

Instruments

2 Separate the panel sections as necessary, taking care not to lose or damage any graphic strips. The instruments are secured to the panel by screws; note the number of different types of screw fitted, and the washers.

Refitting

3 Refitting is the reverse of the removal procedure, noting the following points.
a) *Printed circuit - ensure that the printed circuit is correctly located on its lugs and that the screws are refitted to their original locations, with their washers (where applicable).*
b) *Instruments - ensure that the graphic strips are located correctly and that the screws are refitted to their original locations, with their washers (where applicable).*

8.3a Unscrew the crosshead screws . . .

8.3b . . . and remove the instrument panel surround

8.4 Removing the instrument panel from the facia

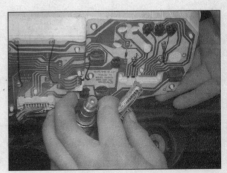

8.5 Disconnecting the wiring from the instrument panel

12

10 "Lights on" warning system - general information

On all models, a lights-on warning buzzer is fitted. The buzzer will sound if the driver's door is opened when the headlights or sidelights are switched on. Where a sunroof is fitted the buzzer will sound when the ignition is switched off with the sunroof open.

The buzzer unit is located behind the heater control panel on the facia.

11 Cigarette lighter - removal and refitting

Removal

1 Remove the centre console as described in Chapter 11.
2 Disconnect the wiring, then push out the cigarette lighter and recover the retaining ring.

Refitting

3 Refitting is a reversal of removal.

12 Horn - removal and refitting

Removal

1 Disconnect the battery negative lead.

14.3a Lift up the cover . . .

14.3b . . . and unscrew the windscreen wiper arm-to-spindle mounting nut

12.3 The horns mounted on the engine compartment front crosspanel

2 Open the bonnet, then remove the radiator grille as described in Chapter 11.
3 Unscrew the mounting bolt, then disconnect the wiring and withdraw the horn complete with its mounting bracket (see illustration).

Refitting

4 Refitting is a reversal of removal.

13 Speedometer speed sensor - removal and refitting

Removal

1 Remove the air inlet duct and air cleaner from the left-hand side of the engine compartment with reference to Chapter 4A.
2 Disconnect the wiring from the speedometer speed sensor located on the rear of the transmission.
3 Unscrew and remove the speed sensor (see illustration).

Refitting

4 Refitting is a reversal of removal.

14 Wiper arm - removal and refitting

Removal

1 Operate the wiper motor, then switch it off

14.3c Unscrewing the tailgate wiper arm-to-spindle mounting nut

13.3 Speed sensor on the transmission

so that the wiper arm returns to the parked position.
2 Stick a piece of tape along the edge of the wiper blade, to use as an alignment aid on refitting.
3 Lift up the wiper arm spindle nut cover, then unscrew and remove the spindle nut (see illustrations). Lift the blade off the glass, and pull the wiper arm off its spindle. If necessary, the arm can be levered off the spindle using a suitable flat-bladed screwdriver. If both windscreen wiper arms are removed, note their locations, as different arms are fitted to the driver's and passenger's sides. The tailgate wiper arms for Hatchback and Estate models are different.

Refitting

4 Refitting is a reversal of removal, but ensure that the wiper arm and spindle splines are clean and dry and align the blades with the tape fitted before removal.

15 Windscreen wiper motor and linkage - removal and refitting

Removal

1 Remove the wiper arms as described in Section 14.
2 Open the bonnet. Make sure the ignition is switched off.
3 Using a screwdriver to release the clips, remove the weatherstrip from the front edge of the bulkhead cowl panel (see illustration).

15.3 Release the weatherstrip and clips from the front edge of the bulkhead cowl panel

15.4a Remove the centre screw . . .

15.4b . . . and side screws . . .

15.4c . . . and remove the cowl panels

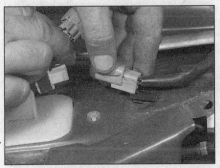

15.5 Disconnecting the windscreen wiper motor wiring

15.6a Unscrew the mounting bolts . . .

15.6b . . . and remove the windscreen wiper motor and linkage

4 Unscrew and remove the screws and remove the cowl panels (see illustrations).
5 Disconnect the wiring at the connector (see illustration).
6 Unscrew the mounting screws and withdraw the windscreen wiper motor and linkage from the bulkhead (see illustrations).
7 If necessary disconnect the operating rods from the crank arm, then unscrew the retaining screws and remove the motor from the linkage bracket (see illustration).

Refitting

9 Refitting is a reversal of removal, but apply a little grease to the crank arm ball before reconnecting the linkage and refer to Section 14 when refitting the wiper arms.

16 Tailgate wiper motor - removal and refitting

Removal

1 Remove the wiper arm as described in Section 14.
2 Unscrew the nut securing the wiper motor spindle body to the tailgate (see illustration).
3 Open the tailgate and remove the inner trim panel.
4 Disconnect the wiring at the connector.
5 Unscrew the mounting bolts noting that the earth lead is attached to one of them (see illustration).
6 Withdraw the wiper motor from the tailgate.
7 If necessary, remove the spindle grommet from the hole in the tailgate (see illustration).

15.7 Windscreen wiper motor crank arm and operating rods

Refitting

8 Refitting is a reversal of removal, but ensure that the grommet is correctly located in the tailgate, and refit the wiper arm (Section 14).

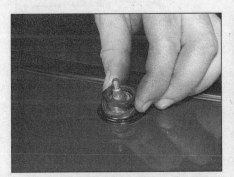

16.2 Unscrewing the nut securing the wiper motor spindle body to the tailgate

16.5 Tailgate wiper motor and mounting bolts (note the earth lead)

16.7 Removing the spindle grommet from the tailgate

17 Washer system components - removal and refitting

Washer fluid reservoir

Removal

1 The washer fluid reservoir is located on the right-hand side of the engine compartment. Before removing it, syphon out all of the fluid using a suitable plastic tube.
2 Unscrew the mounting screws and lift the reservoir from the body, then disconnect the wiring from the pump (see illustration).
3 Loosen the clips and disconnect the tubes.

Refitting

4 Refitting is a reversal of removal.

Washer pump(s)

Removal

5 Proceed as described in paragraphs 1 to 3.
6 Pull the washer pump from the reservoir, and recover the grommet. If the reservoir still contains fluid, be prepared for fluid spillage.

Refitting

8 Refitting is a reversal of removal.

Windscreen washer nozzle

Removal

9 Open the bonnet.
10 Working under the bonnet, release the securing tabs using long-nosed pliers, then push the nozzle from the bonnet. Disconnect the fluid hose, and withdraw the nozzle.

17.2 Removing the washer fluid reservoir

Refitting

11 Refitting is a reversal of removal.

Tailgate washer nozzle

Removal

12 Open the tailgate, and working at the inside top edge, pull the fluid hose from the washer nozzle.
13 Unscrew the securing nut, then withdraw the nozzle from the outside of the tailgate.

Refitting

14 Refitting is a reversal of removal.

18 Radio/cassette player - removal and refitting

Caution: If the radio/cassette player fitted to the vehicle is one with an anti-theft security code, refer to the information given in the Reference Section at the rear of this manual before disconnecting the battery.

Note: *This Section describes the removal and refitting of the standard radio/cassette fitted as original equipment. The procedure may differ for non-standard equipment.*

Removal

1 Disconnect the battery negative lead.
2 Depress the button and remove the security front from the radio (see illustration).
3 Insert a feeler blade through the release slot on the top edge of the radio, and press in to release the retaining peg (see illustrations).
4 Withdraw the radio/cassette from the facia.
5 Disconnect the aerial and the wiring plug (see illustration).
6 If necessary, unbolt the radio/cassette enclosure from the facia (see illustration).

Refitting

7 Refitting is a reversal of removal.

19 Loudspeakers - removal and refitting

Front door-mounted loudspeakers

1 The removal and refitting procedures are included in the door inner trim panel procedures described in Chapter 11.

Rear door-mounted loudspeakers

Removal

2 Remove the door inner trim panel as described in Chapter 11.
3 Unscrew the mounting bolts and withdraw the loudspeaker from the door inner panel (see illustration).

18.2 Removing the security front from the radio

18.3a Insert a feeler blade through the slot in the radio to remove it

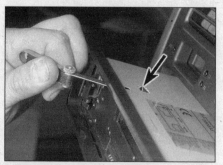

18.3b Showing the radio retaining peg on the top of the radio

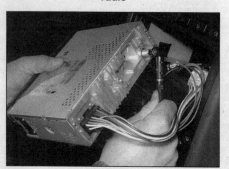

18.5 Disconnecting the aerial from the rear of the radio

18.6 Removing the radio enclosure from the facia

19.3 Removing the rear door-mounted loudspeaker

4 Disconnect the wiring.

Refitting

5 Refitting is a reversal of removal.

20 Radio aerial - removal and refitting

Removal

1 The power aerial is located on the left-hand rear wing, and the standard aerial is located at the top of the right-hand front A pillar.

Power aerial rod

2 To remove the aerial rod and cable from the power aerial, first turn the ignition key to the LOCK position. Unscrew and remove the nut from the top of the aerial unit. Have an assistant press the AM button on the radio and at the same time turn the ignition key to the ACC position - the aerial will extend fully and be released from the top of the aerial together with its cable. Prevent damage to the rear wing paintwork by holding the rod as it is ejected from the aerial body. Leave the ignition key in the ACC position until the new rod is fitted.

3 To fit the aerial rod and cable to the power aerial, insert the cable with the teeth facing rearwards, then insert the rod approximately 290 mm. Turn the ignition key to the LOCK position - the rod will retract into the body. Refit and tighten the retaining nut.

Aerial and lead

4 To remove the aerial and lead, first remove the radio as described in Section 18, and disconnect the aerial lead.

5 Trace the aerial from the radio position to the aerial position, and remove the relevant interior trim with reference to Chapter 11. To reduce the amount of trim removed, tie pieces of string to the aerial as it is being withdrawn through sections of the trim and leave in place to aid refitting.

6 To remove the power aerial, disconnect the wiring then unbolt it and remove from inside the vehicle together with the lead.

7 To remove the standard aerial, unscrew the crosshead screws and withdraw the aerial together with the lead from the roof.

Refitting

8 Refitting is a reversal of removal.

21 Anti-theft alarm system - general information

Some models are fitted with the Toyota Vehicle Security System (TVSS) which is controlled by an ECU located beneath the centre console.

Any suspected faults with the system should be referred to a Toyota dealer.

22 Heated front seat components - general information

Some models are fitted with heated front seats. The seats are heated by electrical elements built into the seat cushions. For access to the heating elements, the seats must be dismantled, and this work should be entrusted to a Toyota dealer.

23 Air bag and Supplementary Restraint System - general information and precautions

General information

1 An air bag and seat belt Supplementary Restraint System (SRS) is fitted to most models to prevent serious chest and head injuries during an accident. The driver's air bag is fitted in the steering wheel centre pad, and the optional passenger's air bag is fitted in the top of the facia panel. Later models are fitted with seat belt tensioners, which automatically tighten the seat belts in the event of an accident. The tensioners form part of the seat belt retractors.

23.2 SRS ECU located beneath the centre console

2 The SRS system is armed when the ignition key is in the ON or START positions, and is activated by a 'g' sensor (deceleration sensor) located in the driver's air bag. The sensor incorporates a floating ball to detect deceleration. The system ECU is located beneath the rear of the centre console **(see illustration)**.

3 The air bag is inflated by a gas generator, which forces the bag out from its location in the steering wheel.

Precautions

The following precautions must be observed when working on vehicles with an air bag system, to prevent the possibility of personal injury.
a) Do not attempt to test any of the air bag system circuits using test meters or any other test equipment.
b) Before working on the air bag and SRS related components (steering wheel and column), switch off the ignition, and disconnect the battery negative lead, then wait for at least 10 MINUTES before carrying out any further work.
c) Do not attempt to turn the steering wheel or column with the steering gear removed.
d) If the air bag warning light comes on, or any fault in the system is suspected, consult a Toyota dealer without delay. Do not attempt to carry out fault diagnosis, or any dismantling of the components.

Key to symbols

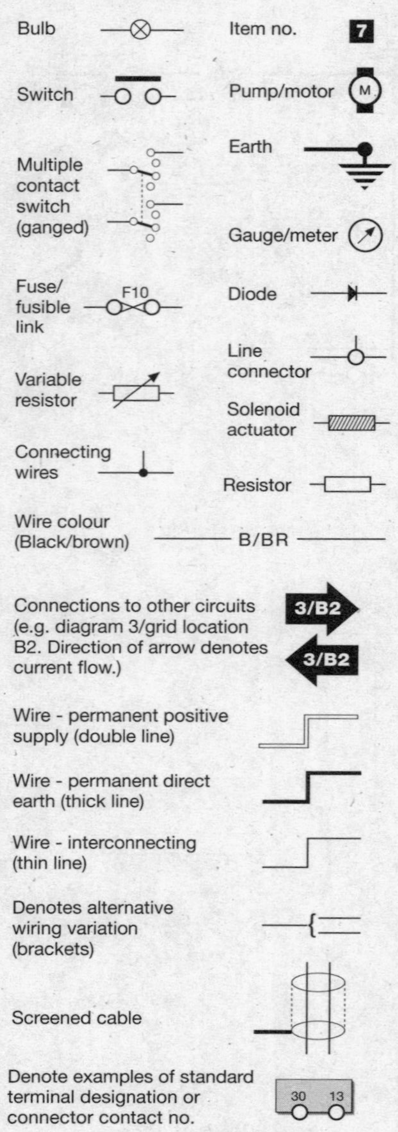

Bulb	
Switch	
Multiple contact switch (ganged)	
Fuse/fusible link	
Variable resistor	
Connecting wires	
Wire colour (Black/brown)	B/BR
Connections to other circuits (e.g. diagram 3/grid location B2. Direction of arrow denotes current flow.)	
Wire - permanent positive supply (double line)	
Wire - permanent direct earth (thick line)	
Wire - interconnecting (thin line)	
Denotes alternative wiring variation (brackets)	
Screened cable	
Denote examples of standard terminal designation or connector contact no.	
Item no.	7
Pump/motor	M
Earth	
Gauge/meter	
Diode	
Line connector	
Solenoid actuator	
Resistor	

Key to fuses

Fuse	Rating	Circuit protected
F1	15A	Power door lock, ABS
F3	7.5A	Interior light, glovebox light, instrument illumination
F4	30A	Heated windscreen and mirrors, engine idle up system
F5	10A	Gauges and meters, service reminder indicators, and warning buzzers (except no charge and door ajar warning lights), econodrive monitor, automatic transmission overdrive system, heated rear window, electric windows, central locking, heated screen, charging system and electric aerial
F6	7.5A	Engine starter system, fuel injection
F7	7.5A	Emission control system, charging system, no charge warning light
F8	15A	Radio/cassette, cigar lighter, clock, shift lock control system (automatic transmission), electric aerial
F9	10A	Direction indicators
F10	15A	Stop lights, ABS, fuel injection, shift lock control system (automatic transmission)
F11	10A	LH side and tail light, number plate lights, headlight levelling
F12	10A	Tail lights, number plate lights, radio/cassette, headlight washer, instrument illumination, rear fog lights, side lights
F13	20A	Supply to F12
F14	15A	Electronic transmission, ABS, shift lock control system (automatic transmission)
F15	20A	Front and rear wash/wipe
F16	15A	Front fog lights
F17	7.5A	Engine idle up system
F18	15A	Engine idle up system
F19	20A	Fuel heater
F20	20A	Heated mirrors
F21	20A	Heated seats
F22	10A	Horns
F23	15A	Hazard warning lights
F24	20A	Fuel injection
F25	15A	Fuel injection
F26	15A	LH headlight
F27	15A	RH headlight
F32	30A	Supply to F6 and F7
F33	20A	Electric mirrors, door ajar, electric sunroof, electric aerial ignition switch light, interior light, luggage compartment light, clock and radio/cassette
F34	7.5A	Charging system
F35	40A	Headlight cleaner, charging system, supply to F5, F8, F9, F14, F15, F16, F20 and F21
F36	30A	Central locking, sunroof and electric windows
F37	40A	Heated rear window
F38	30A	Electric cooling fan
F39	30A	Electric cooling fan
F40	40A	Starting system, supply to F26 and F27
F41	50A	Air conditioning
F42	50A	ABS
F43	100A	Charging system, supply to F1, F10, F13, F18, F35, F36, F37, F38, F39, F41, F42,
F44	80A	Glow plug system (diesel)

Earth locations

E1	In engine compartment, RH inner wing
E2	In engine compartment, on block
E3	In engine compartment, near battery
E4	In engine compartment, LH strut tower
E5	In passenger compartment, LH kick panel
E6	In passenger compartment, behind centre console
E7	In passenger compartment, behind fusebox
E8	In passenger compartment, RH kick panel
E9	LH 'C' pillar (saloon)
E10	LH 'C' pillar (saloon)
E11	In luggage compartment RH side (estate), under parcel shelf (saloon)
E12	In luggage compartment LH side (estate), centre rear panel (saloon)
E13	Under headlining RH rear
E14	Base of RH 'C' pillar
E15	RH tailgate (hatch)
E16	Centre tailgate (hatch)
E17	Centre rear panel (hatch)
E18	LH tailgate (hatch)
E19	In luggage compartment, LH side (hatch)
E20	RH kick panel

Passenger fusebox *(in passenger compartment)*

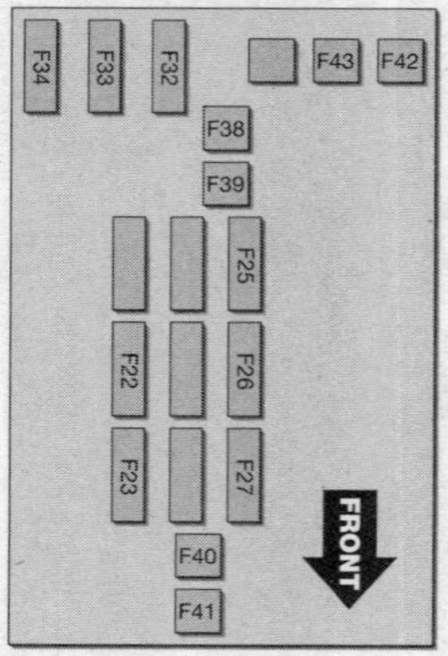

Engine fusebox 4A-FE engine *(in engine compartment)*

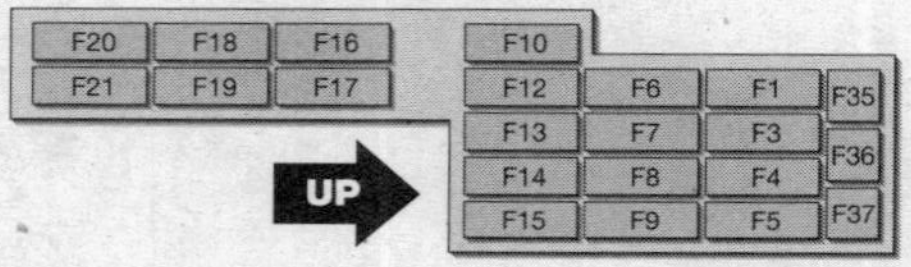

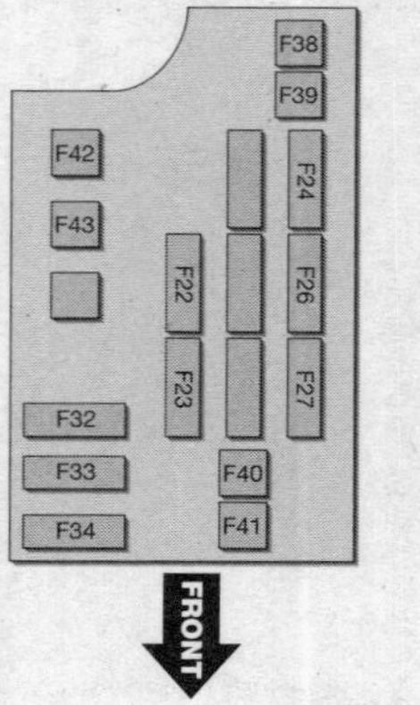

Engine fusebox 3S-FE and 3S-GE engines *(in engine compartment)*

H29400
T.M.Marke

Diagram 1 : Information for wiring diagrams

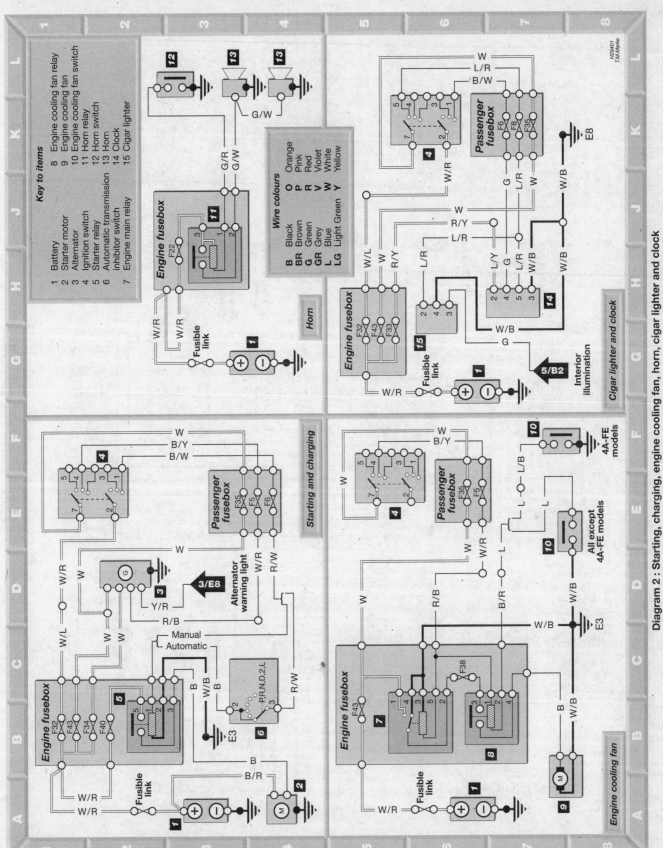

Key to items

1 Battery
2 Starter motor
3 Alternator
4 Ignition switch
5 Starter relay
6 Automatic transmission inhibitor switch
7 Engine main relay
8 Engine cooling fan relay
9 Engine cooling fan
10 Engine cooling fan switch
11 Horn relay
12 Horn switch
13 Horn
14 Clock
15 Cigar lighter

Wire colours

B	Black	O	Orange
BR	Brown	P	Pink
G	Green	R	Red
GR	Grey	V	Violet
L	Blue	W	White
LG	Light Green	Y	Yellow

Horn

Cigar lighter and clock

Interior illumination

Starting and charging

Alternator warning light

Manual
Automatic

P,R,N,D,2,L

Engine cooling fan

All except 4A-FE models

4A-FE models

H29401
T.M.Marie

Diagram 2 : Starting, charging, engine cooling fan, horn, cigar lighter and clock

12

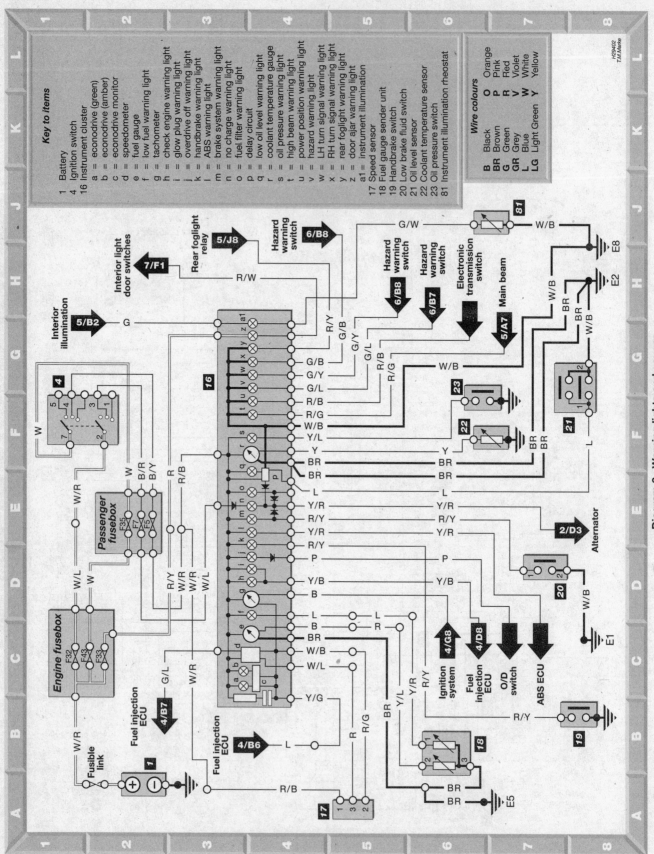

Key to items

1 Battery
4 Ignition switch
16 Instrument cluster
  a = econodrive (green)
  b = econodrive (amber)
  c = econodrive monitor
  d = speedometer
  e = fuel gauge
  f = low fuel warning light
  g = tachometer
  h = check engine warning light
  i = glow plug warning light
  j = overdrive off warning light
  k = handbrake warning light
  l = ABS warning light
  m = brake system warning light
  n = no charge warning light
  o = fuel filter warning light
  p = delay circuit
  q = low oil level warning light
  r = coolant temperature gauge
  s = oil pressure warning light
  t = high beam warning light
  u = power position warning light
  v = hazard warning light
  w = LH turn signal warning light
  x = RH turn signal warning light
  y = rear foglight warning light
  z = door ajar warning light
  a1 = instrument illumination
17 Speed sensor
18 Fuel gauge sender unit
19 Handbrake switch
20 Low brake fluid switch
21 Oil level sensor
22 Coolant temperature sensor
23 Oil pressure switch
81 Instrument illumination rheostat

Wire colours

B	Black	O	Orange
BR	Brown	P	Pink
G	Green	R	Red
GR	Grey	V	Violet
L	Blue	W	White
LG	Light Green	Y	Yellow

H29402
T.M.Marke

Diagram 3 : Warning lights and gauges

Interior light door switches
Interior illumination
Rear foglight relay
Hazard warning switch
Passenger fusebox
Engine fusebox
Fusible link
Fuel injection ECU
Fuel injection ECU

Hazard warning switch
Hazard warning switch
Electronic transmission switch
Main beam
Ignition system
Fuel injection ECU
O/D switch
ABS ECU
Alternator

5/J8
7/F1
6/B8
5/B2
4
16
5/B2
4/B7
4/B6
1
17
18
19
20
21
22
23
81
6/B8
6/B7
5/A7
4/G8
4/D8
2/D3

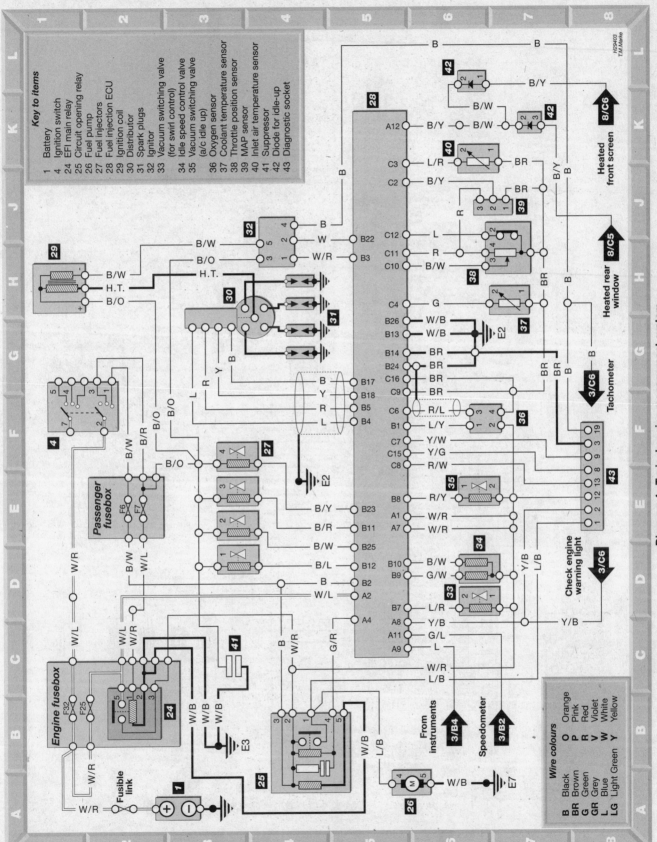

Diagram 4 : Typical engine management system

Key to items

1 Battery
24 Ignition switch
25 EFI main relay
26 Circuit opening relay
27 Fuel pump
28 Fuel injectors
29 Fuel injection ECU
30 Ignition coil
31 Distributor
32 Spark plugs
33 Ignitor
33 Vacuum switching valve (for swirl control)
34 Idle speed control valve
35 Vacuum switching valve (a/c idle up)
36 Oxygen sensor
37 Coolant temperature sensor
38 Throttle position sensor
39 MAP sensor
40 Inlet air temperature sensor
41 Suppressor
42 Diode for idle-up
43 Diagnostic socket

Passenger fusebox

Engine fusebox

Fusible link

Wire colours

B	Black	O	Orange
BR	Brown	P	Pink
G	Green	R	Red
GR	Grey	V	Violet
L	Blue	W	White
LG	Light Green	Y	Yellow

Heated front screen

Heated rear window

Tachometer

Check engine warning light

From instruments

Speedometer

12

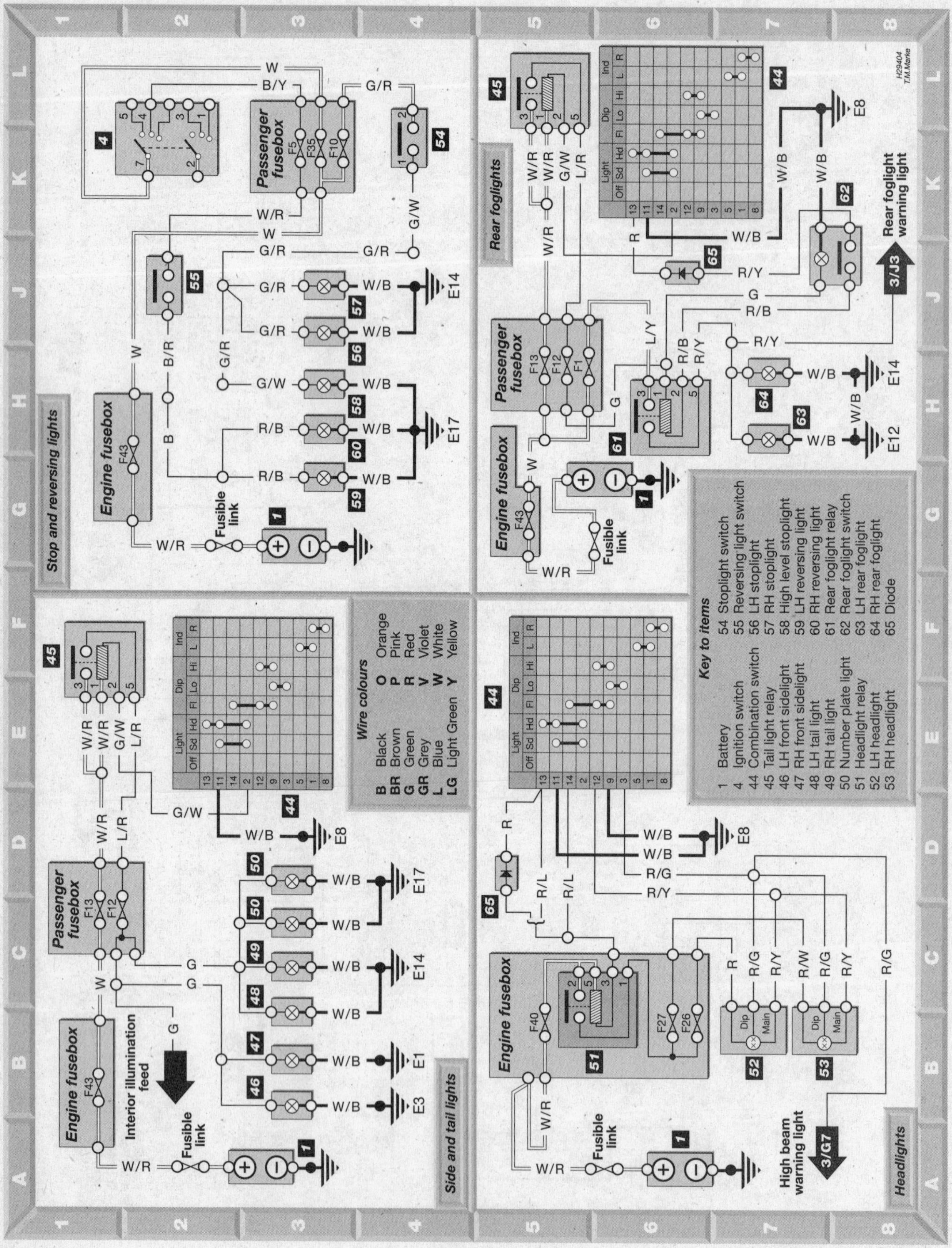

Stop and reversing lights

Rear foglights

Side and tail lights

Headlights

Passenger fusebox

Engine fusebox

Interior illumination feed

Fusible link

Rear foglight warning light

High beam warning light

Wire colours

B	Black	O	Orange
BR	Brown	P	Pink
G	Green	R	Red
GR	Grey	V	Violet
L	Blue	W	White
LG	Light Green	Y	Yellow

Key to items

1 Battery
4 Ignition switch
44 Combination switch
45 Tail light relay
46 LH front sidelight
47 RH front sidelight
48 LH tail light
49 RH tail light
50 Number plate light
51 Headlight relay
52 LH headlight
53 RH headlight
54 Stoplight switch
55 Reversing light switch
56 LH stoplight
57 RH stoplight
58 High level stoplight
59 LH reversing light
60 RH reversing light
61 Rear foglight relay
62 Rear foglight switch
63 LH rear foglight
64 RH rear foglight
65 Diode

Diagram 5 : Exterior lighting

H29404
T.M.Marke

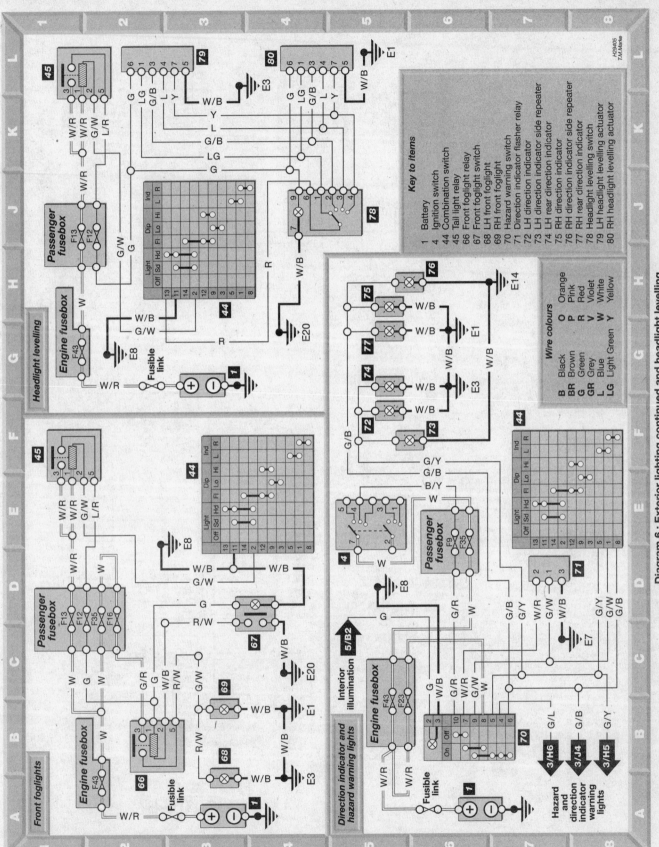

Key to items

1. Battery
4. Ignition switch
44. Combination switch
45. Tail light relay
66. Front foglight relay
67. Front foglight switch
68. LH front foglight
69. RH front foglight
70. Hazard warning switch
71. Direction indicator flasher relay
72. LH direction indicator
73. RH direction indicator
74. LH rear direction indicator
75. LH direction indicator side repeater
76. RH direction indicator side repeater
77. RH rear direction indicator
78. Headlight levelling switch
79. LH headlight levelling actuator
80. RH headlight levelling actuator

Wire colours

B	Black	O	Orange
BR	Brown	P	Pink
G	Green	R	Red
GR	Grey	V	Violet
L	Blue	W	White
LG	Light Green	Y	Yellow

Headlight levelling

Engine fusebox

Passenger fusebox

Front foglights

Direction indicator and hazard warning lights

Interior illumination

Hazard and direction indicator warning lights

Diagram 6 : Exterior lighting continued and headlight levelling

H29405
T.M.Marke

12

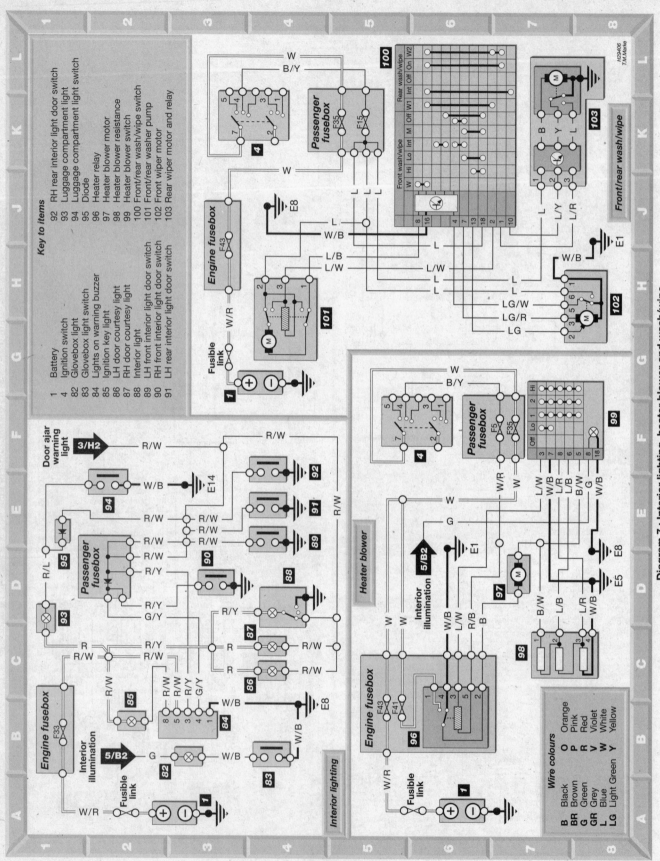

Key to items

1 Battery
4 Ignition switch
82 Glovebox light
83 Glovebox light switch
84 Lights on warning buzzer
85 Ignition key light
86 LH door courtesy light
87 RH door courtesy light
88 Interior light
89 LH front interior light door switch
90 RH front interior light door switch
91 LH rear interior light door switch

92 RH rear interior light door switch
93 Luggage compartment light
94 Luggage compartment light switch
95 Diode
96 Heater relay
97 Heater blower motor
98 Heater blower resistance
99 Heater blower switch
100 Front/rear wash/wipe switch
101 Front/rear washer pump
102 Front wiper motor
103 Rear wiper motor and relay

Wire colours

B	Black	O	Orange
BR	Brown	P	Pink
G	Green	R	Red
GR	Grey	V	Violet
L	Blue	W	White
LG	Light Green	Y	Yellow

Diagram 7 : Interior lighting, heater blower and wash/wipe

Front/rear wash/wipe

Interior lighting

Heater blower

Interior illumination

Door ajar warning light

H29406
T.M.Marke

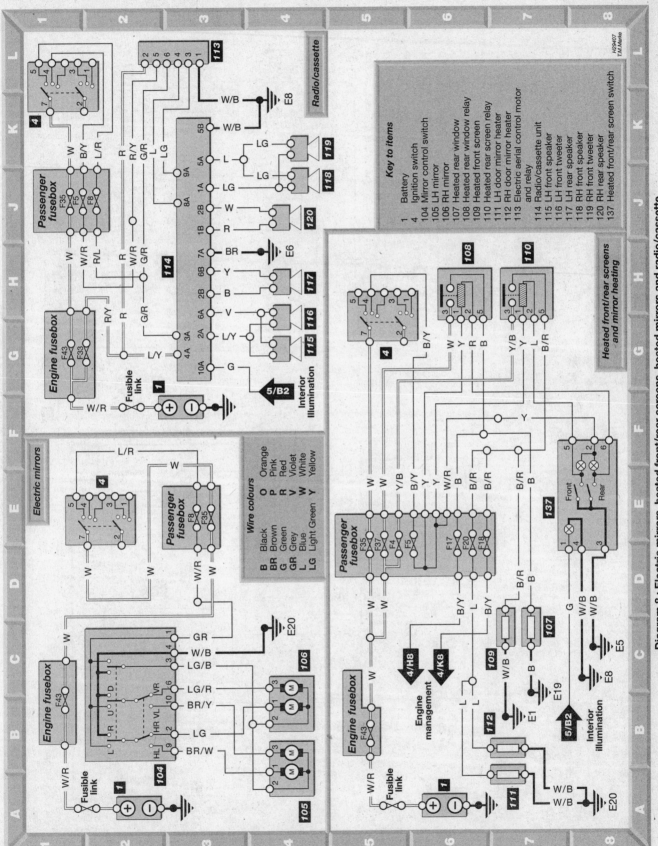

Diagram 8 : Electric mirrors, heated front/rear screens, heated mirrors and radio/cassette

Key to items

1 Battery
4 Ignition switch
104 Mirror control switch
105 LH mirror
106 RH mirror
107 Heated rear window
108 Heated rear window relay
109 Heated front screen
110 Heated rear screen relay
111 LH door mirror heater
112 RH door mirror heater
113 Electric aerial control motor and relay
114 Radio/cassette unit
115 LH front speaker
116 LH front tweeter
117 LH rear speaker
118 RH front speaker
119 RH front tweeter
120 RH rear speaker
137 Heated front/rear screen switch

Wire colours

B	Black	O	Orange
BR	Brown	P	Pink
G	Green	R	Red
GR	Grey	V	Violet
L	Blue	W	White
LG	Light Green	Y	Yellow

Radio/cassette

Heated front/rear screens and mirror heating

Electric mirrors

Interior illumination

Engine management

12

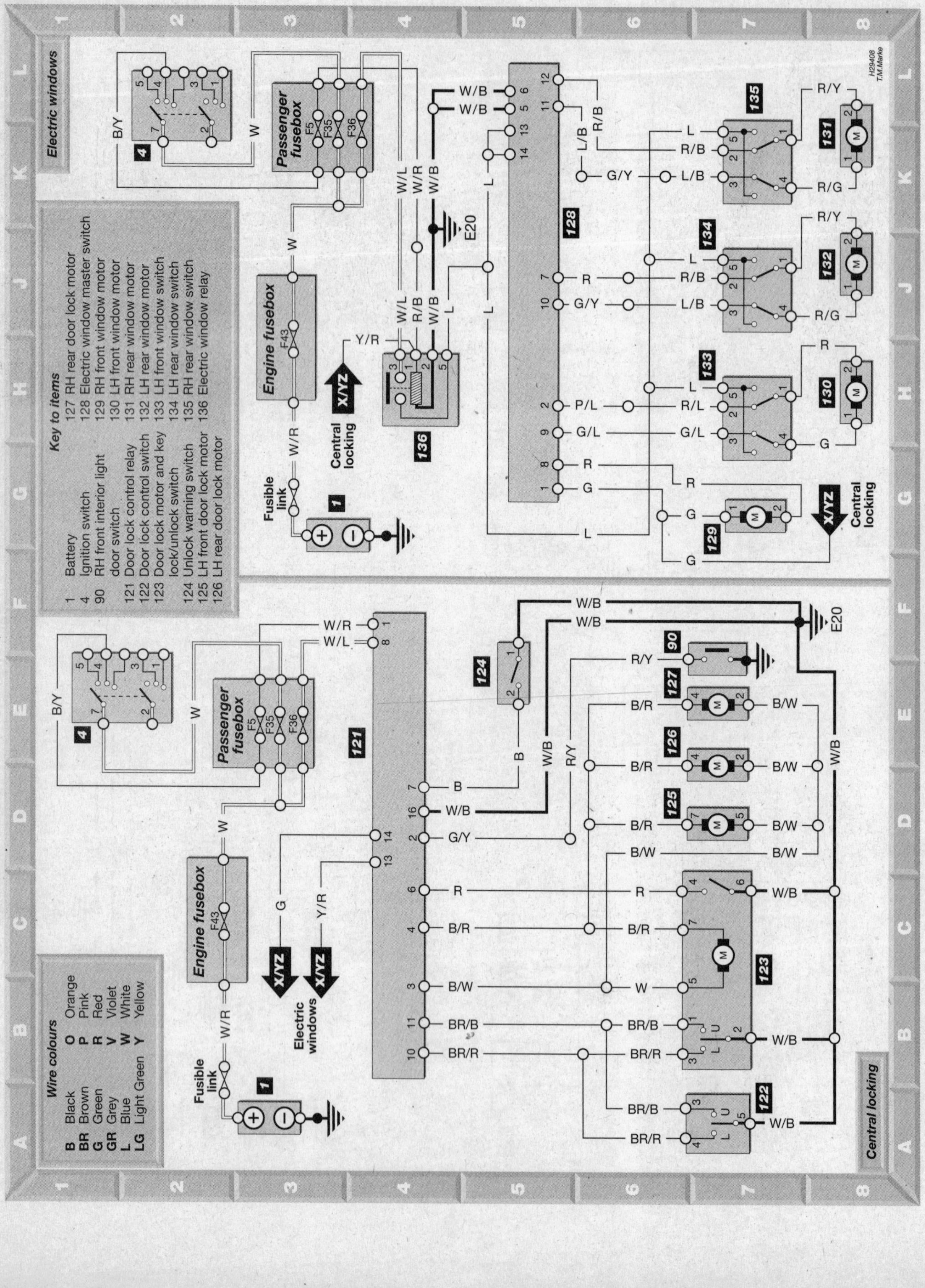

Diagram 9 : Central locking and electric windows

General dimensions and weights

Note: *All figures are approximate, and may vary according to model. Refer to manufacturer's data for exact figures.*

Dimensions

Overall length:
Saloon and Hatchback .... 4530 mm
Estate .... 4545 mm
Overall width .... 1695 mm
Overall height:
Saloon and Hatchback .... 1410 mm
Estate .... 1425 mm
Wheelbase .... 2580 mm

Track:

	Front	Rear
Saloon and Hatchback:		
models without 3S-GE engine	1465 mm	1445 mm
models with 3S-GE engine	1470 mm	1445 mm
Estate	1465 mm	1445 mm

Weights

Kerb weight .... 1185 to 1290 kg
Towing weight .... 1300 kg

Conversion factors

Length (distance)

Inches (in)	x 25.4	=	Millimetres (mm)	x 0.0394 =	Inches (in)
Feet (ft)	x 0.305	=	Metres (m)	x 3.281 =	Feet (ft)
Miles	x 1.609	=	Kilometres (km)	x 0.621 =	Miles

Volume (capacity)

Cubic inches (cu in; in³)	x 16.387	=	Cubic centimetres (cc; cm³)	x 0.061 =	Cubic inches (cu in; in³)
Imperial pints (Imp pt)	x 0.568	=	Litres (l)	x 1.76 =	Imperial pints (Imp pt)
Imperial quarts (Imp qt)	x 1.137	=	Litres (l)	x 0.88 =	Imperial quarts (Imp qt)
Imperial quarts (Imp qt)	x 1.201	=	US quarts (US qt)	x 0.833 =	Imperial quarts (Imp qt)
US quarts (US qt)	x 0.946	=	Litres (l)	x 1.057 =	US quarts (US qt)
Imperial gallons (Imp gal)	x 4.546	=	Litres (l)	x 0.22 =	Imperial gallons (Imp gal)
Imperial gallons (Imp gal)	x 1.201	=	US gallons (US gal)	x 0.833 =	Imperial gallons (Imp gal)
US gallons (US gal)	x 3.785	=	Litres (l)	x 0.264 =	US gallons (US gal)

Mass (weight)

Ounces (oz)	x 28.35	=	Grams (g)	x 0.035 =	Ounces (oz)
Pounds (lb)	x 0.454	=	Kilograms (kg)	x 2.205 =	Pounds (lb)

Force

Ounces-force (ozf; oz)	x 0.278	=	Newtons (N)	x 3.6 =	Ounces-force (ozf; oz)
Pounds-force (lbf; lb)	x 4.448	=	Newtons (N)	x 0.225 =	Pounds-force (lbf; lb)
Newtons (N)	x 0.1	=	Kilograms-force (kgf; kg)	x 9.81 =	Newtons (N)

Pressure

Pounds-force per square inch (psi; lbf/in²; lb/in²)	x 0.070	=	Kilograms-force per square centimetre (kgf/cm²; kg/cm²)	x 14.223 =	Pounds-force per square inch (psi; lbf/in²; lb/in²)
Pounds-force per square inch (psi; lbf/in²; lb/in²)	x 0.068	=	Atmospheres (atm)	x 14.696 =	Pounds-force per square inch (psi; lbf/in²; lb/in²)
Pounds-force per square inch (psi; lbf/in²; lb/in²)	x 0.069	=	Bars	x 14.5 =	Pounds-force per square inch (psi; lbf/in²; lb/in²)
Pounds-force per square inch (psi; lbf/in²; lb/in²)	x 6.895	=	Kilopascals (kPa)	x 0.145 =	Pounds-force per square inch (psi; lbf/in²; lb/in²)
Kilopascals (kPa)	x 0.01	=	Kilograms-force per square centimetre (kgf/cm²; kg/cm²)	x 98.1 =	Kilopascals (kPa)
Millibar (mbar)	x 100	=	Pascals (Pa)	x 0.01 =	Millibar (mbar)
Millibar (mbar)	x 0.0145	=	Pounds-force per square inch (psi; lbf/in²; lb/in²)	x 68.947 =	Millibar (mbar)
Millibar (mbar)	x 0.75	=	Millimetres of mercury (mmHg)	x 1.333 =	Millibar (mbar)
Millibar (mbar)	x 0.401	=	Inches of water (inH₂O)	x 2.491 =	Millibar (mbar)
Millimetres of mercury (mmHg)	x 0.535	=	Inches of water (inH₂O)	x 1.868 =	Millimetres of mercury (mmHg)
Inches of water (inH₂O)	x 0.036	=	Pounds-force per square inch (psi; lbf/in²; lb/in²)	x 27.68 =	Inches of water (inH₂O)

Torque (moment of force)

Pounds-force inches (lbf in; lb in)	x 1.152	=	Kilograms-force centimetre (kgf cm; kg cm)	x 0.868 =	Pounds-force inches (lbf in; lb in)
Pounds-force inches (lbf in; lb in)	x 0.113	=	Newton metres (Nm)	x 8.85 =	Pounds-force inches (lbf in; lb in)
Pounds-force inches (lbf in; lb in)	x 0.083	=	Pounds-force feet (lbf ft; lb ft)	x 12 =	Pounds-force inches (lbf in; lb in)
Pounds-force feet (lbf ft; lb ft)	x 0.138	=	Kilograms-force metres (kgf m; kg m)	x 7.233 =	Pounds-force feet (lbf ft; lb ft)
Pounds-force feet (lbf ft; lb ft)	x 1.356	=	Newton metres (Nm)	x 0.738 =	Pounds-force feet (lbf ft; lb ft)
Newton metres (Nm)	x 0.102	=	Kilograms-force metres (kgf m; kg m)	x 9.804 =	Newton metres (Nm)

Power

Horsepower (hp)	x 745.7	=	Watts (W)	x 0.0013 =	Horsepower (hp)

Velocity (speed)

Miles per hour (miles/hr; mph)	x 1.609	=	Kilometres per hour (km/hr; kph)	x 0.621 =	Miles per hour (miles/hr; mph)

Fuel consumption*

Miles per gallon (mpg)	x 0.354	=	Kilometres per litre (km/l)	x 2.825 =	Miles per gallon (mpg)

Temperature

Degrees Fahrenheit = (°C x 1.8) + 32   Degrees Celsius (Degrees Centigrade; °C) = (°F - 32) x 0.56

* It is common practice to convert from miles per gallon (mpg) to litres/100 kilometres (l/100km), where mpg x l/100 km = 282

Spare parts are available from many sources, including maker's appointed garages, accessory shops, and motor factors. To be sure of obtaining the correct parts, it may sometimes be necessary to quote the vehicle identification number. If possible, it can also be useful to take the old parts along for positive identification. Items such as starter motors and alternators may be available under a service exchange scheme - any parts returned should always be clean.

Our advice regarding spare part sources is as follows.

Officially-appointed garages

This is the best source of parts which are peculiar to your car, and are not otherwise generally available (eg badges, interior trim, certain body panels, etc). It is also the only place at which you should buy parts if the vehicle is still under warranty.

Accessory shops

These are very good places to buy materials and components needed for the maintenance of your car (oil, air and fuel filters, spark plugs, light bulbs, drivebelts, oils and greases, brake pads, touch-up paint, etc). Parts like this sold by a reputable shop are of the same standard as those used by the car manufacturer.

Motor factors

Good factors will stock all the more important components which wear out comparatively quickly and can sometimes supply individual components needed for the overhaul of a larger assembly. They may also handle work such as cylinder block reboring, crankshaft regrinding and balancing, etc.

Tyre and exhaust specialists

These outlets may be independent or members of a local or national chain. They frequently offer competitive prices when compared with a main dealer or local garage, but it will pay to obtain several quotes before making a decision. Also ask what extras may be added to the quote - for instance, fitting a new valve and balancing the wheel are both often charged on top of the price of a new tyre.

Other sources

Beware of parts or materials obtained from market stalls, car boot sales or similar outlets. Such items are not invariably sub-standard, but there is little chance of compensation if they do prove unsatisfactory. In the case of safety-critical components such as brake pads there is the risk not only of financial loss but also of an accident causing injury or death.

Second-hand components or assemblies obtained from a car breaker can be a good buy in some circumstances, but this sort of purchase is best made by the experienced DIY mechanic.

Vehicle identification

The Vehicle Identification (VIN) plate is riveted to the left-hand side of the engine compartment bulkhead

Modifications are a continuing and unpublicised process in vehicle manufacture, quite apart from major model changes. Spare parts lists are compiled upon a numerical basis, the individual vehicle identification numbers being essential to correct identification of the component concerned.

When ordering spare parts, always give as much information as possible. Quote the car model, year of manufacture, body and engine numbers, as appropriate.

The *Vehicle Identification Number* (VIN) plate is riveted to the left-hand side of the engine compartment bulkhead, and can be viewed once the bonnet is open. The plate carries the VIN, vehicle weight information, and paint and trim colour codes. The vehicle identification number is also stamped into the right-hand side of the bulkhead **(see illustrations)**.

The *Engine number* is stamped on a machined surface on the front left-hand side of the cylinder block, at the flywheel end on 4A-FE and 7A-FE engines **(see illustration)**. On 3S-FE and 3S-GE engines it is stamped on a machined surface on the left-hand end of the cylinder block, over the transmission.

The VIN number is also stamped into the bulkhead

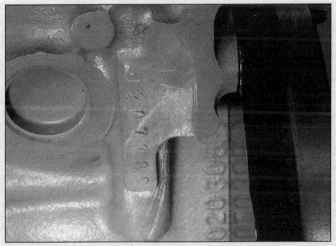

The engine number is stamped on the cylinder block (4A-FE engine shown)

Whenever servicing, repair or overhaul work is carried out on the car or its components, observe the following procedures and instructions. This will assist in carrying out the operation efficiently and to a professional standard of workmanship.

Joint mating faces and gaskets

When separating components at their mating faces, never insert screwdrivers or similar implements into the joint between the faces in order to prise them apart. This can cause severe damage which results in oil leaks, coolant leaks, etc upon reassembly. Separation is usually achieved by tapping along the joint with a soft-faced hammer in order to break the seal. However, note that this method may not be suitable where dowels are used for component location.

Where a gasket is used between the mating faces of two components, a new one must be fitted on reassembly; fit it dry unless otherwise stated in the repair procedure. Make sure that the mating faces are clean and dry, with all traces of old gasket removed. When cleaning a joint face, use a tool which is unlikely to score or damage the face, and remove any burrs or nicks with an oilstone or fine file.

Make sure that tapped holes are cleaned with a pipe cleaner, and keep them free of jointing compound, if this is being used, unless specifically instructed otherwise.

Ensure that all orifices, channels or pipes are clear, and blow through them, preferably using compressed air.

Oil seals

Oil seals can be removed by levering them out with a wide flat-bladed screwdriver or similar implement. Alternatively, a number of self-tapping screws may be screwed into the seal, and these used as a purchase for pliers or some similar device in order to pull the seal free.

Whenever an oil seal is removed from its working location, either individually or as part of an assembly, it should be renewed.

The very fine sealing lip of the seal is easily damaged, and will not seal if the surface it contacts is not completely clean and free from scratches, nicks or grooves. If the original sealing surface of the component cannot be restored, and the manufacturer has not made provision for slight relocation of the seal relative to the sealing surface, the component should be renewed.

Protect the lips of the seal from any surface which may damage them in the course of fitting. Use tape or a conical sleeve where possible. Lubricate the seal lips with oil before fitting and, on dual-lipped seals, fill the space between the lips with grease.

Unless otherwise stated, oil seals must be fitted with their sealing lips toward the lubricant to be sealed.

Use a tubular drift or block of wood of the appropriate size to install the seal and, if the seal housing is shouldered, drive the seal down to the shoulder. If the seal housing is unshouldered, the seal should be fitted with its face flush with the housing top face (unless otherwise instructed).

Screw threads and fastenings

Seized nuts, bolts and screws are quite a common occurrence where corrosion has set in, and the use of penetrating oil or releasing fluid will often overcome this problem if the offending item is soaked for a while before attempting to release it. The use of an impact driver may also provide a means of releasing such stubborn fastening devices, when used in conjunction with the appropriate screwdriver bit or socket. If none of these methods works, it may be necessary to resort to the careful application of heat, or the use of a hacksaw or nut splitter device.

Studs are usually removed by locking two nuts together on the threaded part, and then using a spanner on the lower nut to unscrew the stud. Studs or bolts which have broken off below the surface of the component in which they are mounted can sometimes be removed using a stud extractor. Always ensure that a blind tapped hole is completely free from oil, grease, water or other fluid before installing the bolt or stud. Failure to do this could cause the housing to crack due to the hydraulic action of the bolt or stud as it is screwed in.

When tightening a castellated nut to accept a split pin, tighten the nut to the specified torque, where applicable, and then tighten further to the next split pin hole. Never slacken the nut to align the split pin hole, unless stated in the repair procedure.

When checking or retightening a nut or bolt to a specified torque setting, slacken the nut or bolt by a quarter of a turn, and then retighten to the specified setting. However, this should not be attempted where angular tightening has been used.

For some screw fastenings, notably cylinder head bolts or nuts, torque wrench settings are no longer specified for the latter stages of tightening, "angle-tightening" being called up instead. Typically, a fairly low torque wrench setting will be applied to the bolts/nuts in the correct sequence, followed by one or more stages of tightening through specified angles.

Locknuts, locktabs and washers

Any fastening which will rotate against a component or housing during tightening should always have a washer between it and the relevant component or housing.

Spring or split washers should always be renewed when they are used to lock a critical component such as a big-end bearing retaining bolt or nut. Locktabs which are folded over to retain a nut or bolt should always be renewed.

Self-locking nuts can be re-used in non-critical areas, providing resistance can be felt when the locking portion passes over the bolt or stud thread. However, it should be noted that self-locking stiffnuts tend to lose their effectiveness after long periods of use, and should then be renewed as a matter of course.

Split pins must always be replaced with new ones of the correct size for the hole.

When thread-locking compound is found on the threads of a fastener which is to be re-used, it should be cleaned off with a wire brush and solvent, and fresh compound applied on reassembly.

Special tools

Some repair procedures in this manual entail the use of special tools such as a press, two or three-legged pullers, spring compressors, etc. Wherever possible, suitable readily-available alternatives to the manufacturer's special tools are described, and are shown in use. In some instances, where no alternative is possible, it has been necessary to resort to the use of a manufacturer's tool, and this has been done for reasons of safety as well as the efficient completion of the repair operation. Unless you are highly-skilled and have a thorough understanding of the procedures described, never attempt to bypass the use of any special tool when the procedure described specifies its use. Not only is there a very great risk of personal injury, but expensive damage could be caused to the components involved.

Environmental considerations

When disposing of used engine oil, brake fluid, antifreeze, etc, give due consideration to any detrimental environmental effects. Do not, for instance, pour any of the above liquids down drains into the general sewage system, or onto the ground to soak away. Many local council refuse tips provide a facility for waste oil disposal, as do some garages. If none of these facilities are available, consult your local Environmental Health Department, or the National Rivers Authority, for further advice.

With the universal tightening-up of legislation regarding the emission of environmentally-harmful substances from motor vehicles, most vehicles have tamperproof devices fitted to the main adjustment points of the fuel system. These devices are primarily designed to prevent unqualified persons from adjusting the fuel/air mixture, with the chance of a consequent increase in toxic emissions. If such devices are found during servicing or overhaul, they should, wherever possible, be renewed or refitted in accordance with the manufacturer's requirements or current legislation.

OIL CARE
FOLLOW THE CODE

OIL BANK LINE
0800 66 33 66

Note: It is antisocial and illegal to dump oil down the drain. To find the location of your local oil recycling bank, call this number free.

The jack supplied with the vehicle tool kit should only be used for changing the roadwheels - see *Wheel changing* at the front of this manual. When carrying out any other kind of work, raise the vehicle using a hydraulic (or trolley) jack, and always supplement the jack with axle stands positioned under the vehicle jacking points **(see illustration)**.

When using a hydraulic jack or axle stands, always position the jack head or axle stand head under one of the relevant jacking points (note that the jacking points for use with the vehicle jack are different from those for a hydraulic trolley jack). When jacking up the front of the vehicle with a hydraulic jack, position the jack head under the longitudinal member beneath the engine compartment.

When jacking up the rear of the vehicle, position the jack head under the rear axle beam beneath the inner ends of the rear suspension lower arms. **Do not** jack the vehicle under the sump.

Never work under, around, or near a raised vehicle, unless it is adequately supported on stands.

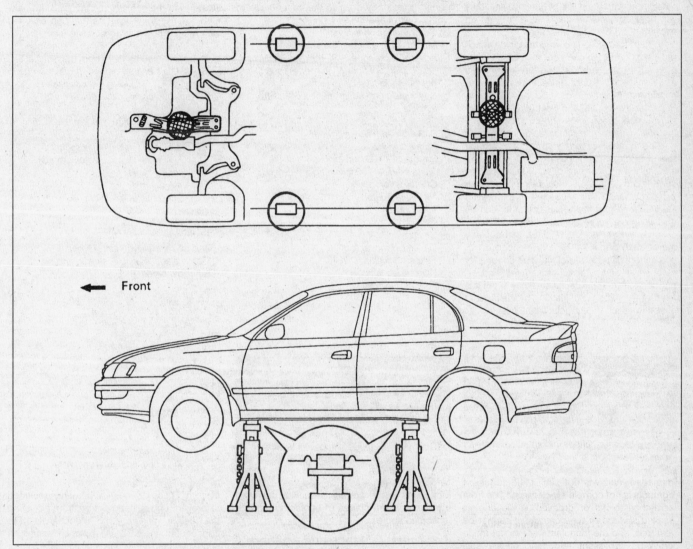

Front

Jacking and Vehicle Support points on the underbody

Radio/cassette unit anti-theft system - precaution

The radio/cassette anti-theft system used by Toyota on most models consists of a front control panel which is removable from the front of the unit, thus rendering the radio/cassette unuseable. If a non-standard unit is fitted, this may have a built-in security code to deter thieves - if the power source to the unit is cut, the anti-theft system will activate. Even if the power source is immediately reconnected, the unit will not function until the correct security code has been entered. Therefore if you do not know the correct security code for the unit, **do not** disconnect the battery negative lead, or remove the unit from the vehicle.

A number of different types of radio/cassette player may be fitted, with different methods of entering the security code. If the incorrect code is entered a number of times, the unit will lock.

Introduction

A selection of good tools is a fundamental requirement for anyone contemplating the maintenance and repair of a motor vehicle. For the owner who does not possess any, their purchase will prove a considerable expense, offsetting some of the savings made by doing-it-yourself. However, provided that the tools purchased meet the relevant national safety standards and are of good quality, they will last for many years and prove an extremely worthwhile investment.

To help the average owner to decide which tools are needed to carry out the various tasks detailed in this manual, we have compiled three lists of tools under the following headings: *Maintenance and minor repair, Repair and overhaul*, and *Special*. Newcomers to practical mechanics should start off with the *Maintenance and minor repair* tool kit, and confine themselves to the simpler jobs around the vehicle. Then, as confidence and experience grow, more difficult tasks can be undertaken, with extra tools being purchased as, and when, they are needed. In this way, a *Maintenance and minor repair* tool kit can be built up into a *Repair and overhaul* tool kit over a considerable period of time, without any major cash outlays. The experienced do-it-yourselfer will have a tool kit good enough for most repair and overhaul procedures, and will add tools from the *Special* category when it is felt that the expense is justified by the amount of use to which these tools will be put.

Maintenance and minor repair tool kit

The tools given in this list should be considered as a minimum requirement if routine maintenance, servicing and minor repair operations are to be undertaken. We recommend the purchase of combination spanners (ring one end, open-ended the other); although more expensive than open-ended ones, they do give the advantages of both types of spanner.

☐ *Combination spanners:*
   Metric - 8 to 19 mm inclusive
☐ *Adjustable spanner - 35 mm jaw (approx.)*
☐ *Spark plug spanner (with rubber insert) - petrol models*
☐ *Spark plug gap adjustment tool - petrol models*
☐ *Set of feeler gauges*
☐ *Brake bleed nipple spanner*
☐ *Screwdrivers:*
   Flat blade - 100 mm long x 6 mm dia
   Cross blade - 100 mm long x 6 mm dia
☐ *Combination pliers*
☐ *Hacksaw (junior)*
☐ *Tyre pump*
☐ *Tyre pressure gauge*
☐ *Oil can*
☐ *Oil filter removal tool*
☐ *Fine emery cloth*
☐ *Wire brush (small)*
☐ *Funnel (medium size)*

Repair and overhaul tool kit

These tools are virtually essential for anyone undertaking any major repairs to a motor vehicle, and are additional to those given in the *Maintenance and minor repair* list. Included in this list is a comprehensive set of sockets. Although these are expensive, they will be found invaluable as they are so versatile - particularly if various drives are included in the set. We recommend the half-inch square-drive type, as this can be used with most proprietary torque wrenches.

The tools in this list will sometimes need to be supplemented by tools from the *Special* list:

☐ *Sockets (or box spanners) to cover range in previous list (including Torx sockets)*
☐ *Reversible ratchet drive (for use with sockets)*
☐ *Extension piece, 250 mm (for use with sockets)*
☐ *Universal joint (for use with sockets)*
☐ *Torque wrench (for use with sockets)*
☐ *Self-locking grips*
☐ *Ball pein hammer*
☐ *Soft-faced mallet (plastic/aluminium or rubber)*
☐ *Screwdrivers:*
   Flat blade - long & sturdy, short (chubby), and narrow (electrician's) types
   Cross blade - Long & sturdy, and short (chubby) types
☐ *Pliers:*
   Long-nosed
   Side cutters (electrician's)
   Circlip (internal and external)
☐ *Cold chisel - 25 mm*
☐ *Scriber*
☐ *Scraper*
☐ *Centre-punch*
☐ *Pin punch*
☐ *Hacksaw*
☐ *Brake hose clamp*
☐ *Brake/clutch bleeding kit*
☐ *Selection of twist drills*
☐ *Steel rule/straight-edge*
☐ *Allen keys (inc. splined/Torx type)*
☐ *Selection of files*
☐ *Wire brush*
☐ *Axle stands*
☐ *Jack (strong trolley or hydraulic type)*
☐ *Light with extension lead*

Sockets and reversible ratchet drive

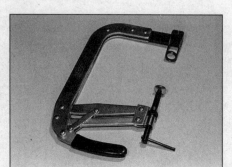

Valve spring compressor

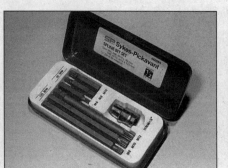

Spline bit set

Piston ring compressor

Clutch plate alignment set

Special tools

The tools in this list are those which are not used regularly, are expensive to buy, or which need to be used in accordance with their manufacturers' instructions. Unless relatively difficult mechanical jobs are undertaken frequently, it will not be economic to buy many of these tools. Where this is the case, you could consider clubbing together with friends (or joining a motorists' club) to make a joint purchase, or borrowing the tools against a deposit from a local garage or tool hire specialist. It is worth noting that many of the larger DIY superstores now carry a large range of special tools for hire at modest rates.

The following list contains only those tools and instruments freely available to the public, and not those special tools produced by the vehicle manufacturer specifically for its dealer network. You will find occasional references to these manufacturers' special tools in the text of this manual. Generally, an alternative method of doing the job without the vehicle manufacturers' special tool is given. However, sometimes there is no alternative to using them. Where this is the case and the relevant tool cannot be bought or borrowed, you will have to entrust the work to a dealer.

☐ Valve spring compressor
☐ Valve grinding tool
☐ Piston ring compressor
☐ Piston ring removal/installation tool
☐ Cylinder bore hone
☐ Balljoint separator
☐ Coil spring compressors (where applicable)
☐ Two/three-legged hub and bearing puller
☐ Impact screwdriver
☐ Micrometer and/or vernier calipers
☐ Dial gauge
☐ Stroboscopic timing light
☐ Dwell angle meter/tachometer
☐ Universal electrical multi-meter
☐ Cylinder compression gauge
☐ Hand-operated vacuum pump and gauge
☐ Clutch plate alignment set
☐ Brake shoe steady spring cup removal tool
☐ Bush and bearing removal/installation set
☐ Stud extractors
☐ Tap and die set
☐ Lifting tackle
☐ Trolley jack

Buying tools

Reputable motor accessory shops and superstores often offer excellent quality tools at discount prices, so it pays to shop around.

Remember, you don't have to buy the most expensive items on the shelf, but it is always advisable to steer clear of the very cheap tools. Beware of 'bargains' offered on market stalls or at car boot sales. There are plenty of good tools around at reasonable prices, but always aim to purchase items which meet the relevant national safety standards. If in doubt, ask the proprietor or manager of the shop for advice before making a purchase.

Care and maintenance of tools

Having purchased a reasonable tool kit, it is necessary to keep the tools in a clean and serviceable condition. After use, always wipe off any dirt, grease and metal particles using a clean, dry cloth, before putting the tools away. Never leave them lying around after they have been used. A simple tool rack on the garage or workshop wall for items such as screwdrivers and pliers is a good idea. Store all normal spanners and sockets in a metal box. Any measuring instruments, gauges, meters, etc, must be carefully stored where they cannot be damaged or become rusty.

Take a little care when tools are used. Hammer heads inevitably become marked, and screwdrivers lose the keen edge on their blades from time to time. A little timely attention with emery cloth or a file will soon restore items like this to a good finish.

Working facilities

Not to be forgotten when discussing tools is the workshop itself. If anything more than routine maintenance is to be carried out, a suitable working area becomes essential.

It is appreciated that many an owner-mechanic is forced by circumstances to remove an engine or similar item without the benefit of a garage or workshop. Having done this, any repairs should always be done under the cover of a roof.

Wherever possible, any dismantling should be done on a clean, flat workbench or table at a suitable working height.

Any workbench needs a vice; one with a jaw opening of 100 mm is suitable for most jobs. As mentioned previously, some clean dry storage space is also required for tools, as well as for any lubricants, cleaning fluids, touch-up paints etc, which become necessary.

Another item which may be required, and which has a much more general usage, is an electric drill with a chuck capacity of at least 8 mm. This, together with a good range of twist drills, is virtually essential for fitting accessories.

Last, but not least, always keep a supply of old newspapers and clean, lint-free rags available, and try to keep any working area as clean as possible.

Micrometer set

Dial test indicator ("dial gauge")

Stroboscopic timing light

Compression tester

Stud extractor set

This is a guide to getting your vehicle through the MOT test. Obviously it will not be possible to examine the vehicle to the same standard as the professional MOT tester. However, working through the following checks will enable you to identify any problem areas before submitting the vehicle for the test.

Where a testable component is in borderline condition, the tester has discretion in deciding whether to pass or fail it. The basis of such discretion is whether the tester would be happy for a close relative or friend to use the vehicle with the component in that condition. If the vehicle presented is clean and evidently well cared for, the tester may be more inclined to pass a borderline component than if the vehicle is scruffy and apparently neglected.

It has only been possible to summarise the test requirements here, based on the regulations in force at the time of printing. Test standards are becoming increasingly stringent, although there are some exemptions for older vehicles. For full details obtain a copy of the Haynes publication Pass the MOT! (available from stockists of Haynes manuals).

An assistant will be needed to help carry out some of these checks.

The checks have been sub-divided into four categories, as follows:

1 Checks carried out **FROM THE DRIVER'S SEAT**

2 Checks carried out **WITH THE VEHICLE ON THE GROUND**

3 Checks carried out **WITH THE VEHICLE RAISED AND THE WHEELS FREE TO TURN**

4 Checks carried out on **YOUR VEHICLE'S EXHAUST EMISSION SYSTEM**

1 Checks carried out **FROM THE DRIVER'S SEAT**

Handbrake

☐ Test the operation of the handbrake. Excessive travel (too many clicks) indicates incorrect brake or cable adjustment.
☐ Check that the handbrake cannot be released by tapping the lever sideways. Check the security of the lever mountings.

Footbrake

☐ Depress the brake pedal and check that it does not creep down to the floor, indicating a master cylinder fault. Release the pedal, wait a few seconds, then depress it again. If the pedal travels nearly to the floor before firm resistance is felt, brake adjustment or repair is necessary. If the pedal feels spongy, there is air in the hydraulic system which must be removed by bleeding.

☐ Check that the brake pedal is secure and in good condition. Check also for signs of fluid leaks on the pedal, floor or carpets, which would indicate failed seals in the brake master cylinder.
☐ Check the servo unit (when applicable) by operating the brake pedal several times, then keeping the pedal depressed and starting the engine. As the engine starts, the pedal will move down slightly. If not, the vacuum hose or the servo itself may be faulty.

Steering wheel and column

☐ Examine the steering wheel for fractures or looseness of the hub, spokes or rim.
☐ Move the steering wheel from side to side and then up and down. Check that the steering wheel is not loose on the column, indicating wear or a loose retaining nut. Continue moving the steering wheel as before, but also turn it slightly from left to right.
☐ Check that the steering wheel is not loose on the column, and that there is no abnormal

movement of the steering wheel, indicating wear in the column support bearings or couplings.

Windscreen and mirrors

☐ The windscreen must be free of cracks or other significant damage within the driver's field of view. (Small stone chips are acceptable.) Rear view mirrors must be secure, intact, and capable of being adjusted.

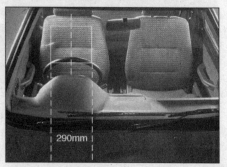

290mm

Seat belts and seats

Note: *The following checks are applicable to all seat belts, front and rear.*

☐ Examine the webbing of all the belts (including rear belts if fitted) for cuts, serious fraying or deterioration. Fasten and unfasten each belt to check the buckles. If applicable, check the retracting mechanism. Check the security of all seat belt mountings accessible from inside the vehicle.

☐ The front seats themselves must be securely attached and the backrests must lock in the upright position.

Doors

☐ Both front doors must be able to be opened and closed from outside and inside, and must latch securely when closed.

2 Checks carried out WITH THE VEHICLE ON THE GROUND

Vehicle identification

☐ Number plates must be in good condition, secure and legible, with letters and numbers correctly spaced – spacing at (A) should be twice that at (B).

☐ The VIN plate and/or homologation plate must be legible.

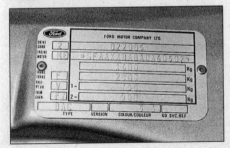

Electrical equipment

☐ Switch on the ignition and check the operation of the horn.

☐ Check the windscreen washers and wipers, examining the wiper blades; renew damaged or perished blades. Also check the operation of the stop-lights.

☐ Check the operation of the sidelights and number plate lights. The lenses and reflectors must be secure, clean and undamaged.

☐ Check the operation and alignment of the headlights. The headlight reflectors must not be tarnished and the lenses must be undamaged.

☐ Switch on the ignition and check the operation of the direction indicators (including the instrument panel tell-tale) and the hazard warning lights. Operation of the sidelights and stop-lights must not affect the indicators - if it does, the cause is usually a bad earth at the rear light cluster.

☐ Check the operation of the rear foglight(s), including the warning light on the instrument panel or in the switch.

Footbrake

☐ Examine the master cylinder, brake pipes and servo unit for leaks, loose mountings, corrosion or other damage.

☐ The fluid reservoir must be secure and the fluid level must be between the upper (A) and lower (B) markings.

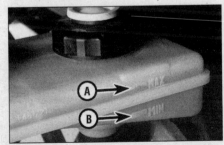

☐ Inspect both front brake flexible hoses for cracks or deterioration of the rubber. Turn the steering from lock to lock, and ensure that the hoses do not contact the wheel, tyre, or any part of the steering or suspension mechanism. With the brake pedal firmly depressed, check the hoses for bulges or leaks under pressure.

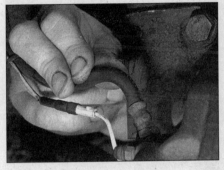

Steering and suspension

☐ Have your assistant turn the steering wheel from side to side slightly, up to the point where the steering gear just begins to transmit this movement to the roadwheels. Check for excessive free play between the steering wheel and the steering gear, indicating wear or insecurity of the steering column joints, the column-to-steering gear coupling, or the steering gear itself.

☐ Have your assistant turn the steering wheel more vigorously in each direction, so that the roadwheels just begin to turn. As this is done, examine all the steering joints, linkages, fittings and attachments. Renew any component that shows signs of wear or damage. On vehicles with power steering, check the security and condition of the steering pump, drivebelt and hoses.

☐ Check that the vehicle is standing level, and at approximately the correct ride height.

Shock absorbers

☐ Depress each corner of the vehicle in turn, then release it. The vehicle should rise and then settle in its normal position. If the vehicle continues to rise and fall, the shock absorber is defective. A shock absorber which has seized will also cause the vehicle to fail.

Exhaust system

☐ Start the engine. With your assistant holding a rag over the tailpipe, check the entire system for leaks. Repair or renew leaking sections.

3 Checks carried out
WITH THE VEHICLE RAISED AND THE WHEELS FREE TO TURN

Jack up the front and rear of the vehicle, and securely support it on axle stands. Position the stands clear of the suspension assemblies. Ensure that the wheels are clear of the ground and that the steering can be turned from lock to lock.

Steering mechanism

☐ Have your assistant turn the steering from lock to lock. Check that the steering turns smoothly, and that no part of the steering mechanism, including a wheel or tyre, fouls any brake hose or pipe or any part of the body structure.
☐ Examine the steering rack rubber gaiters for damage or insecurity of the retaining clips. If power steering is fitted, check for signs of damage or leakage of the fluid hoses, pipes or connections. Also check for excessive stiffness or binding of the steering, a missing split pin or locking device, or severe corrosion of the body structure within 30 cm of any steering component attachment point.

Front and rear suspension and wheel bearings

☐ Starting at the front right-hand side, grasp the roadwheel at the 3 o'clock and 9 o'clock positions and shake it vigorously. Check for free play or insecurity at the wheel bearings, suspension balljoints, or suspension mountings, pivots and attachments.
☐ Now grasp the wheel at the 12 o'clock and 6 o'clock positions and repeat the previous inspection. Spin the wheel, and check for roughness or tightness of the front wheel bearing.

☐ If excess free play is suspected at a component pivot point, this can be confirmed by using a large screwdriver or similar tool and levering between the mounting and the component attachment. This will confirm whether the wear is in the pivot bush, its retaining bolt, or in the mounting itself (the bolt holes can often become elongated).

☐ Carry out all the above checks at the other front wheel, and then at both rear wheels.

Springs and shock absorbers

☐ Examine the suspension struts (when applicable) for serious fluid leakage, corrosion, or damage to the casing. Also check the security of the mounting points.
☐ If coil springs are fitted, check that the spring ends locate in their seats, and that the spring is not corroded, cracked or broken.
☐ If leaf springs are fitted, check that all leaves are intact, that the axle is securely attached to each spring, and that there is no deterioration of the spring eye mountings, bushes, and shackles.

☐ The same general checks apply to vehicles fitted with other suspension types, such as torsion bars, hydraulic displacer units, etc. Ensure that all mountings and attachments are secure, that there are no signs of excessive wear, corrosion or damage, and (on hydraulic types) that there are no fluid leaks or damaged pipes.
☐ Inspect the shock absorbers for signs of serious fluid leakage. Check for wear of the mounting bushes or attachments, or damage to the body of the unit.

Driveshafts
(fwd vehicles only)

☐ Rotate each front wheel in turn and inspect the constant velocity joint gaiters for splits or damage. Also check that each driveshaft is straight and undamaged.

Braking system

☐ If possible without dismantling, check brake pad wear and disc condition. Ensure that the friction lining material has not worn excessively, (A) and that the discs are not fractured, pitted, scored or badly worn (B).

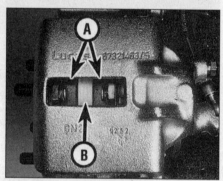

☐ Examine all the rigid brake pipes underneath the vehicle, and the flexible hose(s) at the rear. Look for corrosion, chafing or insecurity of the pipes, and for signs of bulging under pressure, chafing, splits or deterioration of the flexible hoses.
☐ Look for signs of fluid leaks at the brake calipers or on the brake backplates. Repair or renew leaking components.
☐ Slowly spin each wheel, while your assistant depresses and releases the footbrake. Ensure that each brake is operating and does not bind when the pedal is released.

☐ Examine the handbrake mechanism, checking for frayed or broken cables, excessive corrosion, or wear or insecurity of the linkage. Check that the mechanism works on each relevant wheel, and releases fully, without binding.

☐ It is not possible to test brake efficiency without special equipment, but a road test can be carried out later to check that the vehicle pulls up in a straight line.

Fuel and exhaust systems

☐ Inspect the fuel tank (including the filler cap), fuel pipes, hoses and unions. All components must be secure and free from leaks.

☐ Examine the exhaust system over its entire length, checking for any damaged, broken or missing mountings, security of the retaining clamps and rust or corrosion.

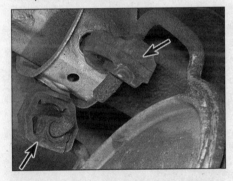

Wheels and tyres

☐ Examine the sidewalls and tread area of each tyre in turn. Check for cuts, tears, lumps, bulges, separation of the tread, and exposure of the ply or cord due to wear or damage. Check that the tyre bead is correctly seated on the wheel rim, that the valve is sound and

properly seated, and that the wheel is not distorted or damaged.

☐ Check that the tyres are of the correct size for the vehicle, that they are of the same size and type on each axle, and that the pressures are correct.

☐ Check the tyre tread depth. The legal minimum at the time of writing is 1.6 mm over at least three-quarters of the tread width. Abnormal tread wear may indicate incorrect front wheel alignment.

Body corrosion

☐ Check the condition of the entire vehicle structure for signs of corrosion in load-bearing areas. (These include chassis box sections, side sills, cross-members, pillars, and all suspension, steering, braking system and seat belt mountings and anchorages.) Any corrosion which has seriously reduced the thickness of a load-bearing area is likely to cause the vehicle to fail. In this case professional repairs are likely to be needed.

☐ Damage or corrosion which causes sharp or otherwise dangerous edges to be exposed will also cause the vehicle to fail.

4 Checks carried out on YOUR VEHICLE'S EXHAUST EMISSION SYSTEM

Petrol models

☐ Have the engine at normal operating temperature, and make sure that it is in good tune (ignition system in good order, air filter element clean, etc).

☐ Before any measurements are carried out, raise the engine speed to around 2500 rpm, and hold it at this speed for 20 seconds. Allow the engine speed to return to idle, and watch for smoke emissions from the exhaust tailpipe. If the idle speed is obviously much too high, or if dense blue or clearly-visible black smoke comes from the tailpipe for more than 5 seconds, the vehicle will fail. As a rule of thumb, blue smoke signifies oil being burnt (engine wear) while black smoke signifies unburnt fuel (dirty air cleaner element, or other carburettor or fuel system fault).

☐ An exhaust gas analyser capable of measuring carbon monoxide (CO) and hydrocarbons (HC) is now needed. If such an instrument cannot be hired or borrowed, a local garage may agree to perform the check for a small fee.

CO emissions (mixture)

☐ At the time of writing, the maximum CO level at idle is 3.5% for vehicles first used after August 1986 and 4.5% for older vehicles. From January 1996 a much tighter limit (around 0.5%) applies to catalyst-equipped vehicles first used from August 1992. If the CO level cannot be reduced far enough to pass the test (and the fuel and ignition systems are otherwise in good condition) then the carburettor is badly worn, or there is some problem in the fuel injection system or catalytic converter (as applicable).

HC emissions

☐ With the CO emissions within limits, HC emissions must be no more than 1200 ppm (parts per million). If the vehicle fails this test at idle, it can be re-tested at around 2000 rpm; if the HC level is then 1200 ppm or less, this counts as a pass.

☐ Excessive HC emissions can be caused by oil being burnt, but they are more likely to be due to unburnt fuel.

Diesel models

☐ The only emission test applicable to Diesel engines is the measuring of exhaust smoke density. The test involves accelerating the engine several times to its maximum unloaded speed.

Note: *It is of the utmost importance that the engine timing belt is in good condition before the test is carried out.*

☐ Excessive smoke can be caused by a dirty air cleaner element. Otherwise, professional advice may be needed to find the cause.

Engine

- ☐ Engine fails to rotate when attempting to start
- ☐ Engine rotates, but will not start
- ☐ Engine difficult to start when cold
- ☐ Engine difficult to start when hot
- ☐ Starter motor noisy or excessively-rough in engagement
- ☐ Engine starts, but stops immediately
- ☐ Engine idles erratically
- ☐ Engine misfires at idle speed
- ☐ Engine misfires throughout the driving speed range
- ☐ Engine hesitates on acceleration
- ☐ Engine stalls
- ☐ Engine lacks power
- ☐ Engine backfires
- ☐ Oil pressure warning light illuminated with engine running
- ☐ Engine runs-on after switching off
- ☐ Engine noises

Cooling system

- ☐ Overheating
- ☐ Overcooling
- ☐ External coolant leakage
- ☐ Internal coolant leakage
- ☐ Corrosion

Fuel and exhaust systems

- ☐ Excessive fuel consumption
- ☐ Fuel leakage and/or fuel odour
- ☐ Excessive noise or fumes from exhaust system

Clutch

- ☐ Pedal travels to floor - no pressure or very little resistance
- ☐ Clutch fails to disengage (unable to select gears)
- ☐ Clutch slips (engine speed increases, with no increase in vehicle speed)
- ☐ Judder as clutch is engaged
- ☐ Noise when depressing or releasing clutch pedal

Manual transmission

- ☐ Noisy in neutral with engine running
- ☐ Noisy in one particular gear
- ☐ Difficulty engaging gears
- ☐ Jumps out of gear
- ☐ Vibration
- ☐ Lubricant leaks

Automatic transmission

- ☐ Fluid leakage
- ☐ Transmission will not downshift (kickdown) with accelerator fully depressed
- ☐ General gear selection problems
- ☐ Engine will not start in any gear, or starts in gears other than Park or Neutral
- ☐ Transmission slips, shifts roughly, is noisy, or has no drive in forward or reverse gears

Driveshafts

- ☐ Clicking or knocking noise on turns (at slow speed on full-lock)
- ☐ Vibration when accelerating or decelerating

Braking system

- ☐ Vehicle pulls to one side under braking
- ☐ Noise (grinding or high-pitched squeal) when brakes applied
- ☐ Excessive brake pedal travel
- ☐ Brake pedal feels spongy when depressed
- ☐ Excessive brake pedal effort required to stop vehicle
- ☐ Judder felt through brake pedal or steering wheel when braking
- ☐ Brakes binding
- ☐ Rear wheels locking under normal braking

Suspension and steering systems

- ☐ Vehicle pulls to one side
- ☐ Wheel wobble and vibration
- ☐ Excessive pitching and/or rolling around corners, or during braking
- ☐ Wandering or general instability
- ☐ Excessively-stiff steering
- ☐ Excessive play in steering
- ☐ Lack of power assistance
- ☐ Tyre wear excessive

Electrical system

- ☐ Battery will not hold a charge for more than a few days
- ☐ Ignition/no-charge warning light remains illuminated with engine running
- ☐ Ignition/no-charge warning light fails to come on
- ☐ Lights inoperative
- ☐ Instrument readings inaccurate or erratic
- ☐ Horn inoperative, or unsatisfactory in operation
- ☐ Windscreen/tailgate wipers inoperative, or unsatisfactory in operation
- ☐ Windscreen/tailgate washers inoperative, or unsatisfactory in operation
- ☐ Electric windows inoperative, or unsatisfactory in operation

Introduction

The vehicle owner who does his or her own maintenance according to the recommended service schedules should not have to use this section of the manual very often. Modern component reliability is such that, provided those items subject to wear or deterioration are inspected or renewed at the specified intervals, sudden failure is comparatively rare. Faults do not usually just happen as a result of sudden failure, but develop over a period of time. Major mechanical failures in particular are usually preceded by characteristic symptoms over hundreds or even thousands of miles. Those components which do occasionally fail without warning are often small and easily carried in the vehicle.

With any fault-finding, the first step is to decide where to begin investigations. Sometimes this is obvious, but on other occasions, a little detective work will be necessary. The owner who makes half a dozen haphazard adjustments or replacements may be successful in curing a fault (or its symptoms), but will be none the wiser if the fault recurs, and ultimately may have spent more time and money than was necessary. A calm and logical approach will be found to be more satisfactory in the long run. Always take into account any warning signs or abnormalities that may have been noticed in the period preceding the fault - power loss, high or low gauge readings, unusual smells, etc - and remember that failure of components such as fuses or spark plugs may only be pointers to some underlying fault.

The pages which follow provide an easy-reference guide to the more common problems which may occur during the operation of the vehicle. These problems and their possible causes are grouped under headings denoting various components or systems, such as Engine, Cooling system, etc. The Chapter and/or Section which deals with the problem is also shown in brackets. Whatever the fault, certain basic principles apply. These are as follows:

Verify the fault. This is simply a matter of being sure that you know what the symptoms are before starting work. This is particularly important if you are investigating a fault for someone else, who may not have described it very accurately.

Don't overlook the obvious. For example, if the vehicle won't start, is there fuel in the tank? (Don't take anyone else's word on this particular point, and don't trust the fuel gauge either!) If an electrical fault is indicated, look for loose or broken wires before digging out the test gear.

Cure the disease, not the symptom. Substituting a flat battery with a fully-charged one will get you off the hard shoulder, but if the underlying cause is not attended to, the new battery will go the same way. Similarly, changing oil-fouled spark plugs for a new set will get you moving again, but remember that the reason for the fouling (if it wasn't simply an incorrect grade of plug) will have to be established and corrected.

Don't take anything for granted. Particularly, don't forget that a new component may itself be defective (especially if it's been rattling around in the boot for months), and don't leave components out of a fault diagnosis sequence just because they are new or recently-fitted. When you do finally diagnose a difficult fault, you'll probably realise that all the evidence was there from the start.

Engine

Engine fails to rotate when attempting to start

- [ ] Battery terminal connections loose or corroded (Chapter 1).
- [ ] Battery discharged or faulty (Chapter 5A).
- [ ] Broken, loose or disconnected wiring in the starting circuit (Chapter 5A).
- [ ] Defective starter solenoid or switch (Chapter 5A).
- [ ] Defective starter motor (Chapter 5A).
- [ ] Starter pinion or flywheel/driveplate ring gear teeth loose or broken (Chapter 2A or 5A).
- [ ] Engine earth strap broken or disconnected (Chapter 2A).
- [ ] Automatic transmission not in Park/Neutral position or starter inhibitor switch faulty (Chapter 7B).

Engine rotates, but will not start

- [ ] Fuel tank empty.
- [ ] Battery discharged (engine rotates slowly) (Chapter 5A).
- [ ] Battery terminal connections loose or corroded (Chapter 5A).
- [ ] Ignition components damp or damaged (Chapter 1 and 5B).
- [ ] Broken, loose or disconnected wiring in the ignition circuit (Chapters 1 and 5B).
- [ ] Worn, faulty or incorrectly-gapped spark plugs (Chapter 1).
- [ ] Fuel injection system fault (Chapter 4A).
- [ ] Major mechanical failure (eg timing belt) (Chapters 2A and 2B).

Engine difficult to start when cold

- [ ] Battery discharged (Chapter 5A).
- [ ] Battery terminal connections loose or corroded (Chapter 1).
- [ ] Worn, faulty or incorrectly-gapped spark plugs (Chapter 1).
- [ ] Fuel injection system fault (Chapter 4A).
- [ ] Other ignition system fault (Chapters 1 and 5B).
- [ ] Low cylinder compressions (Chapter 2A).

Engine difficult to start when hot

- [ ] Air filter element dirty or clogged (Chapter 1).
- [ ] Fuel injection system fault (Chapter 4A).
- [ ] Ignition system fault (Chapters 1 and 5B).
- [ ] Low cylinder compressions (Chapter 2A).

Starter motor noisy or excessively-rough in engagement

- [ ] Starter pinion or flywheel/driveplate ring gear teeth loose or broken (Chapter 2A or 5A).
- [ ] Starter motor mounting bolts loose or missing (Chapter 5A).
- [ ] Starter motor internal components worn or damaged (Chapter 5A).

Engine starts, but stops immediately

- [ ] Loose or faulty electrical connections in the ignition circuit (Chapters 1 and 5B).
- [ ] Vacuum leak at the throttle body or inlet manifold (Chapter 4A).
- [ ] Fuel injection system fault (Chapter 4A).

Engine idles erratically

- [ ] Air filter element clogged (Chapter 1).
- [ ] Vacuum leak at the throttle body, inlet manifold or associated hoses (Chapter 4A).
- [ ] Worn, faulty or incorrectly-gapped spark plugs (Chapter 1).
- [ ] Uneven or low cylinder compressions (Chapter 2A).
- [ ] Camshaft lobes worn (Chapters 2A and 2B).
- [ ] Timing belt incorrectly tensioned (Chapter 2A).
- [ ] Fuel injection system fault (Chapter 4A).

Engine misfires at idle speed

- [ ] Worn, faulty or incorrectly-gapped spark plugs (Chapter 1).
- [ ] Faulty spark plug HT leads (Chapter 1).
- [ ] Vacuum leak at the throttle body, inlet manifold or associated hoses (Chapter 4A).
- [ ] Fuel injection system fault (Chapter 4A).
- [ ] Distributor cap cracked or tracking internally (Chapter 1).
- [ ] Uneven or low cylinder compressions (Chapter 2A).
- [ ] Disconnected, leaking, or perished crankcase ventilation hoses (Chapter 4B).

Engine misfires throughout the driving speed range

- [ ] Fuel filter choked (Chapter 1).
- [ ] Fuel pump faulty, or delivery pressure low (Chapter 4A).
- [ ] Fuel tank vent blocked, or fuel pipes restricted (Chapter 4A).
- [ ] Vacuum leak at the throttle body, inlet manifold or associated hoses (Chapter 4A).
- [ ] Worn, faulty or incorrectly-gapped spark plugs (Chapter 1).
- [ ] Faulty spark plug HT leads (Chapter 1).
- [ ] Distributor cap cracked or tracking internally (Chapter 1).
- [ ] Faulty ignition coil (Chapter 5B).
- [ ] Uneven or low cylinder compressions (Chapter 2A).
- [ ] Fuel injection system fault (Chapter 4A).

Engine hesitates on acceleration

- [ ] Worn, faulty or incorrectly-gapped spark plugs (Chapter 1).
- [ ] Vacuum leak at the throttle body, inlet manifold or associated hoses (Chapter 4A).
- [ ] Fuel injection system fault (Chapter 4A).

Engine (continued)

Engine stalls

- ☐ Vacuum leak at the throttle body, inlet manifold or associated hoses (Chapter 4A).
- ☐ Fuel filter choked (Chapter 1).
- ☐ Fuel pump faulty, or delivery pressure low (Chapter 4A).
- ☐ Fuel tank vent blocked, or fuel pipes restricted (Chapter 4A).
- ☐ Fuel injection system fault (Chapter 4A).

Engine lacks power

- ☐ Fuel filter choked (Chapter 1).
- ☐ Fuel pump faulty, or delivery pressure low (Chapter 4A).
- ☐ Uneven or low cylinder compressions (Chapter 2A).
- ☐ Worn, faulty or incorrectly-gapped spark plugs (Chapter 1).
- ☐ Vacuum leak at the throttle body, inlet manifold or associated hoses (Chapter 4A).
- ☐ Fuel injection system fault (Chapter 4A).
- ☐ Brakes binding (Chapters 1 and 9).
- ☐ Clutch slipping - manual transmission models (Chapter 6).

Engine backfires

- ☐ Vacuum leak at the throttle body, inlet manifold or associated hoses (Chapter 4A).
- ☐ Fuel injection system fault (Chapter 4A).

Oil pressure warning light illuminated with engine running

- ☐ Low oil level, or incorrect oil grade (see Weekly Checks).
- ☐ Faulty oil pressure sensor (Chapter 2A).
- ☐ Worn engine bearings and/or oil pump (Chapter 2A or 2B).
- ☐ Excessively high engine operating temperature (Chapter 3).
- ☐ Oil pressure relief valve defective (Chapter 2A).
- ☐ Oil pick-up strainer clogged (Chapter 2A).

Engine runs-on after switching off

- ☐ Excessive carbon build-up in engine (Chapter 2A or 2B).
- ☐ High engine operating temperature (Chapter 3).
- ☐ Faulty fuel injection system fault (Chapter 4A).

Engine noises

Pre-ignition (pinking) or knocking during acceleration or under load

- ☐ Ignition timing incorrect/ignition system fault (Chapters 1 and 5B).
- ☐ Incorrect grade of spark plug (Chapter 1).
- ☐ Incorrect grade of fuel (Chapter 1).
- ☐ Vacuum leak at throttle body, inlet manifold or associated hoses (Chapter 4A).
- ☐ Excessive carbon build-up in engine (Chapter 2A or 2B).
- ☐ Fuel injection system fault (Chapter 4A).

Whistling or wheezing noises

- ☐ Leaking inlet manifold or throttle body gasket (Chapter 4A).
- ☐ Leaking exhaust manifold gasket or downpipe-to-manifold joint (Chapter 4A).
- ☐ Leaking vacuum hose (Chapters 4A, 4B, and 9).
- ☐ Blowing cylinder head gasket (Chapter 2A).

Tapping or rattling noises

- ☐ Worn valve gear or camshaft (Chapter 2A).
- ☐ Incorrect valve clearances (Chapter 1)
- ☐ Ancillary component fault (water pump, alternator, etc) (Chapters 3, 5A, etc).

Knocking or thumping noises

- ☐ Worn big-end bearings (regular heavy knocking, perhaps less under load) (Chapter 2B).
- ☐ Worn main bearings (rumbling and knocking, perhaps worsening under load) (Chapter 2B).
- ☐ Piston slap (most noticeable when cold) (Chapter 2B).
- ☐ Ancillary component fault (water pump, alternator, etc) (Chapters 3, 5A, etc).

Cooling system

Overheating

- ☐ Auxiliary drivebelt broken - or incorrectly adjusted on 4A-FE and 7A-FE engines only (Chapter 1).
- ☐ Insufficient coolant in system (see Weekly Checks).
- ☐ Thermostat faulty (Chapter 3).
- ☐ Radiator core blocked, or grille restricted (Chapter 3).
- ☐ Electric cooling fan or thermostatic switch faulty (Chapter 3).
- ☐ Radiator pressure cap faulty (Chapter 3).
- ☐ Ignition timing incorrect, or ignition system fault (Chapters 1 and 5B).
- ☐ Inaccurate temperature gauge sender unit (Chapter 3).
- ☐ Airlock in cooling system (Chapter 1).

Overcooling

- ☐ Thermostat faulty (Chapter 3).
- ☐ Inaccurate temperature gauge sender unit (Chapter 3).

External coolant leakage

- ☐ Deteriorated or damaged hoses or hose clips (Chapter 1).
- ☐ Radiator core or heater matrix leaking (Chapter 3).
- ☐ Radiator pressure cap faulty (Chapter 3).
- ☐ Water pump internal seal leaking (Chapter 3).
- ☐ Boiling due to overheating (Chapter 3).
- ☐ Core plug leaking (Chapter 2B).

Internal coolant leakage

- ☐ Leaking cylinder head gasket (Chapter 2A).
- ☐ Cracked cylinder head or cylinder block (Chapter 2A or 2B).

Corrosion

- ☐ Infrequent draining and flushing (Chapter 1).
- ☐ Incorrect coolant mixture or inappropriate coolant type (Chapter 1).

Fuel and exhaust systems

Excessive fuel consumption

☐ Air filter element dirty or clogged (Chapter 1).
☐ Fuel injection system fault (Chapter 4A).
☐ Ignition timing incorrect or ignition system fault (Chapters 1 and 5B).
☐ Tyres under-inflated (Chapter 1).

Fuel leakage and/or fuel odour

☐ Damaged fuel tank, pipes or connections (Chapters 1 and 4A).

Excessive noise or fumes from exhaust system

☐ Leaking exhaust system or manifold joints (Chapters 1 or 4A).
☐ Leaking, corroded or damaged silencers or pipe (Chapters 1 or 4A).
☐ Broken mountings causing body or suspension contact (Chapter 4A).

Clutch

Pedal travels to floor - no pressure or very little resistance

☐ Hydraulic fluid level low/air in the hydraulic system (see Weekly Checks).
☐ Broken clutch release bearing or arm (Chapter 6).
☐ Broken diaphragm spring in clutch pressure plate (Chapter 6).

Clutch fails to disengage (unable to select gears)

☐ Hydraulic fluid level low/air in the hydraulic system (see Weekly Checks).
☐ Clutch disc sticking on splines (Chapter 6).
☐ Clutch disc sticking to flywheel or pressure plate (Chapter 6).
☐ Faulty pressure plate assembly (Chapter 6).
☐ Clutch release mechanism worn or incorrectly assembled (Chapter 6).

Clutch slips (engine speed increases, with no increase in vehicle speed)

☐ Clutch disc linings excessively worn (Chapter 6).
☐ Clutch disc linings contaminated with oil or grease (Chapter 6).
☐ Faulty pressure plate or weak diaphragm spring (Chapter 6).

Judder as clutch is engaged

☐ Clutch disc linings contaminated with oil or grease (Chapter 6).
☐ Clutch disc linings excessively worn (Chapter 6).
☐ Faulty or distorted pressure plate or diaphragm spring (Chapter 6).
☐ Worn or loose engine or transmission mountings (Chapters 2A and 2B).
☐ Clutch disc hub or transmission input shaft splines worn (Chapter 6).

Noise when depressing or releasing clutch pedal

☐ Worn clutch release bearing (Chapter 6).
☐ Worn or dry clutch pedal bushes (Chapter 6).
☐ Faulty pressure plate assembly (Chapter 6).
☐ Pressure plate diaphragm spring broken (Chapter 6).
☐ Broken clutch disc cushioning springs (Chapter 6).

Manual transmission

Noisy in neutral with engine running

☐ Input shaft bearings worn (noise apparent with clutch pedal released, but not when depressed) (Chapter 7A).*
☐ Clutch release bearing worn (noise apparent with clutch pedal depressed, possibly less when released) (Chapter 6).

Noisy in one particular gear

☐ Worn, damaged or chipped gear teeth (Chapter 7A).*

Difficulty engaging gears

☐ Clutch fault (Chapter 6).
☐ Oil level low (Chapter 1).
☐ Worn or damaged gear linkage/cable (Chapter 7A).
☐ Worn synchroniser units (Chapter 7A).*

Jumps out of gear

☐ Worn or damaged gear linkage/cable (Chapter 7A).
☐ Worn synchroniser units (Chapter 7A).*
☐ Worn selector forks (Chapter 7A).*

Vibration

☐ Lack of oil (Chapter 1).
☐ Worn bearings (Chapter 7A).*

Lubricant leaks

☐ Leaking oil seal (Chapter 7A).
☐ Leaking housing joint (Chapter 7A).*
☐ Leaking input shaft oil seal (Chapter 7A).*

*Although the corrective action necessary to remedy the symptoms described is beyond the scope of the home mechanic, the above information should be helpful in isolating the cause of the condition, so that the owner can communicate clearly with a professional mechanic.

Automatic transmission

Note: *Due to the complexity of the automatic transmission, it is difficult for the home mechanic to properly diagnose and service this unit. For problems other than the following, the vehicle should be taken to a dealer service department or automatic transmission specialist.*

Fluid leakage

☐ Automatic transmission fluid is usually deep red in colour. Fluid leaks should not be confused with engine oil, which can easily be blown onto the transmission by air flow.
☐ To determine the source of a leak, first remove all built-up dirt and grime from the transmission housing and surrounding areas, using a degreasing agent or by steam-cleaning. Drive the vehicle at low speed, so that air flow will not blow the leak far from its source. Raise and support the vehicle, and determine where the leak is coming from. The following are common areas of leakage.
a) *Oil pan (Chapter 7B).*
b) *Dipstick tube (Chapter 7B).*
c) *Transmission-to-fluid cooler fluid pipes/unions (Chapter 7B).*

Transmission will not downshift (kickdown) with accelerator pedal fully depressed

☐ Low transmission fluid level (see *Weekly Checks*).
☐ Incorrect selector cable adjustment (Chapter 7B).
☐ Incorrect kickdown cable adjustment (Chapter 7B).

General gear selection problems

☐ The most likely cause of gear selection problems is a faulty or poorly-adjusted gear selector mechanism. The following are common problems associated with a faulty selector mechanism.
a) *Engine starting in gears other than Park or Neutral.*
b) *Indicator on gear selector lever pointing to a gear other than the one actually being used.*
c) *Vehicle moves when in Park or Neutral.*
d) *Poor gear shift quality, or erratic gear changes.*
☐ Refer any problems to a Toyota dealer, or an automatic transmission specialist.

Engine will not start in any gear, or starts in gears other than Park or Neutral

☐ Incorrect starter inhibitor switch adjustment (Chapter 7B).
☐ Incorrect selector cable adjustment (Chapter 7B).

Transmission slips, shifts roughly, is noisy, or has no drive in forward or reverse gears

☐ There are many probable causes for the above problems, but the home mechanic should be concerned with only one possibility - fluid level. Before taking the vehicle to a dealer or transmission specialist, check the fluid level and condition of the fluid as described in Chapter 1. Correct the fluid level as necessary, or change the fluid if needed. If the problem persists, professional help will be necessary.

Driveshafts

Clicking or knocking noise on turns (at slow speed on full-lock)

☐ Lack of constant velocity joint lubricant, possibly due to damaged gaiter (Chapter 8).
☐ Worn outer constant velocity joint (Chapter 8).

Vibration when accelerating or decelerating

☐ Worn inner constant velocity joint (Chapter 8).
☐ Bent or distorted driveshaft (Chapter 8).

Braking system

Note: *Before assuming that a brake problem exists, make sure that the tyres are in good condition and correctly inflated, that the front wheel alignment is correct, and that the vehicle is not loaded with weight in an unequal manner.*

Vehicle pulls to one side under braking

☐ Worn, defective, damaged or contaminated front or rear brake pads/shoes on one side (Chapters 1 and 9).
☐ Seized or partially-seized front or rear brake caliper/wheel cylinder piston (Chapter 9).
☐ A mixture of brake pad/shoe lining materials fitted between sides (Chapter 9).
☐ Brake caliper mounting bolts loose (Chapter 9).
☐ Worn or damaged steering or suspension components (Chapters 1 and 10).

Noise (grinding or high-pitched squeal) when brakes applied

☐ Brake shoe friction lining material worn down to pad wear indicator (Chapter 9).
☐ Brake pad or shoe friction lining material worn down to metal backing (Chapters 1 and 9).
☐ Excessive corrosion of brake disc/drum - may be apparent after the vehicle has been standing for some time (Chapter 9).

Excessive brake pedal travel

☐ Inoperative rear brake self-adjust mechanism - rear drum brake models (Chapter 9).
☐ Faulty master cylinder (Chapter 9).
☐ Air in hydraulic system (Chapter 9).
☐ Faulty vacuum servo unit (Chapter 9).

Brake pedal feels spongy when depressed

☐ Air in hydraulic system (Chapter 9).
☐ Deteriorated flexible rubber brake hoses (Chapters 1 and 9).
☐ Master cylinder mountings loose (Chapter 9).
☐ Faulty master cylinder (Chapter 9).

Excessive brake pedal effort required to stop vehicle

☐ Faulty vacuum servo unit (Chapter 9).
☐ Disconnected, damaged or insecure brake servo vacuum hose (Chapters 1 and 9).
☐ Primary or secondary hydraulic circuit failure (Chapter 9).
☐ Seized brake caliper/wheel cylinder piston(s) (Chapter 9).
☐ Brake pads/shoes incorrectly fitted (Chapter 9).
☐ Incorrect grade of brake pads/shoes fitted (Chapter 9).
☐ Brake pads/shoes contaminated (Chapter 9).

Braking system (continued)

Judder felt through brake pedal or steering wheel when braking

- [ ] Excessive run-out or distortion of brake disc/drum (Chapter 9).
- [ ] Brake pad/shoe linings worn (Chapters 1 and 9).
- [ ] Brake caliper/rear brake backplate mounting bolts loose (Chapter 9).
- [ ] Wear in suspension or steering components or mountings (Chapters 1 and 10).

Brakes binding

- [ ] Seized brake caliper/wheel cylinder piston(s) (Chapter 9).
- [ ] Incorrectly-adjusted handbrake mechanism (Chapter 9).
- [ ] Faulty master cylinder (Chapter 9).

Rear wheels locking under normal braking

- [ ] Rear brake shoe linings contaminated (Chapters 1 and 9).
- [ ] Faulty brake pressure regulator (Chapter 9).

Suspension and steering systems

Note: *Before diagnosing suspension or steering faults, be sure that the trouble is not due to incorrect tyre pressures, mixtures of tyre types, or binding brakes.*

Vehicle pulls to one side

- [ ] Defective tyre (Chapter 1).
- [ ] Excessive wear in suspension or steering components (Chapters 1 and 10).
- [ ] Incorrect front wheel alignment (Chapter 1).
- [ ] Accident damage to steering or suspension components (Chapters 1 and 10).

Wheel wobble and vibration

- [ ] Front roadwheels out of balance (vibration felt mainly through the steering wheel) (Chapter 10).
- [ ] Rear roadwheels out of balance (vibration felt throughout the vehicle) (Chapter 10).
- [ ] Roadwheels damaged or distorted (Chapter 10).
- [ ] Faulty or damaged tyre (Chapter 1).
- [ ] Worn steering or suspension joints, bushes or components (Chapters 1 and 10).
- [ ] Wheel nuts loose (Chapter 10).

Excessive pitching and/or rolling around corners, or during braking

- [ ] Defective shock absorbers (Chapters 1 and 10).
- [ ] Broken or weak coil spring and/or suspension component (Chapters 1 and 10).
- [ ] Worn or damaged anti-roll bar or mountings (Chapter 10).

Wandering or general instability

- [ ] Incorrect front wheel alignment (Chapter 1).
- [ ] Worn steering or suspension joints, bushes or components (Chapters 1 and 10).
- [ ] Roadwheels out of balance (Chapter 10).
- [ ] Faulty or damaged tyre (Chapter 1).
- [ ] Wheel nuts loose (Chapter 10).
- [ ] Defective shock absorbers (Chapters 1 and 10).

Excessively-stiff steering

- [ ] Lack of steering gear lubricant (Chapter 10).
- [ ] Seized track rod end balljoint or suspension balljoint (Chapters 1 and 10).
- [ ] Broken or incorrectly adjusted auxiliary drivebelt on power steering models (Chapter 1).
- [ ] Incorrect front wheel alignment (Chapter 10).
- [ ] Steering rack or column bent or damaged (Chapter 10).

Excessive play in steering

- [ ] Worn steering column universal joint(s) (Chapter 10).
- [ ] Worn steering track rod end balljoints (Chapters 1 and 10).
- [ ] Worn rack-and-pinion steering gear (Chapter 10).
- [ ] Worn steering or suspension joints, bushes or components (Chapters 1 and 10).

Lack of power assistance

- [ ] Broken or incorrectly-adjusted auxiliary drivebelt (Chapter 1).
- [ ] Incorrect power steering fluid level (see *Weekly Checks*).
- [ ] Restriction in power steering fluid hoses (Chapters 1 and 10).
- [ ] Faulty power steering pump (Chapter 10).
- [ ] Faulty rack-and-pinion steering gear (Chapter 10).

Tyre wear excessive

Tyres worn on inside or outside edges

- [ ] Tyres under-inflated (wear on both edges) (Chapter 1).
- [ ] Incorrect camber or castor angles (wear on one edge only) (Chapter 1).
- [ ] Worn steering or suspension joints, bushes or components (Chapters 1 and 10).
- [ ] Excessively-hard cornering.
- [ ] Accident damage.

Tyre treads exhibit feathered edges

- [ ] Incorrect toe setting (Chapter 10).

Tyres worn in centre of tread

- [ ] Tyres over-inflated (see *Weekly Checks*).

Tyres worn on inside and outside edges

- [ ] Tyres under-inflated (see *Weekly Checks*).
- [ ] Worn shock absorbers (Chapters 1 and 10).

Tyres worn unevenly

- [ ] Tyres out of balance (Chapter 10).
- [ ] Excessive wheel or tyre run-out (Chapter 10).
- [ ] Worn shock absorbers (Chapters 1 and 10).
- [ ] Faulty tyre (see *Weekly Checks*).

Electrical system

Note: *For problems associated with the starting system, refer to the faults listed under Engine earlier.*

Battery will not hold a charge for more than a few days

- [ ] Battery defective internally (Chapter 5A).
- [ ] Battery electrolyte level low - where applicable (Chapter 5A).
- [ ] Battery terminal connections loose or corroded (see *Weekly Checks*).
- [ ] Auxiliary drivebelt worn - or incorrectly adjusted (Chapter 1).
- [ ] Alternator not charging at correct output (Chapter 5A).
- [ ] Alternator or voltage regulator faulty (Chapter 5A).
- [ ] Short-circuit causing continual battery drain (Chapters 5A and 12).

Ignition/no-charge warning light remains illuminated with engine running

- [ ] Auxiliary drivebelt broken, worn, or incorrectly adjusted (Chapter 1).
- [ ] Alternator brushes worn, sticking, or dirty (Chapter 5A).
- [ ] Alternator brush springs weak or broken (Chapter 5A).
- [ ] Internal fault in alternator or voltage regulator (Chapter 5A).
- [ ] Broken, disconnected, or loose wiring in charging circuit (Chapter 5A).

Ignition/no-charge warning light fails to come on

- [ ] Warning light bulb blown (Chapter 12).
- [ ] Broken, disconnected, or loose wiring in warning light circuit (Chapter 12).
- [ ] Alternator faulty (Chapter 5A).

Lights inoperative

- [ ] Bulb blown (Chapter 12).
- [ ] Corrosion of bulb or bulbholder contacts (Chapter 12).
- [ ] Blown fuse (Chapter 12).
- [ ] Faulty relay (Chapter 12).
- [ ] Broken, loose, or disconnected wiring (Chapter 12).
- [ ] Faulty switch (Chapter 12).

Instrument readings inaccurate or erratic

Instrument readings increase with engine speed

- [ ] Faulty voltage regulator (Chapter 12).

Fuel or temperature gauges give no reading

- [ ] Faulty gauge sender unit (Chapters 3 and 4A).
- [ ] Wiring open-circuit (Chapter 12).
- [ ] Faulty gauge (Chapter 12).

Fuel or temperature gauges give continuous maximum reading

- [ ] Faulty gauge sender unit (Chapters 3 and 4A).
- [ ] Wiring short-circuit (Chapter 12).
- [ ] Faulty gauge (Chapter 12).

Horn inoperative, or unsatisfactory in operation

Horn operates all the time

- [ ] Horn contacts permanently bridged or horn push stuck down (Chapter 12).

Horn fails to operate

- [ ] Blown fuse (Chapter 12).
- [ ] Wiring or wiring connections loose, broken or disconnected (Chapter 12).
- [ ] Faulty horn (Chapter 12).

Horn emits intermittent or unsatisfactory sound

- [ ] Wiring connections loose (Chapter 12).
- [ ] Horn mountings loose (Chapter 12).
- [ ] Faulty horn (Chapter 12).

Windscreen/tailgate wipers inoperative, or unsatisfactory in operation

Wipers fail to operate, or operate very slowly

- [ ] Wiper blades stuck to screen, or linkage seized or binding (Chapter 12).
- [ ] Blown fuse (Chapter 12).
- [ ] Wiring or wiring connections loose, broken or disconnected (Chapter 12).
- [ ] Faulty relay (Chapter 12).
- [ ] Faulty wiper motor (Chapter 12).

Wiper blades sweep over too large or too small an area of the glass

- [ ] Wiper arms incorrectly positioned on spindles (Chapter 12).
- [ ] Excessive wear of wiper linkage (Chapter 12).
- [ ] Wiper motor or linkage mountings loose or insecure (Chapter 12).

Wiper blades fail to clean the glass effectively

- [ ] Wiper blade rubbers worn or perished (see *Weekly Checks*).
- [ ] Wiper arm tension springs broken, or arm pivots seized (Chapter 12).
- [ ] Insufficient windscreen washer additive to adequately remove road film (see *Weekly Checks*).

Windscreen/tailgate washers inoperative, or unsatisfactory in operation

One or more washer jets inoperative

- [ ] Blocked washer jet (Chapter 1).
- [ ] Disconnected, kinked or restricted fluid hose (Chapter 12).
- [ ] Insufficient fluid in washer reservoir (see *Weekly Checks*).

Washer pump fails to operate

- [ ] Broken or disconnected wiring or connections (Chapter 12).
- [ ] Blown fuse (Chapter 12).
- [ ] Faulty washer switch (Chapter 12).
- [ ] Faulty washer pump (Chapter 12).

Washer pump runs for some time before fluid is emitted from jets

- [ ] Faulty one-way valve in fluid supply hose (Chapter 12).

Electric windows inoperative, or unsatisfactory in operation

Window glass will only move in one direction

- [ ] Faulty switch (Chapter 12).

Window glass slow to move

- [ ] Regulator seized or damaged, or in need of lubrication (Chapter 11).
- [ ] Door internal components or trim fouling regulator (Chapter 11).
- [ ] Faulty motor (Chapter 11).

Window glass fails to move

- [ ] Blown fuse (Chapter 12).
- [ ] Faulty relay (Chapter 12).
- [ ] Broken or disconnected wiring or connections (Chapter 12).
- [ ] Faulty motor (Chapter 11).

A

ABS (Anti-lock brake system) A system, usually electronically controlled, that senses incipient wheel lockup during braking and relieves hydraulic pressure at wheels that are about to skid.

Air bag An inflatable bag hidden in the steering wheel (driver's side) or the dash or glovebox (passenger side). In a head-on collision, the bags inflate, preventing the driver and front passenger from being thrown forward into the steering wheel or windscreen.

Air cleaner A metal or plastic housing, containing a filter element, which removes dust and dirt from the air being drawn into the engine.

Air filter element The actual filter in an air cleaner system, usually manufactured from pleated paper and requiring renewal at regular intervals.

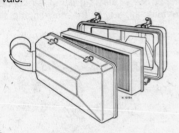

Air filter

Allen key A hexagonal wrench which fits into a recessed hexagonal hole.

Alligator clip A long-nosed spring-loaded metal clip with meshing teeth. Used to make temporary electrical connections.

Alternator A component in the electrical system which converts mechanical energy from a drivebelt into electrical energy to charge the battery and to operate the starting system, ignition system and electrical accessories.

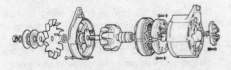

Alternator (exploded view)

Ampere (amp) A unit of measurement for the flow of electric current. One amp is the amount of current produced by one volt acting through a resistance of one ohm.

Anaerobic sealer A substance used to prevent bolts and screws from loosening. Anaerobic means that it does not require oxygen for activation. The Loctite brand is widely used.

Antifreeze A substance (usually ethylene glycol) mixed with water, and added to a vehicle's cooling system, to prevent freezing of the coolant in winter. Antifreeze also contains chemicals to inhibit corrosion and the formation of rust and other deposits that would tend to clog the radiator and coolant passages and reduce cooling efficiency.

Anti-seize compound A coating that reduces the risk of seizing on fasteners that are subjected to high temperatures, such as exhaust manifold bolts and nuts.

Anti-seize compound

Asbestos A natural fibrous mineral with great heat resistance, commonly used in the composition of brake friction materials. Asbestos is a health hazard and the dust created by brake systems should never be inhaled or ingested.

Axle A shaft on which a wheel revolves, or which revolves with a wheel. Also, a solid beam that connects the two wheels at one end of the vehicle. An axle which also transmits power to the wheels is known as a live axle.

Axle assembly

Axleshaft A single rotating shaft, on either side of the differential, which delivers power from the final drive assembly to the drive wheels. Also called a driveshaft or a halfshaft.

B

Ball bearing An anti-friction bearing consisting of a hardened inner and outer race with hardened steel balls between two races.

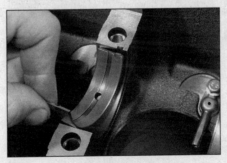

Bearing

Bearing The curved surface on a shaft or in a bore, or the part assembled into either, that permits relative motion between them with minimum wear and friction.

Big-end bearing The bearing in the end of the connecting rod that's attached to the crankshaft.

Bleed nipple A valve on a brake wheel cylinder, caliper or other hydraulic component that is opened to purge the hydraulic system of air. Also called a bleed screw.

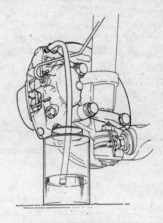

Brake bleeding

Brake bleeding Procedure for removing air from lines of a hydraulic brake system.

Brake disc The component of a disc brake that rotates with the wheels.

Brake drum The component of a drum brake that rotates with the wheels.

Brake linings The friction material which contacts the brake disc or drum to retard the vehicle's speed. The linings are bonded or riveted to the brake pads or shoes.

Brake pads The replaceable friction pads that pinch the brake disc when the brakes are applied. Brake pads consist of a friction material bonded or riveted to a rigid backing plate.

Brake shoe The crescent-shaped carrier to which the brake linings are mounted and which forces the lining against the rotating drum during braking.

Braking systems For more information on braking systems, consult the *Haynes Automotive Brake Manual*.

Breaker bar A long socket wrench handle providing greater leverage.

Bulkhead The insulated partition between the engine and the passenger compartment.

C

Caliper The non-rotating part of a disc-brake assembly that straddles the disc and carries the brake pads. The caliper also contains the hydraulic components that cause the pads to pinch the disc when the brakes are applied. A caliper is also a measuring tool that can be set to measure inside or outside dimensions of an object.

Camshaft A rotating shaft on which a series of cam lobes operate the valve mechanisms. The camshaft may be driven by gears, by sprockets and chain or by sprockets and a belt.

Canister A container in an evaporative emission control system; contains activated charcoal granules to trap vapours from the fuel system.

Canister

Carburettor A device which mixes fuel with air in the proper proportions to provide a desired power output from a spark ignition internal combustion engine.

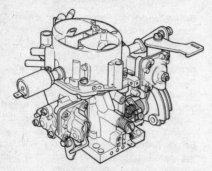

Carburettor

Castellated Resembling the parapets along the top of a castle wall. For example, a castellated balljoint stud nut.

Castellated nut

Castor In wheel alignment, the backward or forward tilt of the steering axis. Castor is positive when the steering axis is inclined rearward at the top.

Catalytic converter A silencer-like device in the exhaust system which converts certain pollutants in the exhaust gases into less harmful substances.

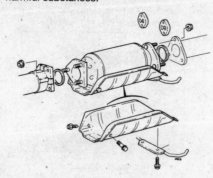

Catalytic converter

Circlip A ring-shaped clip used to prevent endwise movement of cylindrical parts and shafts. An internal circlip is installed in a groove in a housing; an external circlip fits into a groove on the outside of a cylindrical piece such as a shaft.

Clearance The amount of space between two parts. For example, between a piston and a cylinder, between a bearing and a journal, etc.

Coil spring A spiral of elastic steel found in various sizes throughout a vehicle, for example as a springing medium in the suspension and in the valve train.

Compression Reduction in volume, and increase in pressure and temperature, of a gas, caused by squeezing it into a smaller space.

Compression ratio The relationship between cylinder volume when the piston is at top dead centre and cylinder volume when the piston is at bottom dead centre.

Constant velocity (CV) joint A type of universal joint that cancels out vibrations caused by driving power being transmitted through an angle.

Core plug A disc or cup-shaped metal device inserted in a hole in a casting through which core was removed when the casting was formed. Also known as a freeze plug or expansion plug.

Crankcase The lower part of the engine block in which the crankshaft rotates.

Crankshaft The main rotating member, or shaft, running the length of the crankcase, with offset "throws" to which the connecting rods are attached.

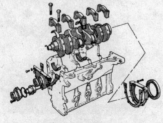

Crankshaft assembly

Crocodile clip See Alligator clip

D

Diagnostic code Code numbers obtained by accessing the diagnostic mode of an engine management computer. This code can be used to determine the area in the system where a malfunction may be located.

Disc brake A brake design incorporating a rotating disc onto which brake pads are squeezed. The resulting friction converts the energy of a moving vehicle into heat.

Double-overhead cam (DOHC) An engine that uses two overhead camshafts, usually one for the intake valves and one for the exhaust valves.

Drivebelt(s) The belt(s) used to drive accessories such as the alternator, water pump, power steering pump, air conditioning compressor, etc. off the crankshaft pulley.

Accessory drivebelts

Driveshaft Any shaft used to transmit motion. Commonly used when referring to the axleshafts on a front wheel drive vehicle.

Driveshaft

Drum brake A type of brake using a drum-shaped metal cylinder attached to the inner surface of the wheel. When the brake pedal is pressed, curved brake shoes with friction linings press against the inside of the drum to slow or stop the vehicle.

Drum brake assembly

E

EGR valve A valve used to introduce exhaust gases into the intake air stream.

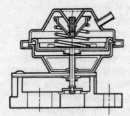

EGR valve

Electronic control unit (ECU) A computer which controls (for instance) ignition and fuel injection systems, or an anti-lock braking system. For more information refer to the *Haynes Automotive Electrical and Electronic Systems Manual.*

Electronic Fuel Injection (EFI) A computer controlled fuel system that distributes fuel through an injector located in each intake port of the engine.

Emergency brake A braking system, independent of the main hydraulic system, that can be used to slow or stop the vehicle if the primary brakes fail, or to hold the vehicle stationary even though the brake pedal isn't depressed. It usually consists of a hand lever that actuates either front or rear brakes mechanically through a series of cables and linkages. Also known as a handbrake or parking brake.

Endfloat The amount of lengthwise movement between two parts. As applied to a crankshaft, the distance that the crankshaft can move forward and back in the cylinder block.

Engine management system (EMS) A computer controlled system which manages the fuel injection and the ignition systems in an integrated fashion.

Exhaust manifold A part with several passages through which exhaust gases leave the engine combustion chambers and enter the exhaust pipe.

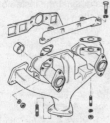

Exhaust manifold

F

Fan clutch A viscous (fluid) drive coupling device which permits variable engine fan speeds in relation to engine speeds.

Feeler blade A thin strip or blade of hardened steel, ground to an exact thickness, used to check or measure clearances between parts.

Feeler blade

Firing order The order in which the engine cylinders fire, or deliver their power strokes, beginning with the number one cylinder.

Flywheel A heavy spinning wheel in which energy is absorbed and stored by means of momentum. On cars, the flywheel is attached to the crankshaft to smooth out firing impulses.

Free play The amount of travel before any action takes place. The "looseness" in a linkage, or an assembly of parts, between the initial application of force and actual movement. For example, the distance the brake pedal moves before the pistons in the master cylinder are actuated.

Fuse An electrical device which protects a circuit against accidental overload. The typical fuse contains a soft piece of metal which is calibrated to melt at a predetermined current flow (expressed as amps) and break the circuit.

Fusible link A circuit protection device consisting of a conductor surrounded by heat-resistant insulation. The conductor is smaller than the wire it protects, so it acts as the weakest link in the circuit. Unlike a blown fuse, a failed fusible link must frequently be cut from the wire for replacement.

G

Gap The distance the spark must travel in jumping from the centre electrode to the side

Adjusting spark plug gap

electrode in a spark plug. Also refers to the spacing between the points in a contact breaker assembly in a conventional points-type ignition, or to the distance between the reluctor or rotor and the pickup coil in an electronic ignition.

Gasket Any thin, soft material - usually cork, cardboard, asbestos or soft metal - installed between two metal surfaces to ensure a good seal. For instance, the cylinder head gasket seals the joint between the block and the cylinder head.

Gasket

Gauge An instrument panel display used to monitor engine conditions. A gauge with a movable pointer on a dial or a fixed scale is an analogue gauge. A gauge with a numerical readout is called a digital gauge.

H

Halfshaft A rotating shaft that transmits power from the final drive unit to a drive wheel, usually when referring to a live rear axle.

Harmonic balancer A device designed to reduce torsion or twisting vibration in the crankshaft. May be incorporated in the crankshaft pulley. Also known as a vibration damper.

Hone An abrasive tool for correcting small irregularities or differences in diameter in an engine cylinder, brake cylinder, etc.

Hydraulic tappet A tappet that utilises hydraulic pressure from the engine's lubrication system to maintain zero clearance (constant contact with both camshaft and valve stem). Automatically adjusts to variation in valve stem length. Hydraulic tappets also reduce valve noise.

I

Ignition timing The moment at which the spark plug fires, usually expressed in the number of crankshaft degrees before the piston reaches the top of its stroke.

Inlet manifold A tube or housing with passages through which flows the air-fuel mixture (carburettor vehicles and vehicles with throttle body injection) or air only (port fuel-injected vehicles) to the port openings in the cylinder head.

J

Jump start Starting the engine of a vehicle with a discharged or weak battery by attaching jump leads from the weak battery to a charged or helper battery.

L

Load Sensing Proportioning Valve (LSPV) A brake hydraulic system control valve that works like a proportioning valve, but also takes into consideration the amount of weight carried by the rear axle.

Locknut A nut used to lock an adjustment nut, or other threaded component, in place. For example, a locknut is employed to keep the adjusting nut on the rocker arm in position.

Lockwasher A form of washer designed to prevent an attaching nut from working loose.

M

MacPherson strut A type of front suspension system devised by Earle MacPherson at Ford of England. In its original form, a simple lateral link with the anti-roll bar creates the lower control arm. A long strut - an integral coil spring and shock absorber - is mounted between the body and the steering knuckle. Many modern so-called MacPherson strut systems use a conventional lower A-arm and don't rely on the anti-roll bar for location.

Multimeter An electrical test instrument with the capability to measure voltage, current and resistance.

N

NOx Oxides of Nitrogen. A common toxic pollutant emitted by petrol and diesel engines at higher temperatures.

O

Ohm The unit of electrical resistance. One volt applied to a resistance of one ohm will produce a current of one amp.

Ohmmeter An instrument for measuring electrical resistance.

O-ring A type of sealing ring made of a special rubber-like material; in use, the O-ring is compressed into a groove to provide the sealing action.

O-ring

Overhead cam (ohc) engine An engine with the camshaft(s) located on top of the cylinder head(s).

Overhead valve (ohv) engine An engine with the valves located in the cylinder head, but with the camshaft located in the engine block.

Oxygen sensor A device installed in the engine exhaust manifold, which senses the oxygen content in the exhaust and converts this information into an electric current. Also called a Lambda sensor.

P

Phillips screw A type of screw head having a cross instead of a slot for a corresponding type of screwdriver.

Plastigage A thin strip of plastic thread, available in different sizes, used for measuring clearances. For example, a strip of Plastigage is laid across a bearing journal. The parts are assembled and dismantled; the width of the crushed strip indicates the clearance between journal and bearing.

Plastigage

Propeller shaft The long hollow tube with universal joints at both ends that carries power from the transmission to the differential on front-engined rear wheel drive vehicles.

Proportioning valve A hydraulic control valve which limits the amount of pressure to the rear brakes during panic stops to prevent wheel lock-up.

R

Rack-and-pinion steering A steering system with a pinion gear on the end of the steering shaft that mates with a rack (think of a geared wheel opened up and laid flat). When the steering wheel is turned, the pinion turns, moving the rack to the left or right. This movement is transmitted through the track rods to the steering arms at the wheels.

Radiator A liquid-to-air heat transfer device designed to reduce the temperature of the coolant in an internal combustion engine cooling system.

Refrigerant Any substance used as a heat transfer agent in an air-conditioning system. R-12 has been the principle refrigerant for many years; recently, however, manufacturers have begun using R-134a, a non-CFC substance that is considered less harmful to the ozone in the upper atmosphere.

Rocker arm A lever arm that rocks on a shaft or pivots on a stud. In an overhead valve engine, the rocker arm converts the upward movement of the pushrod into a downward movement to open a valve.

Rotor In a distributor, the rotating device inside the cap that connects the centre electrode and the outer terminals as it turns, distributing the high voltage from the coil secondary winding to the proper spark plug. Also, that part of an alternator which rotates inside the stator. Also, the rotating assembly of a turbocharger, including the compressor wheel, shaft and turbine wheel.

Runout The amount of wobble (in-and-out movement) of a gear or wheel as it's rotated. The amount a shaft rotates "out-of-true." The out-of-round condition of a rotating part.

S

Sealant A liquid or paste used to prevent leakage at a joint. Sometimes used in conjunction with a gasket.

Sealed beam lamp An older headlight design which integrates the reflector, lens and filaments into a hermetically-sealed one-piece unit. When a filament burns out or the lens cracks, the entire unit is simply replaced.

Serpentine drivebelt A single, long, wide accessory drivebelt that's used on some newer vehicles to drive all the accessories, instead of a series of smaller, shorter belts. Serpentine drivebelts are usually tensioned by an automatic tensioner.

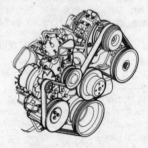

Serpentine drivebelt

Shim Thin spacer, commonly used to adjust the clearance or relative positions between two parts. For example, shims inserted into or under bucket tappets control valve clearances. Clearance is adjusted by changing the thickness of the shim.

Slide hammer A special puller that screws into or hooks onto a component such as a shaft or bearing; a heavy sliding handle on the shaft bottoms against the end of the shaft to knock the component free.

Sprocket A tooth or projection on the periphery of a wheel, shaped to engage with a chain or drivebelt. Commonly used to refer to the sprocket wheel itself.

Starter inhibitor switch On vehicles with an

automatic transmission, a switch that prevents starting if the vehicle is not in Neutral or Park.

Strut See MacPherson strut.

T

Tappet A cylindrical component which transmits motion from the cam to the valve stem, either directly or via a pushrod and rocker arm. Also called a cam follower.

Thermostat A heat-controlled valve that regulates the flow of coolant between the cylinder block and the radiator, so maintaining optimum engine operating temperature. A thermostat is also used in some air cleaners in which the temperature is regulated.

Thrust bearing The bearing in the clutch assembly that is moved in to the release levers by clutch pedal action to disengage the clutch. Also referred to as a release bearing.

Timing belt A toothed belt which drives the camshaft. Serious engine damage may result if it breaks in service.

Timing chain A chain which drives the camshaft.

Toe-in The amount the front wheels are closer together at the front than at the rear. On rear wheel drive vehicles, a slight amount of toe-in is usually specified to keep the front wheels running parallel on the road by offsetting other forces that tend to spread the wheels apart.

Toe-out The amount the front wheels are closer together at the rear than at the front. On front wheel drive vehicles, a slight amount of toe-out is usually specified.

Tools For full information on choosing and using tools, refer to the *Haynes Automotive Tools Manual*.

Tracer A stripe of a second colour applied to a wire insulator to distinguish that wire from another one with the same colour insulator.

Tune-up A process of accurate and careful adjustments and parts replacement to obtain the best possible engine performance.

Turbocharger A centrifugal device, driven by exhaust gases, that pressurises the intake air. Normally used to increase the power output from a given engine displacement, but can also be used primarily to reduce exhaust emissions (as on VW's "Umwelt" Diesel engine).

U

Universal joint or U-joint A double-pivoted connection for transmitting power from a driving to a driven shaft through an angle. A U-joint consists of two Y-shaped yokes and a cross-shaped member called the spider.

V

Valve A device through which the flow of liquid, gas, vacuum, or loose material in bulk may be started, stopped, or regulated by a movable part that opens, shuts, or partially obstructs one or more ports or passageways. A valve is also the movable part of such a device.

Valve clearance The clearance between the valve tip (the end of the valve stem) and the rocker arm or tappet. The valve clearance is measured when the valve is closed.

Vernier caliper A precision measuring instrument that measures inside and outside dimensions. Not quite as accurate as a micrometer, but more convenient.

Viscosity The thickness of a liquid or its resistance to flow.

Volt A unit for expressing electrical "pressure" in a circuit. One volt that will produce a current of one ampere through a resistance of one ohm.

W

Welding Various processes used to join metal items by heating the areas to be joined to a molten state and fusing them together. For more information refer to the *Haynes Automotive Welding Manual*.

Wiring diagram A drawing portraying the components and wires in a vehicle's electrical system, using standardised symbols. For more information refer to the *Haynes Automotive Electrical and Electronic Systems Manual*.

Note: *References throughout this index are in the form "Chapter number"•"page number"*

Notes

Haynes Manuals – The Complete List

Title	Book No.
ALFA ROMEO	
Alfa Romeo Alfasud/Sprint (74 - 88) up to F	0292
Alfa Romeo Alfetta (73 - 87) up to E	0531
AUDI	
Audi 80 (72 - Feb 79) up to T	0207
Audi 80, 90 (79 - Oct 86) up to D & Coupe (81 - Nov 88) up to F	0605
Audi 80, 90 (Oct 86 - 90) D to H & Coupe (Nov 88 - 90) F to H	1491
Audi 100 (Oct 82 - 90) up to H & 200 (Feb 84 - Oct 89) A to G	0907
Audi 100 & A6 Petrol & Diesel (May 91 - May 97) H to P	3504
Audi A4 (95 - Feb 00) M to V	3575
AUSTIN	
Austin A35 & A40 (56 - 67) *	0118
Austin Allegro 1100, 1300, 1.0, 1.1 & 1.3 (73 - 82)*	0164
Austin Healey 100/6 & 3000 (56 - 68) *	0049
Austin/MG/Rover Maestro 1.3 & 1.6 (83 - May 95) up to M	0922
Austin/MG Metro (80 - May 90) up to G	0718
Austin/Rover Montego 1.3 & 1.6 (84 - 94) A to L	1066
Austin/MG/Rover Montego 2.0 (84 - 95) A to M	1067
Mini (59 - 69) up to H	0527
Mini (69 - Oct 96) up to P	0646
Austin/Rover 2.0 litre Diesel Engine (86 - 93) C to L	1857
BEDFORD	
Bedford CF (69 - 87) up to E	0163
Bedford/Vauxhall Rascal & Suzuki Supercarry (86 - Oct 94) C to M	3015
BMW	
BMW 1500, 1502, 1600, 1602, 2000 & 2002 (59 - 77)*	0240
BMW 316, 320 & 320i (4-cyl) (75 - Feb 83) up to Y	0276
BMW 320, 320i, 323i & 325i (6-cyl) (Oct 77 - Sept 87) up to E	0815
BMW 3-Series (Apr 91 - 96) H to N	3210
BMW 3- & 5-Series (sohc) (81 - 91) up to J	1948
BMW 520i & 525e (Oct 81 - June 88) up to E	1560
BMW 525, 528 & 528i (73 - Sept 81) up to X	0632
CITROËN	
Citroën 2CV, Ami & Dyane (67 - 90) up to H	0196
Citroën AX Petrol & Diesel (87 - 97) D to P	3014
Citroën BX (83 - 94) A to L	0908
Citroën C15 Van Petrol & Diesel (89 - Oct 98) F to S	3509
Citroën CX (75 - 88) up to F	0528
Citroën Saxo Petrol & Diesel (96 - 01) N to X	3506
Citroën Visa (79 - 88) up to F	0620
Citroën Xantia Petrol & Diesel (93 - 98) K to S	3082
Citroën XM Petrol & Diesel (89 - 00) G to X	3451
Citroën Xsara Petrol & Diesel (97 - Sept 00) R to W	3751
Citroën ZX Diesel (91 - 98) J to S	1922
Citroën ZX Petrol (91 - 98) H to S	1881
Citroën 1.7 & 1.9 litre Diesel Engine (84 - 96) A to N	1379
FIAT	
Fiat 126 (73 - 87) *	0305
Fiat 500 (57 - 73) up to M	0090
Fiat Bravo & Brava (95 - 00) N to W	3572
Fiat Cinquecento (93 - 98) K to R	3501
Fiat Panda (81 - 95) up to M	0793
Fiat Punto Petrol & Diesel (94 - Oct 99) L to V	3251
Fiat Regata (84 - 88) A to F	1167
Fiat Tipo (88 - 91) E to J	1625
Fiat Uno (83 - 95) up to M	0923
Fiat X1/9 (74 - 89) up to G	0273
FORD	
Ford Anglia (59 - 68) *	0001
Ford Capri II (& III) 1.6 & 2.0 (74 - 87) up to E	0283

Title	Book No.
Ford Capri II (& III) 2.8 & 3.0 (74 - 87) up to E	1309
Ford Cortina Mk III 1300 & 1600 (70 - 76) *	0070
Ford Cortina Mk IV (& V) 1.6 & 2.0 (76 - 83) *	0343
Ford Cortina Mk IV (& V) 2.3 V6 (77 - 83) *	0426
Ford Escort Mk I 1100 & 1300 (68 - 74) *	0171
Ford Escort Mk I Mexico, RS 1600 & RS 2000 (70 - 74)*	0139
Ford Escort Mk II Mexico, RS 1800 & RS 2000 (75 - 80)*	0735
Ford Escort (75 - Aug 80) *	0280
Ford Escort (Sept 80 - Sept 90) up to H	0686
Ford Escort & Orion (Sept 90 - 00) H to X	1737
Ford Fiesta (76 - Aug 83) up to Y	0334
Ford Fiesta (Aug 83 - Feb 89) A to F	1030
Ford Fiesta (Feb 89 - Oct 95) F to N	1595
Ford Fiesta (Oct 95 - 01) N-reg. onwards	3397
Ford Focus (98 - 01) S to Y	3759
Ford Granada (Sept 77 - Feb 85) up to B	0481
Ford Granada & Scorpio (Mar 85 - 94) B to M	1245
Ford Ka (96 - 02) P-reg. onwards	3570
Ford Mondeo Petrol (93 - 99) K to T	1923
Ford Mondeo Diesel (93 - 96) L to N	3465
Ford Orion (83 - Sept 90) up to H	1009
Ford Sierra 4 cyl. (82 - 93) up to K	0903
Ford Sierra V6 (82 - 91) up to J	0904
Ford Transit Petrol (Mk 2) (78 - Jan 86) up to C	0719
Ford Transit Petrol (Mk 3) (Feb 86 - 89) C to G	1468
Ford Transit Diesel (Feb 86 - 99) C to T	3019
Ford 1.6 & 1.8 litre Diesel Engine (84 - 96) A to N	1172
Ford 2.1, 2.3 & 2.5 litre Diesel Engine (77 - 90) up to H	1606
FREIGHT ROVER	
Freight Rover Sherpa (74 - 87) up to E	0463
HILLMAN	
Hillman Avenger (70 - 82) up to Y	0037
Hillman Imp (63 - 76) *	0022
HONDA	
Honda Accord (76 - Feb 84) up to A	0351
Honda Civic (Feb 84 - Oct 87) A to E	1226
Honda Civic (Nov 91 - 96) J to N	3199
HYUNDAI	
Hyundai Pony (85 - 94) C to M	3398
JAGUAR	
Jaguar E Type (61 - 72) up to L	0140
Jaguar MkI & II, 240 & 340 (55 - 69) *	0098
Jaguar XJ6, XJ & Sovereign; Daimler Sovereign (68 - Oct 86) up to D	0242
Jaguar XJ6 & Sovereign (Oct 86 - Sept 94) D to M	3261
Jaguar XJ12, XJS & Sovereign; Daimler Double Six (72 - 88) up to F	0478
JEEP	
Jeep Cherokee Petrol (93 - 96) K to N	1943
LADA	
Lada 1200, 1300, 1500 & 1600 (74 - 91) up to J	0413
Lada Samara (87 - 91) D to J	1610
LAND ROVER	
Land Rover 90, 110 & Defender Diesel (83 - 95) up to N	3017
Land Rover Discovery Petrol & Diesel (89 - 98) G to S	3016
Land Rover Series IIA & III Diesel (58 - 85) up to C	0529
Land Rover Series II, IIA & III Petrol (58 - 85) up to C	0314
MAZDA	
Mazda 323 (Mar 81 - Oct 89) up to G	1608
Mazda 323 (Oct 89 - 98) G to R	3455
Mazda 626 (May 83 - Sept 87) up to E	0929
Mazda B-1600, B-1800 & B-2000 Pick-up (72 - 88) up to F	0267
Mazda RX-7 (79 - 85) *	0460

Title	Book No.
MERCEDES-BENZ	
Mercedes-Benz 190, 190E & 190D Petrol & Diesel (83 - 93) A to L	3450
Mercedes-Benz 200, 240, 300 Diesel (Oct 76 - 85) up to C	1114
Mercedes-Benz 250 & 280 (68 - 72) up to L	0346
Mercedes-Benz 250 & 280 (123 Series) (Oct 76 - 84) up to B	0677
Mercedes-Benz 124 Series (85 - Aug 93) C to K	3253
Mercedes-Benz C-Class Petrol & Diesel (93 - Aug 00) L to W	3511
MG	
MGA (55 - 62) *	0475
MGB (62 - 80) up to W	0111
MG Midget & AH Sprite (58 - 80) up to W	0265
MITSUBISHI	
Mitsubishi Shogun & L200 Pick-Ups (83 - 94) up to M	1944
MORRIS	
Morris Ital 1.3 (80 - 84) up to B	0705
Morris Minor 1000 (56 - 71) up to K	0024
NISSAN	
Nissan Bluebird (May 84 - Mar 86) A to C	1223
Nissan Bluebird (Mar 86 - 90) C to H	1473
Nissan Cherry (Sept 82 - 86) up to D	1031
Nissan Micra (83 - Jan 93) up to K	0931
Nissan Micra (93 - 99) K to T	3254
Nissan Primera (90 - Aug 99) H to T	1851
Nissan Stanza (82 - 86) up to D	0824
Nissan Sunny (May 82 - Oct 86) up to D	0895
Nissan Sunny (Oct 86 - Mar 91) D to H	1378
Nissan Sunny (Apr 91 - 95) H to N	3219
OPEL	
Opel Ascona & Manta (B Series) (Sept 75 - 88) up to F	0316
Opel Ascona (81 - 88) (Not available in UK see Vauxhall Cavalier 0812)	3215
Opel Astra (Oct 91 - Feb 98) (Not available in UK see Vauxhall Astra 1832)	3156
Opel Astra & Zafira Diesel (Feb 98 - Sept 00) (See Astra & Zafira Diesel Book No. 3797)	
Opel Astra & Zafira Petrol (Feb 98 - Sept 00) (See Vauxhall/Opel Astra & Zafira Petrol Book No. 3758)	
Opel Calibra (90 - 98) (See Vauxhall/Opel Calibra Book No. 3502)	
Opel Corsa (83 - Mar 93) (Not available in UK see Vauxhall Nova 0909)	3160
Opel Corsa (Mar 93 - 97) (Not available in UK see Vauxhall Corsa 1985)	3159
Opel Frontera Petrol & Diesel (91 - 98) (See Vauxhall/Opel Frontera Book No. 3454)	
Opel Kadett (Nov 79 - Oct 84) up to B	0634
Opel Kadett (Oct 84 - Oct 91) (Not available in UK see Vauxhall Astra & Belmont 1136)	3196
Opel Omega & Senator (86 - 94) (Not available in UK see Vauxhall Carlton & Senator 1469)	3157
Opel Omega (94 - 99) (See Vauxhall/Opel Omega Book No. 3510)	
Opel Rekord (Feb 78 - Oct 86) up to D	0543
Opel Vectra (Oct 88 - Oct 95) (Not available in UK see Vauxhall Cavalier 1570)	3158
Opel Vectra Petrol & Diesel (95 - 98) (Not available in UK see Vauxhall Vectra 3396)	3523
PEUGEOT	
Peugeot 106 Petrol & Diesel (91 - 01) J to X	1882
Peugeot 205 Petrol (83 - 97) A to P	0932
Peugeot 206 Petrol and Diesel (98 - 01) S to X	3757
Peugeot 305 (78 - 89) up to G	0538

* Classic reprint

Title	Book No.
Peugeot 306 Petrol & Diesel (93 - 99) K to T	3073
Peugeot 309 (86 - 93) C to K	1266
Peugeot 405 Petrol (88 - 97) E to P	1559
Peugeot 405 Diesel (88 - 97) E to P	3198
Peugeot 406 Petrol & Diesel (96 - 97) N to R	3394
Peugeot 505 (79 - 89) up to G	0762
Peugeot 1.7/1.8 & 1.9 litre Diesel Engine (82 - 96) up to N	0950
Peugeot 2.0, 2.1, 2.3 & 2.5 litre Diesel Engines (74 - 90) up to H	1607

PORSCHE
Title	Book No.
Porsche 911 (65 - 85) up to C	0264
Porsche 924 & 924 Turbo (76 - 85) up to C	0397

PROTON
Title	Book No.
Proton (89 - 97) F to P	3255

RANGE ROVER
Title	Book No.
Range Rover V8 (70 - Oct 92) up to K	0606

RELIANT
Title	Book No.
Reliant Robin & Kitten (73 - 83) up to A	0436

RENAULT
Title	Book No.
Renault 4 (61 - 86) *	0072
Renault 5 (Feb 85 - 96) B to N	1219
Renault 9 & 11 (82 - 89) up to F	0822
Renault 18 (79 - 86) up to D	0598
Renault 19 Petrol (89 - 94) F to M	1646
Renault 19 Diesel (89 - 96) F to N	1946
Renault 21 (86 - 94) C to M	1397
Renault 25 (84 - 92) B to K	1228
Renault Clio Petrol (91 - May 98) H to R	1853
Renault Clio Diesel (91 - June 96) H to N	3031
Renault Clio Petrol & Diesel (May 98 - May 01) R to Y	3906
Renault Espace Petrol & Diesel (85 - 96) C to N	3197
Renault Fuego (80 - 86) *	0764
Renault Laguna Petrol & Diesel (94 - 00) L to W	3252
Renault Mégane & Scénic Petrol & Diesel (96 - 98) N to R	3395
Renault Mégane & Scénic (Apr 99 - 02) T-reg onwards	3916

ROVER
Title	Book No.
Rover 213 & 216 (84 - 89) A to G	1116
Rover 214 & 414 (89 - 96) G to N	1689
Rover 216 & 416 (89 - 96) G to N	1830
Rover 211, 214, 216, 218 & 220 Petrol & Diesel (Dec 95 - 98) N to R	3399
Rover 414, 416 & 420 Petrol & Diesel (May 95 - 98) M to R	3453
Rover 618, 620 & 623 (93 - 97) K to P	3257
Rover 820, 825 & 827 (86 - 95) D to N	1380
Rover 3500 (76 - 87) up to E	0365
Rover Metro, 111 & 114 (May 90 - 98) G to S	1711

SAAB
Title	Book No.
Saab 90, 99 & 900 (79 - Oct 93) up to L	0765
Saab 95 & 96 (66 - 76) *	0198
Saab 99 (69 - 79) *	0247
Saab 900 (Oct 93 - 98) L to R	3512
Saab 9000 (4-cyl) (85 - 98) C to S	1686

SEAT
Title	Book No.
Seat Ibiza & Cordoba Petrol & Diesel (Oct 93 - Oct 99) L to V	3571
Seat Ibiza & Malaga (85 - 92) B to K	1609

SKODA
Title	Book No.
Skoda Estelle (77 - 89) up to G	0604
Skoda Favorit (89 - 96) F to N	1801
Skoda Felicia Petrol & Diesel (95 - 01) M to X	3505

SUBARU
Title	Book No.
Subaru 1600 & 1800 (Nov 79 - 90) up to H	0995

SUNBEAM
Title	Book No.
Sunbeam Alpine, Rapier & H120 (67 - 76) *	0051

SUZUKI
Title	Book No.
Suzuki SJ Series, Samurai & Vitara (4-cyl) (82 - 97) up to P	1942
Suzuki Supercarry & Bedford/Vauxhall Rascal (86 - Oct 94) C to M	3015

TALBOT
Title	Book No.
Talbot Alpine, Solara, Minx & Rapier (75 - 86) up to D	0337
Talbot Horizon (78 - 86) up to D	0473
Talbot Samba (82 - 86) up to D	0823

TOYOTA
Title	Book No.
Toyota Carina E (May 92 - 97) J to P	3256
Toyota Corolla (Sept 83 - Sept 87) A to E	1024
Toyota Corolla (80 - 85) up to C	0683
Toyota Corolla (Sept 87 - Aug 92) E to K	1683
Toyota Corolla (Aug 92 - 97) K to P	3259
Toyota Hi-Ace & Hi-Lux (69 - Oct 83) up to A	0304

TRIUMPH
Title	Book No.
Triumph Acclaim (81 - 84) *	0792
Triumph GT6 & Vitesse (62 - 74) *	0112
Triumph Herald (59 - 71) *	0010
Triumph Spitfire (62 - 81) up to X	0113
Triumph Stag (70 - 78) up to T	0441
Triumph TR2, TR3, TR3A, TR4 & TR4A (52 - 67)*	0028
Triumph TR5 & 6 (67 - 75) *	0031
Triumph TR7 (75 - 82) *	0322

VAUXHALL
Title	Book No.
Vauxhall Astra (80 - Oct 84) up to B	0635
Vauxhall Astra & Belmont (Oct 84 - Oct 91) B to J	1136
Vauxhall Astra (Oct 91 - Feb 98) J to R	1832
Vauxhall/Opel Astra & Zafira Diesel (Feb 98 - Sept 00) R to W	3797
Vauxhall/Opel Astra & Zafira Petrol (Feb 98 - Sept 00) R to W	3758
Vauxhall/Opel Calibra (90 - 98) G to S	3502
Vauxhall Carlton (Oct 78 - Oct 86) up to D	0480
Vauxhall Carlton & Senator (Nov 86 - 94) D to L	1469
Vauxhall Cavalier 1300 (77 - July 81) *	0461
Vauxhall Cavalier 1600, 1900 & 2000 (75 - July 81) up to W	0315
Vauxhall Cavalier (81 - Oct 88) up to F	0812
Vauxhall Cavalier (Oct 88 - 95) F to N	1570
Vauxhall Chevette (75 - 84) up to B	0285
Vauxhall Corsa (Mar 93 - 97) K to R	1985
Vauxhall/Opel Corsa (Apr 97 - Oct 00) P to X	3921
Vauxhall/Opel Frontera Petrol & Diesel (91 - Sept 98) J to S	3454
Vauxhall Nova (83 - 93) up to K	0909
Vauxhall/Opel Omega (94 - 99) L to T	3510
Vauxhall Vectra Petrol & Diesel (95 - 98) N to R	3396
Vauxhall/Opel 1.5, 1.6 & 1.7 litre Diesel Engine (82 - 96) up to N	1222

VOLKSWAGEN
Title	Book No.
Volkswagen 411 & 412 (68 - 75) *	0091
Volkswagen Beetle 1200 (54 - 77) up to S	0036
Volkswagen Beetle 1300 & 1500 (65 - 75) up to P	0039
Volkswagen Beetle 1302 & 1302S (70 - 72) up to L	0110
Volkswagen Beetle 1303, 1303S & GT (72 - 75) up to P	0159
Volkswagen Beetle Petrol & Diesel (Apr 99 - 01) T reg onwards	3798
Volkswagen Golf & Bora Petrol & Diesel (April 98 - 00) R to X	3727

Title	Book No.
Volkswagen Golf & Jetta Mk 1 1.1 & 1.3 (74 - 84) up to A	0716
Volkswagen Golf, Jetta & Scirocco Mk 1 1.5, 1.6 & 1.8 (74 - 84) up to A	0726
Volkswagen Golf & Jetta Mk 1 Diesel (78 - 84) up to A	0451
Volkswagen Golf & Jetta Mk 2 (Mar 84 - Feb 92) A to J	1081
Volkswagen Golf & Vento Petrol & Diesel (Feb 92 - 96) J to N	3097
Volkswagen LT vans & light trucks (76 - 87) up to E	0637
Volkswagen Passat & Santana (Sept 81 - May 88) up to E	0814
Volkswagen Passat Petrol & Diesel (May 88 - 96) E to P	3498
Volkswagen Passat 4-cyl Petrol & Diesel (Dec 96 - Nov 00) P to X	3917
Volkswagen Polo & Derby (76 - Jan 82) up to X	0335
Volkswagen Polo (82 - Oct 90) up to H	0813
Volkswagen Polo (Nov 90 - Aug 94) H to L	3245
Volkswagen Polo Hatchback Petrol & Diesel (94 - 99) M to S	3500
Volkswagen Scirocco (82 - 90) up to H	1224
Volkswagen Transporter 1600 (68 - 79) up to V	0082
Volkswagen Transporter 1700, 1800 & 2000 (72 - 79) up to V	0226
Volkswagen Transporter (air-cooled) (79 - 82) up to Y	0638
Volkswagen Transporter (water-cooled) (82 - 90) up to H	3452
Volkswagen Type 3 (63 - 73) *	0084

VOLVO
Title	Book No.
Volvo 120 & 130 Series (& P1800) (61 - 73) *	0203
Volvo 142, 144 & 145 (66 - 74) up to N	0129
Volvo 240 Series (74 - 93) up to K	0270
Volvo 262, 264 & 260/265 (75 - 85) *	0400
Volvo 340, 343, 345 & 360 (76 - 91) up to J	0715
Volvo 440, 460 & 480 (87 - 97) D to P	1691
Volvo 740 & 760 (82 - 91) up to J	1258
Volvo 850 (92 - 96) J to P	3260
Volvo 940 (90 - 96) H to N	3249
Volvo S40 & V40 (96 - 99) N to V	3569
Volvo S70, V70 & C70 (96 - 99) P to V	3573

AUTOMOTIVE TECHBOOKS
Title	Book No.
Automotive Air Conditioning Systems	3740
Automotive Brake Manual	3050
Automotive Carburettor Manual	3288
Automotive Diagnostic Fault Codes Manual	3472
Automotive Diesel Engine Service Guide	3286
Automotive Electrical and Electronic Systems Manual	3049
Automotive Engine Management and Fuel Injection Systems Manual	3344
Automotive Gearbox Overhaul Manual	3473
Automotive Service Summaries Manual	3475
Automotive Timing Belts Manual – Austin/Rover	3549
Automotive Timing Belts Manual – Ford	3474
Automotive Timing Belts Manual – Peugeot/Citroën	3568
Automotive Timing Belts Manual – Vauxhall/Opel	3577
Automotive Welding Manual	3053
In-Car Entertainment Manual (3rd Edition)	3363

* Classic reprint

CL13.4/02